*Poverty Row Studios,*
*1929–1940*

# Poverty Row Studios, 1929–1940

## An Illustrated History of 55 Independent Film Companies, with a Filmography for Each

MICHAEL R. PITTS

McFarland & Company, Inc., Publishers
*Jefferson, North Carolina, and London*

*The present work is a reprint of the library bound edition of*
Poverty Row Studios, 1929–1940: An Illustrated History of
55 Independent Film Companies, with a Filmography for
Each, *first published in 1997 by McFarland.*

LIBRARY OF CONGRESS CATALOGUING-IN-PUBLICATION DATA

Pitts, Michael R.
    Poverty row studios, 1929–1940: an illustrated history of 55
independent film companies, with a filmography for each / Michael R.
Pitts.
        p.   cm.
    Includes index.

    ISBN 0-7864-2319-6 (softcover : 50# alkaline paper) ∞

    1. Motion picture studios—California—Los Angeles—History.
    2. Low budget motion pictures—California—Los Angeles—History.
    I. Title.
    PN1993.5.U65P55   2005
    384'.8'0979494—dc20                                        96-22311

British Library Cataloguing-in-Publication data are available

Cover art ©2005 Photodisc

Manufactured in the United States of America

*McFarland & Company, Inc., Publishers*
  *Box 611, Jefferson, North Carolina 28640*
    *www.mcfarlandpub.com*

# Table of Contents

# Introduction

From the beginning of the sound era until the end of the 1930s, independent movie-making thrived in Hollywood. While it is true that independents have been on the movie scene since the cinema's inception, independent operators reached their peak at the height of the Depression despite its economic horrors and the establishment of radio. While vaudeville deteriorated at this time, movies continued to draw an ever-growing audience, and while the major studios had a hammerlock on most film distribution, the independents still managed to garner enough box-office returns to stay afloat. Yet as independent production reached its zenith at the middle of the 1930s, so it also began its decline, and by 1940 few of these studios were still around.

This book takes a look at over fifty independent movie operations in existence from 1929 to 1940. Most of these were headquartered in a section of Hollywood called Gower Gulch (because of its proclivity for westerns) in an area commonly known as Poverty Row. Here the independents carried out their business affairs, making movies on the cheap, usually at rented facilities where shooting was limited to only a few days. Then the product was peddled on the states' rights market, an intricate distribution system that sold movies in various territories, usually for a fixed fee. The cheapest of westerns, for example, could rent for as low as five dollars, but if made cheaply enough and given quantity bookings in various locales, its makers made a profit.

In discussing the films of Poverty Row, I have tried to provide a history of production companies, a representative sampling of their product and a filmography for each outfit. I should state one qualification however. This volume is not intended to be comprehensive; it is designed to give an overview of the companies and films that have received little or no previous attention. Because they have been covered in other McFarland books, Grand National, Mascot and Monogram are not included in this volume. Neither is Republic, since it too has been covered by other sources and because its history runs well past 1940. Another company not included is Producers Releasing Corporation (P.R.C.) because it was mainly active in the 1940s, although its beginnings took place at the end of the time covered by this book. All titles in the book's filmographies were produced between 1929 and 1940, even though a company may have existed prior to or after those dates.

Why do a study of Poverty Row movies of the 1930s? For one thing, as already noted previous coverage has been minimal. For another, with the proliferation of video many of these old films are now readily available and can be viewed by the public with relative ease. Still another reason is that these movies are fun—many make good viewing and are interesting to research and evaluate. In some ways these Poverty Row affairs reflect their time better than the glossier big studio productions of that era. They certainly provide a wealth of entertainment, and while most are dated, they are not without cinematic merit. This book will certainly reveal a great many run-of-the-mill efforts, but along with these are hidden classics, both features and shorts. It is often said that those who worked on Poverty Row were either on their way up or on their way down. In this context one can watch the evolution of a future star or acclaimed director, writer or photographer or see a has-been making another valiant attempt at a comeback.

This volume is meant to provide the reader with an informative look at low-budget movie production outside the studio system in the 1930s. I hope, too, that the book will stimulate the reader to search out and watch many of these old movies and learn of their charm. While in no way is it meant to lionize the Poverty Row movies of the 1930s or their makers, this book is a salute to those who left us with such a diverse entertainment legacy.

I would like to thank the following for their help in the preparation of this volume: Ann McKee, John R. Cocchi, Gary Kramer, James Robert Parish, Richard Bojarski, Romano Tozzi, Buck Rainey, and the Library of Congress' Motion Picture, Broadcasting and Recorded Sound Division (Patrick J. Sheehan).

Michael R. Pitts
*Fall 1996*

# THE STUDIOS

# Victor Adamson
# Productions

Victor Adamson worked under several names, the best known having been Denver Dixon. Among his other monickers were Art Mix, Art James and Al Mix. In the silent days he created the character of Art Mix, hoping to cash in on the popularity of cowboy hero Tom Mix. The ploy proved successful, but producing, directing and sometimes writing his Art Mix Productions left Adamson little time to star in the features after the initial 1923–24 season. As a result he hired George Kesterson to portray Art Mix, and the actor became so associated with the role that he began to bill himself as Art Mix when he signed for a series of silent westerns with producer J. Charles Davis. Adamson then hired Bob Roberts to play Art Mix, and litigation ensued between Adamson and Kesterson over the use of the name. Kesterson continued to bill himself as Art Mix for the rest of his career, which lasted well into the 1940s. In fact, in the sound era Adamson and Kesterson reteamed for more Art Mix films like *Sagebrush Politics* (1930) and *The Rawhide Terror* (1935).

Adamson's *modus operandi* was to go into a particular scenic area, get the cooperation of locals with financing and quickly make a feature film. In Oregon he did this with *The Old Oregon Trail* (1928), in the Mojave Desert with *Desert Mesa* (1936) and in Utah with *The Mormon Conquest* (1939). Like many *auteurs* Adamson developed a stock company of players like Allen Holbrook, Clyde McClary, Lafe McKee, George Hazel, Bud Osborne, Bob McKenzie, Ernest Scott, William McCall, Merrill McCormack and Horace B. Carpenter. A cowboy star on the downward path like Buddy Roosevelt, Buffalo Bill, Jr., or Bill Patton usually headlined his productions, although toward the end of his "B" western activities in the late 1930s he tried to groom stuntman Wally West as a star, billing him under his real name of Tom Wynn. Often Adamson worked with his wife Delores Booth, who either acted in or scripted a film, sometimes both. His preferred cameraman in the 1930s was Bydron Baker, a superb craftsman whose photography was sometimes the only asset of a Victor Adamson production.

In *Hollywood Corral* (1976), Don Miller's definitive work on the low-budget western, Miller likened Victor Adamson's oaters to adults "having fun

3

playing cowboy in somebody's back yard," and this is probably the best way to approach any assessment of these productions. Certainly there was little to link Adamson's minuscule budgets and daffy scripts to even the most minor of studio offerings. Although mercifully short (usually 50 minutes or less), Adamson's sound efforts are often plodding affairs in which reality is totally suspended. Some have needless sequences or corny comedy to fill the running time, and often the acting is high-school-play level. Most characters are one dimensional at best. Although Buddy Roosevelt tried to make something of the parts he played in the four oaters he did for Adamson, he was almost totally defeated by the scripts. On the other hand, Buffalo Bill, Jr., had trouble delivering even the briefest of dialogue, and his reputation was not helped by films like *Riding Speed* in which a member of the crew ambles into camera range during a scene. For his film *Lightning Bill* the title card is even misspelled! Further, Adamson's westerns tended to employ a certain amount of sadism: crook Allen Holbrook drops a cigar ash in a can of fruit about to be eaten by a child, Bud Osborne plans to roast Lafe McKee alive in his ranch house in *Lightning Bill* and Lew Meehan is a cold-blooded gang leader in *Range Riders*. L.V. Jefferson wrote most of Victor Adamson's scripts, although *Circle Canyon* was based on Burl Tuttle's magazine story "Gun Glory," for which the author did the screen adaptation. Except for some excellent desert photography by Bert Longnecker at the beginning of the film, it is a boring affair with hero Buddy Roosevelt showing as much interest in teenager Clarise Woods (his adopted daughter in the film) as in leading lady June Mathews. Roosevelt's lechery is certainly understandable, however, when one considers the remarkable lack of talent displayed by Mathews. Sheriff Bud Osborne's ride to the rescue at the film's finale seems to take forever. Interestingly, Tuttle's script was also filmed the same year, 1934, at Monogram by producer Paul Malvern in the John Wayne-Lone Star western *'Neath Arizona Skies*. It proved to be one of the shoddiest films in the series.

Born in New Zealand in 1890, Albert Victor Adamson got involved in films in Australia, coming to the U.S. in the teens. He was making his own productions like *The White Rider* in Hollywood by 1918. He remained active in the independent market, gaining some success with his Art Mix Productions in the mid–1920s with films like *Ace of Cactus Range*, *Riders of Mystery Range* and *Terror of Pueblo* (all 1924) and *Desert Vultures* (1928). He also did a few dramas like *Compassion* (1927) and *Sweeping Against the Wind* (1928), which his obituary claimed won the equivalent of the British Academy Award! Adamson often used the name of Denver Dixon either as producer, director, writer or star and he fared well in silents, but a heavy "Down Under" accent limited his sound acting primarily to bit parts. In *Lightning Range*, for example, he sounds decidedly out of place as a townsman telling a woman he cannot marry a girl because he already has a wife.

Victor Adamson Productions was busiest in the mid–1930s when the company made four starrers, each with Buddy Roosevelt and Buffalo Bill, Jr., plus the 1935 features *The Rawhide Terror* with Art Mix, *The Pecos Dandy* with George J. Lewis and *Arizona Trails* with Bill Patton. Alan James is credited with directing *Arizona Trails*, and he is often listed in the same capacity for *Desert Mesa* (1936), but Adamson actually directed it under the Denver Dixon brand. It was shot on the Mojave Desert, and Adamson played the hero's sidekick, using the screen name Art James. Earlier he was billed as Al Mix, the sidekick to Wally Wales in the two-reeler *The Adventures of Texas Jack*, the first of a series that never materialized. Apparently Adamson's final 1930s production was *The Mormon Conquest* (1939), which he made in Kanab, Utah, to exploit the beauties of Zion National Park. During the late 1930s and early 1940s the craftsman could be seen in small roles in various westerns, billed as Denver Dixon.

After a long absence from the screen, Victor Adamson Productions returned in 1961 with *Half Way to Hell*, which was filmed in Mexico and at Capitol Reef National Monument in Utah. Adamson directed as Denver Dixon, while his son Al Adamson coproduced and played a supporting role as Rick Adams. Next the two teamed up for *Two Tickets to Terror* (1963) with Adamson producing and his son directing. New footage was added to the feature in 1969, and it was called *Fiend with the Electronic Brain*. In 1972 it was refashioned again into *Blood of Ghastly Horror* and was released by Independent-International Pictures. That company was formed in 1968 by Victor Adamson, his son Al and *Screen Thrills Illustrated* magazine's editorial director Samuel M. Sherman. They intended to make low-budget features for the small-town and drive-in trade. As Denver Dixon, Victor Adamson served as consultant on the company's *Satan's Sadists* (1968) and *Dracula vs. Frankenstein* (1972), and he played a character role in the horror western *Five Bloody Graves* (1970).

Victor Adamson died November 9, 1972. His obituaries appeared under the name Denver Dixon.

## Sagebrush Politics

Hollywood Pictures, May 15, 1930, 5 reels.

*P-D*: Victor Adamson.

*Cast*: Art Mix, Lillian Bond, Wally Merrill, William Ryno, Pee Wee Holmes, Jack Gordon, Jim Campbell, Tom Forman.

Two drifters aid a lawman in rescuing his son who is held prisoner by the Wolf and his outlaw gang.

## The Fighting Cowboy

Superior Talking Pictures, 1933, 58 minutes.

*P*: Victor Adamson [Denver Dixon]. *D*: Denver Dixon. *SC*: L.V. Jefferson. *PH*: Bydron Baker. *SD*: Herb Eicke. *Tech Dir*: Bart Carre.

*Cast*: Buffalo Bill, Jr., Genee Boutell, Allen Holbrook, William Ryno, Marin Sais, Tom Palky, Bart Carre, Betty Butler, Clyde McClary, Jack Evans, Boris Bullock, Ken Brocker, Ernest Leath, Budd Buster, Jack Bronston, Hamilton Steele.

A range investigator helps a miner and his daughter avoid having their tungsten mine stolen by a crook.

Lyle Felice, Sergio Virell and Carol Montour in *Half Way to Hell* (Victor Adamson Productions, 1961).

## The Boss Cowboy

Superior Talking Pictures, 1934, 51 minutes.

*P-D*: Denver Dixon [Victor Adamson]. *SC*: B. Burbodge [Betty Burbridge]. *PH*: Bydron Baker. *ED*: Frances Burroughs. *Art Dir*: Jack Cook.

*Cast*: Buddy Roosevelt, Frances Morris, Sam Pierce, Fay McKenzie, Bud Osborne, George Chesebro, Lafe McKee, William [Merrill] McCormack, Allen Holbrook, Clyde McClary, Eva McKenzie, Denver Dixon.

A ranch foreman tries to help his girlfriend's sister and her father who are being cheated by their corrupt ranch foreman.

## Circle Canyon

Superior Talking Pictures, 1934, 48 minutes.

*P-D*: Victor Adamson [Denver Dixon]. *SC*: B.R. (Burl) Tuttle, from his story "Gun Glory." *PH*: Bert Longnecker. *SD*: International Studios.

*Cast*: Buddy Roosevelt, June Mathews, Clarise Woods, Bob Williamson, Allen Holbrook, Harry Leland, George Hazel, Clyde McClary, Mark Harrison, Ernest Scott, Johnny Tyke, Bud Osborne, Sherry Tansey, Barney Beasley, Tex Miller, William McCall.

A man searches for his adopted daughter's father and becomes involved with outlaws who want the girl's oil claims.

## Lightning Bill

Superior Talking Pictures, 1934, 46 minutes.

*P-D*: Victor Adamson [Denver Dixon]. *SC*: L.V. Jefferson. *PH*: Frank

**Buddy Roosevelt and June Mathews in** *Circle Canyon* **(Superior Talking Pictures/Victor Adamson Productions, 1934).**

Bender. *ED*: Frances Burroughs. *SD*: National Recording.

*Cast*: Buffalo Bill, Jr., Alma Rayford, Bud Osborne, Allen Holbrook, Bill [William] McCall, Nelson McDowell, George Hazel, Mrs. [Eva] McKenzie, [Black] Jack Ward, Bob McKenzie.

A cowboy and his pal go to work for a rancher whose land is being sought by the crook who murdered the owner's brother.

## Lightning Range

Superior Talking Pictures, 1934, 50 minutes.

*P-D*: Victor Adamson [Denver Dixon]. *SC*: L.V. Jefferson. *PH*: Bydron Baker. *SD*: Herb Eicke. *Tech Dir*: Bart Carre.

*Cast*: Buddy Roosevelt (U.S. Deputy Marshal), Patsy Bellamy (Dor-

othy Horton), Lafe McKee (Judge Williams), Olin Francis (Black Pete), Si Jenks (Hezekiah Simmons), Bart Carre (Jim), Anne Howard (Aunt), Ken Brocker (Sheriff), Boris Bullock (Boob), Clyde McClary (Miner), Betty Butler (Eastern Girl), Jack Evans (Jack Knife), Jack Bronston (Deputy Sheriff), Genee Boutell (Stage Passenger), Denver Dixon (Townsman).

After killing a miner for his poke, outlaw leader Black Pete (Olin Francis) and his gang plan to hold up a stagecoach for its gold shipment. A Deputy Marshal (Buddy Roosevelt) who witnessed the murder trails the gang, and after they carry out the holdup he stalks them to their hideout but is captured. Black Pete learns that Dorothy Horton (Patsy Bellamy) will lose her inheritance if she does not marry by noon that day, so he has one of his men, Jim (Bart Carre), masquerade as her intended, whom she has never seen. In reality the groom is Hezekiah (Si Jenks), the nephew of a scheming woman (Anne Howard) who wants Dorothy's estate for herself. Hezekiah, however, loses his clothes to Boob (Boris Bullock), a member of the gang. When Jim arrives to marry Dorothy, her friend Judge Williams (Lafe McKee) advises her to go through the ceremony so he can annul the proceedings. The lawman, however, arrives in time to stop the wedding, scare Jim away, and take his place as the groom. Black Pete has the deputy marshal's badge, though, and he claims the real lawman is a wanted outlaw. A fight ensues but the local sheriff (Ken Brocker) and his possee arrive, and the real lawman is arrested and taken away. When Dorothy spies Black Pete stealing bonds, she rides to the lawman's rescue and convinces the sheriff of the truth. The deputy marshal then sets out to stop Black Pete and corners the gang. During the fight Dorothy brings the sheriff and the posse, and Black Pete and his gang are arrested. Dorothy and her new husband agree to stay married.

One of four westerns producer-director Victor Adamson made with Buddy Roosevelt, *Lightning Range* is a meager affair that does nothing for its likable star. Roosevelt's nameless character suffers from a severe case of ineptitude, being at one point knocked unconscious by a dynamite blast and at another lassoed off his horse and pulled up the face of a cliff by his dastardly foes. His misidentification at his own wedding and his subsequent rescue by the film's leading lady depict him as more of a buffoon than action hero. The film descends further into silliness with Boris Bullock's over-the-top performance as Boob, the dimwitted

outlaw who steals Hezekiah's fancy duds.

Made by California Motion Picture Enterprises, *Lightning Range* carried a 1933 copyright but apparently saw release in 1934.

## The Pecos Dandy

Security, 1934, 5 reels.

*P-D*: Victor Adamson [Denver Dixon]. *SC*: L.V. Jefferson. *PH*: Tom Galligen. *SD*: Karl Zint.

*Cast*: George J. Lewis, Dorothy Gulliver, Betty Lee, Horace B. Carpenter, Robert Walker, Clyde McClary.

A cowboy is framed on a horse-stealing charge by his romantic rival.

## Range Riders

Superior Talking Pictures, 1934, 46 minutes.

*P-D*: Victor Adamson [Denver Dixon]. *SC*: L.V. Jefferson. *PH*: Bydron Baker. *ED*: Frances Burroughs. *SD*: International Sound Recording.

*Cast*: Buddy Roosevelt, Barbara Starr, Lew Meehan, Merrill McCormack, Horace B. Carpenter, Fred Parker, Herman Hack, Clyde McClary, Bob McKenzie, Denver Dixon.

A young man returns to his home range to clean up a gang of toughs and takes on the guise of a "Texas Terror."

## Rawhide Romance

Superior Talking Pictures, 1934, 47 minutes.

*P-D*: Victor Adamson [Denver Dixon]. *SC*: L.V. Jefferson. *PH*: Bydron Baker. *SD*: Herb Eicke. *Prod Mgr*: Hamilton Steele. *Tech Dir*: Bart Carre.

*Cast*: Buffalo Bill, Jr., Genee Boutell, Lafe McKee, Si Jenks, Boris Bullock, Bart Carre, Jack Evans, Marin Sais, Clyde McClary, Ken Brocker.

Planning to rid a locale of outlaws, a cowboy finds himself involved with a pretty young woman.

# Riding Speed

Superior Talking Pictures, 1934, 50 minutes.

*P*: Victor Adamson [Denver Dixon]. *D*: Jay Wilsey [Buffalo Bill, Jr.]. *SC*: Delores Booth. *ST*: Ella May Cook. *PH*: Bydron Baker. *ED*: Frances Burroughs.

*Cast*: Buffalo Bill, Jr. (Steve Funny), Joile Benet (Gypsy Vale), Bud Osborne (Bill Durkey), Lafe McKee (Dad Vale), Clyde McClary (Bill), Allen Holbrook (Roberts), Ernest Scott (Crooky), Delores Booth (Mrs. Roberts), Denver Dixon (Outlaw).

After thwarting an outlaw gang, Border Patrol agent Steve Funny (Buffalo Bill, Jr.) comes to the rescue of a wild-driving girl, Gypsy Vale (Joile Benet), who has overturned her car. Later at the ranch of the girl's father, Dad Vale (Lafe McKee), Steve enlists his aid in tracking down a gang of alien smugglers and he pretends to be a new hand hired by Vale. Ranch foreman Bill Durkey (Bud Osborne), actually the leader of the outlaws, is suspicious of Steve and he also wants Gypsy for himself. When the young woman gets stranded in a canyon, Steve tries to rescue her and both end up there when Steve's saddle strap breaks as they are being pulled out of the canyon by his horse.

Meanwhile Dad Vale fires Durkey who then knocks him out and robs the place and plans to burn down the homestead. Riding away Durkey spies Gypsy and Steve in the canyon and rescues the girl but leaves Steve there. One of Vale's ranch hands (Ernest Scott) manages to get Steve out of the canyon as Durkey and his gang plan to drive a group of Chinese across the border.

Returning to the ranch, Durkey sets the house on fire to cover his tracks but Steve arrives and saves Dad Vale and then corners the crooks, who hold Gypsy prisoner, in an abandoned house. Ramming the house with a wagon, Steve captures the gang, although Durkey escapes with Gypsy. Steve then overpowers Durkey and saves the girl he loves.

Dedicated to the riders of the U.S. Border Patrol, *Riding Speed* was allegedly directed by star Buffalo Bill, Jr., under his real name of Jay Wilsey. The film, however, appears to be just another in the series Victor Adamson (Denver Dixon) did at the time with both Buffalo Bill, Jr., and Buddy Roosevelt. His wife, Delores Booth, contributed the script and also made a cameo appearance as the unfaithful wife of a bandit who is romancing another outlaw. She pays with her life for her infidelity. The scenes of the two outlaws (Clyde McClary, Allen Holbrook) fighting over her were obviously filler to make up for a short running time.

One wonders how much of the movie, if any, was really directed by Buffalo Bill, Jr. Certainly the feature has the look of a Victor Adamson movie with its plodding direction, drawn out scenes and even a crew member stepping before the camera as the outlaw gang rides away from the hideout. Also the feature contains the usual hard-to-accept plot ploys such as the scene where Crooky (Ernest Scott), who has just been shot by the gang leader, has the strength to pull Buffalo Bill, Jr., out of a canyon with a rope. Later he is shown as an active participant in rounding up the outlaws, so his injury must have been slight indeed.

# The Adventures of Texas Jack

Security, 1935, 18 minutes.

*P*: Richard L. Bare. *D*: Denver Dixon [Victor Adamson]. *PH*: Bert Longnecker.

*Cast*: Wally Wales (Texas Jack), Al Mix [Denver Dixon] (Blister Sanderson), Buffalo Bill, Jr. (Bill Mayberry), Victoria Vinton (Lucy), Jack Evans (Steve Parsons), Duke R. Lee (Colonel Bodie), Bart Carre (Sheriff).

After bringing in prisoners, scouts Texas Jack (Wally Wales) and Blister Sanderson (Al Mix) are assigned to stop the Mayberry gang which has been robbing banks and express offices near the railroad. Mayberry (Buffalo Bill, Jr.) and his henchman hold up an express office, taking money from Lucy (Victoria Vinton) and her brother. Escaping, the outlaws stop Texas Jack and Blister and steal their horses. The two scouts recover their mounts and in his saddlebags Texas Jack finds money bags filled with washers. The two return the bags to the express office, and store owner Steve Parsons (Jack Evans) accuses them of being the robbers. Lucy, however, vindicates them only to have her brother arrested by the sheriff (Bart Carre) for the robbery. Upset at Jack for returning the bags that implicated her brother, Lucy plans to ride to the town of Truckee where she believes the robbers have shipped the gold they took. Parsons rides with her, and Texas Jack and Blister follow. Along the way Mayberry and his partner stop Parsons and Lucy, and he identifies the businessman as his boss. When Lucy tells Mayberry that Parsons doublecrossed him the two men fight and the girl rides away. The other outlaw pursues her but is captured by Texas Jack. The sheriff arrives with a posse and arrests Mayberry, whom Parsons has accused of the robbery. Blister arrives with the other outlaw and identifies Mayberry as a fellow undercover agent and Parsons escapes back to town. There he is caught trying to get away with the stolen gold and is arrested by Texas Jack. As Jack prepares to take Parsons back for trial he promises to return to Lucy.

Apparently intended as the first of a series to star Wally Wales and Victor Adamson, billed here as Al Mix, this western short is badly photographed and staged. Portions of it were shot silent and backed by the "William Tell Overture." Mostly long and medium shots, the movie was obviously done on a shoestring budget and in quick fashion; retakes are not evident. So bad it almost defies description, the movie is even worse than the tacky series of "Bud 'n' Ben" shorts that Imperial (q.v.) was issuing at the time. Of some interest is the fact *The Adventures of Texas Jack* was the first film project for Richard L. Bare, then a 25-year-old Carmel, California, theatre operator. In his book *The Film Director* (1971), Bare noted the movie was filmed as *The Double Cross* and he doubted it was ever released. Bare later created the "Joe McDoakes" short subjects starring George O'Hanlon that Warner Brothers released from 1942 to 1956. Bare also directed feature films like *Flaxy Martin* (1949), *The House Across the Street* (1949), *Shoot-Out at Medicine Bend* (1957) and *This Rebel Breed* (1960) but is probably best known as the director of the "Green Acres" television series (CBS-TV, 1965–71). Despite Bare's contention, *The Adventures of Texas Jack* apparently did get some limited release on the states' rights market, but it was Victor Adamson's only attempt at a short subject series in the sound era.

Lobby card for *The Rawhide Terror* (Security, 1935) picturing William Barrymore (Boris Bullock), Frances Morris, Tommy Bupp and William Desmond.

## Arizona Trails

Superior Talking Pictures, 1935.

*P*: Victor Adamson [Denver Dixon]. *D*: Alan James. *ST*: Tom Camden. *PH*: A.J. Fitzpatrick.

*Cast*: Bill Patton, Edna Aslin, Denver Dixon, Ed Carey, Tom Camden, Herman Hack, Ernest Scott, Fred Parker, Delmar Costello, Wallace Pindell.

In the small town of Red Rock, a cowboy tries to thwart crooks.

## The Rawhide Terror

Security, 1935, 46 minutes.

*P*: Victor Adamson. *D*: Bruce Mitchell & Jack Nelson. *SC*: Jack Nelson. *ST*: A.V. [Victor] Adamson. *PH*: A.J. Fitzpatrick & Burt Longnecker. *SD*: Cineglow System.

*Cast*: Art Mix (Al Blake), Edmond Cobb (Sheriff Luke), William Desmond (Tom Blake), William Barrymore [Boris Bullock] (Brent), Frances Morris (Betty Blake), George Holt (Gang Leader), Bill Patton (Ben), Herman Hack (Ed), Tommy Bupp (Jimmy Brent), Fred Parker (Deputy), Denver Dixon (Townsman); George Gyton, Ed Carey, Ernest Scott.

In the late 1890s renegade whites masquerade as Indians and molest settlers. Two young brothers witness the murder of their parents by a gang of these renegades, and one of the boys becomes mentally unhinged. Years later the raiders have become respectable citizens of Red Dog, a town plagued by a series of killings perpetrated by the mysterious Rawhide Terror. Sheriff Luke (Edmond Cobb) has been unable to bring in the killer despite the protests of the town's banker (George Holt), the one-time leader of the renegades. The sheriff believes the Terror's motives are in revenge for something done a decade before, but after trailing him a number of times to Ghost Mountain, he always loses the Terror's trail. At a nearby ranch, young Jimmy Brent (Tommy Bupp) comes for aid from brothers Al (Art Mix) and Tom Blake (William Desmond) and their sister Betty (Frances Morris), the sheriff's girl-friend. The boy has been beaten by his stepfather Brent (William Barrymore), and when Tom goes after the man he is shot. Al comes to his rescue but Tom is only grazed. The next day, however, Brent captures Tom and stakes him out in the sun to die. Tommy comes along and finds Tom but falls into a trap dug by Brent. Finally the boy manages to escape and sets Tom free. Meanwhile Al sees Brent and chases him. After a fight Al is left to die in a runaway wagon but manages to escape at the last minute. The sheriff arrives and finds both Tom and Al and then con-tinues to hunt the Rawhide Terror. In town the renegades, now the board of directors of the town's bank, hold a meeting and receive word from the Terror that he plans to kill them all. They follow him out of town, and he sets off T.N.T. which destroys the entire gang. The Terror then captures Betty, but the Sheriff and the Blake brothers give chase and the madman leaves the girl behind as Al shoots him. The sheriff then finds the mortally wounded Rawhide Terror and realizes they are brothers since they both have the same birthmark. The killer dies telling his brother he has avenged the death of their parents. The sheriff and Betty decide to go away together.

*The Rawhide Terror* represents a failed experiment in the mixing of two fairly distinct genres. Part western and part horror film, it is largely forgotten today. The title character is a maniac who predates the faceless killers of the cinema of the 1970s and 1980s. He wears a rawhide strip across his face and a sleeveless leather vest. His men-acing appearance is further accentuated by his maniacal laughter after he dis-poses of a victim. In one scene he even laughs fiendishly after killing a rat-tlesnake. The Rawhide Terror uses many methods to kill his victims, but his favorite seems to be staking them in the sun with a leather strip around their necks and letting them strangle to death as the sun's heat tightens the leather. Despite the scary villain, the movie is otherwise a typical Victor Adamson production—a choppy, rag-tag affair with a convoluted plot. Filled with excessive riding sequences, *The Rawhide Terror* is also sloppily made. (In one scene the mike's boom shadow is clearly in evidence.) Plot continuity is greatly hindered by inexplicable changes in character names. At one point Tommy Bupp's little boy is called Jimmy while later he is Tommy and, later still, Jimmy again. The same holds true for Edmond Cobb, who is first called Luke but at the finale has become Tim.

*The Rawhide Terror* does provide starring roles for three silent screen favorites, Art Mix, William Desmond and Edmond Cobb. This trio usually played villains in sound films. It is especially interesting to see Art Mix in a leading role. While he had little to do acting wise, he proved to be a fine horseman and was effective in fight sequences. Advertised as "An Art Mix Production," *The Rawhide Terror* was the final screen collaboration of Victor

Adamson and George Kesterson, who first played the Art Mix character in the mid–1920s after Adamson had abandoned the role to take up producing. Kesterson permanently adopted the screen moniker of Art Mix although he does not play that character in the feature.

While *The Rawhide Terror* carries a 1934 copyright date it apparently had no screenings until the next year.

## Desert Mesa

Security, 1936, 50 minutes.

*P-D*: Victor Adamson [Denver Dixon]. *SC*: Van Johnson. *PH*: A.J. Fitzpatrick. *SD*: Oscar Dowling. *Prod Mgr*: Robert Smith.

*Cast*: Tom Wynn [Wally West], Franklyn Farnum, Bill Patton, Lew Meehan, Tonya Beauford, Allen Greer, William McCall, Horace B. Carpenter, Delores Booth, Art James [Denver Dixon], Harry Keaton, Tex Miller.

A cowboy on the trail of the crook who swindled his father gets a job at a ranch plagued by raiders.

## The Mormon Conquest

Security National Picture Corporation, July 11, 1939, 50 minutes.

*P-D-SC*: Denver Dixon [Victor Adamson]. *AP*: H.J. "Jack" Cook. *PH*: Phil E. Cantonwine.

*Cast*: Tom Wynn [Wally West] (Santa Fe Chris Ferril), Dorothy McKinnon (Lucy Lane), William Wood (Willard Smith), Oscar Gahan (Jud Gunnison), Bonnie Chamberlain (Bonnie).

Late in 1938 Victor Adamson and his associate H.J. "Jack" Cook traveled to the southern Utah community of Kanab to scout locations for Adamson's screenplay *The Mormon Conquest*. There, in association with more than twenty local stockholders, they formed Security National Picture Corporation to produce the movie. At the time Adamson said George O'Brien and Monte Blue would star in the production, which was to be filmed in the Kanab area, where a studio was to be built. The plot was to revolve around the trek of the Mormons to southern Utah, the settlement of Kanab and the discovery of Zion Canyon by Nephi Johnson. "Although the story and some of the characters in the movie are fiction and the doings of the pioneers are portrayed under fictitious names, the theme of this featurette is founded in the early settlement of Kanab," Adamson told *Kane County Standard* weekly newspaper. Production began early in 1939 with filming at the Kanab studio (known as Utah's Hollywood), Robinson Canyon and Zion National Park. The production was finished in Hollywood and debuted in Kanab on July 11, 1939.

A Mormon wagon train led by Willard Smith (William Wood) crosses the Virgin River in southwestern Utah and is sighted by Apache Indians. Jud Gunnison (Oscar Gahan), a saloon owner in Kanab, hates the Mormons and plans to incite the Indians against them by killing a brave. When the Mormons make camp, Lucy Lane (Dorothy McKinnon) goes in search of rabbits and finds Santa Fe Chris Ferril (Tom Wynn) bending over the body of the dead Indian. The two are immediately taken prisoner by the Apaches, but Lucy is set free. That night Smith arrives at the Indian camp and convinces them Chris is innocent. Gunnison then kills more Indians but, in the process, loses his hat. Chris finds it and realizes who is behind the trouble. When the wagon train arrives in Kanab, orphan Bonnie (Bonnie Chamberlain) is kidnapped by Gunnison and locked in the back of his saloon. Chris corners Gunnison in his saloon as the Apaches arrive and burn the building. Chris is able to rescue Bonnie as Gunnison dies in the fire. The next day Chris tells Lucy that he loves her.

Kanab stockholders had hoped *The Mormon Conquest* would bring the movie business to Southern Utah. In reviewing the film the *Kane County Standard* noted it "was well received by large crowds of Kanab theatre goers"

and added, "*The Mormon Conquest* was written with a two-fold purpose, that of portraying the settlement of Kanab and to advertise the scenery in and around Zion national park and Kanab." Unfortunately, the picture remained obscure and apparently has been lost to the ages. More beneficial to the Southern Utah locale was the studio built by Adamson. It was used by other film companies that favored the area because of its wide variety of location scenery.

# Ajax Pictures

By the mid–1930s Hollywood's Poverty Row was at the height of operations, and in 1935 a new studio, Ajax Pictures, emerged, releasing the first of its eight features in January and the last in December. Half of the Ajax product consisted of Harry Carey westerns produced by William Berke and directed by Harry Fraser while Bernard B. Ray and Harry S. Webb's Reliable Pictures, not yet releasing its own product, made two Richard Talmadge starrers. The other two releases consisted of a David Sharpe vehicle and a comeback attempt by silent screen stars Pauline Starke and James Murray. None of these outings made much of a dent in the independent market, and Ajax went under after operating only one year.

Despite the sparsity of its releases, Ajax Pictures produced some memorable films. This is especially true of the Harry Carey westerns. By the 1930s Carey (who had been making oaters since 1910) was well into his fifties but he was still a stalwart hero, and the productions given him by William Berke were solid affairs with plots harkening back to the stark realism informing the William S. Hart westerns of the silent days. In fact, a couple of the films tended toward the sadistic, as noted by the branding scene in *Wild Mustang* and the whipping sequence in *Rustlers' Paradise*. The Carey films were also paced decently and action-filled with good acting by a stock company that appeared in all of the releases. Certainly the Harry Carey galloper quartet was the high point for Ajax.

Also popular in the action market were the two films Richard Talmadge did for Reliable productions. Talmadge had gained fame stunting for Douglas Fairbanks in the silent days and had begun to establish himself as a film star.

Sound, however, made a dent in Talmadge's career in that he was a mediocre actor at best with a somewhat high pitched voice. Thus his action antics were relegated to Poverty Row where he remained through the 1930s before going to the other side of the camera. The two Ajax releases Talmadge did for Reliable were passable, but plotwise they were little more than vehicles for an extended series of stunts performed by the star.

Rounding out the Ajax program were *Adventurous Knights* and *$20 a Week*. The former was scripted by David Sharpe, who starred in it along with former "Our Gang" alumni Mary Kornman and Mickey Daniels. It was a lame farce at best and no doubt one of the reasons Sharpe switched to character roles and stunt work, becoming one of the best stuntmen in the business. *$20 a Week* was a fragile item for Pauline Starke and James Murray, both of whom had fallen on hard times in the sound era. This society drama did nothing for their floundering careers.

With Harry Carey's *The Last of the Clintons*, Ajax folded at the end of 1935.

## $20 a Week

January 22, 1935, 80 minutes.

*P:* Burton King. *D:* Wesley Ford. *SC:* L.V. Jefferson. *ST:* Rob Eden. *PH:* Arthur Martinelli. *ED:* Fred Bain.

*Cast:* James Murray, Pauline Starke, Owen Lee, Dorothy Revier, William Worthington, Bryant Washburn, Gloria Gray, Bartlett (Bart) Carre, Andy Rice, Jr., Noran Hamilton, Paul Ellis, Bessie Farrell.

A wealthy young man is at odds with his family when he falls in love with a secretary.

## The Fighting Pilot

February 14, 1935, 56 minutes.

*P:* Bernard B. Ray. *AP:* Harry S. Webb. *D:* Noel Mason. *SC:* Ralph Cusamano. *PH:* Reggie Lyons & Frank Bender. *ED:* Holbrook N. Todd. *Rec:* Robert Pritchard.

*Cast:* Richard Talmadge (Hal Foster), Gertrude Messinger (Jean Reynolds), Robert Frazer (Cardigan), Eddie Davis (Berty), Victor Mace (Toughy), William Humphrey (F.S.

Reynolds), Rafael Storm (Robert R. Jones), Jack Cheatham (Barnes).

Richard Talmadge's films were noted for their endless action, and this Reliable production is no different. In less than one hour Talmadge engaged in scores of fights and liberated himself from many a precarious situation. Lots of aerial and stunt footage padded the production and among the highlights of the star's antics was a fight between two airplanes with Talmadge dropping from one plane into the other while in mid-air. There was also the usual leap from rooftop to rooftop and then into a moving car in one sequence. While most of these hazardous stunts were well patched by editing work, continuity problems often arose. One scene had the back of the star's pants split while taking a tumble from a speeding car, but for the rest of the movie, while he never changed wardrobe, the trousers were mysteriously mended.

The slim plot for all this action had businessman Robert Jones (Rafael Storm) being told by his boss to buy inventor Reynolds' (William Humph-

Richard Talmadge, Eddie Davis, Gertrude Messinger and William Humphrey in *The Fighting Pilot* (Ajax, 1935).

rey) new aircraft. But crook Cardigan (Robert Frazer) wants the plane and its plans for himself. He enlists Jones' aid in a crooked scheme to steal the plane after Reynolds refuses to sell his invention. Pilot Hal Foster (Richard Talmadge), who loves the inventor's daughter Jean (Gertrude Messinger), successfully tests the new plane and comes to the inventor's rescue when Cardigan and his thugs steal the plane and its blueprints. Foster and dopey pal Berty (Eddie Davis) trail the culprits to Chinatown where they have many close calls before Hal is finally captured by Cardigan's men. Berty, however, is able to rescue him and they eventually escape with the knowledge that Cardigan and Jones have hidden the plane at a remote desert airport. They go to retrieve the plane, called

Silver Wing, when Secret Service Agent Barnes (Jack Cheatham) arrives on the trail of Cardigan. Jean and her father fly with Barnes to the desert airport and arrive just as Hal captures the two crooks.

## Wagon Trail

April 9, 1935, 55 minutes.

*P:* William Berke. *D:* Harry Fraser. *SC:* Monroe Talbot. *PH:* Robert Cline. *ED:* Arthur A. Brooks. *SD:* Terry Kellum. *Asst Dir:* Harry Knight.

*Cast:* Harry Carey, Gertrude Messinger, Edward Norris, Earl Dwire, Roger Williams, Chuck Morrison, Chief Thundercloud, Francis Walker, Silver Tip Baker, Lew Meehan, Allen Greer, John Elliott, Dick Botiller, Sonny the Wonder Horse.

A lobby card for *Rustlers' Paradise* (Ajax, 1935).

Falsely accused of murder, a gambler is aided by his lawman father.

## Rustlers' Paradise

May 1, 1935, 61 minutes.
    *P:* William Berke. *D:* Harry Fraser. *SC:* Weston Edwards. *ST:* Monroe Talbot. *PH:* Robert Cline. *ED:* Arthur A. Brooks. *Sound:* Terry Kellum. *Asst Dir:* William Strohbach.
    *Cast:* Harry Carey (Cheyenne Kincaid), Gertrude Messinger (Connie), Edmund Cobb (Larry Martin), Carmen Bailey (Dolores Romero), Theodore Lorch (El Diablo/Rance Kimbell), Roger Williams (Todd), Chuck Morrison (Henchman), Allen Greer (Antonio), Slim Whitaker (Senor Romero), Sonny the Wonder Horse (Himself).
    During 1935 Ajax Pictures issued

eight films, half of them starring veteran actor Harry Carey, who had been making westerns since 1910. *Rustlers' Paradise* was the fourth of the eight releases, and in many ways it was a throwback to the type of movie Harry Carey did in the silent era. The feature is an austere affair with Carey as an avenging-angel type who takes a terrible revenge on the man who stole his wife and daughter. In this respect the plot borrows somewhat from Edgar G. Ulmer's *The Black Cat,* issued the year before by Universal. A greater similarity exists between the two films in that in both features a man promises to get even with his nemesis by skinning him alive. Here a rather sadistic scene is included at the finale in which Harry Carey flays villain Theodore Lorch with a whip while forcing a confession out of him. On a lighter side, the movie contains a most amusing scene where the tough outlaws are thwarted in their attempt to overtake a hacienda by a pretty senorita wielding a shotgun. Also, usual cowboy villain Slim Whitaker is nicely cast here as a Mexican ranch owner at odds with the outlaws who want to steal his land. In the 1940s *Rustlers' Paradise* was reissued theatrically by Astor Pictures.

Outlaw El Diabo (Theodore Lorch) and his gang is running settlers off their land. On one of their raids they meet Cheyenne Kincaid (Harry Carey), who claims to be on the run from the law. Cheyenne joins up with the outlaws and finds that a young girl Connie (Gertrude Messinger) lives with them at their hideout at Rustlers' Paradise. When El Diablo captures landowner Romero (Slim Whitaker) and tries to torture him in order to obtain his land grants, Cheyenne stops him and he and Romero escape. Later Cheyenne returns to the hideout to get Connie, whom he discovers is really his daughter, as years before his wife ran off with Rance Kimbell, who is really El Diablo. The gang returns and captures Kincaid but when they leave to raid the Romero ranch, Kincaid manages to escape and he takes Connie with him. They ride to Romero's and warn him of the impending raid and Larry Martin (Edmond Cobb), the boyfriend of Romero's daughter Delores (Carmen Bailey), rides to a nearby hacienda to get help. El Diablo and his gang attack the ranch but the vaqueros arrive and the gang flees, with Cheyenne trailing El Diablo, whom he captures. He takes the bad man back to his hideout, ties him up, and flays him with a whip, forcing him to confess that he killed Kincaid's wife and kept Connie a prisoner. The gang arrives but

is captured by Cheyenne and the vaqueros. Cheyenne and Connie then leave for a new life together.

## Adventurous Knights

June 7, 1935, 56 minutes.

*P:* William Berke. *D-SC:* C. Edward Roberts. *ST:* David Sharpe. *PH:* Robert Cline. *ED:* Arthur A. Brooks. *Mus:* Lee Zahler. *SD:* Karl Zindt. *Prod Mgr:* Leslie Simmonds.

*Cast:* David Sharpe, Mary Kornman, Gertrude Messinger, Mickey Daniels.

A young American athlete learns he is actually the heir to the throne of Transylvania. Advertised as the first of six "Our Young Friends" series features.

## Now or Never

July 9, 1935, 63 minutes.

*P-D:* Bernard B. Ray. *AP:* Harry S. Webb. *SC:* C.C. Church. *PH:* J. Henry Kruse. *ED:* Fred Bain. *Prod Mgr:* Leon Metz.

*Cast:* Richard Talmadge, Janet Chandler, Robert Walker, Eddie Davis, Otto Metzetti, Thomas Ricketts, Victor Metz.

A man hired as the double of a crooked jewelry broker finds himself in a quandry when the crook is murdered and he must fight his killers as well as romance the late jeweler's fiancée.

TV title: *Tearing Into Trouble.*

## Wild Mustang

October 22, 1935, 61 minutes.

*P:* William Berke. *D:* Harry Fraser. *SC:* Weston Edwards. *ST:* Monroe Talbot. *PH:* Robert Cline. *ED:* Arthur A. Brooks. *SD:* Corson Jowett. *Asst Dir:* Harry Knight.

*Cast:* Harry Carey, Barbara Fritchie, Del Gordon, Cathryn Johns,

Robert Kortman, George Chesebro, Chuck Morrison, Dick Botiller, George Morrell, Milburn Morante, Francis Walker, Budd Buster, Roger Williams, Phil Dunham, Sonny the Wonder Horse.

An old-time lawman comes to the aid of a young man forced to ride with outlaws.

**Last of the Clintons**

November 12, 1935, 59 minutes.

*P:* William Berke. *D:* Harry Fraser. *SC:* Weston Edwards. *ST:* Monroe Talbot. *PH:* Robert Cline. *ED:* Arthur A. Brooks. *SD:* Cliff Ruberg. *Asst Dir:* William Nolte.

*Cast:* Harry Carey, Betty Mack, Del Gordon, Ruth Findlay, Victor Potel, Earl Dwire, Tom London, Charles "Slim" Whitaker, Lafe Mc-Kee, Allen Greer, William McCall, Lew Meehan, Barney Beasley, Tex Palmer, Francis Walker, Sonny the Wonder Horse.

A range detective takes on the guise of an outlaw to bring in a gang of raiders.

# Allied Pictures Corporation

Independent producer M.H. "Max" Hoffman (1881–1937) had a varied career as a language instructor, painter, singer and lawyer before entering the movie business around 1910. For a time he was general manager of Universal Studios, but by the mid–1920s he was a producer at Tru-Art on films like *Drums of Jeopardy* (1923) and *Daring Love* (1924). By 1927 he was heading Tiffany Pictures, and in 1930 he started Liberty Pictures with the solo effort *Ex-Flame*. In 1931 he formed Allied Pictures Corporation, and in the next three years he produced 22 features for his company, half of them Hoot Gibson westerns. His son Max Hoffman, Jr., served as associate producer and was also often listed as the films' presenter. Hoffman used a stock company of production people that included cameramen Harry Neuman and Tom Galligan, editor Mildred Johnston and directors Albert Ray, George Melford and Otto Brower. Even while associated with Allied, Hoffman also produced two features for Monogram, *The Thirteenth Guest* (1932) and *West of Singapore* (1933). Following the demise of Allied in 1934, Hoffman reactivated Liberty Pictures (q.v.), producing films under that banner from 1934 to 1936.

Evidently M.H. Hoffman was able to launch Allied on the basis of having signed popular cowboy star Hoot Gibson, who had been let go at Universal in an economy move by Carl Laemmle and his son. Gibson still retained a vast popularity among western film fans, and Hoffman no doubt planned to use the profits from the low-budget Gibson oaters to finance his real interest, the filming of famous literary properties. Allied was launched in the spring of 1931 with the Hoot Gibson western *Clearing the Range*, which costarred Gibson's then-wife Sally Eilers, who would soon find stardom at Fox in *Bad Girl* (1931). Two more Gibson vehicles, *Wild Horse* and *Hard Hombre*, filled out the year for Allied. In 1932 Hoffman would make five more Gibson starrers, but of more prestige value were the films made from literary classics. In quick order he starred Lew Cody in *File 113* and *A Parisian Romance*, the former from Emile Gaboriau's detective story and the latter from Octave Feuillet's play. There was also a modern-day version of William Makepeace Thackeray's *Vanity Fair* with Myrna Loy and Conway Tearle. The period costumes were also dropped, apparently to save money, when Gustave Flaubert's *Madame Bovary* became *Unholy Love*, set in modern-day Rye, New York. In 1932 Hoffman was also able to obtain the services of Monte Blue, who starred in *The Stoker*. He also teamed Monte Blue with Lila Lee for two films: *Officer 13* (which saw release late in 1932 and playdates well into the next year) and *The Intruder* (1933). Apparently Hoffman planned a whole series with Monte Blue as several titles were announced but never filmed. Other planned Monte Blue films included *The Nestors* and *Valley of Adventure*. Lila Lee did make *The Iron Master* with Reginald Denny in 1933, and that year also saw Allied's best-known release, *A Shriek in the Night*, starring Ginger Rogers and Lyle Talbot, whom Hoffman had teamed earlier in the big moneymaker *The Thirteenth Guest* (1932) for Monogram.

Three Hoot Gibson films were released in 1933, but relations between producer and star had faded. Carl Laemmle wanted Hooter back at Universal, but Hoffman refused to release him from his Allied contract. Litigation followed, which proved costly to the cowboy star and contributed further to keeping him off the screen. Hoffman issued *One Year Later* late in 1933, but this interesting tale told in flashback proved to be the company's penultimate entry followed by *Picture Brides* in 1934. Hoffman re-formed Liberty Pictures, and Hoot Gibson found himself off the screen for nearly two years before obtaining costarring roles at RKO in *Powdersmoke Range* (1935) and *The Last Outlaw* (1936) and a brief series for Walter Futter's Diversion Pictures (q.v.) at the same time.

While Allied Pictures Corporation did not have a lengthy run in the independent film market of the 1930s, it produced a good, steady product, and exhibitors apparently had little qualms about showing Allied films. With Hoot Gibson for the western trade and established names like Monte Blue, Lew Cody, Lila Lee, Myrna Loy, Reginald Denny, Marian Marsh and H.B. Warner for general audiences, Allied had a saleable product. More releases like *A Shriek in the Night* might well have stabilized Allied for a long run in the independent field, but the squabble with Hoot Gibson prompted M.H. Hoffman to abandon his dependable western income for contemporary films under the Liberty label. Ironically after folding Liberty in 1936, Hoffman went back to the "B" western field, producing the Ken Maynard starrers *Boots of Destiny* and *Trailin' Trouble* for Grand National Pictures before his death in 1937.

# Clearing the Range

April 1, 1931, 61 minutes.

*P:* M.H. Hoffman, Jr. *D:* Otto Brower. *SC:* Jack Natteford. *ST:* Jack Cunningham. *PH:* Ernest Miller. *ED:* Mildred Johnston. *SD:* L.E. Tope.

*Cast:* Hoot Gibson, Sally Eilers, Hooper Atchley, George Mendoza, Robert Homans, Eve Grippon, Maston Williams, Edward Piel, Jack Byron, Edward Hearn, Jim Fremont, Ben Corbett, Jim Corey.

A cowboy pretends to be a coward to find out who murdered his brother.

# Wild Horse

August 2, 1931, 67 minutes.

*P:* M.H. Hoffman. *D:* Richard Thorpe & Sidney Algier. *SC:* Jack Natteford. *ST:* Peter B. Kyne. *PH:* Ernest Miller. *ED:* Mildred Johnston. *Rec:* L.E. Tope.

*Cast:* Hoot Gibson (Jim Wright), Alberta Vaughn (Alice Hall), Stepin Fetchit (Stepin), Neal Hart (Hank Howard), Edmund Cobb (Gil Davis), Skeeter Bill Robbins (Skeeter Burke), George Bunny (Col. Ben Hall), Edward Peil (Sheriff), Joe Rickson (Deputy), Fred Gilman (Drunk), Hank Bell, Slim Whitaker, Glenn Strange, Pete Morrison, Silvertip Baker, Tom Smith (Cowboys).

Cowpokes Jim Wright (Hoot Gibson) and Skeeter Burke (Skeeter Bill Robbins) are hired to work at Col. Ben Hall's (George Bunny) Rodeo Ranch. They capture "The Devil Horse" which has been eluding Hall's wranglers, but later rival Gil Davis (Edmund Cobb) kills Skeeter and steals the horse, claiming he captured it himself. Jim is blamed for Skeeter's murder, but he manages to escape when the sheriff (Edward Peil) is ambushed by wanted outlaw Hank Howard (Neal Hart), who witnessed Skeeter's shooting. Colonel Hall and his daugher Alice (Alberta Vaughn) agree to help Jim get the goods on Davis after Jim is injured saving Alice from Silver Devil, the captured horse. At the colonel's rodeo Davis spots Jim and runs away. Jim takes his place and rides Silver Devil but is then arrested. The sheriff, however, allows Jim to escape and he heads to wild horse country to capture Davis. There Davis ambushes and robs Hank Howard, and when the sheriff and the posse find Howard he rides with them to get Davis. The latter, however, is roped by Jim, and when the law arrives Howard tells about seeing Skeeter murdered. Jim is thus exonerated. Later Jim tames Silver Devil and gives him as a present to his new love, Alice.

The second of eleven series westerns Hoot Gibson did for Allied, *Wild Horse* is one of the best of the lot and certainly an improvement over the opener, *Clearing the Range*. The film's worst drawbacks are its lack of music and too many plot twists, but on the plus side is the fact that the movie is paced well and features a pleasing cast. Certainly an asset is the appearance of Stepin Fetchit as a ranch hand who has considerable troubles with a contrary mule. In an amusing scene, Stepin arrives at the local jail to give an incarcerated Hoot some lunch, but the sheriff and his deputy discover the wrapping contains a blow torch! A frisking of Stepin also reveals such items as a saw, chisel and a file. During the 1940s *Wild Horse* was reissued theatrically by Astor as *Silver Devil*.

# Hard Hombre

September 20, 1931, 65 minutes.

*P:* M.H. Hoffman, Jr. *D:* Otto

Brower. *SC-ST:* Jack Natteford. *PH:* Harry Neuman. *ED:* Mildred Johnston. *SD:* L.E. Tope.

*Cast:* Hoot Gibson, Lina Basquette, Skeeter Bill Robbins, Mathilda Comont, Jesse Arnold, Raymond Nye, Christian Frank, Jack Byron, Frank Winkelman, Fernando Galvez, Rosa Gore, Bob Burns, Glenn Strange, Tiny Sanford, Florence Lawrence, Fred Burns, Clare Hunt.

When thieves try to take over a woman's ranch, her son comes to her rescue.

## Local Bad Man

January 15, 1932, 59 minutes.

*P:* M.H. Hoffman, Jr. *D:* Otto Brower. *SC:* Philip White. *ST:* Peter B. Kyne. *PH:* Harry Neuman & Tom Galligan. *ED:* Mildred Johnston. *SD:* L.E. Tope. *Prod Mgr:* Sidney Algier.

*Cast:* Hoot Gibson, Sally Eilers, Hooper Atchley, Edward Peil, Edward Hearn, Skeeter Bill Robbins, Jack Clifford, Milt Brown, Bud Osborne, Lew Meehan.

Two crooked businessmen try to blame an employee for their express shipment holdups.

## The Gay Buckaroo

January 17, 1932, 61 minutes.

*P:* M.H. Hoffman, Jr. *D:* Phil Rosen. *SC:* Philip White. *PH:* Harry Neuman. *ED:* Mildred Johnston. *SD:* L.E. Tope.

*Cast:* Hoot Gibson, Merna Kennedy, Roy D'Arcy, Edward Peil, Charles King, Lafe McKee, Sidney de Grey, Lafe McKee, The Hoot Gibson Cowboys, Skeeter Bill Robbins.

A cowboy vies with a crooked gambler for the affections of a young lady.

## Spirit of the West

March 1, 1932, 62 minutes.

*P:* M.H. Hoffman, Jr. *D:* Otto Brower. *SC:* Philip White. *ST:* Jack Natteford. *PH:* Harry Neuman & Tom Galligan. *ED:* Mildred Johnston. *SD:* L.E. Tope. *Prod Mgr:* Sidney Algier.

*Cast:* Hoot Gibson, Doris Hill, Hooper Atchley, Al Bridge, Lafe McKee, George Mendoza, Charles Brinley, Walter Perry, Tiny Sanford, Hank Bell, Gordon DeMain, Tex Palmer, Lucio Villegas.

A rodeo performer pretends to be slow-thinking in order to prove his brother did not murder his ranchowner boss.

## Vanity Fair

May 8, 1932, 67 minutes.

*P-D:* Chester M. Franklin. *AP:* M.H. Hoffman. *SC:* F. Hugh Herbert, from the novel by William Makepeace Thackeray. *PH:* Harry Neumann & Tom Galligan. *ED:* Mildred Johnston. *Rec:* L.E. Tope. *Asst Dir:* Wilbur McCaugh.

*Cast:* Myrna Loy (Becky Sharp), Conway Tearle (Rawden Crowley), Barbara Kent (Amelia Sedley), Walter Byron (Dobbin), Anthony Bushell (George Osborne), Billy Bevan (Joseph Sedley), Montagu Love (The Marquis), Herbert Bunston (Mr. Sedley), Mary Forbes (Mrs. Sedley), Lionel Belmore (Sir Pitt Crowley), Lillyan Irene (Polly).

Wealthy and kind-hearted Amelia Sedley (Barbara Kent) brings her friend Becky Sharp (Myrna Loy) home for the Christmas holidays, and Becky makes a play for Amelia's older brother Joseph (Billy Bevan), who has been game hunting in India. When she tries to get Joseph to marry her, he runs away to Scotland and Becky begins making eyes at Amelia's fiancée George Osborne (Anthony Bushell). The snobbish Sedleys turn Becky out, and she takes a job as a governess to the elderly but lecherous Sir Pitt Crowley (Lionel Belmore). She also gains the attentions of his oldest son, Rawden (Conway Tearle). Sir Pitt's invalid wife dies, and he proposes to Becky but finds out she has married Rawden. He disowns them both. To make ends meet, the newlyweds cheat at bridge with their society friends, and Becky secretly has an affair with George, now married to Amelia. During a fox hunt at the Osborne estate George falls from a horse and is killed. Becky gets Rawden the job of administering his estate, but the latter is arrested for writing bad checks. When Rawden finds out Becky has had an affair with an elderly marquis (Montagu Love), he throws her out and she again takes up with Joseph Sedley, now broke and living off his sister who is being romanced by her old boyfriend Dobbin (Walter Byron). Becky also makes a play for Dobbin but he rejects her. She tells Amelia the truth about George as Becky and Joseph are forced to live in a hovel. Finally Joseph too leaves Becky who is no longer desirable.

Allied's 1932 adaptation of William Thackeray's expansive novel takes its place in a fairly extensive line of celluloid adaptations. Helen Gardner had played the character of Becky Sharp in the initial screen version of *Vanity Fair* for Vitagraph in 1911, and four years later the aging Mrs. Fiske essayed the role at Edison. In 1923 Mabel Ballin played Becky in a version issued by Goldwyn, and three years after the Allied venture, Miriam Hopkins earned an Academy Award nomination for her role as *Becky Sharp* at RKO. Although modestly budgeted, Allied's

modern-dress version is a surprisingly good, compact retelling of the Thackeray tale with Chester M. Franklin's smooth direction moving the picture along at a good clip. Myrna Loy shines as Becky Sharp, making the most of her exotic good looks in projecting the sexual magnetism of the protagonist. The supporting cast is fine, too, especially Conway Tearle as the weak-willed man who loves and marries her, and silent screen comedian Billy Bevan as the society chap who first rejects Becky and then lets her drag him down. The rest of the cast is good as well, and despite its modern trappings, the movie retains the nineteenth-century flavor of Thackeray's novel. Of the scores of movies made on Hollywood's Poverty Row in the 1930s, *Vanity Fair* is one of the best and one of the most unjustly neglected.

## Unholy Love

June 1, 1932, 77 minutes.

*P:* M.H. Hoffman. *AP:* M.H. Hoffman, Jr. *D:* Albert Ray. *SC:* Frances Hyland, from the novel *Madame Bovary* by Gustave Flaubert. *PH:* Harry Neuman & Tom Galligan. *ED:* Mildred Johnston. *SD:* A.F. Blinn. *Mus:* Abe Meyer. *Prod Mgr:* Sidney Algier. *Asst Dir:* Gene Anderson.

*Cast:* H.B. Warner, Lila Lee, Beryl Mercer, Joyce Compton, Lyle Talbot, Ivan Lebedeff, Jason Robards, Kathlyn Williams, Frances Rich, Richard Carlyle.

A self-centered young man's father and fiancée try to save him from a selfish flirt.

## A Man's Land

June 11, 1932, 65 minutes.

*P:* M.H. Hoffman, Jr. *D:* Phil Rosen. *SC:* Adele Buffington. *PH:*

**Billy Bevan and Myrna Loy in *Vanity Fair* (Allied, 1932).**

Harry Neuman & Tom Galligan. *SD:* L.E. Tope. *ED:* Mildred Johnston.

*Cast:* Hoot Gibson, Marion Shilling, Ethel Wales, Robert Ellis, Charles King, Bill Nye, Skeeter Bill Robbins, Al Bridge, Hal Burney, Merrill McCormick, Slim Whitaker, Charles K. French, Fred Gilman, Bud Osborne, Hank Bell, Frank Ellis.

Cattle thieves raid a ranch just inherited by its foreman and a young woman.

## The Stoker

June 15, 1932, 70 minutes.

*P:* M.H. Hoffman. *AP:* M.H. Hoffman, Jr. *D:* Chester M. Franklin. *SC:* F. Hugh Herbert. *ST:* Peter B. Kyne. *PH:* Harry Neuman & Tom Galligan. *ED:* Mildred Johnston. *SD:* L.E. Tope. *Prod Mgr:* Sidney Algier.

*Cast:* Monte Blue, Dorothy Burgess, Noah Beery, Natalie Moorhead, Richard Tucker, Charles Stevens, Clarence Geldert, Harry Vejar, Chris-Pin Martin.

On a Nicaraguan coffee plantation, a man whose wife has deserted him saves a girl from an evil bandit.

## The Boiling Point

July 15, 1932, 70 minutes.

*P:* M.H. Hoffman, Jr. *D:* George Melford. *SC:* Donald W. Lee. *PH:* Harry Neuman & Tom Galligan. *SD:* L.E. Tope. *ED:* Mildred Johnston.

*Cast:* Hoot Gibson, Helen Foster, Wheeler Oakman, Skeeter Bill Robbins, Lafe McKee, Billy Bletcher, Tom London, William Nye, George Hayes, Charles Bailey, Hattie McDaniel, Frank Ellis, Lew Meehan, Art Mix,

Merrill McCormack, Bob Burns, Artie Ortego.

To save his inheritance, a young man is sent to a ranch to help control his temper.

## The Cowboy Counsellor

October 15, 1932, 62 minutes.

*P:* M.H. Hoffman, Jr. *D:* George Melford. *SC:* Jack Natteford. *PH:* Harry Neuman & Tom Galligan. *ED:* Mildred Johnston. *SD:* L.E. Tope.

*Cast:* Hoot Gibson, Sheila Mannors, Skeeter Bill Robbins, Bobby Nelson, Fred Gilman, Jack Rutherford, Alan Bridge, William Humphrey, Gordon DeMain, William M. (Merrill) McCormack, Sam Allen, Frank Ellis, Slim Whitaker.

A frontier lawyer works to bring an outlaw gang to justice.

## A Parisian Romance

October 18, 1932, 76 minutes.

*P:* M.H. Hoffman. *AP:* M.H. Hoffman, Jr. *D:* Chester M. Franklin. *SC:* F. Hugh Herbert, from the play by Octave Feuillet. *PH:* Harry Neuman & Tom Galligan. *ED:* Mildred Johnston. *SD:* A.F. Blinn.

*Cast:* Lew Cody, Marion Shilling, Gilbert Roland, Joyce Compton, Yola D'Avril, Nicholas Soussanin, George Lewis, Luis Alberni, James Eagles, Paul Porcasi, Helen Jerome Eddy, Nadine Dore, Bryant Washburn.

A rake in Paris loves a variety of women but finally falls for the girl of his dreams.

## Officer 13

December 15, 1932, 62 minutes.

*P:* M.H. Hoffman. *D:* George Melford. *SC:* Frances Hyland. *ST:* Paul Edwards. *PH:* Harry Neuman & Tom Galligan. *ED:* Leete Brown.

*Cast:* Monte Blue, Lila Lee, Seena Owen, Charles Delaney, Robert Ellis, Frances Rich, Joseph Girard, Jackie Searle, Mickey (Rooney) McGuire, Lloyd Ingraham, Florence Roberts, George Humbert, Dot Meyberg, Charles O'Malley, Alan Cavan, Edward Cooper.

A police officer brings in a woman charged with manslaughter, but he falls in love with her.

## File 113

January 5, 1933, 63 minutes.

*P:* M.H. Hoffman. *AP:* M.H. Hoffman, Jr. *D:* Chester M. Franklin. *SC:* John Francis (Jack) Natteford, from the story by Emile Gaboriau. *PH:* Harry Neuman & Tom Galligan. *SD:* L.E. Tope. *Asst Dir:* Wilbur McGaugh.

*Cast:* Lew Cody, Mary Nolan, William Collier, Jr., Clara Kimball Young, June Clyde, George E. Stone, Roy D'Arcy, Herbert Bunston, Irving Bacon, Crauford Kent, Harry Cording.

A Parisian law enforcer solves a series of crimes, including blackmail and robbery.

## The Iron Master

February 4, 1933, 64 minutes.

*P:* M.H. Hoffman, Jr. *D:* Chester M. Franklin. *SC:* Adele Buffington, from the novel and play by George Ohnet. *PH:* Harry Neuman & Tom Galligan. *ED:* Mildred Johnston. *SD:* Farrell Redd. *Prod Mgr:* Sidney Algier.

*Cast:* Reginald Denny, Lila Lee, J. Farrell MacDonald, Esther Howard, William Janney, Virginia Sale, Richard Tucker, Astrid Allwyn, Tom London, Nola Luxford, Otto Hoffman, Freddie Frederick, Ronnie Cosbey.

A wealthy iron-works owner dies and leaves his foreman in charge of his estate, much to the chagrin of his selfish heirs.

## The Intruder

March 13, 1933, 66 minutes.
P: M.H. Hoffman. AP: M.H. Hoffman, Jr. D: Albert Ray. SC: Frances Hyland. PH: Harry Neuman & Tom Galligan. ED: Mildred Johnston. Mus: Abe Meyer.

Cast: Monte Blue, Lila Lee, Gwen Lee, Arthur Houseman, Sidney Bracey, Mischa Auer, Harry Cording, William B. Davidson, Wilfred Lucas, Lynton Brent, Jack Beck, Alan Cavan.

After being shipwrecked on a tropical isle, the passengers are stalked by a mad killer.

## The Eleventh Commandment

March 25, 1933, 68 minutes.
P: M.H. Hoffman. AP: M.H. Hoffman, Jr. D: George Melford. SC: Adele Buffington & Kurt Kempler, from The Pillory by Brandon Fleming. PH: Harry Neuman. ED: Mildred Johnston. AD: Harold MacArthur. Mus: Abe Meyer.

Cast: Marian Marsh (Corinne Ross), Theodore Von Eltz (Wayne Winters), Alan Hale (Max Stager), Marie Prevost (Tessie Florin), Gloria Shea (Nina Ross), Arthur Hoyt (Charles Moore), William V. Mong (John Ross), Lee Moran (Jerry Trent), Ethel Wales (Mabel Moore), Lyman Williams (Steve).

New York society spinster Annie Bedell dies, leaving an estate of $50 million, which is claimed by her attorney John Ross (William V. Mong) since there are no apparent heirs. In Heidelberg, knife-thrower Max Stager (Alan Hale) reads the story of Annie's death and realizes she is the wife he deserted long ago. In his act he kills his

nagging mate and makes plans to claim the fortune through the daughter he also deserted. Meanwhile Ross' partner Wayne Winters (Theodore Von Eltz), who loves Ross' older daughter Corinne (Marian Marsh), has been willed the Bedell house and Ross terminates their partnership. To get even, Wayne sets up a couple of false claimants to the estate, hooker Tessie Florin (Marie Prevost) and Peter Ross, who is really deceased and is impersonated by his brother Charlie (Arthury Hoyt), who has embezzled money from the bank where he works. By these claimants, Wayne hopes to break Ross' hold on the will. Corinne finds out that her younger sister Nina (Gloria Shea) is really Annie Bedell's daughter, who had been entrusted to Ross' care as an infant, and she is the rightful inheritor of the estate. When Stager arrives at the Bedell mansion, Winters decides to use him to get Ross out of the way but Corinne tries to persuade him to drop the entire matter. Wayne steals Stager's proof of marriage and takes it to Ross, trying to work out a deal, but Stager finds out and arrives at Ross' home. He attempts to knife Wayne but the latter shoots him. Corinne then destroys the proof of the marriage of Annie Bedell and Stager, saying she is really their daughter. Thus Nina is free to marry her society beau Jerry Trent (Lee Moran), Ross inherits the estate with the understanding it will be given to Nina, and Wayne and Corinne are reconciled.

"Thou Shall Not Be Caught" is the Eleventh Commandment referred to in the title of this programmer, which continued producer M.H. Hoffman's penchant for adapting the classics to the screen in modern-day versions. Unfortunately, this predictable drama has little to offer. Despite good direction by George Melford, the plot is so hackneyed that little entertainment value is offered other than offbeat characterizations by Alan Hale as the sadistic and none-too-bright knife-thrower, Arthur Hoyt and Ethel Wales as the scheming couple, and one-time Mack Sennett bathing beauty Marie Prevost as floozie Tessie Florin (perhaps the source of Raymond Chandler's character Jessie Florian in *Farewell, My Lovely* [1941]). Few of the characters in *The Eleventh Commandment* are truly likable until the atonement when most take a sudden turn for the good. Even then, however, a terrible lie is left intact, allowing the "hero" to get away with theft and murder, although the latter could be called self-defense.

## The Dude Bandit

May 1, 1933, 62 minutes.
*P:* M.H. Hoffman, Jr. *D:* George Melford. *SC:* Jack Natteford. *PH:* Harry Neuman & Tom Galligan. *ED:* Mildred Johnston. *SD:* L.E. Tope. *Prod Mgr:* Sidney Algier. *AD:* Gene Hornbostel.

*Cast:* Hoot Gibson, Gloria Shea, Skeeter Bill Robbins, Hooper Atchley, Neal Hart, Lafe McKee, Gordon DeMain, Fred Burns, Fred Gilman, George Morrell, Art Mix, Merrill McCormack, Hank Bell, Horace B. Carpenter, Pete Morrison, Blackie Whiteford, Frank Ellis, Charles Brinley, Charles King, Slim Whitaker, Bill Gillis.

Pretending to be a dimwit, a cowboy tries to find out who killed his pal.

## A Shriek in the Night

July 22, 1933, 70 minutes.
*P:* M.H. Hoffman. *D:* Albert Ray. *SC:* Frances Hyland. *ST:* Kurt Kemplar. *PH:* Harry Neumann & Tom Galligan. *ED:* Leete Brown. *Mus:* Abe Meyer. *Rec:* Homer C. Ellmaker. *Prod Mgr:* Sidney Algier. *AD:* Gene Hornbostel.

*Cast:* Ginger Rogers (Pat Morgan), Lyle Talbot (Ted Rand), Arthur Hoyt (Wilfred), Harvey Clark (Pete), Purnell Pratt (Inspector Russell), Lillian Harmer (Augusta), Maurice Black (Martini), Louise Beavers (Maid), Clarence Wilson (Perkins).

At the Harker Apartments a cry is heard in the night, and when a body is found on the pavement in front of the building, the corpse is identified as Mr. Harker by the janitor Pete (Harvey Clark). Inspector Russell (Purnell Pratt) and his secretary, Wilfred (Arthur Hoyt), learn that Harker resided on the top floor of the building with his secretary, pretty Pat Morgan (Ginger Rogers) and a maid (Lillian Harmer). Reporter Ted Rand (Lyle Talbot) uses the ruse of a borrowed police badge to enter the crime scene and sees Pat, his estranged girlfriend and a reporter for a rival newspaper. He overhears Pat phoning in the story to her editor. He steals it and ends up getting her fired. With Russell's okay, Pat stays on at the apartment to close out Harker's affairs, and she also continues to investigate his murder since the head man received a card in the mail reading "You will hear it" accompanied by a picture of a coiled snake. The same card is found beside the body of a woman murdered in a nearby apartment, and the suspect, her husband, is found drowned in a river. Pat learns the seemingly respectable Harker, whose past she was investigating when he was killed, was in cahoots with gangster Martini (Maurice Black), and when a man is found murdered in the hoodlum's apartment with the same card by his body, Martini is arrested. In the next day's mail Pat also gets one of the cards and decides to vacate the premises when she is captured by the killer and almost incinerated before a suspicious Wilfred comes to her rescue. Pat, Ted and Russell deduce the killer used gas fed through radiator pipes to kill his victims, and Pat and Ted are reunited romantically.

Filmed at Western Service Studios, *A Shriek in the Night* was producer M.H. Hoffman's followup to his highly successful *The Thirteenth Guest*, which he had done for Monogram the previous year. Reuniting stars Ginger Rogers and Lyle Talbot with the same production team, Hoffman made a similar thriller, but this time he kept it for release through his own Allied exchanges. The result is an entertaining mystery-comedy slightly less effective than its predecessor but still a viable product which greatly benefitted from its tongue-in-cheek attitude and the chemistry between the two principals. Ginger Rogers, in fact, is excellent in the lead, and Lyle Talbot is just right as the flippant reporter who loves her. The supporting cast, while small, is also very good, especially Purnell Pratt as the seasoned detective, Lillian Harmer as the dingbat maid, Louise Beavers as another addled maid, and Arthur Hoyt as the seemingly wimpy secretary of the inspector. It is Hoyt who delivers the priceless line, "It must be pleasant having such a secretary living on the premises" when he learns that the heroine resided with the murder victim. The movie's greatest deficit is the fact that the identity of the killer is revealed too early in the proceedings. An added mystery element of having the killer concealed by shadows would have heightened the effect and added to the film's entertainment value.

## The Fighting Parson

August 2, 1933, 61 minutes.

*P:* M.H. Hoffman, Jr. *D:* Harry Fraser. *SC:* Edward Weston. *PH:* Harry Neuman. *ED:* Mildred Johnston. *SD:* Dave Stoner. *Prod Mgr:* Ray Culley. *AD:* Gene Hornbostel.

*Cast:* Hoot Gibson, Marceline Day, Robert Frazer, Stanley Blystone, Skeeter Bill Robbins, Ethel Wales, Phil Dunham, Jules Cowles, Charles King, Frank Nelson, Tex Palmer.

To stop crooks who control a town, a cowboy pretends to be a sky pilot.

## One Year Later

November 16, 1933, 69 minutes.

*P:* M.H. Hoffman. *D:* E. Mason Hopper. *SC:* F. Hugh Herbert & Will Ahern. *PH:* Faxon Dean & Tom Galligan. *ED:* Mildred Johnson. *Rec:* Pete Clark. *Mus:* Abe Meyer. *AD:* Harold H. MacArthur.

*Cast:* Mary Brian, Russell Hopton, Donald Dillaway, George Irving, Will Ahern, Gladys Ahern, DeWitt Jennings, Jackie Searle, Pauline Garon, Pat O'Malley, Marjorie Beebe, Al Hill, Myrtle Steadman, Edward Keane, Harry Holmes, William Humphrey, Lloyd Whitlock, Nina Guilbert, John Ince, James Mack, Walter Brennan, Herbert Evans, Jane Keckley, Kit Guard, Al Klein, Tom London, Virginia True Boardman.

A dying reporter interviews a young bride whose husband is about to die for a crime he did not commit.

## Picture Brides

April 24, 1934, 66 minutes.

*P:* M.H. Hoffman. *AP:* M.H. Hoffman, Jr. *D:* Phil Rosen. *SC:* Adele Buffington & Will Ahern, from the play by Charles E. Blaney & Harry

Poster for *The Fighting Parson* (Allied, 1933).

Clay Blaney. *PH:* Harry Neuman & Tom Galligan. *ED:* Mildred Johnston. *AD:* Harold H. MacArthur. *SD:* L.E. "Pete" Clark. *Mus:* Abe Meyer. *Asst Dir:* J.H. McCloskey. *Prod Mgr:* Ray Culley.

*Cast:* Dorothy Mackaill, Regis Toomey, Dorothy Libaire, Alan Hale, Will & Gladys Ahern, Harvey Clark, Mary Kornman, Esther Muir, Fred Malatesta, Mae Busch, Viva Tattersall, Al Hill, Michael Visaroff, Brooks Benedict, Franklin Parker, Larry McGrath, Jimmie Aubrey.

At a remote mining site in Brazil, several young women arrive to marry miners, and one girl is the object of lust from the sadistic boss.

# Ambassador-Conn-Melody Pictures

Over thirty feature films were produced by Maurice Conn from 1934 to 1937 under the banner of four different picture companies: Ambassador, Conn, Conn-Ambassador and Melody Pictures. Conn was a resourceful producer whose on-location shooting, good casts and crews and minimal stock footage made his productions some of the classier, more entertaining of mid–1930s Poverty Row productions. Three stars dominated Conn's product: Kermit Maynard, Frankie Darro and Pinky Tomlin. Maynard made nine features for Conn, the early ones appealing to the action market as they were allegedly based on the works of James Oliver Curwood. Later, Maynard made straight low-budget westerns as the series deteriorated. Frankie Darro appealed to the youth and action markets, and his ten starrers for Conn were supposed to be based on Peter B. Kyne stories. In both the Curwood and Kyne cases it was often hard to recognize any relationship between film and original work. Darro, who was 18 when his series started in 1935, was paired with two different leading men, Roy [LeRoy] Mason and Kane Richmond. Tomlin's four musicals for Conn were probably his most prestigious features, but they also marked the end of his career as the head of an independent Hollywood film company.

Ambassador Pictures was initiated late in 1934 with the release of *The Fighting Trooper*. Its star, Kermit Maynard, the younger brother of Ken Maynard, was a native of Indiana who came to Hollywood following the success of his sibling and gained success as a stuntman. In 1927, billed as Tex Maynard, he starred in oaters for W. Ray Johnson's Rayart Pictures. Following these cheapies he went back to stunting and supporting and bit roles, and in the early 1930s he twice won world championships for trick and fancy riding. When he signed with Conn to do the Ambassador series, the producer dubbed Maynard's white horse Rocky. To accommodate the claim that the films were based on James Oliver Curwood, filming was done in mountainous terrain away from Hollywood, and the photography by such cameramen as Jack Greenlagh, Earl Lyons and Arthur Reed was a decided plus for the series. The early Maynard efforts were particularly well done with the star often doing his own stunt work, trick riding and roping. For the tenth entry in the series, *Wildcat Trooper* (1936), *Film Daily* enthused, "Kermit Maynard carries the picture in grand style. He handles himself well, he's the center of all activity, his riding stands out and he looks great."

Maurice Conn took care to provide Kermit Maynard with excellent supporting players, and one-time top names like Walter Miller, Monte Blue, Robert Warwick, Hobart Bosworth, J. Farrell MacDonald and Evelyn Brent were assets to these outdoor dramas. Miss Brent also headed a bevy of lovely and talented leading ladies like Ann Sheridan, Andrea Leeds (billed as Antoinette Lees), Eleanor Hunt, Billie Seward, Polly Ann Young, Lucille Lund, Joan Barclay, Beryl Wallace, Beth Marion (billed as Betty Lloyd) and Harley Wood. Several films in the series had comedy support from Fuzzy Knight. As already noted, the series' excellent camera work indicates that Conn also employed top talent behind the camera. Conn was also open for experiment. Forrest Sheldon scripted *The Fighting Trooper* and directed *Wilderness Mail* (1935).

Several films in the series were edited by Jack English, who also made his directorial debut, billed as John English, on *His Fighting Blood* and *Red Blood of Courage* (both 1935). English soon evolved into one of the screen's top action directors in westerns and serials at Republic. Conn also shared producer credit on some of the Maynard films with Sigmund Neufeld, whose brother Sam Newfield directed some of the best of the lot—*Northern Frontier, Code of the Mounted, Trails of the Wild* and *Timber War*—in 1935. Film buffs can spot a very young Tyrone Power in a bit as a Mountie in *Northern Frontier.* Actor Russell Hopton also got behind the camera to direct *Song of the Trail* (1936).

After its initial release in 1934, Ambassador issued seven Kermit Maynard starrers in 1935, a quartet in 1936 and seven final entries in 1937. The 1936 production schedule also called for the release of *Call of the Yukon, Dawn Rider, Klondike Law* and *Legion of the North,* but none of them appeared, at least under those titles. At this point the Kermit Maynard features began a downward trend. The first part of the series had Maynard as a Mountie, but by *Whistling Bullets* (1937) he was a Texas Ranger and later just another cowboy star. Entries like *Galloping Dynamite* (1937) had him crooning in the Gene Autry mode, and several of the last films in the series were not even copyrighted. After *Roaring Six Guns* in 1937, Kermit Maynard returned to stunt work and supporting roles.

The Frankie Darro series, released through Conn Pictures from 1935 to 1937, never had the strong production values of the early Kermit Maynard Ambassador Mountie movies, but they were consistently entertaining and done in a workmanlike fashion. These features were built around Frankie Darro's screen persona, a likable, optimistic, devil-may-care character who always managed to get into various difficulties. Conn smartly paired Darro with a stalwart male lead, not only to extricate Darro from various situations but also for romance with the lovely leading ladies. For the initial three features, Frankie was teamed with Roy Mason, better known as film villain LeRoy Mason. Mason proved to be a most appealing hero and, in fact, may have overshadowed his young costar. Following the second outing, *Men of Action* (1935), *Film Daily* referred to Mason as a "newcomer" (he had actually been on screen for a decade) and called him "a handsome, well-built, clean-cut Gable type." The same reviewer called the film a "fast outdoor action drama," but after two more entries Mason was replaced by Kane Richmond. It was announced that Darro, Mason and Richmond would star in *Phantom of Death Valley,* but it was not filmed.

Themes and genres of the Darro series varied: *Valley of Wanted Men* (1935) was a western; *Born to Fight* (1936) was a boxing melodrama, while *Racing Blood* (1936) dealt with race track corruption; *Headline Crasher* (1937) was a newspaper yarn; *Anything for a Thrill* (1937) was a detective thriller and *Devil Diamond* (1937) was a mystery feature. In the last seven series entries Kane Richmond proved a fine leading man, but he never overshadowed Frankie Darro.

Maurice Conn was also willing to experiment in this series. Actor Russell Hopton again directed, this time handling *Black Gold* (1935), an oil-field actioner, and editor Martin G. Cohn served as associate producer on *Anything for a Thrill.* Unlike the Kermit Maynard series, the Darro films retained a level scale of production throughout the ten outings with the last, *Young Dynamite* (1937), being just as good as the first, *Men of Action* (1935). Following the demise of his Conn Pictures series, Frankie Darro continued to portray the same kind of brash juvenile character in a string of pictures for Monogram from 1938 well into the 1940s.

Truman "Pinky" Tomlin headlined Maurice Conn's final four productions. *With Love and Kisses* was issued late in 1936 by Melody Pictures and cast the bespectacled Tomlin as a rustic songwriter trying to hit the big time in Gotham. The star contributed several tunes to the affair including the title song, "The Trouble with Me Is You," "Sweet," "I'm Right Back Where I Started" and "Don't Ever Lose It." Three more Tomlin features came out in 1937. First there was *Sing While You're Able*, issued under the Melody Pictures banner and coproduced by Tomlin's song collaborator Coy Poe, followed by *Thanks for Listening*, which included Tomlin's popular self-penned hit song "The Love Bug Will Bite You." No Tomlin compositions were among the plethora of songs in Pinky Tomlin's last starrer for Maurice Conn, *Swing It, Professor*, released late in 1937. Although popular on radio and recordings, Pinky Tomlin was always a questionable screen property. Coming across as a somewhat civilized Kay Kyser, he simply lacked screen charisma despite being an acceptable actor and a fine vocalist. Today he is probably best remembered for his composition, "The Object of My Affection." Following the higher budgeted Pinky Tomlin musicals, Maurice Conn abandoned Ambassador-Conn-Melody Pictures.

Born in 1906, Conn had been associated with Olympia and Sterling theatres before coming to Hollywood where he was comptroller and assistant to the president of Mascot Pictures. After running his own studio from 1934 to 1937 he served as the associate producer of the 1938 Grand National western *Frontier Scout*, starring George Houston. That year he formed Concord Productions and produced seven westerns for Monogram. For Conn, Tim McCoy starred in *West of Rainbow's End*, *Code of the Rangers*, *Two Gun Justice* and *Phantom Ranger*, while Jack Randall headlined *Where the West Begins*, *Land of Fighting Men* and *Gunsmoke Trail*. Conn later wrote and produced features such as *The Dragnet* (Fortune, 1947), *The Counterfeiters* (20th Century–Fox, 1948) and *Zamba* (Eagle Lion, 1949). Maurice Conn died October 16, 1973, in Hollywood.

## The Fighting Trooper

November 1, 1934, 63 minutes.

*P:* Maurice Conn. *D:* Ray Taylor. *SC:* Forrest Sheldon, from the story "Footprints" by James Oliver Curwood. *PH:* Edgar Lyons. *ED:* Ted Ballinger.

*Cast:* Kermit Maynard, Barbara Worth, Robert Frazer, LeRoy Mason, Walter Miller, Charles Delaney, George Regas, Joseph W. Girard, Charles King, George Chesebro, Merrill McCormack, Milburn Morante, George Morrell, Nelson McDowell, Artie Ortego, Gordon DeMain, Rocky.

When his comrade is murdered by

bandits, a Mountie pretends to be a trapper in order to capture them.

## Black Gold

1935, 55 minutes.

P: Maurice Conn. D: Russell Hopton. SC: Sacha Baraniey, from the story "The Joy of Living" by Peter B. Kyne. PH: Arthur Reed. ED: Richard Wright. Mus: Stetson Humphrey. Songs: Didheart Conn. SD: Dave Stoner. Sets: Louis Rachmil.

Cast: Frankie Darro (Clifford "Fishtail" O'Riley), Roy [LeRoy] Mason (Henry "Hank" Langford), Gloria Shea (Cynthia Jackson), Berton Churchill (J.G. Anderson), Stanley Fields (Lefty Stevens), Frank Shannon (Dan O'Riley), George Cleveland (Mr. Clemens), Fred "Snowflake" Toones (Snowflake), Dewey Robinson (Homer), Slim Whitaker (Slim).

To make life better for his teenage son Clifford (Frankie Darro), Dan O'Riley (Frank Shannon) tries to borrow money from wealthy banker J.G. Anderson (Berton Churchill) to bring in his oil well. Anderson refuses to lend him the money but offers him one thousand dollars for his lease, which will expire in a few weeks. Anderson is aware that the land on which O'Riley is drilling is rich in oil and he wants it for himself. When Anderson's hoodlums, led by Lefty (Stanley Fields), sabotage the man's drilling operations, O'Riley is about to give in to Anderson's offer when geologist Hank Langford (Roy Mason) convinces him of the worth of the project. Hank is sweet on Cynthia Jackson (Gloria Shea), Clifford's teacher, and to be near her he pretends to help the boy with his studies. When Lefty again sabotages O'Riley's rig, the old man is killed when a chain breaks and he falls to his death. Lefty then abducts Hank and takes him to a remote cabin while Anderson tries to get Clifford to sell him his newly inherited oil lease. Clifford refuses and Hank escapes as the local oilmen unite to stop Anderson. Learning that Anderson and Lefty plan to sabotage Clifford's well with nitro, Hank rushes to the well and saves Clifford from being killed in the explosion. The nitro goes off, however, and a part of the rig hits Anderson's car, crushing him to death. The nitro causes the well to come in, making Clifford and Hank rich. As a result, Hank can marry Cynthia and Clifford goes to military school.

One of a trio of features Maurice Conn made with Frankie Darro and Roy Mason for his newly formed Conn Pictures, *Black Gold* is a fairly interesting affair with Mason, better known as LeRoy Mason, showing just how good he could be in hero parts. The film even gives him a chance to use his fine baritone singing voice in a duet with Frankie Darro, but unfortunately the song was a clinker as was the other tune in the film, both having been written by a composer with the same surname as the producer. Actor Russell Hopton helmed this dual-biller, and he kept it moving at a good clip although his lack of close-ups better fit the silent days. Oil field stock footage was used as a filler as was the final scene of Darro in military school. Frank Shannon, best remembered as Dr. Zharkov in the three Universal "Flash Gordon" serials, here exhibits stage-bound theatrics as the doomed oilman. After this film, *Men of Action* and *Valley of Wanted Men*, LeRoy Mason was replaced by Kane Richmond as Frankie Darro's partner in the Conn series.

# Northern Frontier

January 1, 1935, 56 minutes.

*P:* Maurice Conn. *D:* Sam Newfield. *SC:* Barry Barringer, from the story "Four Minutes Late" by James Oliver Curwood. *PH:* Edgar Lyons. *ED:* Jack English. *SD:* Hans Weeren. *Sets:* Louis Rachmill.

*Cast:* Kermit Maynard, Eleanor Hunt, Russell Hopton, J. Farrell MacDonald, LeRoy Mason, Ben Hendricks, Jr., Gertrude Astor, Lloyd Ingraham, Kernan Cripps, Dick Curtis, Jack Chisholm, Artie Ortego, Charles King, Walter Brennan, Tyrone Power, Rocky.

A Mountie infiltrates a counterfeiting operation and tries to bring the gang members to justice.

# Wilderness Mail

March 9, 1935, 60 minutes.

*P:* Maurice Conn. *D:* Forrest Sheldon. *SC:* Ben Cohen & Robert Dillon. *ST:* James Oliver Curwood. *PH:* Arthur Reed. *ED:* Jack English.

*Cast:* Kermit Maynard, Fred Kohler, Doris Brook, Paul Hurst, Syd Saylor, Dick Curtis, Nelson McDowell, Kernan Cripps, Rocky.

When his brother is blackmailed by crooks, a Mountie comes to his rescue.

# Red Blood of Courage

June 1, 1935, 55 minutes.

*P:* Maurice Conn & Sigmund Neufeld. *D:* Jack English. *SC:* Barry Barringer. *ST:* James Oliver Curwood. *PH:* Arthur Reed. *ED:* Richard G. Wray.

*Cast:* Kermit Maynard, Ann Sheridan, Reginald Barlow, Ben Hendricks, Jr., George Regas, Nat Carr, Charles King, Rocky.

Crooks kidnap a man for his land

and put an imposter in his place but a Mountie investigates.

# Code of the Mounted

June 8, 1935, 60 minutes.

*P:* Maurice Conn & Sigmund Neufeld. *D:* Sam Newfield. *SC:* George Sayre, from the story "Wheels of Fate" by James Oliver Curwood. *PH:* Edgar Lyons. *ED:* Jack English.

*Cast:* Kermit Maynard, Robert Warwick, Lillian Miles, Wheeler Oakman, Jim Thorpe, Syd Saylor, Dick Curtis, Roger Williams, Stanley Blystone, Rocky.

A Mountie tries to stop crooks and their Indian allies from bothering incoming settlers.

# Men of Action

July 13, 1935, 61 minutes.

*P:* Maurice Conn. *D:* Alan James. *SC:* Forrest Sheldon, John W. Krafft & Barry Barringer. *ST:* Peter B. Kyne. *PH:* Arthur Reed. *ED:* Charles Harris.

*Cast:* Frankie Darro, Roy [LeRoy] Mason, Barbara Worth, Fred Kohler, Gloria Shea, Edwin Maxwell, Arthur Hoyt, Syd Saylor, John Ince, Eddie Phillips, Roger Williams, Joseph W. Girard.

A crook and his henchman try to stop an engineer from completing a dam project.

# Trails of the Wild

August 1, 1935, 60 minutes.

*P:* Maurice Conn. *D:* Sam Newfield. *SC:* Joseph O'Donnell, from the story "Caryl of the Mountains" by James Oliver Curwood. *PH:* Jack Greenhalgh. *ED:* Jack English.

*Cast:* Kermit Maynard, Billie Seward, Monte Blue, Fuzzy Knight, Theodore Von Eltz, John Elliott,

Wheeler Oakman, Roger Williams, Robert Frazer, Charles Delaney, Frank Rice, Dick Curtis, Rocky.

A Mountie is on the trail of criminals who killed his best friend.

## His Fighting Blood

October 15, 1935, 60 minutes.

*P:* Maurice Conn & Sigmund Neufeld. *D:* John W. English. *SC:* Joseph O'Donnell. *ST:* James Oliver Curwood. *PH:* Jack Greenhalgh. *ED:* Richard G. Wray.

*Cast:* Kermit Maynard, Polly Ann Young, Paul Fix, Ben Hendricks, Jr., Ted Adams, Joseph W. Girard, Frank LaRue, John McCarthy, Frank O'Connor, Charles King, Jack Cheatham, Ed Cecil, Theodore Lorch, The Singing Constables [Chuck Baldra, Jack Kirk, Glenn Strange], Rocky.

Once saved from jail by his brother, a man becomes a Mountie and hunts the gang his sibling has joined.

## Valley of Wanted Men

October 23, 1935, 63 minutes.

*P:* Maurice Conn. *D:* Alan James. *SC:* Barry Barringer & Forrest Barnes, from the story "All for Love" by Peter B. Kyne. *PH:* Arthur Reed. *ED:* Richard G. Wray. *Songs:* Chantelle & Dukig. *SD:* Hans Weeren. *Sets:* Louis Rachmil.

*Cast:* Frankie Darro, Roy [LeRoy] Mason, Grant Withers, Russell Hopton, Drue Layton, Walter Miller, Paul Fix, Alan Bridge, Fred "Snowflake" Toones, Jack Rockwell, Frank Rice, William Gould.

Outlaws take over a peaceful valley. A young man tries to stop them.

## Timber War

November 1, 1935, 58 minutes.

*P:* Maurice Conn & Sigmund Neufeld. *D:* Sam Newfield. *SC:* Joseph O'Donnell & Barry Barringer. *ST:* James Oliver Curwood. *PH:* Jack Greenhalgh. *ED:* Richard G. Wray. *SD:* Hans Weeren. *Sets:* Harry Lewis.

*Cast:* Kermit Maynard, Lucille Lund, Lawrence Gray, Robert Warwick, Wheeler Oakman, Lloyd Ingraham, Roger Williams, James Pierce, George Morrell, Patricia Royal, Rocky.

A Mountie tries to toughen a playboy as he battles timber thieves.

## Song of the Trail

March 15, 1936, 65 minutes.

*P:* Maurice Conn. *D:* Russell Hopton. *SC:* George Sayre & Barry Barringer, from the story "Playing with Fire" by James Oliver Curwood. *PH:* Arthur Reed. *ED:* Richard G. Wray. *Mus:* Didheart Conn. *Supv:* Charles Hutchison. *SD:* Corson Jowett. *Sets:* Harry Williams.

*Cast:* Kermit Maynard, Evelyn Brent, Antoinette Lees [Andrea Leeds], Fuzzy Knight, Wheeler Oakman, George Hayes, Lynette London, Roger Williams, Lee Shumway, Ray Gallagher, Bob McKenzie, Frank McCarroll, Artie Ortego, Charles McMurphy, Horace Murphy, Rocky.

A rodeo star aids a girl whose father's mine is coveted by outlaws.

## Born to Fight

April 17, 1936, 69 minutes.

*P:* Maurice Conn. *D:* Charles Hutchison. *SC:* Stephen Norris. *ST:* Peter B. Kyne. *PH:* Arthur Reed. *ED:* Richard G. Wray. *Mus:* Didheart Conn. *SD:* Leslie Taft. *Supv:* Martin G. Cohn.

*Cast:* Frankie Darro, Kane Richmond, Jack LaRue, Frances Grant, Sheila Mannors, Monty Collins, Eddie Phillips, Fred "Snowflake" Toones, Hal

Price, Philo McCullough, Donald Kerr, Gino Corrado, Olin Francis, Harry Harvey, Charles McMurphy, Bob Perry.

Forced to hide from gangsters, a fighter meets a younger boxer and becomes his manager.

## Wildcat Trooper

July 1, 1936, 60 minutes.
P: Maurice Conn. D: Elmer Clifton. SC: Joseph O'Donnell, from the story "The Midnight Call" by James Oliver Curwood. PH: Arthur Reed. ED: Richard G. Wray. Mus: Didheart Conn.

Cast: Kermit Maynard, Hobart Bosworth, Lois Wilde, Fuzzy Knight, Yakima Canutt, Jim Thorpe, Eddie Phillips, John Merton, Frank Hagney, Roger Williams, Hal Price, Dick Curtis, Theodore Lorch, Rocky.

A doctor heads an outlaw gang which is stalked by a Mountie.

## Racing Blood

August 13, 1936, 63 minutes.
P: Maurice Conn. D: Rex Hale. SC: Stephen Norris. ST: Peter B. Kyne. PH: Robert Doran, William Hyer & Jack Greenhalgh. Supv-Ed: Martin G. Cohn. Mus: Connie Lee & Tommy Reilly. SD: Hans Weeren. Sets: E.H. Reif.

Cast: Frankie Darro, Kane Richmond, Gladys Blake, Arthur Houseman, James Eagles, Matthew Betz, Si Jenks, Fred "Snowflake" Toones, Bob Tansill, The Jones Quintette.

An amateur detective tries to get the goods on a gang of race-track crooks.

## The Phantom Patrol

September 30, 1936, 60 minutes.
P: Maurice Conn. D: Charles Hutchison. SC: Stephen Norris, from the story "Final Note" by James Oliver Curwood. PH: Arthur Reed. ED: Richard G. Wray. SD: Hans Weeren.

Cast: Kermit Maynard (Sergeant Jim MacGregor), Joan Barclay (Doris McCloud), Harry Worth (Dapper Dan Geary/Stephen Norris), Paul Fix (Joe Joe Regan), George Cleveland (Inspector McCloud), Julian Rivero (Frenchie LaFarge), Eddie Phillips, Roger Williams, Lester Dorr (Gang Members), Richard [Dick] Curtis (Emile), Rocky (Horse).

When producer Maurice Conn signed Kermit Maynard to star in a series of outdoor dramas about the Royal Canadian Mounted Police based on the works of James Oliver Curwood, he was obviously hoping that some of older brother Ken Maynard's popularity would be transferred to Kermit. Although Kermit had starred in five silent oaters in 1927 for Rayart Pictures as Tex Maynard, he had worked primarily in films as a stuntman (in 1933 he became the World's Champion Trick and Fancy Rider). Although Kermit was handsome and more athletic than brother Ken, and many felt he was a better actor, he lacked his older sibling's screen charisma. At any rate he did ten Mountie movies for Conn and then headlined another eight westerns for Ambassador before his starring days ended in 1937. After that he returned to stunt work and supporting parts until the early 1960s. *The Phantom Patrol* is rather typical of his Ambassador Mountie series in that it contained good scenic locales, moved along well and even contained quite a bit of tongue-in-cheek humor. Unfortunately, it was saddled with an overloud music score and in one scene Kermit even played guitar and joined the

Mounties in singing "Be on Your Guard."

Gangster Geary (Harry Worth) is wanted by the law and he heads to Canada with pal Joe Joe (Paul Fix) and finds his look-alike, author Stephen Norris (Harry Worth), with whom he changes identities. The two gangsters then team with local hoodlum Frenchie (Julian Rivero) and his gang, who have murdered a trapper for his pelts. To give Frenchie and his gang a place to hide, Geary leaves Norris' cabin and moves into the village inn where he meets Mountie MacGregor (Kermit Maynard), who is after Frenchie. As Norris, who is being held captive by Frenchie, Geary hires pretty Doris (Joan Barclay) as his secretary, she being the daughter of the commander (George Cleveland) of the local Mountie post. Doris becomes infatuated with Geary in deference to boyfriend MacGregor, who is waylaid by Frenchie's gang during a mail robbery. Later at a masquerade ball, a matron is robbed of her jewelry by Frenchie and Joe Joe, and the Mounties get on the trail of the gang as Doris finds the gems which have been hidden by Joe Joe. Geary and Joe Joe try to escape with Doris as their hostage while MacGregor leads the Mounties to Norris' cabin. A shootout takes place between the lawmen and the outlaws, with the Mounties rounding up the gang as Jim rescues Doris from Geary.

## Wild Horse Roundup

December, 1936, 55 minutes.

*P:* Maurice Conn. *D:* Alan James. *SC:* Joseph O'Donnell. *ST:* James Oliver Curwood. *PH:* Arthur Reed. *ED:* Richard G. Wray.

*Cast:* Kermit Maynard, Betty Lloyd [Beth Marion], Dickie Jones,

John Merton, Roger Williams, Budd Buster, Dick Curtis, Frank Hagney, Jack Ingram, Rocky.

Night riders harass a lady rancher and she is aided by a cowboy and his friends.

## With Love and Kisses

December 7, 1936, 60 minutes.

*P:* Maurice Conn. *AP:* Coy Poe. *D:* Les Goodwins. *SC:* Sherman Lowe. *ST:* Al Martin & Sherman Lowe. *PH:* Arthur Reed. *ED-Supv:* Martin G. Cohn. *AD:* E.H. Reif. *Mus Dir:* Edward J. (Eddie) Kay. *SD:* J.S. Westmoreland. *Songs:* Pinky Tomlin, Coy Poe, Harry Tobias, Connie Lee, Morey Amsterdan, Tony Romano, Paul Parks, Al Heath & Buddy LeRoux.

*Cast:* Pinky Tomlin, Toby Wing, Kane Richmond, Russell Hopton, Arthur Houseman, Jerry Bergen, Billy Gray, The Peters Sisters, Chelito & Gabriel, Fuzzy Knight, Kenneth Thomson, G. Pat Collins, Olaf Hytten, Bob McKenzie, Si Jenks, Jack Ingram, Kernan Cripps, Bruce Mitchell, Eva McKenzie.

A songwriter from Arkansas goes to New York City to become a success and gets mixed up with a dishonest singer and a racketeer.

## Valley of Terror

January 20, 1937, 59 minutes.

*P:* Maurice Conn. *D:* Al Herman. *SC:* Stanley Roberts. *ST:* James Oliver Curwood. *PH:* Arthur Reed. *ED:* Richard G. Wray.

*Cast:* Kermit Maynard, Harley Wood, John Merton, Dick Curtis, Roger Williams, Jack Ingram, Frank McCarroll, Slim Whitaker, Jack Casey, Herman Hack, George Morrell, Blackie Whiteford, Hal Price, Hank Bell, Rocky.

To get the mineral rights to a woman's ranch, a crook has her boyfriend framed on a bogus charge.

## Sing While You're Able

March 24, 1937, 68 minutes.
*P:* Maurice Conn. *AP:* Coy Poe. *D:* Marshall Neilan. *SC:* Sherman Lowe & Charles Condon. *ST:* Stanley Lowenstein & Charles Condon. *PH:* Jack Greenhalgh. *ED-Supv:* Martin G. Cohn. *Mus Dir:* Edward J. Kay. *Songs:* Pinky Tomlin, Harry Tobias, Connie Lee, Paul Parks, Buddy LeRoux, Al Heath, Coy Poe & Roy Ingraham.
*Cast:* Pinky Tomlin, Toby Wing, H.C. Bradley, Monte Collins, Suzanne Kaaren, Sam Wren, Bert Roach, Michael Romanoff, Jimmy Newell [James Newill], The Three Brian Sisters, The Three Mountain Boys, Elma Pappas, Lane Chandler, Fern Emmett, Harry Strang, Rita Carlyle.
A country boy gets involved with a blond and kidnappers when he sings on radio for a toymaker.

## Headline Crasher

April 6, 1937, 59 minutes.
*P:* Maurice Conn. *D:* Les Goodwins. *SC:* Harry O. Hoyt & Sherman Lowe. *ST:* Peter B. Kyne. *PH:* Gilbert Warrenton. *Supv-ED:* Martin G. Cohn. *SD:* Hans Weeren. *Sets:* E.H. Reif.
*Cast:* Frankie Darro, Kane Richmond, Muriel Evans, John Merton, Richard Tucker, Edward Earle, Jack Ingram, Charles King, Dick Curtis, Eddie Kaye, Eleanor Stewart, Harry Harvey, John Ward, Walter Clinton, Henry Hall, Wayne Bumpus, Bunny Bronson, Ray Martin.
A newspaperman romances the secretary of a senator who is running

for re-election and is opposed by gangsters.
Working Title: *Robin Hood Jr.*

## Whistling Bullets

May 3, 1937, 58 minutes.
*P:* Maurice Conn. *D:* John English. *SC:* Joseph O'Donnell. *ST:* James Oliver Curwood. *PH:* Arthur Reed. *ED:* Richard G. Wray.
*Cast:* Kermit Maynard, Harlene [Harley] Wood, Maston Williams, Bruce Mitchell, Karl Hackett, Jack Ingram, Herman Hack, William McCall, Buck Moulton, Cliff Parkinson, Sherry Tansey, Cherokee Alcorn, Rocky.
A Texas Ranger hunts the culprits in a bond theft operation.

## Tough to Handle

May 25, 1937, 61 minutes.
*P:* Maurice Conn. *D:* S. Roy Luby. *SC:* Sherman Lowe & Jack Neville. *ST:* Peter B. Kyne. *PH:* Jack Greenhalgh. *ED:* Martin G. Cohn.
*Cast:* Frankie Darro, Kane Richmond, Phyllis Fraser, Harry Worth, Johnstone White, Lorraine Hayes, Burr Caruth, Jack Ingram, Bill Hunter, Harry Anderson, Stanley Price, Lee Phelps.
A reporter and his younger brother try to break a sweepstakes ticket theft racket.

## The Fighting Texan

June, 1937, 59 minutes.
*P:* Maurice Conn. *D:* Charles Abbott. *SC:* Joseph O'Donnell. *ST:* James Oliver Curwood. *PH:* Arthur Reed. *ED:* Richard G. Wray.
*Cast:* Kermit Maynard, Elaine Shepard, John Merton, Bruce Mitchell, Frank LaRue, Budd Buster, Ed Cassidy, Murdock McQuarrie, Art

Miles, Merrill McCormack, Blackie Whiteford, Bob Woodward, Wally West, Rocky.

A rancher and his daughter are accused in the murder of a rival landowner.

## Devil Diamond

June 30, 1937, 61 minutes.

*P:* Maurice Conn. *D:* Les [Leslie] Goodwins. *SC:* Sherman L. Lowe & Charles Condon. *ST:* Peter B. Kyne. *PH:* Jack Greenlagh. *ED:* Martin G. Cohen. *SD:* Hans Weeren. *Sets:* E.H. Reif.

*Cast:* Frankie Darro (Lee), Kane Richmond (Jerry Carter), June Gale (Dorothy Lanning), Rosita Butler (Yvonne), Robert Fiske (John Henry Moreland), Charles Prince (Al), Edward Earle (Peter Lanning), Fern Emmett (Miss Wallace), Byron Foulger (Ole), George Cleveland (George Davis), Burr Carruth (Stevens), Jack Ingram (Chuck), Frank McCarroll (Dave), Eva McKenzie (Cook).

New York City diamond dealer George Davis (George Cleveland) acquires the notorious Jarvis diamond, which has a history of death and destruction. He plans to have the diamond cut up and sold in pieces, and he hires retired diamond cutter Peter Lanning (Edward Earle) to do the job. Davis' partner Stevens (Burr Carruth) hires gangster John Henry Moreland (Robert Fiske), known as The Professor, to steal the gems once they are cut. As a cover Moreland has his gang pretend to be fight trainers, and they take messenger-boy Lee (Frankie Darro), a would-be boxer, to train in the town where Lanning lives. There Moreland, pretending to be a writer, gets a room at the boarding house run by Lanning's daughter Dorothy (June Gale). Also arriving is Jerry Carter (Kane Rich-

mond), who also claims to be a writer. Other guests include spinster Miss Wallace (Fern Emmett) and her man-hungry niece Yvonne (Rosita Butler), who becomes attached to Lee. Lanning gets the diamond and begins cutting it but when Lee sees Jerry spying on the old man, Jerry tells him he is a special agent from the International Jewelers' Association sent to protect the diamond from thieves. Moreland meanwhile murders Stevens and then steals the cut gems from Lanning. The stones fall into the hands of Miss Wallace and Lee before the gang recovers them. Lee and Jerry pursue Moreland and his gang in a car chase, capture the hoodlums, and recover the precious diamonds.

*Devil Diamond* is probably the weakest in the series of features Frankie Darro made for producer Maurice Conn. Darro's character could easily have been written out of the plot without damaging the storyline. Most of his scenes depict Darro being subjected to harassment from bad guy Chuck (Jack Ingram) or to low-comedy antics from lovestruck Yvonne (Rosita Butler). The film is saddled with a choppy, meandering plot, and tacky sets do not help matters. While the acting is good, the movie has an old fashioned, obtrusive music score, and much of the action is forced, such as a nightclub brawl. Another poor plot ploy has both hero Kane Richmond and villain Robert Fiske claiming to be writers doing research on the life of Joaquin Murietta. Like *Men of Action*, the movie has Frankie Darro as a promising boxer, but in this case he never gets into the ring.

## Anything for a Thrill

June 29, 1937, 60 minutes.

*P:* Maurice Conn. *AP:* Martin G.

Cohn. *D:* Les Goodwins. *SC:* Joseph O'Donnell & Stanley Lowenstein. *ST:* Peter B. Kyne. *PH:* Jack Greenhalgh. *ED:* Richard G. Wray. *SD:* Glen Glenn. *Sets:* E.H. Reif.

*Cast:* Frankie Darro, Kane Richmond, June Johnson, Ann Evers, Johnstone White, Horace Murphy, Edward Hearn, Ernie Adams, Robert Kortman, Frank Marlowe, Charles Dorety, Charles MacAvoy.

A female detective and her partner find themselves involved in a homicide.

## Galloping Dynamite

July 8, 1937, 58 minutes.

*P:* Maurice Conn. *D:* Harry Fraser. *SC:* Sherman Lowe & Charles Condon, from the story "Dawn Rider" by James Oliver Curwood. *PH:* Jack Greenhalgh. *ED:* Robert Jahns. *SD:* Hans Weeren.

*Cast:* Kermit Maynard, Ariane Allen, John Merton, Stanley Blystone, John Ward, David Sharpe, Francis Walker, Earl Dwire, Tracy Layne, Bob Burns, Allen Greer, Budd Buster, Rocky.

A Texas Ranger is out for revenge against the three men who murdered his brother for gold.

## Rough Riding Rhythm

August 15, 1937, 57 minutes.

*P:* Maurice Conn. *AP:* William Berke. *D:* J.P. McGowan. *SC:* Arthur Everett, from the story "Getting a Start in Life" by James Oliver Curwood. *PH:* Jack Greenhalgh. *AD:* E.H. Reif. *ED:* L.R. Brown. *Mus:* Connie Lee. *SD:* Glen Glenn.

*Cast:* Kermit Maynard, Beryl Wallace, Ralph Peters, Olin Francis, Betty Mack, Dave O'Brien, Curley Dresden, Cliff Parkinson, J.P. McGowan, Newt Kirby, Rocky.

A cowboy and his pal hunt the man who killed the friend's sister.

## Roaring Six Guns

September 1, 1937, 55 minutes.

*P:* Maurice Conn. *AP:* William Berke. *D:* J.P. McGowan. *SC:* Arthur Everett. *ST:* James Oliver Curwood. *PH:* Jack Greenhalgh. *ED:* Richard G. Wray. *SD:* Hans Weeren. *AD:* E.H. Reif. *Mus:* Connie Lee.

*Cast:* Kermit Maynard, Mary Hayes, John Merton, Robert Fiske, Budd Buster, Sam Flint, Ed Cassidy, Curley Dresden, Dick Morehead, Slim Whitaker, Earle Hodgins, Rene Stone, Rocky.

A rancher falls for a girl whose father wants him to lose his government grazing land.

## Thanks for Listening

October 21, 1937, 60 minutes.

*P:* Maurice Conn. *D:* Marshall Neilan. *SC:* Rex Hale, Joseph O'Donnell & Stanley Roberts. *PH:* Jack Greenhalgh. *ED-Supv:* Martin G. Cohn. *AD:* E.H. Reif. *SD:* Glen Glenn. *Asst Dir:* Henry Spitz. *Songs:* Pinky Tomlin, Connie Lee, Al Heath & Buddy LeRoux.

*Cast:* Pinky Tomlin, Maxine Doyle, Aileen Pringle, Claire Rochelle, Henry Roquemore, Rafael Storm, Beryl Wallace, Benny Burt, Grace Fields, The Three Brian Sisters, George Lloyd, Eliot Jonah Jones, Charles Prince.

Two female gangsters trick a guitar player into trying to get a rich miner to reveal the location of his gold claim.

## Swing It, Professor

November 13, 1937, 64 minutes.

*P:* Maurice Conn. *AP:* William

Berke. *D:* Marshall Neilan. *SC:* Nicholas H. Barrows & Robert St. Clair. *ST:* Connie Lee. *PH:* Jack Greenhalgh. *ED:* Richard G. Wray. *AD:* E.H. Reif. *SD:* Glen Glenn. *Asst Dir:* Henry Spitz. *Supv:* Martin G. Cohn. *Songs:* Connie Lee, Al Heath & Buddy LeRoux.

*Cast:* Pinky Tomlin, Paula Stone, Mary Kornman, Gordon [Bill] Elliott, Milburn Stone, Pat Gleason, Ralph Peters, George Cleveland, Harry Depp, Harry Semels, The Gentle Maniacs, The Four Squires, The Four Singing Tramps, George Grandee.

After being fired from his job as a college music professor, a man goes to Chicago and is mistaken for a gangster.

British title: *Swing It, Buddy.*

## Young Dynamite

December 15, 1937, 59 minutes.

*P:* Maurice Conn. *AP:* William Berke. *D:* Les Goodwins. *SC:* Arthur Durlam & Joseph O'Donnell. *ST:* Peter B. Kyne. *PH:* John Kline. *ED:* Martin Cohn. *Asst Dir:* Henry Spitz.

*Cast:* Frankie Darro (Freddie Shields), Kane Richmond (Tom Marlin), Charlotte Henry (Jane Shields), David Sharpe (Johnny Shields), William Costello (Flash Slaven), Carlton Young (Spike Dillon), Pat Gleason (Butch Baker), Frank Austin (Mr. Endaberry/Doc Clark), Fred Sarasino (Tony/Rankin).

When the U.S. government calls in all the nation's gold supply, gangster Flash Slaven (William Costello) plans to horde the precious mineral and has his henchmen Spike (Carlton Young) and Butch (Pat Gleason) kill a go-between and steal the loot. Teenager Freddie Shields (Frankie Darro) gets on the trail of the culprits hoping to upstage his older brother Johnny

(David Sharpe), who has just become a state trooper, and roomer Tom Marlin (Kane Richmond), a seasoned trooper engaged to Jane (Charlotte Henry), Freddie's sister. When the two thugs give him the slip, Freddie hitches a ride on a truck the gangsters hijack, and he is able to escape with the money. Meanwhile, the hoodlums stop Johnny, kill him and escape in his car. Freddie hides the money and after hearing about his brother's murder intends to use it to smoke out the culprits. Tom suspects Slaven of masterminding the crime but the latter's influence gets him taken off the case. Freddie goes to Slaven's smelting company, where the gangsters spot him and follow him to his house. Freddie then gets Slaven to try to set up a meeting with Butch and Spike to sell them back the stolen gold and instead leads the trio into a trap which reveals the real boss behind the gold racket.

The last of seven action entries producer Maurice Conn made with Frankie Darro and Kane Richmond for the dual-bill market, *Young Dynamite* is a fast-paced, well-made programmer that belies its low-budget origins. The two stars mesh well together and the topical gold robbery plot adds zest to a well-rounded production. While Kane Richmond had little to do in this effort, the handsome actor was a popular performer in the 1930s and 1940s on the B movie circuit. From the onset of his movie career in 1930 to its demise two decades later, Kane Richmond headlined many Poverty Row outings in the 1930s while in the next decade he was a leading man in dual-billers and serials. Perhaps he is best remembered for having the title role in a trio of Monogram films about "The Shadow" in the mid–1940s.

# Artclass Pictures

The Weiss Brothers (Adolph, Max and Louis) entered the movie production business in 1917 as exhibitors. From 1922 to 1926 they churned out a number of features as Weiss Brothers Artclass Productions, and from 1924 to 1926 they also operated Weiss Brothers Clarion Photoplays. In the late 1920s Louis Weiss took over management of Lee DeForest's DeForest Phonofilm Studios at DeForest, New York, where the famous inventor had been making sound short-subjects for most of the decade. During his brief tenure at Phonofilm, Louis Weiss reactivated Artclass with the production of *Unmasked* in 1929. This stage-bound murder mystery featured Robert Warwick as Arthur B. Reeve's famous scientific detective Craig Kennedy, whose screen career dated back to the Pearl White serial *Exploits of Elaine* in 1915. The fictional character was still popular with readers but *Unmasked* was not a distinguished early sound entry, and it was the final collaboration of the Weiss Brothers. In fact, the film was issued by Weiss Brothers Artclass.

In the fall of 1931 Artclass was reactivated by Louis Weiss and in the next two years issued a dozen feature films, including a reissue of *Unmasked* late in 1931. The studio's initial release was *Maid to Order*, starring famed female impersonator Julian Eltinge. This curio was followed by a series of murder mysteries with varied plots: *Night Life in Reno* involved the divorce capitol; *The Phantom* was basically a horror story with the mind-boggling casting of Guinn "Big Boy" Williams as an ace reporter and plump Allene Ray as an innocent heroine; *Convicted* was set on a cruise liner. Artclass closed out 1931 with the first of four Harry Carey westerns—*Cavalier of the West*—produced by Louis Weiss.

Harry Carey had scored impressively for M.G.M. in 1930 with the immensely popular *Trader Horn*, and for most of the 1930s he would return to the field of the low-budget western, a field in which he had worked in varying degrees since 1910. His 1932 Artclass releases—*Without Honor, Border Devils* and *The Night Rider*—like the initial *Cavalier of the West*, were strong on plot and action, and while sparsely budgeted, they did not look cheap and fared well in the action market. The company also issued two crime melodramas, Regis Toomey in the fight film *They Never Come Back* and H.B. Warner in *Cross-Examination*, a particularly strong courtroom mystery.

Artclass Pictures, which had its main offices at 729 Seventh Avenue in New York City, put out a good product for the independent market, but that market was glutted by 1931–32, the height of the Depression. Following the release of *The Night Rider* in late May, 1932, Artclass folded. Alfred T. Mannon, who produced several of the company's releases, would go on to form Resolute Pictures (q.v.) in 1934, while Louis Weiss would remain in the independent field, making exploitation items like the all-black casted *Drums O'Voodoo* (1934) and the fifteen-chapter serial *The Clutching Hand* (1936) for Stage and Screen [q.v.].

## Unmasked

Weiss Brothers Artclass, August 25, 1929, 62 minutes.

*P:* Louis Weiss. *D:* Edgar Lewis. *SC:* Albert Cowles, Bert Ennis & Edward Clark. *ST:* Arthur B. Reeve. *PH:* Thomas Malloy, Buddy Harris & Irving Browning. *SD:* Martin G. Cohn.

*Cast:* Robert Warwick, Susan Conroy, Milton Krims, Lyons Wickland, Sam Ash, Charles Slattery, William Corbett, Roy Byron, Marie Burke, Waldo Edwards, Kate Roemer, Helen Mitchell, Clyde Dillson.

Scientific detective Craig Kennedy relates a case in which he proved how a young woman was forced to commit murder by being hypnotized by a swami. Reissued by Artclass on December 1, 1931.

## Maid to Order

September 1, 1931, 65 minutes.

*D:* Elmer Clifton. *SC:* Grace Elliott. *ST:* Doris Dembow. *Songs:* Jack Stone, Fred Thompson & George Beauchamp.

*Cast:* Julian Etlinge, Jane Reid, George E. Stone, Betty Boyd, Jack Richardson, Al Hill, Kernan Cripps, Charles Giblin.

Hired to help bring in diamond smugglers, a detective masquerades as a female nightclub singer and ends up rooming with the real warbler.

## Night Life in Reno

October 1, 1931, 58 minutes.

*D:* Ray Cannon. *SC:* Arthur Hoerl. *PH:* M.A. Anderson & M. San-tacross. *ED:* Don Hayes & Martha Dresback. *SD:* L.E. Tope. *Prod Mgr:* George M. Merrick. *Asst Dir:* Harry F. Crist [Harry Fraser].

*Cast:* Virginia Valli, Jameson Thomas, Dixie Lee, Carmelita Geraghty, Dorothy Christy, Pat O'Malley, Arthur Houseman, Clarence Wilson.

When his wife goes to Reno for a divorce, a man proves his love for her by getting involved in a murder case.

## The White Renegade

October 1, 1931, 7 reels.

*P-D-SC:* Jack Irwin.

*Cast:* Tom Santschi, Blanche Mehaffey, Reed Howes, Ted Wells, Marjorie Keyes, Philo McCullough, Donald Keith, Gene Layman, Billy Franey, Tom Murray, Mrs. Ted Wells.

Traveling west with a wagon train, a medicine show pitchman becomes upset when his wife takes up with a gambler who has already taken another woman from her husband.

Working title: *The Empire Builders*.

## Convicted

November 1, 1931, 63 minutes.

*P:* Alfred T. Mannon. *D:* Christy Cabanne. *SC:* Jo Van Ronkel, Barry Barringer & Arthur Hoerl. *ST:* Edward Barry. *PH:* Sidney Hickox. *ED:* Thomas Persons & Don Lindberg. *Asst Dir:* Wilbur McGaugh. *SD:* L.E. Tope. *Prod Mgr:* George M. Merrick.

*Cast:* Aileen Pringle (Claire Norville), Jameson Thomas (Bruce Allen), Harry Meyers (Sturgeon), Richard

Tucker (Tony Blair), Dorothy Christy (Constance Forbes), Niles Welch (Roy Fenton), Jack Mower (Henderson), Wilfred Lucas (Captain Hammond), John Vosburg (Mr. Dayton).

The murder-at-sea mystery motif was used as the basis for this nice-looking Artclass production although the film itself suffered from poor sound and old-fashioned, stage-bound acting. The movie has a fairly interesting plot and director Christy Cabanne keeps the pace moving right up to the climactic moment in which the killer is revealed. Aileen Pringle was still a minor box office force, and she is well cast as the stage star trying to thwart the unwanted advances of her producer. The male lead is played by Jameson Thomas, here an upper crust Englishman-criminologist turned detective to solve the homicide. Harry Meyers adds some life to the proceedings as a tipsy passenger. *Convicted* has a better look to it than most of its contemporaries; unfortunately, it is not an overly interesting feature.

Passengers on an ocean cruise include Broadway star Claire Norville (Aileen Pringle), her producer Tony Blair (Richard Tucker), criminologist Bruce Allen (Jameson Thomas), gambler Roy Fenton (Niles Welch), his drunken friend Sturgeon (Harry Meyers) and Blair's lady friend (Dorothy Christy). Blair, who has lost heavily in the stock market, makes advances to Claire and is stopped by Bruce. That night Blair plays cards with Fenton, Sturgeon, Henderson (Jack Mower)— who is in cahoots with Constance, Blair's lady friend—and the ship's radio operator Dayton (John Vosburg). After heavy losses, Blair accuses Fenton of cheating and says he will get even. After that Claire comes to Blair's cabin and tells him to leave her alone. A few

hours later Blair is found murdered in his cabin, and the ship's captain (Wilfred Lucas) requests that Bruce conduct the investigation into Blair's death. After considerable deduction Bruce is able to gather the passengers together and name the murderer.

The role of the ship's captain was well-acted by Wilfred Lucas, an actor, director and author whose screen career dated back to 1908. From 1910 to 1912 Lucas was a leading player for D.W. Griffith at Biograph, and he developed into one of the silent screen's most versatile character actors, usually playing villain roles. A veteran of the stage, Lucas easily adapted to the sound era and remained quite active until his death in 1940 at the age of 69. During the 1930s he often worked on Poverty Row doing both major and minor parts.

## The Phantom

November 1, 1931, 60 minutes.

*D:* Alan James. *SC:* Alvin J. Neitz [Alan James]. *PH:* Lauron Draper. *ED:* Ethel Davey. *Asst Dir:* Jerry Callahan.

*Cast:* Guinn Williams (Dick Mallory), Allene Ray (Ruth Hampton), Niles Welch (Sam Crandall), Tom O'Brien (Pat Collins), Sheldon Lewis (The Phantom), Wilfred Lucas (John Hampton), Violet Knight (Lucy), William Gould (Dr. Weldon), Bobby Dunn (Shorty), William Jackie (Oscar), Horace Murphy (Police Chief Murphy).

The Phantom (Sheldon Lewis), a condemned murderer, escapes from prison and vows to take revenge on John Hampton (Wilfred Lucas), the district attorney who put him behind bars. Newspaper editor Sam Crandall (Niles Welch) loves Hampton's daughter Ruth (Allene Ray), his society writer, but her affections are for ace reporter Dick Mallory (Guinn Williams). Hoping to get his rival out of the way, Crandall assigns Dick to cover the Hampton house since The Phantom has promised to do in the district attorney that night. A number of mysterious happenings begin to occur in the Hampton house, scaring the butler (Bobby Dunn) and maid (Violet Knight), but the police are unable to catch the culprit, a figure in a black mask and cape. When Ruth is kidnapped, Dick tries to find her. The trail leads to a nearby asylum where The Phantom conducts weird experiments. He plans to operate on Ruth, placing an ape's brain in her head. Dick, however, stops the madman and saves Ruth, and The Phantom is returned to prison to face the electric chair.

One of Poverty Row's more obscure horror-mystery movies from the early 30s, *The Phantom* is a plodding affair with typical character types: a mad, hooded killer, comic domestics (a nervous butler and hysterical maid), a vulnerable heroine and a thick-headed police detective. The casting of the principals—Guinn "Big Boy" Williams as ace reporter Dick Mallory and aging plump serial queen Allene Ray as the innocent heroine—is unlikely to say the least. A bit closer to type is Sheldon Lewis as the mad scientist intent on performing an ape-to-heroine brain transplant in his small but impressive basement laboratory. Lewis was an old hand at such goings-on, having had the role of "The Clutching Hand" in the famous Pearl White silent serial *The Exploits of Elaine*. He also had the title role in the 1920 version of *Dr. Jekyll and Mr. Hyde*. In 1932 he would play another character called "The Phantom" in World

Wide's eerie Ken Maynard western *Tombstone Canyon*. Although far from a classic, *The Phantom* is worth seeing if only to witness the performances of its two unlikely leads.

## Pleasure

November 1, 1931, 70 minutes.

*D:* Otto Brower. *SC:* Jo Van Ronkel & Thomas Thiteley. *ST:* John Varley. *PH:* Sidney Hickox. *ED:* Tom Parsons. *SD:* L.E. Tope.

*Cast:* Conway Tearle, Carmel Myers, Lina Basquette, Frances Dade, Paul Page, Roscoe Karns, Harold Goodwin.

An unhappily married novelist and his younger brother, an artist, both fall in love with the same woman.

## Cavalier of the West

December 5, 1931, 75 minutes.

*P:* Louis Weiss. *AP-Prod Mgr:* George M. Merrick. *D:* John P. McCarthy. *SC:* John P. McCarthy & Harry P. Crist [Harry Fraser]. *PH:* Frank Kesson. *ED:* James Morley. *SD:* B.J. Kroger.

*Cast:* Harry Carey, Carmen LaRoux, Kane Richmond, George F. Hayes, Ted Adams, Maston Williams, Paul Panzer, Carlotta Monti, Ben Corbett, Lew Meehan, P. Narcha.

An army captain tries to keep the peace between Indians and settlers.

## Without Honor

January 10, 1932, 65 minutes.

*P:* Louis Weiss. *D:* William Nigh. *SC:* Harry P. Crist [Harry Fraser] & Lee Sage. *ST:* Lee Sage. *PH:* Edward Lindon. *ED:* Holbrook N. Todd. *SD:* L.E. Tope. *Prod Mgr:* George M. Merrick. *Asst Dir:* Harry P. Crist [Harry Fraser].

*Cast:* Harry Carey, Mae Busch,

Mary Jane Irving, Gibson Gowland, Ed Brady, Lafe McKee, Jack Richardson, Tom London, Lee Sage, Pardner Jones, Maston Williams, Bud McClure, Jim Corey, Roy Bucko, Buck Bucko, Blackjack Ward.

After his brother is murdered, a man becomes a ranger in order to capture the killer.

## Cross-Examination

February 14, 1932, 74 minutes.

*D:* Richard Thorpe. *SC:* Arthur Hoerl. *PH:* A. Anderson. *ED:* Holbrook N. Todd. *SD:* Mark Dalgleish. *Asst Dir:* Melville Shyer.

*Cast:* H.B. Warner (Gerald Waring), Sally Blane (Grace Varney), Natalie Moorhead (Inez Wells), Edmund Breese (Dwight Simpson), William V. Mong (Emory Wells), Donald Dillaway (David Wells), Sarah Padden (Mary Stevens), Wilfred Lucas (Judge Hollister), Niles Welch (Warren Slade), Nita Cavalier (Etta Billings), Margaret Fealy (Martha Good), Alexander Pollard (Boggs), B. Wayne LaMont (Ralph Varney), Frank Clark (Court Clerk), John Webb Dillon (Lt. Elkins), Lee Phelps (Officer Myles).

Noted lawyer Gerald Waring agrees to be the defense attorney for David Wells (Donald Dillaway), who is accused of murdering his rich father Emory (William V. Mong) when the latter refused to let him marry Grace Varney (Sally Blane). During the trial Waring tries to get his client acquitted but the case by the prosecutor (Edmund Breese) is just too tight. David is found guilty and sentenced to die. Waring, however, believes in his client's innocence and he works to get him freed, eventually obtaining a deathbed confession from the murdered man's housekeeper (Sarah Padden) that she committed the crime. Her motive was that years before, she and the elder Wells had been lovers and that David was their son, but that the selfish Emory would never admit she was the mother and cruelly kept her on as his housekeeper. When she saw his refusal to let David find happiness with the girl he loved, the woman killed Emory Wells. As a result of the confession, David is set free and reunited with his fiancée.

*Cross-Examination* is a well-made Poverty Row melodrama that belies its low-budget origins. *Variety* noted, "For an independently made product, much more than the customary value is received. ... In a technical way as well done as most products of major producer-distributors." The acting in the film is quite good, especially H.B. Warner as the lawyer-turned-detective, Edmund Breese as his courtroom adversary and William V. Mong as the hateful Emory Wells. Arthur Hoerl's script is well thought out and Richard Thorpe's direction paces it well, even including courtroom procedures. A high point of the film is the repetition of the murder sequence as shown through the eyes of the various witnesses.

## Border Devils

March 20, 1932, 63 minutes.

*P:* Louis Weiss. *AP-Prod Mgr:* George M. Merrick. *D:* William Nigh. *SC-Asst Dir:* Harry P. Crist [Harry Fraser]. *ST:* Murray Leinster. *PH:* William Dietz. *ED:* Holbrook N. Todd. *SD:* B.J. Kroger.

*Cast:* Harry Carey, Kathleen Collins, Niles Welch, Olive Fuller Golden (Carey), George F. Hayes, Al Smith, Merrill McCormack, Maston

Lobby card for *The Night Rider* (Artclass, 1932).

Williams, Ray Gallagher, Murdock McQuarrie, Art Mix, Frank Ellis, Ketsu Komai.

Arrested for a crime he did not commit, a man escapes from jail to prove his innocence.

## They Never Come Back

May 1, 1932, 67 minutes.
*P:* Louis Weiss. *D:* Fred Newmeyer. *SC:* Arthur Hoerl & Sherman Lowe. *PH:* James Diamond. *ED:* Holbrook N. Todd. *SD:* W.M. Dalgleish. *Prod Mgr:* George M. Merrick.

*Cast:* Regis Toomey, Dorothy Sebastian, Greta Grandstadt, Eddie Woods, Earle Foxe, Gertrude Astor, George Byron, Jack Richardson, Jack Silver, Little Billy, James J. Jeffries.

No longer able to fight, a boxer takes a job at a club but ends up being railroaded into jail by the brother of the girl he loves.

## The Night Rider

May 21, 1932, 72 minutes.
*P:* Alfred T. Mannon. *AP-Prod Mgr:* George M. Merrick. *D:* Fred Newmeyer. *SC-ST-Asst Dir:* Harry P. Crist [Harry Fraser]. *PH:* James R. Diamond. *ED:* Holbrook N. Todd. *SD:* B.J. Kroeger.

*Cast:* Harry Carey (The Stranger/ John Brown), Eleanor Fair (Barbara Rogers), George F. Hayes (The Tourist/Altoona), Julian Rivero (Manuel Alonzo Valdez), Tom London (Jeff Barton), Bob Kortman (Steve), Nadja (Tula Fernandez), Jack Weatherly (David Rogers), Cliff Lyons (Bert Logan), Walter Shumway (Lem, the Sheriff), Hank Bell, Slim Whitaker,

Ben Corbett, Bart Carre (Townsmen), Sonny (Horse).

The mysterious Night Rider is robbing area ranchers and his identity is unknown even to his minions, saloon operator Jack Barton (Tom London) and henchman Steve (Bob Kortman). The Stranger (Harry Carey) arrives in the area, and later his pal (Cliff Lyons) is ambushed and killed by the Night Rider. The Stranger then teams with hard-of-hearing Altoona (George F. Hayes) and verbose caballero Manuel (Julian Rivero) to capture the masked man. Using the guise of gunman Bad Jim Blake, the Stranger ingratiates himself with Barton who recommends him to pretty Barbara Rogers (Eleanor Fair) as the new foreman for the ranch she runs with her crippled half-brother David (Jack Weatherly). The Stranger takes the job but is later arrested by the sheriff (Walter Shumway) who accuses him of being the Night Rider, but it is all a ruse to capture the outlaws. The sheriff lets the Stranger escape, and the latter tells Barton and Steve he is the Night Rider. Later he captures Barbara and hands her over to Barton and Steve with orders to meet him at midnight at the Rogers' ranch. At the appointed time the sheriff and the posse arrive and arrest Barton, Steve and their gang as the Stranger captures the real Night Rider.

The final of a quartet of westerns to be made with Harry Carey by producer Alfred T. Mannon, *The Night Rider* was also Artclass' final release. Even for 1932 it was not a typical matinee galloper with Harry Carey retaining the austere character he had created in the silent days, although here he also adds several doses of subtle humor. The script includes plot twists, and the title character is seen only as a rider wearing a black cape, hat and face mask. Besides the villain, the movie has a flavorful mystery subplot surrounding an old mine and a hidden tunnel that leads to the heroine's ranch house. The theme of triad heroes is developed early in the film when Harry Carey's Stranger teams with Mexican caballero Julian Rivero and tourist George F. Hayes, long before he became "Gabby," to track down and capture the Night Rider. Even the later popular concept of comedy between the characters is used here, especially in the byplay between Hayes and Rivero. Finally, the film ends with a hint of romance between Harry Carey and Eleanor Fair, although there must have been thirty years difference in their ages.

# Atlantic Pictures Corporation

Operating in the last half of the 1930s, Atlantic Pictures Corporation mainly reissued older features licensed from United Artists. The company did, however, distribute a quartet of westerns starring Jack Perrin in 1936 as well as a British import, *The Last Journey*, that same year. Among its United Artists reissues were *Hell Harbor* and *Hell's Angels* (both 1930), *The Front Page* (1931),

*Cock of the Air, Scarface* and *Sky Devils* (all 1932) and another 1932 film, *The Silver Lining*, which Atlantic retitled *Big House for Girls*.

The four cowboy pictures Atlantic distributed were made by Berke-Perrin Productions and dubbed "Blue Ribbon" westerns. The production company was organized by producer William Berke and star Jack Perrin. William Berke (1903–58) worked as a cameraman and writer before becoming an independent producer, releasing his features through the various William Steiner exchanges. Following the Atlantic venture he worked at Republic, and in 1942 he joined Columbia as a director. Later, he made features like *Dark Mountain* (Paramount, 1944), *The Falcon in Mexico* (RKO Radio, 1944) and *Dick Tracy* (RKO Radio, 1945). He continued to work for Paramount, Columbia, Screen Guild, Eagle Lion, Lippert and United Artists until his death during the production of *The Lost Missile* (United Artists, 1958); his son, Lester William Berke, finished the feature. Billed as Lester Williams, William Berke also directed the last two films in the Atlantic series with Jack Perrin, *Desert Justice* and *Gun Grit*.

Jack Perrin (1896–1967) began starring in films in 1917 and worked mostly in westerns for the next two decades, culminating in the Atlantic series. During the 1920s he made many two-reelers for Universal and features for Arrow, and other companies. During this period, he teamed with his beautiful white stallion Starlight, who remained with him for the rest of his starring career. With the coming of sound Jack Perrin continued to star for outfits like Big 4, Robert J. Horner Productions and Reliable (qq.v.), but he also took supporting roles. During this period, the mid-to-late 1930s, Perrin also used the screen names Jack Gable and Richard Terry. After the Atlantic series, Jack Perrin continued to work in films in minor roles before retiring in the early 1960s.

The Berke-Perrin "Blue Ribbon" westerns were filmed at the Talisman Studios (formerly Tiffany [q.v.]), and while done on the cheap they tried to differ from the usual sagebrush fodder flooding the market at the time. For example, *Gun Grit* (1936) sets many of its scenes within the Los Angeles city limits in its modern-day tale of gangsters infiltrating the range. In addition to the four Jack Perrin westerns released by Atlantic, two others—*Song of the Gun* and *Border Ranger*—were announced but apparently were never produced.

Following the brief Berke-Perrin series in 1936, Atlantic Pictures continued to operate as a reissue company, one of its last releases being the 1938 feature *Hell Is a Circus*, originally issued by World Wide (q.v.) in 1933 as *The Constant Woman*.

## Wildcat Saunders

January, 1936, 60 minutes.

*P:* William Berke. *D:* Harry Fraser. *SC:* Miller Easton. *PH:* Robert Cline. *ED:* Arthur A. Brooks. *SD:* T.T. Triplett. *Asst Dir:* William Nolte.

*Cast:* Jack Perrin (Wildcat Saunders), Blanche Mehaffey (June Lawson), William Gould (Joe Pitts), Fred "Snowflake" Toones (Snowflake), Roger Williams (Laramie), Tom London (Pete Hawkins), Edward Cassidy (Lawson), Earl Dwire (Steve), Jim

Corey (Sheriff Townsend), Bud Osborne (Slim Marlin), Tex Palmer, Ray Henderson (Ranch Hands), Starlight (Himself).

Because he is out of shape from chasing "dizzy dames," boxer Wildcat Saunders (Jack Perrin) loses a match, and his disgruntled manager Joe Pitts (William Gould) takes him and handyman Snowflake (Fred "Snowflake" Toones) to the remote ranch of his friend Lawson (Edward Cassidy) to train. There Saunders falls for Lawson's pretty daughter June (Blanche Mehaffey) but has a run-in with foreman Pete Hawkins (Tom London), who has robbed the Wells Fargo of a fortune in precious gems. Hawkins picks on Snowflake, and Saunders, who was raised on a ranch, knocks him down. As Joe sets up a training camp for Wildcat, a stranger, Laramie (Roger Williams), rides to the ranch claiming to be looking for mounts for the army. He meets with Hawkins and pal Steve (Earl Dwire) and tells them he has come for his share of the robbery loot. The three agree to ride across the Mexican border after Hawkins retrieves the package with the gems, having left it with Lawson for safekeeping. Lawson put the package in his riding boots which June loans to Wildcat so they can go riding. Wildcat finds the package and gives it to Joe who, in turn, hands it over to Snowflake. Hawkins confronts Wildcat about the package but learns nothing. While out riding Wildcat and June see the sheriff (Jim Corey) and his men chasing outlaw Slim Marlin (Bud Osborne), and Wildcat captures him. Afraid Slim, his partner, will talk, Hawkins gets the drop on Wildcat, Joe and Snowflake and ties them up after taking a package from Snowflake. Hawkins takes June as hostage and

rides away. Lawson helps the three men get untied and Wildcat rides after Hawkins while Joe and Snowflake follow on foot. Hawkins frees June but is captured by Wildcat, followed by the sheriff and his posse, including Laramie, who is really a representative of the express company. The package Hawkins took from Snowflake turns out to be bogus, but when Snowflake comes up with the real gems, Hawkins is arrested and Wildcat and Snowflake share in the reward for his capture and the return of the gems. Wildcat then asks June to marry him.

The first of a quartet of oaters Jack Perrin made with producer William Berke, *Wildcat Saunders* is a fast-moving affair with both action and comedy. Jack Perrin, who was 40 when the film was released, handles the role of the young boxer in good form, even having a brief ring sequence at the start of the picture. Blanche Mehaffey is good as the leading lady while comedy relief is provided by the always delightful Fred "Snowflake" Toones and, surprisingly by William Gould, who, usually cast as villains, is most amusing as Wildcat's harried manager. Tom London is in his usual good form as the bad guy with an able assist from Earl Dwire as his pal. Appearing in all four films in the series was Jack Perrin's beautiful horse Starlight. In the final two series entries, *Desert Justice* and *Gun Grit*, they are also assisted by canine star Braveheart.

## Hair-Trigger Casey

February 19, 1936, 60 minutes.

*P:* William Berke. *D:* Harry Fraser. *SC:* Monroe Talbot. *PH:* Robert Cline. *ED:* Arthur A. Brooks. *Mus:* Lee Zahler. *SD:* T.T. Triplett. *Asst Dir:* William Nolte.

*Cast:* Jack Perrin, Betty Mack,

WILLIAM BERKE *presents*
*Jack* **PERRIN**
*and* **STARLIGHT** - *The Wonder Horse*

IN A LIGHTNING-TRIGGER ACTION DRAMA OF THE GLORIOUS WEST · · · · PACKED WITH THRILLS AND COLORFUL ADVENTURE!

"Hair-Trigger Casey"

*with*
BETTY MACK · "SNOWFLAKE" WALLY WALES · PHIL DUNHAM ROBERT WALKER · VI WONG *and* DENNY MEADOWS · · ·

*Directed by* HARRY FRASER

*Distributed by* ATLANTIC PICTURES CORP.

Advertisement for *Hair-Trigger Casey* (Atlantic, 1936).

Edward Cassidy, Wally Wales, Fred "Snowflake" Toones, Phil Dunham, Robert Walker, Denny Meadows [Dennis Moore], Victor Wong, Starlight.

An army captain is called home to his border ranch where he finds evidence of alien smuggling.

## Desert Justice

April 22, 1936, 58 minutes.

*P:* William Berke. *D:* Lester Williams [William Berke]. *SC:* Gordon Phillips & Lewis Kingdon. *ST:* Allen Hall. *PH:* Robert Cline. *ED:* Arthur A. Brooks. *Mus:* Lee Zahler. *SD:* Joseph Lapis. *Asst Dir:* King Guidice.

*Cast:* Jack Perrin, Warren Hymer, Maryan Dowling, David Sharpe, Roger Williams, William Gould, Denny Meadows [Dennis Moore],

Fred "Snowflake" Toones, Budd Buster, Earl Dwire, Starlight, Braveheart.

A retired policeman finds out that his younger brother has been sprung from reform school by a gang who uses him in their holdups.

## The Last Journey

April 27, 1936, 66 minutes.

*P:* Julius Hagen. *D:* Bernard Vorhaus. *SC:* John Soutar & H. Fowler Mear. *ST:* J. Jefferson Farjeon. *PH:* William Luff & Percy Strong. *ED:* Lister Laurance.

*Cast:* Hugh Williams, Godfrey Tearle, Judy Gunn, Julien Mitchell, Nielson Keys, Michael Hogan, Frank Pettingell, Olgba Lindo, Sydney Fairbrother, Eliot Markeham, Eve Gray, Mickey Brantford, Sam Wilkinson, Viola Compton, John Lloyd.

When he comes to believe his wife

is having an affair with a fireman, an express train driver loses his sanity. Made in England by Twickenham in 1935; running time, 66 minutes.

## Gun Grit

August 1, 1936, 57 minutes.
    *P:* William Berke. *D:* Lester Williams [William Berke]. *SC:* Gordon Phillips & Lewis Kingdon. *ST:* Allen Hall. *PH:* Robert Cline. *ED:* Arthur A. Brooks. *Mus:* Lee Zahler.

*SD:* Corson Jowett. *Asst Dir:* King Guidice.
    *Cast:* Jack Perrin, Ethel Beck, David Sharpe, Roger Williams, Ralph Peters, Frank Hagney, Jimmy Aubrey, Edward Cassidy, Phil Dunham, Earl Dwire, Oscar Gahan, Horace Murphy, Baby Lester, Budd Buster, Starlight, Braveheart.
    An FBI agent is sent west to investigate gangsters who are stealing cattle shipments and forcing ranchers to pay protection money.

# Beacon Pictures

Brothers Max and Arthur Alexander were longtime independent motion picture producers in Hollywood who during the 1930s briefly had their own companies, Beacon and Colony (q.v.). The Alexander brothers first became associated with movies in their native Germany, and in the late 1920s they worked for Universal in Frankfurt. Nephews of Universal chief Carl Laemmle, they migrated to Hollywood with the coming of sound and eventually formed Beacon. Max Alexander (1904–1964) headed the company and is listed as the producer for the eight films issued during 1934–35 with Arthur Alexander as the company's production manager.

Technically, Beacon's first release was the documentary *Through the Centuries,* which came out late in 1934. The one-hour filler was written by Francis X. Talbot. The company got into gear in the summer of 1934 with the release of *I Can't Escape,* featuring Lila Lee, a star of the silents and early talkies who had been keeping busy on Poverty Row. This film and *Ticket to a Crime* gave employment to another silent-screen hero, Charles Ray, while the latter also starred two other silent movie favorites, Ralph Graves and Lois Wilson. Probably the most profitable series for Beacon was the series of five features done with Guinn "Big Boy" Williams for the Saturday matinee cowboy trade. The first, *Thunder Over Texas* (1934), was directed by Edgar G. Ulmer, who used the pseudonym John Warner. Williams was a likable cowboy hero, able to handle easily the physical action required of a western star, but because the Alexanders gave him minimal budgets, the features look tacky and must rate among the lower grade in the galloper series sweepstakes of the Depression era.

The final three Guinn Williams starrers—*Danger Trails, Big Boy Rides Again* and *Gun Play*—were issued in 1935, but the first two were so obscure that no definite release dates can be found for them. *Gun Play* (better known as *Lucky Boots* on TV) came out at the end of 1935, but by that time the Beacon banner was dim indeed. The only non–Guinn Williams 1935 release from the company was *What Price Crime?*, starring Charles Starrett. Evidently the Alexanders expended a bit more in the way of budget for this programmer but it was still a cheap affair despite a fast-moving plot and a solid supporting cast that included Noel Madison, Virginia Cherrill, Jack Mulhall and Charles Delaney.

Arthur Alexander also used the Beacon monicker, in conjunction with his and his brother's newly formed Normandy Picture Corporation, to make one final Guinn Williams western, *Law of the 45s* in 1935, and it was released through First Division (q.v.) exchanges. In addition Normany also was involved in four Rex Bell oaters (*Idaho Kid, Men of the Plains, Too Much Beef, West of Nevada*) that the Alexander brothers made for their Colony Pictures (q.v.) in 1936. The only film made solely by Normandy was *The Lion Man* (1936) with Charles Lochner (spelled Loucher on screen) in the title role. This states' rights release got new life in the next decade when the leading man became better known as Jon Hall. Based on Edgar Rice Burroughs' "The Lad and the Lion," it was even reissued on a double bill with *Tarzan and the Green Goddess* (1937) in the 1940s by the American Film Company.

# I Can't Escape

July 5, 1934, 60 minutes.

*P:* Max Alexander. *AP:* Sam Weisenthal. *D:* Otto Brower. *SC:* Faith Thomas. *ST:* Jerry Sackheim & Nathan Ash. *PH:* Jerome Ash. *ED:* Lou Sackin & Fred Knudtson. *AD:* Fred Preble. *Prod Mgr:* Charles S. Gould.

*Cast:* Lila Lee, Onslow Stevens, Russell Gleason, Otis Harlan, Hooper Atchley, Clara Kimball Young, Nat Carr, Eddie Gribbon, Kane Richmond, Charles Ray, William Desmond, John Elliott.

Unable to get a decent job because of a prison history, a man gets involved in a phony stock scheme.

# Thunder Over Texas

October 18, 1934, 61 minutes.

*P:* Max Alexander. *D:* John Warner [Edgar G. Ulmer]. *SC:* Eddie Graneman. *ST:* Sherle Castle. *PH:* Harry Forbes. *ED:* George Merrick. *Tech Dir:* Fred Preble. *SD:* Frank McKenzie. *Prod Mgr:* Arthur Alexander.

*Cast:* Guinn "Big Boy" Williams (Ted Wright), Marion Shilling (Helen Mason), Helen Westcott (Betty "Tiny" Norton), Claude Payton (Bruce Laird), Philo McCullough (Sheriff Collier), Robert McKenzie (Judge Blake), Tiny Skelton (Dick), Victor Potel (Gonzales), Benny Corbett (Tom), Dick Botiller (Harry), Eva McKenzie (Town Woman), Jack Kirk (Outlaw/Radio Singer), Hank Bell (Court Spectator).

In what looks like a bank robbery, an engineer for the railroad tries to safeguard right-of-way maps and is killed in an auto accident. His little

*The Lion Man* (Normandy Pictures, 1936) was reissued in the 1940s on a double bill with *Tarzan and the Green Goddess* (Burroughs-Tarzan, 1937). By this time stars Charles Lochner and Herman Brix were better known as Jon Hall and Bruce Bennett.

daughter, Tiny (Helen Westcott), escapes unharmed. Cowboy Ted Wright (Guinn Williams) takes custody of the girl over the protests of crooked banker

Bruce Laird (Claude Payton), who engineered the accident, and his cohort, Sheriff Collier (Philo McCullough). Laird wants Wright's ranch

Helen Westcott, Claude Payton, Guinn Williams and Marion Shilling in *Thunder Over Texas* (Beacon, 1934).

because it is valuable to the railroad, and he tries to keep the local judge (Bob McKenzie) from giving legal custody of Tiny to Ted. Schoolmarm Helen Mason (Marion Shilling), who has rejected Laird's advances in favor of Ted, agrees to live at the latter's ranch and take care of Tiny. In order to pay off his mortgage to Laird, Ted plans to ship a herd of cattle but the banker has his men kidnap Tiny and stampede the herd. The plan fails, however, when Ted's hired hands intercede and stop the bad guys. Ted finds where Tiny has been taken and beats up Collier, saving the girl as the judge arrests Laird. Ted, Helen and Tiny head back to their ranch as Helen has agreed to marry Ted.

The first of five westerns Max Alexander produced for his Beacon Pictures, *Thunder Over Texas* is also worth noting because it was directed by Edgar G. Ulmer under the name of John Warner, although the signature on the screen looks like "Joen Warner." At any rate, Ulmer directed this "B" galloper based on a story by his wife, Sherle Castle. Cinephiles looking for a buried classic will have to go elsewhere because this rough-hewn affair has none of the polish or sophistication of Ulmer's *The Black Cat*, done the same year for Universal. Legend has it that Ulmer refused to be loaned to Fox to do a Shirley Temple film and was suspended by Universal. Another story is that he took Sherle Castle away from her husband, one of the Laemmle relatives. Whatever the case, Ulmer spent the rest of the decade doing mainly ethnic features before reemerging at Producers Releasing Corporation in the 1940s. Outside of a few unusual camera angles, *Thunder Over Texas* has none of Ulmer's typical eccentricities over which film critics have fawned for the last three decades.

Star Guinn Williams made three dozen Poverty Row oaters in the 1920s but this series for Beacon was his only sound-era western package, although he made many genre appearances in character roles. The ingratiating little girl in the movie is played by Helen Westcott, who literally grew up on film and by the 1950s was a leading lady. Although she continued to work in low-budget efforts like *Battles of Chief Pontiac* (1952) and *Invisible Avenger* (1958), her best role was probably Rosamund in *God's Little Acre* (1958). One of the more amusing plot ploys in *Thunder Over Texas* depicts Williams' three ranch hands (Benny Corbett, Tiny Skelton, Dick Botiller) as radio-crazy, constantly doing impersonations of such airwaves personalities as Kate Smith, Rudy Vallee, Joe Penner, Ted Lewis, Amos 'n Andy and Baron Munchausen.

## Ticket to a Crime

December 20, 1934, 67 minutes.

*P:* Max Alexander. *AP:* Peter E. Kassler. *D:* Lewis D. Collins. *SC:* Charles A. Logue. *ST:* Carroll John Daly. *PH:* Gilbert Warrenton. *ED:* Holbrook N. Todd & S. Roy Luby. *SD:* Dave Stoner. *AD:* Fred Preble.

*Cast:* Ralph Graves, Lois Wilson, Lola Lane, James Burke, Charles Ray, Edward Earle, Hy Hoover, John Elliott.

A private detective and a policeman are at odds in several cases, including a murder, the theft of pearls and a big heist.

## Cowboy Holiday

December 26, 1934, 56 minutes.

*P:* Max Alexander. *D:* Bob Hill. *SC:* Rock Hawkey [Bob Hill]. *PH:* Gilbert Warrenton. *ED:* Holbrook N.

Todd. *AD:* Fred Preble. *Asst Dir:* Myron Marsh. *Prod Mgr:* Arthur Alexander.

*Cast:* Guinn Williams, Janet Chandler, Julian Rivero, Dick Alexander, John Elliott, Alma Chester, Frank Ellis, Julia Bejarano, William Gould.

A cowboy tries to bring in an outlaw disguised as a Mexican bandit.

## Big Boy Rides Again

Beacon/First Division, 1935, 60 minutes.

*P:* Max Alexander. *AP:* Peter E. Kassler. *D:* Al Herman. *SC:* William L. Nolte. *PH:* Harry Forbes. *ED:* Ralph Holt. *AD:* Fred Preble. *Prod Mgr:* Arthur Alexander.

*Cast:* Guinn Williams, Connie Bergen, Charles K. French, Victor Potel, Lafe McKee, Augie Gomez, Frank Ellis, William Gould, Bud Osborne, Louis Vincenot.

When his father is killed over buried treasure, a cowboy is kidnapped by crooks.

## Danger Trails

Beacon/First Division, 1935, 55 minutes.

*P:* Max Alexander. *AP:* Peter E. Kassler. *D:* Bob Hill. *SC:* Rock Hawkey [Bob Hill]. *ST:* Guinn Williams. *PH:* William Hyer. *ED:* Holbrook N. Todd. *SD:* Cliff Ruberg. *Prod Mgr:* Arthur Alexander.

*Cast:* Guinn Williams, Marjorie Gordon, Wally Wales, Ace Cain, John Elliott, Edmund Cobb, Steve Clark, George Chesebro, Bob Hill, George Morrell, Francis Walker, Buck Morgan, Ray Henderson, Wally West.

After being educated in the East, a man returns home to get revenge on the killers of his family.

# What Price Crime?

May 28, 1935, 63 minutes.

*P:* Max Alexander. *D:* Albert Herman. *SC:* Al Martin. *PH:* Harry Forbes. *ED:* S. Roy Luby. *Asst Dir:* Myron Marsh. *Prod Mgr:* Arthur Alexander. *Tech Dir:* Fred Preble. *SD:* Cliff Ruberg.

*Cast:* Charles Starrett (Allen Grey), Noel Madison (Douglas Worthington), Virginia Cherrill (Sondra Worthington), Charles Delaney (Jim Armstrong), Jack Mulhall (Hopkins), Nina Guilbert (Mrs. Worthington), Henry Roquemore (Pete Crenshaw), John Elliott (Chief J. Radcliff), Arthur Loft (Donahue), Earl Tree (Graham), Jack Cowell (Henry Davis), Arthur Roland (Red), Edwin Argus (Leroy), Al Baffert (Battling Brennon), Gordon Griffith (Hogan), Monte Carter (Lefty), Lafe McKee (Night Watchman), Fred "Snowflake" Toones (Snowflake).

Burglars rob a warehouse of guns and kill a night watchman (Lafe McKee). Undercover agent Allen Grey (Charles Starrett) is en route to police headquarters to look into the matter when he has a traffic accident with pretty Sondra Worthington (Virginia Cherrill). Federal agents believe nightclub owner Douglas Worthington (Noel Madison), Sondra's brother, is behind the burglaries, and Allen is assigned to masquerade as a boxer in order to get Worthington's attention, since the latter is also a fight manager. Allen wins several bouts and then K.O.'s Worthington's man Battling Brennon (Al Baffert), and Worthington buys his contract. As a result, Allen meets Sondra again and they fall in love, but Allen then finds out that Worthington is the brains behind the burglaries and he vows to get him after the murder of his pal Hopkins (Jack Mulhall). Pretending to be a racketeer, Allen gets in good with Worthington, and despite being seen talking with his boss (John Elliott), Allen is able to convince Worthington he is on the level. When the gangsters plan to take munitions to a gang of counterfeiters, Allen wires a truck and leads the convoy, alerting his superiors to the location of the meeting. In a shootout, the federal men are able to capture the gangsters and counterfeiters, but Worthington and his henchman Armstrong (Charles Delaney) are fatally wounded. Despite the death of her brother, Sondra realizes she loves Allen.

*What Price Crime?* has its best scenes at the beginning, with the Beacon logo flashing across the screen like a searchlight, followed by the heavily backlit sequence showing silhouetted burglars robbing a warehouse. After this promising opening, however, the film moves progressively downhill, with much murky nighttime photography, stock boxing footage and a night club floor show cut from another movie. Fifth-billed Jack Mulhall is given limited screen time (only one scene), and when his character is killed off, the murder is announced, not shown.

For Charles Starrett, *What Price Crime?* was another in a line of Poverty Row productions he did (mostly for Chesterfield) before earning his niche as a cowboy hero at Columbia. This Beacon release preceded by only a few months the rival studio's *The Gallant Defender* (1935), the film that would establish Starrett as a Columbia saddle star from 1935 to 1952. His portrayal in *What Price Crime?* as a handsome government undercover agent is convincing, aided by Starrett's athletic looks and football background.

Also noteworthy is second-billed Noel Madison's performance as the gang leader. During the 1930s and 1940s Madison often played George Raft/Humphrey Bogart types. His fine performances highlighted Poverty Row efforts like *The Cocaine Fiends* (1935), *Nation Aflame* (1937) and *The Black Raven* (1943).

## Gun Play

Beacon/First Division, December 27, 1935, 59 minutes.

*P:* Max Alexander. *D:* Al Herman.

*SC:* William L. Nolte. *PH:* William Hyer. *Asst Dir:* Myron Marsh. *Prod Mgr:* Arthur Alexander.

*Cast:* Guinn Williams, Marion Shilling, Frank Yaconelli, Wally Wales, Charles K. French, Tom London, Roger Williams, Gordon Griffith, Barney Beasley, Julian Rivero, Si Jenks, Dick Botiller, Buck Morgan, George Morrell.

After a Mexican bandit is killed, a cowboy tries to find his buried loot on a ranch. TV title: *Lucky Boots.*

# Beaumont Pictures

Producer Mitchell Leichter's Beaumont Pictures arrived on the Hollywood scene in the mid–1930s and had a short life span, running out of gas after being in operation for only a few months. In that time, however, the company released only westerns—four with Conway Tearle, one each with David Worth and Edmund Cobb. The bulk of these featured the handsome Black King, "The Horse with the Human Brain." Also on the company's agenda was the reissue of the 1933 Monogram horse opera, *Breed of the Border,* starring Bob Steele.

Beaumont kicked off its release schedule in late August, 1935, with a western doubleheader: *Gunners and Guns* and *Trail's End.* The latter was the first of four Beaumont oaters starring Conway Tearle, hardly a likely cowboy star. Tearle, a fifty-six-year-old native of England whose real name was Frederick Levy, did the Beaumont series although he had headlined *The Great Divide* in 1925 and the northwoods actioner *Smoke Bellew* in 1929, at the beginning of the sound era. Due to his age Tearle's leading-man status was confined to Poverty Row, although he worked as a supporting player in big-budget pictures when not appearing on stage. He was a surprisingly effective cowboy star as he retained his handsome features and even did some of his own stunt work and riding in the Beaumont actioners. Unfortunately, *Trail's End,* like the rest of Leichter's productions, had very shoddy production values, which helped to negate the star's otherwise worthy efforts. A glutted western field did not help the Conway Tearle series either, although he went on to make *The Judgement Book* in 1935 and *Desert Guns* and *Señor Jim* in 1936. The latter, however, is so obscure that its release date remains uncertain. The film is often overlooked even in Conway Tearle filmographies. Interestingly, Beaumont announced that Tearle would also star in two other oaters, *Hell's Hacienda* and *Whistling Skull*, but they were never produced.

*Gunners and Guns* has an interesting history in that it was originally released in the early summer of 1934 by Aywon as *Racketeers Round-Up* with Robert Hoyt credited as the director. Seven minutes of new footage were added for the Beaumont reissue, this time crediting Jerry Callahan as the director. *Riddle Ranch*, released late in 1935 and starring David Worth, is possibly a retitling of *Hell's Hacienda* with Worth replacing Conway Tearle in the lead role. It was directed by Charles Hutchison, who also helmed Tearle in *The Judgement Book*. Hutchison had been a favorite serial star and director in the silent days when he was known as "Daredevil Hutch" because of his staging and performing of action sequences. Early in the sound era he directed several interesting Poverty Row efforts like *Out of Singapore* (1932), for Goldsmith Productions [q.v.], and *On Probation* (1935), a Peerless [q.v.] release.

## Gunners and Guns

August 22, 1935, 57 minutes.

*P:* Mitchell Leichter. *D:* Jerry Callahan. *SC:* Ruth Runell. *PH:* William Tuers. *ED:* William Austin. *SD:* Ralph M. Like.

*Cast:* Edmund Cobb, Edna Aslin, Edward Allen Biby, Eddie Davis, Ned Norton, Lois Glaze, Felix Valee, Jack Cheatham, Ruth Runell, Francis Walker, Black King.

A dude ranch owner is murdered and his foreman is unjustly accused of the crime.

## Trail's End

August 22, 1935, 61 minutes.

*P:* Mitchell Leichter. *D:* Al Herman. *SC:* Jack Jevne, from the story "Trail's End" by James Oliver Curwood. *PH:* William Tuers. *ED:* William Austin. *SD:* Ralph M. Like. *Asst Dir:* Jerry Callahan.

*Cast:* Conway Tearle, Claudia Dell, Fred Kohler, Baby Charline Barry, Ernie Adams, Pat Harmon, Victor Potel, Gaylord [Steve] Pendleton, Stanley Blystone, Jack Duffy, Tom London, Hank Bell, Black King.

Out to get revenge on the men who sent him to jail, a cowboy drifts into a small town plagued by the outlaws and is made its lawman.

## The Judgement Book

October 17, 1935, 63 minutes.

*P:* Mitchell Leichter. *D:* Charles Hutchison. *SC:* E.J. Thornton. *ST:* Homer King Gordon. *PH:* Bob Doran. *ED:* James Whitehead. *AD:* Jeanette. *SD:* Cliff Ruberg. *Asst Dir:* Melville DeLay.

*Cast:* Conway Tearle, Bernadine Hayes, Howard Lang, Richard Cramer, William Gould, Roy Rice, James Aubrey, Jack Pendleton, Ray Gallagher, Francis Walker, Philip Keiffer, Dick Rush, Blackie Whiteford, Edward Clayton, Black King.

After the murder of his newspaper-owner uncle, a man takes over the journal and vows to catch the killers.

## Riddle Ranch

December 3, 1935, 59 minutes.

*P:* Mitchell Leichter. *D:* Charles Hutchison. *SC:* E.J. Thornton. *ST:* L.V. Jefferson. *PH:* Bob Doran. *ED:* George Halligan. *AD:* Jeanette. *SD:* Ralph M. Like & T.T. Triplett. *Asst Dir:* Roy Rice.

*Cast:* David Worth, June Marlowe, Baby Charline Barry, Richard Cramer, Julian Rivero, Fred "Snowflake" Toones, Roy Rice, Budd Buster, Arturo [Art] Feliz, Henry Sylvester, Ray Gallagher, Kay Brinker, Ace Cain, Larry Francis, Sue Milford, Black King.

Wanting a man's horse, an outlaw poses as a buyer and has him framed for murder. TV title: *Western Show Down.*

## Senor Jim

1936, 61 minutes.

*P:* Mitchell Leichter. *D:* Jacques Jaccard. *SC:* Celia Jaccard, from her story "I.O.U.'s of Death." *PH:* Ted McCord. *AD:* Jeanette. *Mus:* Hugh Tulane. *SD:* Leslie Taft. *Asst Dir:* William Nolte.

*Cast:* Conway Tearle, Barbara Bedford, Alberta Dugan, Fred Malatesta, Betty Mack, Bob McKenzie, Dirk Thane, Evelyn Hagara, Harrison Greene, Lloyd Brooks, Ashton & Co'ena, Tove Lindan.

A man rescues a young woman and her daughter from the law only to learn his wife is behind a scheme to separate the woman and her child.

## Desert Guns

January 13, 1936, 60 minutes. •

*P:* Mitchell Leichter. *D:* Charles Hutchison. *SC:* Jacques Jaccard & C.C. Cheddon. *PH:* J. Henry Kruse. *ED:* Fred Bain. *Asst Dir:* Roy Rice. *SD:* Cliff Ruberg. *AD:* Jeanette.

*Cast:* Conway Tearle (Kirk Allenby/Bob Enright), Margaret Morris (Roberta Enright), William Gould (Jeff Bagley), Budd Buster (Utah), Kay Brinker (Sherry Molette), Duke R. Lee (Steve Logan), Marie Werner (Mary), Charles K. French (Colonel), Roy Rice (Sheriff), Ray Gallagher (Deputy), Pinky Barnes (Henchman), Horace Murphy (Dr. Jeff D. Stanley).

Lawman Kirk Allenby (Conway Tearle) is hired by the Cattlemen's Association to bring in his look-alike, renegade rancher Bob Enright (Conway Tearle). Allenby carries out the assignment and badly injures Enright in a gun fight but then promises the dying man he will come to the rescue of his sister Roberta Enright (Margaret Morris) who is in trouble. Roberta is about to marry Jeff Bagley (William Gould), the man who framed Bob and who wants the Enright ranch. Tipsy foreman Utah (Budd Buster) thinks Allenby is Bob and takes him to the ranch where, much to the joy of Roberta, he stops the ceremony. Bagley then plots with Logan (Duke R. Lee), the Enright's stepfather, to get Bob out of the way so he can get the ranch through marrying Roberta. Allenby tells Utah the truth about his identity, and Utah informs him that Bagley and Logan are in cahoots. Logan fails in an attempt to kill Allenby and later tells Bagley he will not be a part of murder. Bagley's henchmen knock Allenby out and shoot Logan, placing the blame on the unconscious hero. Bagley then incites the locals to lynch Allenby, whom they think is Bob, but the real Bob Enright arrives as Utah shoots Bagley. Allenby is then free to romance Roberta while Bob has brought along his new bride (Kay Brinker).

Conway Tearle had starred in *The Great Divide* (1925) in the silent days and opened the talkie era with *Smoke*

**Lobby card for *Desert Guns* (Beaumont, 1936) showing Conway Tearle and Budd Buster.**

*Bellew* (1929), but he seemed an unlikely candidate for cowboy stardom, especially since he was well into his fifties and a British cowpoke as well. Tearle, however, turned out to be a very fine western star, and his polished acting style added much to this otherwise routine series for Beaumont Pictures. *Desert Guns* is saddled with a canned dramatic music score and opens with the star viewing a rhumba dance team. Otherwise it is a very acceptable horse opera which gave its star a chance to play dual roles, although the split-screen image used to show the two men together is hardly convincing. Despite his age, Conway Tearle handled the riding and fighting well, and

he is probably the only cowboy star to end up with two lovelies—each character winning a heroine. Budd Buster served as a sidekick of sorts, but his drunk routines are tiring and the best laugh in the feature comes at his expense. During a wedding sequence, the guests are awaiting the arrival of the minister. When tanked up Budd Buster comes whooping and hollering to the ranch, the prospective stepfather of the bride announces, "Here comes the preacher now." One of the more memorable moments in the film comes when Allenby, pretending to be Bob, gives Roberta a brotherly kiss that turns out to be quite passionate.

# Big 4 Film Corporation

New life was breathed into the Western early in 1929 with the success of Fox's *In Old Arizona*, followed by Paramount's *The Virginian* later in the year. Up to that time it was thought the constraints of sound equipment had doomed the Western in the talking era, but these films proved otherwise and as the year ended two independent oaters, Leo Maloney's *Overland Bound* and Davis Production's *West of the Rockies* showed the "B" Western too could prosper in the talkie era. As a result, veteran producer John R. Freuler formed Big 4 Pictures Corporation to provide fodder for the states' rights market which catered to small communities, the same places the "B" Western had thrived in the silent days. With offices at 1501 Broadway in New York City, Big 4 shared space with Educational Film Exchange, Sono Art-World Wide and National Players, a Freuler subsidiary.

Having founded the Theatre Comique in 1905 in Milwaukee, Wisconsin, John R. Freuler was no stranger to the entertainment world. In 1915 he partnered in the American Film Company, which lasted until the end of the silent era. Freuler's 1930 schedule of nine feature releases kicked off with the Edward Everett Horton comedy *Take the Heir*, but excluding the British import *Would You Believe It?*; the rest of the fare was made up of very low-grade "B" Westerns starring silent screen second echelon cowboys like Jack Perrin, Wally Wales, Buffalo Bill, Jr., Franklyn Farnum and Yakima Canutt. These oaters were produced by Flora E. Douglas, and the cowboy stars took turns playing the lead and villain roles. For example Wally Wales was the hero of *Trails of Peril* and *Breed of the West* but the bad guy in *Bar L Ranch*, in which Buffalo Bill, Jr., assumed the hero part. Wales was also the villain in *Canyon Hawks*, which gave Yakima Canutt his only hero role in the sound era. These shoddy offerings, however, found a market and more of the same would come in 1931. In 1930 Big 4 also assumed the distribution of Leo Maloney's *Overland Bound*, which was originally released by Rayton Talking Pictures/Presido and not only featured Maloney but also serial queen Allene Ray, Wally Wales and Jack Perrin, the latter with his horse Starlight. As noted both these cinema cowpokes headlined at Big 4, and adding grace to several of the company's oaters was the beautiful silent star Virginia Browne Faire who costarred with Wally Wales in *Trails of Peril* and *Breed of the West* in 1930 and *Hell's Valley* the next year.

The 1931 film schedule for the company continued with Wally Wales westerns, and toward the end of the year Bob Custer was added to the roster with two releases produced by Burton King and directed by veteran J.P. McGowan. They also teamed growing child star Buzz Barton with stalwart Francis X. Bushman, Jr., and pretty Caryl Lincoln in *Cyclone Kid*, followed by

*Tangled Fortunes* in 1932. The 1931 releases also included a couple of short subjects, *A Radio Razzberry* and *The Wages of Gin*. Outside the Westerns, the company also offered some dramas, including Jobyna Ralston's final film, *Sheer Luck*.

By 1932 Big 4 was about to become a thing of the past although the company offered five releases by spring, two of them being among their best. The year kicked off with Rin-Tin-Tin starring in *Human Targets*, which Burton King produced and J.P. McGowan helmed, with the famous canine star (in his final film role before his death that year) being supported by Francis X. Bushman, Jr., and Buzz Barton. The film had a classier look than most Big 4 fare, as did another Burton King production, *Murder at Dawn*, starring Jack Mulhall and directed by Richard Thorpe in his salad days. This old-house murder mystery certainly supplied plenty of thrills and chills for small-town audiences, but Big 4 bit the dust with two tattered Bob Custer releases, *Mark of the Spur* and *The Scarlet Brand*.

By mid–1932 Big 4 Pictures Corporation was no more, and John R. Freuler formed Freuler Film Associates (q.v.) with offices still at 1501 Broadway in Gotham. This new outfit's release schedule promised "Monarch Melodramas" and Tom Tyler Westerns.

## Take the Heir

January 20, 1930, 6 reels.

*P:* John R. Freuler & C.A. Stinson. *D:* Lloyd Ingraham. *SC:* Beatrice Van. *PH:* Allen Siegler. *Mus:* J.M. Coppersmith.

*Cast:* Edward Everett Horton, Dorothy Devore, Edythe Chapman, Frank Elliott, Otis Harlan, Kay Deslys, Margaret Campbell.

A butler impersonates his tipsy boss and falls for a pretty maid but is pursued by a gold digger.

## Would You Believe It

February 24, 1930, 5 reels.

*P:* Archibald Nettlefold. *D:* Walter Forde. *SC:* Harry Fowler Mear & Walter Forde. *PH:* Geoffrey Faithful.

*Cast:* Walter Forde, Pauline Johnson, Arthur Stratton, Albert Brouett, Anita O'Day, Anita Sharp Bolster.

After inventing a tank controlled by a wireless, a man must thwart foreign spies. This is a British import first issued in that country in 1929 by Butcher as a silent with sound added for rerelease later that year. A clip from the film appears in *Helter-Skelter* (Gainsborough, 1949).

## Beyond the Rio Grande

April 12, 1930, 50 minutes.

*D:* Harry S. Webb. *SC:* Carl Krusada. *PH:* William Nobles. *ED:* Frederick Paine. *SD:* William Garrity & George Lowery. *Song:* Henry Taylor.

*Cast:* Jack Perrin, Franklyn Farnum, Charline Burt, Buffalo Bill, Jr., Pete Morrison, Edmund Cobb, Emma Tansey, Henry Roquemore, Henry Taylor, Starlight.

A cowpoke heads below the border after being blamed for a robbery pulled by his partner.

## Ridin' Law

May 24, 1930, 6 reels.

*D:* Harry S. Webb. *SC:* Carl Kru-

Poster for *Beyond the Rio Grande* (Big 4, 1930). Pictured are Starlight, Jack Perrin and Charline Burt.

sada. *PH:* William Nobles. *ED:* Fred Bain. *SD:* William Garrity.

*Cast:* Jack Perrin, Renee Borden, Yakima Canutt, Jack Mower, Pete Morrison, Ben Corbett, Robert Walker, Fern Emmett, Olive Young, Starlight.

In Mexico smugglers capture a cowboy searching for his father's killer.

## Firebrand Jordan

June 28, 1930, 6 reels.

*P:* Henry Taylor. *D:* Alvin J. Neitz [Alan James]. *SC:* Carl Krusada. *PH:* William Nobles. *SD:* William Garrity.

*Cast:* Lane Chandler, Aline Goodwin, Yakima Canutt, Sheldon Lewis, Marguerite Ainslee, Tom London, Lew Meehan, Frank Yaconelli, Alfred Hewston, Fred Harvey, Cliff Lyons.

A cowboy on the trail of counterfeiters aids a young woman whose father is missing.

## Bar L Ranch

August 4, 1930, 6 reels.

*P:* F.E. Douglas. *D:* Harry S. Webb. *SC:* Carl Krusada. *ST:* Bennett Cohen. *PH:* William Nobles. *ED:* Fred Bain. *SD:* George Lowery.

*Cast:* Buffalo Bill, Jr., Betty Baker, Wally Wales, Yakima Canutt, Ben Corbett, Fern Emmett.

A ranch hand loses his job when he refuses to turn cattle over to a man he suspects is a crook.

## Canyon Hawks

August 26, 1930, 6 reels.

*P:* F.E. Douglas. *D:* Alvin J. Neitz

[Alan James] & J.P. McGowan. *SC:* Alvin J. Neitz. *PH:* William Nobles. *ED:* Fred Bain. *SD:* James Lowrie.

*Cast:* Yakima Canutt, Renee Borden, Buzz Barton, Wally Wales, Robert Walker, Bob Reeves, Cliff Lyons, Bobby Dunn.

After selling a young woman and her brother land for raising sheep, a man tries to rescue the girl when she is kidnapped.

## Trails of Peril

September 30, 1930, 6 reels.

*P:* F.E. Douglas. *D-SC:* Alvin J. Netiz [Alan James]. *ST:* Henry Taylor. *ED:* Ethel Davey. *SD:* James Lowrie.

*Cast:* Wally Wales, Virginia Browne Faire, Jack Perrin, Frank Ellis, Lew Meehan, Pete Morrison, Joe Rickson, Buck Connors, Bobby Dunn, Hank Bell.

When he is mistaken for an outlaw, a cowpoke decides to get the reward by capturing the bad-men. Working Title: *Trails of Danger*.

## Breed of the West

November 1, 1930, 6 reels.

*P:* F.E. Douglas. *D-SC:* Alvin J. Neitz (Alan James). *ST:* Alvin J. Neitz & Henry Taylor. *PH:* William Nobles. *ED:* Ethel Davey. *SD:* Homer Ellmaker.

*Cast:* Wally Wales, Virginia Browne Faire, Buzz Barton, Robert Walker, Edwin [Edmond] Cobb, Lafe McKee, Bobby Dunn, George Gerwing, Hank Bell, Art Mix, Frank Ellis, Slim Andrews, Bud Osborne, Slim Whitaker, Bob Burns, Fred Burns, Ben Corbett.

A crooked ranch foreman plans to rob his boss and steal his daughter, but is opposed by a cowboy sweet on the girl.

## Red Fork Range

January 12, 1931, 59 minutes.

*D:* Alvin J. Neitz [Alan James]. *SC-ST:* Henry Taylor. *PH:* William Nobles. *ED:* Ethel Davey. *SD:* Homer Ellmaker. *Prod Mgr:* Henry Taylor.

*Cast:* Wally Wales, Ruth Mix, Al Ferguson, Bud Osborne, Cliff Lyons, Lafe McKee, Will Armstrong, George Gerwing, Jim Corey, Chief Big Tree.

Outlaws try to stop a cowboy from winning a stagecoach race.

## Sheer Luck

January 26, 1931.

*D:* Bruce Mitchell. *SC:* Brownie Mitchell. *PH:* Paul Allen. *ED:* Viola Roehl.

*Cast:* Jobyna Ralston, Nick Stuart, Bobby Vernon, Reed Howes, Philo McCullough, Margaret Landis, John Ince, Oscar Smith.

A milkman attempts to rescue the girl he loves from the attentions of a corrupt politician.

## Hell's Valley

March 7, 1931, 60 minutes.

*P:* F.E. Douglas. *D-SC:* Alvin J. Neitz [Alan James]. *PH:* William Nobles. *ED:* Ethel Davey.

*Cast:* Wally Wales, Virginia Browne Faire, Walter Miller, Franklyn Farnum, Vivian Rich, Jack Phipps, Frank Lackteen, Bobby Dunn, Lafe McKee, A. McKay.

A ranger searches for a gang of Mexican bandits but falls in love with the sister of the gang leader.

## Trapped

April 14, 1931, 60 minutes.

*D:* Bruce Mitchell. *SC:* Jackson Parks & Edith Brown.

*Cast:* Nick Stuart, Priscilla Dean,

Poster for *Red Fork Range* (Big 4, 1931).

Nena Quartero, Tom Santschi, Reed Howes, George Regas, Tom O'Brien, Jimmy Aubrey, Patsy Daly.

A police captain falls in love with a nightclub woman suspected of involvement with bank robbers.

## So This Is Arizona

April 24, 1931, 60 minutes.

*P-D:* David Kirkland. *SC:* Joe Lawliss. *PH:* R.B. Hooper.

*Cast:* Wally Wales, Lorraine La Val, Fred Church, Buzz Barton, Don Wilson, Tete Brady, Gus Anderson, Jack Russell.

A ranger is forced to arrest the outlaw brother of the girl he loves and she rejects him.

## Riders of the Cactus

July 7, 1931, 60 minutes.

*P:* David Kirkland & Charles Connell. *D-SC:* David Kirkland. *ST:* Charles Connell. *PH:* R.B. Hooper. *SD:* B.I. Kroeger.

*Cast:* Wally Wales, Fred Church, Ed Cartright, Buzz Barton, Don Wilson, Joe Lawliss, Lorraine LaVal, Tete Brady, Etta Delmas, Gus Anderson.

A cowboy trails outlaws who are after a man seeking buried treasure.

## Headin' for Trouble

September 22, 1931, 56 minutes.

*D:* J.P. McGowan. *SC-ST:* George Morgan. *PH:* Edward Kull. *ED:* Fred Bain. *SD:* L. John Myers.

*Cast:* Bob Custer, Betty Mack, Andy Shuford, Robert Walker, Jack Hardey, John Ince, Duke Lee.

A cowboy attempts to save a young woman and a small boy from outlaws.

## Cyclone Kid

October 28, 1931, 60 minutes.

*P:* Burton King. *D:* J.P. McGowan. *SC-ST:* George Morgan. *PH:* Edward Kull. *ED:* Fred Bain. *SD:* George S. Hutchins.

*Cast:* Buzz Barton, Francis X. Bushman, Jr., Caryl Lincoln, Ted Adams, Lafe McKee, Blackie Whiteford, Nadja, Silver Harr.

A boy helps his ranch foreman pal stop outlaws and romance his sister.

## Quick Trigger Lee

November 24, 1931, 59 minutes.

*P:* Burton King. *D:* J.P. Mc-

Gowan. *SC-ST:* George Morgan. *PH:* Edward Kull. *ED:* Fred Bain. *SD:* George S. Hutchins.

*Cast:* Bob Custer, Caryl Lincoln, Monte Montague, Lee Cordova, Richard Carlyle, Frank Ellis, Al Taylor.

A notorious gunman comes to the aid of a miner whose property is sought by crooks.

## Human Targets

January 10, 1932, 61 minutes.

*P:* Burton King. *D:* J.P. Mc-Gowan. *SC-ST:* George Morgan. *PH:* Edward Kull. *ED:* Fred Bain. *SD:* George S. Hutchins.

*Cast:* Rin-Tin-Tin, Francis X. Bushman, Jr., Buzz Barton, Pauline Parker, Franklyn Farnum, Edmund Cobb, Ted Adams, Leon Kent, Nanci Price, Helen Gibson, John Ince, Edgar Lewis, Fred "Snowflake" Toones.

A boy, a cowboy and a dog fight gold claim jumpers.

## Mark of the Spur

February 10, 1932, 58 minutes.

*P:* Burton King. *D:* J.P. Mc-Gowan. *SC-ST:* Frederick Chapin. *PH:* Edward Kull. *ED:* Fred Bain. *SD:* Earl Crain.

*Cast:* Bob Custer, Lillian Rich, George Chesebro, Lafe McKee, Franklyn Farnum, Charles Edler, Ada Bell Driver, Bud Osborne, Blackie Whiteford, Frank Ball, Jack Long, Blackjack Ward, Harry Todd.

A cowboy takes a job on a ranch and exposes a crook, winning the love of the owner's pretty daughter.

## Murder at Dawn

February 22, 1932, 61 minutes.

*P:* Burton King. *D:* Richard Thorpe. *SC-ST:* Barry Barringer. *PH:*

Lobby card for *Human Targets* (Big 4, 1932). Pictured at left are Edmond Cobb and Buzz Barton.

Edward Kull. *ED:* Fred Bain. *SD:* Earl N. Crain.

*Cast:* Jack Mulhall (Danny), Josephine Dunn (Doris Farrington), Marjorie Beebe (Gertrude), Eddie Boland (Freddie), Mischa Auer (Henry), Martha Mattox (Housekeeper), J. Crauford Kent (Arnstein), Phillips Smalley (Judge Folger), Frank Ball (Dr. Farrington), Al Cross (Goddard).

Lovers Danny (Jack Mulhall) and Doris (Josephine Dunn) go along with married friends (Marjorie Beebe and Eddie Boland) to the remote home of Doris' inventor father (Frank Ball) to get permission to wed. They find the locals leery of the Farrington mansion, and once there, the quartet is exposed to some weird goings-on as well as a mysterious housekeeper (Martha Mattox) and her moronic son (Mischa

Auer). They find out Farrington has invented a machine to control solar power, but soon a murder occurs and the professor disappears. After a number of strange incidents, Doris is nearly killed, and it appears the invention may explode and kill everyone in the house. Finally Danny figures out the complicated proceedings and manages to save the day.

Evidently the profits from the Wally Wales, Bob Custer and Buzz Barton westerns were ample enough for John R. Freuler to stretch the budget for *Murder at Dawn*, the best-looking of his Big 4 releases. Jack Mulhall and Josephine Dunn were still box office draws and added to the marquee value of this Poverty Row effort, which properly exploits the old-house murder mystery genre so popular in films from the mid–1920s into the 1940s. Also a definite plus is the use of Kenneth Strickfaden's futuristic laboratory equipment, which is best known from Universal's *Frankenstein* (1931) and *Bride of Frankenstein* (1935) but was also used to advantage in low-budget affairs like *The Lost City* (1934) and *Ghost Patrol* (1936). Overall, *Murder at Dawn* was the best of Big 4's cinematic offerings, and it is too bad it came along so near the time of the company's demise.

## Tangled Fortunes

March 23, 1932, 60 minutes.
*P:* Burton King. *D:* J.P. McGowan. *SC-ST:* Frank Howard Clark. *ED:* Edward Kull. *ED:* Fred Bain. *SD:* Earl N. Crain.
*Cast:* Buzz Barton, Caryl Lincoln, Francis X. Bushman, Jr., Edmund Cobb, Frank Ball, Francis Ford, Charles Hartsinger, Jack Long, Fargo Bussey, Ezell Poole.

Crooks try to terrorize a small boy into telling them the location of a gold mine after they kill his father.

## The Scarlet Brand

May 9, 1932, 55 minutes.
*P:* Burton King. *D:* J.P. McGowan. *SC:* Ethel Hill. *PH:* Edward Kull. *ED:* Fred Bain. *SD:* Earl N. Crain.
*Cast:* Bob Custer (Bud Bryson), Betty Mack (Ellen Walker), Robert Walker (Bill Morris), Frank Ball (John Walker), Duke Lee (Sheriff), Nelson McDowell (Slim Grant), Frederick Ryter (Squint), Blackie Whiteford (Cactus), William Nolte (Lefty), Jack Long (Pete).

Bud Bryson (Bob Custer) is mistaken for a cattle thief and branded but escapes from the law with the aid of stranger Slim Grant (Nelson McDowell). The duo get work at the ranch of John Walker (Frank Ball), and Bud falls for Walker's daughter Ellen (Betty Mack). The actual leader of the rustlers, rancher Bill Morris (Robert Walker), lusts after Ellen and gets her father arrested. Bud vows to clear himself and Mr. Walker, but when Ellen learns he is wanted by the law for rustling she rejects him. Slim overhears Morris plan to kill Bud, and he causes the latter's arrest. Bud, however, escapes again, and at Morris' ranch Slim, who is really an investigator for the Cattlemen's Association, gets the drop on the outlaws, whom he and Bud fight. The sheriff and his posse arrive and arrest Morris and his gang, and Bud and Ellen are reconciled.

The last of a quartet of Bob Custer starrers producer Burton King and director J.P. McGowan did for Big 4, *The Scarlet Brand* was also the company's last gasp. Marred by choppy editing and direction with long, drawn-out chase sequences, the film was bottom-rung but typical of Poverty Row oaters of the period. Its worst detriment, however, came in the person of star Bob Custer, who had been around since the silent days and who would survive well into the mid–1930s. Unfortunately, Custer had minimal acting ability, and he was too often expressionless, speaking in a monotone, even when delivering lines like, "My hands are itching to get hold of Morris." Custer's sole facial expression seemed to be moving his eyes from right to left and back again when given a close-up.

## Flying Lariats

August 23, 1932, 53 minutes.
*P:* Robert Connell. *D-SC:* David

Kirkland. *PH:* R.B. Hooper. *SD:* B.J. Kroeger.

*Cast:* Wally Wales (Wally Dunbar), Sam J. Garrett (Sam Dunbar), Fred Church (Tex Johnson), Don Wilson (Mr. Appleby), Buzz Barton (Buzz), Gus Anderson (Sheriff), Bonnie Jean Gray (Bonnie Starr), Etta Dalmas (Mrs. Murphy), Joe Lawliss (Dad Starr), Tete Brady (Kate Weston), Lorraine LaVal (Telegraph Operator).

The Dunbar brothers (Wally Wales, Sam J. Garrett) both like Bonnie Starr (Bonnie Jean Gray) and try to help her and her father (Joe Lawliss) save their ranch by providing the money for Bonnie to ride in the Sonora Roundup rodeo. Crook Tex Johnson (Fred Church) talks local banker Appleby (Don Wilson) into taking bank funds to support a betting scheme on the rodeo events. Meanwhile Wally and Sam Dunbar end up fighting over Bonnie, who agrees to marry Wally although she really wants Sam. During the rodeo, Johnson holds up the box office and escapes but is spotted by local boy Buzz (Buzz Barton), and the Dunbars and the sheriff (Gus Anderson) get on Johnson's trail and Sam captures him. Then Wally brings his brother and Bonnie together.

One of the worst of early sound westerns, *Flying Lariats* is plagued by poor sound and lighting and is badly photographed. The plot is thin and stock rodeo footage, a rodeo parade, a horse doing tricks and a barn dance are interpolated to pad the running time. A running gag of an over-protective mother (Etta Dalmar) trying to keep her young son (Buzz Barton) from competing in the rodeo is quite tiresome and the script is plagued with bad dialogue, such as star Wally Wales saying of villain Fred Church, "Gosh that fella's got a nasty laugh." Filmed with lots of long shots and mostly outdoor atmosphere, this lumbering affair seems far longer than its less-than-one-hour running time. While star Wally Wales gets sole billing above the title he has less to do than costar Sam J. Garrett, a near nonactor who could accomplish rope and horse tricks. Former silent cowboy star Fred Church handles the bad guy role in an adequate fashion, but it is sad to see him demoted to the wrong side of the law. Finally, the film even has a theme song, "He's Just a Lonely Cowboy," sung over the closing credits by a ghastly noncredited vocalist.

# Biltmore Productions

Throughout the 1920s Harry S. Webb turned out cheap westerns for various companies, including his own Harry Webb Productions in the middle of the decade. With the coming of sound, Webb turned away from horse operas when he became involved in making three releases for the short-lived Biltmore Productions. For Webb, Biltmore was just a hiatus between the silent era and full-fledged sound productions. Biltmore also had money in two Big 4 (q.v.)

Jack Perrin westerns, *Beyond the Rio Grande* and *Ridin' Law*, both 1930 releases directed by Webb. When Biltmore folded he remained with Big 4 before going on to make scores of cheap pictures for his own outfits like Reliable and Metropolitan [qq.v.].

Biltmore's first release was *Untamed Justice*, a movie that recycled a western theme in a modern setting with the hero being an airmail pilot. For box office appeal Webb teamed Arab, a horse, and Muro, a wolf-dog. The two were back in the company's best-known release, *Phantoms of the North*, a north country melodrama noted for its two villains, Boris Karloff and Joe Bonomo. The film claimed it had scenes of wild wolves pursuing a horse herd, but the so-called wolves were actually police dogs.

Despite the film's scenic locales, *Variety* called it "a quickie that a home movie group wouldn't figure good box office, even for their friends in the parlor."

*Dark Skies* was released by Biltmore late in 1929 but got most of its screenings early the next year. Set in a small California coastal community, the movie was an adventure romance starring Wallace MacDonald and Shirley Mason.

The film's chief claim to fame is that it contained the song "Juanita," which has since become a standard, recorded by such diverse performers as organist Jesse Crawford and baritone Robert Merrill. Unlike *Untamed Justice* and *Phantoms of the North*, which were silent films (although the latter had some music sequences), *Dark Skies* was a talkie and was issued through Capital Film Exchange. Historians have sometimes confused the feature with *Darkened Skies* (Paramount, 1929) and mistakenly listed that film's leading lady, Evelyn Brent, as *Dark Skies'* star.

Biltmore's final release, *The Poor Millionaire*, was the sound-film debut of stuntman Richard Talmadge, and he produced the film with veteran George Melford directing. Talmadge had doubled for Douglas Fairbanks in the silent era before starring in movies, but he overextended himself in his first sound feature, playing both hero and villain. When the physical action halted, Talmadge's lack of thespian ability and a heavily accented high-pitched voice precluded any chance for sound stardom although he would work on Poverty Row for the next six years. In fact his last features were for Bernard B. Ray and Harry S. Webb's Reliable Pictures (q.v.).

*The Poor Millionaire* was blessed with direction by George Melford, who began directing in 1914 and was one of the top directors of the silent days. He is probably best remembered for helming Rudolph Valentino in *The Sheik* in 1922.

The sound era found Melford's career at a somewhat low ebb although he did direct the highly praised Spanish version of *Dracula* in 1931 and several good Poverty Row outings like *Officer 13* and *The Eleventh Commandment*, both for Allied in 1933.

## Untamed Justice

January 27, 1929, 7 reels.

*D:* Harry S. Webb. *SC:* John Francis (Jack) Natteford. *PH:* Arthur Reeves.

*Cast:* Gaston Glass, Virginia Browne Faire, David Torrence, Philo McCullough, Allen Lake, Tom London, Sheldon Lewis, Arab, Muro.

At a Nevada ranch, a girl falsely accused of bond theft is aided by an airmail pilot, a dog and a horse.

## Phantoms of the North

June 5, 1929, 5 reels.

*D:* Harry S. Webb. *SC:* George Hull & Carl Krusada. *ST:* Flora E. Douglas. *PH:* Arthur Reeves & William Thornley. *ED:* Fred Bain.

*Cast:* Edith Roberts (Doris Rayburn), Kathleen Key (Colette), Donald Keith (Bob Donald), Josef Swickard (Colonel Rayburn), Boris Karloff (Jules Gregg), Joe Bonomo (Pierre Blanc), Muro (Dog), Arab (Horse).

Trapper Bob Donald (Donald Keith) is robbed by French-Canadian Jules Gregg (Boris Karloff), who later kills another trapper who has abducted Doris Rayburn (Edith Roberts), the daughter of the local Mounties' commander. Bob, however, is blamed for the murder and is arrested. Gregg vows to his Indian girlfriend Colette (Kathleen Key) that Bob will not live to stand trial. When he is thrown from his horse into a river, Bob is saved by his dog Muro, while Doris is kidnapped by Gregg. Colette learns what Gregg has done, and she goes to the cabin where he is holding Doris captive. Bob also arrives and confronts Gregg, defeating him in a fight. With Colette's evidence, Gregg goes to jail and Bob and Doris are reunited.

Pretty Edith Roberts had starred in a string of feature films throughout the 1920s, but her career was coming to a close when she headlined *Phantoms of the North*. Today the film is best remembered for its two bad guys, Boris Karloff and strongman Joe Bonomo. Muro, the Dog Marvel, and Arab, the Wild Horse, had been paired earlier by director Harry S. Webb in Biltmore's first release, *Untamed Justice*. Like that film, *Phantoms of the North* was silent, but a musical score arranged by Gisdon True was available to theatres. The production was a cheap, fast-paced, scenic affair which was passed by quickly in the race for sound movies.

## Dark Skies

December 15, 1929, 8 reels.

*D:* Harry S. Webb. *SC:* John Francis (Jack) Natteford. *PH:* Ray Reis & Harry Fowler. *SD:* Ralph M. Like. *Song:* Walter Sheridan & Lee Zahler.

*Cast:* Shirley Mason, Wallace MacDonald, William V. Mong, Josef Swickard, Tom O'Brien, Larry Steers, Tom Wilson.

A poor girl falls in love with a rum runner and tries to get him to go straight.

## The Poor Millionaire

June 22, 1930, 5 reels.

*P:* Richard Talmadge. *D:* George Melford. *SC:* Henry Lehrman & Ray Taylor.

*Cast:* Richard Talmadge, Constance Howard, George Irving, Frederick Vroom, John Hennings, Fannie Midgley, Jay Hunt.

Trouble ensues when the escaped convict twin of a millionaire impersonates him.

# Burroughs-Tarzan Enterprises

In an effort to get better screen treatment for his Tarzan character, Edgar Rice Burroughs went into partnership with his friend, actor Ashton Dearholt, to form Burroughs-Tarzan Enterprises. Burroughs' intent was to make a Tarzan film annually and to branch out into other screen projects. The new company was launched in 1934, and when attempts to borrow Johnny Weissmuller and Buster Crabbe to play Tarzan proved futile, a talent search was made, and the part was awarded to Olympic star Herman Brix. (Burroughs' son-in-law James Pierce had played the part in the silent *Tarzan and the Golden Lion* in 1927 and had also essayed the role on radio with Burroughs' daughter Joan as Jane, but he was now too old for the part on screen.) The new project was variously titled *Tarzan in Guatemala, Tarzan and the Green Goddess, Tarzan's 1935 Adventure* and *The New Adventures of Tarzan*, the latter title finally getting the nod.

With animal footage already shot at the Selig Zoo in Los Angeles, an expedition to Guatemala to film the storyline was led by Ashton Dearholt late in 1934. On landing the crew encountered a terrible storm, and later in a jungle location another storm put out the company's electrical equipment. The picture, a twelve-chapter serial, took four months to shoot with the production being constantly plagued by bad weather, heat, insects and poisonous reptiles. The company was headquartered in Guatemala City, but shooting was also done at Chichicastenango, an eight-thousand foot plateau town, and at the Mayan temple at Tikal. Actor Don Castello had to be replaced by Ashton Dearholt in the villainous role of Ragland when Costello came down with jungle fever. The result was a scenic but awkward and crude production hampered by poor sound recording and a convoluted plotline. To tangle matters further, Dearholt began an affair with leading lady Ula Holt. When the company returned to Hollywood, Dearholt and his wife Florence separated, and the latter took up with Edgar Rice Burroughs, who was estranged from his alcoholic wife, Emma. Despite the marital difficulties, however, Burroughs and Dearholt maintained their partnership.

Late in the spring of 1935, two months after its completion, *The New Adventures of Tarzan* saw theatrical release. In addition to its dozen episodes, the serial was released by the company as a 75-minute feature a year later. Although not a critical success the chapterplay made money and Burroughs-Tarzan optioned other properties including Willard Mack's play *The Drag Net*, which was filmed under that title and starred silent-screen favorites Rod LaRoque, Marian Nixon and Betty Compson. It was an old-fashioned affair, however. Much better received was the semidocumentary, *Tundra*, released in the late summer of 1936. It told of a doctor (Del Campre) crashlanding in the Arctic while on a mission of mercy and starting a four-hundred-mile journey accompanied by two bear cubs and pursued by their mother. The *Motion Picture Herald* called it "educational entertainment which rates well above the classification of a travelogue ... extraordinary entertainment." Footage from the feature was used later in the 1949 RKO Radio release *Arctic Fury*.

Like most independents, Burroughs-Tarzan always felt the pinch for money, and expenses outraced profits by the end of 1936 when *The Phantom of Santa Fe* was released. This oddity is more interesting for its history than for its entertainment value. It was originally made in 1931 as *The Hawk* and filmed in a two-color process called Multicolor. The finished product, however, was unsaleable due to production problems and the timbre of star Norman Kerry's speaking voice. The film's rough cut lay dormant for five years until Ashton Dearholt saw possibilities in its release value. At considerable expense he had the film re-recorded and re-edited, with the color process being finished by Cinecolor, an outfit which had taken over the Multicolor labs. The result, however, was hardly worth the effort, and *The Phantom of Santa Fe* got sparse showings.

The feature version of *The New Adventures of Tarzan* had proved profitable, so another feature was culled from the serial and issued in the fall of 1937. Called *Tarzan and the Green Goddess*, this second feature used new footage of Ashton Dearholt and Jack Mower and provided a different ending from that of the original serial. This film too proved successful, especially in London, but the handwriting was on the wall. Outstanding debts forced the termination of Burroughs-Tarzan Enterprises and its subsidiary, Burroughs-Tarzan Pictures, in 1938 with *Tarzan and the Green Goddess* being picked up for release by Principal Pictures [q.v.].

## The New Adventures of Tarzan

May 21, 1935, 12 chapters.

*P:* Ashton Dearholt, George W. Stout, Ben S. Cohen & Edgar Rice Burrouhs (uncredited). *D:* Edward Kull. *SC:* Charles F. Royal. *ST:* Charles F. Royal & Edwin F. Blum, from the works of Edgar Rice Burroughs. *PH:* Edward Kull & Ernest F. Smith. *ED:* Edward Schroeder. *Art Dir:* Charles Clague. *Music:* Abe Meyer. *SP Eff:* Ray Mercer & Howard Anderson. *Asst Dir:* Wilbur F. McCaugh. *SD:* Lyle E. Willey.

*Cast:* Herman Brix [Bruce Bennett] (Tarzan), Ula Holt (Ula Vale), Frank Baker (Major Francis Martling), Dale Walsh (Alice Martling), Harry Ernest (Gordon Hamilton), Don Castello (role actually portrayed by Ashton Dearholt) (Ragland), Lewis Sargent (George), Merrill McCormack (Bouchart), Mrs. Gentry (Queen Maya), Earl Dwire (Old Man), Jiggs (Nkima the Chimpanzee).

The title cards for *The New Adventures of Tarzan* noted the movie was made on location in Guatemala and was carried out despite personal danger to cast and crew. It was also noted the sound quality was not overly good due to on-location difficulties.

Poster for *The New Adventures of Tarzan* (Burroughs-Tarzan, 1935).

Ironically, in later years portions of the film were redubbed with another actor mouthing Tarzan's dialogue. With all its technical difficulties, however, the movie is one of the most authentic and scenic of Tarzan films, and for once the Ape Man is shown to be the literate and well-educated Lord Greystoke of the Burroughs novels. There is much footage of many animals (although it is a bit mind-boggling to see elephants and hippos in Central America), and there are some beautiful waterfalls from along the Rio Dulce River. Just as vivid are the Mayan temple at Tikal and the old Spanish ruins at Antigua. There are some goofs in the film, however, as in the scene where Tarzan jumps into the river wearing cut-offs and emerges, after being chased by crocodiles, in a loincloth. Still, Herman Brix, who would go on to make

Advertisement for the serial *The New Adventures of Tarzan* (Burroughs-Tarzan, 1935).

serials and programmers for Republic, Puritan and Victory before emerging as leading man Bruce Bennett in the 1940s, was fine indeed as Tarzan and Ula Holt was a most enticing leading lady.

*The New Adventures of Tarzan* opens in Africa with Tarzan (Herman Brix) being informed that his best friend, Lieutenant D'Arnot, the man who took Tarzan out of the jungle, educated him and established his identity as Lord Greystoke, has crashlanded in the jungles of Guatemala and is held prisoner by Monster Men. Tarzan vows to go to Central America to rescue his pal. Also going there in search of the Mayan artifact the Green Goddess, which houses priceless gems, is Major Martling (Frank Baker), his daughter Alice (Dale Walsh), her fiancé Gordon Hamilton (Harry Ernest) and bungler George (Lewis Sargent). Also on board the ship to Guatemala is ruthless adventurer Ragland (Ashton Dearholt), who also covets the Green Goddess, and the beautiful and mysterious Ula Vale (Ula Holt), whose brother died in the crash with D'Arnot, as both men were also on the trail of the Mayan relic. In Guatemala, Ragland steals a map to the location of the Lost City, which houses the Green Goddess, and Tarzan and the others go in pursuit. Ragland finds a cave filled with vampire bats which leads to the Lost City while Tarzan and his friends also arrive and are captured by the Monster Men. As Tarzan is about to be sacrificed to the Mayan gods, the city's queen (Mrs. Gentry) falls in love with him and spares his life. At the same time Ragland steals the Green Goddess and Tarzan is able to escape. George uses a machine gun to kill many of the Monster Men, and the group escapes while

Ragland hides the Goddess and later rejoins Tarzan and company, pretending to be their friend. Ula and her guides find the Goddess and hide it while Ragland tries to retrieve the relic. Ragland makes several attempts to kill Tarzan, Ula and the others and fails, but he is able to steal Major Martling's codebook, which is needed to open the Goddess. When Ragland attempts to escape on a smuggling boat after obtaining the Goddess he is followed by Tarzan and the Martling party. The entire group is arrested by local police but Ula intercedes and reveals she is a secret agent on Ragland's trail. Ragland is arrested and the Green Goddess is returned to the Guatemalan people.

It should be noted that the role of the Mayan queen was played by Mrs. Gentry, cotrainer of the chimp Jiggs, and that the feature version of *The New Adventures of Tarzan*, released in the summer of 1936, ends with Tarzan defeating Ragland and taking the Green Goddess after their escape from the Mayan ruins.

A second feature, *Tarzan and the Green Goddess*, billed as a sequel to the initial movie, was released in 1937 and in later releases Herman Brix was billed on screen as Bruce Bennett. This version takes up where the feature film leaves off, with Tarzan and the Martling expedition planning to take the Green Goddess to civilization after their daring escape from the Monster Men at the Mayan temple. It is now revealed the Goddess contains a secret Mayan formula for a powerful explosive which is being sought by the world's nations. Ragland too has escaped, and as the party heads to the coast they are attacked by natives. Ragland steals the Goddess and the code book which reveals the formula for the explosive. Tarzan trails the bad man but he escapes to Puerto Barrios where Tarzan manages to recover the codebook but not the Goddess. En route to Quiriquia in the interior, Ragland's men capture Tarzan, but he escapes while Monster Men from the Lost City set out to retrieve their idol. They capture Major Martling and George while Ula saves Tarzan from drowning when the codebook falls into the river rapids. Tarzan, with Ula following, returns to the Lost City and is captured, but Ula manages to help him escape. They rescue the Major and George, and the group heads to Mantique to stop Ragland, who is planning an escape by water. There Tarzan recovers the Goddess while Major Martling charters a sailing ship belonging to Blade (Jack Mower), not realizing he is in cahoots with Ragland. At sea a storm develops. Ula spots Ragland on board, but the latter is shot in a fight with Blade. Tarzan saves Ula, Major Martling and George from the storm and they reach shore with the Goddess. Later at a costume party at Greystoke Manor Ula destroys the explosive formula for the good of humanity, and she and Tarzan find romance.

## The Drag Net

May 13, 1936, 64 minutes.
    *P:* Ashton Dearholt. *AP:* Burton King. *D:* Vin Moore. *SC:* J. Mulhauser, from the play by Willard Mack. *PH:* Edward Kull. *ED:* Donald Briggs & Thomas Neff. *AD:* Charles Clague. *SD:* W.C. Smith. *Asst Dir:* Glenn Cook.
    *Cast:* Rod LaRocque, Marian Nixon, Betty Compson, Jack Adair, Edward LeSaint, Donald Kerr, Edward Keane, Al K. Hall, Joseph Girard, John Dilson, John Bantry, Allen Matthews, Sid Payne.

When a society matron is murdered, a playboy who witnessed the crime seeks the culprit.

## Tundra

August 25, 1936, 78 minutes.
    *P:* George W. Stout. *D:* Norman Dawn. *SC:* Charles F. Royal & Norman S. Parker. *ST:* Norman Dawn. *PH:* Norman Dawn, Jacob Kull & Edward Kull. *ED:* Walter Thompson & Thomas Neff. *AD:* Charles Clague. *Mus:* Abe Meyer. *Asst Dir:* Glenn Cook.
    *Cast:* Del Campre, Merrill McCormack, Earl Dwire, Wally Howe, Jack Santos, Fraser Acosta, Mrs. Elsie Duran, Bertha Maldanado.
    Semidocumentary filmed in the Arctic Circle in a six-month period about a doctor who treks four hundred miles into the wasteland after a plane crash.

## The Phantom of Santa Fe

November, 1936, 73 minutes, color.
    *D:* Jacques Jaccard. *SC:* Charles F. Royal. *PH:* Otto Himm. *ED:* Walter Thompson. *SD:* Dave Stoner & Thomas Neff.
    *Cast:* Norman Kerry, Nena Quartero, Frank Mayo, Monte Montague, Carmelita Geraghty, Jack Mower, Tom O'Brien, Frank Ellis, Merrill McCormack, Fernando Valdez.
    A foppish young man is really the dashing defender of justice who opposes a crook and his renegades. Made in 1931 as *The Hawk.*

## Tarzan and the Green Goddess

1937, 72 minutes.
    *D:* Edward Kull. *SC:* Charles F. Royal, from the story by Edgar Rice

Burroughs. *PH:* Edward Kull & Ernest F. Smith.

    *Cast:* Herman Brix (Bruce Bennett), Ula Holt, Frank Baker, Don Castello (part actually played by Ashton Dearholt), Dale Walsh, Jack Mower, Harry Ernest, Lewis Sargent, Earl Dwire.

    In Guatemala Tarzan tries to stop crooks from stealing a precious Green Goddess. The film was reissued by Principal Exchange on June 3, 1938.

# Capital Film Exchange

    Like First Division (q.v.), Capital Film Exchange was a distributor for small companies that did not want to involve themselves with the various states' rights distribution outfits. Also like First Division, Capital Film Exchange not only released the products of others both domestic and foreign, but it also made its own occasional product. Mainly, though, the company's domestic release schedule was made up of single-shoots by various small-time producers. The exception to this was a trio of action features made by Richard Talmadge Productions starring the famous stuntman of the silent days.

    The producer behind Capital Film Exchange was J.D. "Jack" Trop, who had come to the movie business in 1917 as an editor for National Film Exchanges. From 1930 through 1933 he operated Capital and then joined forces with Harry Sherman to produce the popular "Hopalong Cassidy" series at Paramount in the mid–1930s. When Sherman moved to United Artists, Trop formed his own Este Productions in 1942 and made government and commercial movies.

    Capital Film Exchange's first release was *Romance of the West* in 1930, starring veteran cowboy star Jack Perrin and his horse, Starlight. By 1931 Capital, which had its main headquarters at 630 Ninth Avenue in New York City, was releasing products from Germany with a total of sixteen features that year. From Britain the company presented Conway Tearle in *Captivation*, and Richard Talmadge boosted the company's revenues with his trio of starrers, *Yankee Don*, *Dancing Dynamite* and *Scareheads*. The company also distributed some of the early Allied (q.v.) products like Hoot Gibson in *Clearing the Range*.

    The same pattern continued in 1932 although the Talmadge actioners were replaced by two dramas—*Hell's House* (starring Junior Durkin, with Pat O'Brien and Bette Davis in support) and *Exposure*, starring Lila Lee. Capital also distributed a Willis Kent (q.v.) western called *Wyoming Whirlwind*, with Lane Chandler, but the bulk of its releases came from Germany with twenty imports from that country. By 1933, however, the company imported only two German features and also released only two domestic products, Marian Marsh in *Daring Daughters* and Thelma Todd in *Cheating Blondes*. By now most of the independent domestic product outside the states' rights market belonged to First Division Exchanges while foreign features were being distributed by outfits like Amkino, Kinematrade, Protex and UFA.

Technically, Capital Film Exchange came to an end in 1933, but J.D. Trop remained in the distribution business for one more feature, *Outlaws' Highway*, released in November 1934. This action western featured the dog Kazan and his trainer John King (who produced the feature) as well as a white stallion called Cactus. The feature was later reissued by Samuel S. Krellberg as *Fighting Fury*.

## Romance of the West

August 10, 1930, 53 minutes.
　　*P:* Arthur Hammond. *D-SC-ED:* Robert & John Tansey.
　　*Cast:* Jack Perrin, Edna Marion, Tom London, Henry Roquemore, Ben Corbett, Fern Emmett, Dick Hatton, Edwin August, Starlight.
　　A cowboy and an ex-boxer vie for the affections of a young woman in Mexico.

## Yankee Don

May 17, 1931, 61 minutes.
　　*P:* Richard Talmadge. *D:* Noel Mason. *SC:* Frances Jackson. *ST:* Madeline Allen.
　　*Cast:* Richard Talmadge, Lupita Tovar, Gayne Whitman, Julian Rivero, Sam Appel, Alma Real, Victor Stanford.
　　A New York City crook flees to Mexico where he falls in love with a pretty senorita and helps her father save his hacienda from crooks.

## Dancing Dynamite

August 16, 1931, 63 minutes.
　　*P:* Richard Talmadge. *D:* Noel Mason.
　　*Cast:* Richard Talmadge, Blanche Mehaffey, Robert Ellis, Richard Cramer, Harvey Clark, Dot Farley, Jack Ackroyd, Stanley Blystone, Walter Brennan.

A Catalina Island fisherman tries to break into society and ends up helping a wealthy young lady beset by kidnappers.

## Captivation

September 27, 1931, 76 minutes.
　　*P-D:* John Harvel. *SC:* Edgar Middleton, from his play. *PH:* James Rogers. *ED:* Stewart B. Moss.
　　*Cast:* Conway Tearle, Betty Stockfield, Violet Vamburgh, Robert Farquharson, Marilyn Mawn, A. Bromley Davenport, Louie Tinsley, Frederick Volpe, George DeWarfax, Dorothy Black.
　　A woman decides to teach a snooty novelist a lesson while they are both guests on a yacht. A British import.

## Scareheads

October 25, 1931, 67 minutes.
　　*P:* Richard Talmadge. *D:* Noel Mason.
　　*Cast:* Richard Talmadge, Gareth Hughes, Jacqueline Wells [Julie Bishop], Joseph Girard, Virginia True Boardman, King Baggott, Lloyd Whitlock, Walter James, Edward Lynch, Nancy Caswell, True Boardman.
　　Sent to prison for opposing a crooked mayor, a reporter escapes to prove his innocence.

Pat O'Brien, Bette Davis and Junior Durkin in *Hell's House* (Capital Film Exchange, 1932).

## Hell's House

February 14, 1932, 72 minutes.

*P:* Benjamin F. Zeidman. *D-ST:* Howard Higgin. *SC:* Paul Gangelin & B. Harrison Orkow. *PH:* Allen G. Siegel. *ED:* Edward Schroeder. *Art Dir:* Edward Jewell. *Prod Mgr:* Harry C. Leavitt.

*Cast:* Junior Durkin (Jimmy Mason), Pat O'Brien (Matt Kelly), Bette Davis (Peggy Gardner), Junior Coghlan (Shorty), Charles Grapewin (Henry Clark), Emma Dunn (Emma Clark), Morgan Wallace (Frank Gebhart), Hooper Atchley (Guard), Wallis Clark (Judge), James Marcus (Superintendent Charlie Thompson), Mary Alden (Mrs. Mason).

After his mother (Mary Alden) is killed in a hit-and-run accident, teenager Jimmy Mason (Junior Durkin) comes to the big city to live with his aunt (Emma Dunn) and uncle (Charley Grapewin). There he meets a fast-talking boarder Matt Kelly (Pat O'Brien), whom Jimmy comes to idolize, not realizing Matt is a bootlegger. Jimmy is also befriended by Matt's girlfriend Peggy (Bette Davis), and Matt gives him a job watching his operations, although Jimmy is unaware of the source of Matt's business until the police raid his office. Refusing to squeal on Matt, Jimmy is sentenced to three years at the State Industrial School for Boys where he becomes a victim of the harsh conditions by being forced to work in the brickyard. He becomes pals with another inmate, Shorty (Junior Coughlan), who has a bad heart. When newspaper editor Frank Gebhart (Morgan Wallace) tries to expose the corruption at the school, he is tricked by the superintendent (James Marcus) and a sadistic guard

(Hooper Atchley) and does not get his story. When Jimmy tries to sneak a letter out to Matt asking for help, Shorty is caught trying to pass the missive and takes the blame. He is placed in solitary, where his condition worsens. Jimmy, who had worked his way up to monitor, escapes from the institution in a garbage truck and comes to Matt for help. At Peggy's urging, Matt takes Jimmy to Gebhart with his story. Although Shorty dies, Jimmy's story exposes the corruption at the boy's school and he is set free when Matt admits Jimmy lied to save him.

Intended as an expose of reform schools, *Hell's House* "projects as having been put together in a slipshod manner" (*Variety*). Mordaunt Hall in the *New York Times* said it "has a few moderately interesting interludes. There is, however, insufficient detail on the institutions that appeals to the spectators as being presented without prejudice." The film is poorly photographed and at times the sound is mediocre. For its time the film had the box office appeal of Junior Durkin in the lead role, but today the film's chief interest is costars Pat O'Brien and Bette Davis. In her fifth film appearance, Bette Davis is not made up well but her acting is a plus. Also pleasant is seeing her in the days before alcohol and nicotine addiction and failed personal relationships turned her into the pathetic Baby Jane-like character of her later years. The movie does contain some rather amusing dialogue. In one scene fast-talking Matt Kelly tells gullible Jimmy that he knows Rudy Vallee. "Do I know Rudy Vallee," he exclaims. "Why the megaphone was my idea."

Evidently major script changes were made at the last moment in the quick production of *Hell's House*. The published plot synopsis has Peggy Gardner as Jimmy Mason's girlfriend, who is taken from him by Matt Kelly. In the synopsis Shorty dies before Jimmy escapes from reform school and before the newspaper editor attempts to expose its corruption. Another unfilmed scene has Jimmy's aunt coming to the institution to tell him that Peggy is seeing Matt, this being the impetus for Jimmy to escape. Later Peggy tells Jimmy she befriended Matt only in an effort to make him help Jimmy.

## Cheating Blondes

May 20, 1933, 66 minutes.

*P:* Larry Darmour. *D:* Joseph Levering. *SC:* Lewis R. Foster & Islen Auster. *ST:* Gertie Des Wentworth James. *PH:* James S. Brown, Jr. *ED:* Dwight Caldwell. *Mus:* Lee Zahler. *SD:* Charles Franklin. *Asst Dir:* J.A. Duffy.

*Cast:* Thelma Todd, Ralf Harolde, Inez Courtney, Milton Wallis, Mae Busch, Earl McCarty, William Humphries, Dorothy Gulliver, Brooks Benedict, Eddie Fetherstone, Ben Savage.

A reporter attempts to prove his girl was framed on a fake criminal charge. Also called *House of Chance*. Reissued in 1952 as *Girls in Trouble*.

## Outlaws' Highway

J.D. Trop, November 1, 1934, 61 minutes.

*P:* John [Jack] King. *D:* Bob Hill. *SC:* Myron Dattlebaum. *PH:* Glen Gano. *SD:* Cliff Ruberg. *Supv:* Dave Berg.

*Cast:* Kazan, John [Jack] King, Bonita Baker, Tom London, Philo McCullough, Lafe McKee, Bartlett

[Bart] Carre, Del Morgan, Jack Donovan, Cactus, Teddy.

A lawman is helped by his dog and a white stallion in fighting a gang of outlaws. Reissued as *Fighting Fury* in 1935 by Sherman S. Krellberg.

# Chesterfield-Invincible

The longest running of the Poverty Row motion picture production companies was the Chesterfield Motion Picture Corporation, which had titles in release from 1925 to 1937. The company was run by George R. Batcheller, and in its twelve-year history Chesterfield made over one hundred feature films, including many releases that went out under the Invincible banner, that company having merged with Chesterfield in 1932. The two operations shared offices at 1540 Broadway in New York City, but like most independents Chesterfield-Invincible did not have its own studio. For most of its productions the company leased space at Universal City, later going to both RKO-Pathe and Republic before folding in 1937.

Although made in assembly-line fashion, the Chesterfield-Invincible product had a polished look uncharacteristic of many quickie operators. While their product was made quickly, it was done with efficiency and care, and the studio's features have a quality look that belies their non-major company status. For the most part, Chesterfield-Invincible was almost a family affair. George R. Batcheller took credit for the Chesterfield releases while Maury M. Cohen did the same on the Invincible titles. M.A. Anderson, who came to Chesterfield in 1926 and remained with the studio for a decade, is credited with photographing almost all of the company's features, well over eighty releases. Edward C. Jewell was just as active as the company's more-than-competent art director while Abe Meyer handled the music scores and L.E. (Pete) Clark the sound. Melville Shyer served as assistant director on most Chesterfield-Invincible features. Credit for much of the company's success must go to Lon Young, who came to Chesterfield in 1925 as a supervisor, writer and titler. A former magician, Young was involved in every aspect of film production at Chesterfield although his billing varied from producer to executive producer or supervisor.

Three directors were primarily responsible for the Chesterfield-Invincible films: Richard Thorpe, Frank R. Strayer and Charles Lamont. Thorpe directed over two dozen features for the company and also served as editor on many of his productions. Strayer helmed seventeen releases, mostly under the Invincible banner, while Lamont directed fourteen titles. Another prolific director was Phil Rosen, who brought in nine features.

Chesterfield-Invincible also limited its writers. Those scripting their product included Ewart Adamson, Charles S. Belden, Paul Perez, Robert Ellis, Karl Brown, Karen De Wolf, Arthur Hoerl, Arthur T. Horman and Edward T. Lowe. Ginger Rogers' mother, Lela E. Rogers, wrote *Women Won't Tell* (1932) for the company.

Another prolific studio employee was Roland D. Reed, who edited nearly all of the company's releases after 1934. He started in films as an extra, then became an assistant director before taking over as editor at Chesterfield-Invincible. He made his directorial debut for the company in 1936 with the remake of *The House of Secrets*, and by 1950 he had formed Roland Reed Productions in Beverly Hills, which made television commercials. Soon the company branched out into TV production, and in the 1950s Reed was a highly successful producer with such series as "Trouble with Father," starring husband-and-wife team Stuart Erwin and June Collyer, "My Little Margie," starring Gale Storm and Charles Farrell, "Waterfront," with Preston Foster, "Mystery Theatre," with Tom Conway and "Rocky Jones, Space Ranger," starring Richard Crane. Other Reed-produced programs included "The Beulah Show," starring Hattie McDaniel (and later Louise Beavers), "Alarm," starring Richard Arlen and "Men of Justice."

In front of the camera the studio collected a stock company of top-notch character actors. Among the most active of Chesterfield-Invincible players were Dorothy Christy, Dorothy Revier, Bryant Washburn, Mischa Auer, Matty Kemp, Hale Hamilton, Gwen Lee, Phillips Smalley, Lew Kelly, Robert Frazer, Lafe McKee, Wilson Benge, Gladys Blake, Holmes Herbert, Barbara Bedford, Tom Ricketts, Jack Shutta, Jane Keckley, James Burtis and Lucy Beaumont. Like most independents the company tended to get stars on their way up or down in Hollywood, but a few "names" are associated with the company. Shirley Grey starred in a half-dozen features for Chesterfield-Invincible, and Sally Blane did five movies for them. On the masculine side, Charles Starrett made five features for the studio, while Jameson Thomas and William Bakewell did seven movies each. Unlike many operations, both major and minor, the studio sometimes gave top billing to character stars. Examples include Sarah Padden in *Midnight Lady* and *Women Won't Tell* (1932), Charles Grapewin and Emma Dunn in *The Quitter* (1935), Henrietta Crossman in *The Curtain Falls* (1934) and Donald Meek in *Happiness Came C.O.D.* (1935).

Chesterfield Motion Picture Corporation first saw light in 1925 with westerns starring Bill Patton (*Flashing Steeds, Fangs of Fate*) and Eileen Sedgwick (*Girl of the West, The Sagebrush Lady*). In 1926 George R. Batcheller took his first production credit on the Bill Patton oater *Beyond the Trail*, and the company continued to issue Patton films like *Lucky Spurs* and *The Last Chance* along with Eileen Sedgwick in *Beyond All Odds* and *Thundering Speed*. Chesterfield also offered a couple of action melodramas featuring a dog called Sandow: *Code of the Northwest* (1926) and *Avenging Fang* (1927). The latter title saw release in the summer of 1927 and it was nearly a year before Chesterfield emerged with new titles, but when it did the company fell into the groove in which it would remain for the next decade.

Chesterfield's quartet of 1928 releases typifies the type of product that would ensue. *The Sky Rider*, with Lloyd Hughes and Josephine Hill, and *South of Panama*, with Carmelita Geraghty were actioners photographed by M.A. Anderson and supervised by Lon Young. Young also supervised the Arthur Hoerl-written mystery *The House of Shame*, with Creighton Hale and Virginia Browne Faire, and *The Adorable Cheat*, with Lila Lee and Cornelius Keefe, a comedy also scripted by Hoerl. Both features were directed by Burton King. Thus Chesterfield set its pattern of eschewing westerns and outdoor action-ers for indoor dramas and comedies shot on rented studio space. When the sound era arrived, Chesterfield was rather late in the shuffle, not releasing its first talkie until the late spring of 1929. This was a mystery called *The House of Secrets*, and unlike most of its product the studio filmed it in New York City using the Phonophone process. A trio of silents—*Below the Deadline, Silent Sentinel* and *Campus Knights*—followed before the next Phonophone release, *Love at First Sight*, which came out late in 1929. This was a musical-drama as was 1930's *Jazz Cinderella*. In fact, Chesterfield was still releasing silent films as late as December, 1930, with *The Midnight Special*, long after most studios had made the transition to sound. Apparently the race by the major studios to make sound features shut out small outfits like Chesterfield, who had to rely on rented studio space as well as the use of studio sound equipment.

Richard Thorpe had cut his teeth directing cheap westerns in the silent days, and with the coming of the talkies he had worked at Columbia, Tiffany and World Wide before coming to Chesterfield in 1931. His competent work-manlike style greatly accentuated the company's production quota, and with studio space more readily available with the establishment of sound features in the early 1930s, Chesterfield's output increased dramatically. From a trio of releases in 1930 the company went to five the next year, and after the 1932 merger with Invincible came a total of ten features that year. These features were mainly dramas which tended to mirror contemporary society's problems, but like today's TV soap operas, the mirror was often clouded or out of focus. In his career study of Betty Compson (*Films in Review* [August-September, 1966]) DeWitt Bodeen comments on the company's 1936 release *August Week-end*, claiming that the feature presented "love and life as it never was in high society." This evaluation pretty much sums up the content of the Chesterfield-Invincible product. Like the major studios, Chesterfield films tended to touch on society's problems but only as a facade. Unlike some of the Poverty Row independents who produced gritty looks at contemporary issues, the Chesterfield-Invincible products were strictly entertainment. They tended to move quickly, run slightly over one hour and show in urban areas as the sec-ond feature on double bills. Due to their lower rental, however, they could also work as top features in smaller theatres. Like most other independents, Chesterfield-Invincible had no distribution system of its own. Its product was distributed on a states' rights basis by First Division (q.v.), which not only released some its own productions but also those of Monogram, the British imports of Alliance and the product of other small studios.

While most of the sound era Chesterfield-Invincible features have a similar look about them, some stand out. Among the more notable of the studio's releases are *The King Murder* (1932), a fine mystery starring Conway Tearle; *The Face on the Bar Room Floor* (1932), dealing with alcoholism; *Secrets of Wu Sin* (1932), a Chinatown melodrama; *Strange People* (1932), an old-house murder mystery; *City Park* (1934), which touches on the theme of prostitution; *Fifteen Wives* (1934), about the murder of a man with fifteen ex-wives (again with Conway Tearle as the sleuth); *Green Eyes* (1934), which presents two different and plausible solutions to the same homicide; *Fugitive Road* (1934), a love triangle World War I drama involving Erich von Stroheim; *The World Accuses* (1935) and *Symphony of Living* (1935), both about child exploitation; *Death from a Distance* (1935), which includes fine special effects by Jack Cosgrove in a story about a futuristic weapon; *Murder at Glen Athol* (1936), an exciting mystery chiller; and *Missing Girls* (1936), a gangster kidnapping racket expose. Of the 1936 Invincible mystery *The Shadow Laughs*, starring Hal Skelly and Rose Hobart, *Film Daily* commented, "Quite an original plot that keeps twisting and turning with any number of unexpected surprises right up to the close makes this a good number for general audience appeal." Sadly, today it is one of the rarest of the studio's releases. A couple of oddities in the Chesterfield-Invincible release schedule include the British import *Footsteps in the Night* (1933), a mystery melodrama involving spies, and the documentary *Taming the Jungle* (1933). Outside of these two features, the company did not involve itself with imports or documentaries, nor did it have a short subject schedule.

Richard Thorpe left Chesterfield in 1934 to make a trio of features for Universal before settling into "A" productions at Metro-Goldwyn-Mayer where he would remain into the 1960s. Charles Lamont took his place while Frank R. Strayer continued to turn out features under Invincible's eagle logo. The year 1935 saw the studio with a total of twenty-one releases, but it must have over-extended itself because the schedule was dropped to fifteen in 1936 (seven from Chesterfield and eight from Invincible) and in 1937 there was one lone Chesterfield feature, Andy Clyde in the comedy *Red Lights Ahead*, a remake of the studio's 1933 effort, *In the Money*. The Andy Clyde comedy was made in 1936 but was released nearly a year after the previous entry, *The House of Secrets*. Both features were directed by former studio editor Roland D. Reed. For all practical purposes Chesterfield-Invincible ceased to exist as a production company after 1936.

Although Chesterfield-Invincible dissolved as a production company in 1936, its product continued to be seen in movie theatres well into 1937 and later. Early in 1935 First Division lost the distribution rights to Monogram Pictures, which merged with several other companies to form Republic. By 1936 First Division's release schedule had been absorbed by the newly formed Grand National Pictures. While that studio planned to make its own product to satisfy exhibitor demands for new features it was forced to fall back on the Chesterfield-Invincible, Alliance and a few other independent features to fulfill its obligations until new movies could be produced. Thus, of the more than forty early Grand National releases, the bulk were Chesterfield-Invincible product. While this situation breathed new life into some three dozen 1935–36 Batcheller-Cohen features, it must have been a bit unnerving for theatre audiences to see the Grand National train logo preceding a title card reading "Chesterfield Film Corporation presents ... An Invincible Picture."

Following the demise of Chesterfield-Invincible, George R. Batcheller and Roland Reed produced industrial films, and in 1940 Batcheller was appointed supervisor of all feature film productions at Producers Releasing Corporation (P.R.C.). He held the position until May, 1942, when he resigned to join the armed forces and was replaced by Leon Fromkess who had been P.R.C.'s general sales manager in charge of production.

## Just Off Broadway

January 10, 1929, 7 reels (silent).

*P:* Lon Young. *D:* Frank O'Connor. *SC:* Arthur Hoerl. *Titles:* Arthur Hoerl & Lon Young. *ST:* Fanny D'Morgal. *PH:* M.A. Anderson. *ED:* James Sweeney.

*Cast:* Donald Keith, Ann Christy, Larry Steers, De Sacia Mooers, Jack Tanner, Syd Saylor, Beryl Roberts, Albert Dresden.

When racketeers murder his brother, a college student hunts for the killers and falls in love with a dancer.

## The Peacock Fan

March 17, 1929, 6 reels (silent).

*P:* Lon Young. *D:* Phil Rosen. *SC:* Arthur Hoerl. *Titles:* Lee Authmar. *ST:* Adeline Leitzbach. *PH:* M.A. Anderson. *ED:* James Sweeney.

*Cast:* Lucien Prival, Dorothy Dwan, Tom O'Brien, Rosemary Theby, Carlton King, Gladden James, David Findlay, James Wilcox, Fred Malatesta, Alice True, Spencer Bell, John Fowler, Lotus Long, Fujii Kishii, Wong Foo.

A detective tries to unravel a murder surrounding a peacock fan.

## Circumstantial Evidence

April 7, 1929, 7 reels (silent).

*P:* Lon Young. *D-ST:* Wilfred Noy. *Titles:* Lee Authmar. *PH:* M.A. Anderson. *ED:* James Sweeney.

*Cast:* Cornelius Keefe, Helen Foster, Alice Lake, Charles Gerrard, Ray Hallor, Fred Walton, Jack Tanner.

When the girl he loves is blamed for the murder of a cad, a man goes to trial in her place to uncover the real killer. Remade in 1935.

## The House of Secrets

May 26, 1929, 7 reels.

*P:* George R. Batcheller. *D:* Edmund Lawrence. *SC:* Adeline Leitzbach, from the novel by Sydney Horler. *PH:* George Webber, Irving Browning, George Peters & Lester Lang. *ED:* Selma Rosenbloom.

*Cast:* Joseph Striker, Marcia Manning, Elmer Grandin, Herbert Warren, Francis M. Verdi, Richard Stevenson, Harry Southard, Edward Roseman, Walter Ringham.

An American arrives in London with a detective friend to investigate an old house and the two uncover a strange mystery. Remade in 1936.

## Below the Deadline

June 6, 1929, 6 reels (silent).

*P:* Lon Young. *D:* J.P. McGowan. *SC:* Arthur Hoerl. *Titles:* Lee Authmar. *PH:* M.A. Anderson. *ED:* James Sweeney.

*Cast:* Frank Leigh, Barbara Worth, Arthur Rankin, Walter Merrill, J.P. McGowan, Mike Donlin, Virginia Sale, Bill Patton, Tiny Ward, Charles Hickman, Fred Walton.

To get even with a police detective, jewel thieves set up his buddy for robbery using a girl as a decoy.

## Silent Sentinel

July 21, 1929, 5 reels (silent).

*D-SC-ED:* Alvin J. Neitz [Alan James]. *PH:* M.A. Anderson.

*Cast:* Gareth Hughes, Josephine Hill, Walter Maly, Lew Meehan, Aline Goodwin, Alfred Hewston, Eddie Brownell, Alice Covert, John Tansey, Edward Cecil, Jack Knight, George Morrell, Champion.

A wonder dog aids a young woman in proving that her brother was framed on an embezzling charge by his banker boss.

## Campus Knights

September 29, 1929, 6 reels (silent).

*P:* Lon Young. *D-ST:* Albert Kelly. *SC:* Arthur Hoerl. *Titles:* Lee Authmar, Lon Young & Hoey Lawlor. *PH:* M.A. Anderson. *ED:* Earl Turner.

*Cast:* Raymond McKee, Shirley Palmer, Marie Quillan, J.C. Fowler, Sybil Grove, P.J. Danby, Leo White, Lewis Sargent.

A meek professor at a girls' school gets into all kinds of trouble when his philandering twin brother romances the coeds.

## Love at First Sight

December 15, 1929, 7 reels.

*P:* George B. Batcheller. *D:* Edgar Lewis. *SC-Songs:* Lester Lee & Charles Levison. *PH:* Dal Clawson. *ED:* Russell Shields. *SD:* George Oschman.

*Cast:* Norman Foster, Suzanne Keener, Doris Rankin, Lester Cole, Abe Reynolds, Hooper Atchley, Burt Mathews, Dorothee Adam, Jim Harkins, Paul Specht & His Orchestra, Tracy & Elwood, The Chester Hale Girls.

A musical producer falls in love with his new find but fades into the background when she stars in a night club revue.

## Ladies in Love

May 4, 1930, 7 reels.

*P:* George B. Batcheller. *D:* Edgar Lewis. *SC:* Charles Beahan. *PH:* M.A. Anderson. *ED:* James Morley. *AD:* Lester E. Tope. *Asst Dir:* Melville Shyer.

*Cast:* Alice Day, Johnnie Walker, Freeman Wood, Marjorie "Babe" Kane, James Burtis, Dorothy Gould, Elinor Flynn, Mary Carr, Mary Foy, Bernie Lamont

A young songwriter comes to New York City to sell his tune to a radio star and promptly falls in love with her.

## Jazz Cinderella

September 28, 1930, 7 reels.

*P:* George R. Batcheller. *D:* Scott Pembroke. *SC:* Arthur Hoerl & Adrian Johnson. *ST:* Edwin Johns & Oliver Jones. *PH:* M.A. Anderson. *ED:* Donn Hayes. *Songs:* Jesse Greer & Ray Klages.

*Cast:* Myrna Loy, Jason Robards, Nancy Welford, Dorothy Phillips, David Durand, Freddie Burke Frederick, Frank McGlynn, James Burtis, George Cowl, Murray Smith, William Strauss, Roland Ray, June Gittleson.

A young high society gentleman falls in love with a model much to the dismay of his snobbish mother.

## The Midnight Special

December 7, 1930, 6 reels.

*P:* George R. Batcheller. *D:* Duke Worne. *SC:* Arthur Hoerl. *PH:* M.A. Anderson. *ED:* Tom Persons.

*Cast:* Glenn Tryon, Merna Kennedy, Mary Carr, Phillips Smalley, James Aubrey, Tom O'Brien, Norman Phillips, Jr.

A crooked division superintendent frames a railroad dispatcher for a train crash and robbery, and the accused man and his little brother try to prove his innocence.

## The Lawless Woman

May 5, 1931, 63 minutes.

*P:* George R. Batcheller. *D:* Richard Thorpe. *SC:* Arthur Hoerl, Barney Gerard & Richard Thorpe. *PH:* M.A. Anderson. *ED:* Tom Persons. *SD:* L.E. Tope. *AD:* Mario D'Agostino. *Asst Dir:* Melville Shyer.

*Cast:* Vera Reynolds, Carroll Nye, Thomas Jackson, Wheeler Oakman, James Burtis, Gwen Lee, Phillips Smalley.

A cub reporter gets on the trail of gangsters and falls in love with a young woman involved with the hoodlums. TV title: *Against All Odds.*

## Lady from Nowhere

August 1, 1931, 65 minutes.

*P:* George R. Batcheller. *D-ED:* Richard Thorpe. *SC:* Barney Gerard & Adrian Johnson. *PH:* M.A. Anderson. *SD:* L.E. Tope. *Asst Dir:* Melville Shyer. *Supv:* Barney Gerard.

*Cast:* Alice Day, John Holland, Phillips Smalley, Barbara Bedford, Mischa Auer, James Burtis, Lafe McKee, Bernie Lamont, Ray Largay.

A young man and woman pose as crooks in order to get evidence against their dishonest employers. Also called *The Girl from Nowhere.*

## Grief Street

October 1, 1931, 70 minutes.

*P:* George R. Batcheller. *D-ED:* Richard Thorpe. *SC:* Arthur Hoerl. *PH:* M.A. Anderson.

*Cast:* Barbara Kent, John Holland, Dorothy Christy, Crauford Kent, Lillian Rich, Lloyd Whitlock, Creighton Hale, James Burtis, Larry Steers, Lafe McKee, Ray Largay, Arthur Brennan.

A reporter tries to solve the murder of an actor, leading to the writer's girlfriend being shot.

## Probation

March 15, 1932, 70 minutes.

*P:* George R. Batcheller. *D-ED:* Richard Thorpe. *SC:* Arthur Hoerl & Edward T. Lowe. *PH:* M.A. Anderson. *SD:* Pete Clark.

*Cast:* Sally Blane, John Darrow, J. Farrell MacDonald, Clara Kimball Young, Eddie Phillips, Matty Kemp, Mary Jane Irving, David Rollins, Betty Grable, David Durand.

A judge, the uncle of a reckless society girl, sentences a young offender to be the young woman's chauffeur.

## Escapade

Invincible, April 1, 1932, 67 minutes.

*P:* Maury M. Cohen. *D:* Richard Thorpe. *SC:* Edward T. Lowe. *PH:* M.A. Anderson. *SD:* Pete Clark.

*Cast:* Sally Blane, Anthony Bushell, Jameson Thomas, Thomas Jackson, Walter Long, Carmelita Geraghty, Phillips Smalley, David Mir.

Two brothers—a convict and a lawyer—both love the same woman who is married to the attorney.

## The Devil Plays

April 5, 1932, 60 minutes.
P: George R. Batcheller. D-ED: Richard Thorpe. SC: Arthur Hoerl. PH: M.A. Anderson.

Cast: Jameson Thomas, Florence Britton, Thomas Jackson, Dorothy Christy, Richard Tucker, Lillian Rich, Robert Ellis, Lew Kelly, Carmelita Geraghty, Edmund Burns, Jack Trent, Murdock MacQuarrie.

A magazine writer is one step ahead of a police detective in solving a murder and blackmail scheme.

## Midnight Lady

May 15, 1932, 65 minutes.
P: George R. Batcheller. D: Richard Thorpe. SC: Edward T. Lowe. PH: M.A. Anderson. SD: Pete Clark.

Cast: Sarah Padden, John Darrow, Claudia Dell, Theodore Von Eltz, Montagu Love, Lucy Beaumont, Lina Basquette, Donald Keith, Brandon Hurst, B. Wayne Lamont.

The owner of a speakeasy finds out that one of her customers is in love with the daughter she once deserted.

## Forbidden Company

Invincible, June 15, 1932, 67 minutes.
P: Maury M. Cohen. D: Richard Thorpe. SC: Edward T. Lowe. PH: M.A. Anderson.

Cast: Sally Blane, John Darrow, John St. Polis, Myrtle Stedman, Josephine Dunn, Dorothy Christy, Bryant Washburn, David Durand, Norman Drew.

A rich young man falls for an artist's model but the union is opposed by his father. Working title: *For Value Received*.

## Beauty Parlor

July 15, 1932, 64 minutes.
P: George B. Batcheller. D: Richard Thorpe. SC: Harry Sauber. ST: Marion Orth. PH: M.A. Anderson.

Cast: Barbara Kent, Joyce Compton, John Harron, Dorothy Revier, Albert Gran, Wheeler Oakman, Mischa Auer, Betty Mack, Harry C. Bradley.

Two manicurists at a hotel barbershop find themselves involved in the lives of several of their customers.

## Thrill of Youth

August 15, 1932, 62 minutes.
P: George R. Batcheller. D: Richard Thorpe. SC: Edward T. Lowe. PH: M.A. Anderson. ED: Vera Wade.

Cast: June Clyde, Matty Kemp, Allen Vincent, George Irving, Dorothy Peterson, Lucy Beaumont, Tom Ricketts, Bryant Washburn, Ethel Clayton, Caryl Lincoln.

Two young men try to follow in their father's footsteps when he begins romancing a married woman.

## The King Murder

September 15, 1932, 64 minutes.
P: George R. Batcheller. D: Richard Thorpe. SC: Charles Reed Jones. PH: M.A. Anderson. SD: Pete Clark.

Cast: Conway Tearle, Natalie Moorhead, Dorothy Revier, Don Alvarado, Robert Frazer, Maurice Black, Marceline Day, Huntley Gordon, Rose Dione.

The head of the homicide bureau

tries to unravel the connection between four separate murders.

## The Face on the Barroom Floor

Invincible, October 14, 1932, 66 minutes.

*P:* Maury M. Cohen. *D:* Bert Bracken. *SC:* Bert Bracken & Barry Barringer. *ST:* Aubrey Kennedy. *PH:* Robert Cline. *ED:* Ethel Davey.

*Cast:* Dulcie Cooper, Bramwell Fletcher, Alice Ward, Phillips Smalley, Walter Miller, Maurice Black, Eddie Fetherstone, Patricia Wing.

A man loses control of his alcoholism when his wife gets drunk at a party.

## Slightly Married

October 15, 1932, 65 minutes.

*P:* George R. Batcheller. *D:* Richard Thorpe. *SC:* Mary McCarty. *PH:* M.A. Anderson. *SD:* Pete Clark. *Asst Dir:* Melville Shyer.

*Cast:* Evelyn Knapp, Walter Byron, Marie Prevost, Jason Robards, Robert Ellis, Dorothy Christy, Phillips Smalley, Clarissa Selwynne, Herbert Evans, Lloyd Ingraham, Mary Foy.

When a young woman marries a man to keep out of jail she comes to realize she wants to keep him.

## Women Won't Tell

November 15, 1932, 65 minutes.

*P:* George R. Batcheller. *D:* Richard Thorpe. *SC:* Lela E. Rogers. *PH:* M.A. Anderson. *SD:* Pete Clark. *Asst Dir:* Melville Shyer.

*Cast:* Sarah Padden, Otis Harlan, Gloria Shea, Larry Kent, Edmund Breese, Mae Busch, Walter Long, William V. Mong, Robert Ellis, Tom Ricketts, Isabel Withers, John Hyams, Jane Darwell, Dewey Robinson, Donald Kirke, June Bennett, Charles Mailes, Betty Mack.

Destitute and living at the city dump, a woman tries to claim the estate of a deceased manufacturer for her daughter, the rightful heir. Working title: *The Woman Nobody Knows.*

## Secrets of Wu Sin

Invincible, December 15, 1932, 65 minutes.

*P:* George A. Batcheller. *D:* Richard Thorpe. *SC:* William McGrath & Betty Burbridge. *ST:* Basil Dickey. *PH:* M.A. Anderson. *ED:* Roland D. Reed. *AD:* Edward C. Jewell. *SD:* Pete Clark. *Mus:* Abe Meyer. *Asst Dir:* Melville Shyer.

*Cast:* Lois Wilson, Grant Withers, Dorothy Revier, Robert Warwick, Toshia Mori, Eddie Boland, Tetsu Komai, Richard Loo, Luke Chan, Jimmie Wang.

Two newspaper reporters fall in love as they investigate a coolie-smuggling racket in Chinatown.

## The Shadow Laughs

Invincible, March 27, 1933, 67 minutes.

*P:* Maury M. Cohen. *D-SC:* Arthur Hoerl. *PH:* Nick Rogalli & Don Malkames. *ED:* Bernard Rogan. *SD:* H.E. Reeves & Harry Belock.

*Cast:* Hal Skelly, Rose Hobart, Harry T. Morey, Geoffrey Bryant, Bran Nossen, Hal Short, Walter Fenner, Robert Keith, John Morrissey.

Several murders result after embezzlement by a bank cashier, and a reporter teams with a police inspector to solve the case.

## Love Is Dangerous

April 29, 1933, 67 minutes.

*P:* George R. Batcheller. *D:* Richard Thorpe. *SC:* Stuart Anthony. *ST:* Beulah Poynter. *PH:* M.A. Anderson.

*Cast:* John Warburton, Rochelle Hudson, Bradley Page, Judith Rosselli, Dorothy Revier, Albert Conti, Herta Lind, May Beatty, Lorin Baker, Mary Foy, Betty Mack, Sam Adams.

A woman is forced to contend with a drunken husband and a love-hungry daughter. Reviewed as *Love Is Like That* and rereleased in 1952 as *No Shame.*

## Footsteps in the Night

May 10, 1933, 63 minutes.

*P:* Basil Dean. *D:* Maurice Elvey. *SC:* Rupert Downing & John Paddy Carstairs, from the novel by Cecily Fraser.

*Cast:* Benita Hume, Peter Hannen, Harold Huth, Walter Armitage, Jack Lambert, Pollie Emery, Robert English, Margery Binner, Frances Ross Campbell.

On their honeymoon a bride saves her inventor husband from being kidnapped. A British import.

## Forgotten

Invincible, May 20, 1933, 65 minutes.

*P:* Maury M. Cohen. *D:* Richard Thorpe. *SC:* Harry Sauber. *PH:* M.A. Anderson. *SD:* Pete Clark. *Asst Dir:* Melville Shyer.

*Cast:* June Clyde, Lee Kohlmar, William Collier, Jr., Leon [Ames] Waycoff, Selmar Jackson, Natalie Moorhead, Natalie Kingston, Otto Lederer, Tom Ricketts, Jean Hersholt, Jr.

An elderly gentleman is neglected by his selfish family. Working title: *The Fifth Commandment.*

## Taming the Jungle

Invincible, June 6, 1933, 56 minutes.

*P:* Paul D. Wyman. *D:* Robert Emmett Tansey & John Tansey. *PH:* John Tansey.

*Cast:* Melvin Koontz, Olga Celeste, Chubby Guilfoyle, Dean Fox, John Tansey (narrator).

Training methods of lion-taming are presented as well as four trainers working with tigers, pumas and leopards.

## Strange People

June 17, 1933, 64 minutes.

*P:* George R. Batcheller. *D:* Richard Thorpe. *SC:* Jack Townley. *PH:* M.A. Anderson. *ED:* Vera Ward. *AD:* Edward C. Jewell. *SD:* Richard Tyler. *Mus:* Abe Meyer. *Asst Dir:* Melville Shyer.

*Cast:* John Darrow, Gloria Shea, Hale Hamilton, Wilfred Lucas, J. Frank Glendon, Michael S. Visaroff, Jack Pennick, Jerry Mandy, Lew Kelly, Jane Keckley, Mary Foy, Frank LaRue, Stanley Blystone, Walter Brennan, Jay Wilsey [Buffalo Bill, Jr.], Gordon DeMain.

A car salesman and his fiancée are among a dozen people invited to a remote house where a murder occurs on a stormy night.

## By Appointment Only

Invincible, July 12, 1933, 63 minutes.

*P:* Maury M. Cohen. *D:* Frank R. Strayer. *SC:* Robert Ellis. *PH:* M.A. Anderson. *ED:* Roland Reed. *AD:* Edward C. Jewell. *Asst Dir:* Melville Shyer. *SD:* L.E. Clark.

*Cast:* Lew Cody (Dr. Michael Travers), Aileen Pringle (Diane Manners), Sally O'Neil (Judy Carrol), Edward Morgan (Dick Manners), Edward Martindel (Judge Barry Phelps), Wilson Benge (Withers), Marceline Day (Brownie), Claire McDowell (Mrs. Mary Carrol), Pauline Garon (Gwen Reid), Gladys Blake (Helen).

Society doctor Michael Travers (Lew Cody) is too busy to see a patient (Claire McDowell), who dies of heart failure. Blaming himself for the woman's death he takes an interest in her fourteen-year-old daughter, Judy (Sally O'Neil), and makes her his ward. Judy wins the hearts of Travers' fiancée Diane (Aileen Pringle), her younger brother Dick (Edward Morgan) and stuffy butler Withers (Wilson Benge). Travers and Diane decide to delay their marriage so he can go to Europe to lecture on a new method of heart valve surgery the doctor has developed, and the trip lasts for three seasons. When Travers returns home he finds Judy is now a beautiful young woman, and he falls in love with her, objecting when he finds out she is engaged to Dick. Dick, who was once saved from a forced marriage by Travers who paid off a girl Dick got pregnant, is enraged when Judy delays their engagement and while driving too fast causes an auto crash in which Judy is badly hurt. Travers operates and saves Judy's life, and when she recovers he gives her in marriage to Dick while the doctor is reconciled with Diane.

A somewhat stuffy affair, *By Appointment Only* does benefit from fine acting but its soap-opera plot fails to entertain. The storyline is told around the gossip of the doctor's switchboard operator (Gladys Blake), who goes from single to married to a mother in the film's running time. Around her telephone conversations the plot takes place. Lew Cody is likable as the society doctor (although in today's world it is a bit astounding to see a cigarette-smoking doctor who has developed a new method for heart valve surgery!). Sally O'Neil is quite ingratiating as Judy, who goes from age fourteen to seventeen in the film, although she is definitely too old for the part. Aileen Pringle is harshly photographed and seems much too old to have a younger brother played by Edward Morgan, who appears more like her son. Morgan's acting is also a handicap from which the film fails to recover. Silent screen leading ladies Marceline Day, Claire McDowell and Pauline Garon have small roles with Miss Day particularly effective as the doctor's loyal secretary, Miss Brown, whom he calls Brownie.

In many ways, *By Appointment Only* exemplifies the assets and weaknesses of Chesterfield-Invincible productions. It provides acceptable entertainment without ever trying to rise above its medium-budget station.

# I Have Lived

July 19, 1933, 65 minutes.

*P:* George R. Batcheller. *D:* Richard Thorpe. *SC:* Winifred Dunn. *ST:* Lou Heifetz. *PH:* M.A. Anderson. *SD:* Pete Clark. *Asst Dir:* Melville Shyer.

*Cast:* Alan Dinehart, Anita Page, Allen Vincent, Gertrude Astor, Maude Truax, Matthew Betz, Eddie Boland, Florence Dudley, Gladys Blake, Dell Henderson, Harry Bradley, Edward Keene.

A girl with a dubious past is chosen by a playwright for the lead in his new production. Reissued as *After Midnight* and in 1954 as *Love Life*.

## Notorious but Nice

August 23, 1933, 65 minutes.

*P:* George R. Batcheller. *D:* Richard Thorpe. *SC:* Carol Webster. *ST:* Adeline Leitzbach. *PH:* M.A. Anderson. *SD:* Pete Clark.

*Cast:* Marian Marsh, Betty Compson, Donald Dillaway, Rochelle Hudson, John St. Polis, Henry Kolker, J. Carrol Naish, Dewey Robinson, Robert Ellis, Wilfred Lucas, Jane Keckley, Robert Frazer, Louise Beavers.

A woman befriends a young girl falsely accused of murder.

## Dance, Girl, Dance

Invincible, October 26, 1933, 67 minutes.

*P:* Maury M. Cohen. *D:* Frank R. Strayer. *SC:* Robert Ellis. *PH:* M.A. Anderson. *ED:* Roland D. Reed. *SD:* Pete Clark. *Mus:* Lee Zahler. *SD:* L.E. Clark. *Asst Dir:* Melville Shyer.

*Cast:* Evelyn Knapp, Alan Dinehart, Edward Nugent, Gloria Shea, Ada May, Theodore Von Eltz, George Grandee, Mae Busch.

Deserted by the father of her child, a young woman makes good as a dancing star.

## A Man of Sentiment

November 16, 1933, 62 minutes.

*P:* George R. Batcheller. *D:* Richard Thorpe. *SC:* Robert Ellis. *ST:* Frederick H. Brennan. *PH:* M.A. Anderson. *SD:* L.E. Clark.

*Cast:* Marian Marsh, Owen Moore, William Bakewell, Christian Rub, Edmund Breese, Emma Dunn, Geneva Mitchell, Jack Pennick, Pat O'Malley, Syd Saylor, Lucille Ward, Cornelius Keefe, Sam Adams, Otto Hoffman, Matt McHugh.

The son of rich parents pretends to be poor in order to win the girl he loves.

## Rainbow Over Broadway

December 27, 1933, 72 minutes.

*P:* George R. Batcheller. *D:* Richard Thorpe. *SC:* Winifred Dunn. *ST:* Carol Webster. *PH:* M.A. Anderson. *SD:* Pete Clark. *Mus:* Albert Von Tilzer.

*Cast:* Joan Marsh, Frank Albertson, Lucien Littlefield, Grace Hayes, Gladys Blake, Glen Boles, Dell Henderson, Harry Meyers, Nat Carr, May Beatty, Maxine Lewis, Alice Goodwin.

Members of a family suddenly find themselves in New York City when their self-centered step-mother resumes her singing career.

## In the Money

Chesterfield-Invincible, January 6, 1934, 66 minutes.

*P:* George R. Batcheller. *D:* Frank R. Strayer. *SC:* Robert Ellis. *PH:* M.A. Anderson. *ED:* Roland D. Reed. *SD:* L.E. Clarke.

*Cast:* Skeets Gallagher, Lois Wilson, Warren Hymer, Sally Starr, Arthur Hoyt, Junior Coghlan, Erin La Bissonier, Harold Waldridge, Louise Beavers.

A zany scientist and his devil-may-care son end up losing their fortune. Remade as *Red Lights Ahead* (1937).

## The Quitter

March 14, 1934, 68 mintues.

*P:* George R. Batcheller. *D:* Richard Thorpe. *SC:* Robert Ellis. *PH:* M.A. Anderson. *SD:* Pete Clark.

*Cast:* Charles Grapewin, Emma Dunn, William Bakewell, Barbara Weeks, Hale Hamilton, Glen Boles,

Mary Kornman, Lafe McKee, Aggie Herring, Jane Keckley.

Deserted by her husband, a woman raises two sons by publishing a weekly newspaper which is nearly ruined by the journalistic ideals of the older boy. Working title: *The Understanding Heart.*

## Twin Husbands

May 9, 1934, 68 minutes.
*P:* Maury M. Cohen. *D:* Frank R. Strayer. *SC:* Robert Ellis. *ST:* Robert Ellis & Anthony Coldeway. *PH:* M.A. Anderson. *ED:* Roland Reed. *AD:* Edward C. Jewell. *SD:* L.E. Clark.

*Cast:* John Miljan, Shirley Grey, Monroe Owsley, Hale Hamilton, Robert Elliott, Maurice Black, William Franklin, Wilson Benge.

A couple kidnap a famous crook and force him to impersonate the woman's missing husband in order to obtain bonds.

## In Love with Life

Chesterfield-Invincible, May 12, 1934, 66 minutes.
*P:* George R. Batcheller. *D:* Frank R. Strayer. *SC:* Robert Ellis. *PH:* M.A. Anderson. *ED:* Roland Reed. *SD:* L.E. Clark. *AD:* Edward C. Jewell. *Mus:* Lee Zahler. *Asst Dir:* Melville Shyer.

*Cast:* Lila Lee, Onslow Stevens, Dickie Moore, Claude Gillingwater, Betty Kendig, Clarence Geldert, Tom Ricketts, Rosita Marstini, Milla Davenport, William Arnold, James T. Mack.

A small boy teaches those around him the meaning of life after being adopted by his grandfather who has disowned his mother. Working title: *Reunion.*

## City Park

July 6, 1934, 72 minutes.
*P:* George R. Batcheller. *D:* Ricahrd Thorpe. *SC:* Karl Brown. *PH:* M.A. Anderson. *ED:* Fred Parry. *AD:* Edward C. Jewell. *SD:* Pete Clark.

*Cast:* Sally Blane, Henry B. Walthall, Matty Kemp, Hale Hamilton, John Harron, Clark King, Gwen Lee, Judith Vosselli, Wilson Benge, Lafe McKee, Mary Foy.

Three elderly men rescue a girl from the streets by making her their housekeeper.

## Cross Streets

July 6, 1934, 64 minutes.
*P:* George R. Batcheller. *D:* Frank R. Strayer. *SC:* Anthony Coldeway. *ST:* Gordon Morris. *PH:* M.A. Anderson.

*Cast:* Claire Windsor, John[ny] Mack Brown, Anita Louise, Kenneth Thomson, Matty Kemp, Josef Swickard, Niles Welch, Edith Fellows, Mary Gordon, Jerry Madden.

A man falls in love with the daughter of his ex-sweetheart who jilted him eighteen years before. Working title: *Swan Song.*

## Fifteen Wives

Invincible, July 17, 1934, 65 minutes.
*P:* Maury M. Cohen. *D:* Frank R. Strayer. *SC:* Charles S. Belden. *ST:* Charles S. Belden & Frederick Stephanie. *PH:* M.A. Anderson. *ED:* Roland Reed. *AD:* Edward C. Jewell. *SD:* L.E. Clark. *Mus:* Abe Meyer. *Asst Dir:* Melville Shyer.

*Cast:* Conway Tearle, Natalie Moorhead, Raymond Hatton, Noel Francis, John Wray, Ralf Harolde, Oscar Apfel, Robert Frazer, Margaret Dumont, Harry C. Bradley, Lew Kelly, Clarence Brown, Alex Folette, Alameda Fowler, Slickem, John Elliott,

Sidney Bracy, Dickie Jones, Hal Price, Lynton Brent.

The death of a rich playboy who has been married fifteen times is investigated by a police inspector.

## Stolen Sweets

August 7, 1934, 75 minutes.

*P:* George R. Batcheller. *D:* Richard Thorpe. *SC:* Karl Brown. *PH:* M.A. Anderson. *ED:* Roland Reed. *SD:* Pete Clark. *Asst Dir:* Melville Shyer.

*Cast:* Sally Blane, Charles Starrett, Claude King, Jameson Thomas, Jane Keckley, Phillips Smalley, Tom Ricketts, John Harron, Polly Ann Young, Goodee Montgomery, Maynard Holmes, Aggie Herring.

On an ocean cruise a rich young society woman drops her fiancé for an insurance salesman

## One in a Million

Invincible, September 15, 1934, 66 minutes.

*P:* Maury M. Cohen. *D:* Frank R. Strayer. *SC-ST:* Karl Brown & Robert Ellis. *PH:* M.A. Anderson. *ED:* Roland Reed. *Art Dir:* Edward C. Jewell. *Asst Dir:* Melville Shyer. *SD:* L.E. Clark.

*Cast:* Dorothy Wilson (Dorothy Brooks), Charles Starrett (Donald Cabot), Holmes Herbert (John Cabot), Robert Frazer (Captain of Detectives), Gwen Lee (Kitty Kennedy), Guinn Williams (Spike), Jane Keckley (Miss Van Alston), John Elliott (Boss), Lew Kelly (Roth), Hal Price (Witness), Gladys Blake (Miss Arnold), Barbara Rogers (Patsy Purcell), Fred Santley (Frankie), Eddie Fetherstone, Francis Sayles, Alex Pollett, Leyland Hodgson, Alan Wood, Belle Drube.

When her boss (John Elliott) makes a pass at her, Dorothy (Dorothy Wilson) pushes him away and he falls from his apartment window. Thefts have taken place at the department store owned by John Cabot (Holmes Herbert), and when Dorothy flees she is also blamed for stealing. She goes to her friend Kitty (Gwen Lee) for help, and the two go on a business trip to a hotel where Cabot's son Donald (Charles Starrett) is staying. He has just been jilted by his fiancée and he is attracted to Dorothy, but she will have nothing to do with the playboy. To get close to Dorothy, Donald arranges for her and Kitty to attend a party given by his aunt (Jane Keckley), but Don's father finds out Dorothy is wanted by the police for attempting to kill her boss, who survived the fall, and for the thefts at his store. Realizing that Donald is in love with Dorothy, Cabot refuses to allow them to be married. Dorothy, who by now also loves Donald, turns herself over to the law and at a hearing the captain of police detectives (Robert Frazer) says it was her boss who was doing the stealing and that she is innocent of all charges. Thus Dorothy and Donald are free to wed.

Released to television as *Dangerous Appointment, One in a Million* is a stale semicomedy which barely fulfills its promise of being the lower part of a dual bill program. While it is competently made and acted, the movie simply lacks interest and its TV title makes it even more disappointing, promising an action feature instead of leaden fluff. Had it not been for leading man Charles Starrett, *One in a Million* would be little known today. It was probably Starrett's reputation as a western star that caused the film's title to be changed to the more virile *Dangerous Appointment* when it came to the small screen. In 1934–35 Starrett made a half-dozen features for Chesterfield-Invincible, although this is the only one under the Invincible banner, the others being listed as Chesterfield releases. This 1934 release was preceded by *Murder on the Campus*, *Stolen Sweets* and *Green Eyes* and in all four he was given second billing to his leading lady, evidence that the studio did not consider him a strong enough box office attraction at the time for top billing. For his two 1935 releases for Chesterfield, however, he got top billing in *Sons of Steel* and *A Shot in the Dark*. These assignments, of course, brought him to the attention of Columbia where he became the studio's resident cowboy star (usually as The Durango Kid) for the next seventeen years.

## The Curtain Falls

October 2, 1934, 67 minutes.
P: George R. Batcheller. D: Charles Lamont. SC: Karl Brown. PH: M.A. Anderson. Ed: Roland Reed.
Cast: Henrietta Crossman, Dorothy Lee, Holmes Herbert, Natalie Moorhead, John Darrow, William Bakewell, Jameson Thomas, Dorothy Revier, Edward Kane, Aggie Herring, Tom Ricketts, Wilson Benge, Edward LeSaint, Bryant Washburn, Robert Frazer, Lloyd Ingraham, Jane Keckley, Jack Shutta, Fern Emmett.
Down on her luck, a once-famous actress pretends to be a rich family's aunt and tries to work out their problems.

## Green Eyes

November 3, 1934, 63 minutes.
P: George R. Batcheller. D: Richard Thorpe. SC: Andrew Moses, from the novel *The Murder of Stephen Kester* by Harriett Ashbrook. PH: M.A. Anderson. AD: Edward C. Jew-

ell. *Mus:* Abe Meyer. *SD:* L.E. Clark. *Asst Dir:* Melville Shyer.
Cast: Shirley Grey, Charles Starrett, Claude Gillingwater, John Wray, William Bakewell, Dorothy Revier, Ben Hendricks, Jr., Alden Chase, Andrew Clayton, Aggie Herring, Edward Keane, Edward LeSaint, Robert Frazer, John Elliott, Lloyd Whitlock, Elmer Ballard, Frank Hagney.
During a masquerade party an old man is murdered and a mystery writer tries to solve the crime.

## Fugitive Road

Invincible, November 13, 1934, 66 minutes.
P: Maury M. Cohen. D: Frank R. Strayer. SC: Charles S. Belden & Robert Ellis. PH: Ted McCord. ED: Roland Reed. AD: Edward C. Jewell. SD: L.E. Clark. Asst Dir: Melville Shyer.
Cast: Erich von Stroheim, Wera Engels, Leslie Fenton, George Humbert, Hank Mann, Harry Holman, Ferdinand Schumann-Heink, Michael Visaroff, Bangie Beilly, Hans Ferberg.
At a remote outpost during World War II, a love triangle develops between the commandant, a pretty refugee and a gangster.

## Murder on the Campus

December 27, 1934, 70 minutes.
P: George R. Batcheller. D: Richard Thorpe. SC: Andrew Moses, from the novel *The Campanile Murders* by Whitman Chambers. PH: M.A. Anderson. AD: Edward C. Jewell. SD: Pete (L.E.) Clark. Mus: Abe Meyer. Asst Dir: Melville Shyer.
Cast: Shirley Grey (Lillian Voyne), Charles Starrett (Bill Bartlett), J. Farrell MacDonald (Captain Ed Kyne), Ruth Hall (Ann Michaels), Maurice Black (Blackie Atwater),

William Bakewell, Shirley Grey and Charles Starrett in *Green Eyes* (Chesterfield, 1934).

Dewey Robinson (Sergeant Charlie Lorrimer), Edward Van Sloan (Dr. C. Ebson Hawley), Harrison Greene (Mr. Brock), Jane Keckley (Hilda Lund), Harry Bowen (Spud), Richard Catlett (Wilson), Al Bridge (Grimes).

Newspaper reporter Bill Bartlett (Charles Starrett) is doing a series of feature articles on college girls working their way through school. He takes special interest in coed Lillian Voyne (Shirley Grey), who moonlights as a singer in a cafe run by gambler Blackie Atwater (Maurice Black). Picking Lillian up at Atwater's club, Bill drives her to the campus because she has a date to see athlete Malcolm Jennings, who also works ringing the chimes at the Campanile. A few minutes later a shot is

heard and police Captain Ed Kyne (J. Farrell MacDonald) and his associate Lorrimer (Dewey Robinson), along with Bill, discover the murdered Jennings. The trio go to the Delta Ki house where they question Jennings' fraternity brother Wilson (Richard Catlett), who leads them to Ann Michaels (Ruth Hall), who has dated the dead student. The police question her but learn nothing. Bill goes back to her swank apartment and finds Lillian there. Next, chemistry professor Dr. Hawley (Edward Van Sloan) is questioned at the faculty club, and he admits to driving Ann home at the time the murder was committed. Lorrimer finds a pistol in Lillian's apartment and the police believe it to be the

Charles Starrett, Ruth Hall, Dewey Robinson and J. Farrell MacDonald in *Murder on the Campus* (Chesterfield, 1934).

murder weapon. When lawyer James Smight is found dead, his secretary (Jane Keckley) implicates Atwater in the crime, and Wilson also tells the police that the gambler threatened Jennings. Hawley, who is also a well-known amateur criminologist, agrees to aid the university in solving Jennings' murder, and he tells Bill he believes a woman committed the crime. Atwater manages to escape the police dragnet out on him, and Kyne arrests Lillian for the killings. Meanwhile Smight's partner Brock (Harrison Greene) commits suicide in Hawley's office. That evening Blackie shows up at police headquarters and turns himself in, telling Kyne that Ann is really his daughter and that she was married to Jennings, who was hooked

up with crooked lawyers Smight and Brock in a blackmail scheme to expose him. With this evidence Bill goes to see Hawley, who confesses he committed the crimes since he wanted Ann for himself and Jennings and the lawyers were also trying to blackmail him. He tries to kill Bill with poison gas, but the police arrive in time to save the reporter. Recovered, Bill sets out to romance the now free Lillian.

Filmed at Universal City, *Murder on the Campus* is a taut murder mystery based on Whitman Chambers' 1933 novel *The Campanile Murders*. Although the villain is not too hard to spot, his method of homicide is difficult to decipher. While Shirley Grey and Ruth Hall appear a bit mature to be coeds (one amusing scene has Grey studying for a chemistry test at Blackie's nightclub) the acting is quite good, and Richard Thorpe's direction speeds the action along nicely. Outside of a few shots at the Campanile and Hawley's laboratory, there are few actual campus scenes in the film, which also features a mansion-type frat house and coeds wearing furs and living in swank apartments.

## Port of Lost Dreams

Invincible, March 2, 1935, 68 minutes.
P: Maury M. Cohen. D: Frank R. Strayer. SC: Charles S. Belden. ST: Robert Ellis. PH: M.A. Anderson. ED: Roland D. Reed. SD: L.E. Clark. AD: Edward C. Jewell. Asst Dir: Melville Shyer.

Cast: Bill Boyd (Lars Christensen), Lola Lane (Molly Deshon), George Marion (Captain Morgan Rock), Harold Huber (Louis Constolos), Edward Gargan (Porky), Evelyn Carter Carrington (Mother McGee), Robert Elliott (Lt. Anderson), John Beck (Lawyer), Charles Wilson (Warden), Robert Frazer (Radio Announcer), Harold Berquist, Pat Harmon (Policemen), Lafe McKee (Justice of the Peace), Eddie Phillips (Lawyer), Gordon DeMain (Jenson), Lew Kelly (Detective).

In the early 1930s actor William Boyd made headlines by being involved in a wild party. Unfortunately, there were two William Boyds starring in films at the same time, and the scandal also adversely affected the career of the other Boyd. The one in the scandal had billed himself as William "Stage" Boyd while the other actor was billing himself as Bill Boyd. The latter, once a silent star for Cecil B. DeMille and then in the early sound era for Pathe, now found himself toiling in a

potboiler like *Port of Lost Dreams.* Badly hampered by a weak story, the film did boast a well-staged brawl in a waterfront barroom, and Lola Lane is good as the hard-edged heroine softened by a happy marriage and a baby. Otherwise *Port of Lost Dreams* was not one of Invincible's better products. It did, however, get more mileage than most of the Chesterfield-Invincible releases because after Bill Boyd became popular again as "Hopalong Cassidy" at Paramount, Mayfair reissued the feature with the misleading action title *Captain Danger.*

Gangster's moll Molly Dichon (Lola Lane) is wanted by the police for assisting in a robbery committed by her ex-boyfriend Louis Constolos (Harold Huber). She seeks refuge in a waterfront dive run by Mother McGee (Evelyn Carter Carrington). Captured by the law, Louis refuses to identify Molly, although she was really innocent of any wrongdoing. After a brawl in Mother's establishment, fisherman Lars Christenson (Bill Boyd) and mate Porky (Edward Gargan) head out to sea not knowing that Molly is a stowaway. When Chris finds her he is very upset, but Porky likes the girl, who soon falls in love with Chris. Chris' friend, slightly addled old seaman Morgan Rock (George Marion), also grows fond of Molly, who tries to straighten out the living quarters on Chris' boat to make it livable. When he objects they have a fight and they realize they are in love. Molly tries to tell him about her past, but he refuses to listen and they are married. A year later Chris and Molly have a son just as Louis gets out of prison. He finds Molly just as she, Chris and the baby are about to sell their boat and move to Oregon. He steals Chris' gu and later robs and kills Jenson (Gordon

DeMain), who has just bought the boat. Because of the gun, Chris is blamed for the crime, but Molly clears him by telling the truth about her past. She is tried and sent to prison as Chris rejects her. Trying to leave the country on Rock's boat, Louis is mysteriously found drowned. Realizing he has made a mistake in rejecting the woman he loves, Chris commits a crime in order to go to the same prison as Molly. Thanks to the efforts of the warden, Chris and Molly are reconciled and wait to serve out their sentences so they can return to their son.

## The World Accuses

March 21, 1935, 63 minutes.

*P:* Lon Young. *D:* Charles Lamont. *SC:* Charles S. Belden. *PH:* M.A. Anderson. *ED:* Roland Reed. *AD:* Edward C. Jewell. *SD:* L.E. Clark.

*Cast:* Dickie Moore, Vivian Tobin, Russell Hopton, Cora Sue Collins, Mary Carr, Robert Elliott, Jameson Thomas, Barbara Bedford, Paul Fix, Harold Huber, Bryant Washburn, Jane Keckley, Robert Frazer, Sarah Edwards, Lloyd Ingraham, Broderick O'Farrell.

The small son of a millionaire is used as a pawn by a greedy family

## The Ghost Walks

Invincible, March 30, 1935, 67 minutes.

*P:* Maury M. Cohen. *D:* Frank R. Strayer. *SC:* Charles S. Belden. *PH:* M.A. Anderson. *ED:* Roland D. Reed. *AD:* Edward C. Jewell. *Mus:* Abe Meyer. *SD:* L.E. Clark. *Asst Dir:* Melville Shyer.

*Cast:* John Miljan (Prescott Ames), June Collyer (Gloria Shaw), Richard Carle (Herman Wood), Henry Kolker (Dr. Kent), Johnny Arthur (Erskine), Spencer Charters (The Professor), Donald Kirke (Terry), Eve Southern (Beatrice), Douglas Garrard (Carroway), Wilson Benge (Jarvis), Jack Shutta, Harry Strang (Guards).

On a stormy night Broadway producer Herman Wood (Richard Carle) and his secretary Erskine (Johnny Arthur) are being driven to the village of Cragdale, eighty miles from New York City, to hear Prescott Ames' (John Miljan) new mystery play. During the storm a tree blocks the road and they take shelter in a large house belonging to Dr. Kent (Henry Kolker). While getting dressed for dinner, Wood hears a woman's scream and is told she is one of the doctor's deranged patients. The beautiful Beatrice (Eve Southern) appears, and Wood is told her husband was murdered in the house three years before and that she can communicate with her late spouse. The room goes dark and a spectral hand appears as the woman screams. When the lights come back on she has disappeared, and the distraught Wood goes back to his room to rest. It is now revealed that all the happenings were enactments from Ames' play, since the members of the household are actually actors. Beatrice, however, really has been murdered, and Ames fears for his fiancée Gloria Shaw (June Collyer), who is also staying at his home. Wood refuses to believe that Beatrice has been murdered until everyone in the house learns that a maniac known as The Professor (Spencer Charters) has escaped from a mental institution. Local authorities warn the people in the house to be on the lookout for the madman since the house is in the locale of his crimes. After several attempts are made on the lives of the inhabitants, guards arrive from the

John Miljan, June Collyer, Wilson Benge, Donald Kirke, Eve Southern, Henry Kolker and Douglas Gerrard in *The Ghost Walks* (Invincible, 1935).

insane asylum and capture The Professor. The harried Wood and his associate return to Broadway, but the producer agrees to buy Ames' play.

*The Ghost Walks* is the title of the film and the play which is enacted in its first portion. Director Frank R. Strayer gives the film a good mystery flavor with its setting in a dark, spooky old house on a stormy night. The acting in the feature is also quite good with John Miljan cutting a strikingly handsome figure as the playwright turned sleuth and June Collyer as his lovely fiancée. Henry Kolker too is fine as the bogus doctor while Wilson Benge and Douglas Gerrard contribute their usual finesse as eccentric types. Spencer Charters carries off the difficult role of The Professor, first seen as a constable and later revealed as the loony, but homicidal killer. Johnny Arthur con-

tributes his usual competence in his portrayal as the producer's bullied secretary. But it is Richard Carle who wins the acting honors as the Broadway producer.

The plot ploy of having a dress rehearsal of the mystery play as part of the film's early action gives *The Ghost Walks* a good start. While the remainder of the film does not quite live up to these early scenes, it is a well-modulated melodrama which never seems to take itself too seriously.

It should be noted that when the film's editor, Roland D. Reed, became a TV producer in the 1950s, one of the programs he made was "Trouble with Father," starring Stuart Erwin and his wife June Collyer, the star of *The Ghost Walks*. The film's director, Frank R. Strayer, also helmed episodes of that TV series.

## Sons of Steel

April 13, 1935, 65 minutes.

*P:* George R. Batcheller. *D:* Charles Lamont. *SC:* Charles S. Belden. *PH:* M.A. Anderson. *ED:* Roland Reed. *AD:* Edward C. Jewell. *Asst Dir:* Melville Shyer. *SD:* L.E. Clark. *Sup:* Lon Young.

*Cast:* Charles Starrett (Phillip Mason), Polly Ann Young (Rosa Mason), William Bakewell (Ronald Chadburn), Walter Walker (John Chadburn), Holmes Herbert (Curtis Chadburn), Richard Carlyle (Tom Mason), Florence Roberts (Sarah Mason), Aileen Pringle (Enid Chadburn), Adolf Milar (Stanislaus), Edgar Norton (Higgins), Barbara Bedford (Miss Peters), Tom Ricketts (Williams), Frank LaRue (Foreman), Al Thompson (Carson), Harry Semels (Ryan), Jack Shutta (Grocery Clerk), Lloyd Ingraham (Draftsman), Edward Le Saint (Mr. Herman).

College chums Phillip Mason (Charles Starrett) and Ronald Chadburn (William Bakewell) graduate and return to their home town where Phil is the son of a worker (Richard Carlyle) in the steel mill owned by Ronald's father (Holmes Herbert) and Uncle John (Walter Walker). Phillip has a great deal of trouble finding a job until John Chadburn, who is really his father, gives him a lowly position in the factory, expecting him to work up to a management position. Ronald is given a job in sales by his father, and both young men hate their work. Phillip, who knows he is adopted, loves Rosa (Polly Ann Young), the daughter of his adopted parents, but Ronald also falls for her when she is hired as his secretary. When Ronald loses a big car manufacturer's account, he tries to save the business by convincing his uncle to accept Phillip's new car design. After an accident, however, John fires Phillip, and Ronald also loses his job because of the auto account. The men at the factory are unhappy and plan a walkout and they want Phillip to be their leader. He agrees after a scab beats up his adopted father. In a showdown with John Chadburn, Phillip is told the truth about his heritage, and as a result he gets the men to go back to work and the factory is saved. Phillip, who plans to marry Rosa, becomes head of the business office while Ronald becomes the factory's chief mechanical engineer.

The fifth of a half-dozen features Charles Starrett made for Chesterfield-Invincible, *Sons of Steel* packed a lot of plot in its sixty-five minutes. Its many underlying themes included management versus labor, the class struggle and the love of the hero for his foster sister. While some of the plot ploys are often incredible, they are not without interest, and *Sons of Steel* is well acted and in some respects belies its low-budget origins. For those who might find political implications in the movie, the hero first leads a workers' revolt against the factory run by his father (although he does not know the relationship at the time) only to realize the "men who started this are really radicals and roughnecks." Fortunately, a more-than-capable cast manages to keep *Sons of Steel* afloat, and the movie quickly ties up its plot themes before becoming incredulous. For Charles Starrett this and the other films for Chesterfield helped keep him in the public eye until he gained real stardom as a cowboy hero at Columbia.

## A Shot in the Dark

May 23, 1935, 69 minutes.

*P:* George R. Batcheller. *D:*

Charles Lamont. *SC:* Charles S. Belden, from the novel *The Dartmouth Murders* by Clifford Orr. *PH:* M.A. Anderson. *ED:* Roland D. Reed. *AD:* Edward C. Jewell. *Mus:* Abe Meyer. *SD:* L.E. Clark. *Supv:* Lon Young. *Asst Dir:* Melville Shyer.

*Cast:* Charles Starrett (Ken Harris), Robert Warwick (Joseph Harris), Edward Van Sloan (Professor Bostwick), Marion Shilling (Jean Coates), Doris Lloyd (Miss Lottie Case), Helen Jerome Eddy (Mrs. Lucille Coates), James Bush (Byron Coates/John Meseraux), Julian Madison (Charlie Penlon), Eddie Tamblyn (Bill Smart), Ralph Brooks (Sam Anderson), Bob McKenzie (Sheriff Briggs), George Morrell (Deputy), Broderick O'Farrell (Dr. Howell), Herbert Bunton (College President), John Davidson (Professor Brand), Jane Keckley (Housekeeper).

"The infallible detective meets the perfect crime!" read the ads for *A Shot in the Dark*, based on Clifford Orr's 1929 novel *The Dartmouth Murders*. In truth, the detective was hardly infallible and the crime hardly perfect. Robert Warwick had the lion's share of the footage as the amateur criminologist, but the detective openly named the wrong suspect in the killings and Warwick played the part as a pompous nicotine addict. Even in 1935 Charles Starrett seemed a bit long in the tooth to be a college man although the supporting cast is quite good, especially Marion Shilling as the alluring heroine, Helen Jerome Eddy as the first victim's mother and Bob McKenzie as the country sheriff. Edward Van Sloan, again cast as a college professor as he was previously with Charles Starrett in *Murder on the Campus* the year before, handles his role in good fashion. *A Shot in the Dark* used a sharp prong fired by

a cattle-killing air gun as its instrument of murder. It is the sheriff, not the detective, who deduces the method of killing and later finds the gun buried on campus. Three murders take place before the sleuth is able to identify the killer, and then he is only able to do so by interviewing (offscreen) the adopted parents of the third victim. The film's mystery element is heightened by the villain parading around in a black cape and hat in a couple of scenes, but overall *A Shot in the Dark* is a predictable mystery. The movie's eeriest scene occurs early on when hero Charles Starrett awakes to a thumping sound outside his bedroom window—it is the body of his roommate hanging from a rope and swinging in the wind.

Corporation lawyer and amateur criminologist Joseph Harris (Robert Warwick) comes to visit his son Ken (Charles Starrett), a student at Cornwall College. The next day Ken's roommate, Byron (James Bush), is found hanged, and the college asks Mr. Harris to investigate, aiding the local sheriff (Bob McKenzie) and his deputy (George Morrell). Ken loves the dead man's sister Jean (Marion Shilling), who moves into the home of music instructor Professor Bostwick (Edward Van Sloan) with her companion Miss Case (Doris Lloyd) until the investigation is completed. Another student, Sam Anderson (Ralph Brooks), says he saw a person visit Byron on the night of his death, but Sam is killed during a school convocation. It is deduced an air pistol was used in the crimes, and Mr. Harris suspects another student John Deveraux (James Bush) of the killings because of his uncanny resemblance to Byron. Ken goes to see Byron's mother (Helen Jerome Eddy) but learns little. The police, Mr. Harris and Ken trail Deveraux to a deserted roadhouse, and he admits he was forced to kill Anderson but is shot before he can reveal the other murderer. Later it is Mrs. Coates who is able to place the blame on the killer, a man who once faked a marriage to her and who was trying to steal Byron's inheritance for himself and their son, Deveraux. The mystery solved, Jean admits her love for Ken.

*A Shot in the Dark* has a rather nondescript look although like many Chesterfield-Invincible features it was lensed at Universal City, thus taking advantage of already-standing sets. The decor of Stoneleigh Hall, the dormitory where Ken Harris and Byron Coates lived at Cornwall College, is decidedly plush when compared to such facilities at today's schools of higher learning. Outside of the dormitory setting, however, the movie gives few signs of being on a college campus, the action being confined to the dormitory, Professor Bostwick's home and a few foggy outdoor night shots. The deserted roadhouse sequence near the end of the feature, however, utilized the Carfax Abbey sets from *Dracula* (1931) while the convocation hall seen earlier in the film was once the medical college operating room in *Frankenstein* (1931).

## Symphony of Living

Invincible, June 22, 1935, 75 minutes.

*P:* Maury M. Cohen. *D:* Frank R. Strayer. *SC:* Charles S. Belden. *PH:* M.A. Anderson. *ED:* Roland Reed. *SD:* L.E. Clark. *AD:* Edward C. Jewell. *Mus:* Lee Zahler. *Supv:* Lon Young. *Asst Dir:* Melville Shyer.

*Cast:* Al Shean, Evelyn Brent, Charles Judels, John Darrow, Albert Conti, Lester Lee, Gigi Parrish, Richard Tucker, John Harron, Ferike

Boros, Ferdinand Schumann-Heink, Carl Stockdale, Les Goodwins.

The parents of a young violin prodigy go to court in a fight over his custody. Based on Offenbach's "Orpheus in Hell."

## Circumstantial Evidence

July 17, 1935, 68 minutes.

*P:* George R. Batcheller. *D:* Charles Lamont. *SC:* Ewart Adamson. *ST:* Tom Teriss. *PH:* M.A. Anderson. *ED:* Roland Reed. *AD:* Edward C. Jewell. *Mus:* Abe Meyer. *SD:* L.E. Clark. *Prod Mgr:* Lon Young. *Asst Dir:* Melville Shyer.

*Cast:* Shirley Grey, Chick Chandler, Arthur Vinton, Dorothy Revier, Lee Morgan, Claude King, Edward Keane, Robert Elliott, Carl Stockdale, Barbara Bedford, Huntley Gordon, Robert Frazer, Lloyd Ingraham.

A reporter is aided by his fiancée and a colleague in attempting to expose murder convictions based on circumstantial evidence. First filmed in 1929.

## Condemned to Live

Invincible, September 15, 1935, 65 minutes.

*P:* Maury M. Cohen. *D:* Frank R. Strayer. *SC:* Karen De Wolf. *PH:* M.A. Anderson. *ED:* Roland D. Reed. *AD:* Edward C. Jewell. *Mus:* Abe Meyer. *SD:* Richard Tyler. *Prod Mgr:* Lon Young. *Asst Dir:* Melville Shyer.

*Cast:* Ralph Morgan (Professor Paul Kristan), Maxine Doyle (Marguerite Mane), Russell Gleason (David), Pedro de Cordoba (Dr. Anders Bizet), Mischa Auer (Zan), Lucy Beaumont (Mother Molly), Carl Stockdale (John Mane), Barbara Bedford (Martha), Robert Frazer (Dr. Dupre), Ferdinand Schumann-Heink (Franz), Hedi Shope (Anna), Marilyn

Knowlden (Maria), Edward Cecil (Servant), Paul Weigel (Doctor), Ted Billings (Bell Ringer), Slim Whitaker, Harold Goodwin, Horace B. Carpenter, Frank Brownlee, Dick Curtis (Villagers).

*Condemned to Live* opens with three people stranded in a dark cave surrounded by hostile natives in Africa. The woman (Barbara Bedford) is about to give birth to a child, attended by her husband (Ferdinand Schumann-Heink) and a doctor (Robert Frazer). The natives will not attack the trio because they fear the "night birds" in a cave, actually vampire bats. Just before giving birth to a son the woman is bitten by one of the bats. Forty years later a European seaside village is being plagued by gruesome murders, the villagers believing the fiend to be a vampire. After the murder of a young girl, the hunchback Zan (Mischa Auer) carries the body to a nearby cave and tosses it into a pit. The villagers discover the body and go to Professor Paul Kristan (Ralph Morgan) for help. Kristan, who is Zan's master and protector, is engaged to beautiful young Marguerite Mane (Maxine Doyle), who is also loved by David (Russell Gleason), a man her own age. Marguerite "is very proud of the honor the professor has done me" and agrees to marry him to make him happy as well as her father (Carl Stockdale), who has but a short time to live. David is angry at Marguerite's decision, and he also tells the villagers the killer is not supernatural but is one of them. Arriving in the village is Dr. Anders Bizet (Pedro de Cordoba), who is Kristan's foster father and best friend. He quickly surmises that Marguerite loves David and not Kristan. When Kristan tells Bizet he has terrible headaches which render him unconscious and that he fears he

may be the killer, Bizet advises him to break off his engagement to Marguerite. When a servant (Hedi Shope) is killed at Mane's home, the villagers blame Zan for the tragedy, and Bizet forces the hunchback to tell him that it is Kristan who committed the crimes and that he disposed of the bodies to protect his master. Fearing Kristan has gone to see Marguerite, Bizet follows as the villagers chase Zan. In the dark Kristan tries to attack the girl but Zan arrives in time to save her. Bizet then tells Marguerite that Kristan is the vampire since he was marked at birth when his mother was bitten by the vampire bat. The infant was taken by the doctor after the death of its parents and given over to Bizet to be raised. Kristan, who was knocked out by Zan in the struggle over Marguerite, comes to and goes to the caves to save Zan. There he confesses to the villagers he is the vampire killer and then he jumps to his death into the pit, quickly followed by Zan. David and Marguerite are now free to marry.

The vampire theme in *Condemned to Live* is much different from the one used in *Dracula* (1931). Here Professor Kristan becomes a vampire because of his mother's having been bitten by a vampire bat with the malady coming on him years later due to exhaustion and overwork leading to madness. Filmed on the Universal lot, the movie incorporates sets from *The Bride of Frankenstein* (1935) to create the same nineteenth-century setting. Ted Billings even repeats his role of the bell ringer from that feature. Although a talkie, the movie is very atmospheric, with most of its scenes taking place at night. Included is the mob of torch-carrying villagers which populated a number of horror movies in the 1930s and 1940s. The movie is filmed mostly in long and medium shots with a minimum of close-ups. The protagonist, Dr. Kristan, is shown to be a very kind man who becomes worn out worrying over the problems of the villagers, thus awakening the vampire in this character. His vampiric acts are committed only when there is no light. Unfortunately, Ralph Morgan's Kristan, who is always spouting wise sayings, is a rather tiresome character, as is the love interest David, blandly played by Russell Gleason. On the other hand, Maxine Doyle is justly alluring as the loyal Marguerite, Pedro de Corboda is good as the sympathetic Bizet and Mischa Auer portrays the hideous Zan convincingly. Overall, *Condemned to Live* is a rather interesting attempt at restrained horror and within its modest confines accomplishes its goal.

When Grand National picked up some of the Chesterfield-Invincible product to fill out its release schedule during the 1936–37 season, *Condemned to Live* saw re-release as *Life Sentence*.

## Death from a Distance

Invincible, September 17, 1935, 65 minutes.

*P:* Maury M. Cohen. *D:* Frank R. Strayer. *SC:* John W. Krafft. *PH:* M.A. Anderson. *ED:* Roland Reed. *AD:* Edward C. Jewell. *Mus:* Abe Meyer. *SD:* L.E. Clark. *Asst Dir:* Melville Shyer. *Prod Mgr:* Lon Young. *SP Eff:* Jack Cosgrove.

*Cast:* Russell Hopton, Lola Lane, Lee Kohlmar, Lew Kelly, John St. Polis, George Marion, Wheeler Oakman, Robert Frazer, Cornelius Keefe, E.H. Calvert, John Davidson, John Dilson, Henry Hall, Creighton Hale, Jane Keckley, Eric Mayne, Herbert Vigran, Charles West, Lynton Brent,

Ralph Brooks, Joel Lyon, Frank LaRue, Hal Price.

A pretty newspaper reporter is at odds with a police detective in solving the mysterious shooting of a drug manufacturer.

## Public Opinion

Invincible, September 19, 1935, 66 minutes.

*P:* Maury M. Cohen. *D:* Frank R. Stayer. *SC:* Karen De Wolf. *PH:* M.A. Anderson. *ED:* Roland Reed. *AD:* Edward C. Jewell. *Mus:* Lee Zahler. *SD:* L.E. Clark. *Supv:* Lon Young.

*Cast:* Lois Wilson, Crane Wilbur, Shirley Grey, Luis Alberni, Andres de Segurola, Paul Ellis, Ronnie Cosby, Florence Roberts, Gertrude Sutton, Erville Alderson, Edward Keane, Mildred Gover, Edward LeSaint, Betty Mack, Lew Kelly, Robert Frazer, Richard Carlyle.

Because of his jealousy, a bacteriologist loses the love of his opera singer wife. Working title: *A Gentleman's Agreement*.

## The Girl Who Came Back

September 20, 1935, 65 minutes.

*P:* George R. Batcheller. *D:* Charles Lamont. *SC:* Ewart Adamson. *PH:* M.A. Anderson. *ED:* Roland Reed.

*Cast:* Shirley Grey, Sidney Blackmer, Noel Madison, Matthew Betz, Torben Meyer, May Beatty, Frank LaRue, Robert Adair, Ida Darling, Edward Martindel, Don Brodie, John Dilson, Lou Davis.

A counterfeiter goes straight and gets a job in a bank but her former criminal pals try to blackmail her into helping them rob the establishment. Reissued by Grand National.

# False Pretenses

October 25, 1935, 66 minutes.

*P:* George R. Batcheller. *D:* Charles Lamont. *SC:* Ewart Adamson. *ST:* Betty Burbridge. *PH:* M.A. Anderson. *ED:* Roland D. Reed.

*Cast:* Irene Ware, Sidney Blackmer, Russell Hopton, Betty Compson, Edward Gargan, Ernest Wood, Herbert Clifton, Lucy Beaumont, Marshall Ruth, John Piccori, Dot Farley, William Humphries, Wilson Benge, Al Thompson, Jack Shutta, Frank O'Connor.

Wanting to impress a wealthy young man who wants to marry her, a girl borrows money from a friend. Rereleased by Grand National.

# Society Fever

Invincible, October 30, 1935, 65 minutes.

*P:* Maury M. Cohen. *D:* Frank R. Strayer. *SC:* Karen De Wolf. *PH:* M.A. Anderson. *ED:* Roland Reed. *Supv:* Lon Young.

*Cast:* Lois Wilson, Lloyd Hughes, Hedda Hopper, Guinn Williams, Grant Withers, Marion Shilling, George Irving, Sheila Terry, Maidel Turner, Erville Alderson, Lois January, Katherine Sheldon, Anthony Marsh, Reginal Sheffield, Shirley Hill, Lew Kelly, Richard Hemingway, Bob McKenzie, Roland Reed.

The mother of an eccentric family worries when wealthy friends are invited to dinner. Reissued by Grand National. Made as *Dinner Party* and also called *Love Fever*.

# Happiness Came C.O.D.

December 21, 1935, 66 minutes.

*P:* George R. Batcheller. *D:* Charles Lamont. *SC:* Robert Ellis &

Helen Logan. *PH:* M.A. Anderson. *ED:* Roland Reed.

*Cast:* Donald Meek, Irene Ware, William Bakewell, Maude Eburne, Edwin Maxwell, Lona Andre, Polly Ann Young, Junior Coghlan, Malcolm MacGregor, Jack Shutta, Richard Cramer, Bob McKenzie, Fred Sumner, Richard Carlyle, John Dilson.

In order to pay off his mortgage and support his lazy family a man decides to become dishonest. Rereleased by Grand National.

# The Lady in Scarlet

December 21, 1935, 66 minutes.

*P:* George R. Batcheller. *D:* Charles Lamont. *SC:* Robert Ellis & Helen Logan. *PH:* M.A. Anderson. *ED:* Roland Reed.

*Cast:* Reginald Denny, Patricia Farr, Dorothy Revier, Claudia Dell, James Bush, Jack Adair, Jameson Thomas, John St. Polis, James T. Murray.

A detective is called in to solve the murder of an antique dealer. Reissued by Grand National.

# Tango

Invincible, February 14, 1936, 66 minutes.

*P:* Maury M. Cohen. *AP:* Lon Young. *D:* Phil Rosen. *SC:* Arthur T. Horman, from the book by Vida Hurst. *PH:* M.A. Anderson. *ED:* Roland Reed. *AD:* Edward C. Jewell. *SD:* Richard Tyler. *Asst Dir:* Melville Shyer.

*Cast:* Marion Nixon, Chick Chandler, Warren Hymer, George Meeker, Marie Prevost, Herman Bing, Franklin Pangborn, Matty Kemp, Virginia Howell, Barbara Bedford, Betty Mack, Wilson Benge, Jane Keckley.

Deserted by the husband who

thought her unfaithful, a young woman becomes a tango dancer to support their child. Reissued by Grand National.

## Ring Around the Moon

February 15, 1936, 72 minutes.

*P:* Lon Young. *D:* Charles Lamont. *SC:* Paul Perez, from the novel by Vere Hobart. *PH:* M.A. Anderson. *ED:* Roland Reed. *SD:* Richard Tyler. *AD:* Edward C. Jewell. *Asst Dir:* Melville Shyer.

*Cast:* Donald Cook, Erin O'Brien-Moore, Ann Doran, Alan Edwards, Douglas Fowley, John Qualen, Barbara Bedford, Richard Tucker, Mildred Gover, John Miltern, Dickie Dewar, Carl Stockdale, Dot Farley.

In order to get even with his boss for firing him, a newspaper reporter marries the man's daughter.

## Murder at Glen Athol

Invincible, February 28, 1936, 64 minutes.

*P:* Maury M. Cohen. *D:* Frank R. Strayer. *SC:* John W. Krafft, from the novel by Norman Lippincott. *PH:* M.A. Anderson. *ED:* Roland Reed. *SD:* Richard Tyler. *Supv:* Lon Young. *Asst Dir:* Melville Shyer.

*Cast:* John Miljan, Irene Ware, Betty Blythe, Noel Madison, Barry Norton, Oscar Apfel, Lew Kelly, Robert Frazer, Iris Adrian, Paul Ellis, James Burtis, Harry Holman, Stanley Blystone, Sidney Bracey.

A writer attempts to solve a murder committed in an old house. Reissued by Grand National as *The Criminal Within*.

## Hitchhike to Heaven

Invincible, March 13, 1936, 64 minutes.

*P:* Maury M. Cohen. *D:* Frank R. Strayer. *SC:* Robert Ellis & Helen Logan. *PH:* M.A. Anderson. *ED:* Roland Reed. *Supv:* Lon Young.

*Cast:* Anita Page, Herbert Rawlinson, Henrietta Crossman, Russell Gleason, Polly Ann Young, Al Shean, Harry Holman, Syd Saylor, Crauford Kent, Harry Harvey, Ethel Wykes, Leila Bliss, John Dilson.

When a member of a theatrical family becomes a movie star his attitude nearly causes him to lose his wife and son. Reissued by Grand National.

## The Bridge of Sighs

Invincible, May 1, 1936, 65 minutes.

*P:* Maury M. Cohen. *D:* Phil Rosen. *SC:* Arthur T. Horman. *PH:* M.A. Anderson. *ED:* Ernest J. Nims.

*Cast:* Onslow Stevens (Jeffrey Powell), Dorothy Tree (Marion Courtney), Jack LaRue (Packy Lacy), Mary Doran (Evelyn "Duchess" Thane), Walter Byron (Arny Norman), Oscar Apfel, Maidel Turner, John Kelly, Paul Fix, Bryant Washburn, Robert Homans, Lafe McKee, Selmer Jackson, Phyllis Crane, Lynton Brent, Frances Wright, Dorothy Roberts, George Hayes.

When Marion Courtney's (Dorothy Tree) brother (Paul Fix) is sentenced to die in the electric chair on a murder charge, she tries to do all she can to prove his innocence and prevent the execution. Marion suspects that gangster Packy Lacy (Jack LaRue) and moll Duchess (Mary Doran) know more about the crime than they have told in court, and she goes to the district attorney, Jeffrey Powell (Onslow Stevens), to plead her brother's case. Powell can do nothing to help her, so Marion confesses to a murder for which she is found guilty and sent to prison. Once there she works to obtain the evidence necessary to clear her brother's name.

While economically produced, *The Bridge of Sighs* is a fast-paced and entertaining dual biller which presented its prison themes in a somewhat different light than most such melodramas. Dorothy Tree carries the picture as the determined heroine while Jack LaRue contributes another of his slick gangster portrayals. Top-billed Onslow Stevens as the D.A. has less to do than the heroine, but he handles the assignment convincingly. Paul Fix also was quite good as the cowardly brother; Fix excelled in playing screen weasels.

*Variety* reported, "*Bridge of Sighs* is formula crime material, but it has enough suspense and action interest to pull through for the masses on double bills. Title isn't a bad one for lure purposes…. Story is occasionally a bit slow, and the dialog never brilliant, but with all elements thrown together the results are still rather fair. Among other things in the picture's favor is the fact it sustains suspense very well…. Numerous scenes in prison, others in a courtroom during the murder trial." On the other hand, Jay Robert Nash and Stanley Ralph Ross in *The Motion Picture Guide* (1985) called it "a shallow production lacking in suspense."

## The Little Red Schoolhouse

May 15, 1936, 66 minutes.

*P:* George R. Batcheller. *D:* Charles Lamont. *SC:* Paul Perez. *PH:* M.A. Anderson. *ED:* Roland D. Reed.

*Cast:* Frank [Junior] Coghlan, Jr. (Frank Burke), Dickie Moore (Dickie Burke), Ann Doran (Mary Burke), Lloyd Hughes (Roger Owen), Richard Carle ("The Professor"), Ralf Harolde (Pete Scardoni), Frank Sheridan (War-

den Gail), Matthew Betz (Bill), Kenneth Howell (Schuyler Tree), Sidney Miller (Sidney Levy), Gloria Browne (Shirley), Don Brodie (Ed), Lou Davis (Mac), Corky (himself).

Youngster Frank Burke (Frank Coghlan Jr.) becomes unhappy with his life with his older brother Dickie (Dickie Moore) and school teacher sister Mary (Ann Doran), who is being romanced by the second-class teacher Roger Owen (Lloyd Hughes). With his dog Corky, Frank decides on the romantic life of a hobo and runs away from home. He becomes attached to petty crooks, The Professor (Richard Carle), Pete Scardoni (Ralf Harolde) and Bill (Matthew Betz), who use him in their larceny schemes. When things become too hot for them, the crooks frame Frank on a false charge, and he is sent to reform school where he is forced to endure harsh prison life. Roger, however, learns of Frank's situation and he works to get the boy out from behind bars. Frank is able to return home and go back to school, no longer bored with his small-town existence.

Not a reference to America's educational system, this film is a 1930s reworking of *Oliver Twist*. Ironically costar Dickie Moore had the title role in a modest but well-received version of this Charles Dickens classic done by Monogram in 1934. By now, however, Moore was becoming too old for the part, which was taken over by Frank Coghlan, Jr., who for some years was billed as Junior Coghlan. Still *Variety* noted, "Having only the name of Dickie Moore to brighten the marquee, this curious admixture of school days, cheap melodrama and forced heart-throbs is only for a minor secondary feature spot. Even there it is apt to baffle the average audience." Despite the review, *The Little Red Schoolhouse* is, in reality, a pleasant bucolic drama that warned youngsters to stick close to hearth and home and to eschew becoming vagabonds or ending up in reform school. The highlight of the feature is Richard Carle's work as a modern-day, somewhat good-hearted Fagin. On the other hand, Ralf Harolde and Matthew Betz are their usual slimy selves as his fellow crooks. The stalwart heroics were handled by Lloyd Hughes as the teacher who gets the young hero out of reform school.

## Below the Deadline

June 6, 1936, 64 minutes.

*P:* George R. Batcheller. *D:* Charles Lamont. *SC:* Ewart Adamson. *PH:* M.A. Anderson. *ED:* Roland Reed. *AD:* Edward C. Jewell. *SD:* Richard Tyler. *Supv:* Lon Young.

*Cast:* Cecilia Parker, Theodore Von Eltz, Russell Hopton, Edward LeSaint, John St. Polis, Jack Gardner, Warner Richmond, Robert Frazer, Robert Homans, Charles Delaney, Katherine Selden, Thomas Jackson.

Framed for murder, a man undergoes plastic surgery after a train wreck in order to prove his innocence. Rereleased by Grand National.

## Three of a Kind

Invincible, June 24, 1936, 75 minutes.

*P:* Maury M. Cohen. *D:* Phil Rosen. *SC:* Arthur T. Horman. *PH:* M.A. Anderson. *ED:* Roland Reed. *AD:* Edward C. Jewell. *SD:* Richard Tyler.

*Cast:* Evelyn Knapp, Chick Chandler, Patricia Farr, Berton Churchill, Bradley Page, Richard Carle, Bryant Washburn, Billy Gilbert, Pat West, Lew Kelly, Harry Bradley, John Dilson.

When they meet at a swank hotel a truck driver and a gold-digger each think the other is wealthy. Reissued by Grand National.

## Easy Money

Invincible, July 11, 1936, 65 minutes.

*P:* Maury M. Cohen. *D:* Phil Rosen. *SC:* Arthur T. Horman. *ST:* Paul Perez & Ewart Adamson. *PH:* M.A. Anderson. *ED:* Roland Reed. *SD:* Richard Tyler. *Supv:* Lon Young & Herman S. Cohen.

*Cast:* Onslow Stevens, Kay Linaker, Noel Madison, Allen Vincent, Barbara Barondess, Wallis Clark, Selmer Jackson, Robert Homans, Robert Graves, Robert Frazer, Broderick O'Farrell, Barbara Bedford, Dickie Walters, Betty Mack, Henry Herbert, John Kelly, Monte Vandergrift, Alan Wood.

A district attorney resigns after his brother gets involved with insurance swindlers and he vows to bring them to justice. Rereleased by Grand National. TV title: *Final Payment.*

## August Weekend

July 18, 1936, 67 minutes.

*P:* George R. Batcheller. *D:* Charles Lamont. *SC:* Paul Perez, from the novel by Faith Baldwin. *PH:* M.A. Anderson. *ED:* Roland Reed.

*Cast:* Valerie Hobson, G.P. Huntley, Jr., Paul Harvey, Betty Compson, Claire McDowell, Frank Melton, Gigi Parrish, Howard Hickman, Dorothea Kent, Edgar Norton, Maynard Holmes, Paul Irving, Pat West.

At a society dinner party, a rich married man makes a play for a girl loved by a younger man. Reissued by Grand National.

# The Dark Hour

August 1, 1936, 64 minutes.

*P:* George R. Batcheller. *EP:* Lon Young. *D:* Charles Lamont. *SC:* Ewart Adamson, from the novel *The Last Trap* by Sinclair Gluck. *PH:* M.A. Anderson. *ED:* Roland D. Reed. *SD:* Richard Tyler. *AD:* Edward C. Jewell. *Asst Dir:* Melville Shyer.

*Cast:* Ray Walker (Jim Landis), Irene Ware (Elsa Carson), Berton Churchill (Paul Bernard), Hedda Hopper (Mrs. Tallman), Hobart Bosworth (Charles Carson), E.E. Clive (Foot), William V. Mong (Henry Carson), Harold Goodwin (Blake), Aggie Herring (Mrs. Dubbin), Katherine Sheldon (Helen Smith), Rose Allen (Mrs. Murphy), Miki Morita (Choong), John St. Polis (Dr. Munro), Fred Kelsey (Detective Watson), Lloyd Whitlock (Dr. Bruce), Harry Strange (Policeman), Michael Marks (Arthur Bell).

Pretty Elsa Carson (Irene Ware) fears for the life of her uncles, Henry (William V. Mong) and Charles Carson (Hobart Bosworth), and she goes to see detective Jim Landis (Ray Walker), who is visiting with retired sleuth Paul Bernard (Berton Churchill). Jim agrees to look into the matter, but at the Carson estate he is told by Henry Carson to leave. That night Henry is found dead in his study, and when Jim and Bernard arrive on the scene none of the members of the household cooperate, including Elsa. After questioning all the suspects in the house Jim comes to believe the murderer is Mrs. Tallman (Hedda Hopper), Elsa's aunt, while Bernard thinks Foot (E.E. Clive), the butler, is the culprit. A dress fitting Mrs. Tallman is found in Elsa's closet, but Jim then begins to suspect Blake (Harold Goodwin); a chemist, may have had

something to do with the homicide. Foot too is found murdered, and it is reported that fires have broken out in some of the Carson properties throughout the city. Bernard sets a trap and nabs a cross-dressing Charles Carson, who is then accused of killing his brother for his estate. As it turns out, Carson also murdered the butler to keep him quiet. Jim, however, does not believe Charles is guilty and he proves that Henry died from poison gas made in Blake's laboratory before being stabbed. When Bernard himself is accused of the crimes, he works out a plan which successfully traps the murderer.

*The Dark Hour* is a fairly faithful rendering of Sinclair Gluck's 1928 novel *The Last Trap.* Except for the miscasting of Ray Walker in the title role (someone like Donald Cook or Jack Mulhall would have been better suited) as the detective, the movie has a well-modulated cast. Berton Churchill is especially impressive as the retired detective who eventually becomes a murder suspect himself before bringing the case to a satisfactory close. The old plot ploy of having a male killer dressed in a woman's clothes was not new by any means when this film was produced, but it does provide an offbeat plot twist and makes spotting the murderer more difficult. Actually the problem in revealing the killer is the most enjoyable aspect of *The Dark Hour* since other mystery motifs such as the use of dark shadows, thunderstorms and the spookiness attributed to murder mansions are eschewed in this thriller. Overall, however, the film provides solid entertainment within the confines of its limited budget and script potential.

# It Couldn't Have Happened

Invincible, September 11, 1936, 64 minutes.

*P:* Maury M. Cohen. *D:* Phil Rosen. *SC:* Arthur T. Horman. *PH:* M.A. Anderson. *ED:* Roland D. Reed. *AD:* Edward C. Jewell. *SD:* Richard Tyler.

*Cast:* Reginald Denny, Evelyn Brent, Jack LaRue, Inez Courtney, Bryant Washburn, Crauford Kent, Hugh Marlowe, Claude King, Robert Frazer, Miki Morita, Broderick O'Farrell, Lynton Brent, Henry Herbert, Emily LaRue, Robert Homans.

When two theatrical producers are murdered, a playwright and a gangster are suspects. Working title: *Divided by Two*. Rereleased by Grand National.

# Lady Luck

September 14, 1936, 62 minutes.

*P:* George R. Batcheller. *D:* Charles Lamont. *SC:* John Knight. *ST:* Stuart & Dorrell McGowan. *PH:* M.A. Anderson. *ED:* Roland Reed.

*Cast:* Patricia Farr (Mamie Murphy), William Bakewell (David Haines), Duncan Renaldo (Tony), Iris Adrian (Rita), Lulu McConnell (Aunt Mamie), Jameson Thomas (Jack Conroy), Vivian Oakland (Mrs. Hemingway), Claude Allister (Briggs), Arthur Hoyt (J. Baldwin Hemingway), Lew Kelly (Lt. James Riley), John Kelly, Joe Barton (Bouncers), Lupe Lupien (Maid), Charles Lane (Mr. Fineberg).

Reporter Dave Haines' (William Bakewell) girlfriend, manicurist Mamie Murphy (Patricia Farr), wins a chance in a British horse-racing sweepstakes and is romanced by wealthy playboy Jack Conroy (Jameson Thomas), who takes her to the Blue Moon night club. The club is run by crook Tony (Duncan Renaldo) (who is also after Mamie) and his moll Rita (Iris Adrian). It turns out Conroy is so broke he has to borrow money from his butler, Briggs (Claude Allister), and he plans to wed Mamie if she wins the sweepstakes so he can control her money. Conroy, however, has problems with an old flame (Vivian Oakland) who has a jealous husband (Arthur Hoyt), and at the club he and Dave get into a fight over Mamie, who also has to fend off the advances of Tony. Mamie then finds out that another woman, who has the same name as she, is the real ticket holder, but the two agree to split the rewards if their horse wins—"Aunt" Mamie (Lulu McConnell) will take the money, and Mamie will get all the publicity and a theatrical contract. Lady Luck does indeed win the race, and the two women move into a swanky hotel. Conroy proposes to Mamie, but later that night he is murdered. During the crime investigation conducted by Lt. Riley (Lew Kelly), a friendly rival of Dave's, Mamie tells the truth about the sweepstakes, but it is Rita who tells how the murder was committed. Dave and Mamie are reunited, and Aunt Mamie takes up with Lt. Riley.

Issued near the end of Chesterfield Pictures' lengthy (for Poverty Row) tenure, *Lady Luck* is a likable film which could not decide if it was a drama or a comedy. In the latter vein it has lots of fast patter and some amusing situations, but overall the movie has too many plot ploys, the most grating of which has one of the leading men murdered near the film's finale. Overall *Lady Luck* is a well-acted, fast-paced "B" offering that did not quite jell into a solid entertainment package.

## Brilliant Marriage

Invincible, September 19, 1936, 62 minutes.

*P:* Maury M. Cohen. *D:* Phil Rosen. *SC:* Paul Perez, from the novel by Katherine Ursula Parrott. *PH:* M.A. Anderson. *ED:* Roland Reed. *Supv:* Lon Young. *SD:* Richard Tyler.

*Cast:* Joan Marsh, Ray Walker, Lawson Trent, Inez Courtney, Ann Codee, Doris Lloyd, Olive Tell, Holmes Herbert, Barbara Bedford, Robert Adair, Victor Wong, Katherine Sheldon, Dick Elliott, George Cleveland, Lynton Brent.

Finding out her mother died in prison, a young woman drops plans to marry her rich boyfriend. Reissued by Grand National.

## Missing Girls

October 7, 1936, 66 minutes.

*P:* George R. Batcheller. *D:* Phil Rosen. *SC:* John W. Krafft & Martin Mooney. *ST:* Martin Mooney. *PH:* M.A. Anderson. *ED:* Roland Reed. *SD:* Richard Tyler. *Asst Dir:* Melville Shyer.

*Cast:* Roger Pryor, Muriel Evans, Sidney Blackmer, Noel Madison, Ann Doran, George Cooper, Dewey Robinson, Wallis Clark, Vera Lewis, Oscar Apfel, Robert Fiske, Cornelius Keefe, Warner Richmond, Matty Fain.

After writing an expose about gangsters kidnapping young girls, a reporter learns his fiancée has been abducted and her father murdered.

## The House of Secrets

October 26, 1936, 64 minutes.

*P:* George R. Batcheller. *D:* Roland D. Reed. *SC:* John W. Krafft, from the novel by Sydney Horler. *PH:* M.A. Anderson. *ED:* Dan Milner. *SD:*
Richard Tyler. *Mus:* Abe Meyer. *Asst Dir:* H. Minter.

*Cast:* Leslie Fenton (Barry Wilding), Muriel Evans (Julie Kenmore), Morgan Wallace (Dr. Kenmore), Sidney Blackmer (Tom Starr), Noel Madison (Dan Wharton), Holmes Herbert (Sir Bertram Evans), Ian MacLaren (Commissioner Cross), Jameson Thomas (Coventry), Syd Saylor (Ed), Matty Fain (Jumpy), George Rosener (Hector Munson), Matty Kemp (Passenger), Rita Carlyle (Mrs. Shipman), Tom Ricketts (Peters), David Thursby (Gregory), R. Lancaster (British Policeman), Ramsey Hill (Police Inspector).

After saving a pretty girl from being bothered on board a ship from France to England, Barry Wilding (Leslie Fenton) arrives in London to find out he has inherited an old estate near the city, but a clause forbids him to sell it. When he tries to see the estate he is run away. He also gets offers from interested parties who want to buy it and a warning to leave England. Finally getting into his own home, Barry recognizes the young woman living there as the one he met on the boat. Her name is Julie Kenmore (Muriel Evans), and she asks him to let her and her father (Morgan Wallace) remain there for several months but refuses to tell him the reason for their staying. After gangsters from the United States attack him on the grounds of the estate, Barry goes to Scotland Yard and the Home Secretary (Holmes Herbert) for help, but his pleas are rejected. When American detective Tom Starr (Sidney Blackmer) arrives on the scene, Barry teams with him, and they learn that gangster Dan Wharton (Noel Madison) is holding Julie and her scientist father prisoners. Dr. Kenmore has been working on a secret government project while the gangsters are seeking treasure buried on the property. Barry and Starr rescue Julie and her father and turn the gangsters over to the law. Barry then finds the treasure, and he and Julie realize they are in love.

Roland Reed, who would later become a noted television producer, made his directorial debut with this film. For several years he had been Chesterfield's in-house film editor, having edited more than a score of the company's releases.

But *The House of Secrets*, is on the dull side, and not even a good cast and attractive sets make it interesting. A remake of the studio's first talkie, the film was based on the play and 1926 novel by Sydney Horler. Set in England, the movie does little to capture the flavor of the country except for a few scenes involving stereotyped citizens and the remote estate called "The Hawk's Nest." Although the mystery angle has some intriguing twists, the film simply does not hold viewer interest for long. Leslie Fenton was hardly a box office attraction in 1936, and the film lacks the marquee value needed to make it attractive to moviegoers. Sidney Blackmer appears somewhat out of place as a tough Yankee detective, and heroine Muriel Evans makes no attempt to seem British. On the other hand Noel Madison is in his element as the leader of gangsters searching for hidden treasure in the old mansion. Unlike the 1929 version which was shot in New York City, this remake was shot at the RKO-Pathe Studio and made good use of standing sets.

## Ellis Island

Invincible, December 10, 1936, 65 minutes.

*P:* Maury M. Cohen. *D:* Phil Rosen. *SC:* Arthur T. Horman. *PH:* M.A. Anderson. *ED:* Holbrook N. Todd. *AD:* Edward C. Jewell. *SD:* Richard Tyler. *Asst Dir:* Milton R. Brown. *Supv:* Herbert S. Cohen.

*Cast:* Donald Cook, Peggy Shannon, Jack LaRue, Joyce Compton, Bradley Page, Johnny Arthur, George Rosener, Maurice Black, Matty Fain, Bryant Washburn, Monte Vandergrift, Lew Kelly, Captain E.H. Calvert.

When a convict who is about to be deported through Ellis Island disappears, his niece is suspected of helping him but a government agent believes she is innocent.

## Red Lights Ahead

September 29, 1937, 70 minutes.

*P:* George R. Batcheller. *D:* Roland Reed. *PH:* M.A. Anderson. *ED:* Dan Milner.

*Cast:* Andy Clyde, Lucille Gleason, Paula Stone, Roger Imhoff, Frank [Junior] Coghlan, Jr., Ben Alexander, Ann Doran, Matty Kemp, Sam Flint, Addison [Jack] Randall.

When his son invests money in a gold mine that goes bust, a man comes to his family's rescue. A 1936 remake of *In the Money* (1933).

# Colony Pictures

Max and Arthur Alexander, immigrant siblings from Germany, had founded Beacon Pictures (q.v.) in the mid–1930s, and when that company folded, they put together Colony Pictures for a series of six westerns starring Rex Bell, who had just finished a brief series for Resolute (q.v.). The Colony Pictures were to be distributed on a states' rights basis by First Division (q.v.), but that outfit was absorbed by the newly formed Grand National after only two of the Bell films were distributed. Thus, Grand National released the final four Rex Bell westerns and rereleased the initial two outings. The Rex Bell westerns were fairly entertaining affairs. The handsome star appealed not only to male youngsters but to female moviegoers. Bell, however, was now married to Clara Bow, and he opted to spend more time on his Nevada ranch, eventually going into politics.

As Rex Bell's final Colony film, *Law and Lead*, was being distributed by Grand National in the spring of 1937, veteran cowboy star Ken Maynard came to the studio to make westerns for producer M.H. Hoffman, one-time head of Allied Pictures (q.v.). Maynard did *Boots of Destiny* and *Trailin' Trouble* (both 1937) before Hoffman died in 1938, and the Alexander Brothers took over production of the Maynard series, making two more: *Whirlwind Horseman* and *Six Shootin' Sheriff* in 1938. The producers had made the Maynard films on the cheap, about $15,000 each, but Grand National realized grosses of more than six times that amount. When Grand National folded in 1939, the Alexanders reactivated Colony Pictures and signed Ken Maynard to star in four more series westerns.

Prior to the second group of films with Ken Maynard, however, Colony produced a solo western starring famed crooner Gene Austin. Hoping to imitate the success Gene Autry was having at Republic, the Alexander brothers starred the famed singer of "My Blue Heaven" in a fairly sturdy oater that concentrated on the star's charming personality and fine singing in an attempt to compensate for his lack of thespian and athletic abilities. Road Show Pictures released the western musical mainly in the South where Austin still retained a big following. To bolster the grosses, which were considerable, Gene Austin and his stage show, which included Joan Brooks and his accompanists Candy and Coco, appeared with the film, giving audiences two shows for the price of one: the movie and a live stage appearance by the crooner, who was also recording for Decca Records at the time. *Songs and Saddles*, as the film was titled, got no national release but was nonetheless highly successful in its regional playoff. It was not until 1949 that it was finally released in Great Britain.

With Grand National out of the picture, Max and Arthur Alexander returned to the states' rights field for the release of their final four Ken Maynard

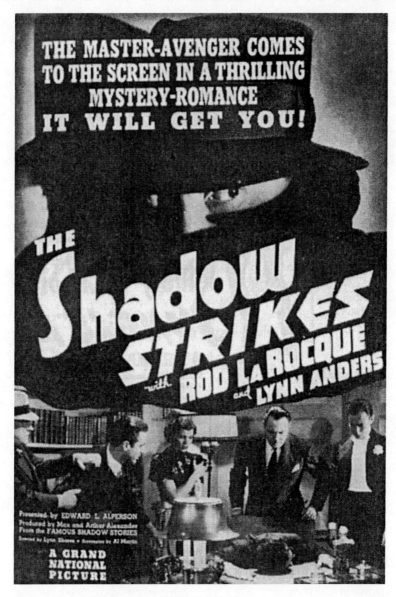

Poster for *The Shadow Strikes* (Grand National, 1937), produced by Colony Pictures.

starrers. Again they kept the budgets in the $10,000 to $20,000 range, but domestic grosses on all four features went to around the $100,000 mark, making them a very profitable venture for their producers. The four Maynard westerns were better than the ones he had done for Grand National with Ken being slimmer and more agile than he had been in the earlier films. Reviewing the first in the series, *Flaming Lead* (1939), *Variety* commented, "Maynard, although he's lost about 25 pounds off his paunch since last seen, could stand a bit more training down to get rid of some unglam midway left." The same reviewer evaluated the film as "...above the Ken Maynard western average." It is interesting to note that the last film in the series, *Lightning Strikes West* (1940), was written by Martha Chapin, who had played the lead in the exploitation melodrama *Gambling with Souls* (1936) for producer J.D. Kendis (q.v.). Following the Colony series, Ken Maynard continued to tour with his circus until returning to films at Monogram in 1943 for six oaters with Hoot Gibson (Bob Steele was in the last three) for producer-director Robert Emmett Tansey, who had scripted the first Rex Bell-Colony, *Men of the Plains*, in 1936.

After the last Colony Pictures series ended in 1940, the Alexander Brothers became producers at Producers Releasing Corporation (P.R.C.) and later in the decade they formed M. & A. Alexander Productions, making series for syndicated television and rereleasing independent movies, including many of their own, to the small screen.

It should be noted that the Alexander brothers, nephews of Universal Pictures founder Carl Laemmle, also used the Colony Pictures banner to produce two mystery features starring Rod La Rocque as The Shadow: *The Shadow Strikes* (1937) and *International Crime* (1938). Both features were distributed by Grand National Pictures and not by Colony.

## Too Much Beef

April 20, 1936, 66 minutes.

*P:* Max & Arthur Alexander. *D:* Robert Hill. *SC:* Rock Hawkey [Robert Hill]. *ST:* William Colt Mac-Donald. *PH:* Harry Forbes. *ED:* Charles Harris. *SD:* Joe Lapis.

*Cast:* Rex Bell, Connie Bergen, Peggy O'Connell, Lloyd Ingraham, Horace Murphy, Jimmie Aubrey, Forrest Taylor, Jack Cowell, Vincent Dennis, George Ball, Fred Burns, Steve Clark, Denny Meadows [Dennis Moore], Jack Kirk, Frank Ellis.

A cowboy aids a rancher whose spread is sought by crooks because the railroad needs the land. Reissued by Grand National.

## West of Nevada

June 22, 1936, 59 minutes.

*P:* Max & Arthur Alexander. *D:* Robert Hill. *SC:* Rock Hawkey [Robert Hill], from the story "Raw Gold" by Charles Kyson. *PH:* Robert Cline. *ED:* Dan Milner. *SD:* Corson Jowett. *Asst Dir:* Glen Cook.

*Cast:* Rex Bell, Joan Barclay, Al St. John, Georgia O'Dell, Steve Clark, Forrest Taylor, Dick Botiller, Frank McCarroll, Bob Woodward.

The son of a senator goes with his comical pal to look into Indian reservation gold mine thefts. Rereleased by Grand National.

## The Idaho Kid

August 6, 1936, 54 minutes.

*P:* Max & Arthur Alexander. *D:* Robert Hill. *SC:* George Plympton, from the story "Idaho" by Paul Evan Lehman. *PH:* Robert Cline. *ED:* Charles Henkel. *SD:* Hans Weeren. *Asst Dir:* Robert Emmett Tansey.

Advertisement for *West of Nevada* (Colony, 1936).

*Cast:* Rex Bell, Marion Shilling, Lane Chandler, Charles King, Dave Sharpe, Phil Dunham, Earl Dwire, Lafe McKee, Dorothy Woods, Dick Botiller, Herman Hack, Edward Cassidy, George Morrell, Jimmie Aubrey, Sherry Tansey.

Returning home a young man tries to stop a feud between his father and another rancher, the father of the girl he loves. Distributed by Grand National.

## Men of the Plains

September 29, 1936, 63 minutes.

*P:* Max & Arthur Alexander. *D:* Robert Hill. *SC-Asst Dir:* Robert Emmett [Tansey]. *PH:* Robert Cline. *ED:* Charles Henkel. *SD:* Hans Weeren.

*Cast:* Rex Bell, Joan Barclay, George Ball, Charles King, Forrest Taylor, Roger Williams, Edward Cassidy, Lafe McKee, Jack Cowell, Jimmie Aubrey.

The government assigns an investigator to look into a series of gold thefts. Distributed by Grand National.

## Stormy Trails

November 11, 1936, 59 minutes.

*P:* Max & Arthur Alexander. *D:* Sam Newfield. *SC:* Phil Dunham, from the story "Stampede" by E.B. Mann. *PH:* Robert Cline. *ED:* Charles Henkel. *SD:* Corson Jowett. *Asst Dir:* Eddie Mull.

*Cast:* Rex Bell (Tom Storm), Bob Hodges (Billy Storm), Lois Wilde (Connie Curlew), Lane Chandler (Dunn), Earl Dwire (Stephen Varick), Lloyd Ingraham (Mr. Curlew), Karl Hackett (Max Durante), Earl Ross (Thurman), Murdock MacQuarrie (Sheriff), Jimmy Aubrey (Shives the Camp Cook), Roger Williams (Dan-

iels), Chuck Morrison, George Morrell.

Siblings Tom (Rex Bell) and Billy Storm (Bob Hodges) own a ranch with valuable gold deposits, and crooked Dunn (Lane Chandler) and his henchmen are out to foreclose on the heavily mortgaged property to get its riches. Tom learns that Billy has become involved with the outlaws and when Billy tries to go straight and turn in the gang, Dunn and his boys attempt to rustle the Storm's cattle herd and Billy dies trying to stop them. Dunn then decides to stampede the cattle so that Tom will not be able to sell them in time to pay off his bank mortgage. The gang captures Tom but he manages to escapes, halt the stampede and round up the outlaws.

*Stormy Trails* was the fifth of six series westerns Rex Bell made for the Alexander brothers, Max and Arthur. He joined up with the Alexander's following his aborted series for Resolute (q.v.) in 1935. *Stormy Trails* is rather typical of the oaters Bell did for Colony. Its plot was on the confused side but the star was able to handle the action sequences in good fashion. The film's biggest detriment was the insertion of some rather poor cattle stampede stock footage which had a mildewed look that did not match the freshness of the rest of the feature. Director Sam Newfield handled the affair in his usual fine fashion, and the supporting cast was typically good for a Alexander brothers production. Following the demise of this series Rex Bell spent more time ranching and in politics, except for costarring with Buck Jones in *Dawn on the Great Divide* for Monogram in 1943.

Like all six of Rex Bell's Colony westerns, *Stormy Trails* was handled on a states' rights basis by First Division and when that exchange was taken over by Grand National the series was reissued through that company.

## Law and Lead

April 21, 1937, 62 minutes.

P: Max & Arthur Alexander. D: Robert Hill. SC: Rock Hawkey [Robert Hill]. ST: Basil Dickey. PH: Robert Cline. ED: Charles Henkel. SD: Hans Weeren. Asst Dir: Jack Korrick.

Cast: Rex Bell, Harley Wood, Wally Wales, Lane Chandler, Earl Dwire, Lloyd Ingraham, Roger Williams, Soledad Jiminez, Donald Reed, Lew Meehan, Karl Hackett, Edward Cassidy, George Morrell.

The Juarez Kid is wanted for criminal acts but the lawman sent to find him thinks the Kid is innocent. Distributed by Grand National.

## Songs and Saddles

Colony/Road Show Pictures, 1938, 65 minutes.

P: Max & Arthur Alexander. AP: Alfred Stein. D: Harry Fraser. SC: Wayne Carter. ST: Arthur Borris. PH: Robert Cline & Harry Forbes. ED: Charles Henkel. Songs: Gene Austin. AD: Fred Preble. Prod Mgr: Clifford Ruberg. Asst Dir: Chuck Wasserman.

Cast: Gene Austin (Himself), Lynne Barkeley (Carol Turner), Charles King (Falcon), Walter Wills (Charlie "Pop" Turner), Henry Roquemore (Jed Hill), Karl Hackett (George Morrow), Joan Brooks (Lucy), Ted Claire (Mark Bowers), John Merton (Rocky Renault), Ben Corbett (Sparks), Bob Terry (Klinker), John Elliott (Sheriff John Lawton), Lloyd Ingraham (Judge Harrison), Russell "Candy" Hall (Slim), Otto "Coco" Heimel (Porky).

Sandwiched between their west-

ern series with Rex Bell in 1936–37 and Ken Maynard from 1939–40, was Colony Pictures' *Songs and Saddles* which was filmed on location in the picturesque High Sierras of California. Unlike Colony's series westerns, *Songs and Saddles* was a one shot effort which was not released on the usual states' rights basis but instead was road shown on a town-to-town, theatre-to-theatre basis. For this particular feature this method was highly successful because of the film's star, Gene Austin. During the 1920s Austin had sold over eighty million records for the Victor Company with major hits like "My Blue Heaven," "Ramona," "Jeanine, I Dream of Lilac Time," "Weary River," "The Lonesome Road" and many more. By this time his career was on the downgrade, and the movie was basically an attempt to parlay box office returns on the type of film Gene Autrey was doing so successfully at Republic. On the other hand, *Songs and Saddles* is not a cheapie western as has often been written, but a solid, well-done little oater with its share of entertainment value. Outside of riding, Gene Austin was not required to do much in the way of fighting or with gunplay, and his easy style, romancing the heroine and crooning five songs, put him over well in the feature. Austin, in fact, composed all five tunes for the film: "Song of the Saddle" (the film's working title), "I Fell Down and Broke My Heart," "I'm Comin' Home," "Why Can't I Be Your Sweetheart Tonight?" and "That Rootin' Tootin' Shootin' Man from Texas." The latter song was refilmed by Gene Austin in 1943 for the Soundies Corporation of America as a three-minute short.

Radio crooner Gene Austin (Himself) is on his way home to see Pop Turner (Walter Wills), the man

IN PERSON!

GENE AUSTIN

America's Song Stylist

ON THE STAGE

*with his* Assisting Artists

ON THE SCREEN

Road Show Pictures, Inc. Present
The Premiere Prevue of

GENE AUSTIN
SONGS and SADDLES
*with an All Star Cast*

Advertisement for *Songs and Saddles* (Colony, 1938), distributed by Road Show Pictures, Inc.

who raised him. Pop's foreman Rocky (John Merton) offers him $3,000 for his ranch, but Pop refuses so Rocky threatens to sue him for back wages. Rocky is in league with corrupt realtor Morrow (Karl Hackett) and contractor Falcon (Charles King) who have hidden the fact that a highway is to be built through Pop's property. To get Pop out of the way Rocky and his men ambush the old man and leave him for dead after his horse plungs off a cliff and into a raging river. Pop, however, manages to escape and Gene finds him and tells him to stay in hiding until the would-be killers show their hand. Jed Hill (Henry Roquemore), a lawyer and Pop's best friend, decides to probate his will which leaves the ranch to Gene and to Pop's granddaughter Carol (Lynn Barkeley). At first Carol does not like Gene, but after he begins to suspect Rocky of trying to kill Pop the two become friendly. At the reading of Pop's will Morrow claims the property should be sold at auction to satisfy debts. Gene gets evidence that Morrow has deliberately kept a public works project a secret to benefit himself, but lacking proof he is jailed for bank robbery. Pop's ranch is sold and the highway project commences. With the aid of Jed Hill, Gene breaks out of jail and proves to the sheriff (John Elliott) that it was Falcon who forged Pop's signature on the fake bank note. He then gets a writ to stop the highway construction, but the work crew turns on him. Carol phones for the sheriff and when the law arrives Morrow and Falcon try to make a getaway but Gene captures them. Pop Turner then goes into the real estate business and reaps a profit off the highway project while Gene and Carol fall in love.

One of the more amusing moments in *Songs and Saddles* occurs when two of the villain's henchmen discuss crooner Gene Austin. One bad guy complains that all his girlfriend can do is talk about Austin. The other replies, "You're lucky you've got a girl that can talk. Mine can't do anything but giggle."

## Flaming Lead

November 15, 1939, 57 minutes.

*P:* Max & Arthur Alexander. *D:* Sam Newfield. *SC:* Joseph O'Donnell. *PH:* Art Reed. *ED:* Holbrook N. Todd. *AD:* Fred Preble. *SD:* Clifford Ruberg. *Mus:* David Chudnow.

*Cast:* Ken Maynard, Eleanor Stewart, Ralph Peters, Dave O'Brien, Walter Long, Tom London, Carleton Young, Reed Howes, Bob Terry, Kenne Duncan, Ethan Allen, John Merton, Joyce Rogers, Carl Mathews, Ernie Adams, Lew Meehan, Budd Buster, Ed Peil, Sr., Chick Hannon, Tex Palmer, Fox O'Callahan, Tarzan.

A rancher about to lose a government contract because of horse thieves is helped by a cowboy.

## Death Rides the Range

January 17, 1940, 58 minutes.

*P:* Max & Arthur Alexander. *D:* Sam Newfield. *SC:* William Lively. *PH:* Art Reed. *ED:* Holbrook N. Todd. *AD:* Fred Preble. *Mus:* Lew Porter. *SD:* Clifford Ruberg. *Song:* Colin Mac-Donald.

*Cast:* Ken Maynard, Fay McKenzie, Ralph Peters, Julian Rivero, Charles King, John Elliott, William Costello, Sven Hugo Borg, Michael Vallon, Julian Madison, Kenneth Rhodes, Murdock McQuarrie, Wally West, Dick Alexander, Bud Osborne, Tarzan.

When foreign agents try to locate helium gas deposits on the range, they are opposed by a cowboy and his pal.

## The Phantom Rancher

March 13, 1940, 61 minutes.

*P:* Max & Arthur Alexander. *D:* Harry Fraser. *SC:* William Lively. *SD:* Clifford Ruberg. *PH:* William Hyer.

*ED:* Fred Bain. *Mus:* Lew Porter. *AD:* Fred Preble.

*Cast:* Ken Maynard (Ken Mitchell), Dorothy Short (Ann Markham), Harry Harvey (Gopher), Dave O'Brien (Luke), Ted Adams (Collins), Tom London (Sheriff Parker), John Elliott (Mr. Markham), Reed Howes (Lon), Steve Clark (Burton), Carl Mathews (Hank), Sherry Tansey (Doc), Herman Hack (Joe), Tarzan (Himself), Wally West, George Morrell.

When rancher Markham (John Elliott) refuses to sell his ranch to crooked realtor Collins (Ted Adams), he is ambushed and killed by Luke (Dave O'Brien), a henchman of Collins. On his way home to take over his late uncle's ranch, cowboy Ken Mitchell (Ken Maynard) witnesses the shooting but later in town Collins accuses him of the crime. Mitchell is absolved of guilt by Markham's foreman Gopher (Harry Harvey). When Ken tells the sheriff (Tom London) his plans, Collins claims the Mitchell spread was left to him, but Ken produces a will that verifies his claim. The sheriff tells Ken that the locals hated his uncle because he destroyed their crops and foreclosed on their mortgages. Ken sets out to find out who killed Markham, and Luke and his men try to drygulch him. Ken, however, gets the upper hand on the gang and then pretends to be in cahoots with them to learn more about their activities. Ken tells Luke he will foreclose on the local ranchers, including the one belonging to Ann Markham (Dorothy Short), the dead man's daughter. Luke then sabotages the girl's water tank so she cannot water her cattle, but Ken, dressed as the Phantom Rider in a cape and mask, gives Ann and the other farmers the

COLONY PICTURES, INC presents

*Ken* **MAYNARD**

*and His Wonder Horse* TARZAN

in

**PHANTOM RANCHER**

with

*Dorothy* *Harry*
**SHORT · HARVEY**

*Produced by*
*Max and Arthur*
**ALEXANDER**

*Directed by*
**HARRY FRASER**

Advertisement for *The Phantom Rancher* (Colony, 1940).

money they need to pay off their mortgages. The Phantom then stops Collins' henchmen from trying to torch the Markham ranch, and Collins vows to put a stop to the masked avenger. Realizing that Collins is behind all the trouble in the area, Ken eventually is able to round up the gang, bring peace to the area and win Ann.

Having made four westerns for Max and Arthur Alexander in 1937–38 which were released by Grand National, Ken Maynard re-signed with the brothers for another four in 1939, receiving $10,000 for all the features, each shot back-to-back on one-week shoots. *The Phantom Rancher* was the third of the quartet and *Variety* termed

it "okay juvenile fodder." Although heavier than in his prime, Ken Maynard was still an agile and ingratiating hero, and the movie is a pleasant one, heightened by its mystery angle of Ken as a masked avenger. During the course of the action when Ken leaves money for the ranchers he signs himself as "The Phantom Rider," but in the movie he is referred to as "The Phantom Rancher." Another hard-to-swallow scene has Ken in his phantom getup getting the draw on the villains, but when he speaks to them he does not disguise his voice! The film, however, does include some amusing dialogue like the verbal sparring between Ken and Gopher in one scene. Gopher tells Ken, "If I was a few years younger I'd take your hide off." Ken counters, "If I was a few years older you could have it."

## Lightning Strikes West

June 19, 1940, 57 minutes.

*P:* Max & Arthur Alexander. *D:* Harry Fraser. *SC:* Martha Chapin. *ST:* Monroe Talbot. *PH:* Elmer Dyer. *ED:* Charles Henkel. *Mus:* Lew Porter. *AD:* Fred Preble. *SD:* Clifford Ruberg.

*Cast:* Ken Maynard, Claire Rochelle, Charles King, Michael Vallon, Bob Terry, Reed Howes, George Chesebro, Dick Dickinson, John Elliott, William Gould, Chick Hannon, Tex Palmer, Carl Mathews, Tarzan.

Pretending to be a hobo, a government agent attempts to bring in crooks responsible for the theft of money from a dam project.

# Commodore Pictures Corporation

William Steiner had been in the movie industry since the teens as an independent producer and distributor. By the early 1930s he was working mainly as a distributor on the states' rights market under the William Steiner banner. As such he handled the product of independents like Reliable (q.v.) and Supreme (q.v.). In 1935 Commodore Pictures Corporation was formed with William Steiner as its president and the company continued to distribute Reliable and Supreme releases. Commodore also released eight features of its own, five produced by William Berke, two by Ray Kirkwood and a solo outing by Fenn Kimball. Although Commodore had more hits than misses in its release schedule, most of the titles were screened in obscure situations and Commodore failed to survive more than one season.

Quality-wise the best of the Commodore releases were the westerns produced by William Berke. The first two to be shown were *Toll of the Desert* and *The Pecos Kid*, both issued in 1935 and starring Fred Kohler, Jr., son of the famous movie badman. Kohler made an acceptable sagebrush hero, and the two features he did for Berke were sombre affairs in the vein of Harry Carey (who appeared in two 1936 Commodore releases as "Cheyenne Harry," a character he had done for William Berke in a quartet of oaters for Ajax [q.v.] the previous year). While Fred Kohler, Jr., made only two starrers for Berke, the Commodore production schedule announced four others that were never filmed: *Call of the Trail, Hand of the Law, Two Gun Justice* and *Trail Blazer*.

In the spring of 1935 Ray Kirkwood Productions announced that Lon Chaney, Jr., had been signed to star in twenty-four action pictures over the next three years, eight of them westerns. Son of the famous "Man of a Thousand Faces," the young Chaney had been in films for several years under his real name of Creighton Chaney, but the lucrative offer from Kirkwood resulted in the name change, something he had resisted for some time. His first scheduled feature under the new contract was a mystery melodrama, *The Riot Squad*, written by Oliver Drake, with Chaney as an undercover agent. That film never materialized, but Chaney did play a similar role in *Scream in the Night*, released late in 1935 to very limited bookings. Norman Springer is credited with this tale of Chaney as a detective in Singapore on the trail of a murderous international gem thief. The plotline had Chaney masquerading as Butch Curtain, a deformed waterfront thug, whose makeup recalled that worn by Lon Chaney, Sr., in *The Road to Mandalay* (1926). Lon Chaney, Jr., was very effective in both roles, and he also did very well with the second Commodore release, *The Shadow of Silk Lennox* (1935). Both features were filmed by Kirkwood at the old Marshall Neilan studios on Glendale Boulevard, but extremely tacky production values and slow pacing negated Chaney's fine portrayals. Both films remained obscure, although *Scream in the Night* was reissued by Astor in 1943 to take advantage of Lon Chaney, Jr.'s, horror-film popularity resulting from *The Wolf Man* (1941) and *The Ghost of Frankenstein* (1942) at Universal. The two films were the only ones made in the Chaney series, but for the 1936–37 season Ray Kirkwood Productions announced it would release twenty features and a serial. "Four Huge Specials"—*Unknown, Black Widow, The Devil's Finger* and *When Hell Breaks Loose* (all written by Zarah Tazil)—were announced as were the release of eight Spanish westerns starring Ernesto Guillen. In addition, Kirkwood promised that Donald Reed and Bobby Nelson would star in eight "B" westerns: *The Valley of Death, The Eagle's Nest, The Masked Devil, Shooting Straight, Adventurous Rogues, The Fighting Vagabonds, Outlaws of Black Butte* and *Across the Black River*. None of these features ever saw the light of day, nor did the promised serial, *Geronimo's Last Raid*.

Two other Commodore releases are worth noting. The comedy-drama *Social Error* (1935) was the third and last of the series "Our Young Friends." The first two entries were *Adventurous Knights*, issued by Ajax, and *Roaring Roads*, distributed by Marcy. Both were 1935 releases that also starred David Sharpe. *Social Error* was probably the best of the trio due to the presence of silent film stars Monte Blue and Jack Mulhall. Commodore's other interesting release was *I Cover Chinatown* (1936), starring Norman Foster, who also made his directorial debut with the melodrama. Bolstered by a good cast, this tale of jewel thieves in Chinatown was made by Banner Productions and filmed at the RKO-Pathe studio, giving it a better look than Commodore's other releases. Norman Foster soon abandoned acting to concentrate on directing, and he later did features like *Journey Into Fear* (1943), *Rachel and the Stranger* (1948) and *Sky Full of Moon* (1952) before working for Walt Disney in the 1960s.

# Toll of the Desert

October 4, 1935, 60 minutes.

*P:* William Berke. *D:* Lester Williams [William Berke]. *SC:* Miller Easton. *ST:* Allen Hall. *PH:* Robert Cline. *ED:* Arthur A. Brooks. *Mus:* Lee Zahler. *SD:* Corson Jowett. *Asst Dir:* William Nolte.

*Cast:* Fred Kohler, Jr. (Bill Carson), Betty Mack (Jean Streeter), Roger Williams (Tom Collins), Earl Dwire (Dad Carson), Tom London (Sheriff Jack Jackson), Ted Adams (Teague), George Chesebro (Carter), John Elliott (Judge), Edward Cassidy (Mr. Streeter), Billy Strange (Little Billy), Herman Hack (One-Eye), Iron Eyes Cody (Indian), Budd Buster (Bartender), Ace Cain, Blackie Whiteford, Blackjack Ward (Gang Members), Steve Clark (Hank).

Renegade Indians attack settlers and a woman is killed in a wagon wreck as she and her family attempt to escape. Her young son (Billy Strange) wanders away while the father is aided in the fight by an outlaw gang. Settler Carson (Earl Dwire) finds the boy in the desert and rescues him. Years later, stage driver Bill Carson (Fred Kohler, Jr.) thwarts a stage holdup and is offered a deputy's job by the sheriff (Tom London) as well as a position driving the stage by owner Streeter (Edward Cassidy), the father of Jean (Betty Mack), the girl Bill loves. The young man, however, wants to resume his schooling and become a lawyer but at his twenty-first birthday party outlaws led by Tom Collins (Roger Williams) hold up the guests and shoot Dad Carson. Bill takes the deputy's job to get the killer, and the next day the gang rides into town to rob the bank but runs off after a gunfight. Bill trails the outlaws to their desert hideout and

is captured. Collins lets Bill go so that he will be ambushed, but when he sees the locket the young man carries he realizes he is the son he lost years before in the Indian attack. He rides to rescue Bill and saves his life but is captured by the young deputy who takes him to town to stand trial for the killing of Carson. Collins is found guilty and sentenced to hang, but he tells Bill he deserves his fate. Returning the locket to Bill, Collins is led off to be hanged.

A leisurely paced western, *Toll of the Desert*'s major flaw is that it lacks action. It was one of two gallopers producer William Berke made starring Fred Kohler, Jr., son of the famous movie villain. Although stalwart and handsome, young Kohler had little of his father's screen savy, appearing awkward and somewhat self-conscious with dialogue. Surrounded by a good supporting cast, acceptable production values and a fine story, Kohler was able to carry off his starring assignment, but it is easy to see why a projected series with him petered out after one more entry, *The Pecos Kid*. Roger Williams, usually cast as a dastardly villain or gang member, is outstanding as the settler who turns to the wrong side of the law after losing his family. At the finale he tells Kohler, "You are what I once started out to be before I got my trails crossed." The downbeat ending with Collins going to be hanged was not typical of "B" westerns of that period, capping the somber mood of the feature. Other assets in this low-budget oater include Robert Cline's scenic desert camera work and the use of the classical "Rubenstein's Romance" as the theme music. It was later reworked into the popular song "If You Are But a Dream." During the birthday party sequence heroine Betty

Mack briefly sings "Just You and I Alone."

## The Pecos Kid

1935, 56 minutes.
P: William Berke. D: Harry Fraser. SC: Henry Hess. ST: Allen Hall. PH: William Nolte. ED: Arthur A. Brooks. SD: T.T. Triplett.
Cast: Fred Kohler, Jr., Ruth Findlay, Roger Williams, Ed Cassidy, Wally Wales, Earl Dwire, Francis Walker, Budd Buster, Rose Plummer, Clyde McClary, Robert Walker, Jack Evans, Milburn Morante, Phil Dunham, Ray Henderson, Tex Palmer.

A young man grows up vowing to take revenge on the outlaws who massacred his family. Reissued by Astor Pictures.

## The Shadow of Silk Lennox

1935, 60 minutes.
P-D: Ray Kirkwood. SC: Norman Springer. PH: Robert Cline. ED: Holbrook N. Todd. AD: Zarah Tazil. Mus: Dean Benton. Orchestrations: Marion Madison.
Cast: Lon Chaney, Jr. (John Arthur "Silk" Lennox), Dean Benton (Jimmy Lambert), Marie Burton (Nola), Jack Mulhall (Fingers Farley/Ferguson), Eddie Gribbon (Lefty Sloan), Larry McGrath (Police Inspector), Allen Greer (Bull), Wally Wales (Inspector Swan), Theodore Lorch (Kennedy), Zarah Tazil (Hostess), Budd Buster (Deacon), Frank Nieman & His Orchestra, Bonnie & Her Boyfriends (Themselves).

When Creighton Chaney agreed to change his name to Lon Chaney, Jr., in 1935 it was because he had signed a contract with Ray Kirkwood Productions which called for him to star in two dozen features in the next three years. Only *The Shadow of Silk Lennox* and *Scream in the Night* materialized, and both of these cheapies got minimal release. It would be another four years before Chaney found real success as Lennie in *Of Mice and Men* (1939) for United Artists. This early starring effort, however, shows the actor to be a self-assured player who neatly handled the difficult role of underworld mobster Silk Lennox. Chaney managed to imbue the homicidal Lennox with many likable characteristics and the gangster dominates an otherwise routine melodrama mixed with music. The latter was provided by bland costar Dean Benton, a fairly good crooner who composed a quartet of tunes for the film, including "Love Is in the Way," "Forgotten Melodies" and "Walkin' in the Dark." Benton and Marie Burton played a musical team in the movie and they do a couple of tunes while Burton also performs an exotic dance. Throughout the feature the title character repeats everything is "fine as silk." Jack Mulhall gives his usual good performance as an undercover man pretending to be a safecracker while Theodore Lorch is justly slimy as a corrupt ward heeler. Unbilled cowboy star Wally Wales is in and out of the plot as a police inspector.

Underworld kingpin and nightclub owner Silk Lennox (Lon Chaney, Jr.) is the brains behind a robbery gang that pulls off a heist while Lennox uses the decoy of having an acetate record played of a gang member's voice while the robbery is in progress. He uses the song-and-dance team of Jimmy (Dean Benton) and Nola (Marie Burton) to help him with the ruse, although they think he is trying to thwart hijackers. When gang member Deacon (Budd Buster) tries to get away with the loot,

**Lon Chaney Jr. and Jack Mulhall are pictured in a lobby card from** *The Shadow of Silk Lennox* **(Commodore, 1935).**

Silk and the gang corner him in a men's room and give him the works. The police arrest Silk for the murder of Deacon, but two witnesses to the crime are scared off by his crooked ward heeler Kennedy (Theodore Lorch). Jimmy and Marie realize they have been duped by Silk, and they vow to keep the record of the gangster's voice to give to the law if Silk gives them any trouble. While in jail Silk meets notorious safecracker Fingers Farley (Jack Mulhall), and Silk promises to try to help him after he is sprung. Later, when Farley breaks out of jail, Silk asks him to join the gang and his first assignment is to take Jimmy "for a ride" after the singer hits Silk for manhandling Nola over her hiding the record. By now Lennox has changed the motif

of his club to Arabian and the police unsuccessfully raid the place looking for Farley. Since the police raid has given him an alibi, Silk decides to rob the express office where Deacon hid the proceeds from the bank robbery, and he asks Farley to open the safe. During the robbery, Farley, actually a G-Man, turns on Lennox. The police arrive, Silk is killed in a shoot-out, and his gang is captured. Jimmy, who was saved by Farley earlier, is cleared by the G-Man and reunited with Nola.

## Social Error

1935, 60 minutes.

*P:* William Berke. *D:* Harry Fraser. *SC:* C. Edward Roberts. *ST:* David Sharpe. *PH:* Robert Cline. *ED:*

Arthur A. Brooks. *Mus:* Lee Zahler. *SD:* Corson Jowett.

*Cast:* David Sharpe, Sheila Terry, Gertrude Messinger, Monte Blue, Jack Mulhall, Roger Williams, Lloyd Hughes, Fred Kohler, Jr., Matty Fain, Fred "Snowflake" Toones, Joe Girard, Earl Dwire.

A former college man gets mixed up in a plot to steal the crown jewels of Russia.

## Scream in the Night

December, 1935, 56 minutes.

*P:* Ray Kirkwood. *D:* Fred Newmeyer. *SC:* Norman Springer. *PH:* Bert Longnecker. *ED:* Fred Bain. *Tech Dir:* Zarah Tazil. *Prod Mgr:* Dick L'Estrange.

*Cast:* Lon Chaney, Jr., Sheila Terry, Dick [Richard] Cramer, Zarah Tazil, Philson [Philip] Ahn, Manuel Lopez, John Ince, Merrill McCormack, John Lester Johnson.

In Singapore, an undercover agent takes on the guise of a disfigured hoodlum to track down an international jewel thief and killer. Reissued by Astor Pictures in 1943.

## Aces Wild

January 2, 1936, 57 minutes.

*P:* William Berke. *D:* Harry Fraser. *SC:* Weston Edwards. *ST:* Monroe Talbot. *PH:* Robert Cline. *ED:* Arthur A. Brooks. *SD:* Corson Jowett. *Asst Dir:* William Nolte.

*Cast:* Harry Carey, Gertrude Messinger, Ted [Theodore] Lorch, Roger Williams, Chuck Morrison, Phil Dunham, Fred "Snowflake" Toones, Sonny the Marvel Horse,

William McCall, Francis Walker, Ed Cassidy, Bill Patton, Jack Evans, Ray Henderson.

Cheyenne Harry comes to the aid of a newspaperman threatened by outlaws. Rereleased by Astor Pictures.

## Ghost Town

February 15, 1936, 60 minutes.

*P:* William Berke. *D:* Harry Fraser. *SC:* Monroe Talbot. *PH:* Robert Cline. *ED:* Arthur A. Brooks. *Asst Dir:* William Nolte. *Mus:* Lee Zahler. *SD:* Cliff Ruberg.

*Cast:* Harry Carey, Ruth Findlay, Jane Novak, David Sharpe, Lee Shumway, Ed Cassidy, Roger Williams, Phil Dunham, Earl Dwire, Chuck Morrison, Sonny the Marvel Horse.

Stranger Cheyenne Harry comes to the rescue of an old miner whose bank loan is coveted by crooks. Reissued by Astor Pictures.

## I Cover Chinatown

August 25, 1936, 65 minutes.

*P:* Fenn Kimball. *D:* Norman Foster. *SC:* Harry Hamilton. *PH:* Art Reed & James V. Murray. *ED:* Carl L. Pierson. *Mus:* Abe Meyer. *AD:* Ralph Berger.

*Cast:* Norman Foster, Elaine Shepard, Theodore von Eltz, Vince Barnett, Eddie Gribbon, Arthur Lake, Polly Ann Young, Edward Emerson, Robert Love, Bruce Mitchell, George Hackathorne, Cherita Alden.

A Chinatown tour guide and his girlfriend find themselves involved in a homicide after getting mixed up with a gang of jewel thieves.

# Continental Talking Pictures

W. Ray Johnston started Rayart Pictures in 1924, naming the company after himself. Throughout the mid-and-late 1920s Rayart released a variety of low-budget efforts, both features and serials. By 1928 Johnston began working under the name Syndicate Film Exchange (q.v.), and by the next year Rayart was phased out. The year 1929 also saw the producer form still another outfit, Continental Talking Pictures, with offices at 1560 Broadway in New York City. During the next two years the company released a total of seven feature films made in the Photophone sound process. When Syndicate became Monogram Pictures Corporation in 1931, Continental Talking Pictures ceased to exist.

Like Chesterfield-Invincible (q.v.), Continental was something of a "family" affair. All of its releases were produced by W. Ray Johnston or Trem Carr. When Johnston served as president of Monogram, he appointed Carr to the position of that company's production chief. The Continental releases were directed by Phil Rosen or Phil Whitman, and most were photographed by Herbert Kirkpatrick. Neil Jack was in charge of sound recording on nearly all the features, and most were edited by Carl Himm. Only the scriptwriters and original story sources varied from film to film with two of the seven releases being based on published novels.

While Syndicate Pictures remained essentially a company issuing silent movies through most of 1930, Continental Talking Pictures lived up to its name by releasing *The Phantom in the House* in the fall of 1929, although it too was available in a silent version. If any film exemplifies the quandary in which low-budget filmmakers found themselves at the beginning of the sound era, *The Phantom of the House* is it. Despite a title promising spooky goings-on in a fog shrouded mansion inhabited by a hooded fiend, audiences found themselves saddled with an inane story about a faithless wife and a man's retribution. Despite the presence of stars Ricardo Cortez, Nancy Welford and Henry B. Walthall, *Photoplay* found it rough going and aptly pronounced, "This murder story fails to provide an alibi for existing."

Things were much better for Continental's next six releases, adequately produced melodramas starring popular players from the silent days like James Murray, Merna Kennedy, Nick Stuart, Josephine Dunn, Bryant Washburn, Lloyd Hughes and Norman Kerry. While none of the last half-dozen Continental's were classics by any means, they fulfilled dutifully their goal of bringing entertainment to the theatres they served. Although the release company title changed to Monogram in 1931, audiences could tell little difference in the fare of that company and Continental. Monogram simply absorbed the Continental melodramas and the Syndicate westerns to form the same type of release schedule W. Ray Johnston had formulated at Rayart in the silent era.

## The Phantom in the House

October 20, 1929, 6 reels.

*P:* W. Ray Johnston. *D:* Phil Rosen. *SC:* Arthur Hoerl, from the novel of Andrew Soutar. *PH:* Herbert Kirkpatrick. *SD:* Neil Jack. *Song:* Abner Silver & Maceo Pinkard.

*Cast:* Ricardo Cortez, Nancy Welford, Henry B. Walthall, Grace Valentine, Thomas A. Curran, Jack Curtis, John Elliott.

An inventor goes to prison for fifteen years for a murder his wife committed. When he gets out he persuades his daughter to marry for love, not money.

## The Rampant Age

January 19, 1930, 60 minutes.

*P:* Trem Carr. *D:* Phil Rosen. *SC:* Harry O. Hoyt & John Elliott. *ST:* Robert S. Carr. *PH:* Herbert Kirkpatrick. *SD:* Neil Jack & C.F. Franklin.

*Cast:* James Murray (Sandy Benton), Merna Kennedy (Doris Lawrence), Eddie Borden (Eddie Mason), Margaret Quimby (Estelle), Florence Turner (Mrs. Lawrence), Patrick Cunning (De Witt), Gertrude Messinger (Julie), John Elliott (Mr. Benton).

The wealthy Benton family throws a big party at their Long Island estate, but son Sandy (James Murray) slips away to visit Mrs. Lawrence (Florence Turner) and her pretty daughter Doris (Merna Kennedy) at their neaby home. Sandy invites Doris to the festivities but the demure girl declines, and Sandy reluctantly returns to his family's guests. Golddigger Estelle (Margaret Quimby) sets her sights on Sandy and during a roughhouse football game she lets herself be tackled by the young man, thus trying to set up a romance. Later Sandy takes Estelle for a ride in his airplane, and she makes him set it down in a field so they can stay the night with some friends. When Doris hears about Estelle and her romantic designs on Sandy, she decides to prove that she too can be modern, hoping to make him jealous. Doris goes to a party with Eddie Mason (Eddie Borden) and while there she also flirts with De Witt (Patrick Cunning), bringing both activities to Sandy's attention. The girl then places herself in a charity slave auction and goes to a late-night beach party with De Witt. Sandy becomes angry with Doris, and she tries to fly away in his airplane but crashes it into an airport hangar. Sandy rescues Doris from the wreckage, and while she is in the hospital the two admit they are in love.

*The Rampant Age* is a typical story of wild-living young people among the upper crust of society at the end of the Jazz Age. *Photoplay* called it a "hackneyed story rendered amusing by lively dialogue and acting." It was the second of Continental's seven releases and certainly far better than its first outing, *The Phantom in the House.* Trem Carr produced this Photophone sound release in good form with Phil Rosen's usual workmanlike directorial style making it a fair hour's entertainment. While *The Rampant Age* had a certain pleasing naivete to it, such stories would soon become old hat with the fast-approaching gloom of the Great Depression.

Like many silent-screen stars, James Murray was on a sea of uncertainty at the beginning of the sound era. Murray had hit the big time in 1928 as the star of King Vidor's highly acclaimed *The Crowd* at M.G.M. and had gone on to costar with Lon Chaney in *The Big City* (1928) and *Thunder* (1929) for the same studio. His voice had registered well in talkies, but a

Lobby card from *The Mystery Train* (Continental Talking Pictures, 1931). Shown from center to right are Joe Girard, Bryant Washburn, Marceline Day, Nick Stuart and Hedda Hopper.

drinking problem was fast bringing James Murray's stardom to a close. By 1931 he was doing supporting parts, and as the decade progressed and his drinking worsened, he drifted into bit roles in major films. He also starred in Poverty Row cheapies like *High Gear* (1933) [q.v.] for Goldsmith, but by 1935 he was doing support in Reliable's (q.v.) *Skull and Crown* (q.v.), his last film before his alcohol-related death in the summer of 1936.

## Worldly Goods

August 3, 1930, 71 minutes.

*P:* Trem Carr. *D:* Phil Rosen. *SC:* John Grey & Scott Littleton. *ST:* Andrew Soutar. *PH:* Herbert Kirkpatrick. *ED:* Carl Himm. *SD:* Neil Jack.

*Cast:* James Kirkwood, Merna Kennedy, Shannon Day, Ferdinand Schumann-Heink, Eddie Featherstone, Thomas A. Curran.

Blinded by an airplane crash, a man vows revenge on the manufacturer who ends up marrying the girl he loves.

## The Fourth Alarm

November 9, 1930, 60 minutes.

*P:* W. Ray Johnston. *D:* Phil Whitman. *SC:* Scott Littleton. *PH:* Herbert Kirkpatrick. *ED:* Carl Himm. *SD:* Neil Jack.

*Cast:* Nick Stuart, Ralph Lewis, Tom Santschi, Ann Christy, Harry Bowen, Jack Richardson.

A fire inspector realizes his manufacturer father is secretly producing nitroglycerin at his warehouse.

## Second Honeymoon

January 11, 1931, 76 minutes.

*P:* Trem Carr. *D:* Phil Rosen. *SC:* Harry O. Hoyt, from the novel by Ruby M. Ayres. *PH:* Herbert Kirkpatrick. *ED:* Charles Hunt. *SD:* Neil Jack & Charles Franklin.

*Cast:* Josephine Dunn, Edward Earle, Ernest Hilliard, Bernice Elliott, Fern Emmett, Harry Allen, Henry Rocquemore.

When a society woman becomes bored with her husband, his pal decides to fake a rendezvous to bring her to her senses.

## Mystery Train

August 23, 1931, 69 minutes.

*P:* W. Ray Johnston. *D:* Phil Whitman. *SC:* Hampton Del Ruth. *ST:* Hampton Del Ruth & Phil Whitman. *PH:* James S. Brown, Jr. *SD:* Neil Jack & Charles Franklin.

*Cast:* Bryant Washburn, Hedda Hopper, Nick Stuart, Marceline Day, Jack Richardson, Al Cooke, Eddie Featherstone, Joe Girard.

A number of people are caught in a runaway Pullman car as a man fights to save the girl he loves.

## Air Eagles

December 27, 1931, 65 minutes.

*P:* W. Ray Johnston. *D:* Phil Whitman. *SC:* James Brown, Jr. & Charles Marshall. *PH:* James S. Brown, Jr. *SD:* Charles Franklin. *ED:* Dwight Caldwell. *Mus:* Lee Zahler.

*Cast:* Lloyd Hughes, Norman Kerry, Shirley Grey, Matty Kemp, Otis Harlan, Berton Churchill, Katherine Ward, Eddie Featherstone.

An airmail pilot matches wits with a crook for the woman they both want.

# Crescent Pictures

Crescent Pictures released eight historical adventure dramas on the states' rights circuit between 1936 and 1938. All of them starred Tom Keene, who was then associated with westerns. The series, in fact, was basically advertised as another Tom Keene western set although only about half the films were actually sagebrush yarns. Seven of the eight, however, did deal with the frontier in some way, and all were supposedly based on various aspects of American history. Unfortunately, nearly all the series entries were on the tired side with minimum budgets. Most were outdoor efforts (an attempt to economize by using few interiors), and the result was a string of features that did little to bolster either American history or Tom Keene's career.

The man behind Crescent Pictures was Edward B. Derr, better known as E.B. Derr. A corporation lawyer, Derr came to Hollywood in the mid–1920s with Joseph P. Kennedy, having been associated with Kennedy since World War I when he was involved in shipbuilding in Massachusetts. Derr worked for Kennedy at Films Booking Office (F.B.O.) and as part of Gloria Productions, the company Kennedy financed with Gloria Swanson. Derr held power of attorney for Gloria Swanson until late in 1930. After that he broke with Kennedy and for a time worked at Metro-Goldwyn-Mayer before becoming an independent producer with the Crescent series.

As noted, all of the Crescent pictures were based on some aspect of American history, but historical facts were usually embellished or clouded to suit the dramatic situation. All of these films had Tom Keene as a hero intervening in the nation's destiny, although the films would probably best be labeled historical fiction. Themes ranged from the Bozeman Massacre in *The Glory Trail* (1936) to the discovery of the Comstock Lode in Virginia City in *Battle of Greed* (1937) to trouble between the Spanish and Americans in Florida in 1815 in *Drums of Destiny* (1937). Only *Raw Timber* (1938) had a modern setting, and it dealt with the Federal Forest Service. Reviews of the films varied. Of *Rebellion* (1936) the *Motion Picture Herald* noted, "Production values of the film are of a high caliber, as is the quality of the acting contributed by the principals." Regarding *Old Louisiana* (1937) *Film Daily* said, "A satisfactory programmer, made doubly interesting, inasmuch as it touches upon history and events leading up to the Louisiana Purchase." On the other hand, *Variety* said of *The Law Commands* (1938), "[This] film is a bad one, made for buttons, and has all the appearances of a quickie. A few more like it and Tom Keene won't mean much."

The Crescent series, which was made in 1936 but strung out for release through the end of 1938, did little for Tom Keene's career. Under his real name of George Duryea, the actor had found success in *The Godless Girl*, a 1929 part-talkie for Cecil B. DeMille. In 1931 RKO changed his name to Tom Keene, and he starred in a highly satisfying series of well-done westerns for that studio through 1933. His best-known role came in King Vidor's *Our Daily Bread* (q.v.) for Viking in 1934, and thereafter he worked on Poverty Row in *Hong Kong Nights* (1935) and a series of westerns at Paramount before the Crescent films. From 1937 to 1942 he starred in gallopers for Monogram with a hiatus from 1939 to 1941 as mayor of Sherman Oaks, California. In 1943 the actor again changed his name, this time to Richard Powers, and he became a character actor in films and, later, television. By the mid–1950s, however, he went back to being Tom Keene and starred in the infamous sci-fi feature *Plan 9 from Outer Space* (1958). In later years the actor turned to real estate and insurance before his death in 1962 at the age of 67.

Following the Tom Keene series, E.B. Derr continued to turn out programmers under the Crescent banner and in the 1938–39 season he produced a half-dozen titles for release by Monogram Pictures: *My Old Kentucky Home* and *Female Fugitive* in 1938 and *Convict's Code*, *Star Reporter*, *Should a Girl Marry?* and *Undercover Agent*, all in 1939. Later Derr turned out features like *Secret Evidence* for P.R.C. in 1941, and in 1946 he briefly reactivated Crescent for a double bill rerelease of *Rebellion* and *Old Louisiana*. The former was retitled *Lady from Frisco* while the latter was dubbed *Louisiana Gal*. The reason for this was the leading lady in both features was Rita Hayworth, although she had originally been billed as Rita Cansino. Since Hayworth was very popular in the mid–1940s, the reissues came about to parlay box office returns based on that vogue. In the new titles Rita Hayworth was given top-star billing while Tom Keene (by then billing himself as Richard Powers) was listed in support.

## The Glory Trail

July 10, 1936, 64 minutes.

*P:* E.B. Derr. *AP:* Bernard A. Moriarty. *D:* Lynn Shores. *SC:* John T. Neville. *PH:* Arthur Martinelli. *ED:* Donald Barrett. *Mus:* Abe Meyer. *AD:* F. Paul Sylos.

*Cast:* Tom Keene, Joan Barclay, James Bush, Frank Melton, Walter Long, E.H. Calvert, Ann Hovey, William Royle, Etta McDaniel, John Lester Johnson, Allen Greer, William Crowell, Harvey Foster, Denver Dixon, Fred Parker, Jack Ingram, Carl Mathews, Tom Steele, Oscar Gahan.

After the Civil War a cowboy goes west to settle and becomes involved in the Bozeman Massacre.

## Rebellion

October 10, 1936, 62 minutes.

*P:* E.B. Derr. *AP:* Bernard A. Moriarty. *D:* Lynn Shores. *SC:* John T. Neville. *PH:* Arthur Martinellli. *ED:* Donald Barrett. *Mus:* Abe Meyer. *AD:* Edward C. Jewell. *Asst Dir:* Fred Spencer. *Prod Supv:* Frank Melford. *SD:* J.S. Westmoreland.

*Cast:* Tom Keene, Rita [Hayworth] Cansino, Duncan Renaldo, William Royle, Gino Corrado, Roger Gray, Bob McKenzie, Allen Cavan, Jack Ingram, Lita Cortez, Theodore Lorch, W.M. [Merrill] McCormack.

A government agent tries to stop the harrassment of Spanish landowners after California becomes a part of the United States. Reissued in 1946 as *Lady from Frisco.*

## Battle of Greed

January 4, 1937, 59 minutes.

*P:* E.B. Derr. *AP:* Bernard A. Moriarty. *D:* Howard Higgin. *SC:* John T. Neville. *PH:* Paul Ivano. *ED:* Donald Barrett. *AD:* Edward C. Jewell. *Mus:* Abe Meyer. *Supv:* Frank Melford. *SD:* Karl Zint.

*Cast:* Tom Keene, Gwynne Shipman, James Bush, Robert Fiske, Jimmy Butler, Carl Stockdale, Rafael Bennett, William Worthington, Henry Rocquemore, Lloyd Ingraham, Bobby Brown.

A young man becomes involved with crooks after the discovery of the Comstock Lode near Virginia City.

## Old Louisiana

March 12, 1937, 60 minutes.

*P:* E.B. Derr. *AP:* Bernard A. Moriarty. *D:* Irvin V. Willatt. *SC:* Mary Ireland. *ST:* John T. Neville. *PH:* Arthur Martinelli. *ED:* Donald Barrett. *Mus:* Abe Meyer. *AD:* Edward C. Jewell. *Asst Dir:* Raoul Pagel. *Supv:* Frank Melford. *SD:* Karl Zink.

*Cast:* Tom Keene, Rita [Hayworth] Cansino, Robert Fiske, Rafael Bennett, Allan Cavan, Will Morgan, Budd Buster, Carlos De Valdez, Wally Albright, Ramsay Hill, Iron Eyes Cody.

A frontiersman tries to stop a crooked trader from causing trouble

Tom Keene and Rita [Hayworth] Cansino in *Old Louisiana* (Crescent, 1937).

between settlers and the Spanish in the Upper Mississippi Valley in the early 1800s. Rereleased in 1946 as *Louisiana Gal.*

## Drums of Destiny

June 15, 1937, 64 minutes.
    *P:* E.B. Derr. *AP:* Bernard A. Moriarty. *D:* Ray Taylor. *SC:* John T. Neville & Roger Whatley. *ST:* Roger Whatley. *PH:* Arthur Martinelli. *ED:* Finn Ulback. *Mus:* Abe Meyer. *SD:* Karl Zink. *Asst Dir:* Theodore Joos. *Supv:* Frank Melford.
    *Cast:* Tom Keene, Edna Lawrence, Budd Buster, Rafael Bennett, Robert Fiske, Carlos De Valdez, Dave Sharpe, John Merton, Chief Flying Cloud, Auroro Navarro, William Hazelwood.

A Cavalry commander goes illegally into west Florida in 1815 to stop Creek Indian attacks on American settlers.

## Under Strange Flags

August 25, 1937, 61 minutes.
    *P:* E.B. Derr. *AP:* Bernard A. Moriarty. *D:* Irvin V. Willat. *SC:* Mary Ireland. *ST:* John Auer. *PH:* Arthur Martinelli. *ED:* Donald Barrett. *Mus:* Abe Meyer. *Prod Mgr:* Frank Melford.
    *Cast:* Tom Keene, Luana Walters, Budd Buster, Maurice Black, Roy D'Arcy, Paul Barrett, Donald Reed, James Wolfe.
    Pancho Villa tries to steal silver shipments from American mines in Mexico.

Advertisement for *Drums of Destiny* (Crescent, 1937).

## My Old Kentucky Home

Monogram, January 26, 1938, 72 minutes.

*P:* E.B. Derr. *AP:* Frank Melford. *D:* Lambert Hillyer. *SC:* John T. Neville. *PH:* Arthur Martinelli. *ED:* Finn Ulback. *Mus:* Abe Meyer. *SD:* Glen Rominger. *Asst Dir:* Edward Stein.

*Cast:* Evelyn Venable, Grant Richards, Clara Blandick, Bernadene Hayes, J. Farrell MacDonald, Margaret Marquis, Cornelius Keefe, Kitty McHugh, Raquel Davido, Paul White, Mildred Glover, The Hall Johnson Choir.

A Southern belle breaks her engagement to her fiancé when she finds out he has a Yankee sweetheart.

## Female Fugitive

Monogram, April 15, 1938, 58 minutes.

*P:* E.B. Derr. *AP:* Frank Melford. *D:* William Nigh. *SC:* John T. Neville.

*ST:* Bennett Cohen. *PH:* Arthur Martinelli. *ED:* Finn Ulback. *Mus:* Abe Meyer. *SD:* Karl Zint. *Asst Dir:* Theodore Joos.

*Cast:* Evelyn Venable, Craig Reynolds, Reed Hadley, John Kelly, Charlotte Treadway, John Merton, Ray Bennett, Reginald Sheffield, Emmett Vogan, Martha Tibbetts, Lee Phelps.

A woman decides to leave her husband when she learns he is behind a hijacking operation.

## The Law Commands

August 17, 1938, 58 minutes.
*P:* E.B. Derr. *AP:* Bernard A. Moriarty. *D:* William Nigh. *SC:* Bennett R. Cohen. *PH:* Arthur Martinelli. *ED:* Donald Barrett. *Mus:* Abe Meyer.

*Cast:* Tom Keene, Lorraine Hayes [Laraine Day], Budd Buster, Robert Fiske, John Merton, Matthew Betz, Dave Sharpe, Carl Stockdale, Marie Stoddard, Horace B. Carpenter, Fred Burns.

A doctor turned lawman aids farmers who have settled in Iowa in 1866 under the Homestead Act when they are harrassed by land grabbers.

## Raw Timber

November 9, 1938, 63 minutes.
*P:* E.B. Derr. *AP:* Bernard A. Moriarty. *D:* Ray Taylor. *SC:* Bennett R. Cohen & John T. Neville. *ST:* Bennett R. Cohen. *PH:* Arthur Martinelli. *ED:* Donald Barrett. *Mus:* Abe Meyer. *Prod Supv:* George Melford. *SD:* Karl Zink.

*Cast:* Tom Keene (Tom Corbin), Peggy Keys (Dale McFarland), Budd Buster (Kentuck), Robert Fiske (Bart Williams), Lee Phelps (Riley), John Rutherford (Supervisor Lane), Rafael Bennett (Hanlin), Charles [Slim] Whitaker (Sheriff), Bart Carre (Coroner), Fred Parker (Secretary).

Forest ranger Tom Corbin (Tom Keene) patrols the Valley of the Moon Forestry Reserve and tries to prevent the Williams-McFarland Lumber Company from cutting more timber than allowed by government regulations. Tom loves Dale McFarland (Peggy Keys), half-owner of the company, but he distrusts her partner Bart Williams (Robert Fiske). When he catches Williams' foreman Riley (Lee Phelps) and his men illegally cutting timber, they drygulch him and he is found by a stranger, Hanlin (Rafael Bennett), who takes him to Dale's house with the help of Tom's old pal, Kentuck (Budd Buster). Forest Supervisor Lane (John Rutherford) is in cahoots with Williams and has been sending false reports to Washington about the company's timber cuttings. When Williams finds out an agent has been sent by the government to investigate the company's activities he orders Riley and Lane to find out who it is and get him out of the way. That night at a party Riley tries to shoot Hanlin but misses. Hanlin tells Tom he is the investigator, and the next day Tom and Kentuck show him how the forest has been ravaged by Williams' lumberjacks. Riley, however, kills Hamlin while Williams forces Lane to make out fake lumber permits. Williams then tells Riley to get rid of Lane who has gone to the ranger station to destroy Tom's reports. There Tom catches him, but Riley ambushes Lane and Tom is blamed for his killing by the sheriff (Slim Whitaker). Kentuck helps Tom to escape from the law, but Riley trails Dale to their hideout. There Riley tries to kill Tom but misses and goes back to Williams with Tom on his trail and the sheriff and his posse after Tom. Riley tells Williams he wants money to get away after helping him in robbery and murder. Tom and the sheriff overhear, and the two crooks are arrested. Dale takes over the lumber company operation, and she and Tom are married.

*Raw Timber* was the eighth and final Crescent historical adventure drama starring Tom Keene. This programmer's link to history is rather tenuous, stopping after the prologue which tells of Theodore Roosevelt getting the government to set up the Forestry Service in 1905 to protect the nation's timberland. Although highlighted by nice photography and locales, the film otherwise is rather bland with too many plot twists and not much interest. Tom Keene handles the role of the forest ranger in good fashion and Robert Fiske is a fine villain, but otherwise the acting is mediocre. There is even the filler of a quartet singing "Long, Long Ago." *Variety* complained, "Paced at a slow trot, this action timberland yarn misses by a considerable margin, amounting to anything but projection machine filler." Outside of being an early ecology statement against timber barons, *Raw Timber* has little to offer.

## Convict's Code

Monogram, February 22, 1939, 63 minutes.

*P:* E.B. Derr. *AP:* Frank Melford. *D:* Lambert Hillyer. *SC:* John W. Krafft. *PH:* Arthur Martinelli. *ED:* Russell Schoengarth. *Mus:* Abe Meyer. *AD:* Frank Dexter. *Asst Dir:* Edward Stein.

*Cast:* Robert Kent, Anne Nagel, Sidney Blackmer, Victor Kilian, Norman Willis, Maude Eburne, Ben Alexander, Pat Flaherty, Carleton Young, Howard Hickman, Joan Barclay, Harry Strang.

When he is framed on a fake

charge and sent to prison, a football hero vows revenge on those behind the scheme.

## Star Reporter

Monogram, April 12, 1939, 62 minutes.

*P:* E.B. Derr. *AP:* Frank Melford. *D:* Howard Bretherton. *SC:* John T. Neville. *PH:* Arthur Martinelli. *ED:* Russell Schoengarth. *Mus:* Abe Meyer. *AD:* Frank Dexter. *SD:* Karl Zint. *Asst Dir-Prod Mgr:* Theodore Joos.

*Cast:* Warren Hull, Marsha Hunt, Morgan Wallace, Clay Clement, Wallis Clark, Virginia Howell, Paul Fix, Joseph Crehan, Lester Dorr, William Ruhl, Effie Anderson, Monty Collins, Dennis Tankard.

When his father is murdered by gangsters, a reporter takes over his job as the publisher in order to bring in the killers.

## Undercover Agent

Monogram, April 19, 1939, 56 minutes.

*P:* E.B. Derr. *AP:* Frank Melford. *D:* Howard Bretherton. *SC:* Milton Raison. *ST:* Martin Mooney. *PH:* Arthur Martinelli. *ED:* Howard Dillinger. *Mus:* Abe Meyer. *SD:* L. John Myers. *AD:* Frank Dexter. *Asst Dir:* Theodore Joos.

*Cast:* Russell Gleason, Shirley Deane, J.M. Kerrigan, Maude Eburne, Oscar O'Shea, Ralf Harolde, Selmer Jackson, Ray Bennett, Ralph Sanford, Max Hoffman, Jr., Walter Wills, Dick Elliott, Lee Phelps.

A mailman and his fiancée, while trying to get enough money to get married, become involved in a crooked sweepstakes operation.

## Should a Girl Marry?

Monogram, July 19, 1939, 61 minutes.

*P:* E.B. Derr. *AP:* Frank Melford.

D: Lambert Hillyer. *SC:* David Silverstein & Gayl Newberry. *PH:* Paul Ivano. *ED:* Russell Schoengarth. *AD:* Frank Dexter. *Mus:* Abe Meyer. *SD:* Karl Zint. *Asst Dir:* Edward Stein.

*Cast:* Warren Hull, Anne Nagel, Mayo Methot, Weldon Heyburn, Aileen Pringle, Lester Mathews, Helen Brown, Sarah Padden, Gordon Hart, Edmund Aleton, Robert Elliott, Claire Rochelle, Harry Hayden, Arthur Loft, Barbara Salisbury.

After getting out of prison a young woman finds out her crooked husband plans to blackmail a society girl whose mother died in jail.

# Diversion Pictures

Walter Futter's Diversion Pictures came into existence like E.B. Derr's Crescent Pictures (q.v.) for the sole purpose of releasing movies by an established western star. In Crescent's case it was Tom Keene, and in Diversion's it was Hoot Gibson. During the silent days at Universal in the 1920s, it was claimed that Hoot Gibson had a salary of $14,500 per week, second only to Tom Mix at Fox, who made $20,000 weekly. Those days, however, were long gone when Hooter signed with Diversion, by which time he was lucky to get $5,000 per picture, not per week. By the mid–1930s Hoot was not alone, however. Only Buck Jones was able to keep his berth at a major studio (Columbia and then Universal), while Tim McCoy signed with Puritan Pictures (q.v.) in 1935. Ken Maynard made a feature and a serial for Mascot in 1934 before signing with producer Larry Darmour's unit, releasing through Columbia in 1935, and Tom Mix retired from films the same year after making the Mascot cliffhanger *The Miracle Rider.*

Edward "Hoot" Gibson had come to movies in the teens from the rodeo circuit, and by 1919 he was starring in two-reelers before gaining his greatest fame at Universal in the 1920s. Hoot's westerns were breezy affairs with much entertainment value but very little overt violence; the star rarely carried a gun. Universal dropped Gibson in 1930 at the beginning of the sound era although he made an easy transition to talkies. From 1931 to 1933 he starred in eleven oaters for Allied (q.v.), but when Universal wanted him back, Allied's owner, M.H. Hoffman, refused to release him. After litigation, Hoffman sold Hooter's contract to First Division Exchanges (q.v.) where the actor made *Sunset Range* and *Rainbow's End* (q.v.) in 1935. The waters become muddy here when one considers that First Division had been releasing the Allied product on a states' rights basis. Hoot was supposed to do four gallopers, but First Division released him from the contract after two features. He then signed with Walter Futter's Diversion Pictures, and his half-dozen westerns for the company were again sold on a states' rights basis by First Division! When Grand

National absorbed the First Division Exchanges in 1936, some of Diversion's were then sent out under the Grand National banner. For Hoot Gibson they marked the end of his solo starring career. After making the Republic serial *The Painted Stallion* in 1937, Hoot was off screen for six years until he did "The Trail Blazers" series with Ken Maynard, and later Bob Steele, for Monogram starting in 1943.

Although Hoot Gibson's First Diversion features were low-budget affairs, they do not look cheap and they do retain viewer interest. In *Hollywood Corral* (1976) Don Miller best summed up the series: "Sometimes, the ambition of the script-writer would be thwarted by the unavailability of funds to execute his work (*Cavalcade of the West*, 1936); at others, plot and execution would be all too familiar (*Swifty*, 1935). But primarily, it would be Gibson operating in a milieu not his own, and trying his best to overcome obstacles over which he had no control." Some sources claim that *Swifty* was released late in 1935 and not after *Frontier Justice* early in 1936 as the official release dates claim. Certainly *Swifty* looks like a series-opener with its strong cast and one-hour plus running time. Even the famous stallion Starlight the Wonder Horse got special billing. The Gibson titles were in release throughout 1936, and unlike most low-budget oaters, half of them were based on magazine stories. Hoot Gibson's current romantic flame June Gale was in *Swifty* and *The Riding Avenger*, and the latter also reunited Ruth Mix and Buzz Barton, who had made a brief series with Rex Bell the year before at Resolute (q.v.). Perhaps the most interesting casting came in the series' finale, *Cavalcade of the West* in which Rex Lease costarred with Hooter. Himself an established western star in the independent market, Lease added some box office draw to the film. He played Hoot's outlaw brother whose sins are forgiven near film's end as the boys are reunited with their mother (Nina Guilbert). In all, the Diversion Pictures were pleasant outings, but their reception was not overwhelming. Lacking decent offers Hooter hit the Sawdust Trail for several years.

Walter Futter, the president of Diversion Pictures, had been an editor in the 1920s working on films like *The Great White Way* and *Janice Meredith* (both 1924). In 1930 he and Lowell Thomas made the acclaimed Columbia documentary *Africa Speaks*, which he directed, wrote the dialogue for and edited. He produced a follow-up in 1932 at RKO Radio called *India Speaks* and prior to that had two short-subject series at Columbia, *Walter Futter's Curiosities* (1930–32) and *Walter Futter's Travelaughs* (1931–32). In 1938 he wrote and produced the British-made feature *Dark Sands* with Henry Wilcoxon, Wallace Ford and Paul Robeson. Although it ceased production of theatrical films after the Hoot Gibson series, Diversion Pictures continued into the 1960s as part of a complex that included an 8mm and 16mm film library and reversible processing laboratory. In later years the operation was run by Fred W. Futter, Walter's younger brother and the man in charge of production on the Gibson features.

Poster for *Frontier Justice* (Diversion, 1936).

# Frontier Justice

January 3, 1936, 58 minutes.

*P:* Walter Futter. *D:* Robert Mc-Gowan. *SC:* W. Scott Darling. *PH:* Paul Ivano. *ED:* Arthur Reed.

*Cast:* Hoot Gibson, Jane Barnes, Richard Cramer, Roger Williams, John Elliott, Franklyn Farnum, Lloyd Ingraham, Joseph Girard, Fred "Snowflake" Toones, George Yoeman, Lafe McKee, Jack Evans, The Beverly Hillbillies.

Returning home, a man finds his father is in an insane asylum and their cattle are being rustled.

# Swifty

January 28, 1936, 62 minutes.

*P:* Walter Futter. *D:* Alan James. *SC:* Bennett Cohen, from the story "Tracks" by Stephen Payne. *PH:* Arthur Reed. *ED:* Carl Himm.

*Cast:* Hoot Gibson, June Gale, George F. Hayes, Ralph Lewis, Wally Wales, Art Mix, Robert Kortman, William Gould, Lafe McKee, Duke R. Lee, Starlight the Wonder Horse.

A stranger is blamed for a rancher's murder and nearly lynched, but the sheriff helps him to escape so he can prove his innocence.

# Lucky Terror

February 20, 1936, 61 minutes.

*P:* Walter Futter. *D-SC:* Alan James. *ST:* Roger Allman. *PH:* Arthur Reed. *ED:* Carl Himm. *Prod Mgr:* F.W. Futter.

*Cast:* Hoot Gibson (Lucky Carson), Charles Hill (Doc Haliday), Lona Andre (Ann Thornton), Jack Rockwell (Bat Moulton), George Chesebro (Jim Thornton), Bob McKenzie (Sheriff Hodges), Wally Wales, Art Mix, Fargo Bussey (Gang Members), Horace B. Carpenter (Coroner), Frank Yaconelli (Tony Garibaldi), Charles King (Wheeler), Hank Bell (Hank), Horace Murphy, Eva McKenzie (Spectators).

Drifter Lucky Carson (Hoot Gibson) sees Jim Thornton (George Chesebro) being chased by Bat Moulton (Jack Rockwell) and his gang (Wally Wales, Art Mix, Fargo Bussey). Later Jim gets the drop on Lucky and attempts to take his horse, but the animal rears and Thornton is dragged over a cliff to his death. Lucky finds gold in Jim's saddlebags and realizes that was the reason he was being chased. Coming upon a medicine show, Lucky hides the gold and then makes friends with the proprietor Doc Haliday (Charles Hill) and his coworkers Ann Thornton (Lona Andre) and Tony Garibaldi (Frank Yaconelli). Moulton and his men show up and tell Ann, who is Jim Thornton's niece, that they have taken possession of the Bonanza Mine that Ann owned with her uncle. Lucky forces the ruffians to leave and then takes a job with the show as a sharpshooter. Later Moulton and his men find Jim's body, and that night in town they tell the sheriff (Robert McKenzie) that Lucky killed Thornton. The sheriff arrests him and the show is closed. At his trial, Lucky is defended by drunken lawyer Wheeler (Charles King), who advises him to flee the scene, which he does. The court, however, finds no evidence against Lucky, declares Thornton's death an accident and orders the mine turned over to Ann. At the Bonanza Mine Ann finds her uncle's diary, which contains evidence that Bat wanted to kill him for the gold he had discovered. Fearing arrest Lucky brings the gold to the mine and hides it. Moulton and his gang arrive and try to capture him, but Ann goes for the sheriff, who comes back with a posse. Jim chases the gang and knocks them all off their horses as the sheriff arrests Moulton and his henchmen. Doc, Tony and Ann find the gold Lucky has hidden and think the mine is still productive.

The third of the six westerns Hoot Gibson did for Diversion, *Lucky Terror* is probably the best. Its title derives from the nickname given to Gibson's character when he works as a sharp-shooter with Doc Haliday's medicine show. The film contains some very impressive desert footage in its early sequences, evidently shot at a high altitude because snow is present in several scenes. The feature exemplifies the type of character Hoot Gibson portrayed best on screen: peaceable, home-spun, resourceful and law-abiding. Gibson's penchant for comedy also comes into play, especially in his dialogue exchanges with villain Jack Rockwell. Rockwell, most often cast as a lawman, is quite good here as the slimy villain with former genre stars Wally Wales and Art Mix as his cohorts. Lona Andre is along for feminine interest while Frank Yaconelli sings the Italian song "Maria." Second billed is Charles Hill as the medicine show huckster, but most amusing is usual villain Charles King, cast here as a tipsy lawyer. The finale of the film includes some impressive trick riding by either Hoot Gibson or his double as the hero overtakes the bad guys by knocking them off their horses.

## Feud of the West

May 19, 1936, 62 minutes.
*P:* Walter Futter. *D:* Harry Fraser. *SC:* Phil Dunham, Walter Farrar & Roger Allman, from the story "Feud of the Rocking U" by Russell A. Bankson. *PH:* Ted McCord. *ED:* Carl Himm.

*Cast:* Hoot Gibson, Joan Barclay, Buzz Barton, Reed Howes, Robert Kortman, Edward Cassidy, Nelson McDowell, Roger Williams, Allen Greer, Richard Cramer, Lew Meehan.

A rodeo rider is forced to run from the law when he is falsely accused of murdering his rancher boss.

## The Riding Avenger

July 14, 1936, 58 minutes.
*P:* Walter Futter. *D:* Harry Fraser. *SC:* Norman Houston, from the story "Big Bend Buckaroo" by Walton West. *PH:* Paul Ivano. *ED:* Carl Himm. *Asst Dir:* William L. Nolte.

*Cast:* Hoot Gibson, Ruth Mix, June Gale, Buzz Barton, Roger Williams, Stanley Blystone, Francis Walker, Slim Whitaker, Budd Buster, Blackie Whiteford, Jack Evans, Tom London, Ed Cassidy, Allen Greer, Herman Hack, Art Dillard.

To bring in a notorious rustling gang, a marshal pretends to be a gunfighter.

## Cavalcade of the West

October 6, 1936, 60 minutes.
*P:* Walter Futter. *D:* Harry Fraser. *SC:* Norman Houston. *PH:* Paul Ivano. *ED:* Arthur Brooks. *Asst Dir:* William L. Nolte.

*Cast:* Hoot Gibson, Rex Lease, Marion Shilling, Adam Goodman, Nina Guilbert, Steve Clark, Earl Dwire, Phil Dunham, Robert McKenzie, Jerry Tucker, Barry Downing, Budd Buster, Blackie Whiteford, Jack Evans, Oscar Gahan, Milburn Morante, Herman Hack, Francis Walker, William McCall, Art Dillard, Dick Morehead.

A Pony Express rider hunts down an outlaw who turns out to be his long lost brother.

# Empire Pictures Corporation

Empire Pictures emerged in the mid–1930s with an ambitious program of action films and westerns from producers like Nathan and Fred Hirsch, Lester F. Scott, Jr., Larry Darmour and Harry S. Knight. Of the company's nine releses, three were directed by Spencer Gordon Bennet. A number of popular film players like Ray Walker, Jack LaRue, Norman Foster, Wallace Ford and Ralph Forbes headlined Empire's action outings, while Lane Chandler and Wally Wales rode the range for the company. Like so many small outfits, however, Empire simply did not have the budget to make anything better than lower-rung efforts, and the company lasted only about eighteen months, from the end of 1934 into the spring of 1936.

Empire's first release was an independent pickup feature, *The Way of the West*, that Robert Emmett Tansey made for Superior Pictures (q.v.), which distributed the western. It headlined Wally Wales, whose decade as a western star came to a close with this cheap outing. Two more westerns were issued by the company, "The Phantom Rider" series made up of two 1935 releases, *The Lone Bandit* and *Outlaw Tamer*, both starring Lane Chandler and directed by J.P. McGowan. Evidently the company had planned more than two entries, but the series failed to take off after the first two releases. Empire was also involved in *Courage of the North* (1935), one of two northwoods dramas Robert Emmett Tansey made, with John Preston as Morton of the Mounted. The second feature, *Timber Terrors* (1935), was also issued by Stage and Screen (q.v.), and both featured Captain, "King of the Dogs," and Dynamite, "The Wonder Horse."

Except for the comedy-mystery *Get That Man* (1935), starring Wallace Ford, Empire's releases were in the action mold, fashioned around either the police or fire departments. *Calling All Cars* (1935) and *The Crime Patrol* (1936) were police action melodramas while *Rescue Squad* and *The Firetrap* (both 1935) dealt with the arson squad and firefighters. *Calling All Cars*, starring Jack LaRue, came in for some special attention as noted by *Film Daily*: "Plenty of nerve tension and genuine amusement in this one. Has everything but the names, starting with the first frame, a breath-taking automobile chase, and winding up with a swell action finish." On the other hand, the general budget deficiencies which plagued most Empire product was noted by *Variety* in its review of *The Crime Patrol*: "Crudely fashioned in all departments ... Mechanics of the plot make for anything but plausibility."

# The Way of the West

Empire/Superior/First Division, 1934, 52 minutes.

*P-D:* Robert Emmett [Tansey]. *SC:* Al Lane. *ST:* Barry Barringer. *PH:* Brydon Baker. *ED:* Arthur Cohen. *Sp Eff:* Ray Mercer.

*Cast:* The American Rough Riders (Themselves), Wally Wales (Wallace "Wally" Gordon), Marla Bratton (Firey Parker), William Desmond (Cash Horton), Little Bobbie Nelson (Bobbie Parker), Art Mix (Tim), Jim Sheridan [Sherry Tansey] (Skippy), Fred Baker (Dad Parker), Billy Patton (Jeff Thompson), Tex Jones (Sheriff), Tiny Skelton (Tiny), Jimmy Aubrey (Jim the Bartender), Harry Beery, Helen Gibson, Gene Laymon.

Cowboy Wally Gordon (Wally Wales), who is really a government agent, arrives in Montana and saves pretty Firey (Marla Bratton) and her little brother Bobbie (Bobbie Nelson) from being molested by cattlemen since their father Dad Parker (Fred Baker) leases government land where he raises sheep. Outlaw Cash Horton (William Desmond) and his henchmen Tim (Art Mix) and Skippy (Jim Sheridan) arrive in town and are paid to run Parker off his land. Parker hires Wally to be his foreman, and when Cash and his men arrive pretending to be government inspectors, Wally runs them off the ranch. Later in the local saloon, Cash murders Dad Parker but claims it is self-defense and then has Wally framed on a stabbing charge. Wally is arrested but shows his credentials to the local sheriff (Tex Jones) as Bobbie overhears the saloon owner (Billy Patton) tell the bartender (Jimmy Aubrey) that it was Horton who did the stabbing and then framed Wally. Bobbie helps Wally escape from jail and the two ride to the ranch to find that Horton and his men are rustling the sheep, planning to drive them across the border. Bobbie rides to get the sheriff and his posse as Wally rounds up Cash and his men. After the gang is captured, Wally decides to give up his job to stay on the ranch with Firey, with whom he has fallen in love.

Wally Wales had been a cowboy star since 1925 when he began in a series of low grade action oaters for producer Lester F. Scott. With the coming of sound he scrambled for any berth he could get, ranging from starring roles with low-budget outfits like Big 4 (q.v.) and Imperial (q.v.) to playing bits and supporting roles at larger studios. For a time he even used the monicker Walt Williams in a couple of 1934 Reliable (q.v.) shorts, *Potluck Pards* and *Nevada Cyclone*. *The Way of the West*—distributed by Superior Talking Pictures (q.v.), but made by Robert Emmett [Tansey] for Empire and released on the First Division Exchanges (q.v.)—which proved to be his final starring effort. By 1937 Wally Wales, whose real name was Floyd Taliaferro Alderson, had changed his name to Hal Taliaferro, and he became an active character actor in Hollywood well into the early 1950s. *The Way of the West* was typical of Wally Wales starrers. It had action but was still somewhat sluggish plotwise, and its finale was padded by drawn-out scenes of the villains rustling sheep and the hero rounding up the bad guys. One dialogue sequence, however, seemed to exemplify the credo of the Poverty Row cowboy star. When asked if he was a cattle or sheep man, Wally Wales replied, "I like to be just a plain human being. Cattle or sheep, we have to live and let live, you know." A more amus-

June Love, William Desmond, John Preston and James Aubrey in *Courage of the North* (Empire, 1935).

ing bit of dialogue occurs when villain William Desmond tries to make a pass at heroine Marla Bratton. When he is rebuffed, henchman Art Mix tells cohort Jim Sheridan, "Cash hasn't made a hit with a woman in the twenty years I've known him."

Although Wally Wales is the star of *The Way of the West*, top billing goes to The American Rough Riders. No such group really makes an appearance in the feature except at the finale when the sheriff and his posse ride to the rescue. Perhaps The American Rough Riders are the posse since some of them are dressed in fancy black outfits. Most likely the group got top billing for helping producer Robert Emmett Tansey finance the feature or for some type of special publicity. At any rate The American Rough Riders have no real involvement in the movie's plot.

## Courage of the North

Empire/Stage & Screen, 1935, 55 minutes.

*P-D-SC:* Robert Emmett [Tansey]. *ST:* Barry Barringer. *Dial:* Al Lane. *PH:* B.B. [Brydon] Baker. *ED:* Arthur Cohen.

*Cast:* John Preston (Sergeant Bruce Morton), William Desmond (Travis), June Love (Yvonne Travis), Tom London (Morgan), Jimmy Aubrey (Constable Jimmy Downs), Jim Sheridan [Sherry Tansey] (Hawk), White Feather (Himself), Dynamite the Wonder Horse (Himself), Captain, King of the Dogs (Himself).

Crooked trader and fur thief Morgan (Tom London) cheats White Feather (Himself) out of his pelts, so the Indian goes to the Mounties for help but is killed by Morgan before he can talk. After Sergeant Bruce Morton (John Preston) and his colleague Constable Jimmy Downs (Jimmy Aubrey) find White Feather's body, Bruce rescues pretty Yvonne Travis (June Love), whose boat capsized in a nearby river. She invites the Mounties to have dinner with her and her trapper father (William Desmond), and while they are there Morgan orders half-breed Hawk (Jim Sheridan) to kill Travis. The attempt fails, however, and when Bruce demands to know who is trying to kill the trapper, Travis refuses to tell. Travis owes money to Morgan, and the next day the trader tells him to pay up or let him marry Yvonne. Travis refuses the latter request. To get the Mounties out of the way, Morgan has his men ambush them and leave them tied up in a shack with dynamite which is set to go off. Bruce's horse Dynamite brings the Mountie's dog Captain, who unties Bruce in time to pull the dynamite fuse. Meanwhile Morgan has his men kidnap Yvonne, and he shoots and kills her father. When Hawk fears he will be blamed for the shooting Morgan stabs him and leaves him for dead, but the half-breed manages to crawl away from the Travis home and is found by Bruce and Jimmy. Before he dies, Hawk tells them that Morgan killed Travis and kidnapped Yvonne. Bruce trails the kidnappers and rescues the girl, placing Morgan under arrest. The two fight and fall in a river as Captain leads Jimmy and a posse in pursuit of Morgan's gang, whom they capture. Bruce subdues Morgan, and the crook and his gang are placed under arrest. Later Bruce and Yvonne are married.

*Timber Terrors* and *Courage of the North* were made by Robert Emmett Tansey for distribution by Stage and Screen (q.v.). Like most films of their ilk photographed in the California high country, *Courage of the North* was a scenic delight, but its plot was slow-moving and its many fistfights routinely staged. In keeping with its budget, most of the film's activities took place outdoors although a brief sequence took place in the Travis home using the same set used in *The Silent Code* (q.v.) that same year. Both films were distributed by Stage and Screen. Star John Preston was a handsome but wooden actor, and leading lady June Love was quite comely but also lacked thespian ability. Old-timers William Desmond, Tom London and Jimmy Aubrey shouldered the bulk of the acting and did so in fine fashion. Special billed were Dynamite, the Wonder Horse, and Captain, King of the Dogs. A running joke in the film had the dog taking the horse for his Saturday bath in the river. Both *Timber Terrors* and *Courage of the North* were part of Tansey's "Morton of the Mounted" series, but the two features proved so pedestrian that no other entries were produced. Stage and Screen ceased releasing features in 1935 although the next year the company did issue a trio of serials.

## Timber Terrors

Empire/Stage & Screen, 1935, 59 minutes.

*P-D-SC:* Robert Emmet(t) [Tansey]. *ST:* Barry Barringer. *Dial:* Al Lane. *PH:* Brydon Baker. *ED:* Arthur Cohen.

*Cast:* John Preston (Sergeant Bruce Morton), Marla Bratton (Mildred Boynton), William Desmond

(Boyd), Tom London (Burke), Harold Berquist (Inspector), Fred Parker (Parker), James Sheridan [Sherry Tansey] (Billy Boynton), Tiny Skelton (Corporal Tiny Anderson), Harry Beery (Simpson), Tex Jones (Henchman), Captain, King of the Dogs (Himself), Dynamite the Wonder Horse (Himself).

When a Mountie catches a group of crooks trying to raid a mine, they kill him. Burke (Tom London) leads the gang, which includes newly arrived Billy Boynton (James Sheridan), who has come to High Point with his sister Mildred (Marla Bratton). The inspector (Harold Berquist) of the local Mounted Police post assigns Sergeant Bruce Morton (John Preston) and his assistant Corporal Tiny Anderson (Tiny Skelton) to investigate the killing. Arriving at High Point, Bruce sees Burke trying to annoy Mildred and stops him. The young woman tells the Mountie she is worried about the company her brother keeps, and he agrees to look into the matter. When Burke finds out his partner Boyd (William Desmond) owns a vicious wolf, he uses the animal to attack Bruce, but the Mountie's loyal dog Captain (Himself) kills the beast. Later Burke and Boyd have a falling out, and in a fight Burke stabs Boyd. Before dying, however, Boyd tells Bruce that Burke plans to carry off a gold shipment robbery. The Mountie trails Burke and his gang and they ambush him. Captain finds his master and goes to Mildred while Billy masquerades as the Mountie in the holdup plans. Billy, however, distrusts Burke, turning on him during the holdup and, in the fight that ensues, is fatally stabbed by Burke. Burke and his gang try to escape with the stolen gold but the Mounties give chase and capture the gang while Morton and Captain subdue Burke. After Burke is sentenced to hang for his crimes, Bruce and Mildred ask permission to wed.

The second of two "Morton of the Mounted" features with John Preston in the title role, *Timber Terrors* is a slow-moving affair highlighted by Brydon Baker's fine camerawork in the north country of California. The real star of the feature, however, is Captain, King of the Dogs, who rescues hero Morton several times in the film: he saves him from being mauled by a savage wolf, he goes for help when his master is ambushed by the villains, he saves the Mountie from drowning when the bad guys tie him up and throw him in a river and he stops murderous Burke (Tom London) from knifing Morton in the finale's fight sequence. Outside of the dog, however, the film has little to offer other than scenic value. John Preston is stalwart but no actor, and leading lady Marla Bratton is high-school-play level throughout the feature. The one surprise, though, comes from James Sheridan (Sherry Tansey), usually an indifferent actor at best, who gives a well-rounded performance as the heroine's cowardly brother. Villains Tom London and William Desmond obviously have fun chewing up the scenery with their verbose acting styles, and a nice sequence has Morton saving a colt from a killer wolf (who looks remarkably like a police dog); otherwise, it is easy to see why the "Morton of the Mounted" series lasted for only two entries.

## Calling All Cars

January 9, 1935, 60 minutes.

*P:* Lester F. Scott, Jr. *D:* Spencer Gordon Bennet. *SC:* Betty Burbridge & George Morgan. *ST:* Homer K.

Lobby card for *The Outlaw Tamer* (Empire, 1935) with Slim Whitaker, Lane Chandler and J.P. McGowan.

Gordon. *PH:* James Brown, Jr. *ED:* Fred Bain. *AD:* Paul Palmentola. *SD:* Tom Lambert. *Asst Dir:* Harry Knight.

*Cast:* Jack LaRue, Lillian Miles, Jack Morton, Harry Holman, Eddie Featherstone.

A newsman tries to bring in a gang of crooks and also romance a gangster's moll.

## The Lone Bandit

February, 1935, 60 minutes.

*P:* Nathan Hirsch. *D:* J.P. Mc-Gowan. *SC:* Ralph Consuman. *ST:* Buck Parsons. *PH:* Leonard Poole. *SD:* Paul Guerin. *Supv:* Robert Curwood.

*Cast:* Lane Chandler, Doris Brook, Wally Wales, Ray Gallagher, Slim Whitaker, Ben Corbett, Jack Prince, Philo McCullough, Frank

Ellis, Horace B. Carpenter, Wally West.

When his horse is stolen by a masked bandit, a man is accused of being an outlaw.

## The Outlaw Tamer

March, 1935, 60 minutes.

*P:* Nathan & Fred Hirsh. *D:* J.P. McGowan. *SC:* J. Wesley Patterson & Kaye Northrup. *PH:* James Diamond. *ED:* Charles Henkel. *SD:* Corson Jowett. *Asst Dir:* Mack V. Wright.

*Cast:* Lane Chandler, Janet Morgan [Blanche Mehaffey], J.P. McGowan, George Hayes, Ben Corbett, Slim Whitaker, Tex Palmer, Herman Hack.

After finding a murdered man, a cowboy tries to locate his killer.

## Rescue Squad

April 3, 1935, 61 minutes.

*P:* Lester F. Scott, Jr. *D:* Spencer Gordon Bennet. *SC:* George Morgan & Betty Burbridge. *ST:* Charles Arthur & Marcel Gluck. *PH:* Gilbert Warrenton. *SD:* Corson Jowett.

*Cast:* Ralph Forbes, Verna Hillie, Leon [Ames] Waycoff, Kate Pentzer, Sheila Terry, Beth Partman, Frank Leigh, Jimmy Aubrey, Catherine Cotter, Catherine Stoker.

Members of a fire-fighting squad work to save the victims of arson.

## Get That Man

July 2, 1935, 57 minutes.

*P:* Lester F. Scott, Jr. *D:* Spencer Gordon Bennet. *SC:* Betty Burbridge. *ST:* Robert Bridgewood. *PH:* James Brown, Jr. *ED:* Grace Davey. *AD:* Paul Palmentola. *SD:* Bert De Sart. *Asst Dir:* Harry Knight.

*Cast:* Wallace Ford, Finis Barton, E. Alyn Warren, Leon [Ames] Waycoff, Lillian Miles, Laura Treadwell, William Humphries, Johnstone White.

Complications develop for a cab driver because he resembles a murdered heir.

## The Firetrap

November 26, 1935, 67 minutes.

*P:* Larry Darmour. *D:* Burt Lynwood. *SC:* Charles Francis Royal. *PH:* Bert Longnecker. *ED:* Earl Turner. *Mus:* Lee Zahler. *SD:* Corson Jowett. *AD:* Paul Palmentola. *Asst Dir:* Harry Knight.

*Cast:* Norman Foster, Evalyn Knapp, Sidney Blackmer, Ben Alexander, Oscar Apfel, Herbert Corthell, Arthur Houseman, Marie Callahan, Corky.

An investigator is on the trail of an arson gang involved in insurance fraud. Reissued by J.H. Hoffberg in 1937.

## Shadows of the Orient

1936, 65 minutes.

*P:* Larry Darmour. *D:* Burt Lynwood. *SC:* Charles Francis Royal. *ST:* L.E. Heifetz. *PH:* James S. Brown, Jr. *ED:* Dwight Caldwell. *Mus:* Lee Zahler. *SD:* Tom Lambert. *AD:* Paul Palmentola. *Asst Dir:* Harry Knight.

*Cast:* Regis Toomey, Esther Ralston, Sidney Blackmer, J. Farrell MacDonald, Oscar Apfel, Matty Fain, Eddie Fetherstone, Kit Guard, James Leong.

An investigator and a young woman become involved in an alien-smuggling racket. Reissued in 1937 by Monogram.

## The Crime Patrol

May 13, 1936, 58 minutes.

*P:* Harry S. Knight. *D:* Eugene Cummings. *SC:* Betty Burbridge. *ST:* Arthur T. Horman. *PH:* Bert Longnecker. *ED:* Earl Neville. *AD:* Paul Palmentola. *SD:* Tom Lambert. *Asst Dir:* J.A. Duffy.

*Cast:* Ray Walker, Geneva Mitchell, Hooper Atchley, Herbert Corthell, Wilbur Mack, Russ Clark, Max Wagner, Virginia True Boardman, Henry Rocquemore, Snub Pollard.

In order to have access to the police gym, a young boxer becomes a cop and ends up foiling a holdup gang. Reissued by Guaranteed in 1938.

# First Division

One of the most successful film laboratory operations in Hollywood was Pathé, which also made feature films and the popular short subjects "Pathé News" and "March of Time" series. In addition to these activities Pathé also had a distribution arm called First Division, which mostly released independent products outside the states' rights market since the company had its own system of exchanges. In the early and mid–1930s First Division released the products of such companies as Monogram, Chesterfield-Invincible, Pinnacle, Alliance, Allied, Liberty and Stage and Screen. The Alliance product was comprised of British imports, but the company also handled documentaries like *Wild Women of Borneo* (1932), *The Big Drive* (1933) and *Hei Tiki* (1935). With offices at 1600 Broadway in New York City, First Division also handled short subjects and serials made by companies like Sol Lesser's Principal Pictures (q.v.).

First Division kicked off its release schedule in 1931 relying mainly on British imports like *The Speckled Band* (1931); *Condemned to Death* (1932), with Arthur Wontner; *The Ringer* (1932); *Hound of the Baskervilles* (1932), with John Stuart; and *Monte Carlo Madness* (1932), with Sari Maritza and Hans Albers. In 1932 the company began distributing solo independent offerings such as the Natural Color western *Tex Takes a Holiday* (1932), starring Virginia Browne Faire and Wallace MacDonald. By 1933 the company was also offering the "Port o' Call" series of thirteen one-reelers as well as the solo three-reeler DASSAN and eight two-reel chapters of the Principal serial *Tarzan the Fearless*, starring Buster Crabbe. The next year the company issued its own cliffhanger, *Young Eagles* (1934), which the Boy Scouts dedicated to President Franklin D. Roosevelt. First Division also released Principal's chapterplay *The Return of Chandu*, starring Bela Lugosi, that year. It also offered eighteen one-reel "Musical Moods" and six one-reel "Thrilling Journeys" short subjects. In 1935 First Division released seven "Musical Moods" one-reelers, six in Technicolor, six more "Thrilling Journeys" one-reelers and six one-reel "Newslaughs."

Probaby the high point of First Division's own filmmaking activity came in 1935 when the company, as First Division Productions, made two fine westerns with Hoot Gibson, *Sunset Range* and *Rainbow's End*. Since the company had been distributing the product of Allied Pictures (q.v.) and Hoot Gibson was under contract to that company's owner, M.H. Hoffman, First Division acquired Gibson's contract from Hoffman after he and the Hooter squabbled over the latter's wanting to return to Universal after Allied went under. The contract called for Gibson to make four westerns for First Division, but after the first two the company released him from the agreement and he signed with Walter Futter's Diversion Pictures (q.v.). Ironically, First Division had just

4

released Walter Futter's production of *Hong Kong Nights* (1935), starring Tom Keene. For its own filmmaking, First Division rented facilities at General Service Studios on Las Palmas Avenue in Hollywood.

Another interesting western distributed by First Division was the Normandy Pictures production of *Law of 45s*, the first film to be based on William Colt MacDonald's famous western characters "The Three Mesquiteers." Actually this low-budget oater contained only two of MacDonald's characters, with Guinn "Big Boy" Williams as Tucson Smith and Al St. John as Stony Burke. The character of Lullaby Joslin was excised.

Since it produced only a handful of films from 1932 to 1935, it is not surprising that First Division's main profit came from its distribution of other companies' product. Much of that profit, however, dwindled in 1935 when Monogram joined Liberty, Mascot and Majestic to form Republic Pictures. With the coming demise of Chesterfield-Invincible, First Division simply had very little product to distribute, since most of the other independent companies were with other exchanges or the states' rights market. In 1936 Grand National Pictures took over the First Division release program and the company was no more. Pathé is known to have had some financial backing in Grand National, and the first forty-six features issued by that company came from First Division.

## Tex Takes a Holiday

Argosy/First Division, December 2, 1932, 60 minutes, color.

*D:* Alvin J. Neitz [Alan James]. *SC:* Robert Walker. *PH:* Otto Himm.

*Cast:* Wallace MacDonald, Virginia Browne Faire, George Chesebro, Olin Francis, Ben Corbett, James Dillon, Claude Payton, Jack Perrin, George Gerwing, Sheldon Lewis, Mary de LaLatta.

When he is blamed for a series of crimes a stranger has to find the real culprit.

## The Big Drive

January 20, 1933, 90 minutes.

*Compiler-Narrator:* A.L. Rule.

Combat footage from the Signal Corps vaults was used in this compilation about World War I.

## Young Eagles

1934, 12 chapters.

*P:* George W. Stout & Harry O. Hoyt. *D:* Spencer Gordon Bennet & Vin Moore. *SC:* Elizabeth Hayter. *PH:* William Hyer & Edward Kull. *ED:* Donn Hayes.

*Cast:* Bob Cox, Jim Vance, Angus McLean, Carter Dixon, Philo McCullough, Frank Lackteen.

After crash landing in the Yucatan Peninsula in Mexico, two Boy Scouts battle crooks over a treasure.

Chapter Titles: The Crash, Drums of Hate, City of the Dead, The Bridge of Doom, Treasure Trails, Fangs of Flame, Tropic Fury, Wings of Terror, The Lost Lagoon, Jungle Outlaws, Trapped, Out of the Sky.

## Sunset Range

May 10, 1935, 60 minutes.

*D:* Ray McCarty. *SC:* Paul

Lobby card for the final chapter of the serial *Young Eagles* (First Division), 1934).

Schofield. *PH:* Gilbert Warrenton. *ED:* Ralph Dietrich. *SD:* Hal Bumbaugh. *Prod Mgr:* Leon D'Usseau. *Asst Dir:* George Sherman.

*Cast:* Hoot Gibson, Mary Doran, James Eagles, Walter McGrail, John Elliott, Eddie Lee, Ralph Lewis, Kitty McHugh, Martha Sleeper, Fred Gilman, Jim Corey, Fred Humes, Horace B. Carpenter, Slim Whitaker, Joe Jackson, George Sowards, Lem Sowards, Bill Gillis.

After giving his sister the title to his ranch, a man is shot and a cowboy tries to find the murderer.

## Convention Girl

May 14, 1935, 60 minutes.

*P:* David M. Thomas. *D:* Luther Reed. *SC:* George Boyle. *PH:* Nicholas Rogalli. *ED:* Emma Hill. *Mus:* Louis Alter & Arthur Swantrom.

*Cast:* Rose Hobart, Weldon Heyburn, Sally O'Neil, Herbert Rawlinson, Shemp Howard, Lucille Mendez, James Spottswood, Nancy Kelly, Alan Brooks, Nell O'Day, Toni Reed, Ruth Gillette, William H. White, Lalive Brownell, Isham Jones & His Orchestra.

A cabaret hostess loves a gambler who does not return her affections.

## Rainbow's End

July 17, 1935, 59 minutes.

*D:* Norman Spencer. *SC:* Rollo Lloyd. *PH:* Gilbert Warrenton. *ED:* Ralph Dietrich. *SD:* Hal Bumbaugh. *Prod Mgr:* Leon D'Usseau.

*Cast:* Hoot Gibson, June Gale,

Advertisement for *Hong Kong Nights* (First Division, 1935).

Warner Richmond, Oscar Apfel, Charles Hill, Buddy Roosevelt, Ada Ince, Stanley Blystone, John Elliott, Henry Rocquemore, Fred Gilman, Jerry Mandy.

Following an argument with his father, a man becomes the foreman on a ranch to which the old man holds the mortgage.

## Law of 45s

Normandy/First Division, December 1, 1935, 57 minutes.

*P:* Arthur Alexander. *D:* John P. McCarthy. *SC:* Robert Emmett Tansey, from the novel by William Colt MacDonald. *PH:* Robert Cline. *ED:* Holbrook N. Todd. *Asst Dir:* Myron Marsh.

*Cast:* Guinn "Big Boy" Williams, Nell O'Day, Al St. John, Ted Adams, Martin Garralaga, Broderick O'Farrell, Curley Dresden, Lafe McKee, Fred Burns, Bill Patton, Francis Walker, Jack Kirk, Glenn Strange, Sherry Tansey, Tex Palmer, Jack Evans,

George Morrell, Merrill McCormack, William McCall, Herman Hack, Ace Cain, Buck Morgan.

Two cowboys are after outlaws who have been terrorizing the territory.

## Hong Kong Nights

December 24, 1935, 59 minutes.
*P:* Walter Futter & Fenn Kimball. *D:* E. Mason Hopper. *SC:* Norman Houston. *ST:* Roger Allman. *PH:* Arthur Reed. *AD:* Charles Gardner.

*Cast:* Tom Keene (Thomas "Tom" Keene), Wera Engels (Trina Vidor), Warren Hymer (Wally), Tetsu Komai (Wong), Cornelius Keefe (Gil Burris), Tom London (Blake), Freeman Lang (Captain Evans).

Customs agent Tom Keene (Tom Keene) and his pal Wally (Warren Hymer) are in Hong Kong when Tom is assigned to go to Macao to find ex-convinct and gunrunner Gil Burris (Cornelius Keefe). Wally meets beautiful Trina (Wera Engels), and later he and Tom see her in Macao with Burris at his gambling club. Wong (Tetsu Komai), who is in cahoots with Burris, finds out Tom's plans and warns the gunrunner, who leaves Macao immediately with Trina. Tom and Wally are on the same boat as Burris and the girl, and when Trina finds out Burris means to do Tom harm, she leaves him and seeks sanctuary in Tom's cabin. That night Tom and Wally sleep on deck, and Wong tries to kill Tom but is overpowered. Tom, however, spares his life.

The next day in Hong Kong Tom takes Trina to the polo matches, where she tells him she met Burris three years before in Vienna and has come East to marry him. She begins to change her mind, however, when Tom tells her that her fiancé is a gunrunner. Trina asks Tom to talk to Burris at his waterfront office and he agrees. Wally has also gone to the waterfront locale and discovers hand grenades in crates supposedly stocked with eggs. When Tom and Trina arrive, Burris asks to see Tom alone. They eventually fight and in the fracas Burris' associate, Blake (Tom London), is killed. Trina too sees the munitions, and Wally escapes after setting off a grenade. Tom is captured and Burris tells Wong to kill him, but Wong lets Tom go free. Tom hides out on the boat Burris uses to take Trina to the island of Tein Chau where he is to get silver from Wong's people for the weapons. On the island Burris gets the silver but says he will deliver the ammunition later when he is safely on his boat. In a fight between Tom and the natives, a fire is started and the island village goes up in flames. Tom escapes back to the boat, but Burris shoots him and then takes Tom and Trina to a deserted island, where he plans to leave them to die. Wong, however, finds out that Burris plans to double-cross him. They fight and both are mortally wounded. Before he dies Wong sets off a blaze that attracts a passing ship, and its captain (Freeman Lang) rescues Tom and Trina, who return to Hong Kong and marry.

Filmed at Mack Sennett Studios, this rough-edged melodrama set in the Orient is chock full of stock footage from that part of the world, not only street scenes with rear projection used to interject characters but also scenes of dancing girls and even a polo game in Hong Kong. Star Tom Keene actually plays a character with that name while costar Wera Engels portrays Trina Vidor, the latter being an inside joke using the surname of director King Vidor, who had directed Keene the previous year in *Our Daily Bread* (q.v.) for Viking Pictures. Third-billed Warren Hymer provides the film's rather mundane comedy, the actor being on the downgrade from the prominence he had earlier in the decade. For no apparent reason he simply disappears from the movie about two-thirds of the way through and is never mentioned again. Ketsu Komai is especially good as the gunrunner's associate who tries to get needed munition for his island

people. Outside of the burning of the native village and the closing scenes on the deserted island, *Hong Kong Nights* is not a visually interesting movie although it moves fairly well. Tom Keene, as usual, is a likable hero, and Wera Engels entrances with her exotic beauty.

# Freuler Film Associates

Following the demise of Big 4 (q.v.), John R. Freuler formed Freuler Film Associates, which announced the ambitious schedule of eighteen "Monarch Melodramas" and six Tom Tyler westerns for the 1932–33 season. What resulted was a dozen feature releases by the company, including a quartet of westerns starring Tom Tyler. F. McGrew Willis and Oliver Drake scripted a number of the Freuler features with Burton King coming over from Big 4 to produce the Tyler sagebrush actioners as well as other Freuler films. Nearly all the releases were photographed by Edward S. Kull and edited by Fred Bain.

The themes of the Monarch melodramas tended to vary from film to film with boxing dominating *The Fighting Gentleman* (1932) while gambling addiction was the concern of *The Gambling Sex* (1932). A good guy gone wrong dominated *The Penal Code* (1932), but despite a fine performance by Regis Toomey in the lead role, it was not a good effort. *Variety* noted, "Not much to offer as novelty in this combination of stressed drama and some rather mawkish attempts at mother love and young romance." The same reviewer labeled the feature "amateurish in plot, development and appeal." Romantic complications highlighted two other Freuler releases, *Marriage on Approval* (1933) and *Love Past Thirty* (1934), while an attempt to revive a desert love story met with middling results in *Kiss of Araby* (1933), starring Walter Byron and Maria Alba.

Tom Tyler starred in his four Freuler westerns, sandwiched between stays at Monogram and Reliable (q.v.). Burton King handled the production chores in much the fashion he did with the Big 4 sagebrush yarns (which is to say they were low-budget indeed). The initial outing, *The Forty-Niners* (1932), was nicely directed by John P. McCarthy and had a fairly interesting historical theme, but the last three—*When a Man Rides Alone, Deadwood Pass* and *War of the Range*—all issued in 1933, were directed in a hurried fashion by J.P. McGowan and scripted just as hurriedly by Oliver Drake. While some viewers feel Tyler took a step down when he joined Reliable after Freuler, there is little visible difference in their product.

Walter Byron, Adolph Milar, Harry Myers and Rochelle Hudson in *Savage Girl* (Freuler Film Associates, 1932).

By early 1934 it was evident that Freuler Film Associates was on the way out, and the company ended business before it could complete its planned program, leaving ten Monarch Melodramas and two Tom Tyler westerns unfilmed.

## The Fighting Gentleman

October 7, 1932, 65 minutes.

*P:* Burton King. *D:* Fred Newmeyer. *SC:* F. McGrew Willis. *ST:* Edward Sinclair. *PH:* Edward S. Kull. *ED:* Fred Bain. *SD:* Theron Kellum.

*Cast:* William Collier, Jr., Josephine Dunn, Natalie Moorhead, Crauford Kent, Lee Moran, Pat O'Malley, James J. Jeffries, Hughie Owens, Mildred Rogers, Peggy Graves, Paddy O'Flynn, Duke Lee.

After losing a fight at a carnival, a young mechanic trains seriously and becomes a boxing contender.

## The Forty-Niners

October 28, 1932, 59 minutes.

*P:* Burton King. *D:* John P. McCarthy. *SC:* F. McGrew Willis. *PH:* Edward S. Kull. *ED:* Fred Bain.

*Cast:* Tom Tyler, Betty Mack, Al Bridge, Fern Emmett, Gordon [De Main] Wood, Mildred Rogers, Fred Ritter, Frank Ball, Florence Wells.

A cowboy comes to the aid of settlers being harassed by outlaws.

# The Gambling Sex

November 21, 1932, 65 minutes.

P: Burton King. D: Fred Newmeyer. SC: F. McGrew Willis. PH: Edward S. Kull. ED: Fred Bain.

Cast: Grant Withers, Ruth Hall, Maston Williams, John St. Polis, Jean Porter, James Eagles, Murdock Mac-Quarrie.

In Miami, a young society woman loses all her money on racing and nearly loses the man she loves.

# The Savage Girl

December 5, 1932, 66 minutes.

P: John R. Freuler. D: Harry S. Fraser. SC: N. Brewster Morse. PH: Edward S. Kull. ED: Fred Bain. Mus: Lee Zahler. SD: Homer Ackerman.

Cast: Rochelle Hudson (The Jungle Goddess), Walter Byron (Jim Franklin), Harry F. Myers (Amos P. Stitch), Adolph Milar (Eric Vernooth), Ted Adams (Cab Driver), Floyd Shackleford (Oscar), Charles Gemora (Gorilla).

At a society party, explorer Jim Franklin (Walter Byron) discusses his latest trip to Africa in search of big game for stateside zoos. At the affair is tipsy millionaire Amos P. Stitch (Harry F. Myers), who not only agrees to finance the expedition but also plans to make the trip. At dockside a cab driver (Ted Adams) tells the two men he always wanted to go to Africa, so they take him and his taxi along on their voyage. When they get to Africa, Franklin engages German big-game hunter Eric Vernooth (Adolph Milar) as his assistant, and their safari heads into the interior with Stitch riding in the taxi. He also takes along Oscar (Floyd Shackleford), a transplanted Harlemite yearning to get back across the Atlantic to home. Franklin wants

to get into unexplored territory but Vernooth tells him the land is "no good for white man" with its tales of natives sacrificing humans to a white female goddess. In the dense jungle they are spotted by the Goddess (Rochelle Hudson), a pretty young white girl, who has befriended the denizens of the area. She sets free all the animals the expedition has captured and is attracted to Franklin who begins to suspect the stories about the girl are true. He sets a trap for her and the Goddess is captured, but when she is placed in a hut Vernooth tries to molest the girl. Franklin orders him out of the camp. He and the girl become friendly, and she tries to kiss him. Meanwhile Vernooth instigates a native uprising by telling them that the white men plan to steal their goddess. The natives capture Franklin, but Stitch and the cab driver take the taxi into the native village and scare away the captors, freeing Franklin. Vernooth corners the girl and tries to rape her, but Franklin arrives to stop him and they fight. The German pulls a gun on Franklin, but a huge gorilla (Charles Gemora), the protector of the Goddess, strangles him. Stitch then wants to go home, but Franklin stays to make love to the beautiful jungle Goddess.

Although cheaply made, *The Savage Girl* is a fun, fairly fast-paced feature that doesn't take itself too seriously. The scenes of the drunken millionaire riding in a taxi on safari are priceless. A running gag in the movie has the millionaire bringing mice to Africa to see if elephants really are afraid of the tiny creatures. Harry T. Myers basically repeats the role of the drunk from *City Lights* (1931) while Walter Byron is somewhat stiff as the Frank Buck-like hero. Adolph Milar, however, exudes lechery as the German hunter who wants to share the jungle girl with Franklin. "She's white, she's beautiful, she's warm, she's smooth," he tells the enraged hero who promptly knocks him down. Both Ted Adams, usually a villain, and Floyd Shackleford have some good comedy moments as somewhat dense characters, but it is comely Rochelle Hudson who attracts all the attention as the leopard-skin-garbed heroine. The costume is rather revealing, and Miss Hudson makes the most of her female Tarzan role, even with lipstick and eye makeup. She is quite an eyeful as she scampers around the jungle.

*Savage Girl* was reissued by Guaranteed Pictures in 1938.

## The Penal Code

December 23, 1932, 67 minutes.

*P:* Burton King. *D:* George Melford. *SC:* F. Hugh Herbert. *ST:* Edward T. Lowe. *PH:* Edward S. Kull. *ED:* Fred Bain. *SD:* Earl Crain.

*Cast:* Regis Toomey, Helene Cohan, Pat O'Malley, Robert Ellis, Virginia True Boardman, Henry Hall, Leander De Cordova, John Ince, Murdock MacQuarrie, Olin Francis, Jack Cheatham, Barney Furey, James Eagles, Julia Griffith, Dorothy Sinclair, Elizabeth Poule, Jean Porter, Albert Richman, Henry Henna, Jack Grant.

When he is pardoned, an ex-convict soon finds himself framed on a bank robbery charge by a romantic rival.

## Kiss of Araby

1933, 62 minutes.

*P:* Burton King. *D:* Phil Rosen. *SC:* F. McGrew Willis. *PH:* Edward Kull. *SD:* Homer Ackerman. *Asst Dir:* Harry Knight.

*Cast:* Walter Byron, Maria Alba,

Claire Windsor, Theodore Von Eltz, Claude King, Frank Leigh.

In the Arabian desert a British army captain fights caravan robbers and romances a dancing girl.

## When a Man Rides Alone

January 29, 1933, 60 minutes.

*P:* Burton King. *D:* J.P. McGowan. *SC:* Oliver Drake. *ST:* F. McGrew Willis. *PH:* Edward S. Kull. *ED:* Fred Bain.

*Cast:* Tom Tyler, Adele Lacey, Alan Bridge, Bob Burns, Frank Ball, Alma Chester, Barney Furey, Leander De Cordova, Lillian Chay, Jack Rockwell, Bud Osborne, Ed Burns, Herman Hack, Jack Kirk.

Settlers cheated in a mine scheme are given gold by a mysterious highwayman.

## Deadwood Pass

June 6, 1933, 61 minutes.

*P:* Burton King. *D:* J.P. McGowan. *SC:* Oliver Drake. *ST:* John Wesley Patterson. *PH:* Edward S. Kull. *ED:* Fred Bain.

*Cast:* Tom Tyler, Alice Dahl, Wally Wales, Lafe McKee, Edmund Cobb, Slim Whitaker, Merrill McCormack, Carlotta Monti, Buffalo Bill, Jr., Duke R. Lee, Blackie Whiteford, Bud Osborne, Bill Nestell, J.P. McGowan, Jack Kirk, Ben Corbett, Chuck Baldra, Bud McClure.

A government agent pretends to be an outlaw called "The Hawk" in order to learn the whereabouts of hidden loot.

## Easy Millions

September 6, 1933, 68 minutes.

*P:* Ralph M. Like. *D:* Fred Newmeyer. *SC:* Jack Jevne. *ST:* Edgar Franklin. *PH:* Jules Cronjager. *ED:*

Byron Robinson. *SD:* Terry Kellum. *Asst Dir:* Harry Knight.

*Cast:* Skeets Gallagher, Dorothy Burgess, Johnny Arthur, Merna Kennedy, Noah Beery, Bert Roach, Walter Long, Arthur Hoyt, Ted Adams, Gay Seabrook, Pauline Garon, Ethel Wales, Henry Roquemore, Virginia Sale, Murdock MacQuarrie, Larry Boles.

After claiming he has inherited a million dollars, a man finds himself with three fiancées.

## War of the Range

September 29, 1933, 59 minutes.

*P:* Burton King. *D:* J.P. McGowan. *SC:* Oliver Drake. *PH:* Edward S. Kull. *ED:* Fred Bain. *SD:* Terry Kellum. *Asst Dir:* Mack V. Wright.

*Cast:* Tom Tyler, Caryl Lincoln, Lane Chandler, Theodore [Ted] Adams, Charles K. French, Lafe McKee, William Nanlan, Wesley Giraud, Slim Whitaker, Fred Burns, Billy Franey.

The son of a cattleman falls in love with the pretty daughter of a nester.

## Marriage on Approval

December 27, 1933, 67 minutes.

*P:* John R. Freuler. *D:* Howard Higgin. *SC:* Olgar Printzlau, Edward Sinclair & Howard Higgin. *ST:* Priscilla Wayne. *PH:* Edward S. Kull. *ED:* Fred Bain.

*Cast:* Barbara Kent, William Farnum, Leila McIntyre, Donald Dillaway, Phyllis Barry, Edward Woods, Dorothy Granger, Otis Harlan, Lucille Ward, Clarence Geldert.

While intoxicated, a young man and woman end up getting married.

## Love Past Thirty

February 14, 1934, 64 minutes.

*P:* John R. Freuler. *D:* Vin Moore. *SC:* Earle Snell, based on the novel by Priscilla Wayne. *PH:* Irving Akers. *ED:* Fred Bain.

*Cast:* Aileen Pringle, Theodore Von Eltz, Phyllis Barry, Robert Frazer, Gertrude Messinger, John Marston, Gaylord [Steve] Pendleton, Mary Carr, Pat O'Malley, Virginia Sale, Dot Farley, Ben Hall.

When she is rejected by her longtime suitor who goes for a younger girl, a woman takes revenge by going after the girl's ex-boyfriend.

# Ken Goldsmith Productions

From 1932 to 1934 Ken Goldsmith Productions turned out six low-budget feature films that were distributed by William Steiner. These features were played off on the states' rights market and quickly forgotten although one of them, *Out of Singapore* (1932), was rereleased by Astor Pictures in 1939 as *Gangsters of the Sea*. Otherwise, these Ken Goldsmith Productions were routine potboilers typifying the type of product churned out on Poverty Row in the mid–1930s.

**Lobby card for** *Out of Singapore* **(Goldsmith Productions, 1932) picturing Noah Beery, Montagu Love and Dorothy Burgess.**

Of the six Goldsmith features, *Out of Singapore* is the best, mainly because of its somewhat sleazy theme and delightfully hammy acting by Noah Beery and Montagu Love as well as Dorothy Burgess and her revealing dancing costume. Not as good, but acceptable entertainment are *High Gear* with its auto racing theme and the circus background drama *Carnival Lady* (both 1933). Mary E. McCarthy scripted both *Woman Unafraid* and *I Hate Women*, two 1934 releases, but by the time William Steiner got them in theatres, Ken Goldsmith Productions had ceased operations.

Following his stint as an independent producer, Ken Goldsmith found a berth at Universal. There he worked on turning out numerous slick programmers such as *His Exciting Night, Little Tough Guy, The Storm* (all 1938), *Hers for a Day, Newboy's Home, Society Smugglers, Unexpected Father* (all 1939), *Honeymoon Deferred, The Invisible Man Returns, I Can't Give You Anything but Love Baby, La Conga Nights, Argentine Nights, Give Us Wings* (all 1940), *San Antonio Rose, Mob Town, Moonlight in Hawaii, Melody Lane* (all 1941), *There's One Born Every Minute, Tough as They Come, You're Telling Me* (all 1942) and *Always a Bridesmaid* and *Mug Town* (both 1943).

# Out of Singapore

September 16, 1932, 61 minutes.

*P:* Ken Goldsmith. *D:* Charles Hutchison. *SC:* John Francis (Jack) Natteford. *ST:* Frederick Chapin. *PH:* Edward S. Kull & Jacob Badaracco. *ED:* S. Roy Luby. *SD:* Freeman Lang. *Asst Dir:* Melville DeLay.

*Cast:* Noah Beery (Woolf Barstow), Dorothy Burgess (Concha Renaldo), Miriam Seegar (Mary Carroll), Montagu Love (Scar Murray), George Walsh (Steve Trent), Jimmy Aubrey (Bloater), William Moran (Captain Carroll), Olin Francis (Bill), Ethan Laidlaw (Second Mate Miller), Leon Wong (Wong), Horace B. Carpenter (Captain Smith), Fred "Snowflake" Toones (Cook), Ernest Butterworth (Sailor).

Needing a first mate for his cargo ship bound for Singapore and Manila, Captain Carroll (William Moran) hires Woolf Barstow (Noah Beery) and his boatswain Scar Murray (Montagu Love). An old seaman (Horace B. Carpenter) warns Carroll that Barstow has a bad reputation and that the last eight ships he was with were destroyed in some manner. It is too late to change his mind, however, and Carroll is forced to sail with Barstow. The captain's pretty daughter, Mary Carroll (Miriam Seegar), is also on board. Barstow and Murray plan to take over the ship and wreck it to collect $80,000 insurance money on the cargo. Second mate Miller (Ethan Laidlaw) overhears their scheme and they drown him. In Singapore, Barstow hires drunken Steve Trent (George Walsh) as his new second mate after seeing the sailor perform well in a fight in a dive run by Wong (Leon Wong), Barstow's partner in insuring the ship's cargo.

Performing at the waterfront saloon is Barstow's ex-lover Concha (Dorothy Burgess), who tries to stab him when he spurns her affections. Steve and pal Bloater (Jimmy Aubrey), who has been hired as the ship's cook, set sail with Barstow while Concha stows away. Captain Carroll has come down with China fever and Barstow pretends to be kind to Mary, but when the captain learns what Barstow is up to with the cargo, they fight and the old man is beaten fatally. Concha resents Mary at first, but she helps her care for her dying father and after his death warns her against Barstow. By now Steve has fallen in love with Mary, and Barstow resents his protection of the girl. When Barstow manhandles Concha, Steve comes to her defense, but the crew overpower him and he is locked up. Barstow then tells Mary she will become his bride and that they will escape when he blows up the ship. Barstow and Murray have a falling out over money as Concha sets Trent free. When Barstow goes below to set off the dynamite to blow up the vessel, Concha locks the door as he tries to go above deck. When Murray attacks the fleeing Steve and Mary, Bloater knocks him out and the three get on a lifeboat and leave the ship. Meanwhile Concha dances for the drunken crew who cannot hear Barstow's cries for help and the ship explodes.

By far the best of Ken Goldsmith's independent productions, *Out of Singapore* is a potboiler imbued with fine entertainment value thanks to the villainy of Noah Beery and Montagu Love and the physical allure of Dorothy Burgess as a sexy half-caste dancer. Beery hams it up beautifully as the lecherous, larcenous and homicidal Woolf Barstow, who has spent three years at sea torching, wrecking and sinking ships for the insurance on their cargo. In several scenes Beery and cohort Montagu Love obviously have a good time as they think up ways to collect on cargo, destroy ships and take innocent lives. Beery, however, also has a yen for Miriam Seegar, the ship captain's blond daughter, whom he plans to seduce. In one scene he tells fellow crook, Wong (Leon Wong), that the girl could not yet be trusted but "after we've been shipwrecked together a couple of weeks on a tropical isle things will be different." In another sequence the sleeping young woman wakes to find Beery bending over her. "It's a cool morning and I just wanted to cover you up, dear," he tells her. Despite the outrageous fun in Beery's hamming, beautiful Dorothy Burgess nearly steals the show as the sexy Concha. She performs a seductive dance wearing only a brief see-through costume with more bare midriff than usually seen in Poverty Row features of this period. The Singapore saloon set later turned up in *Hong Kong Nights* (q.v.) in 1935.

*Out of Singapore* was reissued in 1939 by Astor Pictures as *Gangsters of the Sea.*

## Bachelor Mother

December 14, 1932, 70 minutes.
  *P:* Ken Goldsmith. *D:* Charles Hutchison. *SC:* Paul Gangelin, Luther Reed, John Francis Natteford & Jack Townley. *ST:* Al Boasberg. *PH:* Edward S. Kull. *ED:* Louis Sackin. *SD:* J.S. Westmoreland.
  *Cast:* Evalyn Knapp, James Murray, Margaret Seddon, Astrid Allwyn, Paul Page, Harry Holman, Virginia Sale, Eddie Kane, Jimmy Aubrey, J. Paul Jones, Henry Hall, Margaret Mann, Bess Stafford, Stella Adams.
  After being caught speeding, a young man is forced to adopt a mother from the old folks home and she tries

to change his life. A Spanish language version, *Tres Amores* [Three Loves] (1934), was produced by Moe Sackin. It starred Jose Crespo, Mona Maris and Anita Campillo.

## High Gear

March 22, 1933, 65 minutes.
  *P:* Ken Goldsmith. *D:* Leigh Jason. *SC:* Leigh Jason, Rex Taylor & Charles Saxton. *PH:* Edward S. Kull. *ED:* Louis Sackiln. *AD:* Paul Palmentola. *SD:* J.S. Westmoreland. *Prod Mgr:* Heck Minter.
  *Cast:* James Murray (Marc Shared), Joan Marsh (Ann Merritt), Jackie Searle (Jimmy Evans), Eddie Lambert (Papa Cohen), Ann Brody (Mama Cohen), Theodore Von Eltz (Larry Winston), Lee Moran (Ed Evans), Gordon DeMain (Major), Marion Sayers (Telephone Operator), Winifred Drew (Visiting Mother), Mike Donlin, Douglas Haig, Wesley Giraud, John Sinclair.
  Race driver Marc Shared (James Murray) gets a dinner date with pretty reporter Ann Merritt (Joan Marsh) because she wants to interview him. In order to get the story, though, Ann has to break a date with gossip columnist and radio broadcaster Larry Winston (Theodore Von Eltz). The next day at the big race Marc's mechanic Ed (Lee Moran) warns him not to continue because of a twisted steering gear, but Marc does not listen and Ed is killed in the subsequent crackup. Marc vows to provide for Jimmy (Jackie Searle), Ed's son, and he sends him to military school as the boy's father had intended. Because of the crash Marc loses his nerve, becoming afraid to race, and takes a job as a taxi driver. Not wanting Ann to know his situation, Marc ignores her, but she finds out anyway. She promises, however, not to print the

story. The vindictive Winston, though, does broadcast about Marc's being scared to drive race cars, and Marc blames Ann, thinking she broke her promise. Because of the radio story, Jimmy's fellow students make fun of Marc, and Jimmy runs away from the military school, coming home to Marc, who is living with the Cohen family (Eddie Lambert, Ann Brody). When thugs try to wreck Marc's cab he tries to stop them, and in the fracas Jimmy suffers a severe skull injury. In order to save Jimmy's life Marc drives at breakneck speed to the hospital and the boy recovers. Marc then returns to the racing circuit and wins Ann.

*High Gear* was one of the last starring films of James Murray, who had won fame in the silent days in King Vidor's *The Crowd* (1928). Problems with the bottle brought about the demise of Murray's career and his death at the age of 35, just three years after the release of this feature. Very economically produced, *High Gear* moves at a fairly good clip, but its racing stock footage looks tacky and the overall plotline is very predictable. James Murray, however, does a fine job as race driver Marc "High Gear" Shared, who according to the dialogue, was a one-time winner of the Indianapolis 500. The rest of the cast is more than adequate: Joan Marsh excels as the peppy reporter, Jackie Searle is convincing in his tearful scene and Theodore Von Eltz does his usual fine job as a slick heel. Eddie Lambert's stereotype of Papa Cohen, however, grows tiresome, and too much padding of military school parades is a detriment.

## Carnival Lady

November 11, 1933, 64 minutes.
*P:* Ken Goldsmith. *D:* Howard

Higgin. *SC:* Wellyn Totman. *ST:* Harold E. Tarshis. *PH:* Edward S. Kull. *AD:* Lewis J. Rachmil.

*Cast:* Boots Mallory, Allen Vincent, Donald Kerr, Rollo Lloyd, Jason Robards, Gertrude Astor, Anita Faye, Richard Hayes, Earl McDonald, Kit Guard.

A young man's fiancée deserts him when he loses all his money in a bank crash, so he joins a circus.

## Woman Unafraid

March 27, 1934, 63 minutes.
*P:* Ken Goldsmith. *D:* William J. Cowan. *SC-ST:* Mary E. McCarthy. *PH:* Gilbert Warrenton. *AD:* Lewis J. Rachmil. *Prod Mgr:* Harry J. Takiff.

*Cast:* Lucille Gleason, Skeets Gallagher, Lona Andre, Warren Hymer, Barbara Weeks, Laura Treadwell, Eddie Phillips, Jason Robards, Ruth Clifford, Richard Elliott, Erin LaBissoniere, Julie Kingdon, Joyce Coad, Franklin Parker, Baby Waring.

After getting the goods on a hoodlum, a policewoman tries to reform several young ladies with tainted pasts.

## I Hate Women

July 11, 1934, 70 minutes.
*P:* Ken Goldsmith. *D:* Aubrey H. Scotto. *SC-ST:* Mary E. McCarthy. *PH:* Ernest Miller. *ED:* Louis Sackin. *AD:* Lewis J. Rachmil & Paul Palmentola. *SD:* J.S. Westmoreland. *Asst Dir:* Heck Minter.

*Cast:* Wallace Ford, June Clyde, Bradley Page, Fuzzy Knight, Barbara Rogers, Alexander Carr, Bobby Watson, Eleanor Hunt, Douglas Fowley, Cecilia Parker, Billy Erwin, Margaret Mann, Philo McCullough, Kernan Cripps, James Mack, Fred "Snowflake" Toones, Shirley Lee, Joey Ray, Charles

Saxton, Pat Harmon, James Quinn, Dorothy Vernon.

A woman-hating reporter ends up helping a young lady falsely accused of killing her husband. Working title: *Born to Be Hanged.*

# Hollywood Pictures

At the beginning of the sound film era, Hollywood Pictures was one of the first companies to distribute the product of small outfits outside the traditional states' rights market. With exchanges in many major cities it was able to release various independent productions, affording producers an opportunity to avoid dealing with perhaps dozens of middlemen on the states rights' circuit. With offices at 630 Ninth Avenue in New York City, Hollywood Pictures handled the product of companies like Peerless and Allied as well as many one- and two-shoot operations. The company also distributed imported products in the early sound days, including such East Europe features as *The Wedding on the Volga* (1929) and *Throw of the Dice* (1930). Like most such operations, Hollywood Pictures was mainly an umbrella for independents, but the company did invest its own capital in a few features, none of which had lasting value.

*The Call of the Circus* (1930) brought Francis X. Bushman and Ethel Clayton back to the screen but did nothing to advance their careers. Victor Adamson's *Sagebrush Politics* was one of the first all-talkie independent westerns, and the company also handled some early Willis Kent (q.v.) exploitationers like *Primrose Path* and *Playthings of Hollywood* (1931). *Bachelor Mother* (1932), a Ken Goldsmith (q.v.) production, however, was a dreary affair with James Murray and after *Police Call*, a Showmen's Pictures (q.v.) release, in 1933 with Nick Stuart, the company operated only as a distributor of established independent producers, ceasing to acquire or invest in solo efforts. Hollywood Pictures went out of business in the middle of the decade.

## The Call of the Circus

January 19, 1930, 69 minutes.

*P:* C.C. Burr. *D:* Frank O'Connor. *SC:* Maxine Alton & Jack Townley. *PH:* Louis Physioc. *Mus:* Ralph J. Nase. *Song:* Maxine Alton & Aubrey Stauffer.

*Cast:* Francis X. Bushman (The Man), Ethel Clayton (The Woman), Joan Wyndham (The Girl), William Cotton Kirby (The Boy), Dorothy Gay (The Girl at the Well), Sunburnt Jim Wilson (The Shadow).

At a well, a retired circus clown (Francis X. Bushman) meets a young girl (Dorothy Gay) and tells her he is trying to find a circus. He recounts to

Phyllis Barrington and Charles Delaney in *Playthings of Hollywood* (Hollywood Pictures, 1931).

her how he and his wife (Ethel Clayton) left the circus after years of performing and how her son (William Cotton Kirby) by a previous marriage and a performer called The Shadow (Sunburnt Jim Wilson) lived with them. For a time all is well, but eventually both the boy and The Shadow return to circus life. The man meets a young woman (Joan Wyndham) whom he rescues from an accident, and the two fall in love. Unable to stay with her husband after he has fallen for a younger woman, the wife sends for her son and then leaves home. The boy arrives, and the young accident victim realizes she only felt gratitude, not love, for the stepfather as she and the boy find happiness together. The man realizes he has made a mistake, and he seeks out his wife. They reconcile and return to the circus.

Made by Pickwick Productions, *The Call of the Circus* is a forgotten fantasy film from the early days of sound movies. *Photoplay* said it was "worth seeing because it proves that Francis X. Bushman and Ethel Clayton can still act. Otherwise nil." An all-talkie, the movie appears to have gotten little distribution and except for providing Francis X. Bushman with a starring role in an early sound film it has little merit.

## Primrose Path

January 25, 1931, 71 minutes.

*P:* Willis Kent. *D:* William O'Connor. *PH:* Henry Cronjager & Ernest Laszlo.

*Cast:* Helen Foster, John Darrow, Dorothy Granger, Lane Chandler, DeWitt Jennings, Mary Carr, Virginia Pearson, Julia Swayne Gordon, Gene Darby.

When she goes to college, an innocent young girl is involved in the wild life by a football player.

## Playthings of Hollywood

April 12, 1931, 81 minutes.

*P:* Willis Kent. *D:* William O'Connor. *SC:* Ida May Park. *PH:* Henry Cronjager & James Diamond. *ED:* Tom Persons.

*Cast:* Phyllis Barrington, Rita LaRoy, Sheila Mannors, Edmund Breese, Donald Reed, Charles Delaney, Jack Richardson, Dell Henderson, Syd Saylor.

In Hollywood three sisters look for work and two of them fall in love with the same man. Also called *Sisters of Hollywood*.

# Robert J. Horner Productions

Robert J. Horner garners little esteem from either film critics or fans. His productions are considered among the most rag-tag ever produced on Poverty Row. In his definitive volume on the "B" western, *Hollywood Corral* (1976), Don Miller sums it up best: "Mr. Horner was a man with one leg, small resources and his artistic pretensions were forthrightly nonexistent." Yet from the early 1920s well into the mid–1930s, Robert J. Horner was an active producer of motion pictures, mostly very low-budget gallopers. Among his stars were Jack Perrin, Art Acord, Ted Wells, Fred Church and Buffalo Bill, Jr. Like many low-budget filmmakers, Horner was practically a one-man show, variously operating as producer, director and writer and sometimes as all three. A typical Horner production consisted of lame action, mediocre acting and an implausible script, all done at the lowest possible cost.

During the 1920s Robert J. Horner was involved in the production of low-grade westerns, commencing with *Defying the Law* with Monte Montague in 1922. Thereafter he churned out series oaters with Jack Perrin, George Larkin, Kit Carson, Pawnee Bill, Jr., Montana Bill, William Barrymore, Ted Thompson and Fred Church. It should be noted that Kit Carson and William Barrymore were actually Boris Bullock under assumed names with more box office potential. By the mid–1920s Horner used the Aywon Film Corporation as his production moniker. (Aywon was founded in New York City in 1919 by Nathan Hirsh and operated until the mid–1930s.) He was first located out of a post office box in Hollywood, and during the sound era he used a New York City address. Probably Horner's biggest claim to fame in the silent era was the production of seven westerns starring Art Acord, whose career had nosedived since leaving Universal in 1927. Exhibitors Film Corporation released the Acord series on the states' rights market in 1928–29. By 1931 Art Acord was dead, having met a mysterious end in Mexico after a brief jail sentence for bootlegging.

Robert J. Horner's films saw no improvement with the sound era. A

Horner film still had actors planted firmly in front of a stationary camera, and if lines were muffed or mauled there were no retakes. From 1930 to 1932 Horner made a half-dozen oaters with Jack Perrin for Cosmos/Associated Film Exchange as well as *Pueblo Terror* in 1931 with Buffalo Bill, Jr. In 1934 Horner allegedly used the name of Robert Hoyt to direct *Racketeer Round-Up*, and the same year he committed the indignity of making *Border Menace* and *Border Guns* with Bill Cody for Aywon. They are considered two of the worst "B" westerns ever made. Not much better was a third entry with Cody, *Western Racketeers* (1935).

During the silent period Horner had made a series of cheapjack gallopers headlining one Pawnee Bill, Jr., really Ted Wells. In 1935 Horner starred Wells in two atrocious features, *The Phantom Cowboy* and *Defying the Law*. While Bill Cody was able to land a series with Spectrum (q.v.) after working with Horner, Ted Wells had to call it quits as a movie star. The same fate met the lumbering Buffalo Bill, Jr., in 1935 after making *Trails of Adventure* and *Ranger of the Law (Whirlwind Rider)* for Horner under the American Picutres Corporation banner. The star, under his real name of Jay Wilsey, even got directorial credit for *Trails of Adventure*. Although it was probably Horner who directed, it makes no difference—the films were westerns at their lowest ebb and also marked the end of Robert J. Horner's tattered film career.

## The Apache Kid's Escape

1930, 46 minutes.

*P-D-SC:* Robert J. Horner. *PH:* Ben Baldridge. *ED:* William Austin. *SD:* Dwain Esper.

*Cast:* Jack Perrin (The Apache Kid/Jim), Josephine Hill (June Wilson), Buzz Barton (Tim Wells), Fred Church (Ted Conway), Virginia Ashcroft (Sally Wilson), Henry Rocquemore (King Conway), Bud Osborne (Buck Harris), Fred Burns (Bill Lang), Charles Lemoyne (Sheriff Ward), Starlight (Himself), Horace B. Carpenter.

When his old partner Buck Harris (Bud Osborne) commits a robbery, the Apache Kid (Jack Perrin) is blamed, although he is trying to go straight. The sheriff (Charles Lemoyne) tries to capture Harris, but he and the Kid escape. On a ranch near Mesa City the Kid, now called Jim, gets a job and becomes pals with Ted Conway (Fred Church), who loves June Wilson (Josephine Hill). Ted has been adopted by banker King Conway (Henry Rocquemore), who wants June for himself. Refusing to give up June, Ted masquerades as the Apache Kid, holding up a stage and taking the banker's money. Ted is arrested, however, and Jim vows to help him. Ted tells Jim where the money is hidden and Jim, as the Apache Kid, returns it to King Conway. Ted is then set free. On the run from a posse, the Kid meets Harris, and the two fight, whereupon Harris is killed in a fall from a cliff. The Kid exchanges clothes with the dead man, and when the posse finds Harris they think he is the Apache Kid. Jim then leaves the ranch, leaving Ted and June to find happiness.

Jack Perrin had starred in some low-budget westerns for Robert J. Horner in the 1920s before gaining greater popularity at Universal. Having

Buffalo Bill, Jr., and Jack Harvey in Robert J. Horner's production of *The Pueblo Terror* (Cosmos, 1931).

been in films since 1915, Perrin weathered the transition to sound films but found himself doing supporting roles as well as starring ones. From 1930 to 1932 he headlined a half-dozen oaters for Horner, and technically they were no better than the fare he had done for the producer a decade earlier. Fortunately, Perrin weathered these battered outings and was able to land various western series through 1936 until he settled permanently into character acting. For Horner, the Perrin westerns launched his sound career, but the movie retains some subtitles from the silent era and the soundtrack is poor. Overall the production is a tacky affair obviously made on a shoestring but not without interest thanks to its likable star.

It should be noted that stars Jack Perrin and Josephine Hill were married at the time *The Apache Kid's Escape* was made. Also worth noting is the fact that the star is not the chief romantic interest in the film; instead, second lead Fred Church, who starred for Robert J. Horner in westerns in the silent era, gets the girl. During the course of the film, the Apache Kid shows more interest in Sally Wilson (Virginia Aschcroft), the heroine's young teenage sister, than in the leading lady.

## Wild West Whoopee

Cosmos/Associated Film Exchange, March 8, 1931, 57 minutes.

*P-D-SC:* Robert J. Horner. *PH:* Jules Cronjager. *ED:* Arthur A. Brooks.

*Cast:* Jack Perrin, Josephine Hill, Fred Church, Horace B. Carpenter, George Chesebro, Ben Corbett, John Ince, Henry Rocquemore, Walter Patterson, Charles Austin, Starlight.

A badman has to fight a rodeo rider after he forces his attentions on a young woman.

## Pueblo Terror

Cosmos, April 12, 1931, 59 minutes.
*P:* Robert J. Horner. *D:* Alvin J. Neitz [Alan James]. *SC:* L.V. Jefferson. *PH:* William Thompson.
*Cast:* Buffalo Bill, Jr., Wanda Hawley, Jack Harvey, Yakima Canutt, Art Mix, Aline Goodwin, Jim Spencer, Horace B. Carpenter, Al Ferguson, Hank Bell, Robert Walker.

Returning home, a cowboy finds the area in turmoil and he is blamed for the murder of a cowpuncher.

## The Kid from Arizona

Cosmos, May 10, 1931, 55 minutes.
*P-D-ST:* Robert J. Horner. *SC:* Robert Walker. *PH:* Jules Cronjager.
*Cast:* Jack Perrin, Josephine Hill, Robert Walker, George Chesebro, Ben Corbett, Henry Rocquemore, Starlight.

A lawman is sent into the badlands to stop Indian raids.

## The Sheriff's Secret

Cosmos, June 14, 1931, 58 minutes.
*P:* Robert J. Horner. *D-SC:* Robert J. Hogan. *PH:* Jules Cronjager. *ED:* Henry Adams. *SD:* Ralph M. Like.
*Cast:* Jack Perrin, Dorothy Bauer, George Chesebro, Fred Hargreaves, Joe Marba, Jimmy Aubrey, Billy Franey, Monte Jones, Starlight.

A wanted outlaw adopts an orphan baby but has to remain on the run from the sheriff and his posse.

## Lariats and Sixshooters

Cosmos, October 25, 1931, 65 minutes.
*P:* Robert J. Horner. *D:* Alvin J. Neitz [Alan James]. *SC:* Carl Krusada. *PH:* Edward Kull.
*Cast:* Jack Perrin, Ann Lee, George Chesebro, Art Mix, Richard Cramer, Gloria Joy, Jimmy Aubrey, Lafe McKee, Olin Francis, Virginia Bell, Starlight.

A deputy sheriff is after smugglers who vow revenge when they are forced to flee without the jewels they wanted.

## The .45 Calibre Echo

Robert J. Horner, 1932, 60 minutes.
*P:* Robert J. Horner. *D:* Bruce Mitchell. *SC:* Carl Krusada. *PH:* Edward Kull. *ED:* William Austin.
*Cast:* Jack Perrin, Elinor Fair, George Chesebro, Jimmy Aubrey, Ben Corbett, Alex Francis, Richard Cramer, Ruth Renick, C.H. Bussey, Starlight.

Jack Perrin's last western for producer Robert J. Horner.

## Border Guns

Aywon, 1934, 55 minutes.
*P:* Nathan Hirsh. *D:* Jack Nelson. *SC:* Robert J. Horner. *PH:* Frank Bender. *ED:* William Austin.
*Cast:* Bill Cody, Janet Morgan [Blanche Mehaffey], Franklyn Farnum, William Desmond, George Chesebro, Jim Pierce, Wally Wales, Fred Church, Jimmy Aubrey, Oscar Gahan, Buck Morgan, Fred Parker.

A notorious gunman aids a cowboy in stopping outlaws from taking over range land.

Ted Wells in dual roles with Jimmy Aubrey and Doris Brook in *The Phantom Cowboy* (Aywon, 1935).

## Border Menace

Aywon, 1934, 55 minutes.
P: Nathan Hirsh. D: Jack Nelson. SC: Robert J. Horner. PH: Frank Bender. ED: James Aubrey. SD: Cliff Ruberg. Tech Adv: Ralph Cushman.
Cast: Bill Cody, Miriam Rice, George Chesebro, Jimmy Aubrey, Ben Corbett, Frank Clark, Jim Donnelly, Lafe McKee.

The Shadow, a secret service agent, is out to stop thieves from taking a rancher's rich oil lands.

## The Phantom Cowboy

Aywon, 1935, 56 minutes.
P-D: Robert J. Horner. SC: Carl Krusada. PH: Frank Bender. ED: Sam Hasbold. SD: Ralph M. Like.
Cast: Ted Wells (Bill Collins/Jim Russell), Doris Brook (Ruth Rogers), George Chesebro (Buck Huston),

Jimmy Aubrey (Ptomaine Pete), Lew Meehan (Dick), Allen Greer (Jack Rogers), Oscar Gahan, Milburn Morante, Herman Hack, Sherry Tansey (Henchmen), Richard Cramer (Hank).

A cape-wearing highwayman known as the Phantom Bandit holds up a stagecoach, and during the fracas the horses run away with Ruth Rogers (Doris Brook) still inside the coach. She is rescued by rodeo rider Bill Collins (Ted Wells), and she tells him that she and her brother Jack (Allen Greer) are going to a nearby town where she is to teach school. Later, Bill and his pal Ptomaine Pete (Jimmy Aubrey) go for a swim, and their clothes and horses are stolen by the Phantom. The duo walk to a nearby house where they find their belongings and discover that the Phantom is really prospector Jim Russell (Ted Wells), a

**Jeanne [Genee] Boutell and Buffalo Bill, Jr., in *Whirlwind Rider* (American, 1935), a Robert J. Horner film.**

look-alike for Bill. Russell hires Bill and Pete to find out who is trying to steal his claim, the reason he has been masquerading as the masked man. Later in town, Bill finds Ruth working at Buck Huston's (George Chesebro) saloon, where she is harassed by Huston's partner Hank (Richard Cramer). Buck and his gang plan to rob a nearby ranch with the aid of foreman Dick (Lew Meehan), and they plan to have Jack crack the safe. Buck lusts for Ruth and tells Hank to make her life miserable so she will marry him. When the Phantom empties the safe, Jack is blamed, and the gang attacks Jack in the saloon. Bill comes to his rescue and a shoot-out takes place with Huston and his gang quickly leaving town. Bill takes Ruth and Jack to the safety of the Russell cabin but the Phantom is shot by Huston. At the cabin, the injured Russell is tended by Pete as Bill, Ruth

and Jack arrive. Huston trails them to the cabin and gets the drop on the group but is shot and killed by Russell, who also dies. Bill gets the reward for the Phantom, and he and Ruth plan to wed.

Ted Wells had experienced a brief period of cowboy stardom at Universal in the late 1920s. With the coming of sound, however, Wells wisely retired from the screen, although some silents he did for Robert J. Horner in 1927 as Pawnee Bill, Jr., saw theatrical release in 1928–29. Along with *Defying the Law, The Phantom Cowboy* represents Wells' 1935 screen comeback. He proved a poor actor at best, demonstrating even less ability than Buffalo Bill, Jr. (Jay Wilsey). Admittedly, Wells was not helped by the plot of *The Phantom Cowboy*, which has him and pal Jimmy Aubrey running around in their underwear for nearly a whole reel.

Almost as mind-boggling is the casting of Wells in a dual role, since he is so totally inept at playing a single character, let alone two. Aubrey is bad, too, as a lame comedy sidekick with a particularly appalling drunk scene near the finale. Almost as bad as *Border Menace* (1934) with Bill Cody, this Robert J. Horner effort has little to recommend it.

## Western Racketeers

1935, 48 minutes.

*P:* Nathan Hirsh. *D:* Robert J. Horner. *SC:* James P. Hogan. *PH:* Brydon Baker & Frank Bender. *ED:* Henry Adams. *SD:* Clifford Ruberg. *Tech Dir:* Jules H. Bohnan.

*Cast:* Bill Cody (Bill Bowers), Edna Aslin (Molly Spellman), Wally Wales (Sheriff Rawlins), George Chesebro (Fargo Roberts), Richard Cramer (Coroner), Bud Osborne (Blackie), Frank Clark (Steve Harding), Robert Sands (Molly's Brother), Tom Dwaine (Harding's Brother), Ben Corbett (Jury Foreman), Billy Franey (Townsman), Gilbert [Pee Wee] Holmes (Breed).

Alamo Pass in Southern California near Perdue is used by cattlemen to take their herds to market, and Blackie (Bud Osborne) and his gang start charging a toll for each head of cattle. Steve Harding (Frank Clark) does not have the money to pay the toll so two gang members take him to town to get the money at the bank, but they shoot him when he tries to go to the sheriff (Wally Wales). Another rancher, Bill Bowers (Bill Cody), tries to investigate the killing, and he suspects the fatal shot came from Fargo Roberts' (George Chesebro) saloon. The local cattlemen demand an investigation of the killing and the toll charges as Molly Spellman (Edna Aslin), Bill's

neighbor and rival, decides to take her herd around the pass. Under orders from Fargo, who is the boss of the outlaws, Blackie kidnaps Molly during the drive. Bill is then convinced he will take his herd to market and asks the other cattlemen to aid him in a showdown with the outlaws. During the drive Blackie gets the drop on Bill, but after the two fight Bill forces a confession from the outlaw: Fargo is the brains behind the operation. The cattlemen open fire on the outlaws, but the sheriff arrives with his posse and the gang is captured. Molly escapes and rides to town, as does Bill who is after Fargo. Bill arrives first, has a showdown with Fargo, and the badman is killed. Bill and Molly then ride off together.

Bill Cody had done eight films for Monogram in 1931–32. They had not been well received, and in 1935 he did a trio of westerns for Robert J. Horner. In some circles they are regarded as the nadir of the "B" western in the sound era. Certainly *Border Menace* (1934) is considered one of the worst low-budget westerns ever made, and *Border Guns* (1934) is not much better, although it does benefit from Franklyn Farnum's performance as a good-badman. *Western Racketeers* is perhaps the best of the three, which is not saying much considering its convoluted plot, mediocre acting and mauled lines. Cody wears a fancy black outfit and oversized hat but makes little impression as a cowboy hero. Only villains George Chesebro and Bud Osborne give any life to the dull proceedings, the plotline unreeling at snail's pace. While the climactic gun battle is well staged, there is little else to recommend this arid galloper besides some impressive camera work by Brydon Baker. Unfortunately, most of the feature was staged and shot in a stationary manner by Frank Bender, Horner's usual cameraman.

## Defying the Law

American Pictures Corporation, 1935, 5 reels.

*P-D:* Robert J. Horner. *SC:* Carl Krusada. *PH:* Frank Bender. *ED:* William O'Hara. *Supv:* Captain V.E. Sutton-Mattocks.

*Cast:* Ted Wells, Edna Aslin, George Chesebro, William Desmond, Jimmy Aubrey, Richard Cramer, Bob McKenzie, Doris Brook, Allen Greer, Oscar Gahan, Herman Hack, Milburn Morante.

Two cowboys are befriended by a border patrol agent trying to solve a series of robberies.

## Ranger of the Law

American Pictures Corporation, 1935, 50 minutes.

*P:* Robert J. Horner. *D:* R.J. Renroh [Robert J. Horner]. *SC:* Royal Hampton. *PH:* Brydon Baker. *SD:* Herbert Ficke.

*Cast:* Buffalo Bill, Jr., Jeanne [Genee] Boutell, George Chesebro, Jack Long, Boris Bullock, Ben Corbett, Frank Clark, Duke R. Lee, Lake Reynolds, Tex Palmer, Herman Hack, Clyde McClary.

A rodeo rider is at odds with a crook who wants to steal a girl's ranch. Also called *Whirlwind Rider*.

## Trails of Adventure

American Pictures Corporation, 1935, 57 minutes.

*P:* Robert J. Horner. *D:* Jay Wilsey [Buffalo Bill, Jr.]. *SC:* Donald Kent.

*Cast:* Buffalo Bill, Jr., Edna Aslin, Allen Holbrook, Harry Carter, Raymond B. Wells, Belle D'Arcy, Shorty Hendricks.

A cowboy arrives in a small town where local outlaws are trying to ship out stolen ore.

# Ideal Pictures Corporation

Founded in 1920, Ideal Pictures Corporation was basically a non-theatrical enterprise that by the late 1940s was the country's largest distributor of 16mm motion pictures. The company remained in operation well into the 1970s as a non-theatrical distributor. In the mid–1930s, however, Ideal Pictures did distribute seven feature films to theatres along with several short subjects. Most of the features, however, were not produced by Ideal. They were typically either reissues or acquisitions from various independent producers. This company should not be confused with Ideal Studios, located in Hudson Heights, New Jersey, which was the production site of many low-budget independent productions in the 1930s.

Ideal Pictures got into the theatrical distribution business in 1933 with *Her Secret*, a drama with Sari Maritza, and the next year it distributed the jungle melodrama *Found Alive* with Barbara Bedford. That year the company also turned out a dozen one-reelers in its "Ideal Novelties" short-subject series and thirteen "Ideal Whatnots" one-reel shorts. The company also distributed the two-reelers *Hold That Wild Boar* and *Broadway Nights* and two three-reelers, *River of Death* and *Golden Ghost*. In 1935 the company handled *Manhattan Tower*, which had been made by Remington Pictures president A.E. Lefcourt at a cost of over $50,000. It was the only feature made by Remington, and following Lefcourt's death it was picked up for distribution by Ideal, its budget considerably higher than most features on the independent market. That year Ideal also handled a trio of reissues, *Mad Age*, *Divorce Racket* and *A Jungle Gigolo*, before leaving theatrical distribution with the British import *While London Sleeps* in 1936.

## Her Secret

December 19, 1933, 73 minutes.

*P-SC:* Helen Mitchell. *D:* Warren Millais. *PH:* Peverell Marley. *ED:* M.G. Cohn. *Mus:* James Erickson. *SD:* Corson Jowett. *Asst Dir:* Ray McDevitt.

*Cast:* Sari Maritza, Buster Collier, Alan Mowbray, Ivan Simpson, Monaei Lindley, Rex Armond, Jack De Wees, Barbara Luddy, Johnny Hymes, Lila MacIntire.

A reckless young man falls in love with a waitress who is later accused of contributing to the delinquency of local college students.

## Found Alive

April 11, 1934, 65 minutes.

*P-D:* Charles Hutchison. *SC:* Adrian Johnson. *ST:* Captain Jacob Conn. *PH:* William Thompson. *ED:* Rose Smith. *AD:* Paul Palmentola. *SD:* J.S. Westmoreland. *Asst Dir:* Melville DeLay.

*Cast:* Barbara Bedford (Edith Roberts), Robert Frazer (Harry Roberts), Maurice Murphy (Bobby Roberts), Master Harry Griffin (Little Bobby), Edwin Cross (Brooke), Ernie Adams (C.S. King), Snake King (Snake), Stella Zarco (Stella), Audrey Tallen (Audrey).

Edith Roberts (Barbara Bedford) and her son Bobby (Maurice Murphy) live in the jungles of the delta of the Rio Grande River with their former servant Brooke (Edwin Cross). Now a young man, Bobby is told by his mother how she abducted him from his father, Harry Roberts (Robert Frazer), when the man falsely accused her of adultery. She took the boy when the courts denied her custody and her husband denied her any visitation rights. With the aid of Brooke, they fled their California home and ventured into the Rio Grande jungles, where Edith lived in fear of being found by Robert, who had offered a large reward for the boy's return. Hunters come into the jungle area and capture Bobby's bear, and when he rescues it, the young man meets the outsiders. By accident, King (Ernie Adams), the leader of the expedition discovers Bobby's true identity and that there is a reward for his safe return. King then writes to Harry Roberts that he has found his wife and son. Meanwhile Bobby falls in love with a native girl and fights with one of her tribesmen for her but later learns she does not love him in return. Bro-

Advertisement for *Found Alive* (Ideal Pictures, 1934).

kenhearted, Bobby agrees to leave the jungle with his mother and Brooke, but a jungle cat attacks and kills Brooke. It, in turn, is killed by Bobby's bear. Harry Roberts arrives in the jungle and finds Bobby, asking for his forgiveness. He then tells Edith that he made a mistake and the two are reunited.

Subtitled "Or the Delta of the Rio Grande," *Found Alive* was produced as *Crawling Death*. It contains lots of animal footage, including a two-headed snake and the bear killing the big cat. There are also scenes of snake catching and the capture of an alligator. According to the film's prologue, the cast and crew braved "death and disease" to bring "graphic realism" to theatre viewers in its depiction of the humans and animals of the Rio Grande River delta. One scene, surprising for 1934, had a bathing sequence with young, naked native girls. Unfortunately, *Found Alive* is a threadbare jungle melodrama that stitches together documentary footage with backlot dramatics. Silent stars Barbara Bedford and Robert Frazer do what

they can with their limited roles while the rest of the cast is merely adequate.

Filmed at the Freeman Lang Studios in Los Angeles, *Found Alive* was copyrighted by Olympic Pictures Corporation with domestic release by Ideal Pictures. Overseas it was handled by Excelsior Picture Corporation. *Variety* found it a "better than average indie jungle picture" but noted the plot was "just a frame to hang some wild animal shots, of course, some of it pretty good and some obviously phoney."

Reissued in 1948 as *Ecstasy in the Wilderness*.

## The Divorce Racket

1935, 66 minutes.

*P:* E.H. Goldstein. *D:* Aubrey Scotto. *SC:* James W. Poling. *PH:* Frank Zucker. *ED:* Edna Hill.

*Cast:* James Rennie, Olive Borden, Judith Wood, Wilfred Jessop, Harry Tyler, Adrian Rosley, Charles Easton, Joseph Calleia, Walter Fenner, Harry Short.

A detective is assigned to investigate the murder of a lawyer and the chief suspect is his secretary, who the lawman loves. Originally released by Paradise Pictures in 1932.

## Mad Age

1935, 70 minutes.
*P:* Frederic Ullman, Jr. *SC-ED:* Gilbert Seldes. *Mus:* Dr. Hugo Reisenfeld.
*Cast:* Alois Havrilla (narrator).

Newsreel films are used to cover historic events in the United States from the end of World War I until 1933. Originally released in 1933 as *This Is America* by Beckman Film Corporation.

## Manhattan Tower

1935, 67 minutes.
*P:* A.E. Lefcourt. *D:* Frank R. Strayer. *SC:* Norman Houston. *ST:* David Hempstead. *PH:* Ira Morgan. *ED:* Harry Reynolds. *SD:* Earl Crain.
*Cast:* Mary Brian, Irene Rich, James Hall, Hale Hamilton, Noel Francis, Nydia Westman, Clay Clement, Billy Dooley, Jed Prouty, Wade Boteler.

The lives of tenants in an apartment building are intertwined with the activities of a dishonest investor. Originally released by Remington Pictures in 1932.

## While London Sleeps

July 18, 1936, 58 minutes.
*P:* Norman Loudon. *D:* Adrian Brunel. *SC:* Heinrich Fraenkel & A.R. Rawlinson. *ST:* Victor Varconi. *PH:* Guy Green. *ED:* Michael Hawkinson.
*Cast:* Victor Varconi, Joan Maude, D.A. Clarke-Smith, J. Hubert Leslie, Joan Matheson, J.A. O'Rourke, Shayle Gardner, Wilfred Noy.

Police investigate a series of train crashes, all caused by sabotage. Produced in England and released there by Reunion Films in 1934 as *Menace* but retitled *Sabotage*. The British version ran 70 minutes.

# Imperial Distribution Corporation

Imperial Distribution Corporation, with headquarters at 729 Seventh Avenue in New York City, was formed in 1931 by veteran producer William M. Pizor, who also majored in both the importation of foreign features and the exportation of Hollywood product. Born February 6, 1890, Pizor got started on his own with Pizor Productions in 1926 and stayed with that trademark until 1931 when he launched Imperial. Basically Imperial's release schedule comprised documentaries, cheap westerns, short subjects and melodramas, although by the time the company dissolved in the late 1930s Imperial was relying mostly on British imports and acquiring independent product. Unlike most Poverty Row operations, however, Imperial developed a number of short-subject series, making it the most prolific maker of shorts in the independent field.

William M. Pizor Productions was launched in 1926 with *Gasoline Cowboy*, starring Al Richmond, followed in 1927 with *Was He Guilty?*, a 1919 feature reissued to take advantage of the popularity of William Boyd, who had a supporting role in the movie; this time Boyd was billed as the star. The same thing happened to Boyd in the mid-and-late 1930s when many of his early talkies were reissued to take advantage of his newfound popularity as "Hopalong Cassidy." In 1928 Pizor produced *Flash of the Forest*, starring the popular canine Braveheart, and the same year he financed a group of cheap westerns directed by Robert J. Horner (q.v.), starring Al Hoxie and Montana Bill. Although they were all silents, the Montana Bill features continued to pop up in theatres well into 1930. The Hoxie productions were shot at the La Mesa Studios in San Diego, and some of the leading ladies were furnished by a local acting studio.

*Ubangi*, Pizor's initial sound release in the spring of 1931, was distributed under his own name, but with *Heroes All*, a documentary in the fall of that year, Imperial Distribution Corporation was born. The end of the year saw a spate of Imperial releases including two very cheap westerns made by the Tansey Brothers, *Two Gun Caballero*, with Robert Frazer, and *Riders of the Rio*, starring Lane Chandler. The latter was shot near Palm Springs, and Chandler later reported the producers never paid him the remainder of his salary. *Blonde Captive* (1931) was another in a series of import documentaries released by Imperial, and this Australian feature proved so popular it was still being exhibited well into the mid–1940s. In 1931 Imperial also began its series of short subjects, "Port o' Call," twenty-six one-reelers released through 1932. By 1932, in fact, Imperial was releasing more short subjects and had added six one-reelers in its "Novelties" series and sixteen one-reel "Musical Revue" entries. In 1933 Imperial added thirteen more one-reelers to its "Port O' Call" series as well as three two-reel "Novelties" and six more "Musical Revue" one-reelers. That year the company also acquired two William Berke Productions features, *Corruption* and *The Flaming Signal*, as well as another documentary, *Throne of the Gods*.

William M. Pizor reunited with Robert Emmett Tansey in 1934 for a series of seven featurette westerns starring Wally Wales. In later years the star claimed these were actually features chopped up into small releases but the plots tend to indicate they were made as separate units although the casts and production crews are similar. Sadly, they were a tattered lot with only Brydon Baker's photography and the presence of the late Fred Thompson's beautiful steed Silver King to give them any value. By 1934 Imperial was releasing mostly short subjects, and these included a wretched one-shot western called *Pals of the Prairie* with Buffalo Bill, Jr., two shorts starring Flash the Wonder Dog and David Sharpe (six two-reelers were promised in this series), two three-reel "Special Featurettes," six one-reel "Spring Silhouettes," thirteen one-reel "Imperial Novelties" and a dozen one-reel "World in Color" shorts.

In addition thirteen more one-reelers came out with "Port O'Call" and six more one-reel "Musical Revue." Apparently this large number of shorts was meant to carry over for some time since the company did not issue any new short subjects until 1937. In the interim Imperial released only a few feature films, cheap westerns like *Paradise Valley, Twisted Rails* and *Call of the Coyote* (all 1934) and diverse product like the Russian documentary *Soviet Russia Thru the Eyes of an American* (1935), *Manhattan Butterfly* (1935) and *Forgotten Women* (1936), the latter a rerelease of the 1931 Paramount offering *The Mad Parade.*

In 1935 Pizor became associated with producer-director Clifford Sanforth's Cameo Productions, resulting in Imperial releases like *Murder by Television* (1935), with Bela Lugosi in a non-vampiric, dual-character role, *High Hat* and *I Demand Payment* (both 1938). In 1937 Imperial began distributing British imports such as *Broken Blossoms* (not to be confused with D.W. Griffith's 1919 classic) and *She Shall Have Music.* It also came out with thirteen more one-reel "Port o' Call" shorts in addition to "Poetic Gems" and "Color Classics," both a series of thirteen one-reelers. That year the company also reissued the Wally Wales shorts. By 1938, however, Imperial was on unsteady legs, and it terminated its release schedule at the end of the year with the gangster melodrama *I Demand Payment* with Jack LaRue.

Perhaps the reason for Imperial's somewhat sudden demise was the loss of a lawsuit filed against Pizor by cowboy star Tim McCoy. After finishing a series of gallopers for Puritan (q.v.) in 1936, McCoy signed with Imperial for eight westerns calling for him to receive $4,000 per picture. The series never materialized, and McCoy sued Pizor for breach of contract, as he was off the screen until 1938 when he signed with Monogram. In November, 1939, Tim McCoy was awarded $37,000 in a judgment against Pizor and Imperial, the amount of his salary plus interest.

Although Imperial ceased to exist after the late 1930s, William M. Pizor remained in the motion picture industry. In the mid–1940s he was general sales manager in charge of foreign sales for Screen Guild, and later he was in charge of foreign distribution for Lippert Pictures Corporation.

## Ubangi

William M. Pizor, June 6, 1931, 59 minutes.

*D-PH:* Dr. Louis Neuman & Jacques Maus.

An account of Dr. Louis Neuman's expedition into the Belgian Congo, including cannibals and big game hunting.

## Heroes All

November 11, 1931, 73 minutes.

*D-SC:* Anthony Young. *ED:* Nathan Cy Braunstein. *SD:* George L. Crapp. *Mus:* Emile Velazco.

*Cast:* Emil Gauvreau, General John J. Bradley.

Government newsreels and new footage are combined to tell the story of soldiers in the First World War.

## Two Gun Caballero

December 15, 1931, 58 minutes.
*P:* William M. Pizor. *D-SC:* Jack Nelson. *ST:* B. Wayne Lamont. *PH:* Bert Baldridge.
*Cast:* Robert Frazer, Consuelo Dawn, Bobby Nelson, Carmen La-Roux, Al Ferguson, Pat Harmon, Diane Esmonds.

A cowboy falsely accused of murder takes on the guise of a Mexican friend in order to prove his innocence.

## Secret Menace

December 28, 1931, 59 minutes.
*P:* William M. Pizor. *D-ST:* Richard Kahn. *SC:* B. Wayne Lamont. *PH:* Bert Baldridge. *ED:* Arthur Brooks. *SD:* B.J. Kroger.
*Cast:* Glenn Tryon, Virginia Browne Faire, Arthur Stone, Edward Cecil, John Elliott, Margaret Mann, Joe Savage, Pat Harmon, Pat Cowles, Chuck Baldra.

Crooks want a gold mine located on a dude ranch but the owner refuses to sell.

## Blonde Captive

December 30, 1931, 59 minutes.
*D:* Dr. Paul Withington, Clinton Childs, Ralph P. King & Linus J. Wilson. *Dial-ED:* Lowell Thomas. *PH:* Thornton P. Dewhurst & George L. Crapp. *SD:* Nathan C. Braunstein.
*Cast:* Lowell Thomas (Narrator).

An expedition goes into the Australian outback in search of a lost white woman.

## Riders of the Rio

Imperial/Round-Up, December 31, 1931
*P:* John & Robert Emmett Tansey. *D-SC:* Robert Emmett Tansey. *PH:* Amos Stillman.

*Cast:* Lane Chandler, Karla Cowan, Sheldon Lewis, Fred Parker, Bob Card, Sherry Tansey, Ben Corbett, Jack Kirk, Bud Duncan, Horace B. Carpenter, Lorena Carr, Mary Thompson, Amelio Mio.

Two young rival ranchers are also at odds over the affections of a pretty senorita.

## Virgins of Bali

September, 1932, 46 minutes.
*D-Narr:* Deane H. Dickson. *PH:* Lyman J. Wiggin. *ED:* Nathan Cy Braunstein. *SD:* S. Crawford Ravey.
*Cast:* Ni Wayan Tagai, Ni Wayan Ugembon, T. Kaler, I. Maria.

On the island of Bali two young girls are shown in their daily lives leading up to a wedding ceremony.

## The Galloping Kid

1932, 5 reels.
*P:* William M. Pizor. *D-SC:* Robert Emmett [Tansey].
*Cast:* Al Lane, Karla Cowan, Little Buck Dale, Fred Parker, Horace B. Carpenter, C.E. Anderson, Larry Warner, George Bates.

A stranger aids a young woman and her little brother, whose ranch is being raided by outlaws seeking a mysterious map.

## The Voice of Syama

1933, 51 minutes.
*SC:* Ernest Frederick, Grant Garrett & Chester.

A drama detailing an expedition into the jungles of Siam.

## The Flaming Signal

May 25, 1933, 61 minutes.
*P:* William Berke. *D:* George Jeske & C. Edward Roberts. *SC:* C.

Edward Roberts. *ST:* William G. Steuer. *PH:* Irving Akers. *ED:* Laurence Creutz. *Mus:* Lee Zahler. *SD:* RCA Photophone.

*Cast:* Flash (Himself), John David Horsley (Jim Robbins), Marceline Day (Sally James), Noah Beery (Otto Von Krantz), Carmelita Geraghty (Molly), Henry B. Walthall (Rev. James), Mischa Auer (Manu), Francisco Alonso (Taku), Jan'ne Olmer (Rari), Anya Gamero (Native Girl).

Aviator Jim Robbins (John David Horsley) must leave his dog Flash (Himself) behind as he plans to fly from the West Coast to Hawaii, but the canine becomes a stowaway on the plane. During a bad storm Jim is feared lost. After thirty hours in the air, he is forced to crash land near an island, but first he sees that Flash gets to safety in a parachute. On the island, Jim meets beautiful Sally James (Marceline Day) and finds out she is the daughter of a missionary (Henry B. Walthall). Also on Tabu Island are brutal, drunken trader Otto Von Krantz (Noah Beery) and his mistress, bar-owner Molly (Carmelita Geraghty). Von Krantz cheats native Taku (Francisco Alonso) out of a huge pearl and then gets him drunk so he will spend all of his money. Rev. James gets Jim a room at the trading post, but Von Krantz takes a dislike to Flash. He tries to whip him, but the dog attacks him. Jim saves Von Krantz, who gets drunk and rapes Rari (Jan'ne Olmer), Taku's fiancée. When the natives come to tell Von Krantz to leave the island he shoots high priest Manu (Mischa Auer). The natives take his body to a ceremonial cave in an attempt to resurrect the high priest while Jim, Sally, Rev. James, Molly and Von Krantz barricade themselves in the trading post. Jim sends Flash with a torch to light a warning signal for passing craft as Manu is resurrected. When the natives come to the trading post, Rev. James goes out to talk to them, and Von Krantz shoots and finally kills Manu. In retaliation, the natives murder the missionary. Jim and Sally escape to the beach as Von Krantz turns on Molly and is killed in a fight with Flash. The dog then follows his master, saving Jim and Sally from attack by a native. A sea plane lands near the island and Jim, Sally and Flash make it to safety.

Once *The Flaming Signal* gets away from the flight of *The Spirit of '76* aircraft and to Tabu Island, the plot moves at a good clip. Except for brief fillers of natives hunting oysters and extracting pearls and a few scenes of a shark and an octopus, the movie is an action-filled drama with an appealing cast. While John David Horsley is a bit wooden as the hero, comely Marceline Day is just right as the innocent heroine, despite a couple of brief, darkly lit nude scenes early in the proceedings. Noah Berry has a good time as the vicious, drunken Von Krantz, while Henry B. Walthall and Carmelita Geraghty are a bit more restrained as the missionary and hooker. Mischa Auer is believable as the native high priest and there are some eerie scenes in a cave as the natives try to resurrect him after he is first shot by Von Krantz. Top billing goes to the German shepherd, Flash, who handles the canine heroics quite well. Overall, *The Flaming Signal* is a solid little Poverty Row feature and certainly one of Imperial's best releases. It also contains a most amusing scene near the beginning when the aviator gives a pretty French girl his autograph by signing her leg. How times have changed!

## Corruption

June 21, 1933, 68 minutes.

*P:* William Berke. *D-ST:* C. Edward Roberts. *SC:* C. Edward Roberts & Charles Berner. *PH:* Robert Cline. *ED:* H.W. deBouille & Finn Ulback. *SD:* W.C. Smith.

*Cast:* Evelyn Knapp, Preston Foster, Charles Delaney, Natalie Moorhead, Tully Marshall, Warner Richmond, Lane Chandler, Huntley Gordon, Mischa Auer, Jason Robards, Gwen Lee, Sidney Bracy, Kit Guard, Fred Kohler, Jr., Nick Thompson.

After being elected mayor a young lawyer vows to clean up city hall but must fight the political machine that elected him.

## Throne of the Gods

December 22, 1933, 55 minutes.

*PH:* Chares Du Vanerel. *ED:* Nathan Cy Braunstein.

*Cast:* Lowell Thomas (narrator).

An international expedition headed by Professor Dybrenfurth of Switzerland goes into Central Asia's Himalayan Mountains. Also released in a 39-minute version.

## Call of the Coyote

1934, 50 minutes.

*P:* William M. Pizor. *D:* Patrick [Pat] Carlyle. *PH:* Irving Akers. *ED:* Marshall B. Pollock. *SD:* R.E. Carpenter.

*Cast:* Ken Thomson, Sally Dolling, Merrill McCormick, Patrick Carlyle, Bart Carre, Wallace Shepherd, Jack Pollard, Baby Marie Bracco, Howard Fossett, Morgan Galloway.

The leader of a roving gang comes between two crooks who are after a gold mine.

## Death Fangs

January, 1934, 14 minutes.

*P:* William Berke.

*Cast:* Flash, David Sharpe.

The first of two short subjects starring Flash, a dog.

## Paradise Valley

February, 1934, 51 minutes.

*P-D:* James P. Hogan. *AP:* Joe Wilson. *SC:* Ira Anson, Francis Wheeler & George Dunham. *PH:* Brydon Baker. *ED:* Nathan Cy Braunstein & Henry Adams. *AD:* Walter Cameron & Clyde McClavy. *SD:* Herb Eicke & Vic Fishe. *Mus:* Harry Lygum & Beth Whitney.

*Cast:* Sam Pierce, Jean Chatbourne, Wheeler Oakman, Arthur Loft, Jimmy Aubrey, Si Jenks, Walter Brennan, The Beverly Hillbillies, Zandra the Dog, Donny Baker.

A radio singer tries to quit drinking by going west where he befriends a dog and helps a young woman and her younger brother who are involved in a dispute between sheep raisers and cattlemen.

## Pals of the Prairie

April, 1934, 28 minutes.

*P-D:* Craig Hutchinson. *SC:* Perry Murdock. *PH:* John Badaraco. *ED:* Charles Henkle. *Asst Dir:* Gilbert Hodges.

*Cast:* Buffalo Bill, Jr. (Bob Bently), Buck Owens (Buck), Benny Corbett (Bill), Victoria Vinton (Joan Carter), Charles K. French (Sheriff), Pal (Horse), James Sheridan [Sherry Tansey] (Foreman).

Two broke cowboys, Buck (Buck Owens) and Bill (Benny Corbett), are run out of town by the sheriff (Charles K. French), so they try to wangle food and a job at a local ranch run by pretty

Joan Carter (Victoria Vinton). The foreman (Sherry Tansey) lets Buck do some trick riding, and when he is injured, Joan comes to his aid. Trusting Buck, the young woman asks him to transport needed money from the bank. Her fiancé Bob Bently (Buffalo Bill, Jr.) does not like Buck, and when he gets wind of the situation, he has his men waylay Buck and Bill, and he takes the money. The sheriff talks Joan into marrying Bob, who Bill realizes is actually a notorious wanted criminal. Pal, the horse belonging to Buck and Bill, manages to untie the duo, and they head back to the ranch where the wedding ceremony is about to take place. Using a radio hookup they interrupt the wedding and alert those present to the fact that Bently is a wanted outlaw. When Bob tries to escape, Buck and Bill capture him and turn him over to the sheriff, who retrieves Joan's money. The girl rewards the two men financially, and Buck and Bill ride off to another adventure.

It would be hard to imagine a worse featurette than *Pals of the Prairie*. Badly scripted, filmed and acted, the movie looks more like a rural high school play than a big-screen production. The budget was apparently so impoverished that the hero and his pal are forced to ride the same horse, and many of the interior scenes look stagebound. Although Buffalo Bill, Jr., is given star billing above the title he actually turns out to be the villain of the piece, a dastardly soul wanted for robbery, fraud, bigamy and murder. He drives a big automobile and wants to marry the heroine, a looker whose acting ability is on par with Bill's, both having trouble delivering even the most simple lines. The real hero is a shrimp of a guy named Buck Owens (not the later country singer) whose

principal talent seems to be trick riding. Benny Corbett is the hero's pal, giving his usual mind-boggling attempt at a screen presence. At the finale when the villain tries to escape, the two heroes simply jump on him and hold him down until the aged sheriff (Charles K. French) gets him in handcuffs. Then the heroine hands Owens a wad of money for saving her from the badman, and the two pals ride off together into the sunset on the same horse. (During the course of *Pals of the Prairie* the only horse seen is Pal but in the brief sequence when Buck and Bill ride to the heroine's rescue they are on separate horses. Where did Bill's horse come from? Just another incongruity in this grade-Z production.) While Imperial produced seven featurettes starring Wally Wales in 1934 they made only this solo effort with Buffalo Bill, Jr., and it is easy to see why.

## Arizona Cyclone

May, 1934, 19 minutes.

*P:* William M. Pizor. *D:* Robert Emmett [Tansey]. *SC:* Al Lane. *PH:* Brydon Baker. *ED:* Arthur Cohen.

*Cast:* Wally Wales, Silver King, Karla Cowan, Franklyn Farnum, Jim Sheridan [Sherry Tansey], Fred Parker, Jack Kirk, Barney Beasley, Herman Hack, Bud Pope.

A cowboy tries to help a banker and his daughter oppose outlaws.

## Twisted Rails

May, 1934, 51 minutes.

*P:* Peter White. *D:* Al Herman. *SC:* L.V. Jefferson & James R. Gilbert. *PH:* Ernest Miller. *SD:* Earl Crain.

*Cast:* Jack Donovan, Alice Dahl, Donald Keith, Victor Potel, Tom London, Philo McCullough, Pat Harmon, Henry Rocquemore, Buddy Shaw,

Donald Mack, Annabelle Driver, Laurence Underwood, Bill Patton.

When a railroad man is shot as he is about to reveal the identity of a wrecker, a passenger volunteers to find the killer.

## Sundown Trail

June, 1934, 18 minutes.

*P:* William M. Pizor. *D-ST:* Robert Emmett [Tansey]. *ST:* Al Lane. *PH:* Brydon Baker. *ED:* Arthur Cohen.

*Cast:* Wally Wales, Silver King, Fay McKenzie, Fred Parker, Jim Sheridan [Sherry Tansey], Herman Hack, Ace Cain, Jack Kirk, Barney Beasley.

The son of a cattleman stops his men from running off a sheep herd owned by a pretty young woman.

## Carrying the Mail

July, 1934, 27 minutes.

*P:* William M. Pizor. *D:* Robert Emmett (Tansey). *SC:* Robert Emmett [Tansey] & Al Lane. *PH:* Brydon Baker. *ED:* Arthur Cohen. *SD:* Theron Kellem.

*Cast:* Wally Wales (Wally Reed), Silver King (Horse), Peggy Djarling (Pat West), Fred Parker (Mr. West), Franklyn Farnum (The Boss), Yakima Canutt (Ryan), Jim Sheridan [Sherry Tansey] (Drunk Passenger), Al Hoxie (Charlie), Francis Walker (Sheriff).

After running the stage line and carrying the mail for thirty years, Mr. West (Fred Parker) is about to lose his contract because he has been underbid. The deal was carried out by a nefarious local businessman (Franklyn Farnum) and his henchman Ryan (Yakima Canutt). The two plan to hijack West's motorstage (actually an old car) and steal the mail from the driver (Al Hoxie). Also traveling on the stage are West's daughter Pat (Peggy Djarling), who is going back to college, a cowboy named Wally Reed (Wally Wales) and a drunk (Jim Sheridan). The outlaws stop the motorstage but Wally's horse Silver (Silver King) has followed, and Wally takes the mail and gallops away. Pat, the driver, and the drunk are taken to a nearby shack by Ryan and the gang, where Ryan tries to force his attentions on the girl. Meanwhile, Wally has left the mail at a way station and has sent for the law. He goes to the shack to rescue Pat and a fight ensues. The sheriff (Francis Walker) arrives with his men, and the outlaws are arrested. Wally then tells Pat and her father that he is an undercover agent for the government who has come to investigate the low bid on the mail contract. Since the culprits have been arrested, Mr. West retains his mail contract, and later Wally and Pat are married.

Imperial had announced that Wally Wales would star in eight featurettes in 1934, seven of which were produced. As one of these seven, *Carrying the Mail* was plagued by poor sound and deficient production values; furthermore the featurette tried to pack too much action into less than a half hour, resulting in a tepid attempt at a western. Although *Carrying the Mail* has an interesting cast, it can do little to enliven the affair, which is highly predictable and boring. Fred Thompson's horse Silver King, who gets second billing, highlights an otherwise slow-moving affair in which many of the lines appear to be ad-libbed. There is also some low comedy filler about a drunk throwing explosives to scare the villains, and at the finale star Wally Wales jumps through the roof of a shack in order to save the heroine from villain Yakima Canutt. There are a couple of fight sequences, but they are amateurish indeed. Evidently, little care was taken with these Wally Wales featurettes as they were considered no more than fillers, probably rented in tandem with a feature to small-town theatres. Wally Wales once claimed the movies were made as features and then chopped up into smaller units, but no evidence suggests that this was the case.

## Wild Waters

July, 1934, 16 minutes.

*P:* William Berke. *Mus:* Lee Zahler.

*Cast:* Flash, David Sharpe.

A young man is falsely accused of sabotaging a dam building project.

## The Desert Man

August, 1934, 19 minutes.

*P:* William M. Pizor. *D:* Robert Emmett [Tansey]. *SC:* Al Lane. *PH:* Brydon Baker. *ED:* Arthur Cohen.

*Cast:* Wally Wales, Silver King, Peggy Djarling, Franklyn Farnum, Yakima Canutt, Al Hoxie, Jim Sheridan [Sherry Tansey], Barney Beasley, Tex Miller.

A cowboy aids a young lady whose ranch is coveted by crooks.

## Pals of the West

September, 1934, 27 minutes.

*P:* William M. Pizor. *D-SC:* Robert Emmett [Tansey]. *ST:* Al Lane. *PH:* Brydon Baker. *ED:* Arthur Cohen.

*Cast:* Wally Wales, Silver King, Franklyn Farnum, Yakima Canutt, Al Hoxie, Dorothy Crittin, Jim Sheridan [Sherry Tansey], Francis Walker, Fred Parker, Barney Beasley.

Two soldiers are assigned to bring in a notorious outlaw gang.

## The Woman Who Dared

September 6, 1934, 60 minutes.

*P:* William M. Pizor. *D:* Millard Webb. *SC:* Curtis Kenyon. *ST:* C. Edward Roberts, King Guidice & Robert Webb. *PH:* Robert Cline. *Mus:* Lee Zahler. *SD:* H. Gordon.

*Cast:* Claudia Dell, Monroe Owsley, Lola Lane, Douglas Fowley, Robert Elliott, Matty Fain, Bryant Washburn, Eddie Kane, Esther Muir, Matthew Betz, Paul Fix, Sidney Bracy, Joseph Girard.

After she inherits a textile plant, a young woman refuses to pay protection money and does battle with racketeers who have infiltrated the business.

## The Lone Rider

October, 1934, 27 minutes.

*P:* William M. Pizor. *D-SC:* Robert Emmett [Tansey]. *ST:* Al Lane. *PH:* Brydon Baker. *ED:* Arthur Cohen.

*Cast:* Wally Wales, Silver King, Merla Bratton, Franklyn Farnum, Fred Parker, Jim Sheridan [Sherry Tansey], Barney Beasley.

A cowboy comes to the aid of a man and his daughter whose mine is wanted by outlaws.

## West of the Law

November, 1934, 20 minutes.

*P:* William M. Pizor. *D-SC:* Robert Emmett [Tansey]. *ST:* Al Lane. *PH:* Brydon Baker. *ED:* Arthur Cohen.

*Cast:* Wally Wales, Silver King, Merla Bratton, Franklyn Farnum, Fred Parker, Jim Sheridan [Sherry Tansey], Barney Beasley.

When gangsters use a ranch as their hideout, the foreman sets out to corral them.

# Manhattan Butterfly

Imperial/Cameo; August 14, 1935, 73 minutes.

*P:* Clifford Sanforth. *D:* Lewis D. Collins. *SC:* F. McGrew Willis & Joseph O'Donnell, from the novel *Broadway Virgin* by Lois Bull. *PH:* James Brown, Jr. *Mus:* Ray Golden.

*Cast:* Dorothy Granger, William Bakewell, Betty Compson, Kenneth Thomson, Dorothy Burgess, Carmelita Geraghty, George Meeker, Matty Fain, Harry Holman, Alphonse Martel, Edward Keane, William Arnold, Jack Trent.

A nightclub singer is accused of stealing a rich patron's money after she thwarts his romantic advances.

# Soviet Russia Thru the Eyes of an American

September 30, 1935, 73 minutes.

*P:* Charles E. Stuart. *PH:* M. Gousser & M. Astifier. *ED:* Nathan Cy Braunstein. *Mus:* Constantine Krummel. *SD:* Harry Belock.

*Cast:* Norman Brokenshire (narrator).

A travelogue of the Soviet Union by American engineer Charles E. Stuart showing the political, cultural and everyday life of the country.

# Murder by Television

Imperial/Cameo, October, 1935, 55 minutes.

*EP-D:* Clifford Sanforth. *AP-Tech Supv:* Edward M. Spitz. *SC:* Joseph O'Donnell. *ST:* Joseph O'Donnell, Charles Henncke & Carl Coolidge. *PH:* James S. Brown, Jr. & Arthur Reed. *ED:* Leslie Wilder. *AD:* Louis Rachmil. *Mus:* Oliver Wallace. *SP Eff:* Milton K. Stern. *Prod Mgr:* Melville DeLay.

*Cast:* Bela Lugosi (Arthur Perry/Edwin Perry), June Collyer (June Houghland), Huntley Gordon (Dr. H.M. Scofield), George Meeker (Richard Grayson), Henry Mowbray (Police Chief Nelson), Charles Hill Mailes (Professor James Houghland), Claire McDowell (Mrs. Houghland), Hattie McDaniel (Isabella), Allan Jung (Al Ling), Charles K. French (John M. Jordan), Henry Hall (Hammond), Larry Francis (Reporter), William [Billy] Sullivan (Reardon), Dick Rush (Policeman), William Tooker (Mendoza).

Rival business executives Hammond (Henry Hall) and John Jordan (Charles K. French) both want to obtain Professor Houghland's (Charles Hill Mailes) plans for his new television device. Hammond instructs partner Richard Grayson (George Meeker), who is engaged to Houghland's daughter June (June Collyer), to use any method possible to get the plans. Jordan, on the other hand, offers Arthur Perry (Bela Lugosi) one hundred thousand dollars for them, since Perry has been working as the professor's assistant. When he finds out about the invention, Perry's brother Edwin (Bela Lugosi) masquerades as Perry and accepts the offer from Jordan. Both Edwin and Grayson are at Houghland's home that night to witness a demonstration of the device, and the professor is warned not to proceed with the experiment. During the demonstration Houghland is murdered, and Chief of Police Nelson (Henry Mowbray) investigates. Suspects include Perry, Grayson and Dr. Scofield (Huntley Gordon), a family friend, all of whom were out of the room without alibis at the time of the killing. It is also learned that the plans for the television have been stolen as has an

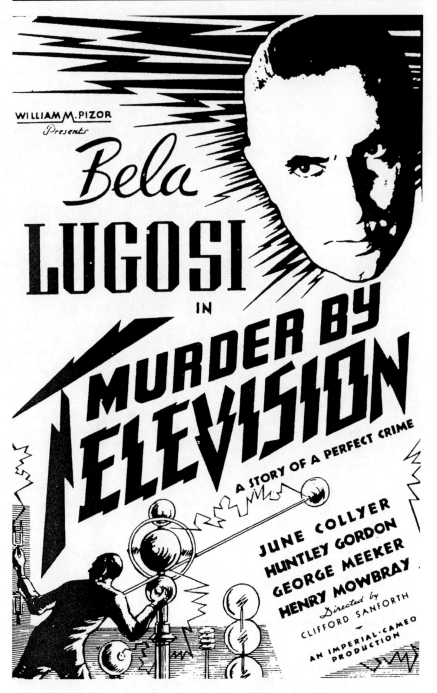

Poster for *Murder by Television* (Imperial/Cameo, 1935).

important tube used in the device. Jordan arrives and tells Nelson about his deal with Perry, who is found murdered, and servant Ahling (Allan Jung) is blamed since his knife was the murder weapon. The crimes, however, are solved by the arrival of secret agent Arthur Perry (Bela Lugosi), who not only reveals that his twin brother was masquerading in his place but also the identify of the murderer.

In their study of Hollywood Poverty Row horror films of the 1930s, George E. Turner and Michael H. Price in *Forgotten Horrors* (1979) complained, "We are hard-put to imagine a film of less merit than *Murder by Television*." A contemporary reviewer in the British *Monthly Film Bulletin* said, "The actors are stiff and appear to be ill at ease with their parts..." but added, "Nevertheless, interest is well maintained...." The latter point is well taken in that *Murder by Television*, while somewhat slow in parts, is overall a fairly interesting murder mystery whose polished look belies its Poverty Row origins. Made as *The Houghland Murder Case* it was filmed at the old Tiffany Studios on Sunset Boulevard, by then called the Talisman Studios. Since television was in its infancy when the movie was made, it contained some sequences showing how the device worked, including a young lady singing "I Had the Right Idea" and sequences broadcast from around the world. For the most part the camerawork and editing is above par for Poverty Row, and the acting is more than passable. It is interesting to see Bela Lugosi in dual roles, and amusement comes from Hattie McDaniel's cook and Allan Jung's Chinese houseboy, the latter spouting both Confucius and Charlie Chan. Besides the T.V. gimmick, some science fiction is thrown in at the finale when Lugosi reveals the murder was committed by an "innerstellar frequency—the death ray."

## The Broken Coin

1936, 50 minutes.
*P:* Gene Laymon. *D:* Al Herman. *SC:* James R. Gilbert, Ellen Hansen & Victor Potel. *PH:* Ernest Miller. *ED:* Dick Fantl. *SD:* Buddy Meyers.
*Cast:* Earle Douglas, Ruth Hiatt, William Desmond, Franklyn Farnum, Donald Keith, Victor Potel, Philo McCullough, Horace B. Carpenter, Henry Roquemore.

A police chief and two protection agency heads try to find out who is behind shipment hijackings.

## Forgotten Women

May 13, 1936, 62 minutes.
*P:* Herman Gumbin. *D:* William Beaudine. *SC:* Gertrude Orr, Doris Malloy, Harry McCarthy & Frank R. Conklin, from the story "Women Like Men" by Gertrude Orr & Doris Malloy. *PH:* Charles Van Enger, Ernest Miller & Clem Kerschner. *ED:* Richard Cahoon. *SD:* William R. Fox. *Supv:* M.H. Hoffman.
*Cast:* Evelyn Brent, Irene Rich, Lilyan Tashman, Marceline Day, Louise Fazenda, Fritzi Ridgeway, June Clyde, Elizabeth Keating, Helen Keating.

The story of eight women who served their country during World War I. Originally released by Paramount in 1931 as *The Mad Parade*.

## Rich Relations

Imperial/Cameo, 1937, 65 minutes.
*P-D:* Clifford Sanforth. *AP:* Edward M. Spitz. *SC:* Joseph O'Donnell. *PH:* James S. Brown, Jr. *ED:* Henry Spitz. *SD:* Hans Weeren. *Prod*

*Mgr:* Melville DeLay. *Tech Supv:* Louis Rachmil.

*Cast:* Ralph Forbes, Frances Grant, Barry Norton, Muriel Evans, Franklyn Pangborn, Wesley Barry, Jeanie Roberts, Crauford Kent, Ethel Clayton, Donald Kirke, Marry Carr, Ed Lawrence, Irving White, Gertrude Astor, Rosemary Theby, Mary MacLaren, Harry Myers.

A secretary is romanced by a lothario although she is really loved by her boss.

## Broken Blossoms

January 15, 1937, 78 minutes.

*P:* Julius Hagen. *D:*Hans [John] Brahm. *SC:* Emlyn Williams, from the story "The Chink and the Child" by Thomas Burke and the screenplay by D.W. Griffith. *PH:* Curt Courant. *ED:* Ralph Kemplen.

*Cast:* Dolly Haas, Emlyn Williams, Arthur Margetson, Ernest Sefton, C.V. France, Ernest Jay, Bertha Belmore, Gibb McLaughlin, Donald Calthrop, Kathleen Harrison, Kenneth Villiers, Jerry Vernon, Basil Radford, Edith Sharpe.

In London's Limehouse a young girl is given shelter by a Chinaman after she is beaten by her brutal boxer father. Made in England and released there in 1936 by Twickenham.

## She Shall Have Music

November 29, 1937, 91 minutes.

*P:* Julius Hagen. *D:* Leslie H. Hiscott. *SC:* Arthur Macrae & H. Fowler Mear. *ST:* Paul England & C. Denier Warren.

*Cast:* Jack Hylton, June Clyde, Marjorie Brooks, Gwen Farrar, Bryan Lawrence, Claude Dampier, Edmond Breon, Felix Aylmer, Ernest Sefton, Freddie Schweitzer, Leslie Carew,

Sonny Farrar, Alec Templeton, Diana Ward, Billie Carlisle, Mathea Merryfield, Madga Neeld, Carmona, Baby Terry, Derek Turner, The Two MacKays, Terry's Juveniles, Dalmora Cancan Dancers, Leon Woizikowski Ballet, Jack Hylton's Orchestra.

The owner of a cruise ship hires Jack Hylton and his orchestra to broadcast during a voyage. Produced in England by Twickenham and released there in December, 1935.

## Dynamite Delaney

January 27, 1938, 77 minutes.

*D:* Joseph Rothman. *SC:* Charles Beahan & Joseph Rothman. *PH:* William J. Miller.

*Cast:* Weldon Heyburn, Eve Farrell, Donald Dillaway, Walter Gilbert, Jane Steele, Jack Squires, Harlan Briggs, Clyde Franklin, Millard Mitchell, Jack Sheehan, Frank Otto, Frank McNellie, Richard Albert.

After being thrown off the force, a highway patrol officer redeems himself by capturing kidnappers.

## High Hat

Imperial/Cameo, March 16, 1938, 90 minutes.

*P-D:* Clifford Sanforth. *SC:* Sherman L. Lowe, from the novel *High Hat* by Alma S. Scarberry. *PH:* Jack Greenhalgh. *ED:* Charles Abbott. *Songs:* Frank Luther. *Prod Mgr:* Henry Spitz.

*Cast:* Frank Luther, Dorothy Dare, Lona Andre, Franklin Pangborn, Gavin Gordon, Esther Muir, Robert Warwick, Clarence Muse, Ferdinand Munier, Sonny & Buddy Edwards, The Downey Sisters, Don Raymond, Kermit Holven, Ted Dawson and His Orchestra, Harry Harvey, Bruce Mitchell.

A noted opera singer nearly loses

her fame before becoming even more popular doing current songs on radio.

## I Demand Payment

December 13, 1938, 55 minutes.
*P-D:* Clifford Sanforth. *AP:* Henry Spitz. *SC:* Sherman L. Lowe, from the novel *Second Choice* by Rob Eden. *PH:* Robert Doran. *ED:* Douglas Biggs.

*Cast:* Jack LaRue, Betty Burgess, Matty Kemp, Guinn Williams, Lloyd Hughes, Sheila Terry, Bryant Washburn, Donald Kirke, Harry Holman, Edward Keane, Norma Taylor.

An innocent young woman finds herself involved with three hoodlums in a loan shark racket.

# Jack Irwin Productions

One of the most obscure moviemakers of the early sound era was Jack Irwin, who wrote, produced and directed several feature films for the states' rights market, including the never-released *Gun Cargo*. Irwin also made a trio of westerns with Buddy Roosevelt plus another oater with Tom Santschi before dropping out of the movie scene. Little is known of Irwin's films although two of them were released by established firms: *Lightnin' Smith's Return* by Syndicate and *The White Renegade* by Artclass, both in 1931. It is not known if Jack Irwin is the same person as actor Jack Irwin, who made a few films in the mid–1930s, or actor John Irwin who worked in features throughout that decade. *Gun Cargo* features actor James Irwin, who may or may not be the man who made the film.

Buddy Roosevelt (real name: Kent Sanderson) had been a Poverty Row cowboy star in the silent era, and like many of his cohorts he found the going rough with the coming of sound. Roosevelt, however, had a pleasing voice and acted well, but he never seemed to get the breaks. An injury cost him the lead as the Cisco Kid in *In Old Arizona* (1929), the part going to Warner Baxter, who won an Academy Award. In 1933 he was about to be signed to a series of westerns for Monogram release when his wife threw a temper tantrum and halted the deal, the contract going to John Wayne. Sandwiched between these episodes was a trio of westerns for Jack Irwin Productions; probably more were planned but only three were filmed. As noted *Lightnin' Smith's Return* (1931) was issued by Syndicate (q.v.), while *The Riding Kid* and *Valley of Bad Men* (both 1931) got few bookings on the states' rights market. *Lightnin' Smith's Return* was remade unofficially in 1934 by Reliable (q.v.) as *Mystery Ranch*, starring Tom Tyler. *The White Renegade* (1931) starred silent screen actor Tom Santschi, who had gained fame in 1914 for his famous brawl with William Farnum in *The Spoilers*, a sequence they repeated for producer Willis Kent in *Ten*

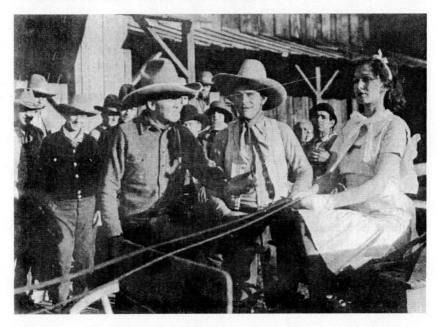

Tom London, Buddy Roosevelt and Barbara Worth in *Valley of Bad Men* (Jack Irwin, 1931).

*Nights in a Bar Room*, also in 1931. Thanks to its release by Artclass (q.v.), *The White Renegade* is probably the best-known of Irwin's productions.

Ironically, Irwin's biggest budgeted film, *Gun Cargo*, never saw theatrical distribution. Apparently, it was started in 1931 under the title *Contraband Cargo*, a period piece about a mutiny aboard a sailing ship, starring Rex Lease and Allene Ray. The feature was not completed until 1939 when new scenes were added along with footage from director Henry King's *Hell Harbor* (1930). Even then, the hybrid movie lay dormant for a decade until Favorite Films released it directly to television. The result is a combination of old and new footage, scenes jumping from modern dress to much earlier times in a strange juxtaposition of general incongruity. One part is played by two different actors, and leading lady Allene Ray is shoved into the background in all the new sequences.

The five feature films made by Jack Irwin Productions in 1931 are among the least seen and hardest to find of all the features from Poverty Row in the early 1930s.

## The Riding Kid

1931, 5 reels.
    *P-D-SC:* Jack Irwin.
    *Cast:* Buddy Roosevelt, Jean Kay, Fred Church, Bill Bertram, Sam Tittley, Nick Dunaev, LaVerne Haag, Mary Martin.
    Pretending to be a hired gunman, a U.S. marshal goes to work for a

rancher who is trying to run his neighbors off the range.

## Valley of Badmen

1931, 5 reels.

*P-D-SC:* Jack Irwin.

*Cast:* Buddy Roosevelt, Barbara Worth, Tom London.

A man tries to take over the family ranch only to be told it has been sold for taxes.

## Gun Cargo

Jack Irwin, 1939, 50 minutes.

*P-D-SC:* Jack Irwin. *PH:* Edward Kull. *ED:* William Austin. *SD:* Clifford Ruberg. *Tech Supv:* Ray Dyer. *Prod Mgr:* Robert Ingledon.

*Cast:* Rex Lease (Jim Parker), Smith Ballew (Singing Sailor), William Farnum (Inquiry Board Chairman), Gibson Gowland (Morgan), Robert Frazer (Fred Winthrop), Allene Ray (Helen), Harry Allen (Peg-Leg), John Ince (Mr. Winthrop), James Irwin (Gimpy), Jack Kirk (Sailor), Rondo Hatton (Cafe Owner), Don Azpiazu and His Casino Orchestra (Themselves).

Sea captain Jim Parker (Rex Lease) is brought before an inquiry board whose chairman (William Farnum) demands to know why charges should not be brought against him for the loss of the three-thousand-ton sailing ship *Black Rover*. Parker tells the inquiry board he was hired to pilot the craft by its owner Mr. Winthrop (John Ince), whose son Fred (Robert Frazer), a friend of Parker's, was the mate. When he took the assignment Parker did not know the ship was carrying contraband guns, nor did he know his girlfriend Helen (Allene Ray) was masquerading as the ship's galley boy. When Jim finds out about the guns, he

attempts to steer the ship to port, but the crew mutinies and he is placed in irons. Fred Winthrop takes over the vessel and when Helen tries to get Jim free during a bad storm, Winthrop attacks her. Jim escapes, and he and Winthrop fight. Jim manages to direct Helen to safety on a lifeboat but is knocked out by Fred and loses his memory. The ship sinks, but Jim is rescued by Peg-Leg (Harry Allen), who finds him washed ashore and clinging to a broken mast. Later at the El Marino Cafe, Peg-Leg is robbed by Fred Winthrop, who is shot trying to escape. In a fight Jim is hit by a bottle and regains his memory. At the hearing Mr. Winthrop intervenes, proclaiming Jim's innocence and offering him the command of his fleet of vessels.

One of the least known of Hollywood's Poverty Row features of the 1930s, *Gun Cargo* was never released theatrically. Originally titled *Contraband* and then *Contraband Cargo*, production began in 1931, but the film remained unfinished until 1939, when a modern-day subplot was added along with footage from the 1930 feature *Hell Harbor*. Still, the movie had no showings until it was issued to television by Favorite Films a decade later.

Jumping from modern-day attire to the days of big sailing ships, *Gun Cargo* is a choppy affair to say the least. Second-billed Smith Ballew makes only a brief appearance as an unnamed sailor who sings "I Dream of Jeannie with the Light Brown Hair." Apparently whatever qualities garnered him second billing were relegated to the cutting room floor at some point in the film's overlong production history. The *Hell Harbor* footage is used for the last part of the film, and Harry Allen and Gibson Gowland even repeat their roles from that feature in order to match the newer footage. Rondo Hatton also shows up from *Hell Harbor*, but unlike *Wolves of the Sea* (1938) (q.v.), which also used *Hell Harbor* footage, Hatton is not in any of the new sequences. Hatton is not in any of the new sequences. But perhaps the most overt casualty of this splicing together of old and new footage is Mr. Winthrop, who is played by two actors. At the beginning of the picture, John Ince portrays the villainous character while at the finale a repentant Winthrop is played by an uncredited actor.

Other deficiencies include performances and plot continuity. Most of the acting in the movie is decidedly old-fashioned, and the film never makes clear how Helen survives the shipwreck, her whereabouts in the interim or how she and Jack are reunited. Although *Gun Cargo* tries to hold together for fifty minutes, it makes little sense and is truly a Hollywood oddity.

# J.D. Kendis

Near the bottom of the rung of cheapie Hollywood film producers was J.D. Kendis, who operated under several names besides his own: Jay Dee Kay Productions, J.D.K. Productions and Continental Pictures, which was not related to the studio of the same name from the early 1930s. From the mid–1930s into the early 1940s, Kendis was involved in the production of a number of feature films, but the waters become muddy because some of them had alternate titles and there are probably others which were not copyrighted or have yet to resurface. Those that are available show that Kendis was the cheapest kind of Hollywood producer. Rarely did his features run more than one hour, most were chock-full of stock footage and musical fillers and few have much in the way of entertainment value. Perhaps Kendis' main claim to fame is his attempt to titillate and bring sexuality to theatrical films in spite of the Hays Office. Since Kendis did not operate through regular distribution channels, choosing instead to go the states' rights circuit, he succeeded in circumventing some of the stringent requirements thrust upon mainstream Hollywood by the censors.

J.D. Kendis entered the exploitation field in 1934 with the plea-for-sex-education feature *Guilty Parents*, followed the next year by the cheap western *The Hawk*. In 1935 he was also the producer of *Jaws of the Jungle*, a documentary-drama filmed in Ceylon and featuring a topless heroine. The producer came into his own in 1936 with *Gambling with Souls*, his tawdry expose of a prostitution racket. It contains all the elements associated with a Kendis production: lots of implied sex but no nudity, sometimes scantily attired young women, oily villains and musical interludes which halt the action but do not advance the plotline. Kendis sometimes had a hand in writing these reverse classics and thanks to the directorial ability of silent film star Elmer Clifton, the features often have a professional quality about them. *Slaves in Bondage* (1937) is a sequel to *Gambling with Souls*, and it even allows Wheeler Oakman to portray the same sleazy pimp in both pictures, although the character names are different.

Kendis and Clifton also teamed for *Wolves of the Sea* (1936) and *Paroled from the Big House* (1938). The former is one of the all-time classic bad films. Few can forget the sequences of comely Jean Carmen stranded on a tropical isle surrounded (via stock footage) by the wildest assortment of flora and fauna ever found in one feature. Also the viewer wonders just when her flimsy costume will fall apart. While *Wolves of the Sea* is wildly entertaining in its ineptitudes, *Paroled from the Big House* is just a big bore. *Variety* noted, "Release hasn't a thing to recommend it.... Sound, photography and dialog just as amateurish as the story and direction, dialog allowing numerous unintended grammatical errors." Its only interest is the presence of Milbourne [Milburn] Stone, cast as a Thomas A. Dewey-type crime-buster.

Even worse was the Sam Newfield-directed *Secrets of a Model* (1940), which told the old wheeze about a naive country girl (Sharon Lee) coming to the big town and being bedded then deserted by a city slicker (Julian Madison). Again *Variety* complained, "Aside from its title, the only secret about this is why anyone should bother to produce it." In the cast was Phyllis Barry who had shown such promise as the jilted shop girl in *Cynara* (1933). Kendis reteamed with Elmer Clifton for *Youth Aflame* in 1941, a Continental release, advertised as "A Shocking Drama of Reckless Youth." The next year he made *Escort Girl* for Continental, starring Betty Compson and Wheeler Oakman, with direction by Eddie Kay.

In 1943 J.D. Kendis popped up again using the Continental Pictures banner for *Teen Age*, the story of an ex-convict (Wheeler Oakman) trying to keep his son from making the same mistakes he did. Wheeler Oakman again plays Jim Murray, the character he portrayed in *Slaves in Bondage* seven years before. The film also included footage from *Gambling with Souls* and other Kendis productions. Elmer Clifton is credited with the script while direction was handled by Dick L'Estrange and Gunther Von Strensch. Filled with shock shots of female acrobats, an Oriental fan dancer and wild youth, *Teen Age* also included seemingly endless flashback sequences. Ironically, it was reissued in 1959 as *Teenage Jungle*.

## Guilty Parents

Syndicate, April 6, 1934, 66 minutes.
    *P:* J.D. Kendis. *D–SC:* Jack Townley. *PH:* Robert Doran. *ED:* Ethel Davey. *Supv:* Nat H. Spitzer.

*Cast:* Jean Lacy, Robert Frazer, Gertrude Astor, Donald Keith, John St. Polis, Isabel Lamal, Lynton Brent, Glen Boles, Leon Holmes, Ima Gilbert, Elen Aristi.

At her murder trial a young woman's past is presented, including how she got into trouble due to lack of sex education.

## The Hawk

Jay Dee Kay Productions/Affiliated Pictures/Herman A. Wohl, May 13, 1935, 55 minutes.

*P:* J.D. Kendis. *D:* Edward Dmytryk. *SC:* Gordon Jay, from the story "The Captive" by James Oliver Curwood. *PH:* Roland Price. *ED:* Moe Miller. *SD:* Herbert Eicke. *Mus:* Hal Chasoff. *Tech Dir:* Jack Corrick. *Asst Dir:* Robert Ray.

*Cast:* Yancy Lane (Jay Price/Jack King), Betty Jordan (Betty), Dickie Jones (Dickie), Lafe McKee (Jim King), Rollo Dix (Jeff Murdock), Don Orlando (Tony), Zandra (Himself), Henry Hall (Sheriff), Edward Foster, Marty Joyce.

On her deathbed a woman makes her son promise to find the father who left him long ago. At the Triple X ranch Jim King (Lafe McKee), with the help of his ward Betty (Betty Jordan), sends out annual letters hoping to find his long lost son. The young man Jay Price (Yancy Lane), steals the letter and learns his real name is Jack King. The local sheriff (Henry Hall) gets on his trail for mail theft, and he runs away, ending up on the Triple X range where he hears the mysterious Hawk making plans to rustle Jim King's cattle. When Betty's little brother Dickie (Dickie Jones) is nearly hurt by a wild horse, Jay saves him, and he meets Betty and they fall in love. Jim gives Jay a job as a cowhand, but Jay is disliked by ranch foreman Jeff Murdock (Rollo Dix), who also wants Betty. When Betty learns Jay is wanted for mail robbery, she becomes upset,

but he asks her to trust him. Later, he is captured by the masked Hawk. Dickie and Jay's dog Zandra (Himself) help Jay to escape, and he warns Jim King and the local vigilantes that the Hawk plans a cattle raid. The sheriff arrives to arrest Jay, but Betty brings in one of the Hawk's men and then proves that Murdock is the Hawk. Jay also gets the proof he needs to show that he is Jim King's son.

*The Hawk* is a cheaply made but competent low-grade western, badly hampered by Yancy Lane's lack of acting ability. The movie is best known today as the directorial debut of film editor Edward Dmytryk, who later directed features like *Tender Comrade* (1943), *Murder, My Sweet* (1945), *Back to Bataan* (1945), *Crossfire* (1947), *The Caine Mutiny* (1954), *Broken Lance* (1954), *Raintree County* (1957), *The Carpetbaggers* (1963), *Mirage* (1965) and *Anzio* (1968). The film also makes good use of music, something not common in very low-budget westerns of that period. In a musical sequence in a bunkhouse costar Dickie Jones does a very lively dance to a western tune. Also of interest is leading lady Betty Jordan, who is as resourceful as she is beautiful. She actually extricates the hero from the grip of the law, her efforts making her an active participant in events, rather than the typically passive damsel-in-distress who must be rescued from the lecherous villain.

In the 1940s the film was reissued as *Trail of the Hawk*. Additional medicine show sequences were added featuring Ramblin' Tommy Scott and his troupe, including Luke McLuke and Frankie and Sandra Scott.

When *The Hawk* was initially released in 1935 *Film Daily* thought it a "good western" adding, "Due to the work of Dickie Jones, a kid actor, who

Advertisement for *Gambling with Souls* (Jay Dee Kay Productions, 1936). Shown are Bryant Washburn and Martha Chapin (left) and Edward Keane, Bryant Washburn, Florence Dudley, Martha Chapin and Robert Frazer (right).

rides, dances, speaks and acts well, this action Western is somewhat different from the usual Western. Yancey [*sic*] Lane has to contend for honors with this kid and on that score his role is smaller than the regular Western Star's."

## Gambling with Souls

Jay Dee Kay Productions, 1936, 67 minutes.

*P-SC:* J.D. Kendis. *D:* Elmer Clifton. *PH:* James Diamond. *ED:* Earl Turner. *Sound:* Clifford Ruberg. *Supv:* Louis Mosher.

*Cast:* Martha Chapin (Mae Miller), Wheeler Oakman (Frank "Lucky" Wilder), Bryant Washburn (Million Dollar Taylor), Gay Sheridan (Carolyn), Robert Frazer (Dr. John Miller), Vera Steadman (Mrs. Simmons), Ed Keane (District Attorney), Gaston Glass (Frenchie Phillips), Florence Dudley (Molly Murdock), Eddie Laughton (Nick).

In an effort "to save other girls from the fool's paradise into which I was lured," prostitute Mae Miller (Martha Chapin) relates to the district attorney (Ed Keane) why she murdered nightclub owner Frank "Lucky" Wilder (Wheeler Oakman). She tells how her life was boring as the young wife of a struggling doctor (Robert Frazer) and how she becomes friends with socialite Molly Murdock (Florence Dudley), not realizing that Murdock was procuring her for a prostitution racket run by allegedly honest businessman

Wilder. Molly takes Mae to Wilder's gambling club, where at first she is allowed to win but eventually loses $10,000. Not wanting her husband to know, Mae agrees to a social date with wealthy Million Dollar Taylor (Bryant Washburn), hoping to borrow the money from him. She gets drunk, however, and he seduces her. The next day Wilder tells Mae he will inform her husband of her activities unless she pays him what she owes. Unable to do so, Mae is forced to work in Wilder's prostitution racket, and she leaves her husband so he won't find out. Both Dr. Miller and Mae's younger sister Carolyn (Gay Sheridan) try to find her, but at a club Wilder sees Carolyn and begins dating her. Some months later Carolyn dies from a botched abortion after being impregnated by Wilder, and Mae finds the bounder at his club and shoots him during a police raid. After telling her story, Mae is handed over for trial, but her husband vows to stand beside her.

Despite its skimpy production trappings, *Gambling with Souls* is an interesting "adults only" feature from the 1930s. As usual, producer J.D. Kendis spared every expense in bringing this "expose" of the call girl racket to the screen, but the story runs smoothly and old-time director Elmer Clifton manages to make it entertaining fare. Acting-wise, Wheeler Oakman is tops as the oily pimp who forces attractive young women to work for him after luring them to his club and causing them to mount huge gambling debts. While Martha Chapin was somewhat lacking in the performance department, she more than made up for it as the sexy housewife gone astray. The seduction scene involving her and Million Dollar Taylor is a classic. Although it contains no nudity, her shadow is seen as Taylor removes her clothing, each garment being thrown to the floor in a frenzy by the slick seducer. "Oh no!" sobs the tearful heroine in a closeup (her regret coming after the fact).

Like most J.D. Kendis productions, *Gambling with Souls* contains some filler material, including a production number probably lifted from another source and several scenes of low comedy, one having a country hick being taken by a group of "party girls."

## Jaws of the Jungle

April, 1936, 60 minutes.

*P:* J.D. Kendis. *ST:* Eddy Graneman. *ED:* Holbrook N. Todd. *ST:* Clifford Ruberg.

*Cast:* Cliff Howell (narrator).

In Ceylon natives are forced into the jungle after an attack by vicious vampire bats. Also called *Jungle Virgin*.

## Slaves in Bondage

Jay Dee Kay Productions/Road Show Attractions, 1937, 65 minutes.

*P:* J.D. Kendis. *D:* Elmer Clifton. *SC:* Robert A. Dillon. *PH:* Eddie Linden. *ED:* Earl Turner. *SD:* Corson Jowett. *Asst Dir:* Mel [Melville] DeLay.

*Cast:* Lona Andre (Donna Lee), Wheeler Oakman (Jim Murray), Donald Reed (Philip Miller), Florence Dudley (Belle Harris), John Merton (Nick), Richard Cramer (Dutch), William Royale (Editor), Ed Peil, Sr. (Chief of Detectives), Louise Small (Mary Lou Smith), Matty Roubert (Good Looking Freddie), Martha Chapin (Lillian).

Pretty Donna Lee (Lona Andre) works at a manicurist shop run by Belle Harris (Florence Dudley), and she is being given the rush by Belle's pal, nightclub owner Jim Murray (Wheeler Oakman). Belle uses the shop as a front for a prostitution racket she runs with Murray, and she procures young girls by taking out want ads in rural newspapers. The girls come to the big city, don't get jobs and after a time end up working as hookers in Murray's posh brothel.

Donna lives at a boarding house, and when Mary Lou (Louise Small), the daughter of the owner, escapes being kidnapped by Murray's white slavers, Donna's boyfriend Philip Miller (Donald Reed) covers the story, hoping to convince the local newspaper editor (William Royale) to give him a job. When Mary Lou identifies Good Looking Freddie (Matty Roubert), one of Murray's henchmen, as a kidnapper, Murray and Belle have hoodlums Nick (John Merton) and Dutch (Richard Cramer) take him for a ride, and Philip and Donna see Freddie's body dumped in the gutter.

Nick and Dutch decide to doublecross Murray and Belle and take over their racket, while Murray plans to seduce Donna by getting Philip out of the way. He has the young man framed and jailed on a charge of passing counterfeit money. Donna convinces the newspaper editor of Philip's innocence, and the newsman calls in the police after Mary Lou tells Donna that Murray was also one of her abductors. Donna agrees to meet Murray at his Bubble Over Cafe. There Belle shows her around, and Donna realizes the place is actually a front for a brothel. Meanwhile, Nick and Dutch take over after a fight with Belle's employees. Murray corners Donna in a locked bedroom and tries to rape her, but Philip and the police arrive in time to save her and round up the racke-

teers. Donna and Philip plan to marry and the groom-to-be gets his newspaper job.

*Slaves in Bondage* continues the Kendis and Clifton "crusade" to expose the prostitution racket. As in the previous year's *Gambling with Souls*, Wheeler Oakman and Florence Dudley team up to victimize naive young girls who come to the big city in search of better lives. Martha Chapin, star of *Gambling with Souls*, shows up in an unbilled part as a country lass lured into prostitution in the big city. Her big scene is a catfight with another hooker. While better made than *Gambling with Souls*, *Slaves in Bondage* is not as titillating and, like the usual Kendis fare, is laden with filler material. Here all action stops while the film unveils an Oriental fan dancer, a tango team, a girl acrobatic dancer and a terrible male duo acrobatic comedy team, plus the expected drunk routines. The dialogue also leaves much to be desired. After being abducted by gangsters a young girl moans, "I want my mother, I want my mother." Another scene has a hooker complaining to a club host, "Say my powderpuff's worn out. When you gonna get me a new one?" Apparently the entire thrust of the film is revealed in a scene when the newspaper editor (William Royale) says he is going to write a series of exposes warning country girls to be careful when they answer big city newspaper job ads.

Although competently made, *Slaves in Bondage* is one of those 1930s adult features that promises a great deal and delivers very little. For the gawker trade there are only a few scenes of comely young ladies in their undergarments. One amusing sequence has them on display as Belle informs Donna how each room in the "club" is set aside for tired businessmen, lawyers, doctors, politicians, etc.

The feature also had some release in the late summer of 1937 as *Crusade Against the Rackets*.

Wheeler Oakman reprised the role of Jim Murray for J.D. Kendis in 1943 in the Continental release *Teen Age*, which used footage from *Slaves in Bondage* and other Kendis productions.

## Wolves of the Sea

Guaranteed, July 4, 1938, 56 minutes. *P:* J.D. Kendis. *D-SC:* Elmer Clifton. *PH:* Eddie Linden. *ED:* Duke Goldstone. *AD:* Fred Preble. *SD:* Corson J. Jowett.

*Cast:* Hobart Bosworth (Captain Wolf Hansen), Jean Carmen (Nadine Miller), Dirk Thane (William Rand), Pat West (Jim Lane), Warner Richmond (Snoden), John Merton (Mitchell), Edward Kay (Frankie), Rondo Hatton (Cafe Owner).

A luxury liner is caught in a storm and sinks at the same time a zoo ship is lost at sea. Wealthy Nadine Miller (Jean Carmen) is the only passenger to survive from the liner and she ends up on a tropical island with the animals from the zoo ship. Meanwhile Captain Wolf Hansen (Hobart Bosworth) pilots his schooner to the spot where the liner sank in order to salvage the treasure it carried. With him are first mate William Rand (Dirk Thane) and his pal Jim Lane (Pat West) along with crooks Snoden (Warner Richmond), Mitchell (John Merton) and Frankie (Edward Kay), who plan to mutiny and take the vessel once the treasure is found. When the spot is found, Rand and Mitchell take turns diving for the treasure, and when Hansen finds out Snoden plans to mutiny, he gives him ten lashes. Getting revenge, Snoden causes a heavy keg to fall on Hansen,

badly injuring him. When Rand and Jim go to a nearby island to get fresh water, they find Nadine, who is exhausted from fever and fighting the animals. They take her aboard ship where she nurses Hansen, who tells her that the treasure he seeks are her jewels, which her father won from him long ago. She tells him they are now his by right of salvage. When Rand goes below to get the treasure, Snoden tries to molest Nadine, but Rand returns in time to stop him. Later Rand sends up the treasure chest, but the crew fights over it and refuses to bring him back up. Using a gun, Nadine forces the crew to rescue Rand. When Rand finds out Nadine is really a rich heiress, he believes he is not good enough for her and becomes cold toward the young woman. When the ship reaches shore Hansen sets the mutinous crew free. Later, they attack Rand and Jim in a dive, and the fight so upsets Nadine that she books passage on a steamer. Also onboard the ship are Rand and Jim as members of the crew, Hansen with his jewels and Snoden and Mitchell, who plan to steal the gems and wreck the ship. Snoden also plans to abduct Nadine. At sea the ship's boiler explodes and the crew and passengers panic. Snoden and Mitchell try to steal a lifeboat and are shot while Hansen drowns rather than leave his treasure. Rand manages to get Nadine on a lifeboat and with Jim they go to a nearby island, the one from which they had originally rescued Nadine. Later the trio is found by a rescue ship.

Kendis' *Wolves of the Sea* is one of the most delightful cheapies to come out of Poverty Row in the 1930s. Packed into its less than one hour running time are a search for undersea treasure, a mutiny, a beautiful girl lost on a tropical isle, a slightly mad sea captain, a singing sailor, a lecherous villain and some of the wildest collection of flora and fauna ever assembled. The movie is filled with stock footage, ranging from the wild animals and reptiles on the tropical island to underwater divers and marine life. Some of the scenes are quite amusing. In one the scantily clad heroine fights off a big cat with a club via stock footage and rear-screen projection. In another scene, lecherous villain Warner Richmond apologizes to hero Dirk Thane for trying to molest heroine Jean Carmen. "I hadn't seen a woman for so long I lost my head," he intones. Through the farrago hero Thane continually sings "King of the Sea" in his best Nelson Eddy manner. Of interest is the jungle footage, which apparently came from Kendis' earlier documentary-drama *Jaws of the Jungle* (1936) filmed in Ceylon. Among the wild creatures menacing the beautiful and sexy heroine are bats, a huge snake, a leopard and even a duck-billed platapus. Performance-wise Hobart Bosworth steals the honors as the sea captain while comely Jean Carmen handles the heroine role in good form. In 1937 she had been known as Julia Thayer when she headlined Republic's serial *The Painted Stallion*. During the course of the feature the story is sometimes punctuated by showing the entries in the captain's log to further the action and most of the dance hall sequence is lifted from director Henry King's *Hell Harbor* (1930). In fact Rondo Hatton not only appears in the original footage but also reprises his role of the cafe owner with new footage to match the eight-year-old celluloid

King shot in Florida. At the time of its release *Variety* complained, "Definitely not for anything above the lower-bracketed duals. Direction, cutting and camera are poor all the way."

## Paroled from the Big House

Syndicate, July 29, 1938, 57 minutes.

*P:* J.D. Kendis. *D:* Elmer Clifton. *SC:* George Plympton. *PH:* Eddie Linden.

*Cast:* Jean Carmen, Richard Adams, George Eldredge, Gwen Lee, Milbourne [Milburn] Stone, Walter Anthony, Ole Olsen, Earl Douglas, Eddie Kaye, Joe Devlin, Eleanor De Van.

When her storekeeper father is murdered for not giving in to a protection racket, a young woman tries to find the killers and is aided by a policeman and the city's district attorney. Reissued in the 1940s as *Main Street Girl.*

## Secrets of a Model

Continental Pictures, April, 1940, 61 minutes.

*P:* J.D. Kendis. *D:* Sam Newfield. *SC:* Sherman Lowe & Arthur St. Claire. *PH:* Jack Greenhalgh. *ED:* George M. Merrick. *SD:* Hans Weeren. *Prod Mgr:* Melville DeLay.

*Cast:* Sharon Lee, Harold Daniels, Julian Madison, Phyllis Barry, Bobby Watson, Eddie Borden, Grace Lenard, Donald Kerr.

A girl from the country comes to the big city to be a model, is seduced by a cad and redeemed by the love of a milkman.

# Willis Kent Productions

From the late 1920s until the early 1940s producer Willis Kent turned out more than three dozen feature films. While most of his product went out under his Willis Kent Productions banner, some of his films were also issued on the states' rights market by outfits like Progressive, Marcy (qq.v.) and True Life Photoplays. Uncredited, Kent sometimes scripted his productions, and like most independents he did not have his own studio but rented space from a variety of outfits like International Studios, Talisman Studios and the Hearst ranches in southern California and at Lone Pine, California. The latter were mainly used for the "B" westerns he made with Lane Chandler and Reb Russell. Kent was also known for exploitation features like *The Pace That Kills* (1928), which he remade in 1936, and his two versions of *The Road to Ruin* with Helen Foster in 1928 and 1934. In addition Kent also turned out a number of other exploitation titles in the early sound era like *Ten Nights in a Barroom* (1931), *Playthings of Hollywood* (1931) and *A Scarlet Week-End* (1932).

Willis Kent began his career as an independent producer in 1928 with his True Life Photoplay's release of *The Road to Ruin*, which he scripted, starring Helen Foster as a teenager who becomes involved in loose sex and dies as a result. Six years later Kent remade this classic exploitation picture under its original title with the same star. Again he issued it under the True Life Photoplay banner. Both pictures proved successful on the states' rights market (particularly the silent version) as both exploited the sex angles to the hilt. Probably Kent's best production as a silent was *Linda*, which was directed by Mrs. Wallace Reid (Dorothy Davenport). It was based on the 1912 novel by Margaret Prescott Montague and starred Warner Baxter (who won an Academy Award in 1929 for *In Old Arizona*), Helen Foster and Noah Beery. Kent also served as the editor of this 1929 release which had music score (including the title song by Al Stewart and Charles and Harry Tobias) and sound effects but no dialogue. *Photoplay* termed it "Maudlin sentimentality." Kent's other silent outing was *The Pace That Kills* (1928) about young people being lured into dope addiction. It too was penned by Kent, and eight years later he remade it.

With the coming of the sound era, Willis Kent worked mainly as a producer of "B" westerns and low-budget, but usually entertaining, melodramas. In many of the latter Phyllis Barrington was the leading lady. While cheaply made, Kent's features retained a professional look about them. He also used familiar names for box-office appeal: William Farnum and Tom Santschi in *Ten Nights in a Barroom* (1931), Jack Mulhall in *Sinister Hands* (1932), William Farnum and Noah Beery in *The Drifter* (1932) and Henry B. Walthall in *Murder in the Museum* (1934). Lane Chandler, who remembered Kent as a "prince" when interviewed in the mid-1960s, starred in eight westerns for the producer in the early 1930s, and football star Reb Russell made nine oaters for Kent during the 1934–35 season. Although low-budget, the Kent westerns were more than competent "B" fare, but like most films of their ilk they often rented for a flat fee, usually around $25 for a weekend. Reviews were often mixed. *Variety* called Lane Chandler's *Texas Tornado* (1932) a "Standard western ... Not up to standard from any angle and for western fans only if they are very fanatic indeed." For *Fighting Through* (1934), starring Reb Russell, *Film Daily* opined, "Lively western with action-filled plot makes good fare for thrill fans."

Reb Russell was offered a second series of westerns for Willis Kent but wisely declined to continue acting. Kent then turned out a couple of oaters: rodeo star Montie Montana in *Circle of Death* (1935) and Buck Coburn in *Gunsmoke on the Guadalupe* (1935). Neither resulted in a series, although the latter was advertised as a Montie Montana Production. It was Kent, however, who financed the western, paying Montie Montana for the use of his name.

Following the demise of his westerns, Willis Kent stayed mainly with exploitation features. He remade *The Pace That Kills* in 1936, still one of the most gritty and unappetizing of anti-drug pictures. Its cheap, tawdry atmosphere heightens the realism of the plot in which Noel Madison is very good as a slick drug pusher. After that film Kent began releasing his features through Real Life Dramas, headquartered at 4376 Sunset Boulevard in Hollywood. In *Smashing the Vice Trust* (1937) Willy Castello created the character of gangster Lucky Lombardo, a role he reprised for Kent five years later in *Confessions of a Vice Baron* (1942), also known as *Skid Row*. Sandwiched between these gangster melodramas were exploitationers like *Race Suicide* (1937), which dealt with abortion (although the word was not used in the movie); *The Wages of Sin* (1938), about a young woman (Constance Worth) who becomes a call girl; *Souls in Pawn* (1940), the story of a teenager (Ginger Britton) forced to give up her child; and *Mad Youth* (1940), starring silent screen star Betty Compson in a tale of a socialite and her daughter who both pursue the same gigolo. *Variety* commented, "Produced in the cheapest manner, poorly directed, tritely written, and amateurishly acted, the indie-made is a first-class collapse. A whole floor show ... is thrown in to help increase the pain."

By the early 1940s it was evident that the major studios had tightened their hold on the distribution market, and with the emergence of conglomerate cheapies like Producers Releasing Corporation (PRC) and the revitalized Monogram, there was simply little room left for solo independent producers like Willis Kent, who died March 11, 1966, at the age of 87.

## Linda

Willis Kent Productions/First Division, March 31, 1929, 70 minutes.

*P-ED:* Willis Kent. *D:* Mrs. Wallace Reid [Dorothy Davenport]. *SC:* Wilfred Noy, Maxine Alton & Frank O'Connor, from the novel by Margaret Prescott Montague. *Titles:* Ruth Todd. *PH:* Henry Cronjager, Bert Baldridge & Ernest Laszlo. *Song:* Al Sherman, Charles & Harry Tobias. *Asst Dir:* Wallace Sheridan. *Prod Mgr:* Cliff Broughton.

*Cast:* Warner Baxter, Helen Foster, Noah Beery, Mitchell Lewis, Kate Price, Allan Connor, Bess Flowers.

A young woman is forced to marry an older man although she really loves a doctor.

## Ten Nights in a Barroom

Road Show Productions, March 1, 1931, 69 minutes.

*P:* Willis Kent. *D:* William O'Connor. *SC:* Norton S. Parker, from the play by Edwin Waugh. *PH:* Verne L. Walker. *SD:* Ernest W. Rovere. *Asst Dir:* Armand L. Schaefer.

*Cast:* William Farnum, Thomas Santschi, Patty Lou Lynd, Robert Frazer, Phyllis Barrington, Rosemary Theby, John Darrow, Lionel Belmore, Thomas Jefferson, Frank Leigh, Kathryn Clare Ward, Sheila Mannors, Fern Emmett, Harry Todd, John Uppman, Daisy Delmore.

Because of his addiction to alcohol, a man alienates his family and nearly loses the little daughter he loves. Stars William Farnum and Thomas Santschi restaged their famous fight sequence from *The Spoilers* (1914) at the film's climax.

## Hurricane Horseman

October 11, 1931, 50 minutes.

*P:* Willis Kent. *D:* Armand L. Schaefer. *SC:* Oliver Drake. *ST:* Douglas Dawson. *PH:* William Nobles. *ED:* Ethel Davey. *Asst Dir:* William O'Connor.

*Cast:* Lane Chandler, Marie Quillan, Walter Miller, Yakima Canutt, Richard Alexander, Lafe McKee, Charles "Rube" Schaefer, Robert Smith, Slim Whitaker, Jack Kirk, Hank Bell, Blackjack Ward, Chuck Baldra, Bill Wolfe, Pascale Perry, Raven.

When a pretty girl is kidnapped and held for ransom by outlaws, a gunsmith comes to her rescue.

## Cheyenne Cyclone

January 10, 1932, 59 minutes.

*P:* Willis Kent. *D:* Armand L. Schaefer. *SC:* Oliver Drake. *PH:* William Nobles. *ED:* Ethel Davey.

*Cast:* Lane Chandler, Marie Quillan, Frankie Darro, Yakima Canutt, Henry Rocquemore, Jay Hunt, Edward Hearn, J. Frank Glendon, Connie Lamont, Slim Whitaker, Jack Kirk, Hank Bell, Josephine Hill, Helen Gibson, Bart Carre, Raven.

Stranded in a small town, a cowboy gets a job with a rancher about to lose his cattle to outlaws. Reissued as *Rustler's Ranch.*

## The Drifter

January 10, 1932, 71 minutes.

*P:* Willis Kent. *D:* William O'Connor. *SC:* Oliver Drake. *PH:* William Nobles. *ED:* Thomas Persons. *Asst Dir:* Melville Shyer.

*Cast:* William Farnum (The Drifter, Louis Valjean), Noah Beery (John McNary), Phyllis Barrington (Bonnie McNary), Charles Sellon (Whitey), Bruce Warren (Paul La Tour), Russell Hopton (Montana), Ann Brody (Marie), Ynez Seabury (Yvonne), Fern Emmett (Woman).

In Canada a man called The Drifter (William Farnum) returns to his family cabin and finds Whitey (Charles Sellon), who has escaped from prison after twenty years. Together, they go to the town of Lebec, and at the saloon The Drifter stops gunman Montana (Russell Hopton) from shooting John McNary (Noah Beery), president of the Canadian Lumber Company. McNary's daughter Bonnie

(Phyllis Barrington) loves Paul La Tour (Bruce Warren), the superintendent of a rival concern, who has hired Montana to protect his interests. McNary hires The Drifter and Whitey, and The Drifter is attracted to Bonnie. When he goes to the village church to see her, Montana corners The Drifter, and in the ensuing gunfight the village priest is killed as is Montana. When Bonnie sticks by The Drifter after the incident, he falls in love with her but realizes her affections are with La Tour. Whitey schemes to have Bonnie run away with La Tour but at the same time makes The Drifter believe he should take the girl for himself. He arranges for Bonnie to meet La Tour at a remote cabin, and he also tells the Drifter to meet the girl there. That night Bonnie runs away to meet Paul, and Whitey surprises McNary and tells him that twenty years before he was the man McNary framed and sent to prison before stealing his wife and child. Whitey stabs McNary with La Tour's knife, but before the lumberman dies he tells Whitey that Bonnie is really his daughter and not McNary's. At the cabin The Drifter tries to seduce Bonnie but realizes she loves Paul. Whitey arrives but is knocked down by a falling tree. As he dies he tells The Drifter the truth about Bonnie being his daughter. Paul comes to the cabin and finds Bonnie with The Drifter and they fight, but the law arrives and arrests Paul for McNary's murder. The Drifter, however, gives Paul the alibi he needs because he realizes La Tour is really his long, lost younger brother. As Paul and Bonnie plan to marry, The Drifter drifts on.

*The Drifter* is probably the best film made by producer Willis Kent. Filmed on location in the California high country, it is a well-produced northwoods drama highlighted by fine performances from William Farnum, Noah Beery, Phyllis Barrington, Charles Sellon and Russell Hopton. William Nobles' photography is especially attractive and Oliver Drake's script is literate and holds audience attention. *The Drifter* presents William Farnum with one of his last starring roles in sound films before developing into a character player, and he makes the most of the opportunity. He has a field day as the French-accented Drifter, often intoning, "Life, she's is one big joke." Watching accomplished hams like Farnum and Noah Beery chew up the scenery is fun as well, although for the most part Beery is more subdued than usual in a semi-sympathetic role. Phyllis Barrington is justly alluring as the beautiful heroine while Russell Hopton is good in his brief scenes as a hired killer. The settings for the feature were done at Tec-Art Studios and *The Drifter* certainly has a classier look about it than most of Kent's productions.

## Battling Buckaroo

1932, 6 reels.

*P:* Willis Kent. *D:* Armand L. Schaefer. *SC:* Oliver Drake. *PH:* William Nobles. *ED:* Ethel Davey. *SD:* Terry Kellum. *Asst Dir:* Bart Carre.

*Cast:* Lane Chandler, Doris Hill, Yakima Canutt, Ted Adams, Bill Patton, Lafe McKee, Olin Francis, Herman Hack, Bart Carre, Raven.

A notorious outlaw rescues a senorita and her father after they are kidnapped by bandits who want their gold. Also called *His Last Adventure*.

## Guns for Hire

1932, 59 minutes.

*P:* Willis Kent. *D:* Lewis D. Collins. *SC:* Oliver Drake. *ST:* E.B. Mann. *PH:* William Nobles. *ED:* Ethel Davey.

*Cast:* Lane Chandler, Sally Darling, Neal Hart, Yakima Canutt, Frances Morris, Jack Rockwell, John Ince, Ben Corbett, Slim Whitaker, Steve Clemento, Bill Patton, Hank Bell, Nelson McDowell, John McGuire, Ed Porter, Roy Bucko, Buck Bucko, Bud McClure, Bart Carre, Gene Alsace, John Bacon, Ray Jones, Jack O'Shea, Bud Pope, Raven.

A gunfighter gets into a range war and finds his mentor on the other side. TV Title: *Blazing Trail.*

## Lawless Valley

1932, 5 reels.

*P:* Willis Kent. *D:* J.P. McGowan. *SC:* Oliver Drake. *PH:* William Nobles. *ED:* Ethel Davey. *SD:* Buddy Myers. *Asst Dir:* Theodore Joos.

*Cast:* Lane Chandler, Gertrude Messinger, Art Mix, Anne Howard, J.P. McGowan, Richard Cramer, Si Jenks, Jack Kirk, Chuck Baldra, Hank Bell, Raven.

A cattlemen's association detective is on the trail of the wanted cattle rustler El Lobo.

## The Reckless Rider

1932, 5 reels.

*P:* Willis Kent. *D:* Armand L. Schaefer. *SC:* Oliver Drake. *PH:* William Nobles. *ED:* Ethel Davey.

*Cast:* Lane Chandler, Phyllis Barrington, Franklyn Farnum, Neal Hart, J. Frank Glendon, Pat Rooney, G. Raymond Nye, Ben Corbett, Bart Carre, Raven.

Masquerading as an outlaw, a marshal helps a man and his daughter plagued by crooks.

## Texas Tornado

1932, 55 minutes.

*P:* Willis Kent. *D-SC:* Oliver Drake. *PH:* James Diamond. *ED:* Ethel Davey. *SD:* Earl Crain. *Asst Dir:* Bart Carre.

*Cast:* Lane Chandler, Doris Hill, Ben Corbett, Mike Brand, J. Frank Glendon, Edward Hearn, Bart Carre, Wes Warner, Yakima Canutt, Fred Burns, Slim Whitaker, Pat Healy, Robert Gale, Buddy Roosevelt, Raven.

A Texas Ranger is on the trail of a kidnapped young woman whose father was murdered by her abductors.

## Sinister Hands

June 5, 1932, 65 minutes.

*P:* Willis Kent. *D:* Armand L. Schaefer. *SC:* Oliver Drake, from the novel *The Seance Mystery* by Norton S. Parker. *PH:* William Nobles. *ED:* Ethel Davey. *AD:* William O'Connor. *SD:* Earl N. Crain.

*Cast:* Jack Mulhall, Phyllis Barrington, Crauford Kent, Mischa Auer, James Burtis, Phillips Smalley, Gertie [Gertrude] Messinger, Nathan Natheaux, Lloyd Ingraham, Helen Foster, Lillian West, Bess Flowers, Fletcher Norton, Russell Collar.

A police inspector must unravel a complicated web surrounding a murder at a seance conducted by a fake swami.

## A Scarlet Week-End

Maxim Productions, September 23, 1932, 63 minutes.

*P:* Willis Kent. *D:* George Melford. *SC:* Oliver Drake, from the novel *The Woman in Purple Pajamas* by Wilson Collison. *PH:* William Nobles. *ED:* Ruth Wright. *Asst Dir:* Melville Shyer.

*Cast:* Dorothy Revier, Theodore

Von Eltz, Phyllis Barrington, Niles Welch, Douglas Cosgrove, William Desmond, Eddie Phillips, Sheila Mannors, Charles K. French, The Aber Twins, Nora Hayden, Vance Carroll.

When her philandering husband is murdered at their country estate a woman is blamed for the crime.

# Wyoming Whirlwind

October 12, 1932, 57 minutes.

*P:* Willis Kent. *D:* Armand L. Schaefer. *SC:* Alan Ludwig, from the story "Shootin' Straight" by William Colt MacDonald. *PH:* William Nobles. *ED:* Ethel Davey.

*Cast:* Lane Chandler (Keen Wallace/The Lone Wolf), Adele Tracy (Judy Flagg), Harry Todd (Sheriff Joe Flagg), Loie Bridges (Molly Flagg), Yakima Canutt (Jackson), Al Bridge (Steve Cantrell), Bob Roper (Brute), Harry Semuels (Pete), Hank Bell (Hank), Jack Rockwell (Henchman), Lafe McKee (Old Man), Jack Kirk (Singer), Fred Burns (Stage Driver), Raven (Himself).

A one thousand dollar reward is offered for the capture of The Lone Wolf (Lane Chandler), really Keen Wallace, who has returned to his home range to get revenge on Steve Cantrell (Al Bridge), who murdered his father and forged a will giving him the Wallace ranch. The Lone Wolf is constantly outfoxing the local lawman, Sheriff Joe Flagg (Harry Todd), and he even saves the man's pretty niece, Judy (Adele Tracy), when drunken Indians attack the stagecoach in which she is riding. Judy is attracted to the Lone Wolf, not realizing he is the young man she was attached to years before. The Lone Wolf confronts Cantrell and his men in the Lone Pine saloon and takes the money they made off a cattle sale. Later he catches Jackson (Yakima

Canutt), one of Steve's cohorts, trying to change the brand on some Flagg cattle, so he takes the outlaw to the sheriff. As a result he is recognized, but Flagg agrees to give him a free hand in proving his case against Cantrell. Jackson tells Keen that it was Cantrell who murdered his father and forged a fake will and that Cantrell carries the real will on his person. Cantrell sets a trap for Keen in the saloon but Judy finds out and rides to the Lone Pine with her uncle and his deputies. At the saloon Keen fights Cantrell's henchman Brute (Bob Roper) and defeats him but Cantrell shoots Brute when he tells Keen the truth about the will. Cantrell escapes and Keen follows. During a fight the bad man is subdued and the real will is found. Keen and Adele are now free to find romance.

Called *Roaring Rider* on television, *Wyoming Whirlwind* was one of eight westerns Lane Chandler starred in for producer Willis Kent during the 1931-32 season. Lane Chandler's real name was Robert Oakes, and he came from North Dakota but grew up on a Montana cattle ranch. He landed in films in 1927 and became a star that year in *Open Range* followed by films like *Red Hair* (1928), with Clara Bow, and *The Single Standard* (1929) starring Greta Garbo. He was dropped by Paramount at the beginning of the sound era but for a time was a western star before moving into character parts in the mid-1930s. Chandler was a tall, handsome actor who nicely fit the mold of a cowboy hero. His acting was more than acceptable, he rode well and he handled himself well in gunplay and fights. *Wyoming Whirlwind* nicely exemplifies its star's talents, and the character he plays, The Lone Wolf, is always playing practical jokes on the local, good-natured sheriff (Harry

Todd) who trails him. Adele Tracy is an attractive leading lady while Al Bridge is the dastardly villain and Yakima Canutt his somewhat cowardly associate. Bob Roper as Brute and Harry Semuels as Pete also do well as villains.

## The Racing Strain

Maxim Productions, December 16, 1932, 58 minutes.

*P:* Willis Kent. *D:* Jerome Storm. *SC:* Betty Burbridge & Willis Kent. *ST:* Mrs. Wallace Reid [Dorothy Davenport]. *PH:* William Nobles. *ED:* Ethel Davey.

*Cast:* Wallace Reid, Jr., Dickie Moore, Phyllis Barrington, J. Farrell MacDonald, Mae Busch, Ethel Wales, J. Frank Glendon, Paul Fix, Eddie Phillips, Otto Yamaoka, Lorin Raker, Donald Reed, James Burtis, Kit Guard.

When he wins the love of a society girl, a drunken race driver decides to resume his profession.

## The Road to Ruin

True Life Photoplays, March 21, 1934, 64 minutes.

*P:* Willis Kent. *D:* Mrs. Wallace Reid [Dorothy Davenport] & Melville Shyer. *PH:* James Diamond. *ED:* S. Roy Luby. *Asst Dir:* George Curtner. *SD:* Homer Ackerman.

*Cast:* Helen Foster (Ann Dixon), Nell O'Day (Eve Monroe), Glen Boles (Tommy), Bobby Quirk (Ed), Paul Page (Ralph Bennett), Virginia True Boardman (Mrs. Martha Dixon), Richard Tucker (Mr. Dixon), Mae Busch (Mrs. Monroe), Richard Hemingway (Brad), Donald Kerr (Mr. Wheeler), Eleanor Thatcher (Mrs. Morrell), Theodore Lorch (Doctor), Neal Pratt, Jimmy Tolson.

Wild teenager Eve (Nell O'Day) invites her innocent friend Ann (Helen Foster) to spend the night with her, and after Eve's high-living mother (Mae Busch) and boyfriend (Donald Kerr) go off to an all-night party, she introduces Ann to alcohol and cigarettes. Soon Ann is dating Tommy (Glen Boles), and the two go to a lake with Eve and her boyfriend Ed (Bobby Quirk). There Ann and Tommy have sex, but they continue to date. At a roadhouse Ann tires of Tommy's drunken attentions and is attracted to Ralph Bennett (Paul Page), an older man, who takes her home when trouble starts. Ann begins seeing Bennett, and at his apartment he drugs the girl and uses her sexually. Later the two go to a wild party, where Eve loses all her clothes playing strip poker. Then most of the party goers go swimming in their underwear, except for Eve, who goes skinny dipping. Neighbors alert the police, and the party is raided. The girls are taken into custody, but Bennett makes a getaway. After a physical, Eve and Ann are labeled sex delinquents, and Eve takes a cure for a sexual disease. Ann, however, learns she is pregnant and goes to Bennett, who takes her to a doctor (Theodore Lorch) for an abortion. Because of the clumsy operation, Ann becomes very sick and dies at home with her parents (Virginia True Boardman, Richard Tucker) beside her.

Although *The Road to Ruin* contains no screenplay credit it was written by producer Willis Kent, who first filmed it with star Helen Foster as a silent in 1928, also releasing it under the True Life Photoplays banner. This version pretty much follows its silent predecessor although the ending is slightly altered. (In the 1928 film the heroine dies from shock brought on by a bungled abortion and being paired with her own father in a brothel.) The sound version is a bit tamer but still carries the warning, "Our boys and girls today need more than truth. They need the armor of sex instruction to protect them." This dialogue was spoken by a social worker after the two leading ladies are examined and labeled "sex delinquents."

Both Helen Foster and Nell O'Day seem a bit old to be playing high school girls, but otherwise, acting in *The Road to Ruin* is more than competent. Nell O'Day is quite attractive as the pert, mature and fun-loving Eve, who straightens out her life after contracting a sexual disease. On the other hand, Helen Foster's Ann is incredibly innocent. "Eve, do you let boys kiss you," she asks her friend in a wide-eyed manner. While much is implied in *The Road to Ruin*, nothing is really shown except for a few young ladies in wet underclothes during the swimming pool sequence. The film is also laced with a trio of songs, "Dearest," "Campus Crawl" and "Join a Fraternity," during the nightclub sequence.

Like all films of its time and ilk, *The Road to Ruin* was marketed as a warning to keep on the straight and narrow path of life.

## Fighting Through

August 29, 1934, 55 minutes.

*P:* Willis Kent. *D-SC:* Harry Fraser. *PH:* James Diamond. *ED:* S. Roy Luby. *SD:* Earl Crain.

*Cast:* Reb Russell, Lucille Lund, Yakima Canutt, Edward Hearn, Frank McCarroll, Wally Wales, Ben Corbett, Bill Patton, Steve Clemento, Chester Gan, Slim Whitaker, Hank Bell, Nelson McDowell, Lee Meehan, Jack Kirk, Chuck Baldra, Ray Jones, Herman Hack, Bart Carre, Buck Morgan, Jack Evans, Ed Rowland, Rebel.

Two buddies get a job on a ranch whose owner is kidnapped by crooks.

## The Man from Hell

Willis Kent/Cristo, August 29, 1934, 58 minutes.

*P:* Willis Kent. *D:* Lew Collins. *SC:* Melville Shyer. *ST:* Ed Earl Repp. *PH:* William Nobles. *ED:* S. Roy Luby. *SD:* Bud Myers. *Asst Dir:* Bart Carre.

*Cast:* Reb Russell (Clint Mason), Fred Kohler (Rance McCloud), Ann D'Arcy (Nancy Campbell), George Hayes (Colonel Campbell), Charles K. French (Sandy), Jack Rockwell (Marshal Lon Kelly), Charles "Slim" Whitaker (Tom Horford), Tommy Bupp (Timmy McCord), Murdock McQuarrie (Sheriff Jake Klein), Yakima Canutt (Yak), Tracy Layne (McCord), Mary Gordon (Mrs. McCord), Rebel (Himself), Ben Corbett (Pete), Jack Kirk (Singer), Hank Bell (Townsman).

Getting out of prison, Clint Mason (Reb Russell) returns to Bonanza City bent on proving he was framed for a stagecoach holdup he did not commit. He finds out the town is under the control of ruthless Rance McCloud (Fred Kohler) who has been romancing Clint's girl Nancy Campbell (Ann D'Arcy). Clint stops bully Yak (Yakima Canutt) from beating up little Timmy McCord's (Tommy Bupp) father (Tracy Layne) and then goes to see the man who raised him, blacksmith Sandy (Charles K. French). The local sheriff (Murdock McQuarrie) does not believe Clint is guilty of the robbery, but he has little power since McCloud has appointed his henchman Lon Kelly (Jack Rockwell) the marshal of the area. When McCloud threatens to bankrupt her father's (George Hayes) bank, Nancy agrees to marry him, but Clint tries to stop her. Clint tells McCloud he believes he is really escaped convict Kelso, and in a fight Clint beats up McCloud, who then tries to have him lynched. Clint goes to Nancy for help after the fight, and later at McCloud's mine hideout, he learns that his gang has been pulling off stage robberies and then pretending the gold they get comes from the worked-out mine. He also hears McCloud and Kelly admit they pulled the robbery for which Clint was imprisoned. Returning to town Timmy tells Clint that McCloud has killed Sandy, and Clint wires the federal prison that McCloud is really Kelso. Hearing this news McCloud plans to escape across the border before the rangers arrive, but the local miners unite and capture Kelly, who tells them that McCloud plans to rob the Bonanza bank. The next day a shootout occurs during the robbery and the gang is captured, but McCloud abducts Nancy and escapes. Clint follows and the two shoot each other. McCloud dies but Clint survives. As a result of killing McCloud, Clint receives a pardon.

*The Man from Hell* was the first entry in the brief series former Northwestern football star Reb Russell did for producer Willis Kent in the 1934-35 series. The title refers to the hero having been in prison. The film is a fairly solid one, benefiting greatly from Fred Kohler's performance as the badman. It is a brutal movie with one man dying of a broken neck after being beaten by McCloud while another innocent man is lynched by the villain's gang who mistake him for the hero. There is an especially well-staged fight sequence between Reb Russell and Fred Kohler. *Film Daily* labeled the film a "Good western" which "unfolds with lots of action and excitement." Jack Kirk sings "That Rocky Trail from Town" as the credits roll, and spotlighted in the movie is the beautiful white stallion Rebel. The main drawback in *The Man from Hell* is the star, a 1930s counterpart of Sunset Carson. Reb Russell handled the action in good fashion but was a terrible actor, who had difficulty with even the simplest dialogue. This lack of thespian ability doomed him to a short career, even in low-budget westerns.

## Arizona Badman

1935, 58 minutes.

*P:* Willis Kent. *D:* S. Roy Luby. *PH:* James S. Brown Jr. *ED:* Roy Claire. *SD:* David Stoner. *Asst Dir:* William O'Connor.

*Cast:* Reb Russell, Lois January, Edmond Cobb, Tommy Bupp, Anne Howard, Tracy Layne, Dick Botiller, Ben Corbett, Slim Whitaker, Walter James, Ray Henderson, Silver Harr, Lionel Backus, Rebel.

The stepdaughter of a cattle rustler falls in love with an agent for the cattleman's association.

## Blazing Guns

Marcy, 1935, 58 minutes.

*P:* Willis Kent. *D:* Ray Heinz. *SC:* Forbes Parkhill. *PH:* James Diamond. *SD:* J.S. Westmoreland.

*Cast:* Reb Russell, Marion Shilling, Joe Girard, Frank McCarroll, Lafe McKee, Slim Whitaker, Rebel.

On his way to Colorado to see his girlfriend, a cowboy is bushwacked and later accused of being a highwayman.

## Border Vengeance

Marcy, 1935, 57 minutes.

*P:* Willis Kent. *D:* Ray Heinz. *PH:* James Diamond. *Asst Dir:* Bart Carre.

Poster for Reb Russell in *Border Vengeance* (Willis Kent, 1935).

*Cast:* Reb Russell, Mary Jane Carey, Kenneth MacDonald, June Bupp, Marty Joyce, Pat Harmon, Norman Feusier, Clarence Geldert, Ed Phillips, Glenn Strange, Fred Burns, Slim Whitaker, Hank Bell, Ben Corbett, Bart Carre, Eddie Parker, Silvertip Baker, Bud Pope, Bill Gillis, Mabel Strickland, Montie Montana, Rex Bell, Rebel, Sunday.

A rodeo rider tries to help a family forced off their land by greedy relatives.

## Cheyenne Tornado

Marcy, 1935, 55 minutes.

*P:* Willis Kent. *D:* William O'Connor. *PH:* Harvey Gould. *ED:* Roy Claire. *SD:* T.T. Triplett. *Asst Dir:* Bart Carre.

*Cast:* Reb Russell, Victoria Vinton, Edmond Cobb, Roger Williams, Dick Botiller, Francis McDonald, Oscar Gahan, Tina Menard, Ed Porter, Winton Perry, Lafe McKee, Clyde McClary, Jack Evans, Hank Bell, Bart Carre, Rebel.

A wanted outlaw tries to persuade a female ranch owner from taking revenge on a family of sheepherders.

## Lightning Triggers

Marcy, 1935, 50 minutes.

*P:* Willis Kent. *D:* S. Roy Luby. *ST:* E.B. Mann. *PH:* James Diamond. *ED:* Roy Claire. *SD:* T.T. Triplett. *Asst Dir:* Bart Carre.

*Cast:* Reb Russell, Yvonne Pelletier, Fred Kohler, Jack Rockwell, Edmond Cobb, Lew Meehan, Olin Francis, Lillian Castle, William McCall, Dick Botiller, Steve Clark,

Artie Ortego, Ed Porter, Smiley Burnette, Rebel.

On the trail of an outlaw gang, a cowboy learns their leader is his father.

## Outlaw Rule

February, 1935, 60 minutes.

*P:* Willis Kent. *D:* S. Roy Luby. *SC:* E.B. Mann. *PH:* James Diamond. *ED:* Roy Claire. *SD:* Buddy Meyers. *Asst Dir:* Bart Carre.

*Cast:* Reb Russell, Betty Mack, Yakima Canutt, John McGuire, Jack Rockwell, Al Bridge, Joe Girard, Jack Kirk, Henry Hall, Ralph Lewis, Bart Carre, Rebel.

A lawman known as The Whistler tries to prove a young rancher is innocent of a murder charge.

## Range Warfare

March, 1935, 60 minutes.

*P:* Willis Kent. *D:* S. Roy Luby. *SC:* E.B. Mann, from his story "The Death Whistler." *PH:* James Diamond. *ED:* Roy Claire.

*Cast:* Reb Russell, Lucille Lund, Wally Wales, Roger Williams, Lafe McKee, Slim Whitaker, Dick Botiller, Chief Blackhawk, Ed Boland, Gene Alsace, Ed Porter, Rebel.

A vengeful cowboy is after an outlaw gang which has rustled cattle and committed murder. Reissued as *Vengeance.*

## Gunsmoke on the Guadalupe

May, 1935, 57 minutes.

*P:* Montie Montana [uncredited Willis Kent]. *D:* Bartlett [Bart] Carre. *SC:* Paul Evan Leahman. *PH:* Harvey Gould. *ED:* Roy Claire. *SD:* J.S. Westmoreland. *Asst Dir:* Richard Sherer.

*Cast:* Buck Coburn [Rocky Cameron/Gene Alsace], Marion Shilling, Phyllis Barrington, Chief Thundercloud, Steve Clark, Lloyd Ingraham, Lafe McKee, Tracy Layne, Henry Hall, Roger Williams, Dick Botiller, Philo McCullough, Nelson McDowell, Bud Osborne, Ben Corbett, Lew Meehan, Roy Bucko, Buck Bucko, Bill Patton, Bud McClure, Bart Carre.

A cowboy gets a job on a ranch where the owner is feuding with an attorney who lusts for his pretty daughter.

## Circle of Death

Syndicate, June 1, 1935, 60 minutes.

*P:* Willis Kent. *D:* J. Frank Glendon. *SC:* Roy Claire. *PH:* James Diamond. *ED:* S. Roy Luby. *SD:* J.S. Westmoreland. *Asst Dir:* Bart Carre.

*Cast:* Montie Montana, Tove Linden, Yakima Canutt, Jack Carson [Gaylord (Steve) Pendleton], J. Frank Glendon, John Ince, Princess Ah-Tee-Ha, Chief Standing Bear, Dick Botiller, Marin Sais, Bob Burns, Slim Whitaker, Olin Francis, George Morrell, Hank Bell, Budd Buster, Bart Carre, Henry Hall, Ben Corbett, Artie Ortego, Jack Kirk, Ray Henderson.

A white man raised by Indians helps a settler thwart thieves after gold on his ranch.

## The Pace That Kills

1936, 64 minutes.

*P-SC:* Willis Kent. *D:* William A. O'Connor. *PH:* Jack Greenhalgh. *ED:* Holbrook N. Todd. *SD:* T.T. Triplett. *Asst Dir:* Louis Goremomprez.

*Cast:* Lois January, Noel Madison, Sheila Mannors, Dean Benton, Lois Lindsay, Charles Delaney, Eddie Phillips, Frank Shannon, Gaby Fay, Maury Peck, Nona Lee, Gay Sheridan, Frank Collins, Mary Gordon, Marin Sais, Richard Botiller.

Poster for *Circle of Death* (Willis Kent, 1935) starring Montie Montana.

A gangster heads a dope ring which leads young girls into a web of addiction. Reissued in 1937 as *The Cocaine Fiends*.

## Race Suicide

Real Life Dramas, 1937, 61 minutes.
  *P:* Willis Kent. *D:* S. Roy Luby. *PH:* Marcel LePicard. *ED:* Robert Jahns. *Mus:* Milton Royce. *SD:* Hans Weeren. *Asst Dir:* Charles Wasserman.
  *Cast:* Willy Castello, Lona Andre, Carleton Young, Erma Deen, Madeline Hunt, Maude Fealy, Bryant Washburn, Lloyd Ingraham, Frank LaRue, Ethel Leopold, Maxine Lewis, Richard Beach, Frances Flavin, Franklyn Farnum, Brown & Brown, Harry Burns.
  An illegal abortion ring preys on young women in a big city but is opposed by an assistant district attorney. Reissued as *What Price Passion?*

## Smashing the Vice Trust

Real Life Dramas, 1937, 60 minutes.
  *P:* Willis Kent. *D:* John Melville. *SC:* Marion Candler. *PH:* Robert Cline. *ED:* Fred Bain. *SD:* Corson Jowett. *Asst Dir:* Lionel Backus.
  *Cast:* Willy Castello, Vyola Vonn, August Anderson, Maude Fealy, Sam Flint, Edward Cassidy, Selmer Jackson, John Belmont, Paul Perry, Ardis May.
  Because his profits are down, a gangster has his minions kidnap high school girls to work in his brothels.

## What Price Ignorance?

1937, 5 reels.

*P:* Willis Kent.

A young woman is coaxed away from her family by a drug dealer and she ends up in the big city dancing in dives.

## The Wages of Sin

Real Life Dramas, 1938, 65 minutes.
*P:* Willis Kent. *D:* Herman E. Webber. *PH:* Harvey Gould. *ED:* Robert Jahns. *SD:* Hans Weeren. *Asst Dir:* Charles Wasserman.

*Cast:* Constance Worth, Willy Castello, Blanche Mehaffey, Bryant Washburn, Kenneth Harlan, Clara Kimball Young, Carleton Young, Frank LaRue, Rose Plummer, Horace Murphy, Jan Duggan, Paula Bromleigh, Martha Chapin, Edward Cassidy, Frank Wayne, Hal Mead, Betty Wonder, Rose LaRose, Edward Argyle, Dave Daggett, Jack Salling, Willa Curtis, Eve Lynn.

Because she has to support her lazy family and cannot keep up her appearance, a hard-working girl drifts into prostitution after getting involved with a pimp.

## Souls in Pawn

Real Life Dramas, 1940, 64 minutes.
*P:* Willis Kent. D: John Melville.
*Cast:* Ginger Britton, Donald Kerr, Richard Beach, Lloyd Ingraham, Beatrice Curtis, Symona Boniface, Evelyn Mulhall, Patti Lacey, Sammy White, Richard Lee Spitz.

Secretly married to a student, a young girl is forced to give up her baby.

## Mad Youth

Atlas/Real Life Dramas, May 20, 1940, 61 minutes.
*P-SC:* Willis Kent. *D:* Melville Shyer. *PH:* Marcel LePicard & Harvey Gould. *ED:* I.R. [Robert] Jahns. *SD:* Corson Jowett.

*Cast:* Mary Ainslee, Betty Compson, Willy Castello, Betty Atkinson, Tommy Wonder, Lorelei Readoux, Maude Fealy, Donald Kerr, Ray Hirsh, Eugene Taylor, Maxine Taylor, Patti Lacey, Aileen Morris, Pearl Tolson, Hal Price, Ethelreada Leopold.

A society woman and her beautiful daughter fall in love with the same gigolo. Also called *Naked Youth.*

# Liberty Pictures Corporation

Unlike most independent Hollywood studios, Liberty Pictures Corporation had two lives. Producer M.H. "Max" Hoffman formed the company in 1930, but after producing only one film, *Ex-Flame*, he switched to the Allied Pictures Corporation (q.v.) monicker under which he operated until the spring of 1934. Less than a month after Allied's last release, Liberty was back in business in May of that year with *Cheaters*, and during the next two years Hoffman would put out a dozen feature films under the Liberty banner. Like the product he made for Allied, Hoffman's Liberty features were B-plus outings with solid production values, good direction and name stars. Unlike the Allieds, however, the Liberty releases contained no westerns or modern-day adaptations of literary classics. In deference to other independent operators, Hoffman's Liberty product was usually based on literary originals, short stories by such noted writers as P.G. Wodehouse, Earl Derr Biggers, Damon Runyon, Dorothy Canfield, Zola Gale and Mrs. Wilson Woodrow.

Although M.H. Hoffman dropped his penchant for modernizing classic literature when he revived Liberty in 1934, the company's first attempt, *Ex-Flame*, in 1930, was based on Mrs. Henry Wood's 1861 chestnut *East Lynn*. It starred Neil Hamilton and Marion Nixon, who would later reteam for Hoffman in the revived Liberty's second release, *Once to Every Bachelor*, in 1934. It should be noted too that Hoffman retained much of his production outfit from the Allied days. His son, M.H. Hoffman, Jr., continued to supervise the Liberty productions, which were photographed by Harry Neumann and Tom Galligan and edited by Mildred Johnston. The Liberty releases, however, stayed mainly with contemporary social problems such as marital infidelity in *Two Heads on a Pillow* (1934) and *Penthouse Party* (1936) or juvenile delinquency as in *School for Girls* (1934). There was also an attempt at medium-budget musicals like *The Old Homestead* (1935) (which introduced The Sons of the Pioneers, including Roy Rogers, to the screen) and *Dizzy Dames* (1936). Among the more interesting releases were *When Strangers Meet* (1934), about the interwoven lives of the residents of a Hollywood bungalow court, and *No Ransom* (1935), which featured Jack LaRue as a hardened gangster who learns humanity while trying not to carry out a job as a hitman.

Despite good releases Liberty Pictures found itself in a shaky financial situation by the summer of 1935 and was purchased by Herbert J. Yates, who merged it with Majestic (q.v.), Monogram and several other smaller outfits to form Republic Pictures Corporation. While Hoffman's productions continued to carry the Liberty banner, they were distributed by Republic, including the New York City-filmed pickup feature, *The Crime of Dr. Crespi* (1935), starring Erich von Stroheim. In 1937 Hoffman produced two Ken Maynard westerns, *Boots of Destiny* and *Trailin' Trouble*, for Grand National. He died later that same year.

## Ex-Flame

December, 1930, 80 minutes.

*P:* M.H. Hoffman & Edward R. Halperin. *D-ST:* Victor Halperin. *SC:* George Draney & Herbert Farjeon, from the novel *East Lynn* by Mrs. Henry Wood. *PH:* Ernest Miller. *ED:* Donn Hayes. *SD:* Harold Hobson. *AD:* Charles Cadwallader. *Prod Mgr:* George Berholon. *Asst Dir:* Gordon Cooper.

*Cast:* Neil Hamilton, Marion Nixon, Judith Barrie, Norman Kerry, Snub Pollard, Roland Drew, Jose Bohr, Joan Standing, Cornelius Keefe, May Beatty, Lorimer Johnson, Joseph North, Charles Crockett, Billy Hagerty, Louis Armstrong and His Orchestra.

Because of her jealousy over her husband's former girlfriend, a young woman not only loses her home but becomes involved in scandal and ends up having her young son taken away from her.

## Cheaters

May 11, 1934, 66 minutes.
　　*P:* M.H. Hoffman. *AP:* M.H. Hoffman Jr. *D:* Phil Rosen. *SC:* Adele Buffington, from the story "The Peacock Screen" by Fanny Heaslip Lea. *PH:* Harry Neumann & Tom Galligan. *ED:* Mildred Johnston. *SD:* L.E. Clarke. *Mus:* Abe Meyer. *Prod Mgr:* Ray Culley.
　　*Cast:* Bill Boyd, June Collyer, Dorothy Mackaill, William Collier, Jr., Alan Mowbray, Guinn Williams, Louise Beavers, John Webb Dillon, Danny Dowling, Bill O'Brien, Francis Ford, Eve Reynolds, Maralyn Young.
　　Crooks are after a rich man's money and one of them, a young woman, plans to marry and then divorce him for a hefty settlement.

## Once to Every Bachelor

August 23, 1934, 67 minutes.
　　*P:* M.H. Hoffman. *AP:* M.H. Hoffman Jr. *D:* William Nigh. *SC:* George Waggner, from the novel *Search for the Spring* by Eleanor Gates. *PH:* Harry Neumann & Tom Galligan. *ED:* Mildred Johnston. *SD:* R.E. Tyler. *Prod Mgr:* Rudolph Flothow.
　　*Cast:* Marion Nixon, Neil Hamilton, Aileen Pringle, William Austin, Raymond Hatton, Bradley Page, Kathleen Howard, George Irving, Ralf Harolde, Don Alvarado.
　　A young woman mixed up with gangsters becomes involved with a society man who seeks a limited marriage.

## Take the Stand

September 5, 1934, 78 minutes.

*P:* M.H. Hoffman. *AP:* M.H. Hoffman Jr. *D:* Phil Rosen. *SC:* Albert DeMond, from the story "The Deuce of Hearts" by Earl Derr Biggers. *PH:* Harry Neumann & Tom Galligan. *ED:* Mildred Johnston. *Mus:* Abe Meyer. *SD:* W.C. Smith. *Prod Mgr:* Ray Culley.
　　*Cast:* Jack LaRue, Thelma Todd, Gail Patrick, Russell Hopton, Berton Churchill, Vince Barnett, Leslie Fenton, Sheila Terry, Paul Hurst, DeWitt Jennings, Bradley Page, Oscar Apfel, Jason Robards, Richard Tucker, Arnold Gray, Edward Kane, Lew Kelly, Al Hill.
　　Suspects in a crime threaten a columnist who is murdered during a broadcast and a detective seeks the killer.

## Two Heads on a Pillow

October 3, 1934, 68 minutes.
　　*P:* M.H. Hoffman. *AP:* M.H. Hoffman, Jr. *D:* William Nigh. *SC:* Albert DeMond, from the story "Eternal Masculine" by Dorothy Canfield. *PH:* Harry Neumann. *ED:* Mildred Johnston. *Mus:* Abe Meyer. *SD:* R.E. Tyler. *Prod Mgr:* Rudolph Flothow.
　　*Cast:* Neil Hamilton, Miriam Jordan, Henry Armetta, Hardie Albright, Dorothy Appleby, Mary Forbes, Ed Martindel, Claude King, Lona Andre, Betty Blythe, Edward Kane, Claire McDowell, Nellie V. Nichols, George Lewis, Emily Fitzroy, Dorothy Granger, Julia Ford, Mary Foy, Jack Kennedy.
　　Two attorneys, once married, are on opposite sides in a divorce case. Reissued as *Love Can't Wait.*

## When Strangers Meet

October 9, 1934, 72 minutes.
　　*P:* M.H. Hoffman. *D:* Christy

Cabanne. *SC:* Adele Buffington, from the story "The Way" by Zola Gale. *PH:* Harry Neumann & Tom Galligan. *ED:* Mildred Johnston. *SD:* W.C. Smith.

*Cast:* Richard Cromwell, Arline Judge, Lucien Littlefield, Hale Hamilton, Charles Middleton, Sarah Padden, Ray Walker, Barbara Weeks, Sheila Terry, Sidney Miller, Bryant Washburn, Vera Gordon, Maude Eburne, Lee Kohlmar, Luis Alberni, Julie Haydon, Herman Bing, Arthur Hoyt, Franklyn Parker.

The story of the lives of the residents of a bungalow court run by a nasty landlord.

## School for Girls

October 16, 1934, 66 minutes.

*P:* M.H. Hoffman. *AP:* M.H. Hoffman, Jr. *D:* William Nigh. *SC:* Albert DeMond, from the story "Our Undisciplined Daughters" by Reginald Wright Kauffman. *PH:* Harry Neumann. *ED:* Mildred Johnston. *SD:* R.E. Tyler. *Prod Mgr:* Rudolph Flothow.

*Cast:* Sidney Fox, Lois Wilson, Paul Kelly, Lucille LaVerne, Dorothy Lee, Toby Wing, Dorothy Appleby, Lona Andre, Russell Hopton, Barbara Weeks, Kathleen Burke, Anna Q. Nilsson, Purnell B. Pratt, Robert Warwick, William Farnum, Charles Ray, Mary Foy, Dawn O'Day [Anne Shirley], Myrtle Stedman, Edward Kane, Gretta Gould, George Cleveland, Helen Chadwick, Helen Foster, Fred Kelsey, Ed LeSaint, Harry Woods, Jack Kennedy.

A young woman is sent to prison for a crime she did not commit and is paroled to the custody of her future husband.

## No Ransom

January 9, 1935, 78 minutes.

*P:* M.H. Hoffman. *AP:* M.H. Hoffman, Jr. *D:* Fred Newmeyer. *SC:* Albert DeMond, from the story "The Big Mitten" by Damon Runyon. *PH:* Harry Neumann. *ED:* Jack [John] English. *Mus:* Abe Meyer. *SD:* R.E. Tyler. *Prod Mgr:* Rudolph Flothow.

*Cast:* Leila Hyams, Phillips Holmes, Jack LaRue, Robert McWade, Hedda Hopper, Vince Barnett, Eddie Nugent, Carl Miller, Irving Baker, Christian Rub, Garry Owen, Fritz Ridgeway, Mary Foy, Arthur Hoyt.

When a rich man hires a hoodlum to kill him because of family problems, the gangster instead tries to make the wayward kin see the light of day. Working title: *The Quitter.*

## Sweepstake Annie

January 30, 1935, 81 minutes.

*P:* M.H. Hoffman. *D:* William Nigh. *SC-ST:* W. Scott Darling. *PH:* Harry Neumann. *ED:* Mildred Johnston. *SD:* Harold Bumbaugh. *Prod Mgr:* Rudolph Flothow.

*Cast:* Marion Nixon, Tom Brown, Wera Engels, Inez Courtney, Ivan Lebedeff, Lucien Littlefield, Dorothy Peterson, William Janney, Carol Tevis.

A Hollywood script girl wins a sweepstakes and moves out on her lazy family but soon becomes the intended victim of a swindle.

## The Crime of Dr. Crespi

Liberty/Republic, September 24, 1935, 63 minutes.

*P-D:* John H. Auer. *AP:* Herb Hayman. *SC:* Lewis Graham & Edwin Olmstead. *ST:* John H. Auer, from "The Premature Burial" by Edgar Allan Poe. *PH:* Larry Williams. *ED:* Leonard Wheeler. *AD:* William

Erich von Stroheim, Harriet Russell and Paul Guilfoyle in *The Crime of Dr. Crespi* (Republic/Liberty, 1935).

Saulter. *Mus:* Milton Schwartzwald. *Makeup:* Fred Ryle. *Prod Sup:* W.T. O'Sullivan.

*Cast:* Erich von Stroheim (Dr. Andre Crespi), Harriet Russell (Estelle Ross), Dwight Frye (Dr. Thomas), Paul Guilfoyle (Dr. John B. Arnold), John Bohn (Dr. Stephen Ross), Geraldine Kay (Miss Rexford), Jeanne Kelly [Jean Brooks] (Miss Gordon), Patsy Bertin (Jeanne), Joe Verdi (Mr. DiAngelo), Dean Raymond (Minister).

Dr. Andre Crespi (Erich von Stroheim) is a famous surgeon who runs a private hospital assisted by doctors Thomas (Dwight Frye) and Arnold (Paul Guilfoyle). Crespi learns that his former colleague and romantic rival Dr. Stephen Ross (John Bohn) has been badly hurt in a car wreck but agrees to help him upon the urging of Estelle Ross (Harriet Russell), the woman Crespi loves. Although the operation is a success, the vengeful Crespi gives Ross a serum that puts him in a cataleptic trance, making him appear dead. That night Crespi not only comforts Estelle over the loss of her husband but goes to the morgue and gloats over Ross telling him he can hear, see and feel but cannot move and that he will witness his own funeral and die trying to escape from his grave. Before the service Dr. Thomas accuses Crespi of murdering Ross and they fight with Crespi tying up Thomas and locking him in a closet. Following the funeral he sets Thomas free but warns him to be quiet or he will have him committed to an observation ward. Thomas, however, goes to Arnold with his story, and that night they dig up Ross and take him back to the hospital where, regaining motor coordination, he goes after Crespi. Estelle arrives at the hospital as her husband

Hugh Farr, Fuzzy Knight, Tim Spencer, Bob Nolan, Mary Carlisle, Len Slye [Roy Rogers] and Lillian Miles in *The Old Homestead* (Republic/Liberty, 1935).

confronts the now drunk Crespi. Realizing he has been exposed and has also lost Estelle for good, Crespi commits suicide. Later Dr. Arnold marries nurse Miss Rexford (Geraldine Kay) and becomes head of the hospital.

By the time Liberty Pictures acquired this Bronx-lensed horror thriller (shot at the old Biograph Studios), the company was on unsteady legs. Almost immediately Liberty was absorbed into the newly formed Republic Pictures Corporation and *The Crime of Dr. Crespi* went into theatres as a Liberty release distributed by Republic. Its chief asset is Erich von Stroheim's wild-eyed portrayal of the mad, sadistic Dr. Crespi and for some rather horrific morgue and graveyard sequences. It also had good dialogue. As Crespi gloats over his helpless victim he trumpets, "You shall experience such horrors as you never imagined in

your wildest nightmares... . You will feel the cold of your own grave." On a lighter side, after a jittery father-to-be (Joe Verdi) finds out he has five new babies, the nurse (Jeanne Kelly) tells him, "Little man you've had a busy day." Horror specialist Dwight Frye costars as the meek associate of Crespi who proves the madman's undoing.

In *The Encyclopedia of Horror Movies* (1986), Phil Hardy writes, "Cheap, lurid and hesitantly directed, it nevertheless can boast moody camerawork and excellent supporting performances to counterbalance Stroheim's over-the-top portrayal of lecherous sadism." The film has many close-ups although its overall photography is murky and darkly lit. Perhaps most unnerving of all is the fact that the famous surgeon Dr. Crespi is a chain smoker.

Despite much publicity about its

Helen Twelvetrees and Donald Cook (as Ellery Queen) in *The Spanish Cape Mystery* (Republic/Liberty, 1935).

relationship to Edgar Allan Poe's story "The Premature Burial," *The Crime of Dr. Crespi* is only faintly reminiscent of that tale.

## Born to Gamble

Liberty/Republic, October 4, 1935, 65 minutes.

*P:* M.H. Hoffman. *D:* Phil Rosen. *SC:* E. Morton Hough, from the story "The Green Poropulos" by Edgar Wallace. *PH:* Gilbert Warrenton. *ED:* Mildred Johnston. *SD:* Harold Bumbaugh. *Prod Mgr:* Rudolph Flothow.

*Cast:* Onslow Stevens, H.B. Warner, Maxine Doyle, Eric Linden, Lois Wilson, William Janney, Ben Alexander, Lucien Prival, Crauford Kent, Norman Phillips, Jr.

A wealthy man recounts how gambling caused tragedy within his own family. Working title: *I'll Bet You.*

## The Old Homestead

October 5, 1935, 72 minutes.

*P:* M.H. Hoffman. *AP:* M.H. Hoffman, Jr. *D:* William Nigh. *SC-ST:* W. Scott Darling, from the novel by John Russell Corvell. *PH:* Harry Neumann. *ED:* Mildred Johnston. *SD:* Harold Bumbaugh. *Prod Mgr:* Rudolph Flothow. *Songs:* John T. Scholl, Louis Alter, J. Keirn Brennan, Ted Snyder, George Waggner, Howard Jackson, Jack Bennett, Neil Moret, Harry Tobias, Charles Rosoff, Manny Stone & The Sons of the Pioneers.

*Cast:* Mary Carlisle, Lawrence Gray, Dorothy Lee, Willard Robertson, Eddie Nugent, Lillian Miles,

Fuzzy Knight, Eddie Kane, Harry Conley, The Sons of the Pioneers [Bob Nolan, Leonard Slye (Roy Rogers), Karl & Hugh Farr, Tim Spencer].

Two lovers come to the big city to become singing stars and they end up having their heads turned by fame.

## The Spanish Cape Mystery

Liberty/Republic, October 9, 1935, 67 minutes.

*P:* M.H. Hoffman. *D:* Lewis D. Collins. *SC:* Albert De Mond, from the novel by Ellery Queen. *PH:* Gilbert Warrenton. *ED:* Ernie Leadley. *SD:* Harold Bumbaugh. *Prod Mgr:* Rudolph Flothow.

*Cast:* Helen Twelvetrees, Donald Cook, Berton Churchill, Frank Sheridan, Harry Stubbs, Guy Usher, Huntley Gordon, Jack LaRue, Betty Blythe, Olaf Hytten, Ruth Gillette, Frank Leigh, Barbara Bedford, George Baxter, Katherine Morrow, Arnold Gray, Donald Kerr, Lee Prather, George Cleveland.

On vacation, detective Ellery Queen becomes involved in two disappearances as a rich family tries to break a will.

## Penthouse Party

January 29, 1936, 81 minutes.

*P:* M.H. Hoffman. *AP:* M.H. Hoffman Jr. *D:* William Nigh. *SC:* Gertrude Orr, from the story "Eyes of Youth" by Mrs. Wilson Woodrow. *PH:* Harry Neumann. *ED:* Mildred Johnston. *Mus:* Abe Meyer. *SD:* R.E. Tyler. *Prod Mgr:* Rudolph Flothow.

*Cast:* Marguerite Churchill, Bruce Cabot, Evelyn Brent, Reginald Denny, Dorothy Lee, William Janney, Dickie Moore, Cora Sue Collins, Lillian Harmer.

A married couple is divorced but years later their children cause them to be reunited. Originally called *Without Children.*

## Dizzy Dames

July 18, 1936, 73 minutes.

*P:* M.H. Hoffman. *D:* William Nigh. *SC:* George Waggner, from the story "The Watch Dog" by P.G. Wodehouse. *PH:* Harry Neumann. *ED:* Mildred Johnston. *Mus:* Howard Jackson. *Songs:* George Waggner, Louis Alter, Edward Heyman, Harry Tobias & Neil Moret.

*Cast:* Marjorie Rambeau, Florine McKinney, Lawrence Gray, Inez Courtney, Berton Churchill, Fuzzy Knight, Kitty Kelly, Lillian Miles, John Warburton, Mary Forbes, Christine Marston, Edward Heyman, Howard Jackson, The [Theodore] Kosloff Dancers.

The owner of a theatrical boardinghouse does not want her daughter to know that she was once an actress.

# Majestic Pictures Corporation

Although it released only about thirty features from 1930 to 1935, several of which were imports, Majestic Pictures Corporation is one of the most fondly remembered of the independent motion picture operations of the 1930s. Majestic's product had a classy look, and overall the company's release schedule was a good one. Some of its most memorable features include *The Crusader* (1932), *The Vampire Bat* (1933), *The World Gone Mad* (1933), *The Sin of Nora Moran* (1933) and *The Scarlet Letter* (1934). Majestic maintained no studio of its own, filming primarily at Universal or the Larry Darmour Studio on Santa Monica Boulevard. At first the company maintained a few film exchanges although its product was mostly released theatrically by Capitol Film Exchange (q.v.). While these two aspects qualify Majestic as a Poverty Row outfit, its movies were above the usual low-budget quality, and some of its releases, like *The World Gone Mad*, played in top theatres.

Majestic first saw the light of day late in 1930 with the release of *Today*, produced by Harry Sherman and Jack T. Trop, later responsible for the "Hopalong Cassidy" series at Paramount. Conrad Nagel toplined this heavy melodrama in which a young wife (Catherine Dale Owen) sells herself when she cannot adapt to poverty after her husband loses his fortune. The producers included two endings, one tragic and one happy, for exploitation appeal. *Photoplay* opined, "One of those sensationals—all hell, sex and box-office. Hokum, but there's Conrad Nagel to hold you." *Today* remained Majestic's sole release for nearly two years until producer Phil Goldstone, a Palm Springs real estate developer, took over the operation. Some two dozen features were produced by the company from 1932 to 1935, most by Goldstone or Larry Darmour. Perhaps the reason Majestic's product managed to look so classy was because the company worked hand-in-hand with the giant Metro-Goldwyn-Mayer, thanks to a business arrangement with Ida Koverman, a close associate of Louis B. Mayer. Many of the early Majestic films were photographed by Ira Morgan and edited by Otis Garrett, both top MGM craftsmen. Also, by the time Majestic got reactivated in 1932, the company was able to maintain twenty-nine film exchanges in major cities, giving the Majestic features assured bookings not generally granted to independent operations. Throughout most of the country, however, the company's product was handled by Capital Film Exchange.

The two producers most associated with Majestic Pictures are Phil Goldstone and Larry Darmour. Phil Goldstone (1893-1963) worked throughout the 1920s as an independent producer who ran Phil Goldstone Productions. He made low-budget westerns with Franklyn Farnum and action pictures with stars like William Fairbanks, Richard Talmadge and Kenneth Harlan. He also produced dramas like *Deserted at the Altar* (1922), with Tully Marshall and Bessie Love, *The Verdict*, a 1925 Truart release with Lou Tellegen and Louise Lorraine, and Tiffany's *Lost at Sea* (1926), starring Jane Novak, Huntley Gordon and Lowell Sherman. Born in 1897, Larry Darmour acquired his studio in the late 1920s, it having once been the headquarters of Ben Wilson Productions. Darmour made comedy shorts with Karl Dane but his most impressive success came with the "Mickey McGuire" short subjects starring Mickey Rooney, which lasted from 1927 to 1934. By then Darmour was making features for other companies, independents such as Empire (q.v.) and majors like Columbia. He was in charge of production on most of the Majestic films during the 1934-35 season with the major effort being a remake of *The Scarlet Letter* in 1934. After Majestic folded, Darmour produced a series of westerns with Ken Maynard for Columbia and then remained with the studio producing "B" features and the "Ellery Queen" series before his death in 1942.

Unlike most independents, many of the Majestic releases came from literary sources. *The Crusader* (1932) and *Sing, Sinner, Sing!* (1933) were based on plays by Wilson Collison, *What Price Decency?* (1933) was from Arthur Gregor's play, and *The Sin of Nora Moran* (1933) was based on the stage play *Burnt Offerings* by Maxwell Goodhue. Octavas Roy Cohen's 1933 novel *The Back Stage Mystery* was the basis for the solid detective thriller *Curtain at Eight* (1934), while *Unknown Blonde* (1934) was based on Theodore I. Irwin's 1932 novel *Collusion*. Regarding this effort *Harrison's Reports* said, "The plot was altered considerably.... . The picture has been produced lavishly. With better material it would be worthy of a release by a major company." Short stories also served as the basis for some Majestic films like *Hearts of Humanity* (1932), from a story by Olga Printzlau, and *The Perfect Clue* (1935), taken from Lolita Ann Westman's story "Lawless Honeymoon."

As noted earlier, Majestic Pictures produced some well remembered features like *The Vampire Bat, The Crusader, The World Gone Mad, The Sin of Nora Moran* and *The Scarlet Letter. The Vampire Bat* was filmed on the Universal lot and reunited Lionel Atwill and Fay Wray, both of whom had starred in *Doctor X* (1932) and *Mystery of the Wax Museum* (1933) at Warner Brothers. The film has such a classy look about it that it is often mistaken for a major studio production, and in her autobiography *On the Other Hand* (1989) Fay Wray identifies it as a Universal picture. Edward T. Lowe scripted the horror effort as he did with two other Majestic successes, *The Crusader* and *The World Gone Mad*, both starring Evelyn Brent. The former is a particularly strong melodrama about gangsters trying to silence a district attorney, and its top-notch cast garnered some major bookings as had *The World Gone Mad*. In his book *Second Feature* (1991), John Cocchi calls *The Sin of Nora Moran* "the best independent feature of the Thirties." Phil Goldstone not only produced this effort but also directed it, one of his few directorial credits. Larry Darmour produced *The Scarlet Letter*, starring Colleen Moore, Hardie Albright and Henry B. Walthall, based on the classic novel by Nathaniel Hawthorne. *Motion Picture Daily* said it was "able to stand alone on any bill" while *Boxoffice* called it "a credit to independent production."

In addition to its schedule of major releases Majestic also made six westerns starring Jack Hoxie for the Saturday matinee market. Henry L. Goldstone produced these polished efforts, which were nicely scripted by Oliver Drake, except for the initial effort *Gold* in 1932. The Hoxies look better than most non-major studio "B" westerns, but they had one drawback—the star. A true westerner, Jack Hoxie had come to stardom in the early 1920s in the independent field and was a major name as a cowboy hero at Universal during the middle of the decade. When sound came along he dropped out of pictures to tour with circuses. Apparently the need for money brought him back to films, but by 1932 he was getting too old and too heavy to carry off the hero role. He also had considerable trouble with dialogue. Thus Jack Hoxie's films are something of an enigma. Entertaining for the most part, they are hurt by what should be their biggest asset, the star. After a few efforts the studio apparently lost interest in Hoxie and it shows in the films. *Variety* noted that in *Via Pony Express* (1933), "Hoxie is double lassoed from above and left suspended by the dual ropes as his captors ride off with the mail," making the star look like a buffoon. The same film also really relegated him to minor status by giving the bulk of the action to the second lead, Lane Chandler. After the six Majestics, Jack Hoxie left the cinema trails forever, going back to the circus for a time and then settling down as a rancher.

By 1934 Majestic began supplementing its release schedule with imports. Like most independents, the company had no short subject or serial program and relied on feature releases. Apparently, too much money had been expended on the prestige films of the previous year, and announced titles like *My Life*, based on Isadora Duncan, *A Laughing Woman*, *Wild Geese* and *The Rosary* failed to materialize. The company did, however, import three British features made by Wardour Films: *The Charming Deceiver* (1933), starring Constance Cummings (called *Heads We Go* in its homeland); *You Made Me Love You* (1934), with Stanley Lupino and Thelma Todd, both directed by Monty Banks; and *The Morning After* (1934), starring Sally Eilers and Ben Lyon, which Allan Dwan had directed and cowritten as *I Spy*. There was also a Polish import, *Szpiez (The Spy)*, a 1934 espionage thriller.

Majestic Pictures came to a close in 1935 with a quartet of Larry Darmour productions, all with considerably lower budgets than had been given the company's 1932-34 features.

## Today

November 1, 1930, 80 minutes.

*P:* Harry Sherman & Jack D. Trop. *D:* William Nigh. *SC:* Seton I. Miller. *PH:* James Wong Howe. *AD:* Albert D'Agostino. *SD:* Lester E. Tope. *Asst Dir:* Melville Shyer. *Prod Mgr:* Walter Ford Tilford. *Prod Asst:* Leonard Ross.

*Cast:* Conrad Nagel, Catherine Dale Owen, Sarah Padden, John Maurice Sullivan, Judith Vosselli, Julia Swayne Gordon, William Bailey, Edna Marion, Robert Thornby, Drew Demarest.

When her husband is forced to go to work after losing his fortune, a beautiful young society woman cannot cope and drifts into prostitution.

## Hearts of Humanity

September 21, 1932, 65 minutes.

*P:* Phil Goldstone. *D:* Christy Cabanne. *SC:* Edward T. Lowe. *ST:* Olga Printzlau. *PH:* Charles Stumar. *ED:* Don Lindberg.

*Cast:* Jean Hersholt, Jackie Searl, J. Farrell MacDonald, Claudia Dell, Charles Delaney, Lucille LaVerne, Richard Wallace, George Humbert,

J. Farrell MacDonald pictured in a lobby card from *The Phantom Express* (Majestic, 1932).

Betty Jane Graham, John Vosburgh, Tom McGuire.

When his policeman friend is shot by a burglar, an antique dealer adopts the dead man's young son.

## The Phantom Express

September 21, 1932, 70 minutes.

*P:* Irving C. Franklin & Donald M. Stone. *D:* Emory Johnson. *SC:* Emory Johnson & Laird Doyle. *PH:* Ross Fisher. *ED:* S. Roy Luby. *SD:* L.E. Tope. *Prod Mgr:* Robert Ross. *AD:* Mack D'Agostino.

*Cast:* William Collier, Jr. (Bruce Harrington), Sally Blane (Carolyn Nolan), J. Farrell MacDonald (D.J. "Smoky" Nolan), Hobart Bosworth (Mr. Harrington), Axel Axelson (Axel), Eddie Phillips (Jack Harrington), Lina Basquette (Betty), Robert Ellis (Rival Owner), Claire McDowell (Mrs. Nolan), David Rollins (Dick), Tom O'Brien (James Callahan), Huntley Gordon (Reynolds), Brady Kline, Jack Pennick (Thugs), Carl Stockdale (Chief Radio Operator), Alice Dahl (Miss Calhoun), Jack Mower, Tom Wilson, Alan Forest, Jack Trent, Bob Littlefield.

Old-time railroad engineer Smoky Nolan (J. Farrell MacDonald) has his train forced off the tracks by a phantom express which disappears. Despite being backed by his fireman Axel (Axel Axelson), he is placed before a board of inquiry run by company president Mr. Harrington (Hobart Bosworth), whose line has had several such crashes in recent months. At the session Harrington's playboy son Bruce (William Collier, Jr.) sees Nolan's pretty daughter Carolyn (Sally Blane) and falls for her. When no decision is reached Bruce asks his dad for the job of investigating the crash. He changes identities with a pal, Dick (David Rollins), and moves into the Nolan home as a boarder with a job as a mechanic at the railroad headquarters. A rival (Robert Ellis) wants to buy Harrington's railroad and is behind the phantom express, actually a plane with a spotlight which flies low on moonless nights, making engineers think there is a train coming from the opposite direction on the tracks. Harrington's secretary Reynolds (Huntley Gordon), who is in cahoots with the rivals, has Smoky fired from his job, and Bruce vows to get to the bottom of the situation. He finds a note threatening Dick, who the rivals think is Bruce, and this leads him and Axel to a remote airfield where they find Dick and Carolyn, who have been kidnapped by the thugs. A fight ensues, and the culprits are rounded up with Bruce getting the evidence he needs to prove the rival buyers are behind the wrecks. In order to stop the sale of the railroad, Bruce has Smoky engineer a speeding train through a storm. They reach their destination in time, the crooks are arrested, and the railroad is saved. Smoky gets his job back as Bruce and Carolyn go on their honeymoon.

A solid story and good special effects highlight *The Phantom Express*, a fast-paced railroad saga that benefits from a good performance by J. Farrell MacDonald as the old engineer who loses his job after the train he is piloting crashes. The Southern Pacific Railroad is named in the film, and its headquarters in Los Angeles provided many of the on-location sites in the feature. Especially impressive are the sequences with the phantom train, and the finale when engineer Smoky Nolan runs a race with a locomotive through a terrible storm to thwart the villains. A number of mudslides and bridge washouts highlight the latter sequence. While William Collier, Jr., is a bit too boyish for the role of the playboy turned undercover operative, Sally Blane is quite comely as the heroine and old-timer Hobart Bosworth hams entertainingly as the harried railroad executive. Lina Basquette has an amusing cameo as Collier's discarded girl-friend.

## The Crusader

October 5, 1932, 78 minutes.

*P:* Phil Goldstone. *D:* Frank R. Strayer. *SC:* Edward T. Lowe, from the play by Wilson Collison. *ED:* Otis Garrett. *SD:* Earl N. Crain.

*Cast:* Evelyn Brent, H.B. Warner, Lew Cody, Ned Sparks, Marceline Day, Walter Byron, John St. Polis, Arthur Hoyt, Ara Haswell, Joe Girard, Syd Saylor, Lloyd Ingraham.

As a reporter tries to bring up his paper's circulation, gangsters plot to get a crusading district attorney out of the way by blackmailing him through his daughter. Also released as *Should a Woman Tell?*

## Gold

October 5, 1932, 58 minutes.

*P:* Henry L. Goldstone. *D:* Otto Brower. *SC:* W. Scott Darling. *ST:* Jack [John Francis] Natteford. *PH:* Arthur Reed & Charles Marshall. *ED:* S. Roy Luby. *SD:* Earl N. Crain.

*Cast:* Jack Hoxie, Alice Day, Hooper Atchley, Matthew Betz, Lafe McKee, Jack Clifford, Tom London,

Robert Kortman, Jack Byron, Hank Bell, Jack Kirk, Harry Todd, Archie Ricks.

A young woman blames her father's partner when the old man is murdered over a gold claim.

## The Unwritten Law

November 26, 1932, 66 minutes.

*P:* Phil Goldstone. *D:* Christy Cabanne. *SC:* Edward T. Lowe. *PH:* Ira Morgan. *ED:* Otis Garrett. *SD:* Earl N. Crain.

*Cast:* Greta Nissen, Skeets Gallagher, Mary Brian, Lew Cody, Louise Fazenda, Hedda Hopper, Purnell B. Pratt, Theodore Von Eltz, Mischa Auer, Arthur Rankin, Wilfred Lucas, Ernie Adams, Howard Forshay, Betty Tyree.

A movie producer is found dead on a steamer and the suspects include an electrician he fired and a young woman whose mother he wronged.

## The Vampire Bat

January 10, 1932, 71 minutes.

*P:* Phil Goldstone. *D:* Frank R. Strayer. *SC:* Edward T. Lowe. *PH:* Ira Morgan. *ED:* Otis Garrett. *AD:* Daniel Hall. *SD:* Richard Tyler.

*Cast:* Lionel Atwill (Dr. Otto von Neimann), Fay Wray (Ruth Berrin), Melvyn Douglas (Karl Brettscheider), Maude Eburne (Gussie Schnappman), George E. Stone (Kringen), Dwight Frye (Herman Gleib), Robert Frazer (Emil Borst), Lionel Belmore (Burgomeister Gustav Schoen), Carl Stockdale (Schmidt, the Morgue Keeper), Harrison Greene (Weingarten), William Humphrey (Dr. Haupt), Fern Emmett (Gertrude), William V. Mong (Sauer), Rita Carlisle (Martha Mueller), Stella Adams (Georgiana), Paul Weigel (Holdstadt).

Vampires are blamed for several deaths in a remote village in Central Europe called Kleinschloss. The townspeople, led by the Burgomeister (Lionel Belmore), believe that since historical records show the area was plagued by vampires several hundred years before, the epidemic has returned. The local police inspector, Karl Brettscheider (Melvyn Douglas), scoffs at the vampire claims but gets little support from scientist Dr. Otto von Neimann (Lionel Atwill), whose assistant Ruth Berrin (Fay Wray) is being romanced by the policeman. Von Neimann lives at a castle with his Aunt Gussie (Maude Eburne), Ruth and another associate, Emil Borst (Robert Frazer). When an old woman (Rita Carlisle) dies, vampires are blamed, and the villagers suspect idiotic Herman Gleib (Dwight Frye) of being involved since he keeps pet bats. The villagers become worked up to a frenzy and chase Herman into a cave where he jumps to his death into a deep gorge. Meanwhile von Neimann uses hypnosis to have Emil murder a servant (Stella Adams) since the scientist needs her body for his experiments. While Herman is implicated in the killing, Karl realizes he was dead when the murder took place. Von Neimann then instructs Emil to kill the policeman and is forced to tie up Ruth in his laboratory when she learns of his plans. He tells her he has been using the vampire killings to mask his experiments in creating life. Karl takes the comatose Emil to the castle and surprises the scientist, who claims Emil was responsible for the murders. Emil awakens, however, and turns on von Neimann, killing him and then himself as Karl and Ruth escape.

Probably Majestic's best-known production, *The Vampire Bat* is a slickly

Lionel Atwill, Maude Eburne and Fay Wray in *The Vampire Bat* (Majestic, 1932).

made but somewhat slow horror film which cashed in on the popularity of the genre brought about by Universal's *Dracula* and *Frankenstein* in 1931. The movie was shot on the Universal lot using several impressive standing sets. It also used the standard scenes of torch-carrying villagers in pursuit of a monster. Horror favorites Lionel Atwill, Fay Wray and Dwight Frye add flavor to the affair, although hero Melvyn Douglas is a bit too flippant for a part that called for David Manners. Much of the comedy relief is supplied by Maude Eburne as the addled Aunt Gussie, while solid work came from Lionel Belmore, Paul Weigel, William V. Mong, Harrison Greene and Carl Stockdale as villagers. Ira Morgan's moody photography and Otis Garrett's fine editing add much to the movie, which is more atmospheric than horrific. Barrie Pattison wrote in *The Seal of Dracula* (1975), "While much of the film is again dull and talk-bound and played in drawing-room interiors, there are a couple of telling scenes: bat-lover Dwight Frye trapped on the cave stairway by an angry mob and the chilling moment when Fay Wray comes on Dr. Neimann, controlling his murderous aide by thought-transference. Such shots reek of the silent German cinema of *The Cabinet of Dr. Caligari* and *Raskolnikov*."

## Outlaw Justice

February 28, 1933, 61 minutes.

*P:* Henry L. Goldstone. *D:* Armand L. Schaefer. *SC:* Oliver Drake. *ST:* W. Scott Darling. *PH:* William Nobles.

*Cast*: Jack Hoxie, Dorothy Gulliver, Donald Keith, Charles King, Chris-Pin Martin, Jack Trent, Walter Shumway, Jack Rockwell, Tom London, Kermit Maynard.

Pretending to be an outlaw, a cowboy is on the trail of a crook.

# What Price Decency?

March 7, 1933, 67 minutes.

*P:* Phil Goldstone. *D:* Arthur Gregor. *SC:* Arthur Gregor, from his play. *PH:* Chester Lyons. *ED:* Otis Garrett. *SD:* Earl N. Crain.

*Cast:* Dorothy Burgess, Alan Hale, Walter Byron, Val Durant, Henry Durant, Zeppo the Monkey.

In the tropics a young woman with a tainted past marries a brutal pearl trader and then falls in love with another man.

# Law and Lawless

April 12, 1933, 58 minutes.

*P:* Henry L. Goldstone. *D:* Armand L. Schaefer. *SC:* Oliver Drake. *PH:* William Nobles. *ED:* S. Roy Luby. *SD:* Earl N. Crain.

*Cast:* Jack Hoxie, Hilda Moreno, Julian Rivero, Yakima Canutt, Edith Fellows, Wally Wales, J. Frank Glendon, Jack Mower, Bob Burns, Helen Gibson, Alma Rayford, Joe de la Cruz, Fred Burns, Elvira Sanchez, William Quinlan, Al Taylor, Dixie Starr, Slim Whitaker, Hank Bell, Ben Corbett, Gracia Granada and his Orchestra.

Riding into a range land plagued by rustlers, a cowboy is determined to stop the lawlessness.

# The World Gone Mad

April 15, 1933, 80 minutes.

*P:* Phil Goldstone. *D:* Christy Cabanne. *SC:* Edward T. Lowe. *PH:* Ira Morgan. *ED:* Otis Garrett. *SD:* Dean C. Daily. *AD:* David Hadon.

*Cast:* Pat O'Brien (Andy Farrell), Evelyn Brent (Carlotta/Nina Lamont), Neil Hamilton (Lionel Houston), Mary Brian (Diane Cromwell), Louis Calhern (Christopher Bruno), J. Carrol Naish (Raymond/Salvatore), Buster Phelps (Ralph Henderson), Richard Tucker (Grant Ames), John St. Polis (Cromwell), Geneva Mitchell (Evelyn Henderson), Wallis Clark (Avery Henderson), Huntley Gordon (Collins), Max Davidson (Abe Cohen), Joe Girard (Nichols), Lloyd Ingraham (Mr. Blair), Inez Courtney (Susie), Hooper Atchley (Harley Kemp), Syd Saylor (Collins).

When District Attorney Avery Henderson (Wallis Clark) gets too close to the truth about a huge investment scandal, its perpetrator, financier Grant Ames (Richard Tucker), has him earmarked for murder. The assignment goes through a chain of command, from gangster-businessman Christopher Bruno (Louis Calhern), to janitor Collins (Syd Saylor) to hitman Raymond (J. Carrol Naish), who uses torch singer Carlotta (Evelyn Brent) to help carry out the hit. It is made to look like Henderson was caught in a love nest but his pals, Andy Farrell (Pat O'Brien), a newspaper reporter, and assistant DA Lionel Houston (Neil Hamilton), do not believe the story. Cromwell (John St. Polis), one of the businessmen in the crooked scheme, is in cahoots with Ames, and his daughter Diane (Mary Brian) is engaged to Lionel, who is made the new district attorney. Andy suspects Raymond of committing the crime and makes up a story to get him out of town so he can go out with Carlotta, Bruno's moll. When Lionel is nearly killed in a car-truck accident,

A lobby card from *The World Gone Mad* (Majestic, 1932) with Louis Calhern and Pat O'Brien.

Andy begins to realize the investment scandal Henderson was looking into is behind his murder. Lionel gets information that Cromwell is involved in the scandal and confronts him with it, and an angry Diane orders him out of the house. When Andy takes Carlotta to bed in order to get information out of her, Raymond walks in on them followed by Bruno. They force Andy to call Lionel to the apartment the two share. Ames and Cromwell meanwhile decide to leave town with a gold shipment that has just arrived but Cromwell leaves a note explaining the situation to his daughter. The two crooks then die in a car-train crash. Lionel returns to the apartment but with the police. Raymond is shot and killed, and Bruno and Carlotta are arrested. Andy's newspaper story exonerates Avery Henderson as Lionel and Diane get married.

*The World Gone Mad* was one of the most lavish and satisfying productions to come out of Majestic. Pat O'Brien repeated his fast-talking newspaperman from *The Front Page* (1931) while Evelyn Brent excelled in her portrayal of the slinky, seductive gangster's moll. Neil Hamilton as the honest public servant and Mary Brian as the fiancée of the DA and daughter of a corrupt businessman are both well above average. The supporting cast is lined with top-notch work: Louis Calhern as the hoodlum who uses an import-export business as a front, J. Carrol Naish as his poetry-reading hired gun and Richard Tucker and

John St. Polis as the corrupt financiers. Profanity is surprisingly prevalent in the feature, and one lengthy and very suggestive scene has Evelyn Brent and Pat O'Brien in bed together, although it is darkly photographed. Another scene has posters from Majestic's *The Vampire Bat* (q.v.) prominently shown. Unlike most independent offerings, *The World Gone Mad* got top bookings in first-run theatres throughout the country.

## Via Pony Express

May 4, 1933, 60 minutes.
*P:* Henry L. Goldstone. *D:* Lewis D. Collins. *SC:* Oliver Drake. *PH:* William Nobles. *ED:* S. Roy Luby. *SD:* Homer Ackerman.
*Cast:* Jack Hoxie, Marceline Day, Lane Chandler, Julian Rivero, Matthew Betz, Doris Hill, Joe Girard, Charles K. French, Yakima Canutt, Bill Quinlan, Ben Corbett.
Outlaws are after a young woman's land grant and a pony express rider tries to help her.

## Gun Law

July 13, 1933, 59 minutes.
*P:* Henry L. Goldstone. *D:* Lewis D. Collins. *SC:* Oliver Drake. *PH:* William Nobles. *ED:* S. Roy Luby. *SD:* Earl N. Crain.
*Cast:* Jack Hoxie, Betty Boyd, Mary Carr, Paul Fix, J. Frank Glendon, Harry Todd, Edmond Cobb, Dick Botiller, Bob Burns, Jack Kirk, Horace B. Carpenter, Ben Corbett, Archie Ricks, William T. Burt, Otto Lederer.
The scourge of the countryside, the Sonora Kid is hunted by lawmen.

## Sing, Sinner, Sing!

August 17, 1933, 74 minutes.
*P:* Phil Goldstone. *D:* Howard Christy. *SC:* Edward T. Lowe, from the play by Wilson Collison. *PH:* Ira Morgan. *ED:* Otis Garrett. *SD:* Dean C. Daily. *AD:* Ralph Oberg. *Mus:* Abe Meyer. *Song:* George Waggner & Howard Jackson.
*Cast:* Paul Lukas, Leila Hyams, Donald Dillaway, Ruth Donnelly, George E. Stone, Joyce Compton, Jill Dennett, Arthur Hoyt, Walter McGrail, Gladys Blake, Arthur Houseman, Edgar Norton, John St. Polis, Stella Adams, Pat O'Malley, Walter Brennan, Walter Humphrey.
A torch singer working on a gambling ship is tried for the murder of her rich playboy husband after he is found shot.

## Trouble Busters

August 30, 1933, 55 minutes.
*P:* Henry L. Goldstone. *D:* Lewis D. Collins. *SC:* Oliver Drake. *PH:* William Nobles. *ED:* S. Roy Luby. *SD:* Earl L. Crain.
*Cast:* Jack Hoxie (Tex Blaine), Lane Chandler (Jim Perkins), Kaye Edwards (Mary Ann Perkins), Harry Todd (Skinny Cassidy), Ben Corbett (Windy Wallace), William T. Burt (Dan Allen), Roger Williams (Sheriff of Plasserville), Slim Whitaker (Big Bill Jarvis), Henry Rocquemore (Doc), Jack Kirk (Cowboy), Bart Carre (Cy), Dynamite the Wonder Horse (Himself).
In Custer City cowboy Tex Blaine (Jack Hoxie) and his pals plan to run crusty store owner Dan Allen (William T. Burt) out of town, but Tex ends up roping Allen's pretty niece Mary Ann (Kaye Edwards). He is smitten with the girl and leaves town in search of her and makes friends with hellraisers Skinny (Harry Todd) and Windy (Ben Corbett), who rescue him

from the arms of the law. The trio go to Plasserville where Tex ends up in a brawl with Big Bill Jarvis (Slim Whitaker), who then hires him to take possession of a strip of oil-rich land. In carrying out the assignment Tex finds out that Skinny and Windy are working for the opposition, having been hired by Jim Perkins (Lane Chandler). Tex, however, joins forces with them when he finds out Jim is Mary Ann's cousin and that the land in question belonged to her late father. Jarvis offers to buy the land but Mary Ann refuses, and Dan Allen, who is there for a visit, informs them that the land was only leased by Mary Ann's father and is open for claim. Both Dan and Jarvis rush to the land office to check on the claim, and on the way back Jarvis waylays Tex. Jarvis arrives back at the strip of land and tries to make claim on it but has to fight Jim. In doing so, he gives Tex the time he needs to make the claim first. The law arrives to inform Tex he has inherited the ranch for which Jarvis works, and Tex promptly fires the badman. He has also filed on the oil land in Mary Ann's name, and at the finale she agrees to marry Tex.

Jack Hoxie's series of six oaters for producer Larry Darmour came to a close with *Trouble Busters*, which lists Henry L. Goldstone as the producer. *Film Daily* labeled it "largely a routine affair... . For the less discriminating family houses, and for the kids, it ought to get by... ." For Jack Hoxie it marked the end of a screen career that began in 1913 with stardom coming in the early 1920s for Sunset Productions. From 1923 to 1927 Hoxie was a big star at Universal, but he left the screen to tour with circuses after the Mascot serial *Heroes of the Wild* in 1927. The Majestic films brought Jack Hoxie back to the screen one last time, and while they are technically better than most "B" westerns of the period, the big, beefy, awkward Hoxie represented an archaic screen image that failed to gain favor with Depression audiences. By the time *Trouble Busters* came along Jack was handling dialogue fairly well, but the scripts still made him look like a bumpkin. He loses his initial screen brawl with villain Slim Whitaker who also lassoes him off his mount, leaving Hoxie tied up and needing rescue by his horse. In another scene the hero's horse is lamed, and when Hoxie tries to ride a jackass, he is promptly thrown. Such scenes got better service from sidekicks, not cowboy stars. Following the Majestic series, Jack Hoxie returned to circus life, remaining on the sawdust trail until 1959.

## The Charming Deceiver

December 9, 1933, 72 minutes.

*D:* Monty Banks. *SC:* Victor Kendall. *ST:* Fred Thompson.

*Cast:* Constance Cummings, Frank Lawton, Binnie Barnes, Claude Hulbert, Gus McNaughton, Fred Duprez, Ellen Pollock, Peter Godfrey, Tonie Edgar Bruce, Iris Ashley.

A model inherits a large fortune and masquerades as a film star. Produced in Great Britain in 1933 by Wardour Films as *Heads We Go*. Original running time: 86 minutes.

## The Sin of Nora Moran

December 14, 1933, 65 minutes.

*P-D:* Phil Goldstone. *SC:* Frances Hyland, from the play *Burnt Offerings* by Willis Maxwell Goodhue. *PH:* Ira Morgan. *ED:* Otis Garrett. *SD:* Earl Crain. *AD:* Ralph Oberg. *Mus:* Abe Meyer. *Asst Dir:* J.H. McCloskey.

*Cast:* Zita Johann, Paul Cavanaugh,

Alan Dinehart, John Miljan, Claire DuBrey, Henry B. Walthall, Sarah Padden, Cora Sue Collins, Aggie Herring, Otis Harlan.

An innocent young woman is accused of a murder she did not commit and is prosecuted by her lover's brother. Filmed as *The Woman in the Chair* and rereleased in a toned version in 1980 by Independent International Pictures called *Voice from the Grave*.

## Curtain at Eight

February 1, 1934, 68 minutes.

*P:* Phil Goldstone. *D:* E. Mason Hopper. *SC:* Edward T. Lowe, from the novel *The Back Stage Mystery* by Octavas Roy Cohen. *PH:* Ira Morgan. *SD:* Earl Crain. *AD:* Ralph Oberg. *Asst Dir:* J.H. McCloskey.

*Cast:* Dorothy Mackaill, C. Aubrey Smith, Paul Cavanaugh, Marion Shilling, Jack Mulhall, Natalie Moorhead, Hale Hamilton, Sam Hardy, Russell Hopton, Ruthelma Stevens, Matthew Betz, Joseph Girard, Syd Saylor, Herman Bing, Dot Farley, William Humphries, Jane Keckley, Cornelius Keefe, Arthur Hoyt.

An aging detective tries to ferret out who killed a stage actor.

## Unknown Blonde

April 19, 1934, 65 minutes.

*P:* Phil Goldstone. *D:* Hobart Henley. *SC:* Leonard Fields & David Silverstein, from the novel *Collusion* by Theodore D. Irwin. *PH:* Ira Morgan. *ED:* Otis Garrett. *AD:* Ralph Oberg. *SD:* Louis Myers.

*Cast:* Edward Arnold, Barbara Barondess, John Miljan, Dorothy Revier, Barry Norton, Leila Bennett, Walter Catlett, Helen Jerome Eddy, Claude Gillingwater, Arletta Duncan, Maidel Turner, Franklin Pangborn, Esther Muir, Clarence Wilson, Arthur Hoyt.

A conniver makes a living obtaining evidence for divorce proceedings and ends up framing his own daughter. Made as *Age of Indiscretion.*

## You Made Me Love You

May 31, 1934, 63 minutes.

*D:* Monty Banks. *SC:* Frank Launder. *ST:* Stanley Lupino. *PH:* John J. Cox. *ED:* A.S. Bates.

*Cast:* Stanley Lupino, Thelma Todd, John Loder, Gerald Rawlinson, James Carew, Charles Mortimer, Hugh E. Wright, Charlotte Parry, Arthur Rigby, Jr., Syd Crossley, Monty Banks.

A wealthy American businessman pretends to be broke so his daughter will marry a composer. Made in Great Britain by Wardour Films and released there in a 70-minute version in 1933.

## The Morning After

August 27, 1934, 62 minutes.

*P:* Walter C. Mycroft. *D:* Allan Dwan. *SC:* Allan Dwan & Arthur Woods. [Fred Thompson]. *ST:* Fred Thompson. *PH:* James Wilson. *Mus:* Sidney Barnes & Joseph Gilbert.

*Cast:* Sally Eilers, Ben Lyon, Harry Tate, H.F. Maltby, Harold Warrender, Andrews Englemann, Dennis Hoey, Henry Victor, Marcelle Rogez.

In England two Americans, a playboy and an actress, team up to thwart international spies. Produced in England in 1933 by Wardour Films as *I Spy.*

## The Scarlet Letter

September 18, 1934, 70 minutes.

*P:* Larry Darmour. *D:* Robert G. Vignola. *SC:* Leonard Fields & David

Cora Sue Collins and Colleen Moore in *The Scarlet Letter* (Majestic, 1934).

Silverstein, from the novel by Nathaniel Hawthorne. *PH:* James S. Brown, Jr. *ED:* Charles Harris. *Asst Dir:* J.A. Duffy. *SD:* Thomas J. Lambert. *Settings:* Frank Dexter. *Mus:* Heinz Roemheld.

*Cast:* Colleen Moore (Hester Prynne), Hardie Albright (Rev. Arthur Dimmesdale), Henry B. Walthall (Roger Prynne/Dr. Roger Chillingworth), Alan Hale (Bartholomew Hockings), Cora Sue Collins (Pearl), Virginia Howell (Abigail Crakstone), William T. Kent (Sampson Goodfellow), William Farnum (Governor Bellingham), Betty Blythe (Innkeeper), Al C. Henderson (Master Wilson), Jules Cowles (Beadle), Mickey Rentschler (Digeure Crakstone), Shirley Jean Rickert (Humility Crakstone), Flora Finch (Gossip), Dorothy Wolbert (Mrs. Allison), Iron Eyes Cody (Indian Guide).

Nathaniel Hawthorne's *The Scar-*

*let Letter* remains one of the classics of American literature. Set a half-century before the infamous Salem witch trials in Puritan Massachusetts, the novel was written in 1850. Kalem made the drama as a one-reeler in 1908, and another version was made by Independent Motion Picture Company three years later. King Baggott and Linda Arvidson (Mrs. D.W. Griffith) starred in a longer version for Biograph in 1913, and in 1917 Fox filmed *The Scarlet Letter* as a feature-length movie, starring Mary Martin and Stuart Holmes. Probably the definitive version came in 1926 when Metro-Goldwyn-Mayer released director Victor Seastrom's classic, starring Lillian Gish, Lars Hanson and Henry B. Walthall. When Majestic made the story as a talkie in 1934, Walthall reprised the role of Roger Chillingworth, the cuckolded husband. In regards to this handsome-looking sound effort, *Photoplay* noted "... director Robert Vignola maintained spirit of times to the letter." *The Motion Picture Herald* noted, "Produced in an atmosphere that faithfully reflects the tone of Nathaniel Hawthorne's story of early New England and Puritanic customs, lives, religions, morals and laws, this picture has showmanship value for intelligent handling.... The picture is well acted." The feature was shot at the Darmour Studios for interiors with exterior filming at RKO's pioneer town near Sherman Oaks, California. Background work on the feature was done at MGM thanks to Majestic's cooperation deal with that studio.

After being shipwrecked and lost among the Indians for two years, Roger Prynne (Henry B. Walthall) returns to the Massachusetts Bay Colony to find that his young wife Hester (Colleen Moore) is about to be publicly condemned for having a child by a man whom she refuses to name. She is ordered to wear the scarlet letter "A" for the rest of her life. Roger joins the colony as a physician but calls himself Roger Chillingworth, and when he confronts Hester she says she will not reveal his identity. Roger vows to find out who wronged them both, but Hester keeps her vow of silence since her lover was the village minister, Arthur Dimmesdale (Hardie Albright), who suffers guilt over what has happened. Five years pass, and Hester makes a living as a seamstress and raises her daughter Pearl (Cora Sue Collins), who is tormented by the village children. The colony's governor, Bellingham (William Farnum), wants to place Pearl in a foster home, but Hester protests and Dimmesdale takes her side in the matter. The child is told to go to the minister for proper teaching. Later, Chillingworth, who boards in the same house as the minister, finds out that Dimmesdale is the child's father. Roger refuses Hester's plea that he leave the ailing reverend alone, so she tells Dimmesdale that Roger is her husband. Hester wants Dimmesdale to go abroad with her and Pearl and he agrees, but during election-day celebrating he breaks down in the public square and confesses his sin to those in the crowd. Dimmesdale dies in Hester's arms as Chillingworth slinks away.

Although a good re-creation of the Puritan period, *The Scarlet Letter* is an old-fashioned film which nonetheless holds viewer interest. Colleen Moore, Hardie Albright and Henry B. Walthall do well by the lead roles, and the tragedy of the story is somewhat relieved by comedy supplied by Alan Hale and William T. Kent as the village blacksmith and his wimpy friend Sampson.

The director of *The Scarlet Letter*, Robert G. Vignola, was a native of Italy who began his directing career for Kalem in 1914. In the ensuing years he became one of the silent screen's most prolific directors with titles like *Great Expectations* (1917), *The Heart of Youth* (1919), *The Thirteenth Commandment* (1920), *The Passionate Pilgrim* (1921), *When Knighthood Was in Flower* (1922), *Yolanda* (1924) and *Tropic Madness* (1928). He directed few films in the sound era with *The Scarlet Letter* being the most notable; he also helmed *The Perfect Clue* (1935) for Majestic. He retired after making *The Girl From Scotland Yard* for Republic in 1937. Probably the best known of Majestic's releases, *The Scarlet Letter* was reissued to theatres in 1964 by Signature Films.

## She Had to Choose

September 18, 1934, 65 minutes.
    *P:* Larry Darmour. *D:* Ralph

Cedar. *SC:* Houston Branch. *ST:* Mann Page & Izola Forrester. *PH:* James S. Brown, Jr. *ED:* Charles Harris. *SD:* Tom Lambert.

*Cast:* Larry "Buster" Crabbe, Sally Blane, Isabel Jewell, Regis Toomey, Fuzzy Knight, Maidel Turner, Wallis Clark, Edward Gargan, Arthur Stone, Huntley Gordon, Kenneth Howell, Eddie Fetherstone, Max Wagner.

A young actress attempts to become a success in Hollywood despite many roadblocks.

## Night Alarm

December 11, 1934, 65 minutes.

*P:* Larry Darmour. *D:* Spencer Gordon Bennet. *SC:* Earl Snell. *ST:* Jack Stanley. *PH:* James S. Brown, Jr. *ED:* Dwight Caldwell. *SD:* Tom Lambert.

*Cast:* Bruce Cabot, Judith Allen, H.B. Warner, Sam Hardy, Betty Blythe, Harry Holman, Harold Minjir, Tom Hanlon, Fuzzy Knight, John Bleifer.

A novice reporter gets on the trail of an arson operation.

## The Perfect Clue

March 13, 1935, 64 minutes.

*P:* Larry Darmour. *D:* Robert Vignola. *SC:* Albert DeMond, from the story "Lawless Honeymoon" by Lolita Ann Westman. *PH:* Herbert Kirkpatrick. *ED:* Dwight Caldwell. *SD:* Thomas Lambert.

*Cast:* David Manners, Skeets Gallagher, Dorothy Libaire, William P. Carleton, Rolf Harolde, Betty Blythe, Ernie Adams, Robert Glecker, Frank Darien, Charles C. Wilson, Jack Richardson, Pat O'Malley.

A society girl jilts her fiancé for a young man with a false criminal record and she tries to clear him of a murder charge.

## Motive for Revenge

May 21, 1935, 60 minutes.

*P:* Larry Darmour. *D:* Burt Lynwood. *SC-ST:* Stuart Anthony. *PH:* Herbert Kirkpatrick. *ED:* Dwight Caldwell. *Mus:* Lee Zahler. *SD:* Thomas Lambert.

*Cast:* Donald Cook, Irene Hervey, Doris Lloyd, Edwin Maxwell, Wheeler Oakman, William LeStrange, Russell Simpson, John Kelly, Edwin Argus, Billy West, Frank LaRue, Fern Emmett, Dorothy Wolbert.

A bank teller, who wants the good life for his wife, is arrested for stealing bank funds.

## Struggle for Life

June 19, 1935, 56 minutes.

*P-D:* Major C. Court Treatt. *PH:* Errol Herds. *Mus:* Adolph Tandler.

Two young boys are raised together as part of an Arab tribe in Central Sudan, facing the hardships of life with their people.

## Mutiny Ahead

July 6, 1935, 65 minutes.

*P:* Larry Darmour. *D:* Tommy Atkins. *SC:* Stuart Anthony. *PH:* Herbert Kirkpatrick. *ED:* Dwight Caldwell. *Mus:* Lee Zahler. *SD:* Tom Lambert.

*Cast:* Neil Hamilton, Kathleen Burke, Leon Ames, Reginald Barlow, Noel Francis, Matthew Betz, Paul Fix, Maidel Turner, Edward Earle, Dick Curtis, Ray Turner, Booth Howard, Katherine Jackson.

A playboy finds himself mixed up with gangsters and the search for buried treasure.

## Reckless Roads

July 30, 1935, 63 minutes.

*P:* Larry Darmour. *D:* Burt Lynwood. *SC:* Betty Burbridge. *ST:* L.E. Heifetz & H.A. Carlisle. *PH:* James S. Brown, Jr. *ED:* Dwight Caldwell. *Mus:* Lee Zahler.

*Cast:* Regis Toomey, Judith Allen, Lloyd Hughes, Gilbert Emery, Ben Alexander, Louise Carter, Matthew Betz, Dorothy Wolbert, Kit Guard.

A newspaper reporter tries to help a young girl who wants to win a big horse race.

# Mayfair Pictures Corporation

In 1927 Ralph M. Like purchased Charles Ray's old studio on Sunset Drive in Los Angeles and renamed it International Film Corporation. When the talkies came along, Like turned the operation into a sound studio. He not only rented out space for film production but also assumed the role of recording engineer on many features, including *Dark Skies* (1929) and the 1930 releases *Alma De Gaucho*, a Spanish language film, and the Syndicate westerns *Phantom of the Desert* and *Westward Bound*. By 1930 Sono Art-World Wide (q.v.) was using the studio for its productions, and Like often worked on the sound for these films. As a result of the income from his studio rental and sound engineering, Ralph M. Like formed his own company, Action Pictures, in 1931 and the next year he changed the name to Mayfair Pictures Corporation.

From the summer of 1931 to the spring of 1932 eleven feature films were released under the Action Pictures, Inc., banner. Despite the studio's title few of the films showed much action; on the contrary, they were mostly studio-bound and on the lethargic side. While Richard Thorpe directed the initial Action release, *The Sky Spider* (1931), most of the company's output was helmed by either Frank R. Strayer or George B. Seitz. Photography was usually done by Jules Cronjager with editing by Byron Robinson. Ralph M. Like continued to handle sound chores on some of the features, but as he got more involved in the production aspects of the movies, Earl Crain and others assumed those responsibilities. The Action releases tended to run around one hour, had contemporary melodramatic stories and were populated by fading names with box-office appeal like Jack Mulhall, Glenn Tryon, Reed Howes, Henry B. Walthall, Blanche Mehaffey, Barbara Kent, Patsy Ruth Miller, Vera Reynolds and Priscilla Dean. *Variety* was not overly kind to the company's releases. The trade paper noted of *Behind Stone Walls* (1932), "The mounting is adequate, but the lighting is frequently poor, which hurts the photographic quality. Sound is often harsh." Regarding *Dragnet Patrol* (1932) the reviewer noted,

"Picture is cheaply made, possessing none of the sea stuff as indicated and confining its marine action to the docks in the dark." On the other hand *Variety* did have some kind words for *Sally of the Subway* (1932): "Photography good, sound satisfactory and production suggests that money has been spent for sets."

Little discernible change took place when Action Pictures became Mayfair Pictures Corporation in the spring of 1932 with the release of *Love in High Gear*, an auto racing drama starring silent screen favorite Harrison Ford. Like its predecessor, Mayfair issued only feature films with no serials or short subjects on its release schedule, and it also avoided "B" westerns and foreign imports. From 1932 to 1934 Mayfair would release thirty-one feature films, all in the contemporary dramatic mold. For the most part Jules Cronjager continued as photographer as did Byron Robinson as editor. Mayfair's screen adaptations came from original stories, and like Action's the releases tended to be headlined by once-famous names like Monte Blue, Jack Mulhall, Kenneth Harlan, Rex Lease, Lloyd Hughes, Claire Windsor, H.B. Warner, Madge Bellamy and Regis Toomey. Directors like E. Mason Hopper, B. Reeves Eason and Spencer Gordon Bennet continued to churn out the Mayfair product in a workman-like manner, and starting in 1932 the production reins of the films were taken over by George W. Weeks while a few were handled by other producers like Fanchon Royer (q.v.) or Golden Arrow Productions.

Mayfair continued the Action credo of providing adequate fodder for dual bills, but the company never really rose above that status. While entertaining, none of Mayfair's product could be called better than mediocre. While *Film Daily* dubbed *The Fighting Rookie* (1934) a "good action drama ... An unusually original plot treatment lifts this out of the ruck of underworld plays," *Variety* called *The Gorilla Ship* (1932) "a pretty insipid piece of film." The same trade paper also took *Woman in Scarlet* (1932) to task: "*The Woman in Scarlet* should serve as another reminder to indie producers that the best sets, sound, photography, as well as some established names of a lesser category, are inconsequential if the story is slipshod."

No releases were forthcoming from Mayfair Pictures for the first three months of 1934, and for the remainder of the year only four films were issued. While *What's Your Racket*, *The Fighting Rookie*, *Badge of Honor* and *The Oil Raider*, the last two starring Buster Crabbe, better fit the Action name than did Like's initial releases, they could not save Mayfair, which ceased to exist following the release of *The Oil Raider* in November. Like so many of its contemporaries, Mayfair simply did not bring in enough revenue to stay afloat in the middle of the Depression. Mayfair-Action had a much longer run, however, than most of its rivals.

### The Sky Spider

Action, June 23, 1931, 69 minutes.
*P-SD:* Ralph M. Like. *D:* Richard

Thorpe. *SC:* Grace Keel Norton. *PH:* Jules Cronjager. *ED:* Viola Roehl. *Supv:* Cliff Broughton.

*Cast:* Glenn Tryon, Blanche

Mehaffey, Pat O'Malley, John Trent, Beryl Mercer, Joseph Girard, George Chesebro, Philo McCullough, Jay Hunt.

An airmail pilot fights hijackers, the leader of the gang being after his girl.

## Chinatown After Dark

Action, October 25, 1931, 59 minutes.
*P:* Ralph M. Like. *D:* Stuart Paton. *SC:* Betty Burbridge. *PH:* Jules Cronjager. *ED:* Viola Roehl. *AD:* Ben Dore. *Mus:* Lee Zahler. *Asst Dir:* Arthur Black. *Supv:* Cliff Broughton.

*Cast:* Barbara Kent, Rex Lease, Carmel Myers, Edmund Breese, Frank Mayo, Billy Gilbert, Lloyd Whitlock, Laska Winter, Michael Visaroff, Charles Murphy, Willie Fung, James B. Leong.

Thieves are on the trail of a sacred dagger, the inheritance of a young woman, which is brought to San Francisco by an adventurer.

## Anybody's Blonde

Action, November 1, 1931, 59 minutes.
*P:* Ralph M. Like. *D:* Frank R. Strayer. *SC:* Betty Burbridge. *PH:* Jules Cronjager. *ED:* Byron Robinson. *SD:* James Stanley & Ralph M. Like. *Supv:* Cliff Broughton. *Asst Dir:* Arthur Black.

*Cast:* Reed Howes, Dorothy Revier, Henry B. Walthall, Edna Murphy, Lloyd Whitlock, Arthur Houseman, Pat O'Malley, Gene Morgan, Nita Marten.

A newspaper reporter tries to set up a nightclub owner for the murder of her boxer brother.

## Soul of the Slums

Action, November 29, 1931, 64 minutes.

*P:* Ralph M. Like. *D:* Frank R. Strayer. *SC:* W. Scott Darling. *PH:* Jules Cronjager. *ED:* Byron Robinson. *SD:* James Stanley. *Supv:* Cliff Broughton. *Asst Dir:* Arthur Black.

*Cast:* William Collier, Jr., Blanche Mehaffey, Walter Long, James Bradbury, Jr., Paul Weigel, Max Asher, Murray Smith.

A man gets out of prison determined to find out who framed him, sets up a slum mission and falls for a young woman.

## The Night Beat

Action, December 27, 1931, 61 minutes.

*P:* Ralph M. Like. *D:* George B. Seitz. *SC:* W. Scott Darling. *PH:* Jules Cronjager. *ED:* Byron Robinson. *SD:* James Stanley & Earl Crain. *Supv:* Cliff Broughton.

*Cast:* Jack Mulhall, Patsy Ruth Miller, Walter McGrail, Harry Cording, Ernie Adams, Richard Cramer, Harry Semels.

A young couple become involved with gangsters planning to rob a warehouse.

## Dragnet Patrol

Action, January 22, 1932, 60 minutes.

*P:* Ralph M. Like. *D:* Frank R. Strayer. *SC:* W. Scott Darling. *PH:* Jules Cronjager. *ED:* Byron Robinson. *SD:* James Stanley. *Supv:* Cliff Broughton.

*Cast:* Glenn Tryon, Vera Reynolds, Marjorie Beebe, Vernon Dent, Symona Boniface, Walter Long, George Hayes, George Chesebro.

A sailor leaves his wife for a gangster's moll and gets mixed up in crime.

## Sally of the Subway

Action, January 22, 1932, 58 minutes.
*P:* Ralph M. Like. *D–SC:* George B. Seitz. *PH:* Jules Cronjager. *ED:* Byron Robinson. *SD:* James Stanley. *Supv:* Cliff Broughton.

*Cast:* Jack Mulhall, Dorothy Revier, Blanche Mehaffey, Huntley Gordon, Harry Semels, Crauford Kent, John Webb Dillon, Bill Burke.

Crooks use a grand duke to swindle a large jewelry business.

## Docks of San Francisco

Action, February 1, 1932, 64 minutes.
*P:* Ralph M. Like. *D:* George B. Seitz. *SC:* H.H. Van Loan. *PH:* Jules Cronjager. *ED:* Ralph Dixon. *SD:* James Stanley. *Supv:* Cliff Broughton.

*Cast:* Mary Nolan, Jason Robards, Marjorie Beebe, John Davidson, William Haynes, Max Davidson.

A writer falls in love with a gangster's moll and tries to win her away from the hoodlum.

## The Monster Walks

Action, February 7, 1932, 63 minutes.
*P:* Ralph M. Like. *D:* Frank R. Strayer. *SC:* Robert Ellis. *PH:* Jules Cronjager. *ED:* Byron Robinson. *Mus:* Lee Zahler. *AD:* Ben Dore. *Supv:* Cliff Broughton. *Sets:* Ralph Black. *SD:* George Hutchins.

*Cast:* Rex Lease (Ted Clayton), Vera Reynolds (Ruth Earlton), Sheldon Lewis (Robert Earlton), Martha Mattox (Mrs. Krug), Sidney Bracy (Herbert Wilkes), Mischa Auer (Hanns Krug), Sleep 'n Eat [Willie Best] (Exodus).

Pretty Ruth Earlton (Vera Reynolds) arrives at her remote home during a terrible storm since she has been called back from a trip to Europe by the death of her father, who lies in state in the mansion. Also arriving are her fiancé Ted Clayton (Rex Lease) and his driver Exodus (Sleep 'n Eat). In the house are lawyer Herbert Wilkes (Sidney Bracy), Ruth's crippled uncle Robert Earlton (Sheldon Lewis), the housekeeper Mrs. Krug (Martha Mattox) and her half-wit son Hanns (Mischa Auer), along with an ape the late Mr. Earlton kept chained in the basement. Ruth does not like being in the house, especially because of the ape, and Ted tries to comfort her. When Ruth says the ape tried to attack her, it is proved it is safely chained. Mrs. Krug decides to stay with Ruth, but during the night she is murdered. Although Uncle Robert is the chief suspect, Ted finds him dying. The man confesses he planned to use the ape as a guise to get rid of Ruth and inherit the estate and that Hanns, who had accidently killed his own mother, was his instrument to carry out the plan. Meanwhile, Hanns has carried Ruth to the basement and tied her to a post. He beats the ape so it will kill the girl. As Ted arrives, the ape pulls Hanns to its cage and strangles him. Ted sets Ruth free.

Contemporary reviewers have not been kind to *The Monster Walks*. Donald C. Willis in *Horror and Science Fiction Films II* (1982) called it, "A long series of awkward dialogue sequences ... deadly film" while Michael J. Weldon in *The Psychotronic Encyclopedia of Film* (1983) thought it "Real old-fashioned stuff." Somewhat mind-boggling is Phil Hardy's assessment in *The Encyclopedia of Horror Movies* (1986). Hardy refers to the film as a "lavish imitation of *The Cat and the Canary* (1927) ... [with] limp thrills." An imitation maybe, but hardly lavish! Perhaps *Video Hound's Golden Movie Retriever* (1991) sums it up best by saying the feature is "Not unique but

**Lobby card from *The Monster Walks* (Action, 1932) showing Sidney Bracey, Mischa Auer and Rex Lease.**

entertaining." What most critics and some viewers tend to miss is that *The Monster Walks* is a tongue-in-cheek takeoff of the old-house murder mystery thrillers so popular at the time. The story is corny, but the cast plays it straight. If taken in this light, the film is highly entertaining. Of special note is the appearance of Willie Best, in his film debut, billed as Sleep 'n Eat. His final lines in the movie have to be ranked among the classic dialogue in cinema history. For the record, the title character is referred to in the film as an ape but in reality it is a chimpanzee.

An interesting footnote to *The Monster Walks* is supplied by Denis Gifford in *A Pictorial History of Horror Movies* (1973). He stated it was "the first of the 'H' B's:" blue pencilled by the British Censor until he had intro-duced his Horror Certificate. Dated in style to start with, by then the poor little picture was so passe that the conscience-stricken distributor retitled it *The Monster Walked.*"

*The Monster Walks* was reissued by Guaranteed Pictures in 1938.

## Sin's Pay Day

Action, March 1, 1932, 61 minutes.

*P:* Ralph M. Like. *D:* George B. Seitz. *SC:* Gene Morgan & Betty Burbridge. *PH:* Jules Cronjager. *ED:* Byron Robinson. *SD:* James Stanley. *Supv:* Cliff Broughton.

*Cast:* Dorothy Revier, Forrest Stanley, Mickey [Rooney] McGuire, Harry Semels, Alfred Cross, Hal Price, Lloyd Whitlock, Bess Flowers.

A young woman leaves her lawyer

husband when he refuses to stop defending the criminal element. Reissued as *Slums of New York*.

## Behind Stone Walls

Action, March 15, 1932, 58 minutes.
*P:* Ralph M. Like. *D:* Frank R. Strayer. *SC:* George B. Seitz. *PH:* Jules Cronjager. *ED:* Byron Robinson. *SD:* Earl Crain. *Supv:* Cliff Broughton.

*Cast:* Robert Elliott, Priscilla Dean, Eddie Nugent, Ann Christy, Robert Ellis, George Chesebro.

When a woman shoots an old lover, her stepson takes the blame and goes to prison.

## Love in High Gear

May 8, 1932, 66 minutes.
*P:* Ralph M. Like. *D:* Frank R. Strayer. *SC:* George B. Seitz & Donald Douglas. *PH:* Jules Cronjager. *ED:* Byron Robinson. *SD:* O.B. Mills. *Prod Mgr:* Vernon Keays. *Asst Dir:* Arthur Black.

*Cast:* Harrison Ford, Alberta Vaughn, Tyrell Davis, Arthur Hoyt, Ethel Wales, Nanette Vallon, Fred Kelsey, Fern Emmett, Jack Duffy, William H. Strauss.

When a young couple plan to elope they are overheard by a jewel thief who plans to take advantage of the situation.

## Hell's Headquarters

May 15, 1932, 63 minutes.
*P:* George Weeks. *D:* Andrew L. Stone. *SC:* Norton S. Parker. *PH:* Jules Cronjager. *ED:* Frank Atkinson. *SD:* Earl Crain. *Supv:* Armand L. Schaefer.

*Cast:* Jack Mulhall (Ross King), Barbara Weeks (Diane Cameron), Frank Mayo (Phil Talbot), Phillips Smalley (Mr. Cameron), Fred Parker (Dr. Smith), Everett Brown (Kuba).

When Jim Jessop dies suddenly in the jungle, his gunboy Kuba (Everett Brown) sends word to his partner, big-game hunter Ross King (Jack Mulhall), in New York City. He asks King to come to Africa to investigate Jessop's death, which he blames on Phil Talbot (Frank Mayo). Meanwhile, Talbot sends a letter to his fiancée Diane Cameron (Barbara Weeks) and her father (Phillips Smalley) asking them to finance an expedition into the Congo for a hidden cache of ivory. With ebbing fortunes, Diane and her father agree, and on the boat to Africa Diane meets Ross King and becomes infatuated with him. In Africa Mr. Cameron and Diane meet with Phil, who tells them about the planned expedition into the Forbidden Country for the ivory. Diane becomes disenchanted with Phil because of his drinking and nasty behavior toward the natives but agrees to go on the expedition. When Talbot learns that King is on his trail, he tries to have him killed, but Kuba saves King's life. The safari into the Congo goes on for two weeks with the natives reluctant to continue. An elephant charges Cameron and Diane, but Kuba kills it. Later, a leopard attacks Diane, but it is mysteriously shot. King then arrives in camp saying he shot the big cat, and Cameron asks him to lead the expedition to the ivory, much to the chagrin of Talbot. They find the place where the ivory is supposed to be, but it is missing and King declares that Talbot killed Jessop. The two fight, and King forces Talbot to confess. As King promises to share the ivory, which he has hidden, with Diane and her father, Talbot runs into the jungle and is devoured by lions. Ross King, Diane, her father and Kuba then return to civilization.

Subtitled "A story of ivory hunt-

Jack Mulhall, Phillips Smalley and Barbara Weeks in *Hell's Headquarters* (Mayfair, 1932).

ing in the Congo," *Hell's Headquarters* opens with a prologue denouncing the decimation of Africa and its people by the ivory trade before telling its tale of a big-game hunter on the trail of a stolen cache of ivory. In one of his several starring films for Action-Mayfair, Jack Mulhall handles impressively the lead of the stalwart hunter while Barbara Weeks is the attractive heroine and Frank Mayo excels as the slimy, cowardly villain. It is Mayo who has the best lines in the film, ranging from "It's Africa, out here life is cheap," to describing the Dark Continent as "scorching heat, day in, day out. Nothing but greasy blacks with their silly superstitions and idols. Sleepless nights, still with death." The most amusing line, however, is delivered by the heroine. In one scene her father announces his respect for the hero by saying, "He's a real man." The heroine, with a dreamy look on her face, replies, "I found that out a long time ago." Saddled with poor sound, non-matching jungle stock footage and some obvious backlot surroundings, *Hell's Headquarters* is a mild jungle thriller at best although its players more than help in making it entertaining. Everett Brown also has considerable footage as the loyal gunboy, Kuba. *Hell's Headquarters* also marked the English-language film directorial debut of Andrew L. Stone, who later helmed such features as *The Great Victor Herbert* (1939), *Stormy Weather* (1943), *Julie* (1956) and *Song of Norway* (1970).

**MAYFAIR PICTURES CO.**
presents
JAY WILSEY in "DYNAMITE DENNY"

Advertisement for *Dynamite Denny* (Mayfair, 1932) starring Jay Wilsey, better known as Buffalo Bill Jr. This is obviously a reissue since the picture of Buffalo Bill Jr. at right is from the John Wayne western *Rainbow Valley* (Monogram, 1934).

## Temptation's Workshop

June 20, 1932, 5 reels.

*P:* George W. Weeks. *D:* George B. Seitz. *SC:* Norman Battle. *PH:* Otto Himm. *ED:* Byron Robinson. *SD:* O.B. Mills. *Prod Mgr:* Vernon Keays. *Asst Dir:* Arthur Black.

*Cast:* Helen Foster, Tyrell Davis, Dorothy Granger, Carroll Nye, John Ince, Stella Adams.

A rich family loses all its money but is aided by a foreign count who has married into the group.

## Dynamite Denny

July 8, 1932, 60 minutes.

*P:* Ralph M. Like. *D:* Frank R. Strayer. *SC:* W. Scott Darling. *PH:* Jules Cronjager. *ED:* Byron Robinson. *SD:* O.B. Mills. *Prod Mgr:* Vernon Keays. *Asst Dir:* Arthur Black.

*Cast:* Jay Wilsey [Buffalo Bill, Jr.], Blanche Mehaffey, William V. Mong, Matthew Betz, Fern Emmett, Walter Perry.

A railroad engineer loses his job when the union drops him after he refuses to participate in a strike.

## Honor of the Press

July 14, 1932, 64 minutes.

*P:* Fanchon Royer. *D:* B. Reeves Eason. *SC:* John Thomas Neville. *ST:* M.L. Simmons & J.K. Foster. *PH:* Ernest Miller. *ED:* Frank Ware. *AD:* Paul Palmentola. *Asst Dir:* Albert Benham.

*Cast:* Eddie Nugent, Rita LaRoy, Wheeler Oakman, Dorothy Gulliver, Russell Simpson, John Ince, Reginald Simpson, Franklin Parker, Franklyn Farnum, Charles K. French, Vivian Fields.

A newspaper reporter on the trail of robbers finds out his boss is behind the operation.

## Passport to Paradise

July 15, 1932, 67 minutes.

*P:* Ralph M. Like. *D-SC:* George B. Seitz. *PH:* Jules Cronjager. *ED:* Byron Robinson. *SD:* Earl Crain.

*Cast:* Jack Mulhall, Blanche Mehaffey, Eddie Phillips, Gloria Roy, William T. Burt, John Ince.

In order to obtain an inheritance, a man must travel around the world and in doing so he meets and falls in love with a deposed princess.

## The Gorilla Ship

July 20, 1932, 60 minutes.

*P:* Ralph M. Like. *D:* Frank R. Strayer. *SC:* George Waggner. *PH:* Jules Cronjager. *ED:* Byron Robinson. *SD:* O.B. Mills. *Supv:* Cliff Broughton. *Asst Dir:* Arthur Black.

*Cast:* Ralph Ince, Vera Reynolds, Reed Howes, Wheeler Oakman, James Bradbury, Jr., George Chesebro, Ben Hall, Erin La Brissoniere.

After a yacht is wrecked a man becomes jealous of the attentions his friend gives to his wife. Also called *Vengeance Rides the Sea.*

## Widow in Scarlet

July 20, 1932, 64 minutes.

*P:* Ralph M. Like. *D:* George B. Seitz. *SC:* Norman Battle. *PH:* Jules Cronjager. *ED:* Byron Robinson. *SD:* O.B. Mills.

*Cast:* Dorothy Revier, Kenneth Harlan, Lloyd Whitlock, Glenn Tryon, Myrtle Stedman, Lloyd Ingraham, Harry Strange, Hal Price, Arthur Millet, William V. Mong, Phillips Smalley, Wilfred North, Erin La Brissoniere.

A countess brags she can pull off a jewel heist but a thief beats her to the gems only to have them taken by a young woman.

## Midnight Morals

August 9, 1932, 61 minutes.

*P:* Ralph M. Like. *D:* E. Mason Hopper. *SC:* Norman Houston. *PH:* Jules Cronjager. *ED:* Byron Robinson.

*Cast:* Rex Lease, Alberta Vaughn, Charles Delaney, Beryl Mercer, DeWitt Jennings, Gwen Lee.

A rookie cop falls in love with a taxi dancer over the objections of his father.

## Trapped in Tia Juana

August 15, 1932, 61 minutes.

*P:* Fanchon Royer. *AP:* Albert Benham. *D:* Wallace W. Fox. *SC:* Bernard McConville, Wallace W. Fox & Carlos Borcosque. *ST:* Rex Lloyd Lease. *PH:* Ernest Miller. *ED:* Jeanne Spencer. *Asst Dir:* Carlos Borcosque. *SD:* Disney Recording.

*Cast:* Edwina Booth (Dorothy Brandon), Duncan Renaldo (Kenneth Holbert/Johnny Holbert, El Zorro), Dot Farley (Aunt Emma Brandon), Joseph Girard (Captain/Colonel Holbert), Manuel Paris (Lopez), Henry Rocquemore (Mr. Lee).

In 1910 Captain Holbert's (Joseph Girard) twin sons are playing near Fort Crockett when one of them, Johnny, is captured by a Yaqui bandit. Twenty years later the other son, Kenneth (Duncan Renaldo), graduates from West Point and requests duty at the fort to be near his father, now a colonel and the commanding officer. Kenneth is in love with beautiful Dorothy Brandon (Edwina Booth), who is traveling to Mexico with her Aunt Emma (Dot Farley). In Mexico they are stopped by the notorious bandit El Zorro (Duncan Renaldo), who takes a money shipment. A little later they are stopped by outlaw Lopez (Manuel Paris) and his gang, who abduct Dorothy and take her to a remote cantina. At the cantina Lopez pretends to sell Dorothy to the highest bidder, but El Zorro rescues the girl and takes her to his home. Dorothy notices the similarity in looks between Kenneth and El Zorro, and she becomes infatuated with the bandit, who takes her across the border to safety the next day. That night El Zorro comes to the fort to give Dorothy a ring and is nearly captured. Angry, Kenneth goes after the outlaw because he thinks he is Dorothy's lover. Kenneth trails El Zorro to his hacienda, but Lopez sees them and tries to kill the American, winging El Zorro instead. Kenneth then realizes that El Zorro is his lost brother, and Dorothy and Colonel Holbert arrive. After twenty years the colonel is reunited with his long, lost son. El Zorro promises his father he will give up banditry and go into mining, Kenneth realizes that Dorothy loves his twin brother and Dorothy stays in Mexico to nurse Johnny back to health.

Old fashioned and slow moving, this obscure feature gave Duncan Renaldo a chance to play dual roles, one of which was good-hearted bandit El Zorro (The Fox). The feature also reunited Renaldo with his *Trader Horn* (1930) costar Edwina Booth, an extremely beautiful actress whose thespian abilities are more refined here than in her most famous role in *Trader*

*Horn* as the white goddess. This early Cisco-Kid type feature is a good showcase for Duncan Renaldo, who seems more at home as the Mexican bandit than as his American twin brother. The boys' parentage is explained by their having a Spanish mother. Their father is played by Joseph Girard, whose hair color changes from dark to white to explain the passage of two decades in the storyline. With stock footage used as filler, a poorly recorded soundtrack and tacky indoor backgrounds, *Trapped in Tia Juana* is for the most part a boring little feature partially saved by the work of Duncan Renaldo and the presence of Edwina Booth. In *Second Feature* (1991), John Cocchi called the film, "Hilariously inept action comedy-drama-romance, with none of the above.... So bad it's a joke."

## Alias Mary Smith

August 24, 1932, 60 minutes.

*P:* Ralph M. Like. *D:* E. Mason Hopper. *SC:* Edward T. Lowe. *PH:* Jules Cronjager. *ED:* Byron Robinson. *Supv:* Cliff Broughton. *Asst Dir:* Arthur Black.

*Cast:* Blanche Mehaffey, John Darrow, Gwen Lee, Henry B. Walthall, Alec B. Francis, Raymond Hatton, Edmund Breese, Myrtle Stedman, Matthew Betz, Jack Grey, Ben Hall, Harry Strang.

A young woman is befriended by a tipsy playboy as she attempts to prove a gangster committed murder.

## No Living Witness

September 13, 1932, 67 minutes.

*P:* George Weeks. *D:* E. Mason Hopper. *SC:* Norman Houston. *PH:* Jules Cronjager. *ED:* Byron Robinson. *SD:* Dean Daly. *Supv:* Cliff Broughton. *Asst Dir:* Vernon Keays.

*Cast:* Gilbert Roland, Barbara Kent, Noah Beery, Dorothy Revier, Carmel Myers, Otis Harlan, J. Carrol Naish, John Ince, Ferike Boris, Monte Carter, Broderick O'Farrell, Arthur Millett, James Conley, Gordon De Main.

An assistant district attorney almost loses the girl he loves when he tries to stop her father from being swindled by a crooked lawyer in a race track scheme.

## Her Mad Night

October 12, 1932, 67 minutes.

*P:* Cliff Broughton. *D:* E. Mason Hopper. *SC:* John Thomas Neville. *PH:* Jules Cronjager. *ED:* Byron Robinson. *SD:* Earl Crain & E.C. Sullivan. *Asst Dir:* Ralph Black.

*Cast:* Conway Tearle (Steven Kennedy), Irene Rich (Joan Manners), Mary Carlisle (Connie Kennedy), Kenneth Thomson (Schuyler Durkin), William B. Davidson (District Attorney).

On an ocean voyage, attorney Steven Kennedy (Conway Tearle) meets and falls in love with Joan Manners (Irene Rich) and after knowing her five days proposes marriage. When she finds out that he is the guardian of the child she once abandoned, Joan agrees to marry him but does not tell him the truth. The child, Connie (Mary Carlisle), is now an adult, and she believes Steven is her older brother. Connie has been flirting with Steven's best friend, ladies' man Schuyler Durkin (Kenneth Thomson), who has had a long-time affair with Joan. When Schuyler finds out about Joan's engagement to Steven, he tells him about their affair, and the lawyer orders him out of the house. Connie goes to see Joan after finding out about the engag-

ment, and Joan is horrified to learn Connie has been seeing Schuyler. Joan goes to Steven and lies about her affair with him, saying it never happened, and then she decides to go to Schuyler's apartment to obtain an incriminating letter she had written him months before. Connie, however, knows about the letter and goes to the apartment first but is found there by Schuyler, who thinks she wants to spend the night. After several drinks Schuyler gets fresh with Connie, and in a fracas she shoots him just as Joan arrives. Joan and Schuyler both tell Connie to leave as his wound is only minor. She leaves so she can go on a planned world tour. Soon the police arrive and find Schuyler has died, and Joan is arrested for killing him. Steven defends Joan in court, but their engagement is made public, as is her letter to the dead man. She is found guilty and sentenced to the electric chair, never telling that Connie shot Schuyler. On the day of the execution Connie returns home, finds out about the trial and goes to the district attorney (William B. Davidson) with the evidence that sets Joan free. Joan tells Steven the truth about being Connie's mother, and the three are reunited.

*Her Mad Night* was a popular grind house item long after its initial release, mainly due to its overt sexual assertions. Unfortunately, except for some good acting the movie has little to offer in its plot about a woman who did not avoid the wild life in her youth and who later paid the price. John Thomas Neville's script is a stilted one, never picking up much interest, and E. Mason Hopper's direction is old-fashioned with most of the scenes photographed in medium and long shots. Except for the courtroom and jail sequences, the cast is a compact one,

**Mary Carlisle and William B. Davidson (center) in** *Her Mad Night* **(Mayfair, 1932), also called** *Held for Murder.*

but the picture is burdened with endless chatter, some of which is laughable. The characters played by Conway Tearle and Irene Rich are referred to as "young" during the proceedings although Tearle was fifty-four and Rich was forty-one when the film was produced. Irene Rich looks too old for the part, although Mary Carlisle is just right as the bouncy ingenue, and Kenneth Thomson provides another of his well-etched portrayals of a cad. Especially good is the scene where he tears Carlisle's dress while trying to force himself upon her. When she tries to leave he notes, "What did you expect coming to a man's apartment after midnight!" *Her Mad Night* is also known as *Held for Murder*, its television title.

## Heart Punch

October 18, 1932, 64 minutes.

*P:* George Weeks. *D:* B. Reeves Eason. *SC:* John Thomas Neville. *ST:* Frank Howard Clark. *PH:* George Meehan. *ED:* Jeanne Spencer. *AD:* Paul Palmentola. *Asst Dir:* Albert Benham.

*Cast:* Lloyd Hughes, Marion Shilling, Walter Miller, George Lewis, Mae Busch, Wheeler Oakman, Gordon DeMain, James Leong.

A boxer who kills an opponent in the ring falls in love with the dead man's sister.

## Tangled Destinies

October 19, 1932, 64 minutes.

*P:* Ralph M. Like. *D:* Frank

Strayer. *SC:* Edward T. Lowe. *PH:* Jules Cronjager. *ED:* Byron Robinson. *AD:* Ben Dore. *Mus:* Lee Zahler. *Asst Dir:* Vernon Keays. *Supv:* Cliff Broughton. *Prod Asst:* O.B. Mills.

*Cast:* Gene Morgan (Captain Randy Gordon), Doris Hill (Doris), Vera Reynolds (Ruth), Glenn Tryon (Tommy Preston), Sidney Bracy (The Professor/McGinnis), Lloyd Whitlock (Floyd Martin), Ethel Wales (Miss Prudence Daggott), Syd Saylor (Mr. Buchanan), Monai Lindley (Monica Van Buren), James B. Leong (Mr. Ling), William Burt (Mr. Forbes), William Humphrey (Mr. Hartley), Henry Hall (Dr. Wingate).

An airplane traveling from Chicago to Los Angeles is forced to set down three hundred miles east of its destination due to fog and an oncoming storm. The crew and passengers find themselves in a rural area and take refuge in a deserted but furnished farm home. Finding a generator for lights and canned food for dinner, the house's new inhabitants are startled when the lights go out and a shot is heard. One of the passengers, Forbes (William Burt), is found shot. Another passenger who has been masquerading as a professor, McGinnis (Sidney Bracy), reveals himself to be a special agent for an insurance company that had insured $500,000 worth of gems that the murdered man was carrying. The gems are now missing, and the other passengers are all suspect. Later, in another blackout, we learn who had the gems when ex-boxer Buchanan (Syd Saylor) is knocked out and they are stolen from him. He too had been hired to protect them. Suspicion falls on Ling (James B. Leong), but eventually the elderly Miss Daggott (Ethel Wales) finds the hiding place of the diamonds and the identity of the killer and thief is

revealed. The culprit pulls a gun on the group and tries to escape but is stopped by the plane's pilot (Gene Morgan).

Although a crackling good mystery is housed within the confines of *Tangled Destinies*, the film is a multilayered affair with several subplots. In addition to the solving of the murder mystery and theft there originally is a three-way romance between the plane's pilot and copilot over stewardess Vera Reynolds, with friction resulting between the two men. Later showgirl Monai Lindley reveals that Lloyd Whitlock is really a bounder who is running away with heiress Doris Hill only for her money. When the young lady finds out, she drops her fiancé and takes up with the pilot, thus leaving the way for the copilot and the stewardess to rekindle their love affair. The background of the murder mystery in an old house on a stormy night is well staged, and the identity of the killer is not easily deduced. The acting is top notch and the production values are more than adequate for Poverty Row with director Frank Strayer and scriptwriter Edward T. Lowe keeping the affair moving at a good pace. Strayer did a number of such mysteries on Poverty Row in the 1930s, including *Murder at Midnight* (1931), *The Monster Walks* (1932), also for Mayfair, *The Vampire Bat* (1932), *Death from a Distance* (1935) and *Murder at Glen Athol* (1936). Of note is the fact that silent screen stars Vera Reynolds and Glenn Tryon were demoted to the second leads in *Tangled Destinies*, the starring roles being taken by lesser known players Gene Morgan and Doris Hill.

## Sister to Judas

January 12, 1933, 64 minutes.

*P:* George Weeks. *D:* E. Mason

Hopper. *SC:* John Thomas Neville. *ST:* Watkins E. Wright. *PH:* Jules Cronjager. *ED:* Byron Robinson. *SD:* Earl N. Crain. *Supv:* Cliff Broughton. *Asst Dir:* Ralph Black.

*Cast:* Claire Windsor, John Harron, Holmes Herbert, Lee Moran, David Callis, Wilfred Lucas, Stella Adams, Virginia True Boardman.

A struggling writer rescues a young woman who tried to commit suicide and they marry but face heavy odds against a happy future.

## Malay Nights

February 1, 1933, 63 minutes.

*P:* George Weeks. *D:* E. Mason Hopper. *SC:* John Thomas Neville. *ST:* Glenn Ellis. *PH:* Jules Cronjager. *ED:* Byron Robinson. *SD:* Dean Daly. *Supv:* Cliff Broughton. *Asst Dir:* William Nolte.

*Cast:* Johnny Mack Brown, Dorothy Burgess, Ralph Ince, Raymond Hatton, Carmelita Geraghty, George Smith, Lionel Belmore, Mary Jane.

A pearl bed operator falls in love with a girl done wrong by a bounder.

## Midnight Warning

March 8, 1933, 63 minutes.

*P:* George Weeks. *D:* Spencer Gordon Bennet. *SC:* John Thomas Neville. *ST:* Norman Battle. *PH:* Jules Cronjager. *ED:* Byron Robinson. *Mus:* Lee Zahler. *SD:* Homer Ackerman. *Asst Dir:* Ralph Black. *Supv:* Cliff Broughton.

*Cast:* William "Stage" Boyd (William Cornish), Claudia Dell (Enid Van Buren), Huntley Gordon (Mr. Gordon), Hooper Atchley (Dr. Stephen Walcott), John Harron (Erich), Lloyd Whitlock (Rankin), Phillips Smalley (Dr. Brown), Lloyd Ingraham (Adolph Klein), Henry Hall (Dr. Barris).

At a visit with his old friend William Cornish (William "Stage" Boyd), a famous detective, Dr. Stephen Walcott (Hooper Atchley), suddenly faints. Cornish calls for the Gotham Hotel's house doctor, Brown (Phillips Smalley), who says the recovered Walcott suffered a slight heat stroke and cut his head as he fell. Both hotel manager Gordon (Huntley Gordon) and clerk Rankin (Lloyd Whitlock) are relieved by the doctor's diagnosis, but Cornish suspects Walcott was shot through an open window. A search leads him to the hotel across the street, where he is able to prove the shot was fired by Erich (John Harron), the boyfriend of Enid Van Buren (Claudia Dell), who has just returned from the Orient with her brother. A few hours before, the siblings had checked into the Gotham Hotel, and the brother has not been seen since that time. Cornish agrees to help the young lovers in finding the missing brother, and in sifting through the ashes in the fireplace in the room where Walcott was shot, he finds a piece of human earbone. Enid is kidnapped and taken to a mortuary run by Adolph Klein (Lloyd Ingraham), where an attempt is made to drive her insane. Cornish, Erich and Dr. Walcott arrive in time to save the young woman, and there they also find Gordon, Brown and Rankin. The three men then tell Cornish that they had tried to cover up the death of Enid's brother, who died at the hotel of bubonic plague. They had incinerated his body in order to protect the hotel's reputation. Cornish then advises the young couple to forget what has happened and to go away to the country.

*The Midnight Warning* is one of the very few Hollywood films from the

1930s where there is no denouement for the crime committed. The film is also filled with horror overtones, punctuated by Jules Cronjager's often darkly-lit photography. Especially chilling are the sequences in the morgue where the heroine begins to unhinge mentally as she runs through a room of sheet-covered corpses, brushing against dangling dead arms and feet, and hearing spectral voices. William "Stage" Boyd is restrained and quite effective as the noted criminologist, while the supporting cast is also very good, especially Hooper Atchley in a non-villainous role for a change. Claudia Dell makes a fetching heroine, and her well-modulated performance in the morgue scenes helps add suspense to the tale.

Allegedly *The Midnight Warning* was based on an actual incident that took place at the World's Fair in Chicago in 1893. The story was later used for the British feature *So Long at the Fair*, starring Jean Simmons and Dirk Bogarde, which United Artists released in the U.S. in 1951.

## Behind Jury Doors

March 15, 1933, 63 minutes.

*P:* George Weeks. *D:* B. Reeves Eason. *SC:* John Thomas Neville. *ST:* Frank E. Fenton. *PH:* Ernest Miller. *ED:* Jeanne Spencer. *SD:* Earl Crain.

*Cast:* Helen Chandler, William Collier, Jr., Walter Miller, Blanche Frederici, Franklin Parker, John Davidson, Richard Cramer, Jessie Arnold, Louis Natheaux, Patsy Cunningham, James Gordon, Arthur Loft, Gordon DeMain.

A doctor is accused of murdering his nurse and a reporter, who likes the doctor's daughter, tries to prove his innocence.

## Justice Takes a Holiday

April 25, 1933, 65 minutes.

*P:* George Weeks. *D:* Spencer Gordon Bennet. *SC:* John Thomas Neville. *ST:* Walter Anthony Merrill. *PH:* Jules Cronjager. *ED:* Byron Robinson.

*Cast:* H.B. Warner, Huntley Gordon, Audrey Ferris, Matty Kemp, Robert Frazer, Patricia O'Brien, Syd Saylor.

A man breaks out of prison to get even with the judge who kept him there after adopting the prisoner's daughter.

## Revenge at Monte Carlo

April 26, 1933, 63 minutes.

*P:* Fanchon Royer. *D:* B. Reeves Eason. *SC:* John Thomas Neville. *ST:* Frank E. Fenton & John Thomas Neville. *PH:* Ernest Miller. *ED:* Jeanne Spencer. *SD:* Earl N. Crain. *AD:* Paul Palmentola. *Asst Dir:* Bill Billings. *Prod Mgr:* Albert Benham.

*Cast:* June Collyer, Jose Crespo, Wheeler Oakman, Dorothy Gulliver, Edward Earle, Lloyd Ingraham, Clarence Geldert, Lloyd Whitlock.

An international crook gets hold of evidence that implicates several important people in crimes.

## Alimony Madness

May 5, 1933, 65 minutes.

*P:* Fanchon Royer. *D:* B. Reeves Eason. *SC:* John Thomas Neville. *PH:* Ernest Miller. *ED:* Jeanne Spencer. *SD:* Earl Crain. *AD:* Paul Palmentola. *Asst Dir:* David Hitchcock. *Prod Mgr:* Albert Benham.

*Cast:* Helen Chandler, Leon [Ames] Waycoff, Alberta Vaughn, Edward Earle, Charlotte Merriam, Blanche Frederici, Arthur Loft.

A woman is put on trial for the murder of her husband's first wife.

## Her Resale Value

June 21, 1933, 63 minutes.

*P:* Fanchon Royer. *D:* B. Reeves Eason. *SC:* John Thomas Neville. *ST:* Horace McCoy. *PH:* Ernest Miller. *ED:* Jeanne Spencer. *SD:* Earl Crain. *AD:* Paul Palmentola. *Prod Mgr:* Albert Benham. *Asst Dir:* David Hitchcock.

*Cast:* June Clyde, George Lewis, Noel Francis, Ralf Harolde, Gladys Hulette, Crauford Kent, Richard Tucker, Franklin Parker.

Unhappy being the wife of a small town doctor, a young woman goes to the big city to become a model and gets mixed up with a lecherous gown shop owner.

## Riot Squad

July 26, 1933, 64 minutes.

*P-D:* Harry S. Webb. *SC:* Jack Natteford & Barney Sarecky. *PH:* Roy Overbaugh. *ED:* Fred Bain. *SD:* Tom Lambert. *Asst Dir:* Harry P. Crist [Harry Fraser] & George Curtner.

*Cast:* Madge Bellamy, James Flavin, Pat O'Malley, Addison Richards, Harrison Greene, Ralph Lewis, Alene Carroll, Bee Eddels, Charles De la Motte, Kit Guard.

Because of their rivalry over a woman, two police detectives are demoted to the riot squad.

## Dos Noches [Two Nights]

July 28, 1933, 62 minutes.

*P:* Jack Gallagher. *D:* Carlos F. Borcosque. *SC:* Albert Benham, Miguel de Zarraga & John Thomas Neville. *ST:* Frank E. Fenton & John Thomas Neville. *PH:* Ernest Miller.

*Cast:* Jose Crespo, Conchita Mon-

tenegro, Carlos Villarias, Romualdo Tirado, Antonio Cumellas, Juan Martinez Pla, Paul Ellis, Enrique Acosta, Martin Garralaga, Lita Santos, Manuel Noriega, Fernando G. Toledo.

Spanish language version of *Revenge at Monte Carlo* (1933).

## Dance Hall Hostess

August 26, 1933, 73 minutes.

*P:* George Weeks. *D:* B. Reeves Eason. *SC:* Betty Burbridge. *ST:* Tom Gibson. *PH:* Jules Cronjager. *ED:* Byron Robinson. *SD:* Homer Ackerman. *Supv:* Lester F. Scott Jr. *Asst Dir:* Leigh Smith.

*Cast:* Helen Chandler, Jason Robards, Eddie Nugent, Natalie Moorhead, Alberta Vaughn, Jack Keckley, Ronnie Cosbey, Clarence Geldert.

A taxi dancer and her boyfriend argue when she attracts the attentions of a bored, heavy-drinking rich man.

## Her Forgotten Past

October 31, 1933, 68 minutes.

*P-D:* Wesley Ford. *SC:* George Morgan. *PH:* James S. Brown, Jr. *ED:* Fred Bain. *SD:* Tom Lambert. *Prod Mgr:* Lee Cordova.

*Cast:* Monte Blue, Barbara Kent, Henry B. Walthall, Eddie Phillips, William V. Mong, Dewey Robinson.

With her district attorney husband running for reelection, a woman is accused of murdering her first husband.

## Secret Sinners

December 13, 1933, 70 minutes.

*P-D:* Wesley Ford. *SC:* F. McGrew Willis. *PH:* James S. Brown, Jr. *ED:* Fred Bain. *SD:* Tom Lambert. *Mus:* Lee Zahler. *Songs:* Lee Zahler & Harry Barris. *Prod Mgr:* Leigh Smith.

*Cast:* Jack Mulhall, Sue Carol, Nick Stuart, Cecilia Parker, Natalie Moorhead, Armand Kaliz, Bert Roach, Eddie Kane, William Humphries, Gertrude Short, Tom Ricketts, Paul Ellis, Phillips Smalley, Harry Barris.

A man nearly loses his wife when he falls for a chorus girl and the wife decides to find other romance.

## What's Your Racket

March 6, 1934, 64 minutes.

*D:* Fred Guiol. *SC:* Barry Barringer. *ST:* George E. Rogan. *PH:* James S. Brown, Jr. *ED:* Dan Milner. *SD:* Earl Crain. *Prod Mgr:* Leigh Smith.

*Cast:* Regis Toomey, Noel Francis, J. Carrol Naish, Creighton Hale, Fred Malatesta, May Wallace, Lew Kelly, David Callis.

Lawmen are out to corral two criminal gangs who are at war with each other.

## Badge of Honor

May 19, 1934, 62 minutes.

*P:* Lester F. Scott, Jr. *D:* Spencer Gordon Bennet. *SC:* George Morgan. *ST:* Robert Emmett [Tansey]. *PH:* James S. Brown, Jr. *ED:* Fred Bain. *AD:* Paul Palmentola. *SD:* Tom Lambert.

*Cast:* Buster Crabbe, Ruth Hall, Ralph Lewis, Betty Blythe, John Trent, Ernie Adams, Alan Cavan,

Charles McAvoy, Broderick O'Farrell, William Arnold.

Posing as an ex-newspaperman, a playboy is after a big story and a pretty girl.

## The Fighting Rookie

July 13, 1934, 67 minutes.

*P:* Lester F. Scott, Jr. *D:* Spencer Gordon Bennet. *SC:* George Morgan. *ST:* Henry King Gordon. *PH:* James S. Brown, Jr. *ED:* Fred Bain. *SD:* Tom Lambert. *AD:* Paul Palmentola.

*Cast:* Jack LaRue, Ada Ince, DeWitt Jennings, Matthew Betz, Arthur Belasco, Thomas Brewer.

Turning his back on his girlfriend and his pals, a rookie policeman goes undercover to bring in a big-time racketeer and his gang.

## The Oil Raider

November 1, 1934, 59 minutes.

*P:* Lester F. Scott, Jr. *D:* Spencer Gordon Bennet. *SC:* George Morgan. *ST:* Rex Taylor. *PH:* Edward Snyder. *ED:* Fred Bain. *AD:* Paul Palmentola. *SD:* C.S. Franklin. *Asst Dir:* Harry Knight.

*Cast:* Buster Crabbe, Gloria Shea, George Irving, Emmett Vogan, Max Wagner, Harold Minjir.

Needing money a banker hires a rival oil driller to sabotage the rig of an oilman who has borrowed funds from him.

# Metropolitan Pictures

After the collapse of their Reliable Pictures (q.v.) in 1937, producers Bernard B. Ray and Harry S. Webb regrouped to form Metropolitan Pictures, which had a release schedule for the 1939–40 theatrical season. This time

Webb produced the nine efforts issued by the company while Ray stayed in the background except for directing the company's second release, *Smoky Trails*. Webb not only produced all of Metropolitan's nine entries, but he also directed four of them, with three others being helmed by brother Ira Webb and two others by Raymond Johnson. Eight of the nine releases were Bob Steele starrers, and *Variety* commented, "No more slipshod westerns were ever ground out than this present Bob Steele series."

Coming to the screen at the twilight of the silent era, Bob Steele had justly earned a reputation for being one of the screen's most popular cowboy stars. Although his series had been for independents like Films Bookings Office (FBO), Tiffany, World Wide, Monogram, Supreme and Republic, his movies were always entertaining and action-filled, and Steele was an actor of considerable ability as he later proved when he moved into character roles. The Metropolitan series, however, was certainly the low point of his starring career. Fortunately, he rebounded to make many more oaters for Republic, Monogram and PRC before his two decades as a saddle star ended in 1946.

Steele's Metropolitan series was ground out quickly by the same crew (Edward Kull on camera, Fred Bain editing, music by Frank Sanucci and scripts by either George Plympton or Carl Krusada), usually in a week's time. Each film ran less than one hour, and about ten minutes or more of that could be counted on for stock footage. *Mesquite Buckaroo* was stuffed with rodeo stock stuff while *Feud of the Range* had clips from a variety of sources, little of which matched the new footage. Bob Steele and his fellow players tried with little success to make something of these outings. When Steele starred next for PRC in 1940 it was a step upward, something few actors can ever claim when working for that company.

*Feud of the Range*, Metropolitan's first production, was filmed on location near Kanab, Utah. Two local men, Chauncey and Whitney Parry, joined Harry S. Webb in financing the production. In return it was originally called *The Kanab Kid*. It was filmed at Cave Lakes, Johnson Canyon and on the Robinson ranch near Kanab. Over fifty locals were hired to appear as extras in the production. One of the actors in the cast, Denver Dixon (Victor Adamson), later returned to Kanab to make his own film, *The Mormon Conquest* (q.v.).

In addition to the Bob Steele series, Harry S. Webb also produced *Fangs of the Wild* for Metropolitan. Rin-Tin-Tin, Jr., was hired for the leading role with Dennis Moore as his human counterpart. By this time, however, the son of the famous canine star had apparently fallen on hard times, and he received last billing in the picture. His part was only incidental to the plot, which dealt with silver-fox fur thieves. Webb did manage to get some of the filming done on location at two actual fox farms.

In 1940 Harry S. Webb moved Metropolitan Pictures Corporation to Monogram where he produced a western series starring Jack Randall. The previous year under the Metropolitan banner he made *Port of Hate* and *Daughter of the Tong*, but both were released by Times (q.v.). Bernard B. Ray followed

Bob Steele to Producers Releasing Corporation (PRC) in 1940 and produced non-westerns for the company.

It should be noted that Harry S. Webb originally used the monicker of Metropolitan Pictures in 1931 for his ten-chapter serial *The Sign of the Wolf*, which he coproduced with Flora E. Douglas, with whom he had worked at Big 4 (q.v.). Top billing was assigned to King, "Emperor of All Dogs," who was actually Muro, the wolf-dog featured in Webb's two features for Biltmore Pictures (q.v.), *Untamed Justice* and *Phantoms of the North*, in 1929. Rex Lease and Virginia Browne Faire were the human stars of this ten-chapter cliffhanger, which was released in a feature version by Syndicate Pictures (q.v.) in 1932. The plotline was dusted off by Webb in 1936 when he and Bernard B. Ray filmed it again for Reliable, this time retitled *Skull and Crown*, a feature vehicle for Rin-Tin-Tin, Jr.

Finally, this studio should not be confused with another Metropolitan Pictures Corporation which existed in the mid–1930s. George Hirliman formed this Metroplitan in 1935 to make Spanish language versions of his own features.

## The Sign of the Wolf

1931, ten chapters.

*P:* Harry S. Webb & Flora E. Douglas. *D:* Harry S. Webb & Forrest Sheldon. *SC:* Elizabeth [Betty] Burbridge. *ST:* Elizabeth Burbridge & Bennett Cohen. *PH:* William Nobles & Herbert Kirkpatrick. *ED:* Fred Bain. *Asst Dir:* Melville DeLay.

*Cast:* King [Muro], Rex Lease, Virginia Browne Faire, Joe Bonomo, Jack Mower, Josephine Hill, Al Ferguson, Robert Walker, Edmund Cobb, Harry Todd, Billy O'Brien, Jack Perrin.

*Chapter Titles:* Drums of Doom, The Dog of Destiny, The Wolf's Fangs, The Fatal Shot, The Well of Terror, The Wolf Dogs, Trapped, The Secret Mark, Tongues of Flame, The Lost Secret.

A ranger and his dog are on the trail of "The Tiger," the gang leader who murdered the lawman's sister. Released in a feature version called *The Lone Trail* in 1932 by Syndicate Pictures (q.v.).

## Fangs of the Wild

1939, 5 reels.

*P:* Harry S. Webb. *D:* Raymond K. Johnson. *SC:* Richard D. Perasall. *ST:* Carl Krusada. *PH:* Edward A. Kull. *Mus:* Frank Sanucci. *Asst Dir:* Adrian Weiss. *Tech Dir:* Raymond V. Le Vay. *ED:* Fred Bain. *SD:* Thomas Lambert.

*Cast:* Dennis Moore (Don Howard), Luana Walters (Carol Dean), Tom London (Larry Dean), Mae Busch (Mae Barton), Theodore [Ted] Adams (Frank Lewis), George Chesebro (Brad Colby), James Aubrey (Pete Ellis), Bud Osborne (Clem), George Morrell (Captain Dwyer), Martin Spellman (Buddy), Rin-Tin-Tin, Jr. (Rinty).

Rangers are on the trail of fox fur thieves and assign Don Howard (Dennis Moore) to the case. At the Silver Tip Fox Farms there are no clues of any kind regarding the thefts as crooks Colby (George Chesebro) and Ellis (James Aubrey) use their dog Queenie to carry off the foxes which they sell for their valuable pelts. The two escape

Poster for the ten chapter serial *The Sign of the Wolf* (Metroplitan, 1931), also released in a feature version in 1932 by Syndicate.

detection and take their furs to dealer Frank Lewis (Ted Adams) who tries to sell a coat to Mae Barton (Mae Busch), actually an undercover agent for the rangers. As a result Don is able to arrest Lewis but Colby and Ellis escape. At Green Valley Fox Farms, the duo plan to renew their thievery as Don arrives on the scene incognito with his nephew Buddy (Martin Spellman) and dog Rinty (Rin-Tin-Tin, Jr.). They make friends with owner Larry Dean (Tom London) and his daughter Carol (Luana Walters), and when the latter sees Queenie carry off a fox she thinks it is Rinty. Meanwhile, Rinty and Queenie have met in the woods and developed a friendship although Queenie still carries out Colby's orders to steal the foxes. Carol tries to shoot Rinty but after seeing

him with Queenie she knows he is innocent of the thefts. Don trails Queenie to the thieves' cabin while Carol and Buddy go for help. In a fight with Colby and Ellis, Don is knocked out, but Rinty attacks Colby as he tries to escape. Don recovers and captures the crooks as the Rangers arrive on the scene. Don and Carol and Rinty and Queenie are now free to carry on their romances.

In addition to the Bob Steele series, Metropolitan turned out this pedestrian programmer centered around thefts in the fox fur industry. Much of the footage was done on actual fox fur farms with lots of stock shots of silver foxes being raised for their pelts. With rather nice scenic locales and some cute scenes of Rin-Tin-Tin, Jr., with his forest pals, *Fangs of the Wild* was an acceptable "B" feature which did not have the tattered look of the Bob Steele entries. Unlike them, however, it seems to have had no official release date and very little theatrical exposure. Acting-wise the film benefits from leads Dennis Moore and Luana Walters, while Mae Busch has a nice cameo as a decoy of the law who helps uncover a crooked fur seller. Ted Adams and George Chesebro handle their villainous assignments in typically fine fashion.

## Feud of the Range

January 15, 1939, 56 minutes.

*P-D:* Harry S. Webb. *AP:* Chauncey & Whitney Parry. *SC:* Carl Krusada. *ST:* George Plympton. *PH:* Edward Kull. *ED:* Fred Bain. *Mus:* Frank Sanucci. *Asst Dir:* William Nolte. *SD:* Clifford Ruberg. *Tech Dir:* Leo Dow.

*Cast:* Bob Steele (Bob Gray), Richard Cramer (Tom Gray), Gertrude Messinger (Madge Allen), Jean Crauford (Helen Wilson), Frank LaRue (Harvey Allen), Robert Burns (Pop Wilson), Budd Buster (Happy), Jack Ingram (Clyde Barton), Charles King (Dirk), Duke R. Lee (Sheriff Cal Waters), Denver Dixon, Carl Mathews (Gunmen).

Crooks Barton (Jack Ingram) and Dirk (Charles King) are forcing ranchers to sell their land cheap in order to get railroad rights-of-way. Barton is romancing Madge Allen (Gertrude Messinger), but he is really behind the range war that has alienated her father (Frank LaRue) and Tom Gray (Richard Cramer), the rancher father of her boyfriend, Bob Gray (Bob Steele). Bob leaves his own spread and returns home with his pal Happy (Budd Buster) to aid his father who has thrown him out for romancing the daughter of his rival. Back home Bob saves Madge from a hired killer and goes with her to Harvey Allen's Bar A Ranch to get his side of the story. Bob and Happy then stop Dirk and his men from trying to harass homesteader Pop Wilson (Robert Burns) and his daughter Helen (Jean Crauford). When Bob and his dad have a falling out on how to stop the range war, Dirk tries to ambush Bob and Happy, and Bob later follows Dirk and finds out he is in cahoots with Barton. Bob and Happy are deputized by the sheriff, but Dirk shoots Mr. Allen and Bob is blamed. Barton then orders his gang to raid all the ranchers before heading below the border while Madge believes Bob shot her father. During the raids, Bob and Happy fight the gang and nearly run out of ammunition but are saved when men from Bob's ranch, who have been sent for by Happy, arrive. The outlaws are captured, and Dirk turns on Barton, saying he is behind the range war and the shooting of Mr. Allen. With peace on the range, Bob and Happy return to their ranch.

The initial entry in eight starrers Bob Steele did for producer Harry S. Webb, *Feud of the Range* is a rough-hewn affair with poor sound and excessive stock footage. Its plot is somewhat involved but drags quite a bit. Filmed around Kanab, Utah, in the fall of 1938 as *The Kanab Kid, Feud of the Range* was a poor launching pad for Bob Steele's last starring series of the 1930s. A strange plot twist of the movie had the heroine more interested in the villain than the hero. Also the plot failed to develop the potential romance between hero Bob Steele and the nestor's daughter played by Jean Crauford. About the only interesting aspect of the movie is its use of flashes of lightning just before scenes of violence.

## Smoky Trails

March 1, 1939, 56 minutes.

*P:* Harry S. Webb. *D:* Bernard B. Ray. *SC:* George Plympton. *PH:* Edward Kull. *ED:* Fred Bain. *Songs:* Dorcas Cochran & Charles Rosoff.

*Cast:* Bob Steele, Jean Carmen, Murdock MacQuarrie, Bruce Dane, Carleton Young, Ted Adams, Frank LaRue, James Aubrey, Bob Terry, Frank Wayne.

After his father is murdered by an outlaw, a man pretends to join the gang to get the culprit.

## Mesquite Buckaroo

May 1, 1939, 59 minutes.

*P-D:* Harry S. Webb. *SC:* George Plympton. *PH:* Edward Kull. *ED:* Fred Bain. *Mus:* Frank Sanucci.

*Cast:* Bob Steele, Carolyn Curtis, Frank LaRue, Charles King, Gordon Roberts [Carleton Young], Ted Adams, James Whitehead, Ed Brady, Bruce Dane, Snub Pollard, John Elliott.

Crooks kidnap a cowboy so he cannot ride in a big rodeo since they are planning to steal the proceeds.

## Riders of the Sage

August 1, 1939, 55 minutes.

*P-D:* Harry S. Webb. *SC:* Carl Krusada. *PH:* Edward Kull. *ED:* Fred Bain. *Mus:* Frank Sanucci.

*Cast:* Bob Steele, Claire Rochelle, Ralph Hoopes, James Whitehead, Earl Douglas, Ted Adams, Dave O'Brien, Frank LaRue, Bruce Dane, Jerry Sheldon, Reed Howes, Bud Osborne, Gordon Roberts [Carleton Young].

When he stops a proposed killing, a cowboy finds himself in the middle of a range war between sheep raisers and cattlemen.

## The Pal from Texas

November 1, 1939, 55 minutes.

*P-D:* Harry S. Webb. *SC:* Carl Krusada. *PH:* Edward Kull. *ED:* Fred Bain. *Mus:* Frank Sanucci.

*Cast:* Bob Steele, Claire Rochelle, Jack Perrin, Josef Swickard, Ted Adams, Betty Mack, Carleton Young, Robert Walker, Jack Ingram, Reed Howes, Art Davis, Milburn Morante, Lew Porter, Tex Palmer, Bud McClure.

A cowboy comes to the aid of a miner who is about to be cheated out of his property by a crook.

## El Diablo Rides

December 5, 1939, 55 minutes.

*P:* Harry S. Webb. *D:* Ira Webb. *SC:* Carl Krusada. *PH:* Edward Kull. *ED:* Fred Bain. *Mus:* Frank Sanucci.

*Cast:* Bob Steele, Claire Rochelle, Carleton Young, Ted Adams, Robert Walker, Kit Guard.

When a range feud erupts between cattle ranchers and sheep herders, a cowboy gets involved.

## Wild Horse Valley

March 1, 1940, 55 minutes.

*P:* Harry S. Webb. *D:* Ira Webb. *SC:* Carl Krusada. *PH:* Edward Kull. *ED:* Fred Bain. *Mus:* Frank Sanucci.

*Cast:* Bob Steele, Phyllis Adair, George Chesebro, Ted Adams, Lafe McKee, Buzz Barton, Bud Osborne, Jimmie Aubrey.

When outlaws steal his Arabian stallion, a cowboy attempts to retrieve the horse.

## Pinto Canyon

May, 1, 1940, 55 minutes.

*P:* Harry S. Webb. *D:* Raymond Johnson. *SC:* Carl Krusada. *PH:*

Poster for *El Diablo Rides* (Metropolitan, 1939).

Edward Kull. *ED:* Fred Bain. *Mus:* Frank Sanucci.

    *Cast:* Bob Steele, Louise Stanley, Kenne Duncan, Ted Adams, Steve Clark, Budd Buster, Murdock Mac-Quarrie, George Chesebro, Jimmie Aubrey, Carl Mathews.

    A lawman is after a gang of cattle thieves.

# Oscar Micheaux Pictures

Operating on approximately the same level as Bud Pollard and Robert J. Horner (qq.v.) was Oscar Micheaux, a one-man organization that made motion pictures for black urban audiences for thirty years. From 1918 to 1948 Micheaux produced around fifty films, nearly all of which he wrote, directed and promoted in the U.S. and abroad. Headquartered on the East Coast and mostly filming in New Jersey and New York City, Micheaux managed to make a suprisingly large number of films on minimal capital, but technically his features were below par. Looking at a Micheaux feature from the early sound era and then one done nearly a decade later, one sees little, if any, technical improvement.

Today Oscar Micheaux is considered a major figure in the black entertainment industry; in 1987 he was honored with a star on Hollywood Boulevard's Walk of Fame. Yet throughout his career Micheaux was controversial in that his films seemed at times to upset both blacks and whites. Controversy surrounded features like *Within Our Gates* (1920), which dealt with a Southern lynching; *Deceit* (1921), about Negroes going North and passing for white; and *The Spider's Web* (1927), in which a black woman is sexually harassed by a white man. These types of situations often led to Micheaux's films failing to get release in various parts of the country. On the other hand, many blacks felt that Micheaux pandered to the black bourgeoisie; often the heroes and heroines of his films were light-skinned, the villains dark.

Born in Illinois in 1884, Oscar Micheaux started working at an early age, and for several years he homesteaded successfully in the Indian Territory of South Dakota. By 1913, however, he had published his first novel, *The Conquest: The Story of Negro Pioneer*, followed by *The Forged Note* (1915) and *The Homesteader* (1917). When he was unable to get *The Homesteader* made into a movie, Micheaux formed his own motion picture and book company, studied the rudimentary techniques of making films and produced *The Homesteader* in 1918. During the next decade he turned out a plethora of black-casted movies like *Symbol of the Unconquered* (1920), *The Gunsaulas Mystery* (1921), *Birthright* (1924), *Body and Soul* (Paul Robeson's film debut, 1924), *The Ghost of Tolston's Manor* (1924), *The Broken Violin* (1926), *The Devil's Disciple* (1926), *Marcus Garland* (1928), *Thirty Years Later* (1928), *Wages of Sin* (1928) and *When Men Betray* (1929). Like many shoestring independents, Micheaux would make a film or two then market it himself, taking it from city to city, obtaining backers for new projects and using marginal profits to make more films. Micheaux knew almost to the penny what his films would clear in profit and he rarely increased the size of his small budgets, an average Micheaux production costing no more than $10,000.

The coming of sound did not hamper Oscar Micheaux although he continued to make silent pictures as long as it was feasible, finally turning out the part-talkie *A Daughter of the Congo* in the spring of 1930. As in the past the film proved controversial because of the color issue. Harlem's *New York Amsterdam News* complained, "The first offense of the new film is its persistent vaunting of the intraracial color fetishism ... All the noble characters are high yellows; all the ignoble ones are black." The stars of the film, Katherine Noisette and Lorenzo Tucker, are light-skinned. In fact, Micheaux billed Tucker, who made eleven films with him, as "The Colored Valentino." The race issue also carried over into *The Exile* (1931), Micheaux's first all-talkie, and a remake of *The Homesteader* (1918). Its plot had a western homesteader, a black man (Stanley Morrell), falling in love with the white daughter (Nora Newsome) of a neighboring farmer. After that, though, Micheaux tended to steer his plots more towards problems and situations involving urban blacks, sometimes creating a monied class that some of his contemporaries claimed did not exist except in Micheaux's celluloid fantasies.

An interesting curio in Oscar Micheaux's filmography is a 1931 ten-minute short called *Darktown Revue*, perhaps the most technically competent of his movies. Its stationary camera recorded in long and medium shots three blackouts. In two The Harlem Chorus, directed by Donald Heywood, sings "My Dixie Home" and "Ain't It a Shame." Sandwiched between these is the comedy skit "Why Leave by the Window?" featuring Tim Moore, who would later achieve celebrity as George "Kingfish" Stevens on CBS-TV's "Amos 'n' Andy" series in the early 1950s. For the rest of the decade, though, Micheaux turned out a series of static, choppy and technically deficient features like *Veiled Aristocrats* (1932), *Harlem After Midnight* (1934), *Lem Hawkins' Confession* (1935), *Temptation* (1936) and *Birthright* (1939). Not only did Micheaux reuse plot material, but he sometimes cannibalized his own films. *Ten Minutes to Live* (1932) contains a great deal of silent footage from one of his earlier features. Films like *Easy Street* (1930) and *Black Magic* (1932) are so obscure they appear to be lost to the ages. In fact, a complete Oscar Micheaux filmography will probably never exist since most of his films were not copyrighted and those that were released got little publicity. Many, especially the silents, were cast off once their box-office potential faded.

"An Epidemic of High-Yallers and Sugar-Cured Browns Straight from Harlem and Sizzlin' Hot!!" read the ad for *Harlem After Midnight* (1934) as Micheaux attempted to sell his features to urban black houses. Controversy continued to follow Micheaux, however. A scene in *God's Stepchildren* (1938), in which a white man knocks down a young woman and spits on her because she has "colored blood," caused the film to be picketed by the National Negro Congress and the Young Communist League. As a result it was withdrawn from the RKO Regent Theatre in New York City and banned from other RKO theatres, thus depriving Micheaux of his biggest release possibilities. As the 30s progressed Micheaux had to give up some of his independence to get financing. *The Underworld* (1937) was cofinanced and distributed by Sack

Amusements, and noted black aviator Hubert Julian coproduced *The Notorious Elinor Lee* (1940). Although Micheaux's film often featured strong heroines, his views toward women were somewhat ambivalent. In *Swing* (1938), the usual Micheaux combination of music and drama, the mouthy leading lady of a stage production is put in her place by her gangster boyfriend with a vicious right cross.

For most of the 1940s Oscar Micheaux was inactive in films, having returned to writing novels. In 1948, however, he made one final feature, *Betrayal*, distributed by Astor Pictures. Taken from his book *Wind from Nowhere*, the film featured Micheaux's wife, Alice B. Russell, whose input had included everything from on-screen heroine to distributor (as A. Burton Russell) since their marriage in 1929. *Betrayal* was essentially the same story he had told in *The Homesteader* (1918) and *The Exile* (1931), and it was just as technically deficient as his earlier works. With the black film market dwindling, the picture failed to reestablish Micheaux as an independent operator, and, plagued with health problems, he moved to Charlotte, North Carolina, where he died in 1951.

While Oscar Micheaux's features may have been poorly made ethnic fantasies (in *The Girl from Chicago* Micheaux can be heard off camera giving direction to players trying to silence him), he did provide work for a number of well-known performers. As noted, Paul Robeson made his film debut in *Body and Soul* in 1925, and famous heavyweight boxer Sam Langford appeared in *The Brute* (1920). Rex Ingram, Juano Hernandez, Oscar Polk, Robert Earl Jones (father of James Earl Jones), Laura Bowman and Amanda Randolph appeared in Micheaux productions and his stock company of players included Lawrence Chenault, Lorenzo Tucker, Ethel Moses, Dorothy Van Engle, Bee (Bea) Freeman, Alec Lovejoy, Andrew Bishop and Alfred "Slick" Chester. Since most of his movies contained music, Micheaux employed many singers and dancers, among them blues recording artist Trixie Smith. Most of the music for his films was done by Donald Heywood.

From the 1920s to the 1940s a number of film companies made movies for the black market, most financed by white producers like Harry Popkins, Richard C. Kahn, Bert and Jack Goldberg and Robert M. Savini, the president of Astor Pictures. There were also a few black producers such as Ralph Cooper, George Randol, Richard Lawrence and Eddie Green. There was even a bi-racial outfit, Million Dollar Productions, organized in 1937 by Harry Popkin and Ralph Cooper, which featured Cooper in films like *Bargain with Bullets*, *The Duke Is Tops* and *Gang War*.

Of all the black motion picture producers, however, Oscar Micheaux proved to be the most prolific and enduring with a career in the film business that spanned three decades.

## A Daughter of the Congo

A. Burton Russell, April, 1930.

*P-D:* Oscar Micheaux. *SC:* Oscar Micheaux, from the novel *Talk of East Africa* by Henry F. Downing.

*Cast:* Katherine Noisette, Lorenzo Tucker, Roland Irving, Alice B. Russell, Salem Tutt Whitney, Joe Byrd, Wilhelmina Williams, Clarence Redd, Charles Moore, Gertrude Snelson, Percy Verwayen, Madame Robinson, Willa Lee Guilford, Speedy Wilson, Daisy Harding, Rudolph Dawson.

A mulatto girl raised in Africa is rescued from slave traders by a U.S. cavalry captain.

## Easy Street

August 1, 1930.
*P-D-SC:* Oscar Micheaux.
*Cast:* Lorenzo Tucker, Willa Lee Guilford, Alice B. Russell, Richard E. Harrison.

Big city crooks try to swindle an elderly man out of his life's savings.

## Darktown Revue

1931, 10 minutes.
*P-D-SC:* Oscar Micheaux.
*Cast:* Tim Moore, Donald Heywood, The Harlem Chorus.

A series of blackouts featuring two songs and a comedy routine.

## The Exile

1931, 64 minutes.
*P-D:* Oscar Micheaux. *SC:* Oscar Micheaux, from his novel *The Confession.* *PH:* Lester Lang & Walter Strenge. *Mus:* Donald Heywood. *Dance Dir:* Leonard Harper.
*Cast:* Stanley Morrell (Jean Baptiste), Eunice Brooks (Edith Duval), Nora Newsome (Agnes Stewart), Katherine Noisette (Madge), George Randol (Bill Prescott), Carl Mahon (Jango), Charles Moore (Jack Stewart), Lou Vernon (Assistant District Attorney), A.B. Comathiere (Outlaw),

Louise Cook (Maid), Roland Holder (Boy), Lorenzo Tucker (Seducer), Celeste Cole (Singer), Donald Heywood and His Band (Themselves), Leonard Harper's Chorines (Themselves).

In Chicago after the First World War, a fancy mansion is occupied by Edith Duval (Eunice Brooks), who operates it as a social club. Jean Baptiste (Stanley Morrell) proposes to Edith but they part after he realizes she wants to make money in the rackets. Jean becomes a successful homesteader in South Dakota and five years later meets pretty Agnes Stewart (Nora Newsome), the daughter of a new neighbor (Charles Moore). When another farmer (George Randol) tries to molest the girl, Jean comes to her rescue and the two fall in love. Feeling guilt over their being of different races, Jean returns to Chicago, where he again meets Edith and they agree to marry. Her former suitor Jango (Carol Mahon), however, overhears their plans and murders Edith with Jean being blamed for the crime. Meanwhile Agnes is heartbroken that Jean has left her, and her father tells Agnes that her late mother was part Negro. When Agnes reads that Jean has been arrested, she goes to Chicago to help him, but in the meantime he has been exonerated. Jean and Agnes meet, and when Agnes tells him of her heritage the two return to homesteading.

Oscar Micheaux's first all-talking feature, and probably the first such movie by a black producer-director, is a dismal affair at best, a reworking of his initial film *The Homesteader* in 1918. Using subtitles to introduce characters and situations, *The Exile* is overly talky with excessive flowery dialogue. In one scene hero Jean Baptiste says to heroine Nora Newsome, "I dreamed of you by night and longed for you by day and you suddenly appeared like an angel." Other dialogue, however, was more pointed. When Baptiste talks to a young white boy about racial differences he says, "If you're part white and part colored you are still considered all colored." Slow-moving and choppy, *The Exile* is filled with music and dance interludes that do not advance the story, and the work by leading man Stanley Morrell is mediocre. It is claimed that Micheaux was unhappy with Morrell's performance and reshot his scenes with Lorenzo Tucker, but apparently that version was never released, although Tucker is given star billing on the movie's posters. Tucker played a small part in the feature as a city slicker who tries to seduce the heroine, but his role is cut from extant prints. Also missing from available prints is the controversial scene where Baptiste beats up a white man interested in the heroine, the scene that caused the feature to be banned in Pittsburgh. Ironically, black actor George Randol played the part of the white villain.

Oscar Micheaux would again use the plot of *The Exile* in his final feature film, *Betrayal*, released by Astor Pictures in 1948.

## Black Magic

1932.

*P-D-SC:* Oscar Micheaux.

Although apparently produced, no credit or plot information is available on this feature film.

## The Girl from Chicago

A. Burton Russell, 1932, 63 minutes.

*P-D:* Oscar Micheaux. *SC:* Oscar Micheaux, from the story "Jeff Ballenger's Woman." *PH:* Sam Orleans.

*ED:* Richard Halpenny. *Asst Dir:* Vere E. Johns.

*Cast:* Carl Mahon (Alonzo White), Starr Calloway (Norma Shepherd), Alice B. Russell (Miss Warren), Eunice Brooks (Mary Austin), Minta Cato (Mary's sister), Grace Smith (Liza Hatfield), Frank Wilson (Wade Washington), Juano Hernandez (Gomez), John Everett (Jeff Ballenger), Edwin Cary (Numbers Collector), Cherokee Thornton ("A Switch"), Alfred "Slick" Chester, Bud Harris, Chick Evans.

After working several months with Scotland Yard, Secret Service Agent Alonzo White (Carl Mahon) returns home and is sent to Batesburg, Mississippi, on an assignment. Also arriving there is pretty Norma Shepherd (Starr Calloway), who has been promised a teaching job. Both Alonzo and Norma take up residence at Mary Austin's (Eunice Brooks) boarding house. Local crook Jeff Ballenger (John Everett) lusts after Mary and shoots his mistress, Liza (Grace Smith), the girlfriend of Wade Washington (Frank Wilson). Liza leaves town as Ballenger goes for Mary, but when he does Alonzo captures him and puts him in jail on various criminal charges. By now Alonzo and Norma are in love and they go to Harlem to see Mary, who has gone there to be with her ailing sister (Minta Cato). They find Mary is addicted to the numbers racket and bets with hoodlum Gomez (Juano Hernandez). When Mary goes to collect her winnings, she finds Gomez dead and is arrested for the crime. Alonzo believes she is innocent and sets out to find the murderer, who turns out to be Liza, now a cabaret singer and Gomez's mistress. Alonzo and Norma then get married and go on a honeymoon to Bermuda.

*The Girl from Chicago* is a typically tacky Oscar Micheaux production— poorly scripted, poorly lit, and poorly acted. In a couple of scenes the director can be heard cueing the actors who, still on camera, try to silence him. Like most Micheaux early talkies the movie uses subtitles to tell its story, and it contains tacky sets and poor filming locations. Again the producer-director pads the proceedings with musical fillers, although not as much as in some of his other features. Minta Cato provides some ear-piercing opera solos while Frank Wilson does a nice job singing "Shout Sister Shout." The movie was a remake of Micheaux's 1926 silent feature *The Spider's Web*.

## Ten Minutes to Live

A. Burton Russell, 1932, 57 minutes.

*P-D:* Oscar Micheaux. *SC:* Oscar Micheaux, from the stories "Harlem After Midnight." *PH:* Lester Lang. *Mus:* Donald Heywood. *Asst Dir:* A.B. Comathiere.

*Cast:* Lawrence Chenault (Jerry Marshall), Willa Lee Guilford (Letha Watkins), A.B. Comatherie (Club Patron), Laura Bowman (Vengeful Woman), Bessie Mitchell (Charlotte Evans), Mabel Garrett (Ida Morton), Donald Heywood (Master of Ceremonies), Carl Mahon (Anthony), William Clayton, Jr. (Morvis), Lorenzo Tucker (Gangster), Galle De Gaston, George Williams (Patrons).

A motion picture producer (Lawrence Chenault) goes to a cabaret to see a young singer (Mabel Garrett) and offer her a part in his new film, although he really wants to sleep with her. The young lady accepts the movie offer and promises to do anything for him in return. Meanwhile Letha Watkins (Willa Lee Guilford) and her fiancé Anthony (Carl Mahon) come to the club where she is given a note telling her that when she receives another missive she will have ten minutes to live. Letha was once the girlfriend of Morvis (William Clayton, Jr.), who turned out to be a criminal, and he plans to get her because he thinks she framed him for a crime. The girl has gone to Westchester, New York, to stay with her aunt, but Morvis follows her. Before he can kill her, Letha leaves with Anthony for the club and Charlotte Evans (Bessie Mitchell), Morvis' new girl, arrives. Although Morvis plans to kill Letha that night, he learns that it was Charlotte who framed him and that she has called the police. In a rage Morvis strangles Charlotte and then takes his own life. As a result, Letha and Anthony are free to return home.

One of Oscar Micheaux's worst films, *Ten Minutes to Live* is a jumbled mess. It is nothing more than a recycled silent film padded with new footage and interspersed with song, dance and comedy numbers. The plot, told in incoherent flashbacks of silent footage, is so muddled it almost defies description. The new scenes are mostly of a musical nature, including a number of songs such as "Home," "Give Me a Man Like That," "Draggin' My Heart Around," "Spirit of the Jungle," "Sweet Georgia Brown" and "You're Driving Me Crazy." One dance sequence was also used in Micheaux's *The Girl from Chicago* (q.v.) issued the same year. The producer-director hired chorus girls from the Cotton Club to work in his films doing the fairly accomplished dance numbers. Overall, the movie would embarrass even Edward D. Wood, Jr. In fact, Wood never made a movie so incongruous in plot or execution. For the record, two stories are told in the feature, "The

Faker" and "The Killer." The former evidently refers to a film director offering a young singer a part in his new film but planning to seduce her; the story is never completed. "The Killer" basically uses the silent film in telling of a young woman being stalked by an escaped convict who thinks she has framed him.

## Veiled Aristocrats

1932.

*P-D-SC:* Oscar Micheaux.

*Cast:* Lorenzo Tucker, Barrington Guy, Laura Bowman, Lawrence Chenault, Walter Fleming, Alice B. Russell.

A lawyer and his mother try to prevent his sister from carrying out her marriage plans to a man they do not like.

## Harlem After Midnight

1934, 8 reels.

*P-D-SC:* Oscar Micheaux.

*Cast:* Lorenzo Tucker, Dorothy Van Engle, Lawrence Chenault, Rex Ingram, Alfred "Slick" Chester, Bee (Bea) Freeman, A.B. Comatheire, Count Le Shine.

The story of gangsters involved in a kidnapping in Harlem.

## Lem Hawkins' Confession

1935, 98 minutes.

*P-D-SC:* Oscar Micheaux. *PH:* Charles Levine. *AD:* Tony Continenta. *SD:* Harry Belock & Armond Schettin. *Prod Mgr:* Charles B. Nason.

*Cast:* Clarence Brooks, Dorothy Van Engle, Alec Lovejoy, Laura Bowman, Alice B. Russell, Bea Freeman, Andrew Bishop, Lionel Monagas, Eunice Wilson, Sandy Burns, Henrietta Loveless.

After leaving the girl he loves over

a misunderstanding, a lawyer meets her again when he defends her brother on a murder charge. Also called *Murder in Harlem.*

## Temptation

1936.

*P-D-SC:* Oscar Micheaux.

*Cast:* Andrew Bishop, Bernice Gray, Ethel Moses, Ida Forest, Lorenzo Tucker, Hilda Rogers, Alfred "Slick" Chester, Larry Seymour.

A young black model wants to give up her underworld connections but is opposed by the gangster who wants her.

## The Underworld

Sack Amusements, 1937, 8 reels.

*P-D-SC:* Oscar Micheaux. *PH:* Lester Lang. *ED:* Nathan Cy Braunstein.

*Cast:* Bee Freeman, Sol Johnson, Oscar Polk, Alfred "Slick" Chester, Ethel Moses, Lorenzo Tucker.

Leaving the South, a young black student gets mixed up in crime in Chicago.

## God's Stepchildren

1938, 105 minutes.

*P-D-SC:* Oscar Micheaux. *PH:* Lester Lang. *ED:* Patricia Rooney & Leonard Weiss. *SD:* E.A. Schabbehor, George Wicker, Ed Fenton & Nelson Minnerly.

*Cast:* Gloria Press, Carmen Newsome, Ethel Moses, Laura Bowman, Alice B. Russell, Trixie Smith, Alec Lovejoy, Columbus Jackson, Charles Moore, Sam Patterson, Jacqueline Lewis, Charlie Thompson, Consuelo Harris, The Tyler Twins, Sammy Gardiner, The Leon Gross Orchestra.

A light-skinned black girl tries to pass for white with tragic results.

## Swing

A. Burton Russell, 1938, 7 reels.

*P-D:* Oscar Micheaux. *SC:* Oscar Micheaux, from the story "Mandy." *PH:* Lester Lang. *ED:* Patricia Rooney. *SD:* Ed Fenton & E.A. Schabbehor.

*Cast:* Cora Green, Hazel Diaz, Carmen Newsome, Dorothy Van Engle, Larry Seymour, Mandy Randolph, Trixie Smith, Nat Reed, Sammy Gardiner, Don Armena, The Tyler Twins, Columbus Jackson, George R. Taylor, The Leon Gross Orchestra.

A young woman is victimized by her dishonest lover in the world of show business.

## Birthright

1939, 9 reels.

*P-D-SC:* Oscar Micheaux. *PH:* Robert Marshall. *SD:* George Wicker.

*Cast:* Alec Lovejoy, Laura Bowman, Ethel Moses, Carmen Newsome, George Vessey, Trixie Smith, Alice B. Russell, Columbus Jackson, Harry Moses, Tom Dillon, Allen Lee, W. Herbert Jelly, Hazel Lisz, John Ward.

Returning South to start a school, a young black man meets resistance from Jim Crow laws as well as a brutal romantic rival.

## Lying Lips

1939, 60 minutes.

*P-D-SC:* Oscar Micheaux. *PH:* Lester Lang. *ED:* Leonard Weiss. *Mus:* Jack Shilkret. *SD:* Nelson Minnerly. *Dial Dir:* John Kollin.

*Cast:* Edna Mae Harris, Carmen Newsome, [Robert] Earl Jones, Frances Williams, Frank Costello, Slim Thompson, Juano Hernandez, Cherokee Thornton, Gladys Williams, Henry "Gang" Gines, Don De Leo, Charles Latorre, Robert Paquin, George Reynolds, Amanda Randolph, Teddy Hall.

After she refuses to date customers, a nightclub singer is framed for the murder of her aunt and sent to prison but her friend, a police detective, tries to prove her innocence.

## The Notorious Elinor Lee

1940, 10 reels.

*P:* Oscar Micheaux & Hubert Julian. *D-SC:* Oscar Micheaux. *PH:* Lester Lang. *ED:* Leonard Weiss. *Mus:* Jack Shilkret. *SD:* Nelson Minnerly.

*Cast:* Edna Mae Harris, Gladys Williams, Carmen Newsome, Robert Earl Jones, Vera Burella, Ella Mae Waters, Sally Gooding, Laura Bowman, Amanda Randolph, O.W. Polk, Juano Hernandez, Eddie Lemons, Columbus Jackson.

Crooks use a woman to soften up a boxing champion so he will throw a big fight.

# Peerless Pictures

Although it had only eight releases, Peerless Pictures operated from 1931 until 1936, initially out of 630 Ninth Street in New York City. The Peerless Pictures banner appeared above a hodge-podge of feature releases during the

1931–32 season, a quartet placed on the independent market mainly for the value of their name stars. James Hall headlined the opener for Peerless, *Sporting Chance*, while its only other 1931 release was Laura LaPlante in *Sea Ghost*, which *Photoplay* dubbed "an old-fashioned melodrama." Two more features came in 1932 with Sally Blane and James Murray in *The Reckoning* and Jack Mulhall and Natalie Moorhead starring in *Love Bound*. None of Peerless's four releases were considered more than fodder for the states' rights circuit, the product being distributed by Hollywood Film Exchange.

After a two-year hiatus, Peerless Pictures rose like the Phoenix, again releasing its product through Hollywood Film Exchange. This time four more features appeared, all produced by Sam Efrus, the president of Peerless, with direction by old-time serial star Charles Hutchison. The first release in this new arrangement was *House of Danger* in late 1934, followed by the rather well modulated *On Probation* in the spring of 1935. This feature was probably Peerless's best, especially for Monte Blue's work as a likable crook who lusts after his pretty charge (Lucille Browne). George E. Turner and Michael H. Price noted in their book *Forgotten Horrors* (1979), "Peerless's product seldom rose above the morass of 'off-brand' films, but *On Probation* is an exception. Suspenseful, beautifully photographed, and boasting a spectacular climax, the picture has the look of a major studio effort." Near the same league was the eerie *Circus Shadows*, released the next month, starring Dorothy Wilson, Kane Richmond and Walter Miller. Peerless's final outing, *Night Cargo*, issued early in 1936 and distributed by Marcy Pictures, starred veteran Lloyd Hughes and beautiful Jacqueline Wells [Julie Bishop] in an actioner set in Singapore.

The product of Peerless Pictures gained new life in the late 1940s when many of the titles (*Sporting Chance, The Reckoning, Love Bound, On Probation, Night Cargo*) were acquired by independent distributor J.H. Hoffberg and reissued theatrically and then sold to television.

An interesting footnote to Peerless's story is that in 1932 the company began production on a feature called *The Warning Shadow* at the Metropolitan Studios in Fort Lee, New Jersey. Adolph Pollak was the producer with direction by Edgar G. Ulmer. Dita Parlo, Tom Moore and William Desmond starred, but apparently the movie, later titled *Love's Interlude*, was never finished. About twenty minutes of its footage later appeared, however, in *Mr. Broadway*, distributed by Arthur Greenblatt in the fall of 1933.

## Sporting Chance

October 25, 1931, 71 minutes.

*P-D:* Al Herman. *SC:* King Baggot & Rex Taylor. *PH:* Earl Fox. *ED:* Earl Neville.

*Cast:* James Hall, Claudia Dell, William Collier, Jr., Mahlon Hamilton, Eugene Jackson, Joseph Lever-ing, Henry Rocquemore, Hedwig Reicher.

A jockey lets success go to his head, losing his job and becoming a vagabond.

## Sea Ghost

November 29, 1931, 73 minutes.

*P:* Alfred T. Mannon. *D:* William Nigh. *SC:* William Nigh & Jo Von Ronbea. *ST:* Burnet Hershey. *PH:* Sidney Hickox. *ED:* Thomas Persons. *SD:* L.E. Tope.

*Cast:* Laura LaPlante, Alan Hale, Claude Allister, Clarence Wilson, Peter Erkelenz.

A crooked lawyer tries to enlist the aid of a sea captain in cheating a young woman out of a fortune. Reissued by Astor Pictures in 1939 as *U-67.*

## The Reckoning

April 3, 1932, 65 minutes.
   *D:* Harry Fraser. *SC:* Leon Lee. *ST:* Dwight Cummings.
   *Cast:* Sally Blane, James Murray, Edmund Breese, Bryant Washburn, Pat O'Malley, Thomas Jackson, Mildred Golden, Douglas Scott.

A young couple, once crooks, fall in love and try to go straight but are suspects in a murder-holdup at the girl's place of employment.

## Love Bound

July 8, 1932, 67 minutes.
   *P:* Albert Herman. *D:* Robert F. Hill. *SC:* George Plympton & Robert F. Hill. *ST:* J. Gilbert. *PH:* E. Fox Walker. *Mus:* Lee Zahler. *Asst Dir:* Gordon S. Griffith. *Lights:* Edward Cox. *Sets:* E.R. Hickson. *SD:* Balsey & Phillips.
   *Cast:* Jack Mulhall (Dick Randolph), Natalie Moorhead (Verna Wilson/Wendell), Clara Kimball Young (Jane Randolph), Montagu Love (John Randolph), Edmund Breese (J.P. "Lucky" Morrison), Alice Day (Claudia Elliott), Roy D'Arcy (Juan De Leon), Bill [William V.] Mong (Mr. Howell), Tom Ricketts (Jimmy), Dick Alexander (Larry), Lynton Brent (Mr. Dillon).
   Golddigger Verna Wilson (Natalie Moorhead) wins a big settlement against wealthy John Randolph (Montagu Love), and his wife Jane (Clara Kimball Young) threatens to leave him. Their son Dick (Jack Mulhall) tells them he will prove his father's innocence. When Verna receives word her ex-husband Jimmy (Tom Ricketts) has escaped from jail and plans to get revenge on her for dropping him for playboy Juan de Leon (Roy D'Arcy), she makes plans to flee the country on the oceanliner *Romania.* When Dick learns of this, he and his chauffeur Larry (Dick Alexander) book passage on the ship with Larry pretending to be rich financier Lucky Morrison and Dick his pal Roland. De Leon also goes on the cruise and convinces Verna to romance Lucky and marry him for his money. Dick, however, plans to trap Verna into a romance with Larry and then expose her for what she did to his father. Larry, however, falls in love with Verna, and Dick too is attracted to her despite being in love with his fiancée, Claudia (Alice Day). Jimmy is on the ship and when Claudia, who is in love with Dick, finds this out, she becomes distraught and plans suicide. She changes her mind, however, when Dick asks her out, and Verna later turns down Lucky's marriage proposal. Jimmy agrees to leave Verna alone if she tells Dick the truth about her relationship with John Randolph, but before she can do this, Dick himself confesses to his real identity and his plans to trap her. Dick and Jimmy then get into a fight, and Jimmy is shot and killed. Dick is blamed for the crime and put under arrest. Verna, however, tells the authorities that it was De Leon who shot Jimmy, so Dick is set free. Verna agrees to clear Mr. Randolph's name and then goes on alone, leaving Dick to return to his fiancée.

*Love Bound* should have been called *Stage Bound* because most of its action takes place aboard an ocean-liner although there is little evidence that the participants are at sea. Outside of some stock boat footage and Dick Alexander's character complaining once of sea sickness, the story could just as easily have taken place at a hotel or country estate. Outside of the opening credits, the film contains no music, and the plot is so convoluted the cast seems to have trouble giving it coherence. Despite prominent billing, Clara Kimball Young and Montagu Love disappear after the first sequences as does Edmund Breese as the financier. Well into his forties, Jack Mulhall handles the role of the avenging son quite well, although Natalie Moorhead appears a cold fish as the tarnished heroine. Dick Alexander is quite good as the chauffeur Larry, the kind of part usually taken by Guinn "Big Boy" Williams. Roy D'Arcy is the typically oily leech attached to the gold digger, but Alice Day is wasted in a smallish role as the hero's virginal fiancée.

In 1949 J.H. Hoffberg breathed new life into this old wheeze by copyrighting and reissuing it as *Murder on the High Seas*.

# House of Danger

November 10, 1934, 63 minutes.

*P:* Sam Efrus. *D:* Charles Hutchison. *SC:* John Francis (Jack) Natteford. *ST:* C.C. Cheddon. *PH:* J. Henry Kruse. *ED:* Fred Bain. *SD:* J.S. Westmoreland.

*Cast:* Onslow Stevens, Janet Chandler, James Bush, Howard Lang, Desmond Roberts, Nina Guilbert, Tove Lindan, Roy Rice, John Andrews.

In order to save a young woman's life, a man pretends to be her wounded friend so he can capture killers.

# On Probation

April 17, 1935, 64 minutes.

*P:* Sam Efrus. *D:* Charles Hutchison. *SC:* Sherman L. Lowe. *ST:* Crane Wilbur. *PH:* J. Henry Kruse. *ED:* Fred Bain. *SD:* J.S. Westmoreland. *Asst Dir:* Melville DeLay. *Mus:* Cecil Stewart. *AD:* Jennett.

*Cast:* Monte Blue, Lucille Browne, William Bakewell, Barbara Bedford, Matthew Betz, Edward LeSaint, Betty Jane Graham, Arthur Loft, Henry Rocquemore, Lloyd Ingraham, Henry Hall, Margaret Fealy, John Webb Dillon, Roy Rice, Gino Corrado, King Kennedy, James Robinson, Marie Werner, Charles Hutchison.

A crooked politician adopts a young girl and as she grows older he falls in love with her only to learn she loves a wealthy bachelor.

# Circus Shadows

May 3, 1935, 65 minutes.

*P:* Sam Efrus. *D:* Charles Hutchison. *SC:* Sherman L. Lowe. *ST:* C.C. Cheddon. *PH:* J. Henry Kruse. *ED:* Fred Bain. *SD:* J.S. Westmoreland.

*Cast:* Dorothy Wilson, Kane Richmond, Russell Hopton, Dorothy Revier, William Ruhl, Sam Ash, Sumner Getchell, Gladys Gale, Ann Hovey, Tove Lindan, John Ince, Roy Rice, Stan Scharling, George Lloyd, Marjorie O'Connell.

A pretty circus performer is tricked into working for a phony spiritualist racket.

# Night Cargo

January 7, 1936, 66 minutes.

*P:* Sam Efrus. *D:* Charles Hutchison. *SC:* Sherman L. Lowe. *PH:* Walter London. *ED:* Fred Bain. *SD:* J.S. Westmoreland. *AD:* Jennett.

*Cast:* Lloyd Hughes, Jacqueline

William Ruhl, Russell Hopton and Dorothy Wilson in *Circus Shadows* (Peerless, 1935).

Wells [Julie Bishop], Walter Miller, Carlotta Monti, Lloyd Whitlock, George Regas, Jimmie Aubrey, John Ince.

In Singapore, a man and a pretty girl find themselves involved in murder and blackmail.

# Bud Pollard Productions

Bud Pollard, the first president of the Screen Directors Guild, spent 42 years in the motion picture business. No relation to silent film comedian Snub Pollard or director Harry Pollard, he was basically a one-man operation who produced, directed, wrote, edited and sometimes acted in his own features. Few of his productions survive, but it is known that he began operating his own company at the beginning of the sound era and that throughout the 1930s he made a diverse group of movies, including documentaries and ethnic features. Pollard had his own studio in New Jersey and offices at 723 Seventh Avenue in New York City. He catered primarily to the exploitation market, occasionally surfacing with minor releases for the general film trade. He died in Hollywood late in 1952 at age 65.

The first feature from Bud Pollard Productions appears to have been *The Danger Man* in 1930, an updated version of the 1926 serial *Lightning Hutch*, starring silent screen cliffhanger favorite Charles Hutchison, who also directed. Released at the beginning of the talkie era, this feature version had a music score and sound effects but no dialogue. In reviewing the original product, Kalton C. Lahue wrote in *Bound and Gagged* (1968), "Time had not treated him (Hutchison) well. He had gained a good deal around the waistline and his features showed considerable age and abuse. His attempts to lead the fast life of the film colony had taken a heavy toll. The pace of *Lightning Hutch* was rapid, but Hutch did few of the action sequences himself.... The finished product could not begin to compare with his Pathé cliffhangers." In 1930 Pollard also produced his first sound film, *Girls for Sale!*, but it ran into censorship problems due to its white slavery theme and did not see even spotty release until 1934.

In 1931 Bud Pollard made a version of Lewis Carroll's *Alice in Wonderland*, but it is extremely obscure, overshadowed by the Paramount version two years later. It is interesting to note, though, that the music in the Pollard version is credited to Irving Berlin due to the inclusion of his song "Alice in Wonderland," which debuted in the 1916 musical "Century Girl." About the only Bud Pollard film from the 1930s to be shown today is *The Black King*, released by Southland Pictures in 1932. It is an all-black cast film (except for Pollard as a judge) made for the urban Negro market, but by today's standards it is old-fashioned. That year Pollard also directed *O Festino o la Legge* at the Metropolitan Studios in Fort Lee, New Jersey. It was supposed to be the first of a series of features made in Italian by producer Clemente Giglio, and its star was Oreste Sandrino. Also announced as the first of a series which failed to materialize was *Victims of Persecution* (1933), starring Mitchell Lewis, which was to be the initial outing in a group of Jewish dramas Pollard was to make with William Goldberg Productions.

Prior to *Victims of Persecution*, Bud Pollard formed F.P. Productions in 1932 and announced an ambitious program of six exploitation titles: *The Horror, Dance Hall Dames, Lunatic at Large, Metropolitan Murders, Framed* and *The Green Jade*. Only *The Horror* appears to have been made; it was shot at Atlas Soundfilm Recording Studios in New York City in the fall of 1932. Promising "Chills and Thrills in a Drama of Mystery and Madness!" *The Horror* is lost to the ages, but surviving stills show intriguing scenes such as a young woman frightened by an ape-like creature, a huge snake and a madman who appears to suffer from acromegaly, the same disease that disfigured Rondo Hatton. Although *Dance Hall Dames* was announced for production at the end of 1932, it apparently was never filmed, nor were any of the other titles advertised by F.P. Productions.

In 1933 Bud Pollard Productions made *Missing Daughters*, an updated version of the 1924 Selznick silent feature of the same title that had starred Pauline Starke and Rockliffe Fellows. Pollard tacked on music and sound effects and a talking prologue to narrate the story of a young woman who gets involved in prostitution. In the 1930s Bud Pollard also directed two theatrical documentaries that incorporated World War I footage, *Forgotten Men* (1933) and *The Dead March* (1937). The latter was released by Imperial (q.v.), and it was shown in New York City in September, 1937, to coincide with the American Legion convention being held at that time. The feature is a hodge-podge of newsreel footage and its leanings are pacific. Not only did it use World War I newsreel film, but it also included the Japanese invasion of Manchuria, Italy's campaign in Ethiopia and the war between Bolivia and Paraguay. The movie included an interesting sequence that reveals the reason for its title. *Variety* noted, "Handling of the Unknown Soldier stuff misses because each national arises from his grave and gives his idealistic ideas which imbued him when he went to fight." The film's music score was by Erno Rapee, the composer of such popular songs as "Charmaine," "Diane" and "Angela Mia."

In the 1940s Bud Pollard returned to directing and made a series of feature films for the urban Negro market for All American News, headquartered at Fort Lee, New Jersey, and Astor Pictures in New York City. For the former company he shot such titles as *Big Timers*, *It Happened in Harlem* and *Romance on the Beat* (all 1945), and for Astor he directed musicals like *Tall, Tan and Terrific* (1946), *Beware* (1946) and *Look Out Sister* (1948), the last two starring bandleader Louis Jordan.

## The Danger Man

Cosmos, May 20, 1930, 60 minutes.

*P-D-SC-ED-Titles:* Bud Pollard. *ST:* Charles Hutchison. *PH:* Charles Levine. *SD:* D. Castagnaro.

*Cast:* Charles Hutchison, Edith Thornton, Sheldon Lewis, Virginia Pearson, Violet Schram, LeRoy Mason, William St. James.

A secret service agent goes through a series of adventures as he tries to capture a blackmail gang. A feature version of the 1926 serial *Lightning Hutch*, originally issued by Hurricane Film Corporation; it was directed by Charles Hutchison and written by John Francis Natteford.

## Alice in Wonderland

Unique-Cosmos, September 20, 1931, 55 minutes.

*P-D-ED:* Bud Pollard. *SC:* John E. Godson & Ashley Ayre Miller, from the novel by Lewis Carroll. *PH:* Charles Levine. *Mus:* Irving Berlin. *SD:* Armand Pehittini & Marc Ash. *Sets:* Charles Nasca.

*Cast:* Ruth Gilbert, Leslie King, Ralph Hertz, Vic Quinn, N.R. Cregan, Tom Corliss, Lillian Ardell, Mabel Wright, Meyer Beresen, Raymond Schultz, Jimmy Rosen, Patrick Glasgow, Gus Alexander, Charles Silvern.

A little girl, Alice, finds herself in a strange world and has many exciting adventures. Reissued in 1933.

## The Black King

Southland Pictures, March 15, 1932, 65 minutes.

*P-D:* Bud Pollard. *SC:* Donald Heywood. *PH:* Dal Clawson & Lester Lang. *ED:* Morris M. Levinson. *SD:* Geree Barton & Armand Schettini. *Tech Dir:* Marc S. Asch. *Costumes:* Brooks. *Asst Dir:* Joseph A. Bannon. *AD:* Anthony Continer.

*Cast:* A.B. Comathiere (Deacon Charcoal Johnson), Vivian Baber (Mary Lou), Knolly Mitchell (Sug), Dan Michaels (Longtree), Mike Jackson (Lawson), Mary Jane Watkins (Mrs. Bottoms), Lorenzo Tucker (Stephen Carmichael), Harry Gray (Deacon Jones), Trixie Smith (Delia), Freeman Fairley (Mob Leader), Ismay Andrews (Mrs. Ashfoot), James Dunmire (Nappy), Bud Pollard (Judge Lee).

At the black Baptist church in Logan, Mississippi, the congregation votes out their old Deacon Jones (Harry Gray) and replaces him with fast-talking Charcoal Johnson (A.B. Comathiere), who advocates a back-to-Africa movement. Jones dies as a result, much to the sadness of pretty Mary Lou (Vivian Baber) and her boyfriend Sug (Knolly Mitchell). Charcoal works the people into a frenzy over the movement, but Sug goes to the law and Deacon Johnson is run out of town (but not before coming between Mary Lou and Sug). In Tulsa Charcoal declares himself the Emperor of the United States of Africa with Mary Lou as his secretary and Longtree (Dan Michaels) and Lawson (Mike Jackson) as his assistants. They travel to Chicago gathering an army of followers and their money, and in the Windy City Johnson plans a parade which is opposed by Sug and lawyer Stephen

Carmichael (Lorenzo Tucker). While the parade is carried out, Charcoal dallies with the wife (Mary Jane Watkins) of an influential newspaper owner. The movement then heads to Harlem where Carmichael, now a lawyer for the Black Eagle Corporation which is to buy the ship to sail to Africa, tells Johnson and his cohorts that they will need a half million dollars to carry out their enterprise. He also tells them they are not welcome in Africa. Undaunted, Johnson throws a ball and hands out medals, but Sug and Carmichael arrive and show him to be a fraud. As a result the movement turns against Charcoal as Sug and Mary Lou are reunited. Charcoal, Longtree and Lawson then walk back to Mississippi.

Made for Southland Pictures Corporation with backing from white investors, *The Black King* is the one Bud Pollard production that remains available for viewing today. Henry T. Sampson in *Blacks in Black and White* (1977) said, "*The Black King* is typical of the racist films produced in the 1930's by independent white companies." It should be noted, however, that the film was scripted by the noted black writer-composer Donald Heywood. Produced at the Metropolitan Studios in New Jersey, the movie is a broad satire on Marcus Garvey and contains a dominating performance by A.B. Comathiere as the corrupt church deacon who aspires to royalty. In fact, the acting in the film is well above par for low-budget ethnic features of the 1930s, and while obviously shot on the cheap, Bud Pollard's production is not tacky. Surprisingly, there is little music, but profanity is sprinkled into the dialogue. Produced as *Empire, Inc.*, the movie got little initial release because Southland Pictures folded soon after its first showings. In 1936 Alfred N.

Sack reissued the movie as *Harlem Big Shot.*

## O Festino o la Legge

Sandrino Giglio, October, 1932, 6 reels.

P: Clemente Giglio. D: Bud Pollard.

*Cast:* Oreste Sandrino.

An Italian language film which was called *Thou Shalt Not Kill* in its English version.

## The Horror

Stanley Distributing Corporation/F.P. Productions, December, 1932, 7 reels.

P-D-ED: Bud Pollard. SC: Basil Smith. PH: Dal Clawson. Mus: William David. SD: Gerre Barton. AD: Lester. Sets: John Alsteadt. Prod Asst: Joseph A. Bannon & Frank Passar.

*Cast:* Leslie King, Myreda Montez, Ilene Meyers, Jimmie Kelso, Raja Rabold, John Gray, Gus Alexander, Reed Brown, Jr.

A young woman is terrorized by a madman and an ape-like monster in a spooky house.

## Missing Daughters

Quality, January, 1933, 60 minutes.

P-D-ED: Bud Pollard. PH: J. Bergi Contner. Mus: William Tuchman. SD: Lyman J. Wiggin.

*Cast:* Pauline Starke, Rockliffe Fellows, Eileen Percy, Sheldon Lewis, Claire Adams, Walter Long, Robert Edeson, Eva Novak, Walt Whitman, Frank Ridge, Chester Bishop.

A Missing Persons Bureau agent relates a decade-old case about a young woman lured into white slavery. An updated version of the 1924 Selznick release *Missing Daughters* with new footage added along with music and sound effects.

## Forgotten Men

Jewell, May 13, 1933, 60 minutes.

*Supv:* Samuel Cummings. *D:* Bud Pollard. *Prod Asst:* Edward A. Gallner & Louis R. Goldberg.

*Cast:* Samuel Cummings, Walter Schellenberg, Al Handy, Gaston Lauryssen, Angelo Giliberti, Miki Donovan.

Several veterans discuss various World War I battles along with current economic conditions.

## Victims of Persecution

June 17, 1933, 62 minutes.

P-D-ED: Bud Pollard. SC: David Leonard. PH: Don Malkames & Frank Zuker.

*Cast:* Mitchell Lewis, Betty Hamilton, Juda Bleich, Shirling Oliver, John A. Willarde, Anne Lewenwirth, Dan Michaels, David Leonard, Bud Pollard, Charles Adler.

A Jewish judge running for governor is faced with a black defendant in a controversial case.

## Girls for Sale!

1934, 6 reels.

P-D-SC-ED: Bud Pollard.

*Cast:* Vivian Gibson, Albert Stienruck, Ernest Deutsch, Suzi Vernon, Juli Serda, Hans Stuwe.

White slavery operators lure young women by advertising for cabaret jobs in Rio de Janiero. Filmed in 1930.

## The Dead March

Imperial, August 19, 1937, 73 minutes.

P-D-ED: Bud Pollard. SC: Samuel Taylor Moore. PH: Dal Clawson. SD: Walter Hicks. Sets: Al Panci. Mus: Erno Rapee & Max Manne.

*Cast:* Boake Carter (narrator),

Scola Doudauz, Al Rigali, Al Ritchie, Don Black, Howard Negley. A compilation of footage from the First World War and other military campaigns combined into a pacifist narrative.

# Principal Distributing Corporation

A native of Spokane, Washington, where he was born in 1890, Sol Lesser entered the motion picture industry as a circuit operator, and he later founded Fox West Coast Theatres. He became an independent motion picture producer and in the early 1930s formed Principal Theatres Corporation. In order to have films for this enterprise he also founded Principal Distributing Corporation, which was intended to handle both his films and other independents as well as imports. (Sol Lesser formed Principal Productions in 1921; in 1917 he was the head of States' Rights Distributors for which Louis B. Mayer was treasurer.) From 1932 to 1938 Principal released a number of feature films and serials, and some of its product is not without interest.

Principal Distributing Corporation kicked off its schedule in 1932 with a series of documentaries, the British import *Blame the Woman*, starring Adolphe Menjou and a two-year-old William Pizor western, *The Texan*, starring Buffalo Bill, Jr. This was only a prelude to the company's own production of *Tarzan the Fearless* (1933), which was filmed in the San Fernando Valley as *Tarzan the Invincible*. Buster Crabbe made a strong impression in the title role while Jacqueline Wells (later Julie Bishop) was a comely leading lady. Lesser had first acquired the rights to an Edgar Rice Burroughs Tarzan story in 1928, but he did not get his production off the ground for five years. The result was big box office with Lesser not only releasing the cliffhanger in twelve chapters, but also distributing it as a seven-reel feature followed by eight two-reel episodes. Many theatres, however, chose to run only the feature, forgoing the remaining chapters.

Principal also released two feature films in 1933: *Thunder Over Mexico* and *Jaws of Justice*. The former was made up of footage filmed in Mexico by Russian director Sergei Eisenstein in 1931 for a proposed feature to be called *Que Viva Mexico!* It was never finished. Sol Lesser's version incorporated the Eisenstein footage into a 71-minute feature. The Russian director shot over 60,000 meters of film for his aborted project, and the same year *Eisenstein in Mexico*, also distributed by Principal, and *Death Day* were released, both being made up of *Que Viva Mexico!* footage. Later, *Time in the Sun* (1939) and *Eisenstein's Mexican Project* (1958) were also compiled from Sergei Eisenstein's unreleased feature. *Jaws of Justice* was a low-budget north woods melodrama starring Jack Perrin, billed as Richard Terry, but its plotline used elements of Edgar Allan Poe's story "The Gold Bug."

In 1934 Principal released the insipid juvenile feature *Fighting to Live*, the British import *The Little Damozel*, starring Anna Neagle, and the Bela Lugosi serial *The Return of Chandu*. In 1932 Bela Lugosi had essayed the role of the evil Roxor in the Fox feature *Chandu the Magician*, starring Edmund Lowe in the title role, but here he took on the part of the hero, the magician Chandu, better known as Frank Chandler. For a dozen fast-paced chapters he sought to protect the beautiful Princess Nadji (Maria Alba) from Lemurian cat worshippers who wanted to use her for sacrifice. Lugosi was a handsome, but decidedly lecherous, hero. The cliffhanger itself was old-fashioned but highly entertaining. Like *Tarzan the Fearless*, *The Return of Chandu* was released as a seven-reel feature followed by eight two-reel chapters. In addition a second feature was edited by Carl Himm from the last eight chapters of the serial and released theatrically as *Chandu on the Magic Isle*.

Early in 1935 Principal released its third and final serial, *The Lost City*, produced by Sherman S. Krellberg. This cliffhanger has to be seen to be believed. Its dozen chapters contain enough plots and subplots to fill a half-dozen serials, and its acting and production values are strictly old-fashioned. In addition, some critics and viewers consider it highly racist. Of special interest is the performance of star William (Stage) Boyd as the mad scientist Zolok, who appears to have been completely intoxicated during the shooting of the film's finale. Several feature versions of this serial have emerged and most leave out some of the plot and characters but, amazingly, remain cohesive.

Toward the end of its existence, Principal Distributing Corporation became known as Principal Exchange, and it issued a couple of Sam Katzman Victory (q.v.) features, *Put on the Spot* (1936), a retitling of *Rio Grande Romance*, and *Lightning Carson Rides Again* (1937), starring Tim McCoy. The company finally ceased to exist after distributing *Convicts at Large* late in 1938. During the 1930s Lesser's Principal Productions made films for major studios.

Sol Lesser joined RKO Radio Pictures in 1941 as executive in charge of feature production, and he purchased the screen rights to the Tarzan character, eventually making 19 Tarzan films before selling the rights to the Edgar Rice Burroughs creation in the late 1950s. A decade later he taught at the University of Southern California's School of Cinema. Lesser died in 1980.

## The Texan

1932, 64 minutes.

*P:* William Pizor. *D:* Cliff Smith. *PH:* Ross Fisher. *ED:* Murray Seldeen. *Supv:* Gene Marcus.

*Cast:* Buffalo Bill, Jr., Lucille Browne, Bobby Nelson, Lafe McKee, Jack Mower, Art Mix, Yakima Canutt, Duke R. Lee.

On the lam from the law, a cowboy plans to aid two others in fixing a horse race but instead falls in love with a local girl. Filmed in 1930.

## South Seas Adventure

April 3, 1932, 50 minutes.

*P:* Sol Lesser. *SC:* Tom J. Geraghty. *PH:* Romer Grey, Bob Carney & Thomas B. Middleton. *ED:* Carl Himm. *SD:* Balsey & Phillips.

*Cast:* Zane Grey, Captain Lawrence Mitchell, R.C. Grey, Romer Grey, Wedgwood Nowell (narrator).

The story of a big game fishing expedition led by writer Zane Grey, from his home on Catalina Island to the South Seas.

## Dangers of the Arctic

July 2, 1932, 58 minutes.

*D-PH:* Earl Rossman. *Mus:* Michael Hoffman.

*Cast:* Earl Rossman (narrator).

A travelog of the Arctic, showing the salmon fishing industry and the lives of the Eskimos.

## Blame the Woman

October 22, 1932, 67 minutes.

*P:* Eric Hakim. *D:* Fred Niblo & Maurice Elvey. *SC:* Viscount Castlerosse.

*Cast:* Adolphe Menjou, Benita Hume, Claude Allister, Kenneth Kove, Desmond Jeans, G.D. Manetta, Roland Gilette, Toni Bruce, Shayle Gardener, Stanley Vilden, Phillip Strange.

At a country house party, a young woman manages to outwit jewel thieves. Produced in Great Britain by Cinema House as *Diamond Cut Diamond* in 1932.

## Devil's Playground

November 12, 1932, 55 minutes.

*P:* Frank R. Wilson. *SC:* Joe Cunningham. *PH:* Paul Burress. *Mus:* J.L. Merker. *SD:* Joe Finston & Max H. Manne.

*Cast:* George Vanderbilt, George Givot, Joe Cunningham (narrator).

A travelog about fishing adventures around the world.

## Amazon Head Hunters

November 17, 1932, 50 minutes.

*P:* Sol Lesser. *SC:* Irene Kuhn. *ED:* Carl Himm. *Mus:* Maurice Jaubert.

*Cast:* Le Marquis de Wavrin, Frederick Shields (narrator).

Belgian explorer Marquis de Wavrin spends four years in the Amazon jungle looking for a friend lost in Ecuador.

## With Williamson Beneath the Sea

November 26, 1932, 59 minutes.

*P-D-PH:* J.E. Williamson. *SC:* A. Hyatt Verrill. *ED:* Wid Gunning & Paul Maschke.

*Cast:* J.E. Williamson, Mrs. J.E. Williamson, Sylvia Williamson.

Undersea explorer-photographer J.E. Williamson relates his adventures as he finds sunken ships and the wonders beneath the ocean.

## A Jungle Gigolo

1933.

*SC:* Allyn B. Carrick & Forrest Izard. *PH:* Sam Besner. *SD:* S. Charles Fillat.

*Cast:* Edward Powell (narrator).

The trials and tribulations of a native in Sumatra who has a plethora of wives he cannot support. Reissued in 1935 by Ideal Pictures.

## Matto-Grasso

January 14, 1933, 50 minutes.

*P:* Sol Lesser. *D:* John S. Clarke, Jr., Floyd Crosby & David M. Newell.

*Cast:* George Rawls, Alexander Siemel, John S. Clarke, Jr. (narrator).

An expedition heads to the Matto-Grosso in Brazil to study primitive people who live there.

## Tarzan the Fearless

August 12, 1933, 12 chapters.

*P:* Sol Lesser. *D:* Robert Hill. *SC:* Basil Dickey, George Plympton, Ford Beebe & Walter Anthony. *ST:* Edgar Rice Burroughs. *PH:* Harry Neumann & Joseph Brotherton. *ED:* Carl Himm. *Mus:* Abe Meyer & Sam K. Wineland. *SD:* Balsley & Phillips. *SD ED:* Charles J. Hunt. *ST Supv:* William Lord Wright.

*Cast:* Buster Crabbe (Tarzan), Jacqueline Wells [Diane Duval/Julie Bishop] (Mary Brooks), E. Alyn Warren (Dr. Brooks), Edward Woods (Bob Hall), Philo McCullough (Jeff Herbert), Matthew Betz (Nick Moran), Frank Lackteen (Abdul), Mischa Auer (Eltar), Carlotta Monti (Princess of Zar), Symonia Boniface (Arab Servant), Darby Jones (Head Bearer), Al Kikume (Warrior), George DeNormand (Guard).

*Chapter Titles:* The Dive of Death, The Storm God Strikes, Thundering Death, The Pit of Peril, Blood Money, Voodoo Vengeance, Caught by Cannibals, The Creeping Terror, Eyes of Evil, The Death Plunge, Harvest of Hate, Jungle Justice.

When archaeologist Dr. Brooks (E. Alyn Warren) is captured by the worshippers of the god Zar in Africa, he is saved from sacrifice before the idol by Tarzan (Buster Crabbe), who takes him to the safety of his hut. Dr. Brooks asks Tarzan to take a message to his daughter Mary (Jacqueline Wells), who has come inland with her fiancé Bob Hall (Edward Woods) to find her father. The two have secured the services of crooks Jeff Herbert (Philo McCullough) and Nick Moran (Matthew Betz) as guides, but the two are really after the legendary emeralds of Zar. Jeff, who falls in love with Mary, has also been commissioned to prove that Tarzan is dead so that his estate in England can be cleared. Tarzan finds Mary and gives her the message and later follows her safari to Dr. Brooks' hut, but he has been kidnapped by the natives of Zar. A terrible storm wrecks the area, and Mary is carried off by Arab slaver Abdul (Frank Lackteen). Bob, thinking that Mary has been taken to Zar, follows a map to the area. Nick doublecrosses Jeff and tries to kill Bob for the map but instead is mauled to death by a lion. Jeff and Bob are lured to Zar by the high priest Eltar (Mischa Auer) and imprisoned with Dr. Brooks. Meanwhile, Tarzan rescues Mary from the Arab slavers and takes her to his cave. Later he rescues Dr. Brooks, Bob and Jeff from Zar, but on leaving, Jeff steals one of the sacred emeralds. When Jeff finds out that Tarzan is Mary's lover, he threatens to kill the jungle man unless Mary promises to marry him, and she reluctantly agrees. The warriors of Zar again capture Dr. Brooks, Jeff and Bob, but they are set free when the emerald is returned and they agree not to reveal the location of the idol. Later Tarzan and Jeff fight over Mary. Jeff is mortally wounded, and Tarzan disappears. Bob knows Mary no longer loves him and returns to the coast as Mary and her father stay to find Tarzan. He is waiting for them at Dr. Brooks' hut, and Tarzan and Mary remain together.

Swimming champion Buster Crabbe had just played a Tarzan-like jungle man in *King of the Jungle* (1933) for Paramount when he starred in this twelve-chapter serial for producer Sol

Lesser. Lesser also released the film as a feature comprising the first four serial chapters followed by weekly installments of the last eight chapters. In addition there was also a 61-minute feature version of the serial, and in Great Britain a 68-minute feature version was released by Wardour Films. Although rough-hewn, *Tarzan the Fearless* is a speedy action-packed cliffhanger which sports some impressive sets and an especially well-staged jungle storm sequence. Tarzan's cave was originally Lazarus's tomb in *King of Kings* (1927) while the statue of the pagan god Zar was the statue of Isis in *The Mummy* (1932). Padded with jungle stock footage, *Tarzan the Fearless* has enough subplots to keep it moving and an appealing cast greatly aids the proceedings. Buster Crabbe is perfectly cast as the handsome inarticulate jungle man while comely Jacqueline Wells nearly steals the show as the Jane substitute, Mary Brooks. Philo McCullough nicely handles the villain role of Jeff Herbert, who repents of his wrongs as he is dying, Mischa Auer makes a good pagan priest and Carlotta Monti (W.C. Fields' girlfriend) is the sexy Priestess of Zar. Although it takes itself entirely seriously, *Tarzan the Fearless* has one unintentionally hilarious scene. At nightfall Tarzan and Mary are standing at the entrance of Tarzan's cave. As the sun sets Tarzan intones "night comes" and with a lustful look in his eyes carries the girl inside.

## Thunder Over Mexico

September 30, 1933, 71 minutes.

    *P:* Sol Lesser. *D:* Sergei Eisenstein. *SC:* Don Hayes & Howard Alices. *PH:* Edouard Tisse. *ED:* Don Hayes & Carl Himm. *Mus:* Abe Meyer, Dr. Hugo Risenfeld, Juan Aguilar & Francisco Comacho. *Titles:* Howard Chandlee.

    Presented by Upton Sinclair, it was produced from footage shot in Mexico in 1931 by Russian director Sergei Eisenstein for an aborted project called *Que Viva Mexico!* The story tells of a young peon who leads a revolt against his master when the young man's bride is raped.

## Russia Today

October 21, 1933, 42 minutes.

    *D:* Carveth Wells.

    *Cast:* Carveth Wells (narrator).

    Various scenes in Russia, ranging from Moscow and other cities to the Caucasus area and Mount Ararat are shown.

## Eisenstein in Mexico

November 2, 1933, 50 minutes.

    *P:* Sol Lesser. *D:* Sergei Eisenstein. *PH:* Edouard Tisse.

    The story of Russian director Sergei Eisenstein filming the unfinished Mexican feature *Que Viva Mexico!*

## Jaws of Justice

December 4, 1933, 54 minutes.

    *P:* Spencer Gordon Bennet & Jack King. *D:* Spencer Gordon Bennet. *SC:* Joseph Anthony Roach, from the story "The Gold Bug" by Edgar Allan Poe. *PH:* Edward Snyder. *ED:* Grace Davey. *SD:* Lew Myers.

    *Cast:* Richard Terry [Jack Perrin] (Sergeant Kincaid), Robert Walker (Boone Jackson), Ruth Sullivan (Judy Dean), Lafe McKee (Seeker Dean), Jean Toler (Kickabout), Kazan (Himself), Lightnin' Teddy (Dog), Starlight (Himself).

    At a remote north woods settlement, a mute boy named Kickabout

Richard Terry [Jack Perrin], Ruth Sullivan and Robert Walker in *Jaws of Justice* (Principal, 1933).

(Jean Toler) has appeared with two dogs, Kazan and Lightnin' Teddy, and he is adopted by old prospector Seeker Dean (Lafe McKee) and his daughter Judy (Ruth Sullivan), who teaches the boy to read and write. Boone Jackson (Robert Walker), who claims to be a writer, romances Judy, but in reality he works for a syndicate that wants a fortune in gold which is secreted in the area. At a village get-together Seeker tells his friends that he has found the treasure and that it will make them all rich after he has talked to government officials. That night a mountie, Sergeant Kincaid (Richard Terry), comes looking for Kickabout and the dogs, since he is the one who sent the boy to the area in the first place. Kickabout tries to initiate a romance between Kincaid and Judy because he and Kazan do not like Jackson. The next day Jackson drives Seeker out of the area so he can talk with the officials, but along the way Seeker finds a letter from Jackson's true employers and a fight ensues. Jackson kills Seeker and leaves his body in a ravine, but Kazan witnesses the crime. One year passes and Kincaid returns to the village, pleased to find that Judy has not married Jackson. Seeker is declared legally dead, but Kazan, who has been with Kincaid, is openly hostile to Jackson. Kickabout, to whom Seeker had confided, shows Kincaid the whereabouts of a cryptograph that will lead him to the gold. Kincaid finds the message buried in a fireplace wall, and in the meantime Jackson shoots but does not kill Kazan. Kincaid tells Ruth that the clue to the gold is in the Edgar Allan Poe story "The Gold Bug." Kincaid suspects Jackson killed Seeker, and when Jackson finds out about the clue, Ruth finally believes the mountie.

When Jackson attacks Ruth, Kazan comes down a chimney and defends her, but Jackson manages to hurl him against a wall and make a getaway. Kazan trails Jackson to the dam where the gold is hidden and chews through a rope Jackson is climbing, with Jackson falling to his death. Kazan then averts the explosion Jackson had set to free the treasure which is now left to the villagers.

Filmed around Lake Tahoe, *Jaws of Justice* is a pretty solid low-budget affair centered around Jack King's wonder dog Kazan, who by this time had had his tail amputated. Nevertheless Kazan was one of the better canine stars of the 1930s, and he went through his paces well in this scenic melodrama. Taking the lead role is cowboy star Jack Perrin, billed here as Richard Terry, and with him (unbilled) is his loyal steed, Starlight. The story makes interesting use of Edgar Allan Poe's story "The Gold Bug," and a subplot has Kazan bringing a dead man's possessions back to his murderer. *Jaws of Justice* is one of the few feature films to give a production credit to ace serial director Spencer Gordon Bennett, who coproduced it with Jack (John) King, the trainer of Kazan, who would costar with the dog in *Fighting Fury* (1934), also called *Outlaws' Highway*.

## Fighting to Live

1934, 60 minutes.

*P:* Sol Lesser. *D:* Eddie [Edward F.] Cline. *SC:* Robert Ives. *PH:* Frank B. Good. *ED:* Carl Himm. *SD:* Harry Belock. *Mus:* Lee Zahler. *Asst Dir:* Theodore Joos. *Prod Mgr:* Frank Medford.

*Cast:* Marion Shilling (Mary Carson), Gaylord [Steve] Pendleton (John Z. Blake), Reb Russell (Reb), Eddie Phillips (Joe Gilmore), Lloyd Ingra-

ham (Judge Simmons), Henry Hall (Mr. Endicott), John Strohback (Frank Gilmore), Bruce Mitchell (Rancher), Captain, Lady (Themselves).

Mary Carson (Marion Shilling) works as a bookkeeper for real estate agent Frank Gilmore (John Strohback) and is fond of his two dogs, Captain and Lady, that he took in a trade deal. Gilmore and his son Joe (Eddie Phillips) do not like the animals, and when Joe gets fresh with Mary, Captain attacks him. A short time later, mailman Reb (Reb Russell) introduces Mary and Joe to John Z. Blake (Gaylord Pendleton), who plans to practice law in the area. Mary and John are immediately attracted to each other, much to Joe's chagrin. Vowing revenge on the dogs, Joe takes them muzzled into the desert and lets them go. Eventually the dogs are able to get rid of their muzzles, but they are forced to forage for food. Captain begins raiding local hen houses. Upset, the ranchers try to hunt down the dog, who saves John when he falls in the river while fishing. Joe captures Captain and tries to shoot him, but John stops Gilmore and demands the dog be given a fair trial. At the trial the judge (Lloyd Ingraham) and the jury are not sympathetic to his case, so John lets the dog escape. The judge orders the lawyer to bring back the dog, and he and Reb find Captain with Lady, who has had four pups. John and Reb return the dogs to court and Mary brings in Joe, who under cross examination by John, admits taking the dogs to the desert. The court dismisses the case against Captain, and John and Mary find romance.

Director Edward F. Cline is known for comedies like *Cracked Nuts* (1932), *Million Dollar Legs* (1932), *My Little Chickadee* (1939), *The Bank Dick*

(1940), *Never Give a Sucker an Even Break* (1941), *Crazy House* (1943) and *The Ghost Catchers* (1943). *Fighting to Live* must certainly rate as the nadir of his directorial career. Cheaply made, poorly photographed and recorded, the movie is a cheapjack juvenile feature which must have looked moth-eaten even when it was first released. Marion Shilling, a one-time cast member of stage plays by Max Reinhardt and the lovely leading lady who graced many Poverty Row movies in the 1930s, here is badly made-up and photographed. Gaylord, later Steve, Pendleton overacts as the leading man and non-actor Reb Russell is plainly out of place as a small-town mail carrier. The supporting cast is adequate, especially Lloyd Ingraham as the judge, but the plot is mundane and production values are practically nil. The most appealing players in the picture are dogs Captain and Lady, but the script permits them very little action in deference to their vapid human counterparts.

## The Little Damozel

1934, 73 minutes.

*P-D:* Herbert Wilcox. *SC:* Donovan Pedlety, from the play by Monckton Hoffe.

*Cast:* Anna Neagle, James Rennie, Benita Hume, Athole Stewart, Alfred Drayton, Clifford Heatherley, Peter Northcote, Franklyn Bellamy, Aubrey Fitzgerald.

After a sea captain pays a sailor to marry a singer, the husband and wife find they are in love. Made in England in 1933 by British and Dominions Film Corporation and reissued there in 1937 by Equity British Film Productions.

## The Ferocious Pal

April, 1934, 55 minutes.

*P:* Sol Lesser. *D:* Spencer Gordon Bennet. *SC:* Joe Roach. *PH:* Edward Kull.

*Cast:* Kazan, Ruth Sullivan, Jean Toler, Robert Manning, Tom London, Grace Wood, Edward Cecil, Henry Rocquemore, Nelson McDowell, Harry Dunkinson, Prince.

A boy and a girl are helped by their dog as they try to fight crooks.

## The Return of Chandu

Principal Pictures Corporation, October 9, 1934, 12 chapters.

*P:* Sol Lesser. *D:* Ray Taylor. *SC:* Barry Barringer. *PH:* John Hickson. *ED:* Carl Himm & Lou Sackin. *Mus:* Abe Meyer. *SD:* Corson Jowett. *Asst Dir:* Harry Knight. *AD:* Robert Ellis. *Prod Supv:* Frank Melford. *Dial Dir:* Cyril Armbrister.

*Cast:* Bela Lugosi, Maria Alba, Clara Kimball Young, Lucien Prival, Dean Benton, Phyllis Ludwig, Cyril Armbrister, Bryant Washburn, Wilfred Lucas, Josef Swickard, Murdock MacQuarrie, Jack Clark, Peggy Montgomery, Dick Botiller, Frazer Acosta, Harry Walker, Elias Lazaroff, Merrill McCormack, Charles Meacham, Isobel LeMall, Don Brodie, Edward Peil, Henry Hall, Beatrice Roberts, Iron Eyes Cody, Elias Schaffer.

Chapter Titles: The Chosen Victim, The House on the Hill, On the High Seas, The Evil Eye, The Invisible Circle, Chandu's False Step, The Mysterious Island, The Edge of the Pit, The Invisible Terror, The Crushing Rock, The Uplifted Knife, The Knife Descends.

Chandu the magician comes to the rescue of the Princess Nadji who is wanted for sacrifice by a cat-worshipping cult. Principal also released the serial in two feature versions in 1934, *The Return of Chandu* (65 min-

Advertisement for the serial *The Return of Chandu* (Principal, 1934).

utes) and *Chandu on the Magic Isle* (60 minutes).

## The Lost City

February, 1935, 12 chapters.

*P:* Sherman S. Krellberg. *D:* Harry C. Revier. *SC:* Perley Poore Sheehan, Eddie Greneman & Leon D'Usseau. *ST:* Zelma Carroll, George M. Merrick & Robert Dillon. *PH:* Eddie Lindon & Roland C. Price. *ED:* Holbrook N. Todd. *Mus:* Lee Zahler. *AD:* Ralph Berger. *SD:* Clifford Ruberg. *Asst Dir:* William Nolte & Dick L'Estrange. *SP Eff:* Norman Dawn & Kenneth Strickfaden. *Prod Mgr:* George M. Merrick.

*Cast:* William (Stage) Boyd, Kane Richmond, Claudia Dell, Josef Swickard, Ralph Lewis, William (Billy) Bletcher, George F. Hayes, Eddie Featherstone, Milburn Morante, Gino Corrado, Henry Hall, Curley Dresden, Sam Baker, Everett Brown, Margo D'Use, Jerry Frank.

Chapter Titles: Living Dead Men, Tunnel of Death, Dagger Rock, Doomed, Tiger Prey, Human Beasts, Spider Men, Human Targets, Jungle Vengeance, The Lion Pit, The Death Ray, The Mad Scientist.

An expedition to Central America tries to find the source of worldwide electrical disturbances and uncovers a hidden city controlled by a mad scientist. Also released in two feature versions and reissued as a feature called *City of Lost Men.*

## Island Captives

July 29, 1937, 53 minutes.

*D:* Glenn Kershner. *SC:* Al Martin. *PH:* William Hyer. *ED:* Dan Milner. *SD:* Dave Stoner.

*Cast:* Eddie Nugent, Joan Barclay, Henry Brandon, Forrest Taylor, Charles King, Carmen LaRoux, Frederick Palmer, John Beck, John Sheehan.

After a shipwreck a lecherous beachcomber pursues a young woman on a South Seas island.

## Convicts at Large

December 13, 1938, 57 minutes.

*P:* Myron G. Nash & Lee K. Chadwick. *D:* Scott E. Beal & David A. Friedman. *SC:* Walter James & Scott E. Beal. *ST:* Ambrose Parker. *PH:* Marcel LePicard. *ED:* Carl L. Pierson. *SD:* Corson Jowett. *Prod Mgr:* Burton King. *AD:* Fred Preble.

*Cast:* Ralph Forbes, Paula Stone, William Royle, John Kelly, George Travell, Charles Brokaw, Florence Lake, James Flavin, Sam Wren.

An architect unwittingly becomes involved with gangsters and falls in love with a nightclub singer.

# Progressive Pictures

Between 1932 and 1938 Progressive Pictures released eight feature films in two time segments. The movies issued by the company during the 1933–34 season were distributed by Marcy Pictures (q.v.), a subsidiary of William Steiner. Most of them were produced by Willis Kent (q.v.) who usually released his own product on the states' rights market. In 1938 Progressive was reactivated by B.N. Judell, who is probably best remembered for his production of *Terror of Tiny Town* (1938), a Columbia release with an all-midget cast.

The initial five Progressive releases are not without interest, with Kent's *Sucker Money* (1933) and *Murder in the Museum* (1934) being the most worthwhile. *Sucker Money* gave Mischa Auer one of his few starring roles. He portrayed a fake swami called Yomurda, the same character he had played the year before in Willis Kent's *Sinister Hands. Sucker Money* was codirected by Dorothy Reid, the widow of Wallace Reid, who starred in the silent era as Dorothy Davenport. *Murder in the Museum* top-billed a second silent screen favorite, Henry B. Walthall, who dominated the proceedings as stage magician Professor Mysto. In spite of somewhat clumsy production, the feature is a taut mystery thriller whose villain is not easily identified. Also of interest is the obscure *Mystic Hour* (1934), which featured Charles Hutchison in the same type of daredevil role that had made him a favorite of serial fans in the 1920s. Although it got few bookings stateside, it was distributed overseas by J.H. Hoffberg.

The trio of 1938 B.N. Judell Progressive productions, all released by Times Pictures (q.v.), contain one hit and two misses. While *Slander House* is an amusing comedy-drama, both *Delinquent Parents* and *Rebellious Daughters* had little to offer outside a good cast. Of the latter *Variety* noted, "The production comes under the heading of inadequate, but at that it's not worse than the script. The photography is weak and the sound is distinctly unrealistic.... It's pretty grim and lurid stuff."

## Her Splendid Folly

January 28, 1933, 63 minutes.

*P:* Willis Kent. *D:* William O'Connor. *SC:* Beulah Poynter. *PH:* James Diamond & Jules Cronjager. *ED:* S. Roy Luby.

*Cast:* Lillian Bond, Theodore Von Eltz, Alexander Carr, Lloyd Whitlock, J. Frank Glendon, Beryl Mercer, Roberta Gale, Frances Lee, Louise Beavers, William Burt, Harry Todd.

In Hollywood a stenographer poses as a film star while her mother works at the studio as a scrubwoman.

## Sucker Money

March 1, 1933, 70 minutes.

*P-SC:* Willis Kent. *D:* Dorothy Reid & Melville Shyer. *PH:* William Nobles. *ED:* S. Roy Luby.

*Cast:* Mischa Auer, Phyllis Barrington, Ralph Lewis, Mae Busch, Al Bridge, Mona Lisa, Earl McCarty, Anita Faye, Fletcher Norton.

A fake swami plans to use a girl to swindle her rich father but a newspaper reporter works undercover to expose the racket.

## Under Secret Orders

December 6, 1933, 60 minutes.

*D:* Sam Newfield. *SC:* Eustace L. Adams. *PH:* Jules Cronjager. *ED:* Walter Thompson.

*Cast:* J. Farrell MacDonald, Phyllis Barrington, Donald Dillaway, Don Alvarado, Nena Quartero, Matthew Betz, Lafe McKee, Paul Ellis, Leon Holmes.

On his first assignment, a novice secret service agent loses important papers after drinking with an exotic woman.

## Mystic Hour

1934, 60 minutes.

*D:* Melville DeLay. *SC:* John Francis Natteford. *ST:* Susan Embry. *PH:* Leon Shamroy & Bernard B. Ray. *ED:* Otis Garrett. *SD:* L.E. Tope.

*Cast:* Montagu Love, Lucille Powers, Charles Middleton, Edith Thornton, Eddie Phillips, James Aubrey, Charles Hutchison.

A wealthy young man teams with a detective to try and capture a thief known as The Fox.

## Woman Condemned

April 20, 1934, 66 minutes.

*P:* Willis Kent. *D:* Mrs. Wallace Reid [Dorothy Davenport]. *PH:* James Diamond. *ED:* S. Roy Luby. *SD:* Earl Crain. *Asst Dir:* Bartlett [Bart] Carre.

*Cast:* Claudia Dell (Barbara Hammond), Lola Lane (Jane Merrick), Richard Hemingway (Jerry Beal), Jason Robards (Jim Wallace), Mischa Auer (Dr. Wagoner), Douglas Cosgrove (Police Chief), Tom O'Brien (Kennedy), Paul Ellis (Dapper Dan), Sheila Mannors (Radio Actress), Louise Beavers (Sally), Neal Pratt

(Harry Benham), Mary Gordon (Night Court Woman).

Radio singer Jane Merrick (Lola Lane) announces she is going on an extended vacation, but her sponsor wants her back as does station manager Jim Wallace (Jason Robards), who loves her. He hires a detective agency to find out why Jane is in hiding, but their agent, Barbara Hammond (Claudia Dell), is caught and taken to night court when she tries to spy on the Merrick apartment. Brash newspaperman Jerry Beal (Richard Hemingway) claims in court that Barbara is his fiancée and the judge promptly marries them. Jerry finds himself falling for his new bride, who will not reveal her past to him. When Barbara again spies on Jane, she sees the singer give money to a man before being shot and killed. When Barbara is found at the scene with the murder weapon, she is arrested for the crime and provides nothing in her own defense. Jerry is convinced of Barbara's innocence and he goes through the murdered woman's apartment, finding a phone number there that leads him to a remote hospital run by Dr. Wagoner (Mischa Auer). He calls Wallace, and the two are captured by the doctor and his associates. There they see Sally (Louise Beavers), Miss Merrick's maid, and they learn the singer is alive, having undergone plastic surgery. The murdered woman was her twin sister. Through a ruse the police make the killer think Barbara has confessed to the crime. When Jane pretends to be her sister's ghost, the murderer cracks and admits the crime. Jerry learns that Barbara is really a detective, and they plan to go on their delayed honeymoon.

Except for some horror elements at Dr. Wagoner's sanitorium, *Woman Condemned* is an old-fashioned, stodgy melodrama. Mischa Auer does the best work in the film as the mysterious surgeon who at one point threatens to use Jason Robards' brain "for the good of science." This, however, is only a joke since the doctor is really a plastic surgeon. Otherwise, the film is slow-moving with a confused plot and weak performances by principals Richard Hemingway and Claudia Dell. Although the picture has no writing credit, it most likely was scripted by producer Willis Kent who sometimes did not take credit for his writing efforts. In this case it is understandable.

*Woman Condemned* was directed by Mrs. Wallace Reid, the widow of screen idol Wallace Reid who died in 1923 at the age of 31 as a result of drug addiction. Mrs. Reid, who starred in the silent days as Dorothy Davenport, became an outspoken anti-drug advocate and starred in such "message" pictures as *Human Wreckage* (1923) and *Broken Laws* (1924), both produced by Thomas H. Ince for Films Booking Office (FBO). Mrs. Reid also codirected the 1934 remake of *Road to Ruin* (q.v.) for Willis Kent, and in the 1940s she wrote scripts under the name Dorothy Reid.

## Murder in the Museum

May 27, 1934, 60 minutes.

*P:* Willis Kent. *D:* Melville Shyer. *SC:* E.B. Crosswhite. *PH:* James Diamond. *ED:* S. Roy Luby. *Asst Dir:* George Curtner.

*Cast:* Henry B. Walthall, Phyllis Barrington, John Harron, Joseph Girard, John Elliott, Donald Kerr, Symona Boniface, Sam Flint, Clinton Lyle, Steve Clemente, Al Hill, Si Jenks, Lynton Brent, Albert Knight.

When the police raid a freak show

in search of illegal liquor, a city councilman is mysteriously murdered.

# Delinquent Parents

July 6, 1938, 62 minutes.

*P:* B.N. Judell. *AP:* Melville Shyer. *D:* Nick Grinde. *SC:* Nick Barrows & Robert St. Clair. *PH:* M.A. Anderson. *ED:* S. Roy Luby. *Asst Dir:* Melville DeLay.

*Cast:* Doris Weston, Maurice Murphy, Helen MacKeller, Terry Walker, Richard Tucker, Morgan Wallace, Carlyle Moore, Jr., Marjorie Reynolds, Theodore Von Eltz, Walter Young, Sybil Harris, Janet Young, Byron Foulger, Virginia Brissac, Harry Hayden, Betty Blythe.

A woman forced to give up her child years before becomes a judge and is forced to handle a case involving the girl when she grows up.

# Rebellious Daughters

September 28, 1938, 65 minutes.

*P:* B.N. Judell. *AP:* Lon Young. *D:* Jean Yarbrough. *SC:* John W. Krafft. *PH:* M.A. Anderson. *ED:* Carl L. Pierson. *AD:* Edward C. Jewell. *Mus:* Lee Zahler. *SD:* Tom Carmen. *Asst Dir:* Herman E. Webber.

*Cast:* Marjorie Reynolds, Verna Hillie, Sheila Bromley, George Douglas, Dennis Moore, Oscar O'Shea, Irene Franklin, Monte Blue, Nick Lukats, Lita Chevret, Dell Henderson, Vivian Oakland.

A young woman is driven from home by her parents and nearly comes to a bad end before being saved by a newspaperman. Working title: *Wayward Daughters*.

# Slander House

October 4, 1938, 65 minutes.

*P:* B.N. Judell. *AP:* Melville Shyer. *D:* Charles Lamont. *SC:* Gertrude Orr & John W. Krafft, from the novel *Scandal House* by Madeline Woods. *PH:* M.A. Anderson. *ED:* S. Roy Luby. *AD:* Edward C. Jewell. *Asst Dir:* Mel DeLay. *Mus:* Lee Zahler. *SD:* William Fox.

*Cast:* Adrianne Ames (Madame Helene/Helen Smith), Craig Reynolds (Pat Fenton), Esther Ralston (Ruth De Milo), George Meeker (Dr. Herbert Stallings), Pert Kelton (Mazie), William Newell (Terry Kent), Dorothy Vaughn (Mrs. Louise Horton), Edward Keane (George Horton), Vivien Oakland (Mrs. Conway), Ruth Gillette (Madame Renault), Mary Field (Bessie), Blanche Payson (Maude).

One-time slum girl Helen Smith, now calling herself Madame Helene (Adrianne Ames), runs the swank Helen's Rejuvenating Salon which caters to rich, overweight society women. She is romanced by wealthy Dr. Stallings (George Meeker), who sends her all his Park Avenue clients, but she does not love him. Gambler Pat Fenton (Craig Reynolds) falls for Helene and makes a play for her, but when they go out on the town, he causes a scandal by getting into a fight with his lawyer George Horton (Edward Keane), the husband of one of Helene's customers (Dorothy Vaughn). Out with Horton is another customer, show girl Ruth De Milo (Esther Ralston), who wants Pat for herself. Although she knows her husband was out with Ruth, Mrs. Horton thinks he is really after Helene, and later when Helene lets Horton give her a ride home after she has a row with Pat, they are involved in an accident which makes the headlines. Both Stalling and Pat, who has sold his racing stable, want to marry Helene, who tries to tell Mrs. Horton the truth

Esther Ralston, Dorothy Vaughn, Vivien Oakland, Adrianne Ames and William Newell in *Slander House* (Progressive, 1938).

about her husband and the accident. Mrs. Horton, however, hears Ruth and the other women at the salon making fun of her and she takes poison. Helene calls Stallings to save Mrs. Horton, and Pat brings her husband. Mrs. Horton recovers and is reconciled with her husband while Stallings realizes that Helene loves Pat. Ruth admits she deceived Helene into thinking Pat loved her, and Pat and Helene are united.

*Slander House* is one of the very few features to be made by Progressive Pictures, and its production crew looks like old-home week from Chesterfield-Invincible (q.v.). Director Charles Lamont, writers Gertrude Orr and John W. Krafft, cameraman M.A. Anderson, art director Edward C. Jewell and assistant director Melville DeLay were all alumni of Chesterfield-

Invincible, which ceased operations the year before. Understandably, the film has the look of a Chesterfield release, and like many of that company's efforts, it derives from a literary source, in this case Madeline Wood's 1933 novel *Scandal House*. A pleasant comedy-drama, the movie's greatest asset is its beautiful star Adrianne Ames, who is aided by a fine supporting cast, including Esther Ralston as a bitchy show girl and George Meeker, usually cast as a bounder, as a kindly doctor. Basically a satire on overweight, pampered society women and their useless lives, *Slander House* milks its comedy for all it's worth and to good effect. In one scene wisecracking receptionist Pert Kelton says one of the customers "eats like a bird—a peck at a time." In the supporting cast Vivien Oakland as a tipsy customer and Ruth Gillette as an opera singing matron who needs to lose fifty pounds are quite effective. Other amusing scenes have a big dog and later a monkey causing havoc in the beauty salon and hero Craig Reynolds getting caught in the reducing room with a number of flabby matrons.

# Puritan Pictures Corporation

With the emblem of its religious counterpart, Puritan Pictures Corporation burst onto the movie scene in 1935 and over two years released a total of twenty feature films, the main body made up of Tim McCoy westerns. When McCoy failed to renew with the company after making ten features, Puritan floundered and soon disappeared. It should be noted, though, that the bulk of the Puritans were well made, and in addition to the sturdy Tim McCoy series, the company also turned out a superb old-house murder mystery, *The Rogues Tavern* (1936).

As with most Poverty Row outfits of the mid–1930s, Puritan was mainly a clearinghouse for the product of independent filmmakers. Its initial three releases in 1935—*Kentucky Blue Streak, Rip Roaring Riley* and *Skybound*—were action melodramas produced by C.C. Burr, who also produced the second Tim McCoy series entry, *The Outlaw Deputy* (1935). Starting with the third film in the McCoy series, *Bulldog Courage* (1935), the Tim McCoy westerns were produced by Sigmund Neufeld and Leslie Simmonds and directed by the former's brother, Sam Newfield. The star was paid $4,000 each for the ten westerns he made for Puritan, films that were budgeted at between $10,000 and $12,000 each. Despite the low budgets, the Tim McCoy westerns for Puritan had a sturdy look about them, and overall the series was above par for a Poverty Row company. Thus the McCoys for Puritan fared quite well in the states' rights market, bringing in a domestic gross of between $65,000 and $80,000 per picture.

Tim McCoy began starring in westerns at MGM in 1926 and remained with that company into 1929. The next two years found him doing the serials *The Indians Are Coming* (1930) and *Heroes of the Flames* (1931) for Universal before going to Columbia in 1931, where he remained until 1935 when he signed with Puritan. Although the Puritan films lacked the slick production values of his Columbia product, McCoy felt that working for the independent company would give him more artistic freedom and a wider variety of roles. *Bulldog Courage* (1935) is considered the best of the McCoy-Puritan features, but most of the ten outings the star did for the company are quite entertaining, especially *Aces and Eights* (1936) and *Ghost Patrol* (1936), which featured a science fiction motif that utilized Kenneth Strickfadden's electrical equipment made famous in *Frankenstein* (1931) and *The Bride of Frankenstein* (1935). Although offered a renewal of his Puritan contract in 1936, Tim McCoy signed instead with William Pizor's Imperial Pictures (q.v.) for a series of features that were never made, thus resulting in legal action which McCoy won in 1939.

When Tim McCoy left Puritan the company was not able to fill the gap created by the loss of revenue from his features. The company struggled briefly along with independents like C. Burr's *The Reckless Way* (1936) and Fanchon Royer's *Death in the Air* (1937) and *A Million to One* (1938). The second was so loaded with stock footage that one reviewer complained it showed the same plane falling in flames at least five different times.

## Kentucky Blue Streak

June 7, 1935, 60 minutes.
*P:* C.C. Burr. *D:* Raymond K. Johnson. *SC:* Homer King Gordon. *PH:* I.W. Akers. *ED:* Tony Martinelli. *Mus:* Ben Carter. *SD:* Terry Kellum. *AD:* Vin Taylor. *Asst Dir:* George Jeske.
*Cast:* Eddie Nugent, Patricia Scott, Junior Coghlan, Margaret Mann, Cornelius Keefe, Roy D'Arcy, Roy Watson, Joseph Girard, Harry Harvey, Ben Holmes, Roger Williams, Ben Carter's Colored Octette.

A jockey is sent to jail on a false charge but escapes to win the big race and clear himself.

## Rip Roaring Riley

October 24, 1935, 57 minutes.
*P:* C.C. Burr. *D:* Elmer Clifton. *SC:* Homer King Gordon.
*Cast:* Lloyd Hughes, Grant Withers, Marion Burns, John Cowell, Paul Ellis, Eddie Gribbon, Kit Guard, Joe Hiakawa.

Federal agents are sent to a remote island to look into a report of poison gas production.

## Skybound

November 12, 1935, 55 minutes.
*P:* C.C. Burr. *D:* Raymond K. Johnson. *SC:* C. Edward Roberts. *ST-*
*Asst Dir:* George Jeske. *PH:* Irving Akers. *ED:* Anthony Martinelli. *AD:* Vin Taylor. *SD:* Corson Jowett.
*Cast:* Lloyd Hughes, Lona Andre, Eddie Nugent, Grant Withers, Mildred Clare, John Cowell, Duvaland Tregg, Harry Harvey, Dick Curtis, Bill Fleck & His Orchestra, Sam Lufkin, Loren Rowell, Mabel Mason.

A special agent and a runaway heiress team to oppose air mail robbers.

## The Man from Guntown

November 30, 1935, 58 minutes.
*P:* Nat Ross. *D-ST:* Ford Beebe. *SC:* Ford Beebe & Thomas H. Ince, Jr. *PH:* James Diamond. *ED:* Robert Jahns. *Mus:* Lee Zahler. *SD:* T.T. Triplett. *Prod Mgr:* Norman Deming.
*Cast:* Tim McCoy, Billie Seward, Rex Lease, Wheeler Oakman, Jack Clifford, Bob McKenzie, Jack Rockwell, George Chesebro, Hank Bell, Horace B. Carpenter, Ella McKenzie, Charles King, Bud Pope, Oscar Gahan.

A lawman helps a falsely accused cowboy clear himself of a crime.

## The Outlaw Deputy

December 3, 1935, 58 minutes.
*P:* C.C. Burr. *D:* Otto Brower. *SC:* Ford Beebe & Dell Andrews, from the

Advertisement for *The Man from Guntown* (Puritan, 1935).

story "King of Cactusville" by Johnston McCulley. *PH:* James Diamond. *ED:* Robert Jahns. *SD:* Hans Weeren.

*Cast:* Tim McCoy, Nora Lane, Bud Osborne, George Offerman, Jr., Joseph Girard, Si Jenks, Hooper Atchley, Dick Botiller, Charles Brinley, Jack Montgomery, George Holtz, Jim Corey, Tex Cooper, Ray Jones, Bud Pope, Tom Smith, Buck Morgan, Bob Card.

When his friend is murdered a cowboy rides to a lawless town seeking revenge.

Poster for *Bulldog Courage* (Puritan, 1935).

## Bulldog Courage

December 30, 1935, 60 minutes.

*P:* Sigmund Neufeld & Leslie Simmonds. *D:* Sam Newfield. *SC:* Joseph O'Donnell & Frances Guihan. *PH:* Jack Greenhalgh. *ED:* S. Roy Luby. *SD:* Hans Weeren. *Asst Dir:* William O'Connor. *AD:* Harry Lewis.

*Cast:* Tim McCoy, Joan Woodbury, Karl Hackett, John Cowell, Eddie Buzzard, John Elliott, Edward Cassidy, Jack Rockwell, Edmond Cobb, Paul Fix, George Morrell, Bud Osborne, Art Mix, Slim Whitaker, Frank Ellis, Jack Mower, Edward Hearn, Buck Bucko.

A man returns home after twenty years to get even with the crook who stole his father's gold mine.

## The Reckless Way

1936, 72 minutes.

*P:* C.C. Burr. *D:* Raymond K. Johnson. *SC:* Raymond K. Johnson & Philip Dunham. *ST:* C.E. Roberts. *PH:* James Diamond. *ED:* Charles Henkel. *AD:* Vin Taylor. *Mus:* Gene Johnston. *SD:* Tom Lambert. *Prod Mgr-Asst Dir:* George Jeske.

*Cast:* Marion Nixon (Helen Rogers), Kane Richmond (Jim Morgan), Inez Courtney (Laura Jones), Malcolm MacGregor (Don Reynolds), Harry Harvey (Joe), Art Howard (Martin Stoner), Gloria Gordon (Birdie Stoner), William Strauss (Karl Blatz), John Peters (Von Berg).

Hotel stenographer Helen Rogers (Marion Nixon) longs to break into the movies, and she models for a hosiery ad for Don Reynolds (Malcolm MacGregor) who wants to marry her. Helen is also loved by Jim Morgan (Kane Richmond), a hotel clerk who wants to become a screenwriter. By mistake Helen is named as part of a divorce action, and she decides to make the most of the publicity. Jim convinces motion picture executive Karl Blatz (William Strauss) that his Apex Studios should give Helen a screen test. Self-centered director Von Berg (John Peters) is assigned to the test and Reynolds pays him to sabotage it so he can have Helen for himself. The test is a flop, but recovering his investment, Blatz hires a British writer to do a script for Helen. It is Jim, however, who secretly ends up doing the screenplay, which is based on Helen's life at the hotel. This time Helen proves to be quite good, and hoping to stop the production, Reynolds has the British writer arrested in Mexico, but Jim finishes the script. Helen, however, begins to grow tired of all the work and exploitation in the movies as well as the back-biting attitude of its denizens. Blatz finds out Jim actually wrote the script to *Million Dollar Legs*, Helen's film. Upon its completion she agrees to marry Reynolds, but at a party Von Berg tells her the truth about how he and Don tried to ruin her screen test. At the same time Jim learns it was Don who shanghaied the British writer to Mexico and confronts him about it in front of Helen. Helen then tells Reynolds and Von Berg she is finished with Hollywood and goes back to the hotel and agrees to marry Jim, who informs her he has a five year writing contract with Apex Studios.

One of the most obscure of Puritan Pictures' releases, *The Reckless Way* appears to have had no definite release date despite the presence of Marion Nixon in the starring role. Filled with stilted scenes and dialogue, a meandering plot and choppy editing, the movie grows tiresome as it attempts to rib Hollywood by chronicling the rise of a starlet. Cute Marion Nixon is a definite plus as the starry-eyed aspirant for movie stardom, and she is ably assisted by Inez Courtney as her wisecracking pal and Kane Richmond as the stalwart leading man. In the supporting cast, John Peters is especially good as he satirizes Erich von Stroheim. Marion Nixon is allowed to sing the drab tune "I Spoke Out of Turn," and her flop screen test scenes are quite amusing, as is the sequence when prop man Harry Harvey refers to the bounders who try to sabotage Nixon's career as "Hollywood heels." Otherwise *The Reckless Way* is a lacklustre, tacky attempt at Poverty Row Hollywood taking satiric aim at the big studio system.

## I'll Name the Murderer

January, 1936, 66 minutes.

*P:* C.C. Burr. *D:* Raymond K. Johnson. *SC:* Philip Dunham. *PH:* James Diamond. *ED:* Charles Henkel. *AD:* Vin Taylor. *Mus:* Gene Johnston. *SD:* Cliff Ruberg. *Asst Dir:* George Jeske.

*Cast:* Ralph Forbes, Marion Shilling, Malcolm MacGregor, James Guifoyle, John Cowell, William Norton Bailey, Agnes Anderson, Charlotte Barr-Smith, Mildred Claire, Gayne Kinney, Harry Semels, Al Klein.

A Broadway gossip columnist investigates the murder of a nightclub singer killed in her dressing room.

## Suicide Squad

January, 1936, 60 minutes.

*P:* C.C. Burr. *D:* Raymond K. Johnson. *SC:* Homer King Gordon. *ST:*

C.E. Roberts & Ray Nazarro. *PH:* James Diamond. *ED:* Arthur Brooks. *AD:* Vin Taylor. *Mus:* Abe Meyer. *SD:* Corson Jowett. *Asst Dir:* George Jeske.

*Cast:* Norman Foster, Joyce Compton, Robert Homans, Aggie Herring, Peter Warren, Jack Luden, Phil Kramer.

Two members of the fire department's suicide squad both love the same girl, the daughter of their chief.

# Border Caballero

May 26, 1936, 54 minutes.

*P:* Sigmund Neufeld & Leslie Simmonds. *D:* Sam Newfield. *SC:* Joseph O'Donnell. *ST:* Norman S. Hall. *PH:* Jack Greenhalgh. *ED:* Holbrook N. Todd. *SD:* Hans Weeren. *Asst Dir:* William O'Connor.

*Cast:* Tim McCoy, Lois January, Ralph Byrd, Ted Adams, J. Frank Glendon, Earle Hodgins, John Merton, Oscar Gahan, Bob McKenzie, Jack Evans, Tex Phelps, Ray Henderson, George Morrell, Frank McCarroll, Bill Patton, Si Jenks, Steve Clark, Harrison Greene, Jack Rockwell, Slim Whitaker, Dick Botiller, Artie Ortego, Henry Hall, Sherry Tansey, Wally West, Ben Corbett, Bud McClure, Herman Hack, Bill Wolfe.

An ex-federal agent agrees to bring in the gang who murdered his former partner.

# The Rogues Tavern

June 4, 1936, 67 minutes.

*D:* Robert Hill. *SC:* Al Martin. *PH:* William Hyer. *ED:* Dan Milner. *Mus:* Abe Meyer. *Settings:* Fred Preble. *SD:* J.S. Westmoreland. *Prod Mgr:* Edward W. Rote.

*Cast:* Wallace Ford (Jimmy Kelly), Barbara Pepper (Marjorie Burns), Joan Woodbury (Gloria Rohloff), Clara Kimball Young (Mrs. Jamison), Jack Mulhall (Bill), John Elliott (Mr. Jamison), Earl Dwire (Morgan), John W. Cowell (Bert), Vincent Dennis (Hughes), Arthur Loft (Wentworth), Ivo Henderson (Harrison), Ed Cassidy (Mason), Bob McKenzie (Marriage License Official), Silver Wolf (Himself).

Unable to get married at the marriage license bureau, detective Jimmy Kelly (Wallace Ford) and fiancée Marjorie Burns (Barbara Pepper), a former department store sleuth, go to the Red Rock Tavern to await the arrival of a justice of the peace. The place is run by Mrs. Jamison (Clara Kimball Young) and her wheel-chair-ridden husband (John Elliott), the couple renting the place from an inventor named Morgan (Earl Dwire). Also staying at the inn are exotic Gloria Rohloff (Joan Woodbury) and four men, Bill (Jack Mulhall), Hughes (Vincent Dennis), Harrison (Ivo Henderson) and Mason (Ed Cassidy), along with the dim-witted handyman Bert (John W. Cowell). Harrison is found murdered with teeth marks on his neck and a dog, Silver Wolf (himself), is blamed since he was seen in the room where the crime was committed. Later, Hughes is killed in the same manner, and Jimmy deduces the murderer used a set of false dog teeth to tear the victims' throats. After the dog is found Mason too is murdered after the arrival of Wentworth (Arthur Loft). Gloria, Wentworth and Bill try to escape from the inn but find all the windows barred. They admit to Jimmy that they are jewel smugglers. Marjorie sees Jamison leave his wheel chair, and she later follows Mrs. Jamison to the cellar where Morgan is hiding. A mysterious voice draws the guests to the cellar where they discover

Morgan, who says Wentworth stole an invention from him. Morgan, however, denies any knowledge of the murders. Trapped in the basement, the group is confronted by Mrs. Jamison, who says she will murder them all with poison gas because Wentworth and his gang blackmailed her sister into smuggling jewels and because the girl committed suicide rather than go to jail after being caught. Just before she can carry out her plan, Mrs. Jamison is waylaid by Jimmy. The police arrive and Wentworth, Gloria and Bill are arrested along with Mrs. Jamison. Also arriving is the justice of the peace, who marries Jimmy and Marjorie.

Quite polished for an independent production, this Mercury Pictures/Carmel Products murder mystery was filmed at Pathé Studios, giving it a classy look. The original script had Wallace Ford playing a character called Jimmy Flavin but probably in deference to the actor of the same name it was changed to Jimmy Kelly. He and Barbara Pepper make a good team as the wisecracking lover sleuths, and director Robert Hill sustains an overall good mystery aura throughout the proceedings. During the action, Jack Mulhall announces the killings to be "the work of a maniac," and a good exchange of dialogue takes place between Wallace Ford and Ed Cassidy. "How did you know I was a cop," Ford asks Cassidy, who replies, "Your feet gave you away."

## Lightnin' Bill Carson

June 9, 1936, 71 minutes.

*P:* Sigmund Neufeld & Leslie Simmonds. *D:* Sam Newfield. *SC:* Joseph O'Donnell. *PH:* Jack Greenhalgh. *ED:* Jack [John] English. *SD:* Hans Weeren. *Asst Dir:* William O'Connor.

*Cast:* Tim McCoy, Lois January, Rex Lease, Harry Worth, Karl Hackett, John Merton, Edmond Cobb, Jack Rockwell, Oscar Gahan, Lafe McKee, Frank Ellis, Slim Whitaker, Jimmy Aubrey, Artie Ortego, Joseph Girard, Franklyn Farnum, Roger Williams, Francis Walker, Herman Hack, George Morrell, Tom Smith, Dick Botiller, Ray Henderson, Jack Evans.

A lawman is hunted by a gunman as he tracks a wanted outlaw, the brother of the girl he loves.

## Roarin' Guns

July 7, 1936, 60 minutes.

*P:* Sigmund Neufeld & Leslie Simmonds. *D:* Sam Newfield. *SC:* Joseph O'Donnell. *PH:* Jack Greenhalgh. *ED:* S. Roy Luby. *SD:* Hans Weeren. *Asst Dir:* William O'Connor.

*Cast:* Tim McCoy, Rosalinda Price, Rex Lease, Wheeler Oakman, Karl Hackett, John Elliott, Tommy Bupp, Jack Rockwell, Lew Meehan, Frank Ellis, Edward Cassidy, Richard Alexander, Artie Ortego, Al Taylor, Jack Evans, Tex Phelps, Roger Williams, Wally West, Slim Whitaker, Hank Bell, Milburn Morante, Art Dillard.

A cowboy comes to the aid of ranchers being defrauded by a cattle combine.

## Aces and Eights

August 8, 1936, 62 minutes.

*P:* Sigmund Neufeld & Leslie Simmonds. *D:* Sam Newfield. *SC:* George Arthur Durlam. *ST:* Joseph O'Donnell. *PH:* Jack Greenhalgh. *ED:* Jack [John] English. *SD:* Hans Weeren. *Asst Dir:* William O'Connor.

*Cast:* Tim McCoy (Gentleman Tim Madigan), Luana Walters (Juanita Hernandez), Rex Lease (Jose Hernandez), Wheeler Oakman (Ace

Morgan), Jimmy Aubrey (Lucky), Charles Stevens (Captain Felipe De Lopez), Earle Hodgins (Marshal), J. Frank Glendon (Amos Harden), Joseph Girard (Colonel Julio Hernandez), John Merton (Gambler), Frank Ellis (Deputy Sheriff).

Gentleman Tim Madigan (Tim McCoy), a noted gambler, and his pal Lucky (Jimmy Aubrey) ride into a small town where Tim's reputation has preceded him. He warns a crooked gambler (John Merton) who has cheated Jose Hernandez (Rex Lease), and later, when the gambler is shot, Tim is blamed and Jose thinks he pulled the trigger. The marshal (Earle Hodgins) gets on Tim's trail and enlists the aid of the local commandant (Charles Stevens) in bringing in the gambler. Tim meanwhile changes his name to Tim Harrington. He again meets Jose, who invites him to visit Rancho Hernandez, which is coveted by crooked Ace Morgan (Wheeler Oakman), the real killer of the gambler. Jose is estranged from his father (Joseph Girard) and sister Juanita (Luana Walters), who both give Tim a warm welcome. Gambling house boss Amos Harden (J. Frank Glendon), Ace's partner, gives Jose gambling credit, and the latter runs up a huge debt. Tim reunites Jose with his family and Harden demands that Señor Hernandez pay his son's gambling debts with the money he borrowed to save his ranch from Morgan. Tim borrows money Hernandez leaves out for strangers and goes to town where he stops Jose from shooting Harden. Tim then gambles with Harden and wins everything, including the man's gambling house. Tim then takes the gold Harden took from Señor Hernandez and goes to the hacienda where he meets Morgan. The two fight. Tim

wins the brawl, and the marshal arrives to hear Jose clear Tim of the charge of killing the gambler. The marshal then reveals it was Ace Morgan who committed the crime. Tim, now a free man, decides to remain with Juanita.

The seventh of ten westerns Tim McCoy did for Puritan Pictures, *Aces and Eights* is a complicated and slow-moving affair whose limited budget and production values do not mar its overall appearance. Tim McCoy is again the stalwart hero, this time an honest gambler who protects a Spanish family from being robbed by crooks. Luana Walters is the attractive heroine who has little to do, while faded western star Rex Lease takes on the role of a compulsive gambler. The villains parts fall on Wheeler Oakman, J. Frank Glendon and John Merton, who handle them with relish, although Merton is killed off early in the proceedings. What comedy relief is to be found is in the none-too-steady hands of Jimmy Aubrey as McCoy's dice-carrying sidekick Lucky. Charles Stevens (Geronimo's grandson) also has a few amusing moments as the local commandant. Earle Hodgins nearly steals the show as the lawman on McCoy's trail. Here hero Tim McCoy uses strength and not guns to bring about justice; most of the shooting is left up to the bad guys.

## The Lion's Den

August 25, 1936, 59 minutes.

*P:* Sigmund Neufeld & Leslie Simmonds. *D:* Sam Newfield. *SC:* John T. Neville. *ST:* L.V. Jefferson. *PH:* Jack Greenhalgh. *ED:* John English. *SD:* Hans Weeren. *Asst Dir:* William O'Connor.

*Cast:* Tim McCoy, Joan Woodbury, Don Barclay, John Merton, Dick Curtis, J. Frank Glendon, Arthur Millett, Jack Rockwell, Karl Hackett, Jack Evans, Art Felix, Bud McClure, Frank Ellis.

After agreeing to aid terrorized ranchers, a sharpshooter is mistaken for a gunman.

## Ghost Patrol

September 10, 1936, 56 minutes.

*P:* Sigmund Neufeld & Leslie Simmonds. *D:* Sam Newfield. *SC:* Wyndham Gittens. *ST:* Joseph O'Donnell. *PH:* Jack Greenhalgh. *SP Eff:* Kenneth Strickfaden. *Asst Dir-Prod Mgr:* William O'Connor. *SD:* Hans Weeren.

*Cast:* Tim McCoy, Claudia Dell, Walter Miller, Wheeler Oakman, James Curtis, Dick Curtis, Lloyd Ingraham, Jack Casey, Slim Whitaker, Artie Ortego, Art Dillard, Fargo Bussey, Frank Ellis, Bruce Mitchell, Jack Cheatham, Blackie Whiteford.

An FBI agent investigates the mysterious crashes and robberies of several mail plaines.

## The Traitor

November 6, 1936, 58 minutes.

*P:* Sigmund Neufeld & Leslie Simmonds. *D:* Sam Newfield. *SC:* John T. Neville. *PH:* Jack Greenhalgh. *ED:* Jack [John] English. *SD:* Hans Weeren. *Asst Dir:* William O'Connor.

*Cast:* Tim McCoy, Frances Grant, Karl Hackett, Jack Rockwell, Edmond Cobb, Pedro Regas, Frank Melton, Dick Curtis, Wally Wales, Dick Botiller, Tina Menard, Soledad Jiminez, J. Frank Glendon, Wally West, Frank McCarroll, Jimmy Aubrey, Slim Whitaker, George Chesebro, Frank Ellis, Art Dillard, Oscar Gahan, Julian

Rivero, Jack Kirk, Al Taylor, Buck Morgan, Ray Henderson, Jack King.

Tossed out of the service, an ex–Texas Ranger infiltrates a gang south of the Mexican border.

## Death in the Air

February 15, 1937.

*P:* Fanchon Royer. *D:* Elmer Clifton. *SC:* Charles R. Condon. *ST:* Bernard McConville. *PH:* James Diamond & Arthur Reed. *ED:* Carl Himm. *AD:* F. Paul Sylos. *SD:* Carson Jowett. *Asst Dir:* Wilfred Black.

*Cast:* Lona Andre, John Carroll, Leon Ames, Wheeler Oakman, Reed Howes, Henry Hall, Gaston Glass, Pat Somerset, John S. Peters, Willard Kent, John Elliott.

A power-mad pilot goes on a spree destroying planes and is hunted by a fellow aviator. Also called *Pilot X* and reissued in 1943 as *Mysterious Bombardier.*

## A Million to One

June 1, 1938, 59 minutes.

*P:* Fanchon Royer. *D:* Lynn Shores. *SC:* John T. Neville. *PH:* James Diamond. *ED:* Edward Schroeder. *SD:* Cliff Ruberg. *Prod Mgr:* Gaston Glass. *AD:* James Riemer. *Asst Dir:* Vin Taylor.

*Cast:* Herman Brix [Bruce Bennett], Joan Fontaine, Monte Blue, Kenneth Harlan, Suzanne Kaaren, Reed Howes.

A man trains his son to win the decathlon he once lost, only to have him fall in love with the daughter of the winner, his rival. Working title: *Olympic Champ.*

# Regal Distributing Corporation

Regal Distributing Corporation was operated by producer Sherman S. Krellberg from 1934 to 1939, and in the 1935-36 period it may have been associated with Regal Productions, Inc., an outfit run by George A. Hirliman. Those companies, should not be confused with Regal Talking Pictures, which made *Enemies of the Law* with Mary Noland in 1931 and also imported the British feature *Should a Doctor Tell?* that year. Krellberg's shoestring operation turned out minimal-budget features aimed at kiddie audiences, featuring canine stars like Lightning the Wonder Dog, Kazan, and Lobo the Marvel Dog, although none of them lasted very long under Krellberg's slim budget limitations. The movies done by George A. Hirliman had bigger budgets and were shot in color, but Hirliman soon joined Grand National Pictures, which took over the distribution of his productions. By the end of the 1930s Regal operated as an importer of foreign films.

The initial releases for Regal Distributing Corporation were in 1934 with *Hollywood Hoodlum*, a Franchon Royer Production (q.v.), and Krellberg's *When Lightning Strikes* starring Lightning the Wonder Dog. While announced as the first of a series with the canine star, no other features followed with Lightning for Regal. Krellberg did, however, make *Man's Best Friend* (1935) with the dog, but that film went out on the states' rights market via Royal Releasing Corporation, that company's sole effort. In 1935 Krellberg made the twelve-chapter cliffhanger *The Lost City*, starring William (Stage) Boyd, Kane Richmond and Claudia Dell under the Regal Pictures-Super Serial Productions, Inc., banner, but it was distributed by Principal Distributing Corporation (q.v.). Krellberg's final Regal offering came in 1936 with *Thunderbolt*, which teamed Kane Richmond with Lobo the Marvel Dog. It should be noted that for the 1934-35 season Regal announced that John "Jack" King and his dog Kazan would star in a quartet of features: *Fighting Fury, Honor Badge, The Law Rides West* and *Special Duty*. Regal never distributed these films because only *Fighting Fury* was made, and it was issued in 1934 by J.D. Trop as *Outlaws' Highway*. In 1935 Sherman S. Krellberg reissued it under his own banner using its original title.

George A. Hirliman perfected the process called MagnaColor, which at one time rivaled Technicolor; it was later dubbed HirliColor. George A. Hirliman Enterprises had several subsidiary companies, Condor and Pacific, in addition to Regal Productions, Inc. He also formed Metropolitan Pictures Corporation (no relation to the studio of the same name formed by Bernard B. Ray and Harry S. Webb) to make Spanish-language versions of his movies.

For Regal, Hirliman made a trio of 1936 features, *Captain Calamity, The Devil on Horseback* and *The Rest Cure* and their Spanish-language counterparts. His association with Regal, however, was brief since Hirliman soon joined Grand National as a producer. He also made films with George O'Brien and Richard Dix at RKO Radio and was involved in some of the "Hopalong Cassidy" westerns at Paramount. In 1943 he formed Film Classics.

By the late 1930s Regal Distributing Corporation no longer made films, but it did continue to exist by importing foreign features. In 1938 it distributed two French Films, *Advocate D'Amour* and *Rothschild*, and the next year it handled the British feature *The Mutiny of the Elsinore.*

## When Lightning Strikes

1934, 53 minutes.

*P:* Sherman S. Krellberg. *D:* Burton King. *SC:* J.P. McGowan. *PH:* Edward Kull. *ED:* Rena Roberts. *Mus:* Lee Zahler. *SD:* Harry Belock. *Asst Dir:* Bartlett [Bart] Carre.

*Cast:* Lightning the Wonder Dog (Himself), Francis X. Bushman, Jr. (Matt Caldwell), Alice Dahl (Helen Stevens), J.P. McGowan (Broderick), Tom London (Wolf), Blackie Whiteford (Hunky), William Desmond (Marshall Jack Stevens), Marin Sais (Mrs. Stevens), Murdock MacQuarrie (Jim Caldwell), Bart Carre (Townsman), Shaggy (Dog).

In the north country Jim Caldwell (Murdock MacQuarrie) and his son Matt (Francis X. Bushman, Jr.) have secured the timber rights on some two thousand acres of land, thanks to their friendly dealings with the local Indians. Dishonest lumberman Broderick (J.P. McGowan) hires thugs Wolf (Tom London) and Hunky (Blackie Whiteford) to steal the timber lease before it is registered. Fearing trouble, Jim sends faithful dog Lightning (Himself) with the lease, and the dog buries it in the woods before Wolf and Hunky can find it. While Lightning fights with Wolf, Hunky shoots Jim and leaves him for dead. Lightning,

however, finds Jim and gets him to the Indian camp where he is nursed back to health. Broderick orders Wolf and Hunky to live in the Caldwell cabin until the deadline on their lease expires so he can lay claim to the land. Matt returns home to find the two on his property and promptly throws them out. Lightning, who has been shot by Wolf when looking for Matt, is found by Helen Stevens (Alice Dahl), Matt's fiancée and the daughter of the local sheriff (William Desmond). She takes the dog home where he recovers and then leads Matt to his father. Both men worry that their timber lease is lost forever, but Lightning shows them the place in the woods where it is buried. Later Broderick comes to the Caldwell cabin and tries to kill Matt, and during a fight a stove is overturned, setting the cabin on fire. Matt manages to rescue the beaten Broderick as the sheriff comes to arrest him. Matt and Lightning then corner Wolf and Hunky in the local saloon, and the dog defeats the two thugs. Matt and Helen decide to build a new home on their land.

Crudely filmed and photographed, *When Lightning Strikes* was the first of a proposed series to star Lightning, the Wonder Dog. This was, however, the animal's only film for Regal. Hampered by choppy editing and many scenes shot silent with added music background, the feature overworked a music score which included the song "Love Makes the World Go Round" at the end. The soundtrack music was performed by the Regal Serenaders. Lightning handled his heroic chores in good fashion as did Francis X. Bushman, Jr., his human counterpart. Alice Dahl made a comely heroine while silent screen stars William Desmond and Marin Sais had only limited footage as her parents. Tom London and Blackie Whiteford made an entertaining pair of dastardly villains. Overall, though, *When Lightning Strikes* was only a minor entry in the juvenile oriented field and one which had only limited distribution on the states' rights market. Like many features of its ilk the movie was never copyrighted.

It did, however, mark the film debut of Lightning the Wonder Dog who went on to appear in such features as *A Dog of Flanders* and *Man's Best Friend* (both 1935), *Two in Revolt* and *White Fang* (both 1936) and *Renfrew of the Royal Mounted* (1937).

## Hollywood Hoodlum

June 21, 1934, 61 minutes.

*P:* Fanchon Royer. *D:* B. Reeves "Breezy" Eason. *SC:* John Thomas Neville. *ST:* William Bloecher. *PH:* Ernest Miller. *ED:* Jeanne Spencer. *SD:* Terry Kellum.

*Cast:* June Clyde, Frank Albertson, Jose Crespo, Tenen Holtz, John Davidson, Stanley Price, Cyril Ring, Edith Terry Preuss.

A Hollywood publicist gets into real trouble when he hires an actor to pretend to be a gunman who has been cast in the lead role in a new movie.

## De la Sarten al Fuego

December, 1935, 82 minutes. Color.

*P:* George A. Hirliman. *AP:* Louis Rantz. *D:* John Reinhardt. *SC:* Roger Whately. *ST:* J.D. Newsom. *PH:* Mack Stengler. *AD:* Lewis J. Rachmil. *ED:* Tony Martinelli. *Prod Mgr:* Sam Diege.

*Cast:* Rosita Moreno, Juan Torena, Romualdo Tirado, Jose Luis Tortosa, Corazon Montes, Rudolph Amendt, Martin Garralaga, Lou Hicks, Elisa Muriel.

Spanish language version of *The Rest Cure* (1936) with Spanish dialogue written by Jose Luis Tortosa.

## Scandals of Paris

December 31, 1935, 63 minutes.

*P-D:* John Stafford & W. Victor Hanbury. *PH:* Jack Beaver. *Mus:* Otto Strosky, Nikolas Schwalb & Sonny Miller.

*Cast:* Wendy Barrie, Gene Gerrard, Zelma O'Neal, Gus McNaughton, Henry Wenman, Bobbie Comber, Gibb McLaughlin, Mark Daly.

After she poses for a painting, the daughter of a soap manufacturer finds the picture is being used to promote a rival product. Made in England in 1934 as *There Goes Susie* with a running time of 79 minutes.

## Captain Calamity

April 17, 1936, 65 minutes. Color.

*P:* George A. Hirliman. *AP:* Charles Hunt & Louis Rantz. *D:* John Reinhardt. *SC:* Crane Wilbur. *ST:* Gordon Young. *PH:* Mack Stengler. *ED:* Tony Martinelli. *Asst Dir:* Bobby Ray.

*Cast:* George Houston, Marion Nixon, Vince Barnett, Juan Torena, Movita, Crane Wilbur, Roy D'Arcy,

**Marion Nixon and George Houston in** *Captain Calamity* **(Regal Productions, 1936), which was reissued by Grand National.**

George Lewis, Margaret Irving, Barry Norton, Louis Natheaux, Lloyd Ingraham, Maria Kalamo.

A sea captain falls in love with a young woman while fighting pirates in the South Seas. Also called *Captain Hurricane* and produced in a Spanish language version called *El Capitan Tormenta* (1936). Reissued late in 1936 by Grand National.

## El Capitan Tormenta

July 2, 1936, 75 minutes. Color.

*P:* George A. Hirliman. *AP:* Louis Rantz. *D:* John Reinhardt. *SC:* Crane Wilbur. *ST:* Gordon Young. *PH:* Mack Stengler. *SD:* Glen Glenn. *Prod Mgr:* Sam Diege.

*Cast:* Lupita Tovar, Fortunio Bonanova, Juan Torena, Movita,

Romualdo Tirado, Jose Louis Tortosa, Roy D'Arcy, George Lewis, Barry Norton, Paco Moreno, Agostino Borgato, Jose Pena Pepet, Rosa Rey.

Spanish language version of *Captain Calamity* (1936) with Spanish dialogue written by Jose Luis Tortosa.

## Thunderbolt

September 9, 1936, 55 minutes.

*P:* Sherman S. Krellberg. *D:* Stuart Paton. *SC:* Jack Jevne. *PH:* Roland Price. *ED:* Charles Craft. *Asst Dir:* Eddy Graneman.

*Cast:* Kane Richmond, Lobo the Marvel Dog, Bobby Nelson, Fay McKenzie, Lafe McKee, Frank Ellis, Wally West, George Morrell, Hank Bell, Frank Hagney, Barney Furey, Blackie Whiteford, Jack Kirk, Bob Burns.

A prospector is arrested for killings committed by crooked lawmen, but he is rescued by his dog and the son of one of the victims.

## The Devil on Horseback

September 30, 1936, 67 minutes. Color.
*P:* George A. Hirliman. *AP:* Louis Rantz & Charles Hunt. *D-SC:* Crane Wilbur. *PH:* Mack Stengler. *ED:* Ralph Dixon & Joseph H. Lewis. *AD:* Frank Sylos. *Mus:* Hugo Riesenfeld & Abe Meyer. *SD:* Fred Stahl.

*Cast:* Lily Damita, Fred Keating, Del Campo, Jean Chatburn, Tiffany Thayer, Renee Torres, Juan Torena, Blanca Vischer, Enrique de Rosas, Jack Stegall, Ann Miller.

When a movie star and her fiancé tour a foreign republic, her press agent puts out a false story that the actress has been kidnapped. Also filmed in a Spanish-language version called *El Carnaval del Diablo* (1936).

## El Carnaval del Diablo

December 3, 1936, 65 minutes. Color.
*P:* George A. Hirliman. *AP:* Louis Rantz. *D-SC:* Crane Wilbur. *PH:* Mack Stengler. *SD:* Fred Stahl.

*Cast:* Fortunio Bonanova, Blanca de Castejon, Enrique de Rosas, Juan Torena, Romualdo Tirado, George Lewis, Blanca Vischer, Jinx Falkenberg, Carlos Montalban, Anita Gordiano.

Spanish language version of *The Devil on Horseback* (1936) with Spanish dialogue written by Carlos F. Borcosque.

## The Rest Cure

December 13, 1936, 64 minutes. Color.
*P:* George A. Hirliman. *AP:* Louis Rantz & Charles Hunt. *D:* Crane Wilbur. *SC:* Roger Whately & Crane Wilbur. *ST:* J.D. Newsom. *PH:* Mack Stengler. *Mus:* Abe Meyer. *Prod Mgr:* Sam Diege.

*Cast:* Reginald Denny, Esther Ralston, Eleanor Hunt, Vince Barnett, Claudia Dell, Robert Frazer, Rudolph Amendt, Francisco Maran, Merrill McCormack, Manuel Peluffo, John Reinhardt, Crane Wilbur, Grace Cunard, Lou Hicks, Charles Mayer, Frank Hoyt.

Two former American gangsters in Paris decide to get away from their enemies by joining the Foreign Legion. Also filmed in a Spanish-language version called *De la Sarten al Fuego* (1935).

## Avocate D'Amour

September 14, 1938, 90 minutes.
*D:* Raoul Ploquin. *SC:* Jean Boyer. *Mus:* George Van Parys.

*Cast:* Danielle Darrieux, Henry Garat, Alerme, Marguerite Templey, Suffel, Pasquali, R. Casa, Arvel, Emile Prud'homme, Jean Hebey.

A young woman wants to become a lawyer while her father wants her to get married. A French import with English subtitles by Mark A. Brum and Charles Jahrblum.

## Rothschild

October 20, 1938, 78 minutes.
*D:* Marco de Gastyne. *SC:* Jean Guitton & E.R. Escalmel, from the novel by Paul Lafitte. *PH:* Gaston Nrun. *Mus:* Guido Curto.

*Cast:* Harry Bauer, Pasquali, Pauley, Casadensus, Claudie Cleaves, Germaine Michel, Germaine Auger, Philip Heriat, Georges Paulais, Jean d'Yd.

Two hobos use the famous name of one of them to rise in the financial world before being exposed by a banker. A French import with English subtitles by Mark A. Brum and Charles Jahrblum.

## The Mutiny of the Elsinore

February 17, 1939, 79 minutes.

*P:* John Argyle. *D:* Roy Lockwood. *SC:* Walter Summers & Beaufoy Milton, from the novel by Jack London. *PH:* Byron Langley. *ED:* F.H. Bickerton.

*Cast:* Paul Lukas, Lyn Harding, Kathleen Kelly, Clifford Evans, Michael Martin-Harvey, Pat Noonan, Hamilton Keane, William Devlin, Ben Soutten, Conway Dixon, Tony Sympson, Alec Fraser, Jiro Soneya.

While a passenger on a sailing ship, a reporter gets involved in a mutiny. Produced in Great Britain and issued there in 1937 by Argyle British; reissued there in 1948.

# Reliable Pictures Corporation

Bernard B. Ray began his film career in 1911 after finishing college. He first worked as a laboratory technician at Biograph, and six years later he was a laboratory supervisor. Ray also worked as a cameraman, editor, assistant director and miniatures and special-effects man before the coming of the sound era. In the early 1930s he partnered with veteran low-budget director Harry S. Webb to form Bernard B. Ray Productions, and in 1934 the two opened their own studio, Reliable Pictures (originally called Rayliable), at the corner of Sunset Boulevard and Beachwood Drive, near Columbia Pictures. Reliable promised to produce some twenty feature films in 1934 and thirty features in 1935. In truth Reliable Pictures was in existence from late 1933 to early 1937, and in that four-year period the studio produced some 45 features. It eschewed serials and imports, and except for its "Bud'n Ben" series it did not bother with short subjects.

Being veteran filmmakers, Bernard B. Ray and Harry S. Webb knew how to turn out acceptable feature film fodder on the lowest possible budget. Reliable's offerings were aimed mainly at filling dual bills on the states' rights market, and little of its product was copyrighted and even less contained music outside of canned scores over the opening credits. Through the summer of 1935 Reliable films were distributed by William Steiner and thus not only appeared under the Reliable banner but also such Steiner subsidiaries as Ajax, Astor, Commodore, Marcy and William Steiner. Billing for the Reliables stated they were presented by Bernard B. Ray with Harry S. Webb listed as associate producer. Both Ray and Webb directed, sometimes under their own names and sometimes using pseudonyms. Ray sometimes called himself Ray Bernard or Franklyn Shamray while Webb would use the nom-de-plume Henri Semuels. Most of the films were written by Bennett Cohen, Rose Gordon or Carl Krusada, while J. Henry Kruse and Pliny Goodfriend handled the photography, Fred Bain edited and William Nolte served as assistant director.

Because of its limited budget range and basic appeal to small-town audiences, Reliable counted on action and western stars to carry its product. Richard Talmadge and canine star Rin-Tin-Tin, Jr., headlined several features for the studio while its sagebrush stars included Tom Tyler, Jack Perrin and Bob Custer. There were also a couple of somewhat out-of-place modern-day films: Reginald Denny in the suspenseful mystery *The Midnight Phantom* (1935) and Betty Compson and Bryant Washburn headlining *Millionaire Kid* (1936). Actually Reliable got its start late in 1933 with *Girl Trouble*, the first of seven entries in its "Bud'n Ben" featurette series. These half-hour westerns concerned the adventures of two cowpoke pals with Ben Corbett playing Ben while Bud was portrayed mostly by Jack Perrin but also by Walt Williams [Wally Wales], Denny Meadows [Dennis Moore] and Fred Humes in one entry each. These tattered affairs were financed by William Steiner (who probably had a hand in all Reliable financing through the summer of 1935 when he stopped distributing the company's product) and were released through his Astor exchanges. In addition to the "Bud'n Ben" series Jack Perrin also starred in a half-dozen western features for Reliable; William Steiner distributed the first three, *Ridin' Gents*, *Loser's End* and *The Cactus Kid* in 1934, while three 1935 Perrin westerns—*North of Arizona*, *Texas Jack* and *Wolf Riders*—were distributed by Cosmos/Associated Film Exchange.

Tom Tyler came to Reliable in 1934 after making the serial *Clancy of the Mounted* for Universal the previous year. An established cowboy star at FBO since the latter days of the silents, Tyler was a stalwart, handsome hero who could ride and fight with the best of them and whose Thespian abilities were certainly passable. Between 1934 and 1936 Tyler made eighteen oaters for Reliable, and while they kept his face in front of the public, they did not aid his flagging career. Don Miller noted in *Hollywood Corral* (1976) that the series mainly "... consisted of bottom of the barrel caliber in every respect, save perhaps the photography.... Unfortunately, the pleasing eye appeal was vitiated by jumbled storylines, aimless meandering about in quest of an excuse to start the action, and supporting performances of often amateur stature." Miller further noted, "Through it all, Tyler's manly presence did much, if not enough, to overcome the pall. Even Tyler was victimized by sloppy staging of the action scenes." It should be noted that the Tyler Reliables, if taken in small doses, can entertain, but the same casts, locales and plots quickly become monotonous. As noted earlier, William Steiner distributed the first 12 Tylers through his various exchanges but the last six in the series went out solely under the Reliable banner. Probably the best offerings of the Tom Tyler Reliables are early entries like *The Unconquered Bandit*, *Tracy Rides* and *The Silver Bullet* (all 1935) while later features looked quite tattered.

Richard Talmadge (real name: Dick Metzetti) was a famous silent screen stuntman who also headlined many low-budget features during the 1920s and into the sound era. In the 1935-36 season he had his final starring series for Reliable. Actually *The Fighting Pilot* and *Now or Never* were released by Ajax (q.v.) in 1935 although they are listed on the credits as Reliable products. *Never Too Late* and *The Live Wire* in 1935 and *The Speed Reporter* and *Step on It* in 1936 are Reliable releases, but they are so obscure that little can be found out about them. After the series ended Richard Talmadge mainly worked as a second unit director in Hollywood and later on big-budget items like *North to Alaska* (1960) and *Circus World* (1964).

Another star who toiled for Reliable was Rin-Tin-Tin, Jr., the alleged son of the great canine star. Junior, however, was nowhere near the Thespian that his father had been and his trainer, Lee Duncan, was forced to hire him out to low-budget studios like Mascot and Reliable. Rin-Tin-Tin, Jr., headlined several acceptable north woods dramas, allegedly based on the works of James Oliver Curwood, like *Skull and Crown* and *The Test* in 1935 and *Caryl of the Mountains* in 1936. He was also teamed with Bob Custer for *Vengeance of Rannah* in 1936 and Rex Lease in *The Silver Trail* in 1937 but four announced starrers for the dog—*Timber Patrol, Outlaw River, Speck on the Wall* and *Mystery of the Seven Chests*—never materialized.

As noted both Bob Custer and Rex Lease made westerns for Reliable, apparently an attempt by the company to fill the void made by Tom Tyler who moved over to Sam Katzman's Victory Pictures (q.v.) in 1936. The stoic Bob Custer had not had a western series since working at Big 4 (q.v.) in 1932 although he and Rin-Tin-Tin, Jr., had starred in the Mascot serial *The Law of the Wild* in 1934. He and the dog were reunited for the feature *Vengeance of Rannah* in 1936 by Reliable, and it was probably the best of the three westerns he did for the studio. Evidently Custer's appeal was lacking because Rex Lease was called in to headline *The Silver Trail* with Rin-Tin-Tin, Jr., in 1937, Reliable's final release.

Bernard B. Ray and Harry S. Webb continued to make motion pictures, sometimes as a team, sometimes separately. Ray produced, directed and distributed the comedy *It's All in Your Mind*, starring Byron Foulger in 1938, and by 1941 he was a producer at Producers Releasing Corporation (PRC) with his Beaumont Productions. After Reliable folded, Harry S. Webb reactivated Metropolitan Pictures (q.v.). The Reliable studios also remained active. Monogram Pictures used the site as its headquarters in the late 1930s and then Max and Arthur Alexander produced westerns there under the M & A Alexander banner. In the 1940s and 1950s Columbia Pictures used the site to make shorts, and today the locale is used by various production outfits.

## Girl Trouble

December 15, 1933, 31 minutes.
P-D: Bernard B. Ray. SC: Bennett Cohen.

*Cast:* Jack Perrin, Ben Corbett, Lola Tate, Mary Draper, Wally Turner.

## The Cactus Kid

1934, 56 minutes.

P: Bernard B. Ray. AP-D: Harry S. Webb. SC: Carl Krusada & Rose Gordon. ST: William Nolte. PH: J. Henry Kruse. ED: Fred Bain. SD: Oscar Lagerstrom.

Cast: Jack Perrin, Jayne Regan, Tom London, Slim Whitaker, Fred Humes, Philo McCullough, Joe de la Cruz, Lew Meehan, Kit Guard, Tina Menard, Wally Wales, George Chesebro, George Morrell, Gordon DeMain, Starlight.

A cowboy plots to get even for the murder of his best friend.

## Loser's End

1934, 60 minutes.

P-D: Bernard B. Ray. AP: Harry S. Webb. SC: Rose Gordon & Carl Krusada. ST: Harry Samuels [Harry S. Webb]. PH: J. Henry Kruse. ED: Fred Bain. SD: J.S. Westmoreland. Asst Dir: William Nolte.

Cast: Jack Perrin, Rosemary Joyce, Tina Menard, William Gould, Frank Rice, Fern Emmett, Slim Whitaker, Jimmy Aubrey, Robert Walker, Elias Lazaroff, Starlight.

A cowboy gets mixed up with a pretty dancer and a gang of contraband smugglers.

## Potluck Pards

January 15, 1934, 30 minutes.

P-D: Bernard B. Ray. SC: Bennett Cohen.

Cast: Walt Williams [Wally Wales/Hal Taliaferro], Ben Corbett, Josephine Hill, Harry Maoris, George Chesebro, Robert Walker, Jimmy Aubrey, Murdock McQuarrie.

A couple of happy-go-lucky cowboys decide to live a life of crime.

## Nevada Cyclone

March 15, 1934, 26 minutes.

P-D: Bernard B. Ray. SC: Rose Gordon & Carl Krusada. PH: J. Henry Kruse. ED: Fred Bain. Asst Dir: William Nolte. SD: Bud Myers.

Cast: Fred Humes (Bud Jackson), Ben Corbett (Ben), Frances Morris (Joyce Hammond), Lafe McKee (Mr. Hammond), Walt Williams [Wally Wales] (Dick), George Chesebro (Lafe Doragan), Lew Meehan (Henchman), Jimmy Aubrey (Cowhand).

Dick (Walt Williams), one of the wranglers who works for rancher Hammond (Lafe McKee), owes money to outlaw gang leader Lafe Doragan (George Chesebro). Lafe wants Dick to join the gang and give him information about a cattle drive Hammond is planning. Dick is sweet on Hammond's daughter Joyce (Frances Morris), and he tells Lafe that after he marries her he will have the money to pay off his debts. That night at a dance Dick proposes to Joyce but she turns him down, and he realizes she loves his pal Bud Jackson (Fred Humes), a bashful cowpoke who thinks Joyce really loves Dick. Upset, Dick agrees to join Lafe's gang as Hammond runs Lafe off his property. Bud and sidekick Ben (Ben Corbett) catch Lafe's men trying to change brands on cattle but they get away. Bud rides to Lafe's hideout and there is a fight but Bud gets the drop on the outlaws and they escape with Dick who is shot as the crooks ride after them. When the gang corners the trio in some rocks, Bud sends his horse with a message for help. Hammond spies the horse, reads the note, and he and Joyce and his men ride to Ben, Bud and Dick's rescue, corraling Lafe and his gang. Bud is then free to romance Joyce.

Fred Humes' one talking starring

role came in this "Bud'n Ben" series western, the third of seven shorts. William Steiner financed for Astor release. Humes had reached his greatest popularity in the late 1920s when he starred in "Blue Streak" westerns at Universal. Coming to movies after a career as a trick rider in rodeos and wild west shows, he was relegated to supporting and bit parts in talkies due to a lack of charisma and Thespian ability. A dull and dense hero, Humes failed to click in talkies. While he appears to try and emulate Hoot Gibson's screen persona, he fails miserably, and it is easy to see why he lasted for only one film. Wally Wales, billed here as Walt Williams, plays a semi-bad buy, and for the sake of the movie he and Humes should have traded roles. As Walt Williams, Wally Wales did star in the second series entry, *Potluck Pards* (1934). In all seven outings in the series Ben Corbett essayed the role of Ben; here his hair is darkened but his acting (?) style is hardly improved. Overall, *Nevada Cyclone* is a mildly interesting featurette with George Chesebro being especially good as villain Lafe Doragan, the first name probably an inside joke since venerable Lafe McKee played the heroine's father.

## Arizona Nights

April 15, 1934, 20 minutes.

*P-D:* Bernard B. Ray. *SC:* Bennett Cohen.

*Cast:* Jack Perrin (Bud Regan), Ben Corbett (Ben), Marie Quillan (Ann Cavanaugh), Gloria Joy (Tucker), Al Ferguson (Professor Valeski), Jimmy Aubrey (Haley), Charles K. French (Captain Smalley), Robert Walker (Private Trent), Bud Osborne (Servant), Slim Whitaker (Informant), Starlight (Himself).

The Border Patrol sends Bud Regan (Jack Perrin) and his pal Ben (Ben Corbett) to stop alien smuggling along the line between Mexico and the United States. They are also assigned to look into the disappearance of Private Trent (Robert Walker) who earlier had been sent to investigate the smuggling. The two learn Trent's horse Starlight (Himself) is running loose, and they decide to find the animal since he might provide a clue to his owner's whereabouts. Meanwhile Professor Valeski (Al Ferguson), an archaeologist, and his team, including Tucker (Gloria Joy) and Haley (Jimmy Aubrey), bring some ancient mummies across the border from a dig in Mexico. Wrapped in the mummy disguises are two aliens, since Valeski and his gang operate the alien smuggling racket. Bud and Ben find Starlight injured and nurse him back to health. The horse then leads them to Valeski's hacienda. There Bud pretends to be a drunk Mexican and is given the guest room. He learns that Anne Cavanaugh (Marie Quillan) is being held and that Valeski plans to kill her after she finds out about his racket. Valeski and Tucker wrap Anne as a mummy and put her in a mummy case, but Ben rescues her and he and Bud overpower the gang. Valeski tries to escape but Starlight corners him, and remembering it was Valeski who murdered his master, the horse kicks the smuggler to death.

Although some sources list *Arizona Nights* as a feature film running in excess of one hour, it is most likely a featurette since it was the fourth of seven "Bud'n Ben" westerns produced by Bernard B. Ray and financed by William Steiner, who released them through his Astor Exchanges. The print viewed ran twenty minutes but it was choppy and somewhat incoherent plotwise, so one can surmise the film runs about three reels as do most of the other movies in the series. As in the majority of the "Bud'n Ben" films, Jack Perrin plays Bud while Ben Corbett is Ben, a part he enacted in all seven entries. The movie is fast-paced and fairly well-produced and Perrin is a stalwart, likable sagebrush hero. For fans of the genre hybrid, the horror western, *Arizona Nights* is an obscure addition. Its plot of a supposed archaeologist (played by Al Ferguson!) smuggling aliens across the U.S.-Mexican border wrapped as mummies is a delightful departure from the usual outdoor yarns and the professor's hacienda, with its many relics, is surprisingly elaborate. The real star of the film, however, is Jack Perrin's faithful old horse Starlight, a beautiful white stallion, who takes revenge on the bad guy who murdered his owner. The film's most memorable line occurs as Bud and Ben ride across the plains. They stop and Bud says to Ben, "Did you hear that? It sounds like a horse in trouble."

## Rawhide Mail

June 8, 1934, 59 minutes.

*P-D:* Bernard B. Ray. *AP:* Harry S. Webb. *SC:* Rose Gordon & Betty Burbridge. *ST:* Bennett Cohen. *PH:* J. Henry Kruse. *ED:* Fred Bain. *SD:* Oscar Lagerstrom.

*Cast:* Jack Perrin, Lillian Gilmore, Richard Cramer, George Chesebro, Lafe McKee, Nelson McDowell, Robert Walker, Jimmy Aubrey, Lew Meehan, Chris-Pin Martin, Tom London, Blackie Whiteford, Jack Evans, Barney Beasley, Starlight.

An outlaw is befriended by a young lady who steers him to the right side of the law.

## Rainbow Riders

June 15, 1934, 30 minutes.

*P-D:* Bernard B. Ray. *SC:* Bennett Cohen.

*Cast:* Jack Perrin, Ben Corbett, Virginia Brown Faire, Ethan Laidlaw, Mack V. Wright, Grace Woods, Jim Corey, Blackjack Ward, Starlight.

A female ranch owner is aided by two cowpokes when rustlers try to steal her cattle.

## Fighting Hero

July 17, 1934, 55 minutes.

*P:* Bernard B. Ray. *AP-D:* Harry S. Webb. *SC:* Carl Krusada & Rose Gordon. *ST:* Charles E. Roberts. *PH:* J. Henry Kruse. *ED:* Fred Bain.

*Cast:* Tom Tyler, Renee Borden, Edward Hearn, Dick Botiller, Ralph Lewis, Murdock McQuarrie, Nelson McDowell, Tom London, George Chesebro, Rosa Rosanova, J.P. McGowan, Lew Meehan, Jimmy Aubrey, Chuck Baldra.

A wanted outlaw tries to help a young woman falsely accused of murder.

## Ridin' Gents

August 15, 1934, 30 minutes.

*P-D:* Bernard B. Ray. *SC:* Bennett Cohen.

*Cast:* Jack Perrin, Ben Corbett, Doris Hill, George Chesebro, Harry Maoris, Lafe · McKee, Charles K. French, Slim Whitaker, Alex Franks, Starlight.

When a fixed jury convicts an innocent man of murder two pals come to his rescue.

## West on Parade

October 15, 1934, 30 minutes.

*P-D:* Bernard B. Ray. *SC:* Bennett Cohen.

Cast: Denny Meadows [Dennis Moore], Ben Corbett, Jayne Regan, Franklyn Farnum, Fern Emmett, Jimmy Aubrey, Philo McCullough, Merrill McCormack.

## Ridin' Thru

November 26, 1934, 55 minutes.

P: Bernard B. Ray. AP-D: Harry S. Webb. SC: Rose Gordon & Carl Krusada. ST: Carol Shandrew. PH: J. Henry Kruse. ED: Fred Bain. Asst Dir: Bobby Ray.

Cast: Tom Tyler, Ruth Hiatt, Lafe McKee, Philo McCullough, Ben Corbett, Lew Meehan, Bud Osborne, Jayne Regan, Colin Chase, Buck Morgan.

Two cowboys investigate horse thefts from a friend who has been forced to turn his spread into a dude ranch.

## The Live Wire

1935, 60 minutes.

P: Bernard B. Ray. AP-D: Harry S. Webb. SC: Carl Krusada & Carl Hartman. ST: Leon Metz. PH: J. Henry Kruse & Abe Scholtz. ED: Fred Bain. SD: J.S. Westmoreland. Asst Dir: William Nolte

Cast: Richard Talmadge, Alberta Vaughn, George Walsh, Henry Rocquemore, Jimmy Aubrey, Charles K. French, George Chesebro, Ben Hall, Martin Turner.

A seaman is hired by two archaeologists to take them to a remote island to find a priceless vase.

## North of Arizona

1935, 60 minutes.

P: Bernard B. Ray AP-D: Harry S. Webb. SC: Carl Krusada & Rose Gordon. PH: J. Henry Kruse. ED: William Austin. Asst Dir: William Nolte.

Cast: Jack Perrin, Blanche Mehaffey, Lane Chandler, Al Bridge, Murdock MacQuarrie, George Chesebro, Artie Ortego, Budd Buster, Frank Ellis, Blackie Whiteford, Ray Henderson, Oscar Gahan, Steve Clark, George Morrell, Hank Bell, Barney Beasley, Starlight.

When crooks cheat Indians and steal gold shipments, a cowboy infiltrates the gang.

## The Test

1935, 55 minutes.

P-D: Bernard B. Ray. AP: Harry S. Webb. SC: L.V. Jefferson. ST: James Oliver Curwood. PH: J. Henry Kruse & Abe Scholtz. ED: Fred Bain. Asst Dir: William Nolte. SD: J.S. Westmoreland. AD: Jerry Kumler.

Cast: Rin-Tin-Tin, Jr. (Rinnie), Grant Withers (Brule Conway), Grace Ford (Beth McVey), Monte Blue (Pepite La Joir), Lafayette [Lafe] McKee (Dad McVey), Art Ortego (Black Wolf), Jimmie Aubrey (Donovan), Tom London, Jack Evans (Trappers), Dorothy Vernon (Woman), Nanette (Dog).

Returning from trapping with his dog Rinnie (Rin-Tin-Tin, Jr.), Brule Conway (Grant Withers) accuses Pepite La Joir (Monte Blue) and his cohorts Black Wolf (Art Ortego) and Donovan (Jimmie Aubrey) of stealing his animal skins. A fight takes place at the trading post of Dad McVey ( Lafe McKee), whose daughter Beth (Grace Ford) loves Conway. La Joir is beaten in the fight and admits the thefts, whereupon he and his men are ordered out of the settlement. Rinnie is left to guard the pelts belonging to Conway. To get revenge, La Joir and his pals lure him away from them with a female dog Nanette (Herself). La Joir steals the furs, and when Conway sees they are missing, he orders Rinnie to find them. He then organizes a search party. Rinnie trails La Joir, who tries to kill him with an oar but fails. To get the dog, La Joir sets a trap, but when Rinnie attacks him it is the thief who gets caught. Rinnie then takes the boat with the pelts while Black Wolf and Donovan extricate La Joir from the trap. Meanwhile, Conway and his men find Rinnie and the boat and retrieve the pelts. Rinnie leads his master to La Joir, and a fight breaks out before the fur thieves are captured. Back in the settlement Conway and Beth are reunited as are Rinnie and Nanette.

Reliable Pictures produced three northwoods melodramas starring Rin-Tin-Tin, Jr., allegedly based on the stories of James Oliver Curwood. While Rin-Tin-Tin, Jr., never measured up to his famous father as a film star, he probably was best showcased in this trio of inexpensive but fairly entertaining features. *The Test* gave the canine star quite a bit of footage, as well as a girlfriend, and he is shown to advantage as he tracks the villain and brings him to justice. Veteran star Monte Blue has a good time as the French-Canadian bad guy, and usual villain Grant Withers is a somewhat bland hero. Grace Ford is the female lead but has little to do while Artie Ortego and Jimmie Aubrey are Monte Blue's henchmen; Aubrey, in particular, is a comic bad guy. The title has two meanings. First, the villains refuse to take the test of tasting pelts they have stolen since the animals died immediately after being caught in poisoned traps. Secondly, the title refers to Rinnie's need to redeem himself after he lets romance get in the way of duty when the crooks steal his master's furs.

## Texas Jack

1935, 52 minutes.
*P-D:* Bernard B. Ray. *AP:* Harry S.

Webb. *SC:* Carl Krusada, Rose Gordon & Carl Hartman. *PH:* J. Henry Kruse. *ED:* Fred Bain. *SD:* J.S. Westmoreland. *Asst Dir:* William Nolte.

*Cast:* Jack Perrin, Jayne Regan, Robert Walker, Lew Meehan, Nelson McDowell, Budd Buster, Cope Borden, Oscar Gahan, Jim Oates, Steve Clark, Blackie Whiteford, Clyde McClary, Buck Morgan, Jack Evans, Starlight.

Wanting to get revenge for his sister's death, a man uses a medicine show as a front.

## Wolf Riders

1935, 56 minutes.
*P:* Bernard B. Ray. *AP-D:* Harry S. Webb. *SC:* Carl Krusada, Lewis C. Borden & Rose Gordon. *PH:* J. Henry Kruse. *ED:* Fred Bain.

*Cast:* Jack Perrin, Lillian Gilmore, Lafe McKee, Nancy DeShon, William Gould, George Chesebro, Earl Dwire, Slim Whitaker, Budd Buster, Frank Ellis, George Morrell, Robert Walker, Blackie Whiteford, Starlight.

Fur thieves take advantage of Indians and a government agent tries to stop them.

## The Unconquered Bandit

January 8, 1935, 57 minutes.
*P:* Bernard B. Ray. *AP-D:* Harry S. Webb. *SC:* Rose Gordon & Lou C. Borden. *ST:* Carl Krusada. *PH:* J. Henry Kruse. *ED:* Fred Bain. *Asst Dir:* William Nolte.

*Cast:* Tom Tyler, Lillian Gilmore, Charles "Slim" Whitaker, William Gould, John Elliott, Earl Dwire, Joe De La Cruz, George Chesebro, Lew Meehan, Dick Alexander, George Hazel, Wally Wales, Ben Corbett, Colin Chase.

THE INDOMITABLE COURAGE AND FATAL FEUDS OF REDSKINS AND PIONEERS

BERNARD B. RAY
*presents*

# Jack PERRIN

IN

## "Wolf Riders"

Directed by
HARRY S. WEBB

Distributed by
WILLIAM STEINER

*with*
LILLIAN GILMORE
LAFE McKEE
NANCY DESHON
WILLIAM GOULD
GEORGE CHESEBRO
EARL DWIRE
*and*
STARLIGHT
( *The Wonder Horse* )

Advertisement for *Wolf Riders* (Reliable, 1935).

In order to get revenge on the man who was responsible for his father's death, a cowboy begins to court the man's niece.

## Coyote Trails

February, 1935, 60 minutes.
*P-D:* Bernard B. Ray. *AP:* Harry S. Webb. *SC:* Rose Gordon & Lou C. Borden. *ST:* Carl Krusada. *PH:* J. Henry Kruse. *ED:* Fred Bain. *Asst Dir:* Edward Mull.
*Cast:* Tom Tyler, Alice Dahl, Dick Alexander, George Chesebro, Charles "Slim" Whitaker, Ben Corbett, Lafe McKee, Lew Meehan, Jack Evans, Art Dillard, Jimmy Aubrey, Bud McClure, Tex Palmer, Phantom.
A cowboy tries to prove a wild stallion is not responsible for a series of horse thefts plaguing a rancher.

## Tracy Rides

February 26, 1935, 59 minutes.
*P:* Bernard B Ray. *AP-D:* Harry S. Webb. *SC:* Rose Gordon & Betty Burbridge. *ST:* Norman Hughes. *PH:* J. Henry Kruse. *ED:* Fred Bain. *Asst Dir:* Bobby Ray.
*Cast:* Tom Tyler, Virginia Brown Faire, Edmund Cobb, Charles K. French, Carol Shandrew, Lafe McKee, Jimmy Aubrey, Art Dillard, Jack Evans.
A lawman must bring in the brother of the girl he loves.

## Mystery Ranch

April 12, 1935, 56 minutes.
*P:* Bernard B. Ray. *AP:* Harry S. Webb. *D:* Ray Bernard (Bernard B. Ray). *SC:* Carl Krusada & Rose Gordon. *ST:* J.K. Henry. *PH:* J. Henry

Advertisement for *The Unconquered Bandit* (Reliable, 1935).

Kruse. *ED:* Fred Bain. *Asst Dir:* William Nolte.

*Cast:* Tom Tyler, Roberta Gale, Jack Gable [Jack Perrin], Louise Gabo, Frank Hall Crane, Charles King, Tom London, George Chesebro, Lafe McKee, Jimmy Aubrey.

A western novelist comes to a real ranch where he runs up against two crooks.

## Born to Battle

April, 1935, 58 minutes.

*P:* Bernard B. Ray. *AP-D:* Harry S. Webb. *SC:* Rose Gordon & Carl [Krusada] Hartman. *ST:* Oliver Drake. *PH:* J. Henry Kruse. *ED:* Fred Bain. *Asst Dir:* William Nolte.

*Cast:* Tom Tyler, Jean Carmen, Earl Dwire, Julian Rivero, Nelson McDowell, William Desmond, Dick Alexander, Charles King, Ralph Lewis, Ben Corbett, Blackie Whiteford, Robert Walker, Jimmy Aubrey, George Morrell, Roger Williams.

A rip-roaring cowboy is saved from jail by a cattle association representative who sends him on an undercover job.

## Silent Valley

May, 1935, 56 minutes.

*P-D:* Bernard B. Ray. *AP:* Harry S. Webb. *SC:* Rose Gordon. *ST:* Carl Krusada. *PH:* J. Henry Kruse. *ED:* Fred Bain. *Asst Dir:* William Nolte.

*Cast:* Tom Tyler, Nancy DeShon, Al Bridge, Wally Wales, Charles King, Charles "Slim" Whitaker, Art Miles, Murdock McQuarrie, Jimmy Aubrey, Frank Ellis, Budd Buster, George Morrell, Lew Meehan, Tex Palmer, Herman Hack, Art Dillard.

After cattle rustlers, a lawman sus-

BERNARD B. RAY *presents*

*Tom* **TYLER**

IN

*"Terror of the Plains"*

*PACKED WITH STARTLING AND UNUSUAL ADVENTURES!*

*with*
BILL GOULD
ROBERTA GALE
CHARLES WHITAKER
FERN EMMETT
NELSON McDOWELL
FRANK RICE
RALPH LEWIS
ROBERT WALKER
MURDOCK McQUARRIE

Advertisement for *Terror of the Plains* (Reliable, 1934).

pects his girlfriend's brother of being a part of the gang.

## The Silver Bullet

May 11, 1935, 59 minutes.

*P-D:* Bernard B. Ray. *AP:* Harry S. Webb. *SC:* Rose Gordon & Carl Krusada. *ST:* William Nolte. *PH:* J. Henry Kruse. *ED:* Fred Bain. *Asst Dir:* Gene George.

*Cast:* Tom Tyler, Jayne Regan, Lafe McKee, Charles King, George Chesebro, Slim Whitaker, Lew Meehan, Walt Williams [Wally Wales], Franklyn Farnum, Allen Greer, Blackie Whiteford, Hank Bell, Nelson McDowell, Robert Brower, Tex Palmer, Jack Evans, Fern Emmett, Tom Smith.

A prospector becomes the sheriff of a small town and tries to find out who is behind an outlaw gang.

## The Laramie Kid

June, 1935, 57 minutes.

*P:* Bernard B. Ray. *AP-D:* Harry S. Webb. *SC:* Carl Krusada & Rose Gordon. *ST:* C.C. Church. *PH:* J. Henry Kruse. *ED:* Fred Bain. *Asst Dir:* William Nolte.

*Cast:* Tom Tyler, Alberta Vaughn, Al Ferguson, Murdock McQuarrie, George Chesebro, Snub Pollard, Steve Clark, Wally Wales, Jimmy Aubrey, Nelson McDowell, Artie Ortego, Budd Buster.

A cowboy lets himself go to prison so his girl's father can collect the reward but he breaks out to prove his innocence.

## Terror of the Plains

June 27, 1934, 58 minutes.

*P:* Bernard B. Ray. *AP-D:* Harry S. Webb. *SC:* Carl Krusada & Jayne

Regan. *ST:* Rose Gordon. *PH:* J. Henry Kruse. *ED:* Fred Bain. *Asst Dir:* William Nolte.

*Cast:* Tom Tyler, Roberta Gale, William Gould, Charles "Slim" Whitaker, Fern Emmett, Nelson McDowell, Frank Rice, Ralph Lewis, Robert Walker, Murdock McQuarrie, Budd Buster, Jimmy Aubrey, Herman Hack, Jack Kirk, Jack Evans.

A cowboy vows to capture the real killer when his father is falsely jailed for murder.

# Rio Rattler

August, 1935, 58 minutes.

*P:* Bernard B. Ray. *AP:* Harry S. Webb. *D:* Franklyn Shamray [Bernard B. Ray]. *SC:* Carl Krusada. *ST:* Bennett Cohen. *PH:* Pliny Goodfriend. *ED:* William Austin. *Asst Dir:* William Nolte. *SD:* J.S. Westmoreland.

*Cast:* Tom Tyler (Tom Denton), Harry Gribbon (Soapy), Marion Shilling (Mary Adams), William Gould (Mason), Tom London (Bob Adams), Slim Whitaker (Rattler Brown), Lafe McKee (Pop), Ace Cain (Sam Hall), Frank Ellis (Tonto), Blackie Whiteford (Bartender), Jimmy Aubrey (Jeff Davis), Nelson McDowell (Undertaker).

When a bartender (Blackie Whiteford) tries to cheat his sidekick Soapy (Eddie Gribbon), cowboy Tom Denton (Tom Tyler) comes to the rescue, aided by stranger Bob Adams (Tom London). The two part company with Adams promising to meet him in a nearby town, but the man is soon ambushed and mortally wounded. Before dying he gives Tom his credentials as an undercover agent, and the cowboy decides to assume his identity to find the killer. In town they soon learn the killer is the Rattler (Slim Whitaker), but they do not know he is in cahoots with banker Mason (William Gould). The latter pretends to make the new marshal welcome but plots with the Rattler to get him out of the way. Mary Adams (Marion Shilling) arrives in town looking for her brother, and Tom tries to keep out of her way so she will not learn his true identity. Later the Rattler, who planned to ambush Tom, overhears him tell Mary the truth, and he tells Mason, who then frames Tom for Adams' murder. Tom and Soapy escape but Tom later returns to convince Mary of his innocence. When Mason and his men arrive, Soapy leads them away but is captured. Tom goes to the Rattler's hideout to rescue Soapy, but in a shootout his pal is wounded and later dies. Tom then sets a trap for the outlaws by declaring he will meet them in the saloon, but when Mason walks through the front door, Rattler shoots him thinking it is Tom. The Rattler then blames Mason for the lawlessness and tries to escape, but Tom kills him in a shootout. The townspeople and Mary then persuade Tom to stay on as marshal.

The twelfth of eighteen westerns Tom Tyler made for Reliable Pictures in the mid-1930s, *Rio Rattler* was the last to be distributed by William Steiner. Like most of the Tyler Reliables it had threadbare production values and tacky sets. The star, however, was ably supported by Harry Gribbon as his sidekick and Marion Shilling as the love interest. Gribbon, a popular silent screen comedian, still had enough box-office pull to warrant second billing although, surprisingly, his character is killed off at the finale. The title role goes to Slim Whitaker, as a hired killer, although the chief villain is banker William Gould. One scene has Tyler getting bad guy Frank Ellis'

Poster for *Skull and Crown* (Reliable, 1935).

attention by throwing a burning match on his hand while a continuing gag has undertaker Nelson McDowell measuring various prospective clients.

## The Midnight Phantom

November 21, 1935, 63 minutes.

*P-D:* Bernard B. Ray. *AP:* Harry S. Webb. *SC:* Jack Neville. *PH:* Pliny Goodfriend. *ED:* Arthur Hilton. *SD:* J.S. Westmoreland. *AD:* Ira Webb. *Asst Dir:* S. Gordon. *Prod Mgr:* Moe Sackin.

*Cast:* Reginald Denny, Claudia Dell, Lloyd Hughes, James Farley, Barbara Bedford, Mary Foy, John Elliott, Francis Sayles, Al St. John, Henry Rocquemore, Lee Prather, Robert Walker, Jack Kenny.

During a midnight lecture to the police department by a famed criminologist, the police chief is found murdered. Spanish language version: *El Crimen de Media Noche* (1936).

## Never Too Late

November 27, 1935, 59 minutes.

*P:* Bernard B. Ray. *AP:* Harry S. Webb. *D:* Franklin Shamroy [Bernard B. Ray]. *SC:* Carl Krusada & Jack Natteford. *PH:* Pliny Goodfriend. *ED:* Frank Atkinson. *Tech Adv:* Robert Frazer.

*Cast:* Richard Talmadge, Thelma White, Robert Frazer, Mildred Harris, Vera Lewis, Robert Walker, George Chesebro, Bull Montana, Paul Ellis.

A police detective is assigned to find a necklace stolen from his boss' wife.

## Skull and Crown

December 17, 1935, 56 minutes.

*P:* Bernard B. Ray. *AP:* Harry S. Webb. *D:* Elmer Clifton. *SC:* Carl Krusada & Bennett Cohen. *ST:* James Oliver Curwood. *PH:* Pliny Goodfriend. *ED:* Fred Bain.

*Cast:* Rin-Tin-Tin, Jr., Regis Toomey, Molly O'Day, Jack Mulhall, Jack Mower, James Murray, Lois January, Tom London, John Elliott, Robert Walker, Milburn Morante.

While after a notorious bandit, a Customs Patrol officer learns that the outlaw has murdered his sister.

## Step On It

1936, 5 reels.

*P:* Bernard B. Ray. *AP:* Harry S. Webb. *D:* Henri G. Samuels [Harry S. Webb]. *SC:* Herbert Stanton. *PH:* William Hyer. *ED:* Fred Bain. *Asst Dir:* R.G. Springsteen. *SD:* Johnny Eilers. *Prod Mgr:* Ira Webb.

*Cast:* Richard Talmadge, Lois Wilde, George Walsh, Roger Williams, Eddie Davis, Earl Dwire, Robert Walker, Frank Hall Crane, Lafe McKee, Fred Parker.

After losing his job for arresting a speeding heiress, a motorcycle cop rounds up a hijacking gang. TV title: *Hunting Trouble.*

## Trigger Tom

1936, 57 minutes.

*P:* Bernard B. Ray. *AP:* Harry S. Webb. *D:* Henri G. Samuels [Harry S. Webb]. *SC:* Tom Gibson, from the story "The Swimming Herd" by George Cory Franklin. *PH:* Pliny Goodfriend. *ED:* William Austin. *SD:*
J.S. Westmoreland. *Asst Dir:* William Nolte.

*Cast:* Tom Tyler, Bernadine Hayes, Al St. John, William Gould, John Elliott, Lloyd Ingraham, Wally Wales, Bud Osborne, Jack Evans.

A cattle buyer and his sidekick are at odds with an outlaw pretending to be a lawman.

## El Crimen de Media Noche (The Crime at Midnight)

February, 1936, 63 minutes.

*P:* Bernard B. Ray & Harry S. Webb. *AP:* Moe Sackin. *D:* Bernard B. Ray. *SC:* John Thomas [Jack] Neville & Rene Borgia. *PH:* Pliny Goodfriend. *ED:* William Austin. *Asst Dir:* Ira Webb.

*Cast:* Ramon Pereda, Adriana Lamar, Juan Torena, Jose Luis Tortosa, Aura de Silva, Jaime Devesa, Rosa Rey, Jose Pefia, Lucio Villegas, Carlos Montalban, Jesus Topete, Ramon Munoz, Gerardo Gomez, Raul Lechuga, Israel Garcia, Agustin Guzman, Carlos de la Paz, Antonio Manfredi.

Spanish language version of *The Midnight Phanton* (1935). Also called *El Fantasma de Media Noche (The Midnight Phantom).*

## Ridin' On

February, 1936, 60 minutes.

*P-D:* Bernard B. Ray. *AP:* Harry S. Webb. *SC:* John Thomas [Jack] Neville, from the story "Feud of the Jay Bar Dee" by Arthur Cahard. *PH:* Pliny Goodfriend. *ED:* Fred Bain. *Asst Dir:* William Nolte. *SD:* Clarence S. Cobb.

*Cast:* Tom Tyler, Geraine Greear [Joan Barclay], Rex Lease, John Elliott, Bob McKenzie, Earl Dwire, Roger Williams, Slim Whitaker, Jimmy Aubrey, Richard Cramer, Francis Walker, Wally West, Milburn Morante, Jack Evans, Chuck Morrison.

Two young people fall in love despite the fact their families are involved in a range war.

## Fast Bullets

February 24, 1936, 59 minutes.
*P:* Bernard B. Ray. *AP:* Harry S. Webb. *D:* Henri Samuels [Harry S. Webb]. *SC:* Rose Gordon & Carl Krusada. *ST:* Jay J. Bryan. *PH:* Pliny Goodfriend. *ED:* Fred Bain. *SD:* J.S. Westmoreland. *AD:* Ira Webb. *Asst Dir:* R.G. Springsteen.

*Cast:* Tom Tyler, Rex Lease, Margaret Nearing, Al Bridge, William Gould, Robert Walker, Charles King, George Chesebro, Slim Whitaker, Lew Meehan, James Aubrey, Nelson McDowell, Jack Evans, Frank Ellis.

A ranger seeks the aid of an outlaw in bringing in smugglers.

## Millionaire Kid

April 1, 1936, 50 minutes.
*P-D:* Bernard B. Ray. *AP:* Harry S. Webb. *SC:* Jack Natteford & Blanche Church. *PH:* William Hyer. *ED:* Fred Bain. *SD:* Johnny Eilers. *Asst Dir:* William Nolte. *Prod Mgr:* Ira Webb.

*Cast:* Betty Compson, Bryant Washburn, Lois Wilde, Charles Delaney, Creighton Hale, Bradley Metcalfe, Eddie Gribbon, Al St. John, Josef Swickard, John Elliott, Earl Dwire, Edward Cassidy, Arthur Thalasso, Roger Williams.

Ignored by his divorcing parents, a little rich boy runs away from home and gets involved with a gang.

## Roamin' Wild

April 29, 1936, 58 minutes.
*P-D:* Bernard B. Ray. *AP:* Harry S. Webb. *SC:* Robert Emmett Tansey. *PH:* William Hyer. *ED:* Fred Bain.

*AD:* Ira Webb. *Asst Dir:* R.G Springsteen.

*Cast:* Tom Tyler, Carol Wyndham, Max Davidson, Al Ferguson, George Chesebro, Slim Whitaker, Bud Osborne, Earl Dwire, Lafe McKee, Fred Parker, John Elliott, Wally West, Frank Ellis, Sherry Tansey, Jimmy Aubrey, Buck Morgan.

A U.S. marshal investigates a gang of crooks who are fleecing miners.

## The Speed Reporter

May 15, 1936, 58 minutes.
*P-D:* Bernard B. Ray. *AP:* Harry S. Webb. *SC:* Rose Gordon. *ST:* Henri Samuels [Harry S. Webb]. *PH:* William Hyer. *ED:* Carl Himm. *SD:* Johnny Eilers. *Prod Mgr:* Ira Webb. *Asst Dir:* R.G. Springsteen.

*Cast:* Richard Talmadge, Luana Walters, Richard Cramer, Robert Walker, Frank Hall Crane, Earl Dwire, John Ince, George Chesebro, Edward Cassidy.

A reporter tries to uncover a crime operation which masquerades behind a reform group. Also called *Dead Line.*

## Pinto Rustlers

May, 1936, 56 minutes.
*P:* Bernard B. Ray. *AP:* Harry S. Webb. *D:* Henri Samuels [Harry S. Webb]. *SC:* Robert Emmett Tansey. *PH:* William Hyer. *ED:* Fred Bain. *Asst Dir:* R.G. Springsteen. *SD:* Johnny Eilers. *Prod Mgr:* Ira Webb.

*Cast:* Tom Tyler, George Walsh, Al St. John, Catherine Cotter, Earl Dwire, William Gould, George Chesebro, Roger Williams, Bud Osborne, Slim Whitaker, Murdock McQuarrie, Milburn Morante, Sherry Tansey, Richard Cramer, Bob Burns, Charles King, Wally West.

A man joins the gang responsible

for his father's death in order to get revenge on them.

## Santa Fe Bound

August, 1936, 56 minutes.

*P:* Bernard B. Ray. *AP:* Harry S. Webb. *D:* Henri Samuels [Harry S. Webb]. *SC:* Carl Krusada. *ST:* Rose Gordon. *PH:* William Hyer. *ED:* Carl Himm. *SD:* Johnny Eilers. *Asst Dir:* Ira Webb.

*Cast:* Tom Tyler, Jeanne Martel, Charles "Slim" Whitaker, Edward Cassidy, Lafe McKee, Dorothy Woods, Wally Wales, Earl Dwire.

When he is falsely accused of murder, a cowboy joins outlaws to prove his innocence.

## Caryl of the Mountains

September, 1936, 60 minutes.

*P-D:* Bernard B. Ray. *AP:* Harry S. Webb. *SC:* Tom Gibson. *ST:* James Oliver Curwood. *PH:* William Hyer. *ED:* Fred Bain. *SD:* Johnny Eilers. *Prod Mgr:* Ira Webb.

*Cast:* Rin-Tin-Tin, Jr., Francis X. Bushman, Jr., Lois Wild(e), Josef Swickard, Earl Dwire, Robert Walker, George Chesebro, Steve Clark, Jack Hendricks.

Victimized by embezzlers, a young woman is aided by a mountie and her murdered uncle's loyal dog.

## Ambush Valley

October 24, 1936, 57 minutes.

*P:* Bernard B. Ray. *AP:* Harry S. Webb. *D:* Raymond Samuels [Harry S. Webb]. *SC:* Bennett Cohen & Forrest Sheldon. *PH:* Paul Ivano. *ED:* Fred Bain. *SD:* Hans Weeren. *Asst Dir:* William Nolte. *Prod Mgr:* Lew Dow.

*Cast:* Bob Custer, Victoria Vinton, Vane Calvert, Eddie Phillips, Wally Wales, Oscar Gahan, Edward Cassidy, Denver Dixon, Roger Williams, Wally West, John Elliott, The Oklahoma Rangers, Jack Evans, Jimmy Aubrey, Jack Gilman, Herman Hack, George Morrell, Milburn Morante, Jack Anderson.

A lawman must stop a rancher, father of the girl he loves, from killing a nester.

## Vengeance of Rannah

November 6, 1936, 59 minutes.

*P:* Bernard B. Ray. *AP:* Harry S. Webb. *D:* Franklin Shamray [Bernard B. Ray]. *SC:* Joseph O'Donnell. *ST:* James Oliver Curwood. *PH:* Paul Ivano. *ED:* Holbrook N. Todd. *SD:* Hans Weeren. *Asst Dir:* William Nolte.

*Cast:* Bob Custer, Rin-Tin-Tin, Jr., Victoria Vinton, Roger Williams, Eddie Phillips, John Elliott, George Chesebro, Jimmy Aubrey, Oscar Gahan, Wally West, Edward Cassidy.

A detective investigates the murder of a stage driver and the theft of his cargo.

## Santa Fe Rides

February, 1937, 58 minutes.

*P:* Bernard B. Ray. *AP:* Harry S. Webb. *D:* Raymond Samuels [Harry S. Webb]. *SC:* Tom Gibson. *PH:* Pliny Goodfriend.

*Cast:* Bob Custer, Eleanor Stewart, David Sharpe, Snub Pollard, Lafe McKee, Roger Williams, Oscar Gahan, Nelson McDowell, John Elliott, Slim Whitaker, Ed Cassidy, The Singing Cowboys (Lloyd Perryman, Curley Hoag, Rudy Sooter).

A crook frames a rancher on a cattle theft charge and then tries to cheat a romantic rival out of radio contest winnings.

## The Silver Trail

February, 1937, 58 minutes.

*P:* Bernard B. Ray. *AP:* Harry S.

RELIABLE PICTURES CORP.
( BERNARD B. RAY )
*presents*

A NEW MUSICAL WESTERN

BRONZED SONS OF THE WEST IN A SERIES OF PULSE-QUICKENING ADVENTURES!

BOB CUSTER IN "Santa Fe Rides"

*Directed by* RAYMOND SAMUELS
*Distributed by* RELIABLE PICTURES CORP.

*with* ELEANOR STEWART · ED CASSIDY
DAVID SHARP · ROGER WILLIAMS
SLIM WHITTAKER · LAFE McKEE
SNUB POLLARD · "THE SINGING COWBOYS"

Poster for *Santa Fe Rides* (Reliable, 1937).

Webb. *D:* Raymond Samuels [Harry S. Webb]. *SC:* Bennett Cohen & Forrest Sheldon. *ST:* James Oliver Curwood. *PH:* Pliny Goodfriend.

*Cast:* Rex Lease, Rin-Tin-Tin, Jr., Mary Russell, Roger Williams, Edward Cassidy, Slim Whitaker, Steve Clark, Oscar Gahan, Tom London, Sherry Tansey.

A silver combine murders miners and is opposed by a man and his dog.

# Resolute Pictures

Like most independents, Resolute Pictures arrived on the scene in the mid-1930s with a fairly ambitious program that failed to materialize. The company announced a half-dozen titles in a series to star Rex Bell with Ruth Mix and Buzz Barton, but only a quartet of these developed before the company run by producer Alfred T. Mannon folded. Coming as it did at a time when the "B" Western field was glutted, it is not surprising that Resolute, which released its product through the First Division exchanges, failed to make the grade. On the other hand, it is somewhat surprising that the promised six Red Bell starrers were not all made, given Bell's track record with his 1932-33 series at Monogram produced by Paul Malvern. Evidently the revenues from the first four releases were not enough to keep Resolute afloat.

Press releases at the start of Resolute Pictures promised that Rex Bell, Ruth Mix and Buzz Barton would star in *The Tonto Kid, Gunsmoke, Rodeo Rustlers, Roped, Riders of the Law* and *The Lumber Hawk*. Since only the first title materialized it can be presumed that some of the others were working titles for the three films that followed in the series. The company also claimed it was going to launch a twelve-chapter serial called *Sky Fighters*, an aviation adventure, but that too failed to appear. In the year of its existence, Resolute did issue *The Tonto Kid*, followed by *Gunfire* late in 1934 and by *Fighting Pioneers* and *Saddle Aces*, which saw release early in the summer of 1935.

The four Resolute oaters were made well enough, thanks to direction by Harry S. Fraser, who also did the screenplays using the name Harry C. Crist on all but *Fighting Pioneers*, where he used his own name in collaborating with Charles E. "Chuck" Roberts. This title was the only one in the series not based on a literary source, something uncommon for low-budget horse operas.

For Rex Bell, the Resolute series marked the mid-point in his career as a cowboy star. Following this quartet of oaters he starred in a half-dozen films for producers Max and Arthur Alexander for Colony (q.v.) release before he settled down to ranching in Nevada with wife Clara Bow and their two sons. He did support Buck Jones in *Dawn on the Great Divide* for Monogram in 1942, but politics became a dominating force in his life, and after a small part in *Lone Star* in 1953, he retired from the screen and was later elected lieutenant governor of Nevada. He was campaigning for the state's top office in 1963 when he died from a heart attack. Ruth Mix and Buzz Barton reteamed to support Hoot Gibson in *The Riding Avenger* (Diversion, 1936) but neither did a Western series again.

## The Tonto Kid

August, 1934, 61 minutes.

*P:* Alfred T. Mannon. *D:* Harry Fraser. *SC:* Harry C. Crist (Harry Fraser), from the novel *The Daughter of Diamond D* by Christopher B. Booth. *PH:* James Diamond & Robert Cline. *ED:* Holbrook N. Todd. *Prod Mgr:* Marion H. Kohn & Ben Hersh.

*Cast:* Rex Bell, Ruth Mix, Buzz Barton, Theodore Lorch, Joseph W. Girard, Barbara Roberts, Jack Rockwell, Murdock McQuarrie, Bert Lindley, Jane Keckley, Stella Adams, Bud Pope.

In trying to seize a ranch from its rightful owners, a dishonest lawyer places the blame for the rancher's killing on The Tonto Kid, who must prove his innocence.

## Gunfire

December, 1934, 56 minutes.

*P:* Alfred T. Mannon. *D:* Harry Fraser. *SC:* Harry C. Crist (Harry Fraser), from the story "Pards in Paradise" by Eric Howard. *PH:* James Diamond. *ED:* Holbrook N. Todd. *Prod Mgr:* Marion H. Kohn.

*Cast:* Rex Bell, Ruth Mix, Buzz Barton, Milburn Morante, Theodore

Lorch, Philo McCullough, Ted Adams, Mary Jo Ellis, Lew Meehan, Willie Fung, Mary Jane Irving, Jack Baston, Fern Emmett, Howard Hickey, Chuck Morrison, William DeMarest, Slim Whitaker.

When the co-owner of a ranch is falsely accused of murder, he is aided by his female partner and a young cowboy.

# Fighting Pioneers

May 21, 1935, 58 minutes.

*P:* Alfred T. Mannon. *D:* Harry Fraser. *SC:* Harry Fraser & Chuck (Charles E.) Roberts. *PH:* Robert Cline. *ED:* Logan Pearson. *Asst Dir:* Harry Knight. *SD:* Ralph G. Fear.

*Cast:* Rex Bell (Lieutenant Bentley), Ruth Mix (Wa-No-Na), Buzz Barton (Splinters), Stanley Blystone (Hadley), Earl Dwire (Sergeant Luke), Chuck Morrison (Sergeant O'Shaughnessy), Chief Thundercloud (Eagle Feathers), Chief Standing Bear (Chief Blackhawk), Guate Mozin (Crazy Horse), John Elliott (Major Denton), Roger Williams (Captain Burton), Francis Walker (Soldier), Blackjack Ward, Bob Burns, Barney Beasley, Fred Burns (Men at Fort).

The Crow Indians, led by Chief Blackhawk (Chief Standing Bear), try to attack a wagon train, and the chief is badly wounded. Cavalry Lieutenant Bentley (Rex Bell) permits the chief's daughter, Wa-No-Na (Ruth Mix), to take her father back to camp, and before he dies, Blackhawk makes his daughter the leader of the tribe, to the chagrin of Eagle Feathers (Chief Thundercloud), who wants the position. Bentley discovers someone has been selling government rifles to the Indians, and he and Sergeant Luke (Earl Dwire) are suspects since they are the only two that have keys to the gun cabinet at the fort. Luke is in league

with corrupt trading post operator Hadley (Stanley Blystone), who plans to take the Indians' gold and run out on them without delivering more promised guns. The Crows, however, take both Hadley and Luke prisoner, but Bentley, in scout's garb, rescues them. The Indians chase the trio on their way back to the fort and recapture Hadley and Luke, but Bentley manages to take Wa-No-Na prisoner. The commander of the fort, Major Denton (John Elliott), plans to use the Indian princess as a lever in freeing Hadley and Luke and signing a peace treaty with the Crows. Hadley and Eagle Feathers come to the fort at night and get Wa-No-Na, taking Bentley as their prisoner. The Indians then plan to raid an incoming wagon train, but the princess sets Bentley free. He goes back to the fort and captures Hadley and Luke. Bentley then leads the troops in stopping the raid, and as a result Wa-No-Na agrees to take her people to a new land.

The second of Resolute's four releases with Rex Bell, Ruth Mix and Buzz Barton, *Fighting Pioneers*, is a crude affair. Awkwardly acted it contains stock footage of wagon trains, soldiers and Indian attacks. The fort and trading post set is rather impressive, as is the appearance of Guate Mozin, an Indian who performs actual war dances and drumming. Surprisingly, the film has no romantic interest as hero Rex Bell and Indian princess Ruth Mix are barely civil to each other for most of the feature. Stanley Blystone does add a good touch as the rough-hewn villain, but third-billed Buzz Barton has little to do as a young scout anxious to join the cavalry. Although a typical Cowboys vs. Indians drama, *Fighting Pioneers* is a threadbare western that shows no pioneers outside of stock footage.

## Saddle Aces

June, 1935, 56 minutes.
   *P:* Alfred T. Mannon. *D:* Harry Fraser. *SC:* Harry C. Crist (Harry Fraser), from the story "Dueces Wild" by Jay J. Kaley. *PH:* Robert Cline. *ED:* Logan Pierson. *Asst Dir:* Harry Knight.
   *Cast:* Rex Bell, Ruth Mix, Buzz Barton, Stanley Blystone, Earl Dwire, Chuck Morrison, Mary MacLaren, John Elliott, Roger Williams, Chief Thundercloud, Allen Greer, Bud Osborne, Francis Walker, Bob Burns, Blackjack Ward, Chief Standing Bear, Guate Mozin.
   Falsely convicted of murder, two escaped prisoners aid a girl in saving her ranch from the crook who framed them.

# Road Show Attractions

   Producer-director Dwain Esper formed Road Show Attractions in 1934 to distribute his own feature films, which were not approved by the Hollywood Production Code. Esper formed the company after having used the monicker of Hollywood Producers and Distributors for his initial productions, *The Seventh Commandment* (1932) and *Narcotic* (1934). Known both as Road Show Attractions Company and Road Show Attractions, Inc., Esper's operation was not related to Roadshow Productions, which released Willis Kent's (q.v.) *Ten Nights in a Barroom* in 1931, or Road Show Pictures, Inc. It is not known if it is the same company as Road Show Attraction which released such exploitation items as *Liquored Ladies* in 1935.
   Dwain Esper (1893-1982) was considered one of the founding fathers of the exploitation feature. Having found success as a building contractor, Esper entered the movie business in 1932. For the next six years he made a handful of features so controversial they bypassed the Hays Office and were mostly distributed by Esper himself, who would take prints to various communities and advertise them in a manner that would draw quick and lucrative payoffs. On several occasions his method of sensational newspaper and lobby display advertising drew protests from various groups as well as patrons. Since Esper's movies were not approved by the Production Code, little could be done, but the added publicity did not hinder box-office returns. Each of Esper's features had some type of sensational drawing card, usually footage of an actual birth or then-forbidden glimpses of female nudity. In small communities Esper's films played the midnight marquees, while in bigger towns and cities they were exhibited in burlesque theatres and road houses. Some of his features were scripted by his wife Hildagarde Stadie, who also lectured at the film showings.
   *The Seventh Commandment* in 1932, a diatribe against loose living that included footage of a caesarean operation, was Dwain Esper's initial feature film. Ironically, it was directed by James P. Hogan, who worked steadily in the 1920s but whose career halted in the early 1930s. Later in the decade, how-

ever, Hogan directed such sturdy Paramount efforts as *Desert Gold* (1936), *The Accusing Finger* (1936), *Last Train from Madrid* (1937), *Ebb Tide* (1937), *The Texans* (1938) and *The Farmer's Daughter* (1940). Next Esper made *Narcotic* (1934), dealing with the evils of opium addiction. Both features ran into problems with the Production Code, thus fostering Esper's decision to market his films himself.

In 1934 Dwain Esper formed Road Show Attractions to distribute his features, beginning with *Modern Motherhood* that year, which caused a sensation by including footage of an actual childbirth as well as scenes "denouncing" promiscuity and venereal disease. That year the Espers also distributed their delirious horror feature *Maniac*, which thematized mental illness and criminal behavior. The assistant director on *Maniac* was J. Stuart Blackton, Jr., son of movie pioneer J. Stuart Blackton, one of the founders of the Vitagraph Company. Blackton's sister Marion also had a role in the film as Blackton himself had earlier acted in *Narcotic*. *Maniac* was issued in some areas as *Sex Maniac*, and it contained a brief rape sequence as well as nudity.

In terms of production, Dwain Esper's best feature is probably *Marihuana* (1936), which tells the story of a young girl (Harley Wood) who goes down the wrong path after being turned on to smoking dope by a drug peddler, played by Pat Carlyle. The latter also was involved in non-Production Code exploitation features in the 1930s, directing such seedy fare as *Polygamy* and *Honky Tonk Girl* (*Highway Hell*), both 1937 states' rights releases. Carlyle also wrote, produced and played the title role in the obscure 1935 western *The Irish Gringo* and had the lead in cheap oaters like *Call of the Coyote* (1934) and *The Tia Juana Kid* (1936). *Marihuana* is a fairly professional feature which saw revival in the 1970s and 1980s due to its campy appeal following the popularity of its marijuana-themed successor *Tell Your Children* (better known as *The Burning Question*, 1938) and the cult classic, *Reefer Madness*. Esper also got a lot of box-office mileage out of the short subject he made in 1937, *How to Undress in Front of Your Husband*, starring Elaine Barrie, the last wife of John Barrymore. Their marital situation greatly added to the film's grosses.

Dwain Esper also distributed two documentaries, *Forbidden Adventure* (1934) and *Angkor* (1937). Both were shot abroad and exploited for maximum box-office appeal by Esper. *Angkor* used wrap-around footage of distinguished actor and traveler Wilfred Lucas, who also narrated the documentary sequences. The feature ran into censorship problems due to its theme of native women mating with apes and for above-the-waist nudity. Both features were recycled by Esper under new titles in the late 1930s and early 1940s when reissued by Road Show Attractions successor, Esper's Maple Attractions.

In 1948 Dwain Esper acquired the distribution rights to Tod Browning's 1932 Metro-Goldwyn-Mayer feature *Freaks*, and he roadshowed it under various titles like *Forbidden Love*, *The Monster Show* and *Nature's Mistakes*. Esper filmed a written prologue about nature's freaks for the showings to beef up the film's original 64-minute running time. Esper handled *Freaks* for a decade before retiring to work on improving movie sound and projection equipment. He also collected World War II movie footage and films on the Nuremberg trials.

Perhaps Dwain Esper's moviemaking viewpoint is best summed up by Jim Morton in *Incredibly Strange Films* (1986): "Esper defended his films and supported the movie code as well, reasoning that adults could see adult films and then ascertain whether a film should be seen by children. It is ironic that the very code Dwain Esper defended would eventually cause the deterioration of the adult movie industry." George E. Turner and Michael H. Price noted in *Forgotten Horrors: Early Talkie Chillers from Poverty Row* (1979) that Esper "reaped healthy profits from unhealthy pictures ... but Esper publicized his company as a practitioner of taste and a proponent of a cinema rating system for audience suitability."

## The Seventh Commandment

Hollywood Producers and Distributors, October, 1932, 65 minutes.

*P:* Dwain Esper. *D:* James P. Hogan.

A young man goes to the big city, gets mixed up with a rough crowd and ends up contacting syphilis.

## Maniac

Roadshow Attractions, 1934, 57 minutes.

*P-D:* Dwain Esper. *SC:* Hildagarde Stadie, based on "The Black Cat" by Edgar Allan Poe. *PH:* William Thompson. *ED:* William Austin. *Asst Dir:* J. Stuart Blackton, Jr.

*Cast:* Bill Woods (Don Maxwell), Horace B. Carpenter (Dr. Meirschultz), Ted Edwards (Buckley), Phyllis Diller (Mrs. Buckley), Thea Ramsey (Alice Maxwell), Jennie Dark (Maize), Marvel Andre (Marvel), Celia McGann (Jo), J.P. Wade (Mike, the Morgue Attendant), Marion Blackton (Neighbor).

Following a long written prologue on fear and how criminals suffer from mental illness, *Maniac* begins in the laboratory of Dr. Meirschultz (Horace B. Carpenter), who is working on a formula to revive the dead, aided by his assistant Don Maxwell (Bill Woods), a one-time vaudeville impersonation performer now on the lam from the law. They go to the city morgue where Don impersonates the coroner, and they revive a comely young lady, a suicide victim, and take her back to the lab. Wanting to revive a dead person with a heart transplant, the scientist sends Don to a funeral home for another body, but he is frightened away and comes back without a corpse. Angry, Meirschultz orders Don to kill himself so he can revive him, but Don turns the gun on the doctor and shoots him. Madness overtakes Don, and he assumes the identity of the scientist, putting on makeup to look like the dead man. He is consulted by Mrs. Buckley (Phyllis Diller—not the commedienne), who claims her husband (Ted Edwards) is under the delusion he is the killer simian from Edgar Allan Poe's "Murders in the Rue Morgue." Don plans to give him a hypo of plain water but confuses syringes and gives Buckley a chemical that turns him into a raving lunatic. When the revived girl from the morgue comes into the laboratory, Buckley attacks her and carries her off, tearing off her clothes and molesting her. Mrs. Buckley makes Don agree to help her husband, and after she leaves he walls up the body of Dr. Meirschultz in the basement, not knowing a black cat (whose eye the madman has just gouged out and eaten) is beside the corpse. While the police investigate the disappearance of the girl from the morgue, Don continues to impersonate the scientist and performs an examination on an attractive young woman. Meanwhile Don's wife, Alice (Thea Ramsey), learns he has an inheritance, and she comes to see Dr. Meirschultz, unaware that she is talking to her husband. Don decides to get both Alice and Mrs. Buckley out of the way by telling each that the other is mad. He ends up locking the two women in the basement, going into hysterical laughter as he hears them fight. The police arrive, hear the women and rescue them as Don is taken to the basement. There they hear the cat crying behind the mortared wall, and, tearing it down, they find the body of Dr. Meirschultz. Don is then taken to an asylum.

One of the looniest motion pictures ever made, *Maniac* remains a mind-boggling experience despite having been done for the exploitation trade a half century ago. Cheap in the extreme with acting of the old touring-company variety, *Maniac* defies logic at every turn, yet, for the most part, the film is great fun. Where else can one see two cats fight under a coffin or a black cat (named Satan) try to hear a human heart? Perhaps the movie's best-known scene is where the madman gouges out the cat's eye and eats it! For unintentional mirth there is the sequence where the madman mixes up syringes and gives a psychotic the wrong shot, turning him into a sex fiend who immediately carries off a near-catatonic young woman who has just been revived from the dead. Add to this some scenes of nudity, two women locked in a cellar fighting and a bunch of inserted subtitles describing such mental illnesses as dementia praecox, paresis, paranoia and manic-depression. Also not to be overlooked is some classic dialogue. In one scene the mad scientist tells his convict assistant, a former stage impersonator, "Once a ham always a ham." In another scene the assistant tells the doctor, "Between the gangsters and auto drivers we don't need another world war to kill off the population."

The husband and wife team of Dwain Esper and Hildagarde Stadie made *Maniac* and ducked the Hollywood Production Code by four-walling the production through their own Roadshow Attractions. They inserted footage from the silent features *Haxan (Witchcraft Through the Ages)* (1921) and *Siegfried* (1923) to illustrate madness.

*Maniac* was hardly the type of feature to attract reviews in the mid-1930s, but in recent years the film has been written about extensively. "Thoroughly crude, reprehensible exploitation film of the 1930s, fascinating today for shedding insight into how schlock producers of the period pandered to unsophisticated audiences ... The forerunner of bargain-basement sleaze, unforgettable in its ineptitude," wrote John Stanley in *Revenge of the Creature Features Movie Guide* (1988). *The Phantom's Ultimate Video Guide* (1989) noted, "*Maniac* is rife with memorable sequences ... one of the strangest sustained hallucinations ever to flicker before a grindhouse audience's disbelieving eyes." Phil Hardy said in *The Encyclopedia of Horror Movies* (1986), "Aside from the fact that it features little or no blood, the film is very much a precursor of what was to come, exploiting some mild nudity and offering several gleeful examples of 'bad taste' ... A curiosity more than anything else, it is abominably acted and distinctly poor in all technical departments."

Dwain Esper is sometimes called the 1930s counterpart to Edward D. Wood, Jr., and it is interesting to note that the photographer of *Maniac*, William Thompson, later shot such Wood "classics" as *Glen or Glenda?* (1952), *Bride of the Monster* (1955), *Plan 9 from Outer Space* (1958) and *Night of the Ghouls* (1959).

## Narcotic

Hollywood Producers and Distributors, March, 1934, 69 minutes.

*P:* Dwain Esper. *D:* Vival Sodar't. *SC:* A.J. Karnopp. *Prod Mgr:* Robert Farlan.

*Cast:* Harry Cording, Joan Dix, Paul Panzer, Jean Lacey, Patricia Farley, J. Stuart Blackton, Jr., Mimi Alvarez, Charles Bennett.

Beset by personal problems, a young medical student turns to opium for diversion.

## Modern Motherhood

April, 1934, 60 minutes.

*P-D:* Dwain Esper. *ST:* Gardner Bradford.

A young married couple decide they do not want children but as time passes the wife changes her mind.

## Forbidden Adventure

July, 1934, 70 minutes.

*P:* Dwain Esper. *D:* J.C. "Doc" Cook. *ED:* Grace McKee. *Mus:* C. Sharpe Minor (sic).

*Cast:* Gayne Whitman (narrator).

Two explorers in Borneo are saved from a savage tribe by its ruler, a white goddess. Reissued by J.H. Hoffberg in 1936 as *Inyaah the Jungle Goddess* and rereleased in the early 1940s by Maple

Attractions as *Strange Adventures, The Virgin of Sarawak* and *Jungle Virgin*.

## Marihuana

May, 1936, 56 minutes.

*P:* Rex Elgin. *D:* Dwain Esper. *SC:* Hildagarde Stadie & Rex Elgin. *PH:* Roland Price. *ED:* Carl Himm. *Dial Dir:* Alexander Leftwich.

*Cast:* Harley Wood, Hugh MacArthur, Pat Carlyle, Paul Ellis, Dorothy Dehn, Richard Erskine, Juanita Crossman, Gloria Brown, Hal Taggart.

Neglected by her mother and sister, a teenager is turned on to reefers by a drug pusher and gets pregnant by her boyfriend. Also called *Marijuana—The Devil's Weed*.

## How to Undress in Front of Your Husband

Hollywood Producers & Distributors, 1937, 2 reels.

*P-D:* Dwain Esper. *SC:* Hildagarde Stadie.

*Cast:* Elaine Barrie [Barrymore], Albert Van Antwerp (narrator).

Mrs. John Barrymore undresses and puts on a nightgown. Copyrighted as *How to Undress*.

## Angkor

June, 1937, 80 minutes.

*P-ST:* Henry Warner & Roy Purdon. *D:* George M Merrick. *SC:* Armine Von Tempski & Minnie F. Shrope. *ED:* Grace McKee. *Mus:* Dominic McBride. *Sp Eff:* Ray Smallwood. *Asst Dir:* Harry P. Crist [Harry Fraser]. *Research:* Gladys McConnell.

*Cast:* Wilfred Lucas, J.S. Horne.

At the Los Angeles Adventurer's Club, actor Wilfred Lucas, a noted world traveler, tells the story of a 1912 expedition to Cambodia's lost city of

Angkor and the discovery of native girls mating with apes. Also called *Forbidden Adventure in Angkor* and reissued in 1938 as *Forbidden Adventure* by Maple Attractions.

## Horrors of War

Maple Attractions/Merit Pictures, February 14, 1940, 51 minutes.

*P:* Dwain Esper.

Newsreels and movie footage are used to show how the munitions industry got the U.S. into the First World War.

# Fanchon Royer

Noted primarily as an independent producer and one of the few women producers in Hollywood in the 1930s, Fanchon Royer was also associated with Poverty Row studios like Sono Art-World Wide, Mayfair (qq.v.) and Mascot. Born in Des Moines, Iowa, in 1902 Fanchon Royer attended the University of Southern California and began working in the motion picture industry in 1917 as an actor. Later she edited camera trade magazines and also worked as a publicist and artists' agent. In 1928 she produced the "Life's Like That" series of short subjects and with the coming of sound began producing feature films. For Sono Art-World Wide she produced *Cannonball Express* (1932), and for Mayfair she did features like *Behind Jury Doors*, *Heart Punch*, *Honor of the Press* and *Trapped in Tia Juana* (all 1932), and *Alimony Madness*, *Her Resale Value* and *Revenge at Monte Carlo* (all 1933). By 1936 Fanchon Royer was a production assistant to Nat Levine at Republic Pictures but resigned in 1937 to form Fanchon Royer Features, Inc.

Prior to forming that company, Fanchon Royer had been the guiding force behind several motion pictures released on the states' rights market under the banner Fanchon Royer Pictures, Inc. The first of these was *Neighbors' Wives* in 1932 with Dorothy Mackaill, followed by *Fighting Lady* (1935) starring Jack Mulhall. Announced, but apparently unfilmed, during this time were *For Value Received* and *Trouble Doubles*. From 1937 to 1938 Royer operated Fanchon Royer Features, Inc., which made such states' rights releases as *Mile a Minute Love* in 1937, reissued the next year as *Crime Afloat*. Royer's films were of the shoestring-budget variety—cheap sets, lots of talk and plenty of stock footage.

In 1938 Fanchon Royer Productions was formed, but its sole theatrical release was *Religious Racketeers*, the story of a fake swami (Robert Fiske) and the victims he bilked. The movie was tradeshown throughout the country, and in 1939 it was reissued by Merit Pictures as *The Mystic Circle Murder*. An exploitation gimmick had Mme. Harry Houdini appearing in the feature to expose corrupt spiritualists.

After *Religious Racketeers*, Fanchon Royer formed Way of Life Films which produced and released religious movies between 1940 and 1945. In 1943 she became president of the Catholic Film and Radio Guild and later became director of Guardian Films, a religious movie production company associated with the Catachetical Guild of St. Paul, Minnesota.

## Neighbors' Wives

September 20, 1933, 61 minutes.
   *P:* Fanchon Royer. *D:* B. Reeves Eason. *SC:* John Francis Natteford. *PH:* Ernest Miller. *ED:* Jeanne Spencer. *SD:* Charles O'Loughlin. *AD:* Paul Palmentola. *Prod Mgr:* Albert Benham. *Asst Dir:* Tito Davison.
   *Cast:* Dorothy Mackaill, Tom Moore, Mary Kornman, Vivien Oakland, Cyril Ring, Emerson Treacy, James Gordon, Mabel Van Buren, Paul Wigal.
   A detective is forced to arrest his wife for the murder of her younger sister's seducer.

## Fighting Lady

April 16, 1935, 50 minutes.
   *P:* Fanchon Royer. *D:* Carlos Borcosque. *SC:* John Francis Natteford. *ST:* Robert Ober. *PH:* Ernest Miller. *ED:* Jeanne Spencer. *SD:* Terry Kellum. *Prod Mgr:* Albert Benham. *Asst Dir:* Tito Davison. *Dial Dir:* Edward Earle.
   *Cast:* Jack Mulhall, Peggy Shannon, Marion Lessing, Mary Carr, Edward Woods, Edward Earle, Betty Blythe, Alice Moore, David Hitchcock, John Horsley.
   A self-centered young woman romances several men in an effort to find wealth and happiness.

## Ten Laps to Go

Ace Pictures Corporation, June, 1936, 67 minutes.
   *P:* Fanchon Royer. *D:* Elmer Clifton. *SC:* Charles R. Condon. *ST:* William F. Bleecher. *ED:* Edward Schroeder. *AD:* Paul Palmentola. *Prod Mgr:* Gaston Glass. *Asst Dir:* Bobby Ray. *SD:* Corson Jowett.
   *Cast:* Rex Lease (Larry Evans), Muriel Evans (Norma Corbett), Duncan Renaldo (Eddie DeSylva), Charles Delaney (Steve), Marie Prevost (Elsie), Tom Moore (Corbett), Walter McGrail (Drake), Edward Davis (Adams), Yakima Canutt (Barney Smith), John Elliott (Dad).
   Self-centered race car driver Larry Evans (Rex Lease) drives for car builder Corbett (Tom Moore). He falls for the latter's pretty daughter Norma (Muriel Evans), but she refuses his proposal of marriage because he is publicity-hungry. Having beaten the time of rival DeSylva (Duncan Renaldo) in the trials, Larry races Corbett's new car in the big race, but DeSylva purposely hits Larry's car causing a crash in which Evans is injured and loses the use of his legs. Not wanting to be a burden to Norma, Larry rejects her love. Larry's mechanic buddy, Steve (Charles Delaney), gets a job with Corbett, who has moved to California and is building midget racing cars. Back on his feet, Larry also takes a job as a mechanic with Corbett and finds out Norma is dating DeSylva. Now afraid to drive because of his crash, Larry refuses Corbett's offer to drive his new auto in a race, and DeSylva plants another driver (Edward Davis) in the national championship race in order to sabotage

Wilfred Lucas, Vivien Oakland, William Bakewell, Duncan Renaldo and Arletta Duncan in *Mile a Minute Love* (Fanchon Royer Productions, 1937), also called *Crime Afloat* and *Roaring Speedboats*.

Corbett's operation and have Norma for himself. Larry finds out the truth and gets proof of DeSylva's duplicity from gangsters who have been aiding him. Rushing to the race, Larry takes Davis' place and in the last ten laps wins the championship for Corbett, and he also rewins Norma's love.

Producer Fanchon Royer spared every expense in putting together this auto racing melodrama, which is sometimes falsely associated with the Indianapolis 500. Actually the racing sequences take place on both coasts and not in the Midwest. A puny story holds this overlong tale together pumped up with lots of racing stock footage interspersed with closeups of stars Rex Lease and Duncan Renaldo. Other fillers include footage of a parade and

an Hawaiian band complete with a plump hula dancer in a nightclub sequence. While the acting is uniformly good, the overall production is frail with minor entertainment value. Of interest is the fact that speeds of 116–117 miles per hour are emphasized in the film as being spectacular, compared with the 200-plus speeds of today. Also the film includes a rather cruel sequence, meant to be funny, of former Mack Sennett bathing beauty Marie Prevost getting stuck in a race car. Of note is the fact that there is no photography credit on *Ten Laps to Go* and the production manager is former silent screen star Gaston Glass.

## Mile a Minute Love

April 6, 1937, 70 minutes.

Lobby card for *The Mystic Circle Murder* (Fanchon Royer Features, 1939), reissued by Continental Pictures. Pictured are Helen Le Berthon, Robert Fiske and Betty Compson (left); Robert Fiske (center); and Helen Le Berthon and Betty Compson (right).

*P:* Fanchon Royer. *D:* Elmer Clifton. *SC:* Edwin Anthony. *ST:* Duncan Renaldo. *PH:* Arthur Martinelli. *ED:* Edward Schroeder. *SD:* Cliff Ruberg. *AD:* Vin Taylor. *Prod Mgr:* Gaston Glass. *Asst Dir:* Melville DeLay.

*Cast:* William Bakewell, Arletta Duncan, Duncan Renaldo, Vivien Oakland, Wilfred Lucas, Earle Douglas, Etta McDaniel.

Crooks try to get a young inventor to tamper with an entry in a big boat race. Reissued in 1938 as *Crime Afloat.*

## The Mystic Circle Murder

Merit Pictures; October 13, 1939, 66 minutes.

*P:* Fanchon Royer. *D-ST:* Frank O'Connor. *SC:* Frank O'Connor & Charles R. Condon. *PH:* Jack Greenhalgh. *ED:* George Halligan. *AD:* Paul Palmentola. *Prod Mgr:* Ray Nazarro. *SD:* Cliff Ruberg. *Dial Dir:* Don Gallaher. *Tech Dir:* Dr. Edward Saint & Bhogwan Singh.

*Cast:* Robert Fiske (The Great La Gagge), Helen Le Berthon (Martha Morgan), Arthur Gardner (Elliott Cole), Betty Compson (Ada Bernard), David Kerman (Harvey Wilson), Mme. Harry [Beatrice] Houdini (Herself).

Society matron Ada Bernard (Betty Compson) is in love with mystic The Great La Gagge (Robert Fiske), and she has him display his powers before some of her friends, including pretty Martha Morgan (Helen Le Berthon) and her skeptical newspaperman boyfriend Elliott Cole (Arthur Gardner). The police, led by Inspector Burke (Robert Frazer), get after La Gagge when a woman dies of heart failure during one of his seances. As a result of Elliott doing a story on Martha, the girl's grief over the loss of her mother comes to La Gagge's attention. He intends to bilk the young woman out of part of her fortune. Before escaping from the law, La Gagge tells Ada to go to Egypt. She and Martha make the voyage, and there La Gagge masquerades as The Great Prophet, who tells Martha to donate money to build a temple to the goddess Isis, where he will reunite her with her mother. When the mystic's assistant, Harvey Wilson (David Kerman), tells him that Elliott has arrived in Egypt, La Gagge has the women go to India. There he pretends to be a prophet with a white beard, but by now Ada suspects it is really La Gagge, and she is also aware that Martha has fallen in love with the spiritualist. Elliott comes to India and finds out La Gagge's true identity but is captured by the mystic, placed in a block of ice and dumped in the Ganges River. When La Gagge, who has claimed to have materialized in India, holds a seance to call up Martha's mother, Elliott, who has escaped from the ice block, arrives to expose the fakir. Martha and Ada realize they have been duped although La Gagge reveals his love for Martha. Wilson kills La Gagge over Martha's money but is soon captured, and a reunited Elliott and Martha return home.

Despite its title, *The Mystic Circle Murder* contains no homicide except for the villain getting his comeuppance at the finale. A woman does die of heart failure during a seance and the hero is tossed into the Ganges River encased in a block of ice, but he lives to save the heroine from the fake mystic. The theme of the film is the exposing of spiritualism, but the overall effect is nullified by the shoddy production. *Variety* declared, "The story, framed to carry forth the propaganda intended, is ordinary and the dialog lifeless.... Production details also suggest carelessness. The acting, in addition to being stilted, is handicapped by the generally sloppy direction of Frank O'Connor." It should be noted the movie does contain some spooky scenes of seances in the mystic's temple, and Robert Fiske handles the villainous part well, although he is handicapped by several disguises. But with dialogue like "never fall in love with your victims" and "influence your subjects with selling themselves on your game," the movie's preaching becomes hard to swallow. Also a detriment is the phony backscreen projection used in a cemetery and for locales in India. The scenes where the fakir jumps around the world disguised as two different holy men are laughable. While the horror element could have been accentuated for entertainment value, its lack makes the feature a chore even at just over one hour.

For box office allure Mme. Harry Houdini is used at the beginning and end of the film to espouse her belief in the phoniness of spiritualism. For ten years following the death of her husband, famed magician Harry Houdini, Mme. Houdini held seances in an attempt to reach him in the afterworld. Following ten failures she gave up the attempts and thereafter lectured on the fakery of mystics. She continued to do so until her death early in 1943. In the film Mme. Houdini has only two scenes. She appears frail and uncomfortable with her brief dialogue.

*The Mystic Circle Murder* was first tradeshown in the spring of 1938 as *Religious Racketeers* and in the 1940s it was reissued by Continental Pictures.

# Showmen's Pictures

Between 1933 and 1935 Showmen's Pictures released nine feature films on the states' rights market, their product going out through Marcy Pictures (q.v.), an affiliate of William Steiner. None of the company's releases are particularly impressive with the possible exception of the documentary *Beyond Bengal*, released in the spring of 1934. Showmen's releases were mainly from D.J. Mountan's Screencraft Productions and were supervised by Al Alt with Sam Katzman serving as production manager. Since none of its productions were impressive, or overly successful at the box office, Showmen's Pictures passed into obscurity after only eighteen months.

*His Private Secretary*, the first Showmen's release in the early summer of 1933, is probably its best-known production. The reason? The male lead was played by John Wayne (in the period between his westerns for Warner Brothers and Monogram). Thanks to Wayne's continued popularity *His Private Secretary* has resurfaced both on TV and video. The rest of the company's product has some interest, particularly the brawling melodrama *Ship of Wanted Men* (1933), which the *Motion Picture Herald* dubbed "an hour of plentiful action." Thanks to the talents of Nick Stuart in *Police Call* (1933) and pert Sally O'Neil in *The Moth* (1934), both films are worth watching. On the other hand there is little to recommend the musical drama *St. Louis Woman* (1935), starring Jeanette Loff and Johnny Mack Brown. The former was a fading star of the late silent and early sound era while Johnny Mack Brown had yet to come into his own as a cowboy star. As Showmen's Productions, the company made *The Marriage Bargain* (1935) with Lila Lee and Creighton Chaney (later Lon Chaney, Jr.), but it proved to be its final effort.

## His Private Secretary

June 6, 1933, 60 minutes.

*D:* Philip H. Whitman. *SC:* John Francis Natteford. *ST:* Lew Collins. *PH:* Abe Scholtz. *ED:* Bobby Ray. *SD:* Oscar Lagerstrom. *Supv:* Al Alt. *Prod*

*Mgr:* Sam Katzman. *Tech Dir:* Paul Palmantello. *Settings:* Fred Preble.

*Cast:* Evelyn Knapp (Marion Boyd), John Wayne (Dick Wallace), Alec B. Francis (Rev. Hall), Reginald Barlow (Mr. Wallace), Arthur Hoyt (Mr. Little), Natalie Kingston (Polly),

HiS
PRiVATE SECRETARY

Lobby card for *His Private Secretary* (Showmen's Pictures, 1933) with John Wayne, Evalyn Knapp and Mickey Rentschler.

Patrick Cunning (Dan), Al St. John (Tom the Garage Owner), Hugh Kidder (Jenks the Butler), Mickey Rentschler (Bill).

Wealthy businessman Mr. Wallace (Reginald Barlow) is fed up with his son Dick's (John Wayne) playboy ways. He tells him to take the job of collections manager in his business not knowing Dick is being pursued by gold digger Polly (Natalie Kingston), who is being egged on by Dick's supposed pal Dan (Patrick Cunning). Dick is sent to the town of Sommerville to collect a debt, and along the way he meets attractive Marion Boyd (Evelyn Knapp), giving her a lift. When she rejects his advances, he learns the man from whom he is to collect the debt is her minister grandfather Rev. Hall (Alec B. Francis). Finding out the

money has been used to feed hungry children, Dick extends the minister's credit and Mr. Wallace fires him. To be near Marion, Dick purchases a service station in Sommerville, but she will have nothing to do with him until she learns he lost his job because of his extension of the debt. As a result Dick and Marion fall in love and get married. When Dick tells his father he has married, Mr. Wallace throws him out of his office. Marion goes to straighten out the matter and not knowing her identity Mr. Wallace hires her as his secretary. Marion is a big success in her new job, but Dick starts going out with a fast crowd and Polly tries to seduce him away from his wife. When Marion finds Dick has been involved in an all-night party with Polly she leaves him. He goes to his father and tells him the truth about his marriage to Marion. Both men regret she has gone, but after a vacation with her grandfather Marion returns home and finds out that Dick is not involved with Polly. Dick and Marion are reunited much to the relief of both Dick and his father.

This Screencraft Productions feature is best remembered today for giving a lead to John Wayne at the time when his career was on the downslide after his initial starring role in *The Big Trail* in 1930. Thanks to Wayne's appearance, *His Private Secretary* is available on video and has also had some small screen revival. Technically it is an average Poverty Row outing with a rather contrived story, good acting and acceptable production values. Evelyn Knapp, who appeared in many low-budget features throughout the 1930s, is an appealing actress who handles the lead role in good form while John Wayne exudes the boyish charm needed for his harmless playboy role. Reginald Barlow gives the film's best performance as Wayne's crusty businessman father while Arthur Hoyt does some scene stealing as the office manager. Natalie Kingston is quite appealing as the gold digger after Wayne's money and Al St. John and Mickey Rentschler have amusing cameos. Third-billed Alec B. Francis has little to do as the heroine's hard-of-hearing minister grandfather. *His Private Secretary* was issued in Great Britain early in 1934 by Gaumont Ideal.

## Police Call

August 29, 1933, 63 minutes.

*D:* Philip H. Whitman. *SC:* Norman Keene & Jean Hartley. *ST:* Norman Keene. *PH:* Abe Scholtz. *ED:* Rose Smith. *SD:* Robert Quirk. *Supv:* Al Alt. *Prod Mgr:* Sam Katzman.

*Cast:* Nick Stuart, Merna Kennedy, Roberta Gale, Mary Carr, Walter McGrail, Warner Richmond, Robert Ellis, Eddie Phillips, Harry Myers, Ralph Freud, Charles Stevens.

A boxer quits the ring to go to college but finds out his sister is involved with racketeers.

## Ship of Wanted Men

September 9, 1933, 63 minutes.

*D:* Lew Collins. *SC:* Ethel Hill. *PH:* George Meehan. *ED:* Rose Smith. *SD:* Oscar Lagerstrom. *Tech Dir:* Fred Preble. *Supv:* Al Alt. *Prod Mgr:* Sam Katzman.

*Cast:* Dorothy Sebastian, Fred Kohler, Leon [Ames] Waycoff, Gertrude Astor, Maurice Black, Jason Robards, James Flavin, Herbert Evans, John Ince, Kit Guard.

A group of convicts commandeer a ship and head to a remote island and along the way they pick up a shipwrecked young woman.

## Public Stenographer

January 10, 1934, 64 minutes.

*D:* Lew Collins. *SC:* Joseph O'Donnell & Lew Collins. *ST:* Ellwood Ullman. *Supv:* Al Alt.

*Cast:* Lola Lane, William Collier, Jr., Esther Muir, Jason Robards, Duncan Renaldo, Richard Tucker, Al St. John, Bryant Washburn, Al Bridge.

When her car stalls on the highway, a stenographer meets a young man who begins romancing her.

## The Big Race

February 14, 1934, 68 minutes.

*D:* Fred Newmeyer. *SC:* Hugh Cummings. *PH:* George Meehan. *ED:* S. Roy Luby. *SD:* Lew Myers. *Supv:* Al Alt. *Prod Mgr:* Sam Katzman. *Tech Dir:* Fred Preble.

*Cast:* Boots Mallory, John Darrow,

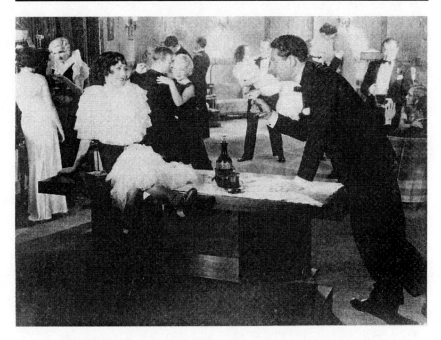

Sally O'Neil and Paul Page in *The Moth* (Showmen's Pictures, 1934).

Frankie Darro, Phillips Smalley, Katherine Williams, Paul Hurst, Georgia O'Dell, James Flavin, Richard Terry, Oscar, Skipper Zeliff.

As a race track employee fixes a big race by drugging a favorite, father and son trainers compete to win the event.

## The Moth

March 9, 1934, 64 minutes.

*D:* Fred Newmeyer. *SC:* Joseph O'Donnell. *PH:* George Meehan. *ED:* S. Roy Luby. *SD:* J.S. Westmoreland. *Supv:* Al Alt. *Tech Dir:* Fred Preble. *Prod Mgr:* Sam Katzman.

*Cast:* Sally O'Neil (Diana Wyman), Paul Page (George Duncan), Wilfred Lucas (John Gale), Fred Kelsey (Detective Blake), Duncan Renaldo (Don Pedro), Rae Daggert (Marie LaMare), Nina Guilbert (Aunt Jane Stevens), Georgia O'Dell.

After squandering the fortune she inherited, socialite Diana Wyman (Sally O'Neil) gets caught in a raid on a private party, and a picture of her dancing in her underwear makes the front page. Her guardian, aging lawyer John Gale (Wilfred Lucas), who has a yen for her, hires engineer George Duncan (Paul Page) to spy on Diana. He follows her on a train to New Orleans, and Diana realizes she is being tailed. On the train she befriends Marie LaMare (Rae Daggert), a dancer who is actually a famous female criminal known as "The Moth," who is also being followed by Blake (Fred Kelsey), a detective. The two young women give their followers the slip in New Orleans, and Marie meets up with her lover Don Pedro (Duncan Renaldo), a pickpocket. George and Blake find Diana in the club where Marie dances while Gale heads to New Orleans with Diana's Aunt Jane (Nina Guilbert).

While Marie dances Don Pedro steals valuables from wealthy customers, and Marie then hides the loot in Diana's room. That night Marie pretends to have a sprained ankle to fool Blake, and a masked Diana takes her place on the dance floor as Don Pedro passes her more stolen merchandise. Blake then finds the jewels on Diana and arrests both her and George, but they lead him and the police to the hotel where Marie and Don Pedro are captured. Marie than clears Diana, and she and George are released in Gale's custody. Gale realizes he likes Aunt Jane while Diana follows after George.

Cute, petite Sally O'Neil had scored a sensation in her film debut in 1925 in *Sally, Irene and Mary*. She continued playing flapper roles successfully through the silent days before finding success in talkies in 1931 in *Brat*, repeating her successful stage role of the previous year. By 1934, however, her film career was definitely on the wane, and *The Moth* was one of several Poverty Row outings for her. *Variety* complained, "Cheaply produced and poorly acted, *The Moth* is the kind of picture that has two strikes on it at the beginning. In story, it is banal. In casting, it's poor as they come. In adaptation and direction, it is no better." Actually Sally O'Neil is okay in the leading role as the feather-headed socialite, but overall the film is poorly photographed, stodgy and slow-moving. There is even a filler with Mardi Gras parade footage. The title refers to the nickname of a female criminal with whom Sally O'Neil becomes entangled.

## Beyond Bengal

April 25, 1934, 70 minutes.

*P-D-SC:* Harry Schenck.

*Cast:* John Martin (narrator), Harry Schenck, John Baldwin, Captain Nain Sei, Ali, Bee.

Harry Schenck's expedition into the jungles of Malaya with fourteen cameras and an elephant convoy.

## St. Louis Woman

January 3, 1935, 68 minutes.

*D:* Albert Ray. *SC:* Jack Natteford. *ST:* Elwood Ullman. *Mus:* Betty Laidlaw & Bob Lively. *Supv:* Al Alt.

*Cast:* Jeanette Loff, John[ny] Mack Brown, Earle Foxe, Roberta Gale.

A woman with a shady past falls for a football star down on his luck and she helps him get reinstated in college.

## The Marriage Bargain

February 20, 1935, 62 minutes.

*D:* Albert Ray. *SC:* Betty Laidlaw & Bob Lively. *PH:* George Meehan. *ED:* S. Roy Luby. *SD:* Frank MacKenzie. *AD:* Fred Preble. *Asst Dir:* Bobby Ray. *Supv:* Al Alt.

*Cast:* Lila Lee, Creighton [Lon, Jr.] Chaney, Edmund Breese, Francis McDonald, Audrey Ferris, Fern Emmett, Victor Potel, Tommy Bond.

To protect her father from a murder charge, a young woman marries a man she despises. Working and TV title: *Within the Rock*.

# Sono Art–World
# Wide Pictures

Sono Art-World Wide Pictures was formed at the beginning of the sound era. It was headed by J. Douglas Watson, and in its five years of existence the studio turned out over 60 feature films, eschewing short subjects and serials. The company's product was competently made and generally regarded as B-plus productions, satisfying either solo or double-bill bookings. Headquartered at 1501 Broadway in New York City, Sono Art-World Wide Pictures made most of its product at Ralph M. Like's International Film Studios, located on Sunset Drive in Los Angeles.

Actually the company kicked off in the spring of 1929 with the Sono Art production of *The Rainbow Man*, a musical starring Eddie Dowling and Marian Nixon. It was released by Paramount Pictures. The film set a trend for the studio in that it was supervised by George W. Weeks and O.E. Goebel, both of whom were involved in many of the studio's early productions. James Cruze Productions added prestige to the fledgling company when the noted director of the classic *The Covered Wagon* (1923) made a number of features for them, including Sono Art-World Wide's first official release, *The Great Gabbo*. Starring Erich von Stroheim and Betty Compson, this was a strange combination of drama and backstage musical numbers hampered by poor sound recording. Although it contained a Technicolor sequence, the film almost sank the infant studio, which rallied with documentaries like *Fighting for the Fatherland* (1929) and *Up the Congo* (1930) plus another Eddie Dowling musical, *Blaze O' Glory* (1930), costarring Betty Compson. It contained songs like "Welcome Home," "The Doughboy's Lullaby" and "Wrapped in a Red, Red Rose." More importantly it was the basis for another Sono Art-World Wide production, *Sombras de Gloria* (1930), the first Hollywood feature film to be entirely in Spanish. Up to this time major studios had little success in dubbing or using off-screen narration for foreign consumption and the company's success with *Sombras de Gloria* not only led to its making other Spanish language films, but it was the impetus for the major companies to follow suit, making Spanish, French and German language versions of their productions. Thus Sono Art-World Wide Pictures has a place in Hollywood history as the first studio to make foreign-language feature films.

By early in 1930 Sono Art-World Wide had settled into the pattern of turning out competent programmers augmented by a few major productions. The latter included James Cruze Productions like *Hello Sister, Cock O' the Walk, The Big Fight* and *Once a Gentleman* (all 1930), while double-bill fare often included above-average westerns like *The Dude Wrangler* and *Rogue of the Rio Grande* (both 1930). In 1930 the company also began importing Michael Balcon productions from England and for a season peppered its release schedule with British films. In addition the studio continued to make Spanish language versions of features like *What a Man!* (1930), filmed in Spanish as *Asi es la Vida* (1930), and *The Big Fight* (1930), which became *La Fuerza del Querer* (1930) in Spanish. Nineteen thirty also found the company with somewhat of a prestige item in *Reno*, a drama marking the sound debut of famed serial queen Ruth Roland. The company also had a solid success that year with the James Cruze murder mystery *The Costello Case*, starring Tom Moore.

By 1931 Sono Art-World Wide began concentrating on program features in deference to bigger budget efforts. Most of these efforts were produced by George W. Weeks and directed by Stuart Paton with *Swanee River* being a good case in point. Dealing with an engineer (Grant Withers) working for a power company in rural Tennessee, the feature was billed as the first "Thrill-O-Drama" from the company, which promised to revert back to the old-time thrills and simplistic plots of the silent era. Thus the studio churned out action dramas like *Air Police*, starring Kenneth Harlan; *First Aid*, with Grant Withers; *Hell Bent for Frisco* with Vera Reynolds; *Is There Justice?* with Rex Lease; *Neck and Neck* with Glenn Tryon and Vera Reynolds; *In Old Cheyenne*, a Rex Lease western; and the north woods adventure, *Mounted Fury*, with John Bowers (whose suicide inspired the finale for *A Star is Born* [1937]). In 1931 George J. Crone, who often handled various production aspects of Sono Art-World Wide product, directed the Spanish-language feature *Hollywood, Ciudad de Ensueno* [Hollywood, City of Illusion], which, unlike the company's other Spanish features, was not based on an English-language original. Starring Jose Bohr, it would be reissued on the independent market in 1934.

Nineteen thirty-two saw major changes in Sono Art-World Wide Pictures. Tiffany Productions (q.v.) ceased operations that year and Sono Art-World Wide picked up their remaining features for distribution, including a series of profitable westerns starring Ken Maynard. The company also launched its own western series with Bob Steele, who had previously been on the Tiffany roster. Produced by Trem Carr, the Bob Steele features proved good box office and helped to enhance the studio's waning profits as did the acquisition of the Ken Maynard westerns. By the summer of 1932 the studio dropped the Sono Art banner, calling itself World Wide Pictures, and by the end of the year E.W. Hammons, the president of Educational Pictures, Inc., took over as the chief at World Wide.

With E.W. Hammons in control, World Wide Pictures returned to the production of high-quality programmers augmented by series westerns and the distribution of the remainder of the Tiffany productions. When Bob Steele and producer Trem Carr signed with Monogram Pictures in 1932, Hammons contracted with Ken Maynard for a series of eight westerns filmed at the Tiffany lot on Sunset Boulevard. Hammons personally produced features like *False Faces*, with Lowell Sherman, *Breach of Promise*, starring Chester Morris and *Uptown New York*, with Jack Oakie (all 1932). All three were solid melodramas with good entertainment values. Less can be said for a studio pickup, *Hypnotized*, released for the 1932 Christmas trade. Made by M.H.S. Productions it proved to be the screen swan song for comedy genius Mack Sennett, who coscripted and then directed this forgettable mixture of comedy and fantasy. It starred Moran and Mack, "The Two Black Crows," who had sold millions of records for Columbia in the 1920s. It was sad at best, with dated humor and a muddled plot.

By 1933 World Wide Pictures was on its last legs, but the company did not go down without a fight. Its Ken Maynard series proved solid with especially interesting entries such as *Drum Taps*, which incorporated a Boy Scout troop in its plot, the action-filled *Fargo Express* and the horrorific *Tombstone Canyon*, which featured Sheldon Lewis as a murderous masked phantom. There was also a flavorful Sherlock Holmes mystery, *A Study in Scarlet*, with Reginald Owen (who also penned the dialogue) as the master sleuth, and a racing drama, *Race Track*, which was greatly enhanced by the work of Leo Carrillo as a gambler with a heart of gold. *The Constant Woman* was also released in the spring of 1933, although it had been turned out the year before as *Auction in Souls*.

Following the demise of World Wide, George W. Weeks joined Ralph M. Like's Mayfair Pictures (q.v.) as a producer, and E.W. Hammons continued to run Educational Pictures until it closed its doors in 1940 after being in operation for a quarter of a century.

## The Rainbow Man

Sono Art Productions/Paramount, April 14, 1929, 10 reels.

*D:* Fred Newmeyer. *SC:* George J. Crone, Frances Agnew & Eddie Dowling. *ST:* Eddie Dowling. *PH:* Jack McKenzie. *ED & Prod Mgr:* J.R. Crone. *Supv:* George W. Weeks & O.E. Goebel. *Songs:* Eddie Dowling, James F. Hanley & Andrew B. Sterling.

*Cast:* Eddie Dowling, Marian Nixon, Frankie Darro, Sam Hardy, Lloyd Ingraham, George Hayes.

A minstrel man falls in love with a young woman whose family disapproves of theatrical folk.

## Fighting for the Fatherland

September 1, 1929, 58 minutes.

*ED:* Walter Futter.

Old newsreel footage and German battle scenes make up this World War I documentary which shows the Axis side of the conflict.

## The Great Gabbo

September 15, 1929, 10 reels.

*D:* James Cruze. *SC:* Hugh Herbert. *ST:* Ben Hecht. *PH:* Ira H. Morgan. *Prod Mgr:* Vernon Keays. *Dance Dir:* Maurice L. Russell. *SD:* Helmer Bergman. *Songs:* Paul Titsworth, Lynn Cowan, Donald McNamee & King Zany.

*Cast:* Erich von Stroheim, Betty Compson, Donald Douglas, Marjorie "Babe" Kane, Otto the Dummy.

A self-centered ventriloquist realizes he loves his loyal assistant after she leaves him to work in another act.

## Asi es la Vida

1930, 7 reels.

*P:* George W. Weeks & O.E. Goebel. *D:* George J. Crone. *SC:* Tom Gibson & Jose Crespo. *PH:* Arthur Todd. *ED:* Arturo Tavares. *Supv-Prod Mgr:* J.R. Crone. *Songs:* Jose Bohr & Eva Bohr. *Mus Dir:* Carlos Molina. *Tech Dir:* Charles Cadwallader. *SD:* J.G. Gregor. *Prod Asst:* A.S. Black.

*Cast:* Jose Bohr, Delia Magana, Lola Vendrill, Cesar Vanoni, Enrique Acosta, Marcela Nivon, Tito Davison, Myrta Bonillas, Julian Rivero, Ernesto Piedra, Rosita Gil.

Spanish language version of *What a Man!* (1930).

## La Fuerza del Queres

1930.

*P:* James Cruze. *D:* Ralph Ince. *SC:* Andres de Segurola, from the play by Milton Herbert Gropper & Max Marcin.

*Cast:* Andres de Segurola, Maria Alba, Carlos Barbe, Stepin Fetchit, Vicente Padula, Tito Davison, Manuel Conesa, Rafael Valverde.

Spanish language version of *The Big Fight* (1930).

## Blaze O' Glory

January 5, 1930, 10 reels.

*P:* George W. Weeks & O.E. Goebel. *D:* Renaud Hoffman & George J. Crone. *SC:* Henry McCarthy & Renaud Hoffman, from the story "The Long Shot" by Thomas A. Boyd. *PH:* Harry Jackson. *ED:* Arthur Huffsmith. *Mus:* James F. Hanley. *Songs:* Eddie Dowling, James Brockman, Ballard MacDonald & Joseph McCarthy. *SD:* Ben Harper.

*Cast:* Eddie Dowling, Betty Compson, Frankie Darro, Henry B. Walthall, William Davidson, Ferdi-nand Schumann-Heink, Eddie Conrad, Frank Sabini, Broderick O'Farrell, The Rounders.

An entertainer is charged with the murder of his wartime friend whom he thought was his wife's lover. Spanish version: *Sombras de Gloria* (1930).

## Up the Congo

January 26, 1930, 6 reels.

*P-D:* Alice O'Brien. *SC:* Harry Chandlee. *ST:* Grace Flandreau. *PH:* Charles Bell.

The story of three explorers on an expedition up the Congo River in Africa. Released in versions with synchronized lectures in English, French, Spanish, Italian and German.

## Sombras de Gloria

February 16, 1930, 11 reels.

*P:* George W Weeks & O.E. Goebel. *D:* Andrew L. Stone & Fernando C. Tamayo. *PH:* Arthur Martinelli. *ED:* Arthur Tavers. *SD:* Ben Harper & J.G. Gregor. *Prod Mgr:* J.R. Crone. *Tech Dir:* Charles Cadwallader. *Songs:* James F. Hanley, Fernand C. Tamayo, Jose Bohr, Jose C. Barreto & Charles Tobias. *Choreography:* Don Summers.

*Cast:* Jose Bohr, Mona Rico, Francisco Maran, Cesar Vanoni, Ricardo Cayol, Demetrius Alexis, Juan Torena, Enrique Acosta, Tito Davison, Roberto Saso Silva, Federico Goday.

Spanish language version of *Blaze O' Glory* (1930).

## Hello Sister

March 9, 1930, 8 reels.

*P:* James Cruze. *D:* Walter Lang. *SC:* Brian Marlow, from the story "Clipped Wings" by Rita Lambert. *PH:* Hal Rosson. *AD:* Robert E. Lee.

*Mus:* Russ Columbo & Howard Jackson. *Dance Dir:* Maurice L. Russell.

*Cast:* Olive Borden, Lloyd Hughes, George Fawcett, Bodil Rosing, Norman Peck, Howard Hickman, Raymond Keane, Wilfred Lucas, James T. Mack, Harry MacDonald.

In order to obtain an inheritance, a young woman is forced to give up the wild party life and she falls in love with an attorney.

## The Talk of Hollywood

March 20, 1930, 7 reels.

*D:* Mark Sandrich. *SC:* Darby Aaronson, Mark Sandrich & Nat Carr. *PH:* Walter Strenge. *ED:* Russell Shields. *SD:* George Osthmann & John Dolan.

*Cast:* Nat Carr, Fay Marble, Hope Sutherland, Sherling Oliver, Edward Le Saint, Gilbert Marble, John Troughton, Al Goodman & His Orchestra, The Leonidoff Ballet, Sam Levene.

A movie producer tries to make a talking picture but runs into all kinds of trouble.

## What a Man!

March 20, 1930, 7 reels.

*D:* George J. Crone. *SC:* A.A. Kline & Harvey Gates, from the novel *The Dark Chapter* by E.J. Rath and the play *They All Want Something* by Courtenay Savage. *PH:* Arthur Todd. *ED:* Harry Chandlee. *Tech Dir:* Charles Cadwallader. *SD:* J.G. McGregor.

*Cast:* Reginald Denny, Miriam Seegar, Harvey Clark, Lucille Ward, Carlyle Moore, Anita Louise, Norma Drew, Christiane Yves, Charles Coleman, Greta Granstedt.

A wealthy family hires a chauffeur who falls in love with the oldest daughter. Spanish version: *Asi de la Vida* (1930).

## Cock O' the Walk

April 13, 1930, 7 reels.

*P:* James Cruze. *D:* Roy William Neill. *SC:* Nagene Searle, Frances Guihan & Brian Marlow. *ST:* Arturo S. Mom. *Song:* Paul Titsworth & Ralph Bell.

*Cast:* Joseph Schildkraut, Myrna Loy, Philip Sleeman, Edward Peil, John Beck, Olive Tell, Wilfred Lucas, Frank Jonasson, Sally Long, Natalie Joyce.

A cafe violinist saves a rich girl from suicide by proposing marriage despite involvements with other women.

## The Big Fight

May 11, 1930, 7 reels.

*P:* James Cruze. *D:* Walter Lang. *SC:* Walter Woods, from the play by Milton Herbert Gropper & Max Marcin. *PH:* Jackson Rose. *Mus:* Lynn Cowan & Paul Titsworth. *SD:* Fred J. Lau & W.C. Smith.

*Cast:* Lola Lane, Ralph Ince, Guinn Williams, Stepin Fetchit, Wheeler Oakman, James Eagles, Robert Emmett O'Connor, Edna Bennett, Tony Stabeneau, Larry McGrath, Frank Jonasson.

When her brother gets involved with gangsters they try to get a manicurist to cause her boxer-lover to lose a big fight. Spanish version: *La Fuerza del Querer* (1930).

## The Dude Wrangler

May 25, 1930, 6 reels.

*P:* Mrs. Wallace Reid [Dorothy Davenport] & Cliff Broughton. *D:* Richard Thorpe. *SC:* Robert N. Lee, from the book by Caroline Lockhart.

*Cast:* Lina Basquette, George Duryea [Tom Keene/Richard Powers], Francis X. Bushman, Clyde Cook, Margaret Seddon, Ethel Wales, Wilfred North, Alice Davenport, Virginia Sale, Julia Swayne Gordon, Louis Payne, Fred Parker, Aileen Carlyle, Jack Richardson.

The owner of a dude ranch and a guest are at odds over a pretty girl who breeds polo ponies. Reissued by Pathe.

## Rogue of the Rio Grande

July 7, 1930, 7 reels.

*P:* George W. Weeks. *D:* Spencer Gordon Bennet. *SC:* Oliver Drake. *Songs:* Herbert Meyers & Oliver Drake. *Supv:* Cliff Broughton. *SD:* Alfred M. Granich & Jack Gregor.

*Cast:* Jose Bohr, Myrna Loy, Raymond Hatton, Carmelita Geraghty, Walter Miller, Gene Morgan, William T. Burt, Florence Dudley.

The notorious bandit El Malo romances a pretty dancer and proves the local sheriff is a crook.

## Once a Gentleman

July 13, 1930, 9 reels

*P-D:* James Cruze. *SC:* Walter Woods & Maude Fulton. *ST:* Frank Worts. *PH:* Jackson Rose. *SD:* W.C. Smith & Fred J. Lau.

*Cast:* Edward Everett Horton, Lois Wilson, Francis X. Bushman, King Baggot, Emerson Treacy, George Fawcett, Frederick Sullivan, Gertrude Short, Estelle Bradley, William J. Holmes, Cyril Chadwick, Evelyn Pierce, William O'Brien, Charles Coleman.

A butler goes on vacation, is mistaken for a rich man and falls in love with a pretty widow.

## Symphony of Two Flats

July 30, 1930, 86 minutes.

*P:* Michael Balcon. *D:* V. Gareth Gundry. *SC:* V. Gareth Gundry & Angus Macphail, from the play by Ivor Novello.

*Cast:* Ivor Novello, Jacqueline Logan, Cyril Ritchard, Rene Clama, Minnie Rayner, Maidel Anderson, Clifford Heatherly, Ernest A. Dagnoll, Alex Scott-Gatty, Jack Payne & BBC Dance Band.

A blind composer enters a music contest and his wife will not tell him he lost. Filmed in England in American and British versions and in the latter the leading lady was Benita Hume.

## Reno

October 12, 1930, 7 reels.

*P:* George W. Weeks. *D:* George J. Crone. *SC:* Harry Chandlee & Douglas W. Churchill, from the novel by Cornelius Vanderbilt, Jr. *Song:* Ben Bard & Leslie Barton. *SD:* Jack Gregor.

*Cast:* Ruth Roland, Montagu Love, Kenneth Thomson, Sam Hardy, Alyce McCormick, Edward Hearn, Doris Lloyd, Judith Vosselli, Virginia Ainsworth, Beulah Monroe, Douglas Scott, Emmett King, Henry Hall, Gayne Whitman.

On her way to Reno with her small son to get a divorce, a woman meets a former sweetheart.

## The Costello Case

October 19, 1930, 7 reels.

*P:* James Cruze & Samuel Zierler. *D:* Walter Lang. *SC:* F. McGrew Willis. *PH:* Harry Jackson. *AD:* Robert E. Lee. *SD:* W.C. Smith. *Asst Dir:* Bernard McEveety.

*Cast:* Tom Moore, Lola Lane, Roscoe Karns, Wheeler Oakman,

Dorothy Vernon, Jack Richardson, William Lawrence, M.K. Wilson

A policeman tries to solve a murder case and he helps the chief suspect to get a job and go straight.

## Hollywood, Ciudad De Ensueno

Hollywood, City of Illusion, 1931. *D:* George J. Crone. *SC:* Miguel de Zarranga. *ST-Supv:* Jose Bohr. *PH:* Harry Jackson. *Asst Dir:* Arthur Black. *Mus Dir:* Carlos Molina.

*Cast:* Jose Bohr, Lia Tora, Donald Reed, Nancy Drexel, Enrique Acosta, Elena Landeros, Cesar Vanoni, Lloyd Ingraham.

Because of his resemblance to a film favorite, a South American actor cannot get work in Hollywood. Reissued in 1934. Filmed in Hollywood with a Spanish soundtrack.

## Jaws of Hell

January 11, 1931, 72 minutes. *P:* Michael Balcon. *D:* Maurice Elvey & Milton Rosmer. *SC:* Robert Stevenson, Milton Rosmer & Angus Mcphail. *ST:* W.P. Lipscomb, V. Gareth Gundry & Boyd Cable, from the poem "The Charge of the Light Brigade" by Alfred Lord Tennyson. *PH:* James Wilson & Percy Strong.

*Cast:* Cyril McLaughlin, Benita Hume, Alf Goddard, Miles Mander, Robert Holmes, Betty Bolton, Walt Patch, Harold Huth, J. Fisher White, Henry Mollison, H. St. Barbe West, Ros Ranevsky, Wallace Bosco, Marian Drada, Eugene Leahy.

In 1854 a disgraced army man reenlists as a private and captures a spy. Filmed in Great Britain and released there in 1928 as *Balaclava* and reissued there in April, 1930, with sound.

## Damaged Love

January 25, 1931, 69 minutes. *P:* Louis Weiss. *D:* Irvin Willat. *SC:* Frederick & Fanny Hatton & Thomas W. Broadhurst, from the play by Thomas W. Broadhurst.

*Cast:* June Collyer, Charles Starrett, Eloise Taylor, Betty Garde, Charles Trowbridge.

When his wife lavishes her affections on their new baby, a husband finds a lover.

## Swanee River

February 8, 1931, 50 minutes. *P:* George W. Weeks. *D:* Raymond Cannon. *SC:* Arthur Hoerl. *ST:* Barbara Chambers Wood. *PH:* William Nobles. *ED:* Harry Webb-Douglas. *Supv:* Harry S. Webb. *Song:* Harry Woods & Mort Dixon.

*Cast:* Grant Withers, Thelma Todd, Philo McCullough, Walter Miller, Palmer Morrison, Robert Frazer, The Jubilee Singers.

A northern engineer working on a dam project in Tennessee is falsely accused of murder.

## Mounted Fury

February 20, 1931, 63 minutes. *P:* George W. Weeks. *D:* Stuart Paton. *SC:* Betty Burbridge. *SD:* Earl N. Crane. *Supv:* Roy Davidge.

*Cast:* John Bowers, Blanche Mehaffey, Robert Ellis, Frank Rice, Lina Basquette, John Ince, George Regas, Lloyd Whitlock, Jack Trent.

A mountie loses his sweetheart to his best buddy, who is later accused of murdering a trapper for his wife.

## Air Police

March 22, 1931, 63 minutes. *P:* George W. Weeks. *D:* Stuart

Charles Starrett, Eloise Taylor and Betty Garde in *Damaged Love* (Sono Art–World Wide, 1931).

Paton. *SC:* Bennett Cohen. *ST:* Arthur Hoerl. *PH:* William Nobles. *ED:* Harry Webb-Douglas.

    *Cast:* Kenneth Harlan, Charles Delaney, Josephine Dunn, Richard Cramer, Tom London, George Chesebro, Arthur Thalasso.

    A lawman plans to avenge the death of his partner who was killed by smugglers.

## Just for a Song

April 26, 1931, 56 minutes.

    *P:* Michael Balcon. *D-SC:* V. Gareth Gundrey. *ST:* Desmond Carter.

    *Cast:* Lillian Davies, Roy Royston, Constance Carpenter, Cyril Ritchard, Nick Adams, Dick Henderson, Syd Crossley, Rebla, Mangan Tillerettes, Syd Seymour's Mad Hatters.

A singer is used by a jealous agent to break up another act. Produced in England in 1930 by Gainsborough with a color sequence.

## In Old Cheyenne

May 3, 1931, 60 minutes.

    *P:* George W. Weeks. *D:* Stuart Paton. *SC:* Betty Burbridge. *ST:* Bennett Cohen. *PH:* William Nobles. *ED:* Carl Himm. *SD:* Ralph M. Like.

    *Cast:* Rex Lease, Dorothy Gulliver, Jay Hunt, Harry Woods, Harry Todd, Slim Whitaker, Pete Morrison, Ben Corbett, Pee Wee Holmes, Hank Bell, Blackie Whiteford.

    A horse is blamed for the rustling actually done by a dishonest ranch foreman.

# First Aid

July 12, 1931, 82 minutes.

*P:* Ralph M. Like. *D:* Stuart Paton. *SC:* Michael L. Simmons. *PH:* Jules Cronjager. *ED:* Carl Himm. *SD:* Earl M. Crane & Ralph M. Like. *Supv:* Cliff Broughton. *Asst Dir:* Wilfred E. Black.

*Cast:* Grant Withers, Marjorie Beebe, Wheeler Oakman, Donald Keith, William Desmond, Paul Panzer, George Chesebro, Ernie Adams, Billy Gilbert, Stuart Hall, Harry Shutan.

Trying to reform, an alcoholic doctor falls in love with a taxi dancer whose brother is mixed up with gangsters.

# Hell Bent for Frisco

July 12, 1931, 71 minutes.

*P:* George W. Weeks. *D:* Stuart Paton. *SC:* Arthur Hoerl. *PH:* Jules Cronjager. *ED:* Carl Himm. *SD:* Earl M. Crane & Ralph M. Like.

*Cast:* Vera Reynolds, Charles Delaney, Carroll Nye, Wesley Barry, William Desmond, Edmund Burns, Reed Howes, Richard Cramer, George Regas, Tom O'Brien, Charles Craig.

A gangster frames a policeman who has fallen in love with his girlfriend and the lawman plots revenge.

# Is There Justice?

September 20, 1931, 60 minutes.

*P:* George W. Weeks. *D:* Stuart Paton. *SC:* Betty Burbridge. *SD:* Ralph M. Like. *Supv:* Cliff Broughton.

*Cast:* Rex Lease, Blanche Mehaffey, Henry B. Walthall, Robert Ellis, Helen Foster, Joseph Girard, Ernie Adams, Richard Cramer, John Ince, Walter Brennan.

When his innocent sister dies in jail, a reporter sets out to frame the judge's daughter.

# Neck and Neck

November 8, 1931, 63 minutes.

*P:* George W. Weeks. *D:* Richard Thorpe. *SC:* Betty Burbridge. *PH:* Jules Cronjager. *ED:* Viola Roehl. *SD:* Earl M. Crane & Ralph M. Like.

*Cast:* Glenn Tryon, Vera Reynolds, Stepin Fetchit, Walter Brennan, Lafe McKee, Fern Emmett, Rosita Butler, Carroll Nye, Richard Cramer, Gene Morgan, Lloyd Whitlock.

Trying to impress a girl, a salesman claims he is wealthy and the owner of a famous racehorse.

# South of Santa Fe

January 8, 1932, 60 minutes.

*P:* Trem Carr. *D-ED:* Bert Glennon. *SC:* George A. Durlam. *PH:* Archie Stout. *Asst Dir:* Paul Malvern. *Sets:* E.R. Hickson.

*Cast:* Bob Steele, Janis Elliott, Eddie Dunn, Chris-Pin Martin, Allan Garcia, Jack Clifford, Bob Burns, Hank Bell, Ed Brady, Slim Whitaker, John Elliott, Buddy Wood [Gordon DeMain].

A cowboy fights an outlaw gang on the Mexican border and falls in love with a murdered rancher's daughter.

# Law of the West

March 20, 1932, 50 minutes.

*P:* Trem Carr. *D-SC:* Robert North Bradbury. *PH:* Archie Stout & William Cline. *ED:* Charles Hunt. *SD:* John Stransky. *Prod Mgr:* Paul Malvern. *Tech Dir:* E.R. Hickson.

*Cast:* Bob Steele, Nancy Drexel, Ed Brady, Hank Bell, Charles West, Earl Dwire, Dick Dickinson, Rose Plummer, Frank Ellis.

Kidnapped by outlaws as a boy, a young man ends up facing his lawman father in a showdown.

# Riders of the Desert

May 27, 1932, 63 minutes.

*P:* Trem Carr. *D:* Robert North Bradbury. *SC:* Wellwyn Totman. *PH:* Archie Stout. *ED:* Carl L. Pierson. *SD:* John Stransky. *Prod Mgr:* Paul Malvern. *Tech Dir:* E.R. Hickson.

*Cast:* Bob Steele, Gertrude Messinger, Al St. John, George Hayes, John Elliott, Horace B. Carpenter, Joe Dominguez, Greg Whitespear, Louise Craver, Tex O'Neil, Earl Dwire.

A ranger goes after an outlaw gang plaguing ranchers.

# The Man from Hell's Edges

May 29, 1932, 63 minutes.

*P:* Trem Carr. *D-SC:* Robert North Bradbury. *PH:* William Cline. *ED:* Carl L. Pierson. *SD:* John Stransky. *Prod Mgr:* Paul Malvern. *Sets:* E.R. Hickson.

*Cast:* Bob Steele, Nancy Drexel, Julian Rivero, Robert Homans, George Hayes, Pee Wee Holmes, Earl Dwire, Dick Dickinson, Blackie Whiteford, Bud Osborne, Blackjack Ward, Roy Bucko, Ray Henderson, Jack Evans, Duke Green, Buck Carey.

After he gets out of prison a young man goes to a remote town where he becomes the deputy sheriff.

# Bachelor's Folly

June 24, 1932, 70 minutes.

*P:* Michael Balcon. *D:* T. Hayes Hunter. *SC:* Angus McPhail & Robert Stevenson, from the play *The Calendar* by Edgar Wallace. *PH:* Bernard J. Knowles & Alex Bryce. *ED:* Bryan Wallace & Ivan Dalrymple. *SD:* Harold King.

*Cast:* Herbert Marshall, Edna Best, Gordon Harker, Anne Gray, Nigel Bruce, Alfred Drayton, Leslie Perrins, Allan Aynesworth, Melville Cooper.

Blamed for losing a big race, a horseman is aided by his ex-convict butler in proving his innocence. Produced in Great Britain and released there in 1931 by Gainsborough-British Lion.

# The Sign of Four

July 22, 1932, 74 minutes.

*P:* Basil Dean. *D:* Rowland V. Lee & Graham Cutts. *SC:* W.P. Lipscomb, from the novel by Arthur Conan Doyle. *PH:* Robert G. Martin & Robert De Grass. *ED:* Otto Ludwig.

*Cast:* Arthur Wontner, Isla Bevan, Ian Fleming, Gilbert Davis, Graham Soutten, Edgar Norfolk, Herbert Lomas, Claire Greet, Miles Malleson, Roy Emerton, Togo, Kynaston Reeves, Ben Soutten, Moore Marriott, Mr. Burnhett.

Sherlock Holmes and Dr. Watson investigate a murder perpetrated for revenge and jewels. Produced in Great Britain by ARP (Radio).

# The Last Mile

August 26, 1932, 75 minutes.

*P:* E.W. Hammons. *D:* Sam Bischoff. *SC:* Seton I. Miller, from the play by John Wexley. *PH:* Arthur Edeson. *ED:* Rose Loewinger. *AD:* Ralph DeLacy. *Mus:* Val Burton. *Asst Dir:* Edwin L. Marin.

*Cast:* Preston Foster (John "Killer" Mears), Harold Phillips (Richard Walters), George E. Stone (Joe Berg), Noel Madison (D'Amoro), Alan Roscoe (Kirby), Paul Fix (Eddie Werner), Al Hill (Fred Major), Daniel L. Haynes (Vincent "Sonny" Jackson), Frank Sheridan (Warden Frank Lewis), Alec B. Francis (Father O'Connor), Edward Van Sloan (Rabbi), Louise Carter

(Mrs. Walters), Ralph Theodore (Principal Keeper Pat Callahan), Jack Kennedy (Michael O'Flaherty), Albert J. Smith (Deathouse Guard Drake), William Scott (Peddie), Kenneth Mac-Donald (Guard Harris), Walter Walker (Governor Blaine), Francis McDonald (Holdup Man).

Circumstantial evidence has sent Richard Walters (Harold Phillips) to death row after he accidentally shot his partner during a gas station holdup. The holdup men got away, and the shooting was made to appear that Walters and his partner had quarreled. Walters arrives at the death house and is introduced to the other inmates: Killer Mears (Preston Foster), D'Amoro (Noel Madison), Kirby (Alan Roscoe), Major (Al Hill), insane Eddie Werner (Paul Fix), Sonny Jackson (Daniel L. Haynes), a black man, and Joe Berg (George E. Stone), who is about to be electrocuted. A Rabbi (Edward Van Sloan) prepares Berg for the electric chair, but Walters loses control when the execution occurs. As time passes Walters hopes for a reprieve, but none arrives, and on the day of his scheduled execution, he is visited by a priest (Alec B. Francis). As the priest is leaving Mears is able to overpower sadistic guard Drake (Albert J. Smith) and take his gun. He sets all the other men free except Werner and he holds the priest hostage as well as the other guards he captures, including the warden's (Frank Sheridan) brother-in-law Pat Callahan (Ralph Theodore), the chief death-house guard. In the fracas Jackson is killed by one of the guards. Mears demands a car and four hours head-start, promising the warden he will set his hostages free when he makes a clean getaway. As the uprising is taking place two holdup men are chased by the police and killed when their car crashes, but the law finds the evidence on them to clear Walters. Meanwhile Majors is killed by machine gun fire, and as a warning to the warden that he means business Mears shoots Drake. When the warden refuses to give into his demands, Mears kills Callahan although he has set free another guard, Flaherty (Jack Kennedy). The warden then uses bombs to blow up the cell-block, and more prisoners and guards are killed. When Mears threatens to kill the priest, D'Amoro (Noel Madison) tries to stop him, and Mears shoots him as Walters gets in the line of fire from the police to protect Mears. By now the warden has received a reprieve for Walters and when Mears hears the news he voluntarily lets himself be shot by the guards in order to stop the bloodshed so that Walters can be set free.

Although this "Powerful, if shuddery" (*Photoplay*) version of the 1930 John Wexley play was a grim affair, it greatly toned down the material from the original stage work. Wexley had based his play on executed death-row inmate Robert Blake's essay "The Law Takes Its Toll," and it opened on Broadway early in 1930, making a star of Spencer Tracy as Killer Mears. James Bell played Richard Walters while Howard Phillips, who played Walters in the screen version, was Fred Mayor. When the play opened that summer in San Francisco, it helped launch Clark Gable to stardom for his work as Mears while Paul Fix played the insane Eddie Werner, a part he repeated in the movie.

*The Last Mile* is the only sound film directed by Sam Bischoff, who functioned as a producer at World Wide, and earlier at Tiffany, and was a partner in K.B.S. Productions. Preston

Foster deftly handled the role of the complex Killer Mears, and the rest of the cast is admirable. There are many memorable moments in the film: Joe Berg (George E. Stone) trying to sing "My Blue Heaven" as he walks to the electric chair; guards Drake (Albert J. Smith) and Callahan (Ralph Theodore) pleading for their lives; and the warden (Frank Sheridan) questioning the death penalty by asking, "I wonder if they know afterwards if they've been punished?" When the movie was first released it contained a self-penned prologue by Sing Sing Prison warden Lewis E. Lawes condemning capital punishment. The prologue was dropped when the film was reissued by Astor Pictures in the late 1940s.

In 1952 Robert Keith played Killer Mears in a "Kraft Theatre" presentation of *The Last Mile* on NBC-TV, and in 1959 Vanguard Pictures remade *The Last Mile* with Mickey Rooney as Mears; it was released through United Artists. Finally the play, which was banned in England in 1931, was done there on TV in 1967 starring Harry H. Corbett and Neil McCallum.

## Texas Buddies

October 19, 1932, 63 minutes.
*P:* Trem Carr. *D-SC:* Robert North Bradbury. *PH:* Archie Stout. *ED:* Carl L. Pierson. *Prod Mgr:* Paul Malvern. *SD:* John Stransky. *Sets:* E.R. Hickson.
*Cast:* Bob Steele, Nancy Drexel, Francis McDonald, Harry Semels, George Hayes, Dick Dickinson, Slade Hurlbert, Bill Dyer, Earl Dwire, Henry Rocquemore, Si Jenks, Artie Ortego, Herman Hack.

Returning home from the war, a man ends up tracking down payroll robbers.

## Those We Love

September 13, 1932, 76 minutes.
*D:* Robert Florey. *SC: F.* Hugh Herbert, from the play by George Abbott & S.K. Lauren. *PH:* Arthur Edeson. *ED:* Rose Loewinger. *Mus:* Val Burton.
*Cast:* Mary Astor, Kenneth MacKenna, Lilyan Tashman, Hale Hamilton, Earle Foxe, Tommy Conlan, Forrester Harvey, Virginia Sale, Pat O'Malley, Harvey Clark, Cecil Cunningham, Edwin Maxwell.

A young wife stands by her husband despite his affair with another woman.

## The Crooked Circle

September 23, 1932, 70 minutes.
*P:* William Sistrom. *D:* H. Bruce Humberstone. *SC:* Ralph Spence & Tim Whelan. *PH:* Robert B. Kurrle. *ED:* Doane Harrison. *AD:* Paul Roe Crawley. *Mus:* Val Burton. *SD:* William Fox.
*Cast:* Ben Lyon, ZaSu Pitts, James Gleason, Irene Purcell, C. Henry Gordon, Raymond Hatton, Roscoe Karns, Berton Churchill, Spencer Charters, Robert Frazer, Ethel Clayton, Frank Reicher, Christian Rub, Paul Panzer, Tom Kennedy.

When a secret society meets to act on a resignation, their senior member is found murdered.

## Son of Oklahoma

October 26, 1932, 63 minutes.
*P:* Trem Carr. *D:* Robert North Bradbury. *SC:* Burl Tuttle & George Hull. *PH:* Archie Stout. *ED:* Carl L. Pierson. *SD:* John Stransky. *Prod Mgr:* Paul Malvern. *Sets:* E.R. Hickson.
*Cast:* Bob Steele, Josie Sedgwick, Robert Homans, Julian Rivero, Carmen LaRoux, Earl Dwire, Henry Rocquemore, Jack Perrin, Si Jenks, Jack

Kirk, Herman Hack, Dick Dickinson, Jack Evans, Silvertip Baker.

A cowpoke searches for his parents, a lawman and a saloon woman.

## False Faces

November 3, 1932, 83 minutes.
*P:* E.W. Hammons. *D:* Lowell Sherman. *SC:* Kubec Glamon & Llewellyn Hughes. *PH:* R.O. Singer & Theodore McCord. *ED:* Rose Loewinger. *Mus:* Val Burton. *Sets:* Ralph DeLacy.

*Cast:* Lowell Sherman, Peggy Shannon, Lila Lee, Berton Churchill, David Landau, Harold Waldridge, Geneva Mitchell, Oscar Apfel, Miriam Seegar, Joyce Compton, Nance O'Neil, Edward Martindel, Purnell B. Pratt, Ken Maynard, Barbara Bedford, Olive Tell.

A noted surgeon bungles a major operation and is exposed as a quack.

## Breach of Promise

November 23, 1932, 67 minutes.
*P:* E.W. Hammons. *D:* Paul Stein. *SC:* Benjamin Verscheser, John Goodrich & Anthony Veiller, from the story "Obscurity" by Rupert Hughes. *PH:* Art Miller. *ED:* Charles Kraft. *SD:* William Fox.

*Cast:* Chester Morris, Mae Clarke, Mary Doran, Theodore Von Eltz, Elizabeth Patterson, Charles Middleton, Lucille La Verne, Eddie Borden, Edward LeSaint, Alan Roscoe, Harriett Lorraine, Philo McCullough, Tom McGuire.

An abused young girl falsely accuses a politician of molesting her.

## Trailing the Killer

December 2, 1932, 64 minutes.
*P:* B.F. Zeidman. *AP:* Charles Hunt. *D:* Herman C. Raymaker. *SC:* Jackson Richards. *SD:* W.C. Smith. *PH:* Pliny Goodfriend. *Mus:* Oscar Potoker. *Prod Mgr:* Louis Rantz.

*Cast:* Francis McDonald, Heinie Conklin, Jose De La Cruz, Pedro Regas, Tom London, Caesar the Wolf Dog.

Canadian made story of a wolf dog falsely accused of killing his master. Also known as *Call of the Wilderness*.

## Uptown New York

December 10, 1932, 80 minutes.
*P:* E.W. Hammons. *D:* Victor Schertzinger. *SC:* Warren B. Duff, from the story "Uptown Woman" by Vina Delmar. *PH:* Norbert Brodine. *ED:* Rose Loewinger. *SD:* Hans Weeren. *Mus:* Val Burton.

*Cast:* Jack Oakie, Shirley Grey, Leon [Ames] Waycoff, George Cooper, Lee Moran, Alexander Carr, Raymond Hatton, Henry Armetta.

A vending machine owner marries a girl not realizing she loves a doctor.

## Hypnotized

December 17, 1932, 70 minutes.
*D:* Mack Sennett. *SC:* John A. Waldron, Harry McCoy, Earle Rodney & Gene Towne. *ST:* Mack Sennett & Arthur Ripley. *PH:* John W. Boyle & George Unhotz. *ED:* William Hornbeck & Francis Lyon.

*Cast:* Moran & Mack, Charlie Murray, Maria Alba, Wallace Ford, Ernest Torrence, Marjorie Beebe, Herman Bing, Alexander Carr, Luis Alberni, Harry Schultz, Matt McHugh, Mitchell Harris, Nona Mozelle, Hattie McDaniel, Genee Boutell, Anne Nagel, Marion Weldon.

An elephant trainer wins a sweepstakes ticket coveted by a wicked professor.

Poster for *Come On, Tarzan* (World Wide, 1932).

## Dynamite Ranch

December 22, 1932, 60 minutes.
   *P:* Burt Kelly, Sam Bischoff &

William Saal. *D:* Forrest Sheldon. *SC:*
Barry Barringer. *PH:* Ted McCord.
*ED:* David Berg. *Sets:* Ralph DeLacy.
   *Cast:* Ken Maynard, Ruth Hall,

Alan Roscoe, Arthur Hoyt, Martha Mattox, Al Smith, George Pearce, John Beck, Jack Perrin, Edmund Cobb, Lafe McKee, Cliff Lyons, Charles LeMoyne, Kermit Maynard, Tarzan.

After he is blamed for a train robbery, a cowboy breaks out of jail to catch the culprits.

## Come on, Tarzan

January 4, 1932, 61 minutes.

*P:* Burt Kelly, Sam Bischoff & William Saal. *D-SC:* Alan James. *PH:* Ted McCord. *ED:* Dave Berg. *Sets:* Ralph DeLacy. *Supv:* Irving Starr.

*Cast:* Ken Maynard, Merna Kennedy, Kate Campbell, Roy Stewart, Bob Kortman, Niles Welch, Ben Corbett, Jack Rockwell, Nelson McDowell, Jack Mower, Edmund Cobb, Robert Walker, Slim Whitaker, Hank Bell, Jim Corey, Bud McClure, Al Taylor, Blackjack Ward, Tarzan.

A ranch foreman feuds with his female boss and tries to track horse thieves.

## The Death Kiss

January 28, 1933, 75 minutes.

*P:* Burt Kelly, Samuel Bishoff & William Saal. *D:* Edwin L. Marin. *SC:* Barry Barringer & Gordon Kahn, from the novel by Madelon St. Denis. *PH:* Norbert Brodine. *ED:* Rose Loewinger. *AD:* Ralph DeLacy. *SD:* Hans Weeren. *Mus:* Val Burton.

*Cast:* David Manners (Franklyn Drew), Adrienne Ames (Marcia Lane), Bela Lugosi (Joseph Steiner), John Wray (Detective Lieutenant Sheehan), Vince Barnett (Officer Gulliver), Alexander Carr (Leoinid Grossmith), Edward Van Sloan (Tom Avery), Harold Minjir (Howell), Barbara Bedford (Script Girl), Al Hill (Assistant Director), Wade Boteler (Sergeant Hilliker), Lee Moran (Todd), Alan Roscoe (Chambers), Mona Maris (Agnes Avery), Edmund Burns (Myles Brent), James Donlan (Hill), King Baggott (Head Juicer), Wilson Benge (Doorman), Eddy Chandler (Mechanic), Harry Strang (Gaffer), Eddie Roland (Bill), Frank O'Connor (Policeman), Paul Porcasi (Makeup Man), Clarence Muse (Shoe Shine Man), Albert Conti (Florist).

Movie actor Myles Brent (Edmund Burns) is killed on the set of a film called *The Death Kiss* being shot at Ton Art Studios. Policeman Sheehan (John Wray) is called into the case, and the leading suspect is costar Marcia Lane (Adrienne Ames), Brent's ex-wife and beneficiary of his $200,000 insurance policy. The film's author, mystery writer Franklyn Drew (David Manners), is in love with Marcia and tries to get the lawman off her trail to little avail. Meanwhile studio chief Grossmith (Alexander Carr), who also loves Marcia, is worried about getting the picture finished, as is studio manager Joseph Steiner (Bela Lugosi). The film's director, Tom Avery (Edward Van Sloan), is reluctant to reshoot the final scene with a double but finally agrees to do so. Studio guard Gulliver (Vince Barnett) catches Chalmers (Alan Roscoe)—a former employee with a grudge against Brent—with a gun, but it has not been fired. Later he is found dead at his bungalow by Drew and Gulliver and the police arrest Marcia for the crimes, saying she hired Chalmers to kill Brent and then murdered Chalmers herself. Going through Brent's clothes, Drew learns he was having an affair with a married woman and traces them to the Cliffside Inn the night before, where the late actor had a fight with the woman's irate husband. Back on the set, Marcia, in police custody, is prepared to redo the final scene in the picture when Drew deduces who committed the murders. He tells his suspicions to Sheehan but is overheard by the killer over an open microphone. When the killer has the lights extinguished on the set and tries to escape, he is trapped in the catwalks above the studio and falls to his death. The motive for the killings was his wife's affair with Brent. Marcia is set free, and Drew asks Steiner for a new contract for having solved the case.

With its title and three cast members (Bela Lugosi, David Manners, Edward Van Sloan) from *Dracula* (1931), *The Death Kiss* was advertised as a horror film when, in fact, it is a slow-moving but meticulous murder mystery. Today its chief interest lies in the fact that it was filmed at the California Tiffany Studios, whose backlot became the chief set of the picture itself. The film is actually as much of a spoof on movie-making as it is a who-dunit. Alexander Carr as the studio chief exclaims "that's gonna cost me a fortune—what a calamity" when he learns that his leading man has been murdered. When the police want to interview the leading lady, the call to her goes through a chain of command from studio manager to gaffer. The movie also abounds with red herrings although the actual killer is not easily spotted.

## Drum Taps

February 26, 1933, 61 minutes.

*P:* Burt Kelly, Sam Bischoff & William Saal. *D:* J.P. McGowan. *SC:* Alan James. *PH:* Jack Young. *ED:* Dave Berg. *SD:* Hans Weeren. *Sets:* Ralph DeLacy. *Supv:* Irving Starr.

*Cast:* Ken Maynard, Dorothy Dix, Junior Coghlan, Hooper Atchley, Charles Stevens, Al Bridge, Harry Semels, Jim Mason, Slim Whitaker, Kermit Maynard, Neal Hart, Art Mix, Leo Willis, Los Angeles Boy Scout Troop 107, Lloyd Ingraham, Merrill McCormack, Jack Rockwell, Fred Burns, Blackjack Ward, Bud McClure, Pascale Perry, Tex Palmer, Tarzan.

A cowboy helps a Boy Scout troop oppose crooks after valuable land.

## Fargo Express

March 1, 1933, 61 minutes.

*P:* Burt Kelly, Sam Bischoff & William Saal. *D:* Alan James. *SC:* Alan James & Earle Snell. *PH:* Ted McCord. *ED:* Dave Berg. *Sets:* Ralph DeLacy. *Supv:* Irving Starr.

*Cast:* Ken Maynard, Helen Mack, Roy Stewart, Paul Fix, William Desmond, Jack Rockwell, Claude Payton, Joe Rickson, Charles King, Ben Corbett, Pat Harmon, Blackjack Ward, Buck Bucko, Bud McClure, Hank Bell, Tarzan.

A cowboy tries to help a robber because he loves the young man's sister.

## Race Track

March 7, 1933, 79 minutes.

*P:* Samuel Zierler. *D:* James Cruze. *SC:* Walter Lang, Douglas Doty, Gaston Glass, Claire Carvaho & Ernest Pagano. *ST:* J. Walter Ruben & Wells Root. *PH:* Charles Schoenbaum. *ED:* Rose Loewinger. *SD:* W.C. Smith & Frederick Lau. *Assit Dir:* Gaston Glass. *Second Unit Dir:* B. Reeves Eason.

*Cast:* Leo Carrillo, Junior Coghlan, Kay Hammond, Lee Moran, Huntley Gordon, Wilfred Lucas, Joseph Girard.

A gambler becomes foster father to a boy deserted by his parents.

# The Constant Woman

May 23, 1933, 76 minutes.

*P:* E.W. Hammons. *D:* Victor Schertzinger. *SC:* Warren B. Duff & F. Hugh Herbert, from the play *Recklessness* by Eugene O'Neill. *PH:* Arthur Edeson. *ED:* Rose Loewinger. *Sets:* Ralph DeLacy.

*Cast:* Conrad Nagel, Leila Hyams, Tommy Conlan, Claire Windsor, Stanley Fields, Fred Kohler, Robert Ellis, Lionel Belmore, Alexander Carr, The Three Ambassadors, Ruth Clifford.

An actress deserts her husband and son to go East for a play and the man later learns the boy was fathered by another man. Originally called *Auction in Souls*. Reissued in 1938 by Atlantic Pictures as *Hell in a Circus*.

# A Study in Scarlet

May 26, 1933, 73 minutes.

*P:* Sam Bischoff, Burt Kelly & William Saal. *D:* Edwin L. Marin. *SC:* Robert Florey & Reginald Owen. *PH:* Arthur Edeson. *ED:* Rose Loewinger. *AD:* Ralph DeLacy. *SD:* Hans Weeren. *Mus:* Val Burton.

*Cast:* Reginald Owen (Sherlock Holmes), Anna May Wong (Mrs. Pyke), June Clyde (Eileen Forrester), Alan Dinehart (Thaddeus Merrydew), John Warburton (John Stanford), Alan Mowbray (Inspector Lestrade), Warburton Gamble (Dr. John H. Watson), J.M. Kerrigan (Jabez Wilson), Doris Lloyd (Mrs. Murphy), Billy Bevan (Will Swallow), Leila Bennett (Daffy Dolly), Wyndham Standing (Captain Pyke), Halliwell Hobbes (Dearing), Cecil Reynolds (Baker), Tetsu Komai (Ah Yet), Timpe Pigott (Mrs. Hudson).

When a member of a secret society called The Scarlet Ring commits suicide, Eileen Forrester (June Clyde) joins the group, replacing her father. At the group's meeting, led by barrister Thaddeus Merrydew (Alan Dinehart), another member, Captain Pyke (Wyndham Standing), is shot and killed and his body disappears. The next day Inspector Lestrade (Alan Mowbray) of Scotland Yard asks consulting detective Sherlock Holmes (Reginald Owen) and his associate Dr. Watson (Warburton Gamble) to look into the affair when another group member, Dearing (Halliwell Hobbes), dies and Pyke's body is recovered from the Thames River. Pyke's widow (Anna May Wong) identifies him by the ring he wore. Holmes is already involved in the case since the widow (Doris Lloyd) of the first society victim has hired him to find out why she was excluded from membership in The Scarlet Ring. When the society meets again Merrydew informs those present the Ring will disband, but since Eileen is not present Holmes and her fiancé, John Stanford (John Warburton), look for her and save her from being killed by poison gas. Baker (Cecil Reynolds), another Ring member, is killed at Pyke's remote country estate, the Grange, and Eileen receives a telegram asking her to come to the Grange. Holmes, Watson, Lestrade and Stanford follow the girl to the country house and rescue her from imprisonment there. When a servant (Tetsu Komai) tries to kill another Ring member, Jabez Wilson (J.M. Kerrigan), Holmes is able to unmask the killer.

Several writers have commented that World Wide's production of *A Study in Scarlet*, from the 1888 novel by Sir Arthur Conan Doyle, is more like an Edgar Wallace thriller than a Sherlock Holmes story. This is not far from the truth since only the Doyle characters remain in a story written by Robert Florey and actor Reginald Owen. Florey was supposed to direct the project but dropped out and was replaced by Edwin L. Marin, who had done a fine job in his directorial debut with *The Death Kiss* (q.v.). Owen, who had portrayed Dr. Watson in *Sherlock Holmes* (Fox, 1932), had hoped to play Holmes in a series of features, but by the time *A Study in Scarlet* was released, World Wide had ceased distribution of films and the feature was picked up by Fox. Despite its title, the movie is basically an original Holmes outing and a flavorful one at that. At the time of its release *Harrison's Reports* noted, "The picture has turned out a pretty good murder-mystery melodrama." The mystery motif highlights the feature and is ably supported by a fine series of performances by an outstanding cast. While purists may not be overly fond of Reginald Owen and Warburton Gamble as Holmes and Watson, there can be little argument with Alan Mowbray's work as Inspector Lestrade. June Clyde and John Warburton do well as the romantic leads, while Anna May Wong is alluring as the mysterious widow and silent screen comic Billy Bevan provides amusement as an opinionated Cockney. The movie is quite atmospheric, especially the eerie scenes at the remote Grange, country home of one of the alleged victims.

In the mid-1970s the soundtrack of *A Study in Scarlet* was released on a long-play record album on the Hudson House label, number ASIS-221. It was produced for the Adelphi Holmes Society of London, England and released in this country by Amalgamated Records.

The film's working title was *The Scarlet Ring*. When World Wide bought the rights to the Conan Doyle work it obtained only the use of the title, thus the need for an entirely new script.

## Phantom Thunderbolt

June 14, 1933, 62 minutes.

*P:* Burt Kelly, Sam Bischoff & William Saal. *D:* Alan James. *SC:* Forrest Sheldon & Betty Burbridge. *PH:* Jackson Rose. *ED:* Dave Berg. *SD:* Hans Weeren. *AD:* Ralph DeLacy. *Asst Dir:* Mike Eason. *Supv:* Irving Starr.

*Cast:* Ken Maynard (Ken Peters, the Thunderbolt Kid), Frances Lee (Judy Lane), Frank Rice (Nevady), William Gould (Red Matthews), Robert Kortman (One Shot Mallory), Frank Beal (Oldham), Bill Robyns (Norton), Wilfred Lucas (Mr. Eaton), Harry Holman (Judge Jobias Wingate), Nelson McDowell (McTavish the Undertaker), Lew Meehan, Horace B. Carpenter, Frank Ellis, Jack Rockwell (Townsmen), Tarzan (Himself).

Riding into the town of Coyote Gulch, stranger Nevady (Frank Rice) warns the locals to beware of the Thunderbolt Kid (Ken Maynard), who soon arrives riding wildly and shooting off his guns. At the Gem Restaurant, nasty One Shot Mallory (Robert Kortman) is unkind to the owner, pretty Judy Lane (Frances Lee), and he and the Kid fight. Mallory ends up being dunked in a drinking trough for horses. The town's leaders, led by Judge Wingate (Harry Holman), ask the Kid to protect their town from the marauding Matthews gang, which has been hired by a rival community, Spotted Horse, that wants a railroad franchise which will make Coyote Gulch the county seat. The Kid, whose real name is Ken Peters, agrees to take the job if Judy, who is upset at him for wrecking her cafe in the fight with Mallory, will give him three kisses. For the good of the town she finally agrees, and Ken goes to the saloon to have a showdown with Red Matthews (William Gould), leader of the gang. Red gets the drop on Ken, but Nevady, who is really Ken's partner, comes to his rescue and they run the gang out of town. Later Mallory pretends to be Ken's friend and tells him more of the gang is arriving on the stage although the passenger, whom Ken forces to strip and run away, is really Mr. Eaton (Wilfred Lucas), head of the railroad. Later, Ken tries to romance Judy, but the Matthews gang ambush him and in the fight Nevady is injured. The gang then lassoes Ken off his horse and ties him up in a shack, but he is aided in escaping by his horse Tarzan. In town Eaton, who has arrived to retrieve his clothes, agrees to give the railroad to Coyote Gulch, but Red and Mallory show up with the gang and cause a disturbance. Ken fights with Red while Eaton and the townspeople subdue the gang. When Ken whips Red, Eaton asks him to stay in town and he does so because he has won Judy's love.

*Phantom Thunderbolt* was the fifth of eight westerns Ken Maynard did for World Wide Pictures. He had just finished a series at Tiffany and this new set of sagebrush yarns were also shot on the Tiffany lot. Plotwise the movie does not take itself too seriously. At the beginning, comedy-relief Frank Rice tells a crowd that the title character, the Thunderbolt Kid already had four graveyards named after him while the local undertaker (Nelson McDowell) looks on in anticipation. Another amusing scene has Ken escaping from the bad guys by rolling down a hill in a barrel. Moving along at a fairly good clip, *Phantom Thunderbolt* gives its star plenty of time for acting, fighting, riding and romancing. This last activity is ably aided by lovely heroine Frances Lee. In fact there is a bit more romance in this outing than most of Ken's westerns. A particularly well-staged fight sequence between Maynard and villain Robert Kortman highlights the first part of the feature, and the finale fight scenes are also quite exciting. Overall, the movie is a pleasant diversion for Ken Maynard followers.

## The Lone Avenger

June 30, 1933, 61 minutes.

*P:* Burt Kelly, Sam Bischoff & William Saal. *D:* Alan James. *SC:* Forrest Sheldon & Betty Burbridge. *PH:* William Nobles. *ED:* Dave Berg. *SD:* Hans Weeren. *Sets:* Ralph DeLacy. *Supv:* Irving Starr.

*Cast:* Ken Maynard, Muriel Gordon, James Marcus, Alan Bridge, Niles Welch, William Norton Bailey, Ed Brady, Charles King, Jack Rockwell, Clarence Geldert, Lew Meehan, Horace B. Carpenter, Blackjack Ward, Bud McClure, Merrill McCormick, Robert Walker, Olin Francis, Fern Emmett, Jack Kirk, Herman Hack, Buck Morgan, Tarzan.

When crooks plan a bank panic a cowboy tries to stop them from taking over a town.

## Tombstone Canyon

July 3, 1933, 62 minutes.

*P:* Burt Kelly, Sam Bischoff & William Saal. *D:* Alan James. *SC:* Claude Rister & Earle Snell. *PH:* Ted McCord. *ED:* Dave Berg. *SD:* Hans Weeren. *Mus:* Val Burton. *Sets:* Eddie Boyle. *Settings:* Ralph DeLacy.

*Cast:* Ken Maynard, Cecilia Parker, Sheldon Lewis, Bob [Bazooka] Burns, Jack Clifford, Frank Brownlee, George Gerwing, Lafe McKee, Ed Peil Sr., George Chesebro, Tarzan.

Looking into his family background, a cowboy arrives in a locale terrorized by a masked phantom.

## Between Fighting Men

October 16, 1933, 60 minutes.
*P:* Burt Kelly, Sam Bischoff & William Saal. *D:* Forrest Sheldon. *SC:* Betty Burbridge & Forrest Sheldon. *PH:* Ted McCord. *ED:* Dave Berg. *Settings:* Ralph DeLacy.

*Cast:* Ken Maynard, Ruth Hall, Josephine Dunn, Wallace MacDonald, Albert J. Smith, Walter Law, James Bradbury, Jr., John Pratt, Jack Perrin, Charles King, Edmund Cobb, Jack Kirk, Bud McClure, Roy Bucko, Blackjack Ward, Slim Whitaker, Robert Kortman, Tarzan.

Two pals, rivals over a pretty girl, try to stop a range war between cattlemen and sheep herders.

# Spectrum Pictures

Although Spectrum Pictures was around for more than half of the 1930s, the company released only twenty-two feature films in its six-year existence. All but one of these, a French import, starred either Bill Cody or Fred Scott. Cody headlined nine features for Spectrum between 1934 and 1936, and Fred Scott did a dozen musical westerns for the company from 1936 through 1939. The twenty-one westerns done with these cowboy stars were produced by independent units and released on a states' rights basis under the Spectrum Pictures banner.

Although he had been a fairly popular second-string western star in the silent days, Bill Cody's career had declined with the talkies. It sank to its lowest ebb in the mid-1930s when he starred in a trio of wretched oaters for Robert J. Horner Productions (q.v.). Surprisingly, Cody was able to improve his genre status with the nine westerns he did for producer Ray Kirkwood, released by Spectrum. In four of these films he costarred with his young son, Bill Cody, Jr. Cheaply but competently made, the Cody westerns were fair enough entertainment, but by this time the star no longer could compete with such stalwarts as Buck Jones and Ken Maynard. Cody appeared emaciated, and the outfits he wore were too big, being crowned by an oversized stetson. His efforts in the action department were dubious, nor did he cut any kind of a romantic figure with his leading ladies. Cody was a likable enough cowboy, and it is nice to see his starring career end on a fairly upbeat note with the Spectrum series.

When Bill Cody's series for Spectrum faded into the proverbial sunset, he was replaced by singing buckaroo Fred Scott in a series initially produced by George H. Callaghan and Jed Buell. Born in 1902, Scott had been in films since 1920, and after making early talkies like *Rio Rita* (1929) and *The Grand*

*Parade* (1930), he became resident baritone at the San Francisco Opera. Through his friendship with Jed Buell, one-time head of publicity for Mack Sennett Studios, Scott landed the lead in the Spectrum series that began in the fall of 1936 with *Romance Rides the Range*, costarring Cliff Nazarro as his comedy sidekick. Nazarro was also in *The Singing Buckaroo* (1937), but for the next seven films in the series Al St. John costarred. In reviewing *The Roaming Cowboy* (1937), *Variety* noted, "Fred Scott is one of the newer western heroes, but if the pace of *Cowboy* is maintained in his subsequent efforts, it won't be difficult to build a following." Like the Cody series, the Fred Scott features were shot on the cheap, with lots of outdoor sequences, but steady direction (mostly by Sam Newfield), Scott's likable personality (abetted by Al St. John's comedy), and the star's magnificent singing voice made the Fred Scott series an entertaining one. Faulty dubbing of some of Scott's vocals mar their affect somewhat, but it is still highly pleasurable to hear him sing such songs as "Prairie Moon," "Wilder Than the Woolly West," "The Old Home Ranch," "Yellow Mellow Moon" and "Ridin' Down the Trail to Albuquerque."

Late in 1937 Jed Buell formed an association with screen comic Stan Laurel, and two of Fred Scott's starrers, *Knight of the Plains* and *Songs and Bullets* (both 1938), were billed as Stan Laurel Productions. Laurel not only served as executive producer on these oaters but also suggested comedy ideas for the scripts. By 1939, however, Buell and Laurel were no longer associated with the series, which was taken over by producer C.C. Burr, who installed Harry Harvey as Scott's sidekick in place of Al St. John. The series, however, maintained a following, and in *Two Gun Troubadour* (1939) Scott played a Zorro-like character. This plot ploy proved a success and Burr made *Ridin' the Trail* in 1939, but by the time it was ready for release Spectrum had folded. Arthur Ziehm, Inc., picked up the feature for distribution in 1940. In 1948 Scott's Spectrum features were rereleased to theatres by Albert Dezel and have been staples on television since the 1950s.

In addition to its two western series, Spectrum Pictures also released one French import, *Heroes of the Marne*, in 1939. It starred the popular actor Raimu, but Spectrum cut it by twenty-five minutes before its stateside issuance. Most likely the cuts were to make it more palatable for U.S. audiences and to somewhat muffle its anti-Teutonic sentiments.

## Frontier Days

November 15, 1934, 61 minutes.

*P:* Al Alt. *D:* Bob Hill. *SC:* James Shawkey. *ST:* Norman Springer. *PH:* Brydon Baker. *ED:* S. Roy Luby. *SD:* Frank McKenzie. *Sp Eff:* Ray Mercer. *Prog Mgr:* Ben Berk.

*Cast:* Bill Cody, Ada Ince, Wheeler Oakman, William Desmond, Bill Cody, Jr., Victor Potel, Franklyn Farnum, Lafe McKee, Bob McKenzie, Harrison Martel, Chico.

The Pinto Kid is falsely blamed for the death of a rancher.

## Reckless Buckaroo

Spectrum/Crescent, 1935, 57 minutes.

*P:* Ray Kirkwood. *D:* Harry Fraser.

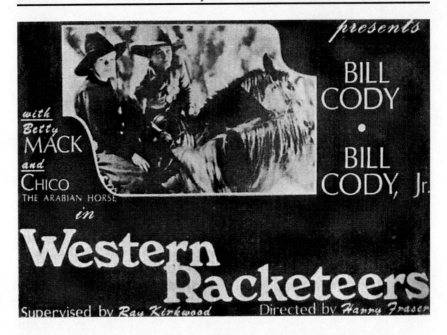

*Western Racketeers* was the title of a film Bill Cody starred in for Robert J. Horner Productions in 1935. Here the title is used on a lobby card for another Bill Cody feature, *Reckless Buckaroo* (Spectrum/Crescent, 1935). Shown are Bill Cody and his son, Bill Cody, Jr.

*SC:* Zara Tazil. *PH:* James Diamond. *ED:* Holbrook N. Todd.

    *Cast:* Bill Cody, Betty Mack, Bill Cody, Jr., Buzz Barton, Roger Williams, Edward Cassidy, Lew Meehan, Francis Walker, Budd Buster, Milburn Morante, Jack Nelson, Allen Greer, Chico.

    A prospector and a young boy aid a lawman in tracking down a gang of smugglers. Also called *Reckless Buckaroos* and sometimes advertised as *Western Racketeers*.

## Six Gun Justice

January 1, 1935, 57 minutes.
    *P:* Ray Kirkwood. *D:* Bob Hill. *SC:* Oliver Drake.

    *Cast:* Bill Cody, Ethel Jackson, Wally Wales, Donald Reed, Budd Buster, Jimmy Aubrey, Frank Moran, Ace Cain, Bud Pope, Roger Williams, Bert Young, Buck Morgan, Blackie Whiteford, Chico.

    An outlaw gang is after one of their members who has reformed and the man is helped by a marshal after the robbers.

## The Cyclone Ranger

March 20, 1935, 60 minutes.
    *P:* Ray Kirkwood. *D:* Bob Hill. *SC:* Oliver Drake. *PH:* Donald Keyes.

    *Cast:* Bill Cody, Nena Quartero, Eddie Gribbon, Solidad Jiminez, Earle Hodgins, Zara Tazil, Donald Reed,

For the 1936–37 season Ray Kirkwood Productions promised eight westerns starring Bill Cody and his son Bill Cody, Jr., for Spectrum release. When the series fizzled after *Outlaws of the Range* (1936), Kirkwood announced a series starring Donald Reed and Bobby Nelson through Gemini Pictures but it failed to materialize.

Colin Chase, Budd Buster, Jerry Ellis, Anthony Natale, Buck Morgan, Herman Hack, Chico.

An outlaw pretends to be the son of a blind woman who has befriended him.

## The Texas Rambler

May 7, 1935, 59 minutes.
*P:* Ray Kirkwood. *D:* Bob Hill. *SC:* Oliver Drake. *PH:* William Hyer.
*Cast:* Bill Cody, Catherine Cotter, Earle Hodgins, Stuart James, Mildred Rogers, Budd Buster, Roger Williams, Ace Cain, Buck Morgan, Allen Greer, Bud Pope, Chico.

A cowboy tries to aid a young woman whose ranch is coveted by crooks.

## The Vanishing Riders

July 2, 1935, 58 minutes.
*P:* Ray Kirkwood. *D:* Bob Hill. *SC:* Oliver Drake. *PH:* William Hyer. *ED:* Holbrook N. Todd.
*Cast:* Bill Cody, Ethel Jackson, Bill Cody, Jr., Wally Wales, Roger Williams, Donald Reed, Buck Morgan, Budd Buster, Ace Cain, Milburn Morante, Francis Walker, Colin Chase, Bert Young, Oscar Gahan, Bud Pope, Barney Beasley, Chico.

A cowboy and his young pal team to round up cattle rustlers.

## Lawless Border

December 11, 1935, 58 minutes.
*P:* Ray Kirkwood. *D:* John P. McCarthy. *SC:* Zara Tazil. *PH:* Robert Cline.

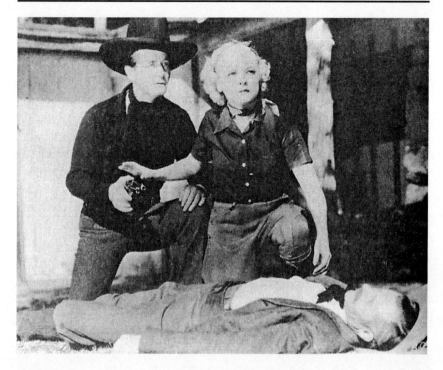

Bill Cody, Gertrude Messinger and Budd Buster in *Blazing Justice* (Spectrum, 1936).

*Cast:* Bill Cody, Molly O'Day, Martin Garralaga, Ted Adams, Jose De La Cruz, John Elliott, Merrill McCormack, Roger Williams, Wally West, Budd Buster, William McCall, Curley Baldwin, Chico.

A government agent teams with a Mexican counterpart to track down smugglers with the U.S. agent falling in love with the gang leader's sister.

## Blazing Justice

January 29, 1936, 60 minutes.

*P:* Ray Kirkwood. *D:* Al Herman. *SC:* Zarah Tazil. *PH:* Bill Hires [William Hyer]. *ED:* Holbrook N. Todd.

*Cast:* Bill Cody (Ray Healy), Gertrude Messinger (Virginia Peterson), Milt Moranti [Milburn Morante] (Pop), Budd Buster (Ed Peterson), Gordon Griffith (Max), Charles Tannen (Lew), Curley Baldwin (Sheriff), Buck Morgan (Pete), Art Mix (Shorty), Horace B. Carpenter (Marshal).

When cowboy Ray Healy (Bill Cody) sees gang leader Max (Gordon Griffith) kill a lawman following a robbery, he tries to stop his gang and ends up capturing Pete (Buck Morgan) and Shorty (Art Mix) while Max and Lew (Charles Tannen) escape. Ray is to get a $5,000 reward for catching the two outlaws and his boss gives him a $1,000 advance so he can take a holiday. As Max and Lew scheme to rob rancher Ed Peterson (Budd Buster) of the money he plans to use to pay off his ranch mortgage, Bill stops along the trail to relax. Max knocks out Peterson and takes his money and is pursued by the man's daughter Virginia (Gertrude Messinger). Max changes horses with Ray, and the girl mistakes the cowboy for the killer of her father and turns him over to the law. In town Ray is able to identify his horse and proves Max is the robber, but the badman escapes after a tussle with Ray. The cowboy decides to stay and help Virginia regain the Peterson money, coming up with a scheme to smoke Max out of hiding. A newspaper article announcing plans for Ed Peterson's funeral states that his daughter will receive a $10,000 insurance settlement at the time of the burial. Ray correctly believes this will lure Max to the Peterson ranch where he can be captured. Max and Lew arrive and try to take the money, but Bill is there with the law and, after a chase, finally subdues the badman. It is then proven the obituary was a hoax and that Ed Peterson is alive, having only been injured in the fracas with the holdup man. With the Peterson mortgage paid off, Ray proposes marriage to Virginia and she accepts.

*Blazing Justice* was the eighth of nine westerns Bill Cody did for producer Ray Kirkwood with release through Spectrum Pictures Corporation. Although somewhat crudely made on a minimal budget, the feature is a fairly pleasant one thanks to a straightforward plot, a likable cast and enough action to satisfy matinee audiences of the 1930s. Bill Cody hardly cut an impressive figure as the hero, twice beaten in fights with the much more virile villain, Gordon Griffith. At the finale fisticuffs were avoided and Cody ends up capturing Griffith by hog-tying him with a rope. Milburn Morante, billed here as Milt Moranti, supplies some vapid comedy relief as a barfly who keeps trying to capture the bad guy without success. The film is further hampered by awkward dialogue and there is little evidence that more than one take per scene was shot in putting the feature together. *Outlaws of the Range* followed *Blazing Justice* in the spring of 1936, but earlier in the year it was announced Ray Kirkwood was about to produce a new series of Bill Cody westerns. That series, however, failed to materialize and Spectrum switched its cowboy hero spot to crooner Fred Scott. One of the backers of the Cody-Spectrum series was Monarch laboratory, which apparently had a falling out with Kirkwood during the production of *Reckless Buckaroo* (1935).

## Outlaws of the Range

April 8, 1936, 59 minutes.

*P:* Ray Kirkwood. *D:* Al Herman. *SC:* Zara Tazil. *PH:* Bill Hyer. *ED:* Holbrook N. Todd.

*Cast:* Bill Cody, Catherine Cotter, Bill Cody, Jr., Gordon Griffith, William McCall, Wally West, Dick Strong, Chico.

When a rancher is murdered by rivals a drifter gets the blame.

## Romance Rides the Range

September 22, 1936, 59 minutes.

*P:* George H. Callaghan & Jed Buell. *D:* Harry Fraser. *SC:* Tom Gibson. *PH:* Robert Cline. *ED:* Arthur Brooks. *Mus:* Abe Meyer. *Songs:* Fred Stryker & Johnny Lange. *SD:* Glen Glenn.

*Cast:* Fred Scott, Marion Shilling, Cliff Nazarro, Buzz Barton, Robert Kortman, Theodore Lorch, Frank Yaconelli, Phil Dunham, Jack Evans, William Steele, Allen Greer, White King.

On a tour in the west an opera singer ends up opposing outlaws.

## The Fighting Deputy

1937, 60 minutes.

*P:* Jed Buell. *D:* Sam Newfield. *SC:* William Lively. *ST:* Bennett Cohen. *ED:* William Hess. *Mus:* Abe Meyer. *SD:* Hans Weeren. *Prod Mgr:* Bert Sternbach.

*Cast:* Fred Scott, Marjorie Beebe, Al St. John, Eddie Hollen, Charles King, Frank LaRue, Lafe McKee, Phoebe Logan, Sherry Tansey, Jack C. Smith, Jack Evans, Chick Hannon, White King.

When his lawman father is abducted, a cowboy takes over his job to round up the culprits.

## The Singing Buckaroo

March 24, 1937, 60 minutes.

*P:* George H. Callaghan & Jed Buell. *D-SC:* Tom Gibson. *PH:* Robert Domn. *ED:* Dan Milner. *Mus:* Abe Meyer. *Prod Mgr:* Lawrence Le Baron. *Asst Dir:* Gordon S. Griffith.

*Cast:* Fred Scott, William Faversham, Victoria Vinton, Cliff Nazarro, Howard Hill, Charles Kaley, Roger Williams, Dick Curtis, Lawrence LeBaron, Rose Caprino, Pinky Barnes, Carl Mathews, Slim Carey, Augie Gomez, The Singing Buckaroos, White King.

A cowboy aids a young woman whose father has been kidnapped by crooks.

## Melody of the Plains

July 7, 1937, 58 minutes.

*P:* Jed Buell. *D:* Sam Newfield. *SC:* Bennett Cohen. *PH:* Robert Cline. *ED:* William Hess. *Mus:* Abe Meyer. *Songs:* Don Swander & June Hershey. *SD:* Corson Jowett. *Prod Mgr:* William Nolte.

*Cast:* Fred Scott, Louise Small, Al St. John, Billy Lenhart, David Sharpe, Slim Whitaker, Lew Meehan, Lafe McKee, Hal Price, Bud Jamison, Carl Mathews, George Morrell, George Fiske, White King.

Thinking he has killed a rancher's son, a cowboy goes to work for the man.

## Moonlight on the Range

October 6, 1937, 60 minutes.

*P:* George H. Callaghan & Jed Buell. *D:* Sam Newfield. *SC:* Fred Myton. *ST:* Witney Williams. *ED:* William Hess. *Mus:* Abe Meyer. *SD:* Hans Weeren. *Prod Mgr:* Bert Sternbach.

*Cast:* Fred Scott, Lois January, Al St. John, Dick Curtis, Frank LaRue, Oscar Gahan, Forrest Taylor, Lew Meehan, Jimmy Aubrey, Carl Mathews, Wade Walker, William McCall, Shorty Miller, Jack Evans, Rudy Sooter, Edward Cassidy, Tex Palmer, George Morrell, Sherry Tansey, Steve Clark, Hank Worden, Herman Hack.

After his half-brother kills his best friend, a man hunts down the rustler.

## The Roaming Cowboy

December 1, 1937, 60 minutes.

*P:* Jed Buell. *AP:* George H. Callahan. *SC:* Fred Myton. *PH:* William Hyer. *ED:* William Hess. *Mus:* Abe Meyer. *Prod Mgr:* Bert Sternbach.

*Cast:* Fred Scott, Lois January, Al St. John, Forrest Taylor, Roger Williams, Richard Cramer, Oscar Gahan, Buddy Cox, Art Miles, George Chesebro, Rudy Sooter, Lew Meehan, Slim Whitaker, Edward Cassidy, Carl Mathews, Jack Evans.

When a rancher is murdered, two cowboys find themselves in the middle of a range war.

# The Ranger's Roundup

February 9, 1938, 57 minutes.
> *P:* Jed Buell. *AP:* Bert Sternbach. *D:* Sam Newfield. *SC:* George Plympton. *PH:* William Hyer. *ED:* Robert Jahns. *Mus:* Lew Porter. *SD:* Hans Weeren.
> *Cast:* Fred Scott, Al St. John, Christine McIntyre, Earle Hodgins, Syd Chatan, Steve Ryan, Karl Hackett, Carl Mathews, Dick Cramer, Lew Porter, Jimmy Aubrey, Taylor MacPeters [Cactus Mack], Steve Clark, Sherry Tansey, Milburn Morante, Chick Hannon.

An undercover agent hopes to stop outlaws by joining a medicine show.

# Knight of the Plains

March 29, 1938, 57 minutes.
> *P:* Jed Buell. AP: Bert Sternbach. *EP:* Stan Laurel. *D:* Sam Newfield. *SC:* Fred Myton. *PH:* Mack Stengler. *ED:* Robert Jahns. *Mus:* Lew Porter. *SD:* Hans Weeren.
> *Cast:* Fred Scott, Al St. John, Marion Weldon, John Merton, Richard Cramer, Frank LaRue, Lafe McKee, Emma Tansey, Steve Clark, Budd Buster, Carl Mathews, Jimmy Aubrey, Sherry Tansey, Bob Burns, Cactus Mack, Olin Francis, George Morrell, Tex Palmer.

When land grabbers and rustlers harass settlers a cowboy comes to their rescue.

# Songs and Bullets

May 20, 1938, 58 minutes.
> *P:* Jed Buell. *AP:* Bert Sternbach. *EP:* Stan Laurel. *D:* Sam Newfield. *SC:* George Plympton & Joseph O'Donnell. *ST:* George Plympton. *PH:* Mack Stengler. *ED:* Robert Jahns. *Mus:* Abe Meyer. *SD:* Hans Weeren. *Songs:* Johnny Lange & Lew Porter.

> *Cast:* Fred Scott (Melody Smith), Al St. John (Fuzzy), Alice Ardell (Jeanette Du Mont), Charles King (Sheriff), Karl Hackett (Harry Skelton), Frank LaRue (Morgan), Richard Cramer (Kelly), Sherry Tansey, Carl Mathews (Gang Members), Jimmy Aubrey (Pete), Budd Buster (Zeke), Lew Porter (Piano Player).

Riding into the town of Dry Gulch, Melody Smith (Fred Scott) and his pal Fuzzy (Al St. John) are accused of cattle rustling by the local sheriff (Charles King). Their innocence is proved, however, by the owner of the local hotel, Morgan (Frank LaRue), who has hired them as musicians to entertain his guests. Melody confides to Morgan that he has really come to the area to investigate the murder of his uncle, who was killed by a highly unusual kind of bullet. These bullets were split and were known as "dumdum 45s." When the new school teacher, Jeanette Du Mont (Alice Ardell) arrives in town most of the men turn out to greet her, leaving the bank virtually untended. It is robbed by town boss Harry Skelton (Karl Hackett), who also controls the sheriff. When the sheriff sends the posse in the wrong direction after the holdup men, Melody realizes he is involved in the plot. Fuzzy follows the holdup men to their hideout and then reports to Melody. Skelton orders his men to shoot Melody, but he outdraws them. He finds a tally book with the number of cattle Skelton's gang has stolen, but later, Melody is arrested in Skelton's office as he tries to get evidence against him. He is jailed, but Fuzzy helps his pal to get free.

Meanwhile, Jeanette, who has come to town to find out who killed her father, Henri Dumont, becomes convinced of Skelton's guilt and

A lobby card from *Songs and Bullets* (Spectrum, 1938). Shown are Fred Scott, Alice Ardell, Charles King, Karl Hackett, Al St. John and Lew Porter.

demands the sheriff arrest him. When he refuses, she goes to get a warrant and is abducted by Skelton and his men and taken to their hideout. Melody comes alone to rescue the girl and is captured and shot by Skelton. When Fuzzy arrives with a posse, Melody gets the drop on the gang, having put the dumdum 45 bullets in Skelton's gun. The gang is arrested and Melody makes love to Jeanette.

Songs and Bullets is a fairly good Fred Scott series entry, the eighth of twelve westerns he did for Spectrum and one of the two Stan Laurel Productions made for the company. Scott is in good form as the handsome singing hero, and in the movie he croons five sagebrush ditties by Johnny Lange and Lew Porter, including

"Prairie Moon," one of the finest songs to ever be used in a "B" western. Al St. John, who first created his popular Fuzzy character in the Spectrum series, adds some good comedy relief, including pratfalls. Karl Hackett, Charles King and Richard Cramer are a slick trio of villain and Frank LaRue, for a change, has a role on the side of the law. Some amusing dialogue occurs when villain Skelton is introduced to the new school marm and is obviously charmed. One of his cohorts tells another, "That's the first time Skelton's smiled since he dispossessed the Higgins family." Another scene has both the good and bad guys occupying the pretty new teacher's class on the first day of school.

## Code of the Fearless

January 16, 1939, 56 minutes.

*P:* C.C. Burr. *D:* Raymond K. Johnson. *SC:* Fred Myton. *PH:* Elmer Dyer. *ED:* Charles Henkel. *AD:* Vin Taylor. *SD:* Hans Weeren. *Asst Dir:* Henry Spitz.

*Cast:* Fred Scott, Claire Rochelle, John Merton, Walter McGrail, George Sherwood, Harry Harvey, William Woods, Don Gallaher, Carl Mathews, Frank LaRue, Gene Howard, James "Buddy" Kelly, Art Mix, Phil Dunham, Denver Dixon, George Morrell.

In order to infiltrate an outlaw gang, a ranger pretends to be on the wrong side of the law.

## In Old Montana

April 6, 1939, 60 minutes.

*P:* C.C. Burr. *D:* Raymond K. Johnson. *SC:* Jackson Parks, Homer King Gordon, Raymond K. Johnson & Barney Hutchison. *PH:* Marcel Picard & Harvey Gould. *ED:* Charles Henkel. *Asst Dir:* Gordon S. Griffith & Ray Nazarro. *SD:* Hans Weeren. *AD:* Ben Berk.

*Cast:* Fred Scott, Jean Carmen [Julia Thayer], John Merton, Wheeler Oakman, Harry Harvey, Walter McGrail, Frank LaRue, Allan Cavan, Jane Keckley, Richard Cramer, James "Buddy" Kelly, Cactus Mack, Carl Mathews.

A medicine show performer tries to stop a range war between cattlemen and sheepherders.

## Heroes of the Marne

April 26, 1939, 68 minutes.

*P-D:* Andre Hugon. *SC:* Andre Hugon & Paul Archard. *PH:* Bujart. *Mus:* Jacques Ibert.

*Cast:* Raimu, Germaine Dermon, Jacqueline Porel, Bernard Lancret, Paul Carabo, Albert Basserman, Delmont, Georges Ferlet, Phillipe Janvier, Jean Toulout, Catherine Fonteney, Poulaia, Camille Bert.

The effects of the First World War change a hardened man after he is blinded and his son is killed. Filmed in France and released there early in 1939 as *Heroes de la Marne*, running 95 minutes.

## Two Gun Troubadour

July 12, 1939, 58 minutes.

*P:* C.C. Burr. *D:* Raymond K. Johnson. *SC:* Richard L. Bare & Phil Dunham. *PH:* Elmer Dyer. *ED:* Charles Henkel. *SD:* Hans Weeren. *AD:* Vin Taylor. *Asst Dir:* William Sheldon.

*Cast:* Fred Scott, Claire Rochelle, Harry Harvey, John Merton, Billy Lenhart, Jack Ingram, Frank Ellis, Harry Harvey, Jr., James "Buddy" Kelly, Carl Mathews, Gene Howard, William Woods, Bud Osborne, John Ward, Cactus Mack, Elias Gamboa.

A young man returns home as a masked avenger to take the property that was stolen when his father was murdered.

# Stage and Screen
# Productions

Stage and Screen Productions, which was associated with Superior Talking Pictures Corporation (q.v.), released eleven movies, three of which were serials also made available in feature versions. While Superior was operational from 1933 to 1935, Stage and Screen outlasted it a year into 1936 although in the first two years of its existence the company only produced two features.

Stage and Screen's first production was *Before Morning*, a 1933 murder mystery distributed by Arthur Greenblatt and starring Leo Carrillo. The next year Stage and Screen released *Inside Information*, a Bert Sternbach production in his "A Police Melodrama" series starring Tarzan the Police Dog. Actually the movie was more of a featurette, running only 38 minutes with some obvious padding. In 1935 Sternbach turned out two more melodramas with the canine star: *Captured in Chinatown*, released through Superior, and *Million Dollar Haul*, distributed by First Division (q.v.). Both features were definitely on the tacky side, but Tarzan the Police Dog proved a likable hero in the Rin-Tin-Tin vein.

Stage and Screen's 1935 releases were mainly northwoods-Mountie melodramas, two produced by Robert Emmett Tansey and one by Louis Weiss, who at the same time made a series of six Rex Lease westerns for Superior. In fact, his feature *The Silent Code* was billed as an International Production as was *The Cowboy and the Bandit* (1935), one of Weiss' starrers with Lease. In addition to Kane Richmond as the mountie lead, *The Silent Code* featured another canine hero, Wolfgang.

Robert Emmett Tansey, billed as Robert Emmett, wrote, produced and directed *Courage of the North* and *Timber Terrors* (both 1935) for Stage and Screen with both features being distributed by Empire Pictures (q.v.). John Preston played the same character in the films, a mountie hero, and he was aided by two animal stars, Dynamite the Wonder Horse and Captain, King of the Dogs. Both features were shot in the California north country. Because of tepid plots, however, they failed to catch on with the public, and no series ensued.

By 1936 Stage and Screen Productions was solely a property of the Weiss-Mintz production unit, and it was announced the company would make a half-dozen serials for the 1936-37 season. Three serials actually appeared, all running fifteen chapters; they were presented by George M. Merrick and supervised by Louis Weiss. All three had surprisingly elaborate production values and good casts. *The Clutching Hand* (1936), based on a novel by Arthur B. Reeve, was probably the best of the lot with its science fiction plot and Jack

Mulhall's portrayal of supersleuth Craig Kennedy. The title character dated back to the 1914 Pearl White serial *The Exploits of Elaine*, which had also been penned by Arthur B. Reeve. *The Black Coin* (1936), starring Ralph Graves, was also an action cliffhanger, costarring Tom Mix's daughter Ruth, who appeared in all three of the Weiss-Mintz serials for Stage and Screen.

The third Stage and Screen serial was the historical production *Custer's Last Stand* (1936), which starred Rex Lease as a psuedo-Kit Carson with Frank McGlynn, Jr., as Custer. The serial assembled one of the finest casts ever in a cliffhanger, a who's who of western and "B" movie players. The serial was really a large scale effort for an independent of the period. It featured some unusually elaborate sets, particularly of Fort Henry, which were generously filled with players. Indian camps and wagon trains were also used effectively for the picture's bigger action scenes. The cast was outstanding, and the serial drew enthusiastic reviews on its first three chapters. "Unfortunately, there were another twelve to go," wrote James Stringham in his serialized article "The Independent Sound Serial" in *Film Fan Monthly* (February, 1968). Sadly the remainder of the serial is leaden although the finale at the Little Big Horn is well-staged. While feature versions of most serials run at a fast clip, the 90 minute condensation of *Custer's Last Stand* seems more like nine hours!

Although Stage and Screen announced it would make the serials *Jungle Perils*, *The Phantom Railroad*, *The Police Reporter* and *The Pony Express*, none appeared and the company was dissolved late in 1936.

## Before Morning

Arthur Greenblatt, October 19, 1933, 56 minutes.

*P:* Louis Weiss. *D:* Arthur Hoerl. *SC:* Arthur Hoerl, from the play by Edna Riley & Edward R. Riley. *PH:* Frank Zukor & Walter Strenge. *ED:* Joseph Silverman. *SD:* Lyman J. Wiggin & Nelson Nunnerly.

*Cast:* Leo Carrillo, Lora Baxter, Taylor Holmes, Louise Prussing, Russell Hicks, Blaine Cordner, Louis Jean Heydt, Jules Epailly, Terry Carroll, Constance Bretrand.

A police investigator poses as a blackmailer in order to find out which of two women murdered a wealthy man.

## Inside Information

September 25, 1934, 38 minutes.

*P:* Bert Sternbach. *D:* Robert Hill. *SC:* Betty Laidlaw & Robert Lively. *ST:* Bert Ennis & Victor Potel. *PH:* George Meehan. *Asst Dir:* William Nolte. *SD:* Tom Lambert. *AD:* Fred Preble.

*Cast:* Rex Lease, Marion Shilling, Tarzan the Police Dog, Philo McCullough, Charles King, Robert McKenzie, Victor Potel, Jimmy Aubrey, Jean Porter, Henry Hall, Henry Rocquemore, Robert Hill, Vance Carroll, Charles Berner.

A lawman recounts how a police dog earned a medal by rounding up a gang of crooks.

## Million Dollar Haul

1935, 63 minutes.

*P:* Bert Sternbach. *D:* Albert Herman. *SC:* Robert Walker & Victor Potel. *ST:* Robert Walker. *PH:* Harry

Kane Richmond in *The Silent Code* (Stage & Screen, 1935).

Forbes. *ED:* Ralph Holt. *AD:* Fred Preble. *Asst Dir:* Bobby Ray.

Cast: Tarzan the Police Dog, Reed Howes, Janet Chandler, William Farnum, Robert Frazer, Charles King, Creighton Hale, John Ince, Tom London, Dick Botiller, Tiny Skelton, Margaret McConnell, Dick Rush, Thelma Marland, Vance Carroll, Jack Grant, Bruce Randall.

When his warehouses are robbed, a businessman calls in a special investigator and his dog to catch the thieves.

## The Silent Code

International/Stage & Screen, 1935, 60 minutes.

*P:* Louis Weiss. *D:* Stuart Paton. *SC:* George Morgan. *PH:* Roland Price. *ED:* Charles Craft. *SD:* Corson Jowett. *Asst Dir:* Dick L'Estrange.

*Cast:* Kane Richmond (Corporal Jerry Hale), Blanche Mehaffey (Helen Brent), Barney Furey (Peter Barkley), Pat Harmon (Carny), Benny Corbett (Breen), Carl Mathews (Lobo), Eddie Coxen (Nathan Brent), J.P. McGowan (Commissioner), Joseph Girard (Superintendent Manning), Ted Mapes (Ted), Rose Higgins (Indian Woman), Wolfgang (Rex, King of the Dogs), Clarence Davis (Red Wing), Douglas Ross.

Mountie Jerry Hale (Kane Richmond) is assigned to patrol the area around the Hudson Bay Company trading post run by Peter Barkley (Barney Furey). Hale is sweet on Barkley's niece, Helen Brent (Blanche Mehaffey), but is disliked by Barkley who secretly is $10,000 short in his accounts. To get the money, Barkley and cohorts Carny (Pat Harmon), Breen (Benny Corbett) and Lobo (Carl Mathews), an

Indian, attack Helen's prospector father (Eddie Coxen) for his gold and the latter is accidentally shot. The four escape just as Jerry arrives on the scene, and the dying man gives him a map to where his gold is buried. Barkley waylays Jerry and steals the map, making it look like the Mountie murdered the prospector. Jerry is arrested for the crime as Barkley finds the gold and brings it back to the trading post. Helen comes to see Jerry and at first does not believe his story, but she decides to help him escape in order to prove his innocence. When Lobo spies Barkley hiding the gold at the trading post he demands money but is rebuffed. Jerry and Helen arrive at the post for the girl to get her belongings. She and her uncle scuffle, and Rex (Wolfgang), her father's dog, attacks Barkley. In the fight Helen throws a knife at her uncle. He falls dead, but the death weapon was actually thrown by Lobo, who watched the fight from an open window. Jerry and Helen escape as the Mounties arrive, and Rex leads them to the hidden gold, thus vindicating Jerry. At Barkley's cabin, Jerry and Helen are surprised by the arrival of Carny, Breen and Lobo, and a fight ensues with the Mounties arriving to arrest the crooks The sergeant (Bud Osborne) proves to Helen that it was Lobo, not she, who killed her uncle. With Jerry exonerated of the murder charge, he and Helen are free to be together.

Like most Royal Canadian Mounted Police movies, *The Silent Code* has some beautiful northwoods locales that belie its Poverty Row origins. A handsome trading post set also adds some class to the proceedings as does a nicely paced story set in modern times. Kane Richmond is justly stalwart as the falsely accused Mountie, and the supporting cast is good,

especially Barney Furey as the villainous Barkley. Leading lady Blanche Mehaffey, however, lacks the verve necessary to carry off the heroine's role; she seems tired after years of toiling on Poverty Row. *The Silent Code* was one of a trio of RCMP movies Stage and Screen released in 1935, and it is certainly superior to Robert Emmett Tansey's productions *Timber Terrors* and *Courage of the North* starring John Preston.

## The Drunkard

September 2, 1935, 63 minutes.

*P:* Bert Sternbach. *D:* Albert Herman. *SC:* Al Martin. *PH:* Edward Linden. *ED:* Holbrook N. Todd. *Mus:* Lee Zahler. *SD:* Cliff Ruberg. *Asst Dir:* Gordon S. Griffith. *Supv:* Louis Weiss.

*Cast:* James Murray, Janet Chandler, Clara Kimball Young, Bryant Washburn, Theodore Lorch, George Stewart, Eric Mayne, Shirley Jean, Snub Pollard, Victor Potel, Lafe McKee, Rosemary Theby, Vera Steadman, Pat O'Malley, Bobby Nelson, Gertrude Astor, John Elliott, Helen Gibson, Ruth Hiatt, Jerome Storm, Joe de Grasse, Geri Foster, Vena Calvert, Joey Ray, Monty Carter, Jack Lipson.

In order to make money and put their lazy relatives to work, hard luck theatrical producers decide to stage the 1843 play *The Drunkard*.

## The Black Coin

1936, 15 chapters.

*P:* Louis Weiss. *D:* Albert Herman. *SC:* Eddy Graneman, Dallas Fitzgerald, Bob Lively & Albert Herman. *ST:* George M. Merrick. *PH:* James Diamond. *ED:* Earl Turner. *Mus:* Lee Zahler. *SD:* Corson Jowett. *Asst Dir:* Gordon S. Griffith.

*Cast:* Ralph Graves, Ruth Mix,

Lobby card for the serial *The Black Coin* (Stage & Screen, 1936). Shown are Robert Frazer, Roger Williams, Ruth Mix and Ralph Graves.

Dave O'Brien, Constance Bergen, Mathew Betz, Robert Frazer, Snub Pollard, Robert Walker, Bryant Washburn, Clara Kimball Young, Josef Swickard, Blackie Whiteford, Yakima Canutt, Jackie Miller, Lane Chandler, Pete de Grasse, Roger Williams, Walter Taylor, Richard Cramer, Joe Garcia, Juan Duval, Lew Meehan, Carter Wayne, William Desmond, Milburn Morante, Carl Mathews.

*Chapter Titles:* Dangerous Men, The Missing Ship, The Fatal Plunge, Monster of the Deep, Wolves of the Night, Shark's Fang, Midnight Menace, Flames of Death, Smuggler's Lair, Flaming Guns, Wheels of Death, The Crash, Danger Ahead, Hidden Peril, The Phantom Treasure.

Two federal agents are on the trail of smugglers while the chief crook seeks several black coins which form a treasure map. Also released in a feature version.

## Custer's Last Stand

April 1, 1936, 15 chapters.

*P:* George M. Merrick. *D:* Elmer Clifton. *SC:* G.A. Durlam, Eddy Graneman & Bob Lively. *PH:* Bert Longnecker. *ED:* Holbrook N. Todd & George M. Merrick. *Mus:* Hal Chanoff. *Sup:* Louis Weiss. *Asst Dir:* Adrian Weiss. *SD:* T. Triplett. *Prod Mgr:* George M. Merrick & William Salzman.

*Cast:* Rex Lease, Ruth Mix, Jack Mulhall, William Farnum, Dorothy Gulliver, Reed Howes, Frank McGlynn, Jr., Josef Swickard, Creighton Hale, Lona Andre, Nancy Caswell, Helen Gibson, Chief Thundercloud,

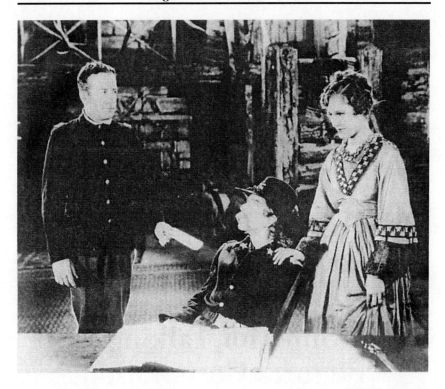

**Jack Mulhall, Frank McGlynn, Jr., and Ruth Mix in** *Custer's Last Stand* **(Stage & Screen, 1936).**

Bobby Nelson, Marty Joyce, William Desmond, George Chesebro, Milburn Morante, George Morrell, Howling Wolf, Robert Walker, Walter James, Mabel Strickland, Sunday, Ted Adams, Carl Mathews, Allen Greer, Budd Buster, Barney Furey, James Sheridan [Sherry Tansey], Chick Davis, Ken Cooper, Chief Big Tree, Iron Eyes Cody, Ed Withrow, Patter Poe, High Eagle, Cactus Mack, Carter Wayne.

*Chapter Titles:* Perils of the Plains, Thundering Hoofs, Fires of Vengeance, The Ghost Dancers, Trapped, Human Wolves, Demons of Disaster, White Treachery, Circle of Death, Flaming Arrow, Warpath, Firing Squad, Red Panthers, Custer's Last Ride, The Last Stand.

A presentation of the events leading up to the showdown between General Custer and the Indian nations at the Little Big Horn. Also released in a 90-minute feature version.

## The Clutching Hand

April 18, 1936, 15 chapters.

*P:* Louis Weiss. *D:* Albert Herman. *SC:* Leon D'Usseau, Dallas Fitzgerald, George M. Merrick & Eddy Graneman, from the novel by Arthur B. Reeve. *PH:* James Diamond. *ED:* Earl Turner. *Mus:* Lee Zahler. *SD:* Cliff Ruberg. *Asst Dir:* Gordon S. Griffith. *Sp Eff:* Kenneth Strickfaden. *Prod Mgr:* Adrian Weiss.

*Cast:* Jack Mulhall, William Farnum, Ruth Mix, Marion Shilling, Rex

Lease, Mae Busch, Yakima Canutt, Reed Howes, Bryant Washburn, Mahlon Hamilton, Robert Frazer, Gaston Glass, Robert Walker, Joseph W. Girard, Frank Leigh, Charles Locher [Jon Hall], Franklyn Farnum, William Desmond, Richard Alexander, Knute Erickson, Milburn Morante, John Elliott, Snub Pollard, Olin Francis, Henry Hall, Robert Russell, Artemus Nigolian, Ethel Grove, Gordon S. Griffith, Roger Williams, George Morrell, Vera Steadman, Robert Kortman, Bull Montana, Slim Whitaker, Tom London, John Cowell, John Ince, Art Felix, George Allen, Roy Cardona, Art Howard, Eugene Burr, Bert Howard, Gil Patrick, Willard Kent.

*Chapter Titles:* Who is the Clutching Hand?, Shadow, House of Mystery, The Phantom Car, The Double Trap, Steps of Doom, The Invisible Enemy, A Cry in the Night, Evil Eyes, A Desperate Chance, The Ship of Peril, Hidden Danger, The Mystic Menace, The Silent Spectre, The Lone Hand.

Scientific detective Craig Kennedy tries to track down the mysterious Clutching Hand who has kidnapped a scientist, the inventor of a formula for synthetic gold. Also called *The Amazing Exploits of the Clutching Hand* and released in a 70-minute feature version.

# Superior Talking Pictures Corporation

Superior Talking Pictures first came on the scene in 1933-34 when it released eight Victor Adamson Productions (q.v.)—four westerns starring Buddy Roosevelt and another quartet headlining Buffalo Bill, Jr. Superior was also the parent company of such outfits as Exploitation Pictures and International Stageplay Pictures, and it was a sister company of Stage and Screen (q.v.). Exploitation released a few adult oriented features like *Enlighten Thy Daughter* (1934) while International Stageplay had only one release, the all-black-casted *Drums O'VooDoo* in 1934. Superior also issued six westerns starring Rex Lease in 1935, and these were made by Weiss Productions, Inc. In addition, Bert Sternbach turned out a Superior feature as did Robert Emmett Tansey, but his western, *Way of the West* (1934), was distributed by Empire Pictures (q.v.).

The close association between Superior and Stage and Screen is evident by the 1935 Bert Sternbach production *Captured in Chinatown* (subtitled "A Police Melodrama"), which starred canine Thespian Tarzan the Police Dog. The feature was produced by Sternbach's Consolidated Pictures Corporation and distributed by Stage and Screen but released through Superior. The previous year Sternbach did a "Police Melodrama" with Tarzan called *Inside Infor-*

*mation*, and in 1935 he did another entitled *Million Dollar Haul*. Both were released through Stage and Screen.

Superior is best remembered today for the half dozen westerns it did with Rex Lease, all produced by Louis Weiss. Although cheaply made, the series is fairly entertaining, and it interpolated cowboy music, emerging at that time as a popular vogue in westerns thanks to Gene Autry. To save money Jack Kirk and various other vocalists usually crooned public domain range tunes. Elmer Clifton directed the bulk of the Lease series and also had a hand in writing most of them. Several of the outings team Rex Lease with juvenile Bobby Nelson, and all are on the action-oriented side. *The Ghost Rider* (1935), written and directed by Jack Jevne, is particularly appealing, buoyed by its mystery plot. A couple of the outings, *Cyclone of the Saddle* and *The Ghost Rider*, with Lease and Nelson, are billed as part of the "Rough Riders" series.

Although Weiss Productions made all the Rex Lease westerns, financial backing apparently came from various quarters. *The Cowboy and the Bandit* is listed as an International Production; *Cyclone of the Saddle* and *The Ghost Rider* are Argosy Productions; *Pals of the Range, Fighting Caballero* and *Rough Riding Ranger* were coproduced with George M. Merrick, who also worked with Louis Weiss on several Stage and Screen releases.

Both Superior Talking Pictures and Stage and Screen Productions ceased feature operations in 1935, although the latter survived another year with a trio of cliffhangers.

## Fighting Caballero

1935, 59 minutes.

*P:* Louis Weiss. *D:* Elmer Clifton. *SC:* Elmer Clifton & George M. Merrick. *PH:* Bert Longnecker. *SD:* Cliff Ruberg.

*Cast:* Rex Lease, Dorothy Gulliver, George Chesebro, Wally Wales, Franklyn Farnum, Earl Douglas, Robert Walker, Milburn Morante, George Morrell, Pinky Barnes, Carl Mathews, Barney Furey, Marty Joyce, Paul Ellis, Jack Kirk.

When outlaws try to take a man's silver mine, a cowboy comes to his defense.

## The Ghost Rider

1935, 56 minutes.

*P:* Louis Weiss. *D:* Jack [Jevne] Levine. *SC:* John West [Jack Jevne].

*PH:* Arthur Reed & James Diamond. *ED:* Arthur Brooks & Tom Neff. *SD:* Corson Jowett. *Asst Dir:* William O'Connor & Harry S. Knight.

*Cast:* Rex Lease, Ann Carol, Bobby Nelson, William Desmond, Franklyn Farnum, Lafe McKee, Art Mix, Roger Williams, Bill Patton, Blackie Whiteford, John Alexander, Blackjack Ward, Denver Dixon, Ed Coxen, Eddie Parker.

A masked phantom aids a lawman who is after a gang of outlaws.

## Rough Riding Ranger

1935, 57 minutes.

*P:* Louis Weiss. *D:* Elmer Clifton. *SC:* Elmer Clifton & George M. Merrick. *PH:* Eddie Linden. *SD:* Cliff Ruberg.

*Cast:* Rex Lease (Corporal Daniels/The Tombstone Kid), Bobby Nelson (Bobby Francis), Janet Chandler (Dorothy White), Yakima Canutt (Draw), Mabel Strickland (Mrs. Francis), David Horsley (Slim), George Chesebro (Bald), Robert Walker (Ram Hansen), Carl Mathews (Cinch), Artie Ortego (Duce), William Desmond (Major Wright), Allen Greer (Lieutenant Rodriguez), Milburn Morante (Town Drunk), Jack Kirk, Clyde McClary, Jack Evans, Cactus Mack, George Morrell (Henchmen), Johnny Luther's Cowboy Band (Themselves), Sunday (The Knowing One/Horse).

A smuggling operation is working the Mexican border, and Major Wright (William Desmond) of the U.S. Border Patrol and his Mexican counterpart Lieutenant Rodriguez (Allen Greer) vow to stop the gang. Assigned to the case is Ranger Corporal Daniels (Rex Lease), who spies a pigeon being shot, and when he finds the bird he notices strange hoofprints beside it. He follows the trail to a saloon where he hears Draw (Yakima Canutt) and Slim (David Horsley) talking about shooting the bird for the message it was carrying as they are part of the smuggling gang. The two, however, get into a fight and Draw breaks Slim's arm. This upsets gang leader Ram Hansen (Robert Walker), who was using Slim to shoot down the pigeons. Daniels then pretends to be drunk and calls himself the Tombstone Kid. He shows off his shooting abilities and Ram hires him to work for an oil company run by Dorothy White (Janet Chandler). Ram plans to use Tombstone to shoot down the next pigeon. Dorothy gets a letter containing a threat to blow up her oil wells if she does not pay protection money, not knowing her foreman Cinch (Carl Mathews) also works for Ram. Later, Daniels captures another gang member, Bald (George

Chesebro), and forces him to confess that Ram wrote the blackmail letter to Dorothy. When Cinch orders Daniels to shoot a pigeon he deliberately misses and then finds the bird, which belongs to Bobby, and gets its coded message. He sends Bobby's mother (Mabel Strickland) after the rangers, but Draw and Cinch tie her up. Her horse, Sunday, helps her to escape and she goes to Major Wright for help. Meanwhile Daniels, Dorothy and Bobby are cornered at the ranch house by Ram and his gang, but the ranger arrives to save them and route the gang. Dorothy, who is Bobby's aunt, then invites Daniels to the boy's birthday party.

*Rough Riding Ranger* is typical of the six westerns Rex Lease made for Weiss Productions in 1935. It is rather slow moving, choppily edited and fairly predictable in plot. Rex Lease appears to have a good time, especially in the scenes where he pretends to be a drunk and in romancing the pretty heroine. Costar Bobby Nelson has little to do as a ranch boy who raises pigeons, while his mother is played by trick rider Mabel Strickland, who shows her rodeo abilities in a few scenes. The film spotlights a good lineup of shady villains, including Yakima Canutt, George Chesebro, Robert Walker, Carl Mathews and David Horsley. Silent star William Desmond has a brief part as Lease's boss, the ranger chief. One of the best scenes in the film has Rex Lease demonstrating his sharpshooting abilities to scare a confession out of George Chesebro. Johnny Luther's Cowboy Band sings a song over the opening credits and during a brief barroom sequence. Still, the film is hampered by stock footage of rangers to the rescue and some comedy between a drunk and a yodeling bartender.

William Desmond and Rex Lease in *Cyclone of the Saddle* (Superior, 1935).

## The Cowboy and the Bandit

April, 1935, 57 minutes.
*P:* Louis Weiss. *D:* Albert Herman. *SC:* Jack Jevne. *PH:* Arthur Reed. *ED:* Carl Himm. *SD:* Corson Jowett. *Asst Dir:* William O'Connor.

*Cast:* Rex Lease, Janet Morgan [Blanche Mehaffey], Bobby Nelson, Dick Alexander, Wally Wales, William Desmond, Franklyn Farnum, George Chesebro, Art Mix, Bill Patton, Lafe McKee, Ben Corbett, Alphonse Martel, Jack Kirk, Fred Parker, Ada Belle Driver, George Morrell, Herman Hack, Bud Pope, Victor Potel.

A cowboy comes to the aid of a young widow whose ranch is coveted by crooks.

## Cyclone of the Saddle

April, 1935, 53 minutes.
*P:* Louis Weiss. *D:* Elmer Clifton. *SC:* Elmer Clifton & George M. Merrick. *PH:* Eddie Linden. *SD:* Cliff Ruberg.

*Cast:* Rex Lease, Janet Morgan [Blanche Mehaffey], Bobby Nelson, William Desmond, Yakima Canutt, Art Mix, George Chesebro, Chief Thundercloud, Milburn Morante, Chief Standing Bear, Helen Gibson, Chick Davis, The Range Ranglers, George Morrell, Glenn Strange, Black Fox.

An army officer is assigned to stop troubles between settlers and Indians caused by outlaws.

## Pals of the Range

April, 1935, 57 minutes.
*P:* Louis Weiss & George M. Merrick. *D:* Elmer Clifton. *SC:* Elmer

Clifton & George M. Merrick. *PH:* Eddie Linden. *SD:* Cliff Ruberg.

*Cast:* Rex Lease, Frances [Morris] Wright, Yakima Canutt, Robert [Blackie] Whiteford, George Chesebro, Milburn Morante, Tom Forman, Joey Ray, Art Mix, Bill Patton, Artie Ortego, Bud Osborne, George Morrell, Ben Corbett, John I. Luther's Cowboy Band.

A rancher is forced to break out of jail after he is falsely accused of cattle theft.

## Captured in Chinatown

July 30, 1935, 50 minutes.

*P:* Bert Sternbach. *D:* Elmer Clifton. *SC:* Elmer Clifton & G.A. Durlam. *PH:* Harry Forbes. *ED:* Ralph Holt. *SD:* Cliff Ruberg. *Asst Dir:* Gordon S. Griffith.

*Cast:* Tarzan the Police Dog, Marion Shilling, Charles Delaney, Philo McCullough, Robert Ellis, Robert Walker, Bobby Nelson, John Elliott, James B. Leong, Paul C. Fong, Wing Foo, Bo Ling.

Sent to cover a big wedding in Chinatown, two reporters find themselves in the middle of a tong war.

# Supreme Pictures Corporation

When A.W. Hackel formed Supreme Pictures Corporation in 1934, he assured himself success on the states' rights market by signing popular cowboy star Bob Steele and launching a western series starring Johnny Mack Brown. The combination of the two brought success to Supreme, and in the next four years Hackel would turn out four dozen program westerns, thirty-two with Bob Steele and sixteen with Johnny Mack Brown. Filmed at rented facilities like Talisman and Reliable studios and at such California locations as Lone Pine, Newhall and Chatsworth, the Hackel features were entertaining affairs that Don Miller described in *Hollywood Coral* (1976) as having "… generally sturdy plots, capable direction and a goodly share of range action." *Variety* in its review of the 1937 Johnny Mack Brown starrer *Trail of Vengeance* noted, "Gunning and suspense are the prevalent ingredients which is all these pics take for good reception."

Bob Steele had launched his western career in 1927 for Films Booking Offices (FBO) and easily weathered the coming of sound at Tiffany (q.v.) before doing series at World Wide (q.v.) and Monogram. The budgets for Hackel's westerns were lower than Steele's previous studio outings, but the thirty-two movies he did for the producer are uniformly good with the first half being a bit rougher around the edges than the last sets. The reason for this is that Supreme joined other studios like Monogram and Liberty (q.v.) and Herbert J. Yates' Consolidated Film Industries, a film laboratory service, in forming Republic Pictures in 1935. Thus by 1936 the Steele and Brown efforts had a much more polished look. Prior to the merger, Supreme Pictures had been released on the states' rights market by William Steiner, and some even carried the Commodore Pictures (q.v.) banner.

Although "B" westerns of the 1930s were aimed mainly at the juvenile trade, the Hackel productions also appealed to adults, and several had offbeat plots. Bob Steele's *Big Calibre* (1935), for example, contains a grotesque villain who uses poison gas to dispose of his victims. Robert North Bradbury, Bob Steele's father, directed and scripted several of his Supreme outings, and he also helmed a sturdy entry in the Brown series, *Between Men* (1935). Supervising editor S. Roy Luby directed some of the Supremes as did Sam Newfield, who took over most of the Steele and Brown films following the Republic merger. After his series for Hackel ended in 1937 Johnny Mack Brown was in three Universal serials and two Paramount features (*Born to the West* and *Wells Fargo*) before resuming series work at Universal in 1939. Bob Steele, on the other hand, stayed with Hackel through 1938, turning out some polished productions like *Cavalry* (1936), *Border Phantom* and *Arizona Gunfighter* (both 1937) and *Thunder in the Desert* (1938). After his thirty-two Hackel outings Steele made eight westerns for Metropolitan Pictures (q.v.).

In 1940 A.W. Hackel made *Am I Guilty?* for Supreme Pictures, the first of a series of features aimed at the Negro film market. Starring Ralph Cooper, this feature gained good reviews in metropolitan areas with its straightforward accounting of a doctor who, by accident, gets involved with hoodlums. No further entries in the proposed series materialized. In 1941 Hackel joined Monogram Pictures as a producer, making such features as *Murder by Invitation* and *Borrowed Hero* (1941), *Man with Two Lives*, *One Thrilling Night*, *The Phantom Killer* and *The Living Ghost* (1943) and *Shadows of Suspicion* (1945). A.W. Hackel died October 21, 1959, at age 76.

## A Demon for Trouble

August 10, 1934, 58 minutes.

*P:* A.W. Hackel. *D:* Bob Hill. *SC:* Jack [John Francis] Natteford. *PH:* William Thompson. *ED:* William Austin. *SD:* Herbert Eicke. *Prod Mgr:* Bobby Ray. *Supv:* Sam Katzman.

*Cast:* Bob Steele, Don Alvarado, Gloria Shea, Nick Stuart, Carmen LaRoux, Walter McGrail, Lafe McKee, Perry Murdock, Blackie Whiteford, Jimmy Aubrey.

When settlers are killed after pur-chasing property, a cowboy investigates and uncovers a land grab scheme.

## The Brand of Hate

November 7, 1934, 63 minutes.

*P:* A.W. Hackel. *D:* Lew Collins. *SC:* Jack [John Francis] Natteford. *PH:* William Thompson. *ED:* S. Roy Luby. *SD:* Herbert Eicke. *Prod Mgr:* Harry Knight. *Supv:* Sam Katzman.

*Cast:* Bob Steele, Lucille Browne, William Farnum, Mickey Rentschler, James Flavin, George F. Hayes,

Charles K. French, Jack Rockwell, Blackie Whiteford, Bill Patton, Rose Plummer, Archie Ricks, Bob Burns, Fred Burns, Roy Bucko, Lionel Backus, Al Haskell, Bob Card, Pardner.

A cowboy investigates cattle thefts which are carried out by a gang led by the brother of the girl he loves.

## The Big Calibre

March 8, 1935, 58 minutes.

*P:* A.W. Hackel. *D:* Robert North Bradbury. *SC:* Perry Murdock. *PH:* William Hyer. *ED:* S. Roy Luby. *SD:* Herbert Eicke. *Prod Mgr:* Glenn Cook. *Supv:* Sam Katzman.

*Cast:* Bob Steele, Peggy Campbell, Forrest Taylor, John Elliott, Georgia O'Dell, Bill Quinn, Perry Murdock, Earl Dwire, Frank Ball, Si Jenks, Frank McCarroll, Blackie Whiteford.

A cowboy tries to find the murderer of his father, a crime committed by a madman using poison gas.

## Tombstone Terror

April 25, 1935, 58 minutes.

*P:* A.W. Hackel. *D:* Robert North Bradbury. *SC:* Perry Murdock. *PH:* Harry Forbes. *ED:* S. Roy Luby. *SD:* Herbert Eicke. *Prod Mgr:* Glenn Cook. *Supv:* Sam Katzman.

*Cast:* Bob Steele, Kay McCoy, George Hayes, Earl Dwire, John Elliott, Ann Howard, Nancy DeShon, Hortense Petra, Frank McCarroll, George Morrell, Artie Ortego, Herman Hack.

Mistaken for a wanted outlaw, a cowboy tries to prove his innocence.

## Western Justice

June 14, 1935, 56 minutes.

*P:* A.W. Hackel. *D-SC:* Robert North Bradbury. *PH:* William Hyer. *ED:* S. Roy Luby. *SD:* Herbert Eicke.

*Prod Mgr:* Glenn Cook. *Supv:* Sam Katzman.

*Cast:* Bob Steele (Jim/Ace), Renee Borden (Beatrice Brent), Julian Rivero (Pancho Lopez/Jack), Arthur Loft (Clem Slade), Lafe McKee (Sheriff/King), Jack Cowell (John Brent), Perry Murdock (Rufe), Vane Calvert (Aunt Emma), Earl Dwire (Doctor), Chief (Horse).

Coming home to visit his daughter, Pancho Lopez (Julian Rivero) finds the girl has been tricked into a fake marriage with crook Clem Slade (Arthur Loft) who has deserted her, taking all her money. Pancho vows to bring him back as the girl later dies. Meanwhile, cowboy Jim (Bob Steele) arrives to visit his aunt (Vane Calvert) and her son Rufe (Perry Murdock). Rufe rides to town for supplies and catches Clem robbing the local store after having killed the owner. The two fight but Clem gets away, and, feeling he will be implicated, Rufe returns home. The sheriff (Lafe McKee), however, sees Rufe ride away on Jim's horse and thinks he is the murderer. When Jim hears Rufe's story, he goes after the robber and is pursued by the sheriff but gives him the slip. Later, in a deserted cabin Jim, Pancho and the sheriff all meet and call themselves Ace, Jack and King. They agree to go to the gold strike at Red Fork, Arizona, but along the way stop at Mirage City to water their horses. They find the people there in a water dispute with businessman John Brent (Jack Cowell), who is also at odds with his niece Beatrice (Renee Borden). The girl is upset with her uncle for withholding needed water from the local ranchers. Jim is attracted to Beatrice, who asks his help in getting water for the locals. He opens a reservoir gate that helps the ranchers and later learns that an underground river is the water supply for the area. Jack finds out that Brent's henchman is Slade, and he follows him to his cave hideout. When Brent orders Slade to take Beatrice prisoner, Jack lets her go and then kills Slade by skinning him alive. Taking ammunition Brent's gang has collected, Ace, Jack and King free the underground river. They also catch Brent and his gang in an ambush by dynamiting a mountain, which falls on the outlaws. The trio then celebrates and Ace/Jim calls Beatrice his queen.

Released in the early summer of 1935, *Western Justice* was the fifth of thirty-two westerns Bob Steele made for A.W. Hackel's Supreme Pictures. Filmed at Reliable Studios, it was shot simultaneously with *Kid Courageous* (1935), released the next month. Bob Steele was a well established and popular sagebrush star who had headlined westerns since 1927. This series for Supreme reunited him with his father, Robert North Bradbury, who also scripted this somewhat awkward but fast-paced and fairly interesting outing. Bradbury had a penchant for imbuing his westerns with touches of the bizarre, and *Western Justice* is no exception. In addition to a cave with a secret tunnel and door, the film has villain Arthur Loft being skinned alive for the seduction of Julian Rivero's daughter. This retribution is the same as that given to Boris Karloff by Bela Lugosi the year before in Universal's *The Black Cat*. The feature also contains an early example of the triad hero concept, and the scene where the trio first meet in a deserted shack on a windy night is somewhat eerie. Offbeat is the finale, in which the heroes blow up the bad guys in an ambush and then are struck by a huge piece of flying timber.

## Kid Courageous

July 5, 1935, 53 minutes.

*P:* A.W. Hackel. *D-SC:* Robert North Bradbury. *PH:* William Hyer. *ED:* S. Roy Luby. *SD:* Herbert Eicke. *Prod Mgr:* Glenn Cook.

*Cast:* Bob Steele, Renee Borden, Arthur Loft, Jack Cowell, Vane Calvert, Lafe McKee, Kit Guard, Perry Murdock, John Elliott, Barney Furey.

Forced to change clothes with an escaped outlaw, a young man tries to clear his name and save a young lady from an unwanted marriage.

## Smokey Smith

July 30, 1935, 58 minutes.

*P:* A.W. Hackel. *D-SC:* Robert North Bradbury. *PH:* William Nobles. *ED:* S. Roy Luby. *SD:* Terry Kellum. *Prod Mgr:* Glenn Cook.

*Cast:* Bob Steele, Mary Kornman, Warner Richmond, George F. Hayes, Earl Dwire, Horace B. Carpenter, Vane Calvert, Archie Hicks, Tex Palmer, Bert Dillard, Herman Hack, Tex Phelps.

A cowboy seeks revenge on the outlaws who ambushed and murdered his parents.

## No Man's Range

September 5, 1935, 56 minutes.

*P:* A.W. Hackel. *D:* Robert North Bradbury. *SC:* Forbes Parkhill. *PH:* William Nobles. *ED:* S. Roy Luby. *SD:* Corson Jowett. *Prod Mgr:* William Strohbach.

*Cast:* Bob Steele, Roberta Gale, Buck Connors, Charles K. French, Jack Rockwell, Roger Williams, Earl Dwire, Forrest Taylor, Art Dillard, Herman Hack, Ed Cassidy, Jim Corey, Clyde McClary.

On his way to take over a ranch he has inherited, a cowboy and his pal agree to help a young woman whose herd is being blocked by an outlaw gang. Working title: *No Man's Land.*

## The Rider of the Law

October 19, 1935, 56 minutes.
*P:* A.W. Hackel. *D:* Robert North Bradbury. *SC:* Jack [John Francis] Natteford. *PH:* Gus Peterson. *ED:* S. Roy Luby. *Prod Mgr:* William Remeck.

*Cast:* Bob Steele, Gertrude Messinger, Si Jenks, Lloyd Ingraham, John Elliott, Earl Dwire, Forrest Taylor, Bud Osborne, Jack Kirk, Steve Clark, Tex Palmer, Sherry Tansey, Art Dillard, Ray Henderson, Chuck Baldra.

A state detective is sent to a mining town to round up a gang of bandits and he poses as a dude.

## Branded a Coward

October 23, 1935, 57 minutes.
*P:* A.W. Hackel. *D:* Sam Newfield. *SC:* Earl Snell. *ST:* Richard Martinsen. *PH:* William Nobles. *ED:* Earl Turner. *SD:* Corson Jowett. *Prod Mgr:* Sam Diege.

*Cast:* Johnny Mack Brown, Billie Seward, Syd Saylor, Lloyd Ingraham, Lee Shumway, Roger Willliams, Mickey Rentschler, Yakima Canutt, Frank McCarroll, Rex Downing, Robert Kortman, Joe Girard, Ed Piel, Sr.

Out to avenge the murder of his parents, a man overcomes his fear of gunmen and sets out to find the killers.

## Between Men

October 29, 1935, 59 minutes.
*P:* A.W. Hackel. *D-ST:* Robert North Bradbury. *SC:* Charles Francis Royal. *PH:* Bert Longnecker. *ED:* S. Roy Luby. *SD:* Corson Jowett. *Asst Dir:* Harry S. Knight.

*Cast:* Johnny Mack Brown

(Johnny Wellington), Beth Marion (Gale Winters), William Farnum (John Wellington/Rand), Earl Dwire (Trent), Lloyd Ingraham (Sir George Thorne), Frank Ball (Gentry Winters), Horace B. Carpenter (Dr. Strong), Barry Downing (Young Johnny Wellington), Forrest Taylor (Lawyer Wyndham), Milburn Morante (Pete), Horace Murphy (Mr. Burton), Sherry Tansey (Tampas), Silver Tip Baker (Dobson), Wally Wales (Luke the Blacksmith), Bud Osborne (Bartender), Jim Corey, Budd Buster, Clyde McClary (Townsmen), Francis Walker, Tex Phelps, Artie Ortego, Archie Ricks, George Morrell (Trent's Henchmen), Jack Kirk (Joe).

In Virginia little Johnny Wellington (Barry Downing) suffers a life-long scar on his chest due to a burn. When townsmen make accusations against Sir George Thorne's (Lloyd Ingraham) daughter, Johnny's father, blacksmith John Wellington (William Farnum), comes to her defense and in a fight the little boy is shot. Believing his son has been killed, Wellington shoots the culprits and then flees. The boy, however, survives and is raised by Thorne. Eighteen years later Johnny Wellington (Johnny Mack Brown) tells Thorne he will find his granddaughter and bring her home since her mother died in childbirth. Going to New Mexico to find the girl, Johnny is befriended by vagabond Pete (Milburn Morante), and the two rescue pretty Gale Gentry (Beth Marion) after her father is shot by Trent (Earl Dwire), an outlaw who has evil designs on her. Trent is a member of a gang led by Rand, the alias of John Wellington. When Rand finds out what Trent has done, he vows revenge and in a showdown is aided by Johnny. Gale comes to live with Rand, and Johnny hires on as his new foreman. Rand, however, is unhappy when a romance develops between the two young people and he forbids them to marry. Johnny and Gale come to realize she is the girl he is seeking and attempt to tell Rand, but two cowboys try to molest the girl and Johnny saves her. Rand, however, thinks Johnny has tried to abduct Gale after he has been ambushed by Trent and his gang. Rand finds Johnny and Gale in a remote shack and the two men fight, but in the fracas Johnny's shirt is torn and Rand sees the scar and realizes the young man is his son. Rand gives the young people his blessing and then deliberately steps outside to be ambushed by Trent, who is out to kill Johnny over Gale. Johnny then kills Trent in a showdown as the dying Rand tells the two young people they have a clear trail ahead.

The second entry in Johnny Mack Brown's Series for A.W. Hackel, *Between Men* is a well-acted programmer which moves along at a steady clip, thanks to Robert North Bradbury's direction. Bert Longnecker's desert photography is appealing, and Beth Marion makes a desirable heroine. Johnny Mack Brown carries the heroics well, and Earl Dwire is an especially slimy villain. William Farnum, however, steals the acting honors, and his fight sequence with Brown is particularly well-staged. A surprising plot element has two randy cowboys trying to rape the heroine. *Variety* reported, "Inexpensively made western which crams a lot of action into its comparatively short running time."

## The Courageous Avenger

October 30, 1935, 58 minutes.

*P:* A.W. Hackel. *D:* Robert North Bradbury. *SC:* Charles Francis Royal. *PH:* E.L. McManigal. *ED:* S. Roy Luby. *SD:* T.T. Triplett. *Prod Mgr:* Jerome S. Bressler. *Asst Dir:* Glenn Cook.

*Cast:* Johnny Mack Brown, Helen Ericson, Warner Richmond, Eddie Parker, Frank Ball, Forrest Taylor, Earl Dwire, Bob Burns, Francis Walker, George Morrell, Art Dillard, Wally West, Fred Parker, Herman Hack.

While investigating a murder, a lawman finds crooks are using forced labor to work a silver mine.

## Alias John Law

November 5, 1935, 54 minutes.

*P:* A.W. Hackel. *D:* Robert North Bradbury. *SC:* Forbes Parkhill. *PH:* William Nobles. *ED:* S. Roy Luby. *SD:* Corson Jowett. *Prod Mgr:* William Strohbach.

*Cast:* Bob Steele, Roberta Gale, Buck Connors, Earl Dwire, Bob McKenzie, Steve Clark, Jack Rockwell, Roger Williams, Jack Cowell, Horace Murphy.

Returning home to claim an oil rich property, a young man finds a crook is also posing as an heir.

## Trail of Terror

December 20, 1935, 59 minutes.

*P:* A.W. Hackel. *D-SC:* Robert North Bradbury. *PH:* E.L. McManigal. *ED:* S. Roy Luby. *SD:* T.T. Triplett. *Asst Dir:* Glenn Cook.

*Cast:* Bob Steele, Beth Marion, Forrest Taylor, Charles King, Frank Lyman, Jr., Charles K. French, Lloyd Ingraham, Richard Cramer, Nancy DeShon, Dr. Barney Cossack, Budd Buster, Ed Cassidy, Wally West, Bob McKenzie, Herman Hack, Clyde McClary.

A government agent pretends to be wanted in order to bring in an outlaw gang.

## Valley of the Lawless

January 25, 1936, 59 minutes.

*P:* A.W. Hackel. *D:* Robert North Bradbury. *SC:* Charles Francis Royal. *PH:* Bert Longnecker. *ED:* S. Roy Luby. *SD:* Corson Jowett. *Asst Dir:* Glenn Cook.

*Cast:* Johnny Mack Brown, Joyce Compton, George F. Hayes, Frank Hagney, Denny Meadows [Dennis Moore], Bobby Nelson, Charles King, Jack Rockwell, Frank Ball, Milburn Morante, Anita Campello, Bob Mc-Kenzie, George Morrell, Forrest Taylor, Jack Evans, Tex Phelps, Rube Dalroy, Horace Murphy, Steve Clark, Francis Walker, Ed Cassidy, Blackie Whiteford, Clyde McClary, Jack Kirk, Buck Morgan, Fred Parker, Bud Pope.

A marksman tries to locate a map stolen years before from his grandparents by an outlaw and his gang.

## The Kid Ranger

February 5, 1936, 57 minutes.

*P:* A.W. Hackel. *D-SC:* Robert North Bradbury. *PH:* E.L. McManigal. *ED:* S. Roy Luby. *SD:* Corson Jowett. *Asst Dir:* Glenn Cook.

*Cast:* Bob Steele, William Farnum, Geraine Greear [Joan Barclay], Charles King, Earl Dwire, Frank Ball, Reetsy Adams, Lafe McKee, Paul & Paulina, Buck Moulton.

A lawman is in love with a girl whose father, an outlaw, was killed by her adopted parent, an ex-sheriff.

## Desert Phantom

March 21, 1936, 66 minutes.

*P:* A.W. Hackel. *D:* S. Roy Luby. *SC:* Earl Snell. *ST:* E.B. Mann. *PH:* Bert Longnecker. *ED:* Roy Claire. *SD:* Corson Jowett. *Prod Mgr:* Jerome S. Bressler. *Asst Dir:* Harry Knight.

*Cast:* Johnny Mack Brown, Sheila Mannors, Ted Adams, Karl Hackett, Hal Price, Nelson McDowell, Charles King, Forrest Taylor, Roger Williams, George Morrell, Fred Parker, Frank Ball, Art Dillard.

A young woman hires a sharpshooter to find the mysterious outlaw who has been terrorizing her ranch.

## Sundown Saunders

April 13, 1936, 64 minutes.

*P:* A.W. Hackel. *D-SC:* Robert North Bradbury. *PH:* Bert Longnecker. *ED:* S. Roy Luby. *SD:* Corson Jowett. *Prod Mgr:* Jerome S. Bressler. *Asst Dir:* Harry S. Knight.

*Cast:* Bob Steele, Catherine Cotter, Earl Dwire, Ed Cassidy, Jack Rockwell, Milt [Milburn] Morante, Hal Price, Charles King, Frank Ball, Edmund Cobb, Horace Murphy, Bob McKenzie, Jack Kirk, Herman Hack.

Crooks try to cheat a cowboy out of a ranch he won in a horse race.

## Rogue of the Range

May 20, 1936, 60 minutes.

*P:* A.W. Hackel. *D:* S. Roy Luby. *SC:* Earle Snell. *PH:* Jack Greenhalgh. *ED:* Roy Claire. *SD:* Corson Jowett. *Prod Mgr:* Jerome S. Bressler. *Asst Dir:* Harry S. Knight.

*Cast:* Johnny Mack Brown, Lois January, Alden Chase, Phyllis Hume, George Ball, Jack Rockwell, Horace Murphy, Frank Ball, Lloyd Ingraham, Slim Whitaker, Horace B. Carpenter, Max Davidson, Blackie Whiteford, Forrest Taylor, George Morrell, Art Dillard, Oscar Gahan, Herman Hack, Tex Palmer, Wally West, Fred Hoose.

A secret service agent pretends to be a gunman to bring in an outlaw gang.

## The Law Rides

June 25, 1936, 57 minutes.

*P:* A.W. Hackel. *D:* Robert North Bradbury. *SC:* Forbes Parkhill & Al Martin. *PH:* Bert Longnecker. *ED:* Dan Milner. *SD:* Corson Jowett. *Prod Mgr:* Jerome S. Bressler. *Asst Dir:* Edward Tyler.

*Cast:* Bob Steele, Harley Wood, Buck Connors, Charles King, Margaret Mann, Jack Rockwell, Norman Nielsen, Barney Furey, Horace Murphy, Budd Buster, Ted Mapes, George Morrell, Ray Henderson, George Ball, Blackie Whiteford, Tex Palmer, Art Dillard.

A cowboy is on the trail of an outlaw gang that ambushes and murders miners.

## Last of the Warrens

July 2, 1936, 56 minutes.

*P:* A.W. Hackel. *D-SC:* Robert N. Bradbury. *PH:* Bert Longnecker. *ED:* S. Roy Luby. *SD:* Corson Jowett. *Prod Mgr:* Jerome S. Bressler. *Asst Dir:* Harry S. Knight.

*Cast:* Bob Steele, Margaret Marquis, Charles King, Horace Murphy, Charles K. French, Blackie Whiteford, Steve Clark, Julian Madison, Art Dillard, Horace B. Carpenter, Jim Corey, Herman Hack, Frank Ball, Tex Palmer, Chuck Baldra.

A World War I flying ace returns home to find a crook has taken over his ranch.

## Everyman's Law

July 21, 1936, 61 minutes.

*P:* A.W. Hackel. *D:* Albert Ray. *SC:* Earle Snell. *PH:* Jack Greenhalgh. *ED:* L.R. Brown. *SD:* Corson Jowett. *Prod Mgr:* Jerome S. Bressler. *Asst Dir:* William O'Connor.

*Cast:* Johnny Mack Brown, Beth Marion, Frank Campeau, Roger Gray, Lloyd Ingraham, John Beck, Horace Murphy, Dick Alexander, Slim Whitaker, Francis Walker, Art Dillard, George Morrell, Jim Corey, Ed Cassidy, Tex Palmer, Jack Evans, Herman Hack, Buck Bucko.

A lawman pretending to be a killer teams with two gunmen to take on a corrupt cattleman.

## The Crooked Trail

July 25, 1936, 60 minutes.

*P:* A.W. Hackel. *D:* S. Roy Luby. *SC:* George Plympton. *PH:* Jack Greenhalgh. *ED:* Roy Claire. *SD:* Cliff Ruberg. *Prod Mgr:* Jerome S. Bressler. *Asst Dir:* Edwin Tyler.

*Cast:* Johnny Mack Brown, Lucille Browne, John Merton, Charles King, Ted Adams, John Van Pelt, Ed Cassidy, Horace Murphy, Dick Curtis, Roger Williams, Earl Dwire, Artie Ortego, Hal Price, Fred Parker, Tex Palmer.

After rescuing two men from the desert, a lawman is faced with the problem that one of them may be a crook.

## Brand of the Outlaws

August 15, 1936, 60 minutes.

*P:* A.W. Hackel. *D-SC:* Robert North Bradbury. *PH:* Bert Longnecker. *ED:* Dan Milner. *SD:* Cliff Ruberg. *Prod Mgr:* Jerome S. Bressler. *Asst Dir:* Edwin Tyler.

*Cast:* Bob Steele, Margaret Marquis, Jack Rockwell, Charles King, Virginia True Boardman, Ed Cassidy, Frank Ball, Horace Murphy, Bob Reeves, Budd Buster, Bud Osborne, Clyde McClary.

Falsely branded as an outlaw, a cowboy tries to prove he is innocent of the charges.

# Undercover Man

Republic, September 24, 1936, 56 minutes.

*P:* A.W. Hackel. *D:* Albert Ray. *SC:* Andrew Bennison. *PH:* Jack Greenhalgh. *ED:* Dan Milner. *SD:* Cliff Ruberg.

*Cast:* Johnny Mack Brown, Suzanne Kaaren, Ted Adams, Frank Darien, Horace Murphy, Lloyd Ingraham, Dick Moorehead, Ed Cassidy, Frank Ball, Margaret Mann, George Morrell.

When a Wells Fargo agent saves a gold shipment, a local businessman who was behind the robbery plans revenge.

# Calvary

Republic, October 5, 1936, 63 minutes.

*P:* A.W. Hackel. *D-ST:* Robert North Bradbury. *SC:* George Plympton. *PH:* Bert Longnecker. *ED:* Roy Claire. *SD:* Cliff Ruberg.

*Cast:* Bob Steele, Frances Grant, Karl Hackett, Hal Price, Earl Ross, Ed Cassidy, William Welsh, Budd Buster, William Desmond, Perry Murdock, Horace B. Carpenter, Earl Dwire, Martin Turner.

A cavalry officer is sent by the army to thwart an attempt by separatists to form a new state after the Civil War.

# The Gun Ranger

Republic, February 9, 1937, 60 minutes.

*P:* A.W. Hackel. *D:* Robert North Bradbury. *SC:* George Plympton. *ST:* Homer Gordon. *PH:* Bert Longnecker. *ED:* Roy Claire. *SD:* Cliff Ruberg. *Asst Dir:* Edwin Tyler.

*Cast:* Bob Steele, Eleanor Stewart, John Merton, Ernie Adams, Earl Dwire, Budd Buster, Frank Ball,

Horace Murphy, Wally Wales, Lew Meehan, Horace B. Carpenter, George Morrell, Tex Palmer, Jack Kirk.

A ranger leaves the force when a murderer is set free and he vows to the dead man's daughter to get revenge on the culprit.

# Lawless Land

Republic, April 6, 1937, 55 minutes.

*P:* A.W. Hackel. *D:* Albert Ray. *SC:* Andrew Bennison. *PH:* Jack Greenhalgh. *ED:* Roy Claire. *SD:* Cliff Ruberg. *Asst Dir:* William O'Connor.

*Cast:* Johnny Mack Brown, Louise Stanley, Ted Adams, Julian Rivero, Horace Murphy, Frank Ball, Ed Cassidy, Ana Camargo, Frances Kellogg, Chiquita Hernandez Orchestra.

A ranger arrives in a small town to find his lawman friend has been murdered and a local businessman has taken over his job.

# Bar-Z Badmen

Republic, April 22, 1937, 57 minutes.

*P:* A.W. Hackel. *D:* Sam Newfield. *SC:* George Plympton. *ST:* James P. Olsen. *PH:* Bert Longnecker. *ED:* Roy Claire. *SD:* Cliff Ruberg. *Asst Dir:* William O'Connor.

*Cast:* Johnny Mack Brown, Lois January, Tom London, Frank LaRue, Ernie Adams, Dick Curtis, Milburn Morante, Jack Rockwell, Budd Buster, Horace Murphy, Frank Ball, Horace B. Carpenter, Art Dillard, George Morrell, Tex Palmer, Oscar Gahan.

A cowboy buys half a ranch where the other owner is being made to look like a cattle thief.

# The Gambling Terror

Republic, March 10, 1937, 60 minutes.

*P:* A.W. Hackel. *D:* Sam Newfield. *SC:* George Plympton & Fred

Myton. *PH:* Bert Longnecker. *ED:* Roy Claire. *SD:* Cliff Ruberg.

*Cast:* Johnny Mack Brown, Iris Meredith, Charles King, Ted Adams, Horace Murphy, Earl Dwire, Frank Ball, Bobby Nelson, Lloyd Ingraham, Emma Tansey, Budd Buster, Frank Ellis, Steve Clark, Sherry Tansey, Oscar Gahan, Clyde McClary, Roy Bucko, George Morrell, Art Dillard, Jack Montgomery, Tex Palmer, Buck Morgan, Herman Hack.

A gambler rescues a small boy from a gang of roughnecks and then sets out to free a town of protection operators.

## The Trusted Outlaw

Republic, May 4, 1937, 60 minutes.

*P:* A.W. Hackel. *D:* Robert North Bradbury. *SC:* George Plympton & Fred Myton. *ST:* Johnston McCulley. *PH:* Bert Longnecker. *ED:* S. Roy Luby. *SD:* Cliff Ruberg. *Asst Dir:* William Nolte.

*Cast:* Bob Steele, Lois January, Joan Barclay, Charles King, Earl Dwire, Richard Cramer, Hal Price, Budd Buster, Frank Ball, Jack Rockwell, Jack C. Smith, Oscar Gahan, Wally West, George Morrell, Sherry Tansey, Chick Hannon, Clyde McClary, Al Taylor, Ray Henderson, Fred Parker.

The last member of an outlaw family vows to go straight and takes a job hauling a payroll through a pass controlled by bandits.

## Guns in the Dark

May 13, 1937, 56 minutes.

*P:* A.W. Hackel. *D:* Sam Newfield. *SC:* Charles Francis Royal. *ST:* E.B. Mann. *PH:* Bert Longnecker. *ED:* Roy Claire. *SD:* Cliff Ruberg. *Asst Dir:* Bobby Ray.

*Cast:* Johnny Mack Brown, Claire Rochelle, Syd Saylor, Ted Adams, Dick Curtis, Steve Clark, Jim Corey, Julian Madison, Roger Williams, Lew Meehan, Slim Whitaker, Francis Walker, Budd Buster, Frank Ellis, Sherry Tansey, Tex Palmer, Oscar Gahan, Merrill McCormack, Richard Cramer, Jack C. Smith, Chick Hannon.

A cowboy who thinks he has killed his pal takes a job working for a young woman whose dam project is being sabotaged.

## Gun Lords of Stirrup Gulch

Republic, May 18, 1937, 60 minutes.

*P:* A.W. Hackel. *D:* Sam Newfield. *SC:* George Plympton & Fred Myton. *ST:* Harry F. Olmstead. *PH:* Bert Longnecker. *ED:* Roy Claire. *SD:* Cliff Ruberg.

*Cast:* Bob Steele, Louise Stanley, Karl Hackett, Ernie Adams, Frank LaRue, Frank Ball, Steve Clark, Lew Meehan, Frank Ellis, Jim Corey, Budd Buster, Jack Kirk, Tex Palmer, Margaret Mann, Lloyd Ingraham, Bobby Nelson, Horace Murphy, Emma Tansey, Milburn Morante, Sherry Tansey, Horace B. Carpenter, Herman Hack.

Although cattlemen and homesteaders feud, a young man and woman from each side fall in love and try to thwart a range war. TV title: *Gunlords of Stirrup Basin.*

## Border Phantom

Republic, June 7, 1937, 58 minutes.

*P:* A.W. Hackel. *D:* S. Roy Luby. *SC:* Fred Myton. *PH:* Jack Greenhalgh. *ED:* Roy Claire. *SD:* Cliff Ruberg.

*Cast:* Bob Steele, Harley Wood, Don Barclay, Karl Hackett, Horace Murphy, Miki Morita, Perry Murdock, John Peters, Frank Ball, Horace B. Carpenter, Budd Buster, Clyde McClary.

Syd Saylor, Johnny Mack Brown and Claire Rochelle in *Guns in the Dark* (Supreme 1937), distributed by Republic.

Two roving cowboys discover a young lady who is being held prisoner following the murder of her scientist uncle on the Mexican border.

## Trail of Vengeance

Republic, June 23, 1937, 60 minutes.
*P:* A.W. Hackel. *D:* Sam Newfield. *SC:* George Plympton & Fred Myton. *ST:* E.B. Mann. *PH:* Bert Longnecker. *ED:* Robert Jahns. *SD:* Cliff Ruberg. *Asst Dir:* William O'Connor.

*Cast:* Johnny Mack Brown, Iris Meredith, Warner Richmond, Karl Hackett, Earle Hodgins, Frank LaRue, Frank Ellis, Lew Meehan, Frank Ball, Dick Curtis, Budd Buster, Horace B. Carpenter, Francis Walker, Richard Cramer, Jim Corey, Steve Clark, Merrill McCormack, Ray Henderson, Horace Murphy, Jack C. Smith, Tex Palmer, Wally West, Herman Hack, Clyde McClary, Jack Kirk.

A wanted outlaw becomes involved in a range war and tries to claim a mine which has been left to him.

## A Lawman Is Born

Republic, June 28, 1937, 61 minutes.
*P:* A.W. Hackel. *D:* Sam Newfield. *SC:* George Plympton. *ST:* Harry F. Olmstead. *PH:* Bert Longnecker. *ED:* Roy Claire. *SD:* Cliff Ruberg. *Asst Dir:* William Nolte.

*Cast:* Johnny Mack Brown, Iris Meredith, Warner Richmond, Mary MacLaren, Dick Curtis, Earle Hodgins, Charles King, Frank LaRue, Al St. John, Steve Clark, Jack C. Smith, Lew Meehan, Tex Palmer, Wally West, Oscar Gahan, Budd Buster, Sherry Tansey.

In trying to help small ranchers

being harassed by rustlers, a man becomes convinced a corrupt cattle buyer is behind the trouble.

## Doomed at Sundown

Republic, July 7, 1937, 60 minutes.
*P:* A.W. Hackel. *D:* Sam Newfield. *SC:* George Plympton. *ST:* Fred Myton. *PH:* Bert Longnecker. *ED:* Roy Claire. *SD:* Cliff Ruberg. *Asst Dir:* William Nolte.
*Cast:* Bob Steele, Lorraine Hayes [Laraine Day], Warner Richmond, Earl Dwire, Harold Daniels, David Sharpe, Horace B. Carpenter, Charles King, Horace Murphy, Jack C. Smith, Lew Meehan, Jack Ingram, Budd Buster, Jack Kirk, Sherry Tansey.
When his lawman father is murdered, a young man becomes a deputy in order to capture the killer.

## The Red Rope

Republic, July 19, 1937, 60 minutes.
*P:* A.W. Hackel. *D:* S. Roy Luby. *SC:* George Plympton. *ST:* Johnston McCulley. *PH:* Bert Longnecker. *ED:* Roy Claire. *SD:* Cliff Ruberg. *Asst Dir:* Bobby Ray.
*Cast:* Bob Steele, Lois January, Forrest Taylor, Charles King, Karl Hackett, Bobby Nelson, Ed Cassidy, Lew Meehan, Frank Ball, Jack Rockwell, Horace Murphy, Lionel Belmore, Horace B. Carpenter, Richard Cramer, Willie Fung, Ray Henderson, Oscar Gahan, Wally West, Emma Tansey, Tex Palmer, Sherry Tansey, Fred Parker.
A notorious outlaw tries to stop the wedding of a ranch foreman and his fiancée because the bad man wants the girl for himself.

## Boothill Brigade

Republic, August 11, 1937, 58 minutes.
*P:* A.W. Hackel. *D:* Sam New-

field. *SC:* George Plympton. *ST:* Harry F. Olmstead. *PH:* Bert Longnecker. *ED:* Roy Claire. *SD:* Cliff Ruberg. *Asst Dir:* Bobby Ray.
*Cast:* Johnny Mack Brown, Claire Rochelle, Dick Curtis, Horace Murphy, Frank LaRue, Bobby Nelson, Frank Ball, Steve Clark, Frank Ellis, Lew Meehan, Tex Palmer, Jim Corey, Sherry Tansey.
A rancher becomes suspicious when the father of his fiancée hires gunmen and begins evicting squatters from the range.

## Ridin' the Lone Trail

Republic, August 28, 1937, 56 minutes.
*P:* A.W. Hackel. *D:* Sam Newfield. *SC:* Charles Francis Royal. *ST:* E.B. Mann. *PH:* Robert Cline. *ED:* Roy Claire. *SD:* Glen Glenn. *Asst Dir:* Bobby Ray.
*Cast:* Bob Steele, Claire Rochelle, Charles King, Ernie Adams, Lew Meehan, Julian Rivero, Hal Price, Frank Ball, Steve Clark, Jack Kirk.
Working undercover as a cowboy, a lawman helps the local sheriff capture a gang of road agents.

## Arizona Gunfighter

Republic, September 24, 1937, 58 minutes.
*P:* A.W. Hackel. *D:* Sam Newfield. *SC:* George Plympton. *ST:* Harry F. Olmstead. *PH:* Robert Cline. *ED:* Roy Claire. *SD:* Glen Glenn. *Asst Dir:* Bobby Ray.
*Cast:* Bob Steele, Jean Carmen, Ted Adams, Ernie Adams, Lew Meehan, Steve Clark, John Merton, Karl Hackett, A.C. Henderson, Frank Ball, Tex Palmer, Horace B. Carpenter, Budd Buster, Archie Ricks, Oscar Gahan, Allen Greer, Sherry Tansey, Silver Tip Baker, Jack Kirk, Hal Price, Roy Bucko.

After taking revenge on the men who murdered his father, a young man joins an outlaw gang which takes from the rich and helps the needy.

## Lightnin' Crandall

Republic, November 17, 1937, 60 minutes.

*P:* A.W. Hackel. *D:* Sam Newfield. *SC:* Charles Francis Royal. *ST:* E.B. Mann. *PH:* Bert Longnecker. *ED:* Roy Claire. *SD:* Cliff Ruberg.

*Cast:* Bob Steele, Lois January, Charles King, Earl Dwire, Ernie Adams, Frank LaRue, Horace Murphy, Lloyd Ingraham, Lew Meehan, Dave O'Brien, Richard Cramer, Jack C. Smith, Tex Palmer, Sherry Tansey, Art Felix, Ed Carey.

A noted gunman leaves Texas and goes to Arizona where he aids a young woman and her family in a range war.

## The Colorado Kid

Republic, December 11, 1937, 60 minutes.

*P:* A.W. Hackel. *D:* Sam Newfield. *SC:* Charles Francis Royal. *ST:* Harry F. Olmstead. *PH:* Robert Cline. *ED:* Roy Claire. *SD:* Cliff Ruberg. *Asst Dir:* William Nolte.

*Cast:* Bob Steele, Marion Weldon, Karl Hackett, Ernie Adams, Ted Adams, Frank LaRue, Horace Murphy, Kenne Duncan, Budd Buster, Frank Ball, John Melton, Horace B. Carpenter, Wally West.

After being falsely convicted for the murder of his rancher boss, a man escapes from jail to prove his innocence.

## Paroled to Die

Republic, January 11, 1938, 55 minutes.

*P:* A.W. Hackel. *D:* Sam Newfield. *SC:* George Plympton. *ST:* Harry F. Olmstead. *PH:* Robert Cline. *ED:* Roy Claire. *SD:* Cliff Ruberg. *Asst Dir:* Jerome S. Bressler.

*Cast:* Bob Steele, Kathleen Eliot, Karl Hackett, Horace Murphy, Steve Clark, Budd Buster, Sherry Tansey, Frank Ball, Jack C. Smith, Horace B. Carpenter.

Paroled from prison for a crime he did not commit, a cowboy returns home to find the real criminal and marry the girl he loves.

## Thunder in the Desert

Republic, May 18, 1938, 60 minutes.

*P:* A.W. Hackel. *D:* Sam Newfield. *SC:* George Plympton. *PH:* Robert Cline. *ED:* Roy Claire. *SD:* Cliff Ruberg. *Prod Mgr:* Jerome S. Bressler.

*Cast:* Bob Steele, Louise Stanley, Don Barclay, Ed Brady, Charles King, Horace Murphy, Steve Clark, Lew Meehan, Ernie Adams, Richard Cramer, Budd Buster, Sherry Tansey.

A man returns home to claim a ranch he has inherited and to find out who murdered its owner, his uncle.

## Desert Patrol

Republic, June 6, 1938, 60 minutes.

*P:* A.W. Hackel. *D:* Sam Newfield. *SC:* Fred Myton. *PH:* Robert Cline. *ED:* Roy Claire. *SD:* Cliff Ruberg. *Prod Mgr:* Jerome S. Bressler.

*Cast:* Bob Steele, Marion Weldon, Rex Lease, Ted Adams, Forrest Taylor, Budd Buster, Steve Clark, Jack Ingram, Julian Madison, Tex Palmer.

When he learns that his best friend has been killed by outlaws, a ranger pretends to be one of them to infiltrate the gang.

## The Feud Maker

Republic, July 20, 1938, 60 minutes.

Poster for *The Colorado Kid* (Supreme, 1937), released by Republic.

*P:* A.W. Hackel. *D:* Sam New-field. *SC:* George Plympton. *ST:* Harry F. Olmstead. *PH:* Robert Cline. *ED:* Roy Claire. *SD:* Cliff Ruberg. *Prod Mgr:* Jerome S. Bressler.

*Cast:* Bob Steele, Marion Weldon, Karl Hackett, Frank Ball, Budd Buster, Lew Meehan, Roger Williams, Forrest Taylor, Steve Clark, Jack C. Smith, Lloyd Ingraham, Wally West, Tex Palmer, Sherry Tansey.

A cowboy goes to his uncle's ranch to help him in a range war with nesters.

## Durango Valley Raiders

Republic, November 2, 1938, 60 minutes.

*P:* A.W. Hackel. *D:* Sam New-field. *SC:* George Plympton. *ST:* Harry F. Olmstead. *PH:* Robert Cline. *ED:* Roy Claire. *SD:* Cliff Ruberg. *Prod Mgr:* Jerome S. Bressler.

*Cast:* Bob Steele, Louise Stanley, Karl Hackett, Ted Adams, Forrest Taylor, Steve Clark, Horace Murphy, Jack Ingram, Julian Madison, Ernie Adams, Budd Buster, Frank Ball.

An outlaw known as The Shadow is terrorizing a valley and a young stranger arrives and is suspected of being the bad man.

## Am I Guilty?

October 2, 1940, 70 minutes.

*P:* A.W. Hackel. *D:* Samuel Neufeld [Sam Newfield]. *SC:* George Sayre & Earle Snell. *ST:* Sherman Lowe. *PH:* Robert Cline. *ED:* S. Roy Luby. *SD:* Cliff Ruberg.

*Cast:* Ralph Cooper, Sybil Lewis, Sam McDaniel, Lawrence Criner, Marcella Moreland, Arthur Ray, Reginald Fenderson, Monte Hawley, Tia Juana Matthew Jons, Pigmeat Markham, Jesse Brooks, Napoleon Simpson, Clarence Brooks, Cleo Desmond, Ida Coffin, Lillian Randolph, Vernon McCalla, Eddie Thompson, Mae Turner, Alfred Grant, Guernsey Morrow.

A black doctor starts a clinic to help the poor but innocently becomes involved with gangsters. Reissued in the late 1940s as *Racket Doctor* by Toddy Pictures.

# Syndicate Film Exchange

Although Syndicate Film Exchange operated as a producer of motion pictures from 1928 to 1932, it was part of a much larger movie corporation. It all began in 1924 with the formation of Rayart Pictures by W. Ray Johnston. This firm lasted into 1929, but by that time Syndicate Film Exchange had been set up by Johnston the previous year. Syndicate survived the coming of sound and continued to produce films into 1932 before becoming solely a distribution outfit which lasted until 1939. Johnston also had Continental Talking Pictures (q.v.) in 1929 and 1930, and in 1931 he and Trem Carr formed Monogram Pictures Corporation. In 1935 Monogram was one of the companies that became part of Republic Pictures Corporation, but in 1937 Monogram was revitalized and lasted under that name until 1952. By 1947 the company also adopted the name Allied Artists for its more prestigious features and managed to survive in various forms until 1980, although 1978 was the last year it released movies.

The founder of this movie empire, W. Ray Johnston, was from Bristow, Iowa, and after college became the treasurer of Syndicate Pictures in the early teens. He later used that name for his own Syndicate Film Exchange when it was launched in 1928. Between 1924 and 1929 Johnston's Rayart Pictures released scores of low-budget features and serials, and he became a major producer on the states' rights market, handling many independents as well as his own product. Syndicate was formed to handle westerns in deference to Rayart which had released all types of features. Between 1928 and 1932, Syndicate released over fifty westerns starring Bob Custer, Tom Tyler and Bob Steele, all of whom had started their cowboy careers at Films Booking Offices (FBO). All of these oaters were churned out by producer-director-actor J.P. McGowan through his various corporations: Big Productions, El Dorado and J.P. McGowan Productions. All were cheaply made using the same sets, locales and similar casts; nearly all were scripted by Sally Winters and photographed by Hap Depew. The films themselves relied on the personalities and established popularity of their stars to carry them through, although most were certainly passable fodder for general audiences. Some, like *Call of the Desert* (1930), a Tom Tyler starrer, are a bit different since this one was filmed after a desert snowfall, giving it more scenic value than usual.

With the coming of sound Syndicate continued to churn out non-talking westerns although by 1930 their product did contain music and sound effects. While Bob Steele waited to make his talking debut by joining Tiffany (q.v.) in 1930, Tom Tyler and Bob Custer did make their first sound films for the McGowan unit. Other names also began to appear in Syndicate westerns: Charles Delaney talked and sang in *The Lonesome Trail* (1930), and *Beyond the Law* (1930), billed as a Raytone Talking Picture, with Robert Frazer, also contained music. Other western stars to do solo efforts for Syndicate included Jack Perrin in *The Phantom of the Desert* (1930) with his beautiful horse Starlight, Mahlon Hamilton in *Code of Honor* (1930), Buffalo Bill, Jr., in *Westward Bound* (1931), Buddy Roosevelt in *Lightnin' Smith Returns* (1931) and Rex Lease in *The Lone Trail* (1932), a feature version of the Metropolitan (q.v.) serial *The Sign of the Wolf*, released the same year.

Between the fall of 1930 and the winter of 1931 Syndicate released twelve westerns starring Jack Hoxie, all edited versions of silent films he had done for Arrow Films in 1921-22. Synchronized music and sound effects were added to these two-reelers (the Arrow features had run five reels each), all of which were originally produced by Ben Wilson. The titles were *Two-Fisted Jefferson*, *The Marshal of Money Mint*, *The Desert's Crucible*, *Cyclone Bliss*, *Rider from Nowhere* (original title: *The Man from Nowhere*), *Dead or Alive*, *The Double O* and *Western Romance* (original title: *Cupid's Brand*), all released in 1930; and *The Romantic Sheriff* (original title: *The Sheriff of Hope Eternal*), *Desert Bridegroom*, *The Broken Spur* and *Sparks of Flint*, released in 1931. In addition, Syndicate released eighteen one-reelers in its "Alice" short-subject series during the 1930-31 movie season.

Regarding cliffhangers, Rayart had turned out several in the silent days, but Syndicate made only one, *The Mystery Trooper*, in 1931. Like *The Sign of the Wolf* it was produced by Harry S. Webb and F.E. Douglas, and Syndicate released it on two occasions. Later it was reissued again as *Trail of the Royal Mounted* with all new chapter titles. Even more of a curio is *Call of the Rockies* (1931), an independent feature Syndicate acquired for release. Evidently it was made toward the close of the silent era and never issued. Syndicate tacked a talking prologue on the movie and added music and sound effects to the silent portion. Even with stars like Ben Lyon and Marie Prevost, *Call of the Rockies* remained an obscure item. Another independent pickup was Willis Kent's *Law of the Tong* (1931), and by the time of its release late in the year Syndicate no longer produced movies, that job having been usurped by the newly formed Monogram.

Syndicate Film Exchange, however, continued to exist as a movie distributor. From 1933 to 1939 Syndicate released a few features on the states' rights market (films made by various independent producers) as well as British imports like *Money Talks* (1933) and *The Merry Monarch* (1935). Three of these releases were made by producer Kenneth J. Bishop in Canada: *Secrets of Chinatown* (1935), *Manhattan Shakedown* and *Special Inspector* (both 1939), the latter with Rita Hayworth. By 1939, however, Monogram was back in full production and Syndicate Film Exchange faded away for good.

## Law of the Plains

August 19, 1929, 48 minutes.

*P-D:* J.P. McGowan.

*Cast:* Tom Tyler, Natalie Joyce, J.P. McGowan, Robert Walker, William Nolte.

Years after his father is killed for the possession of his ranch, a young man vows revenge.

## The Last Roundup

August 25, 1929, 5 reels.

*P-D:* J.P. McGowan. *SC:* Sally Winters. *PH:* Hap Depew.

*Cast:* Bob Custer. Hazel Mills, Bud Osborne, Cliff Lyons, Hank Bell, J.P. McGowan, Adabelle Driver.

A ranch foreman has a falling out with a cowboy over a pretty girl causing his boss' cattle to be rustled.

## The Man from Nevada

September 22, 1929, 48 minutes.

*P-D:* J.P. McGowan. *SC:* Sally Winters. *PH:* Hap Depew.

*Cast:* Tom Tyler, Natalie Joyce, Al Ferguson, Alfred Hewston, Kip Cooper, Godfrey Craig, Frank Crane, William Nolte.

A cowboy aids the father of the girl he loves in keeping his ranch from crooks.

## The Phantom Rider

October 2, 1929, 48 minutes.

*P-D:* J.P. McGowan. *PH:* Frank Cotner.

*Cast:* Tom Tyler, Lotus Thompson, J.P. McGowan, Harry Woods.

Despite a family feud, two young people fall in love but are menaced by a mysterious rider.

## The Invaders

November 24, 1929, 62 minutes.

*P-D:* J.P. McGowan. *SC:* Walter Sterret. *Titles:* William Stratton. *ST:* Sally Winters. *PH:* Hap Depew.

*Cast:* Bob Steele, Edna Aslin, Tom Lingham, J.P. McGowan, Celeste Rush, Tom Smith, Bud Osborne, Chief Yowalchie.

Separated when their parents were killed by Indians, a brother and sister grow up on opposite sides of a conflict.

## The Fighting Terror

December 8, 1929, 5 reels.

*P-D:* J.P. McGowan. *SC:* Sally Winters. *PH:* Hap Depew.

*Cast:* Bob Custer, Hazel Mills, J.P. McGowan, Bud Osborne, Hank Bell, Adabelle Driver, Cliff Lyons, Tom Bay.

In cahoots with a dishonest sheriff an outlaw gang raids the California-Nevada border but is hunted by a man whose brother they killed.

## The Lone Horseman

December 8, 1929, 5 reels.

*P-D:* J.P. McGowan. *SC:* Sally Winters. *PH:* Hap Depew.

*Cast:* Tom Tyler, Charlotte Winn, J.P. McGowan, Mack V. Wright, Tom Bay, Mrs. B. Tansey, Blackjack Ward.

A cowboy tries to recover his ranch which was accidentally sold to a woman and her niece.

## 'Neath Western Skies

December 15, 1929, 49 minutes.

*P-D:* J.P. McGowan. *SC:* Sally Winters. *PH:* Frank Cotner & Hap Depew.

*Cast:* Tom Tyler, Lotus Thompson, J.P. McGowan, Harry Woods, Barney Furey, Hank Bell, Alfred Hewston, Bobby Dunn.

Harassed by outlaws trying to steal their oil rights, a young man and woman plot to stop the gang.

## The Oklahoma Kid

December 15, 1929, 5 reels.

*P-D:* J.P. McGowan. *SC:* Walter Sterret. *Titles:* William Stratton. *ST:* Sally Winters. *PH:* Hap Depew.

*Cast:* Bob Custer, Vivian Ray, J.P. McGowan, Henry Rocquemore, Tommy Bay, Walter Patterson.

Taking his boss' cattle to market, a cowboy is waylaid by an outlaw gang and the herd is stolen.

## A Texas Cowboy

December 21, 1929, 50 minutes.

*P-D:* J.P. McGowan. *SC:* Sally Winters.

*Cast:* Bob Steele, Edna Aslin, J.P. McGowan, Bud Osborne, Perry Murdock, Alfred Hewston, Grace Stevens, Cliff Lyons.

Returning home, a young man learns his widowed mother has married a man who is trying to take control of her ranch.

## The Parting of the Trails

January 15, 1930, 5 reels.

*P-D:* J.P. McGowan. *SC:* Sally Winters. *PH:* Hap Depew.

*Cast:* Bob Custer, Vivian Ray, Bobby Dunn, Henry Rocquemore, Tommy Bay, George A. Miller.

When a millionaire is kidnapped by an outlaw, a cowboy tries to find him and also romance his daughter.

## Pioneers of the West

January 19, 1930, 5 reels.

*P-D:* J.P. McGowan. *SC:* Sally Winters. *PH:* Hap Depew.

*Cast:* Tom Tyler, Charlotte Winn,

J.P. McGowan, Mack V. Wright, Tommy Bay, George Brownhill.

An express company agent tries to protect a young woman who is threatened by train robbers.

## Riders of the Rio Grande

January 26, 1930, 5 reels.
*P-D:* J.P. McGowan. *SC:* Sally Winters. *PH:* Hap Depew.
*Cast:* Bob Custer, Edna Aslin, Horace B. Carpenter, Kip Cooper, Bob Erickson, Martin Cichy, Merrill McCormack.

A cowboy aids a girl who has been kidnapped by a counterfeiting gang.

## O'Malley Rides Alone

February 5, 1930, 5 reels.
*P-D:* J.P. McGowan. *SC:* Sally Winters. *PH:* Hal Depew.
*Cast:* Bob Custer, Phyllis Bainbridge, J.P. McGowan, Perry Murdock, Bud Osborne, Cliff Lyons, Martin Cichy.

Crooks steal a prospector's gold and his daughter summons the aid of a Mountie.

## The Cowboy and the Outlaw

March 23, 1930, 48 minutes.
*P-D:* J.P. McGowan. *SC:* Sally Winters. *PH:* Hal Depew.
*Cast:* Bob Steele, Edna Aslin, Bud Osborne, Tom Lingham, Cliff Lyons, J.P. McGowan, Alfred Hewston.

When his rancher father is murdered, a young man tries to find the killer.

## The Man from Nowhere

April 9, 1930, 49 minutes.
*P-D:* J.P. McGowan. *SC:* Sally Winters. *PH:* Hal Depew.
*Cast:* Bob Steele, Ione Reed, Clark

Comstock, William Nestel, Perry Murdock, Tom Forman, Clark Coffey.

A rambling cowboy comes upon a family feud and helps a girl and her sick father stop a relative from taking the old man's range. Alternate title: *Western Honor.*

## Call of the Desert

May 18, 1930, 48 minutes.
*P-D:* J.P. McGowan. *SC:* Sally Winters. *ST:* Barney Williams. *PH:* Harry Fowler.
*Cast:* Tom Tyler, Sheila Le Gay, Bud Osborne, Cliff Lyons, Bobby Dunn.

A man goes into the desert to find a mine claim left to him by his father only to have his pal steal the claim from him.

## Covered Wagon Trails

May 18, 1930, 5 reels.
*P-D:* J.P. McGowan. *SC:* Sally Winters. *PH:* Hap Depew.
*Cast:* Bob Custer, Phyllis Bainbridge, Perry Murdock, Charles Brinley, Martin Cichy, J.P. McGowan.

A deputy sheriff is after a gang, one of the members being the brother of the girl he loves.

## The Canyon of Missing Men

June 1, 1930, 48 minutes.
*P-D:* J.P. McGowan. *SC:* Sally Winters. *ST:* George H. Williams. *PH:* Hap Depew.
*Cast:* Tom Tyler (Dave Brandon), Sheila Le Gay (Inez Sepulveda), Tom Forman (Juan Sepulveda), Bud Osborne (Slug Slagel), J.P. McGowan (Sheriff), Cliff Lyons (Brill Lonergan), Bobby Dunn (Gimpy Lamb), Arden Ellis (Peg Slagel).

A rustling gang has its hideout in a remote canyon but one of the members, Dave Brandon (Tom Tyler), decides to lead an honest life after falling in love with pretty Inez (Sheila Le Gay), the daughter of rancher Juan Sepulveda (Tom Forman). To get even with Dave for skipping out, gang leader Slug (Bud Osborne) plans to kidnap Inez, but Dave stops him. The gang, however, returns and abducts both Inez and her father and holds them for ransom while planning to rustle their cattle herd. Dave has been arrested for his part in the gang's previous activities, but he manages to escape in order to try and free Inez. After rustling the cattle, the gang plans to blow up the entrance to their hidden canyon as they make their escape but the plan is thwarted by Dave who arrives in time to stop them. A posse follows Dave and rounds up the fleeing outlaws as Dave rescues his sweetheart and her father. For his part in capturing the gang, Dave is placed in Inez' custody and the two plan to wed.

Tom Tyler began his starring career in westerns at Films Booking Offices (FBO) in 1925 and stayed with the operation into 1929 when he switched to Syndicate Film Exchange. For Syndicate he starred in eight silent westerns, some with music and sound effects, and then did three talkies for the company in 1931 before it became Monogram Pictures. He did another eight westerns for Monogram for the 1931-32 film season. All total, Tom Tyler starred in nineteen westerns for Syndicate-Monogram between 1929 and 1932. *The Canyon of Missing Men* was the penultimate silent he did for the company, issued with music and sound effects. The film's title refers to an outlaw hideout and the picture itself is fairly representative of the westerns Tom Tyler did for producer-director J.P. McGowan's Big Productions, Inc.

Plotwise it is only fair, and many of the settings in the film also show up in McGowan's other Syndicate releases. As is to be expected, the tight-fisted McGowan unit shot mostly outdoor sequences, but the overall feature is speedy and action-filled enough to have satisfied its intended audience. Besides making serials for Universal in the 1930s Tom Tyler went on to do series for Freuler Film Associates, Reliable and Victory (qq.v.) in addition to two top-notch westerns at RKO, *Powdersmoke Range* (1935) and *The Last Outlaw* (1936).

## The Oklahoma Sheriff

July 16, 1930, 49 minutes.

*P-D:* J.P. McGowan. *SC:* Sally Winters. *PH:* Herbert Kirkpatrick.

*Cast:* Bob Steele, Jean Reno, Perry Murdock, Cliff Lyons, Mack V. Wright, Tom Lingham, Clark Comstock.

A lawman is murdered by his corrupt deputy and the killer also wants the dead man's daughter, whose boyfriend tries to solve the crime.

## Code of the West

July 27, 1930, 5 reels.

*P-D:* J.P. McGowan. *SC:* Sally Winters. *PH:* Hap Depew.

*Cast:* Bob Custer, Vivian Ray, Bobby Dunn, Bud Osborne, Martin Cichy, Cliff Lyons, Tom Bay, Buck Bucko.

The railroad sends a special investigator to capture a gang behind the theft of insured packages.

## The Lonesome Trail

August 17, 1930, 60 minutes

*P-SC-ED:* George A. Durlam. *D:* Bruce Mitchell. *SD:* J.R. Balsley.

*Cast:* Charles Delaney, Virginia

Brown Faire, Ben Corbett, Jimmy Aubrey, Yakima Canutt, Bob Reeves, Art Mix, Lafe McKee, George Regas, William Von Brincken, William Mc-Call, George Hackathorne, Monte Montague, George Berliner.

A cowboy has to prove his innocence when he is suspected of being the bandit robbing express shipments.

## Breezy Bill

September 14, 1930, 46 minutes.
*P-D:* J.P.. McGowan. *SC:* Sally Winters. *PH:* Hap Depew.

*Cast:* Bob Steele, Edna Aslin, Alfred Hewston, George Hewston, Bud Osborne, J.P. McGowan, Perry Murdock, Cliff Lyons.

When he is blamed for the kidnapping of his rich stepfather, a young man seeks to find the real culprits.

## The Convict's Code

October 5, 1930, 66 minutes.
*P:* W. Ray Johnston. *D:* Harry Revier. *SC:* Mabel Z. Carroll & Vincent Valentini. *PH:* George Peters & Al Harsten. *SD:* George Luckey & T. Dewhurst.

*Cast:* Cullen Landis, Eloise Taylor, William Morris, Robert Cummings, Lyle Evans, Mabel Z. Carroll, John Irwin, John Burkell.

As a man is about to be executed for murder, a young woman makes one last plea in order to save his life.

## The Phantom of the Desert

November 1, 1930, 55 minutes.
*P:* Harry S. Webb & F.E. Douglas. *D:* Harry S. Webb. *SC:* Carl Krusada. *PH:* William Nobles. *ED:* Fred Bain. *SD:* Ralph M. Like.

*Cast:* Jack Perrin, Eva Novak, Josef Swickard, Lila Eccles, Ben Cor-

bett, Edward Earle, Robert Walker, Pete Morrison, Starlight.

When a wild horse is blamed for rustling, a cowboy believes in his innocence.

## Beyond the Law

November 2, 1930, 56 minutes.
*P:* W. Ray Johnston. *D:* J.P. McGowan. *SC:* George A. Durlam. *PH:* Frank Newman. *ED:* Arthur Brooks.

*Cast:* Robert Frazer, Louise Lorraine, Lane Chandler, Jimmy Kane, Charles King, Edward Lynch, William Walling, George Hackathorne, Franklyn Farnum, Robert Graves, Al St. John, Bob Reeves, Harry Holden, Blackie Whiteford, Tex Phelps.

Two drifters stop three crooks from taking over a town on the California-Nevada border.

## Code of Honor

November 16, 1930, 55 minutes.
*P-SC:* George Arthur Durlam. *D:* J.P. McGowan. *PH:* Otto Himm. *ED:* Arthur Brooks.

*Cast:* Mahlon Hamilton, Doris Hill, Robert Graves, Stanley Taylor, Lafe McKee, Jimmy Aubrey, Harry Holden, William Dyer.

A reformed gambler must revive his card tricks to save the ranch of his girlfriend's father from crooks.

## The Mystery Trooper

1931, 10 chapters.
*P:* Harry S. Webb & F.E. Douglas. *D:* Stuart Paton. *SC:* Carl Krusada. *ST:* F.E. Douglas. *PH:* Edward Kull. *ED:* Fred Bain. *SD:* Ralph M. Like. *Asst Dir:* Raymond Hines & Armand L. Schaefer.

*Cast:* Buzz Barton, Robert Frazer, Blanche Mehaffey, Al Ferguson, Charles King, William Von Brincken,

Lobby card for the final chapter of the serial *The Mystery Trooper* (Syndicate, 1931) showing Robert Frazer embracing Blanche Mehaffey.

William Bertram, White Cloud, Henry Rocquemore.

A mysterious Mountie protects a group of people from outlaws as they try to find a lost gold mine.

*Chapter titles:* The Trap of Terror, Paths of Peril, Fighting Fate, The Cave of Horror, The House of Hate, The Day of Doom, The Death Trail, The Killer Dogs, The Ghost City, The Lost Treasure.

*Note:* This serial was reissued as *Trail of the Royal Mounted* with the following chapter titles: Clutches of Death, The Perilous Trail, Shadows of Evil, The Fit of Doom, Escape from Danger, The Devil's Warning, Path of Fate, Fangs of the Killer, The Phantom Warning, Fight to the Finish. The reissue was by Guaranteed Pictures Corporation in 1938.

## Westward Bound

January 25, 1931, 60 minutes.

*P:* Harry W. Webb & F.E. Douglas. *D:* Harry S. Webb. *SC:* Carl Krusada. *PH:* William Nobles. *ED:* Fred Bain. *SD:* Ralph M. Like.

*Cast:* Buffalo Bill, Jr., Allene Ray, Buddy Roosevelt, Yakima Canutt, Pete Morrison, Robert Walker, Wally Wales, Henry Rocquemore, Ben Corbett, Fern Emmett, Tom London.

A tenderfoot and his chauffeur go west and end up infiltrating and bringing to justice an outlaw gang.

## Under Texas Skies

February 1, 1931, 6 reels.

*P:* W. Ray Johnston. *D:* J.P. McGowan. *SC:* George A. Durlam. *PH:* Otto Himm. *ED:* Alfred Brook.

*Cast:* Bob Custer, Natalie Kingston, Bill Cody, Tom London, Lane Chandler, Bob Roper, William McCall, Joseph Marks, Ted Adams.

A Secret Service agent is on the trail of horse rustlers working along the Mexican border.

## West of Cheyenne

March 1, 1931, 56 minutes.

*P:* Harry S. Webb & F.E. Douglas. *D:* Harry S. Webb. *SC:* Oliver Drake & Bennett Cohen. *PH:* William Nobles. *ED:* Carl Himm.

*Cast:* Tom Tyler, Josephine Hill, Harry Woods, Ben Corbett, Robert Walker, Lafe McKee, Fern Emmett, Murdock McQuarrie, Lew Meehan, Slim Whitaker, Frank Ellis, Tex Palmer, Henry Rocquemore.

To clear his father of a murder charge, a man pretends to be an outlaw and goes to a fugitive hideout.

## Riders of the North

April 5, 1931, 59 minutes

*P-SC:* George A. Durlam. *D:* J.P. McGowan. *PH:* Otto Himm. *ED:* Charles Hunt. *SD:* Joe Phillips.

*Cast:* Bob Custer, Blanche Mehaffey, Eddie Dunn, William Walling, Frank Rice, George Regas, Buddy Shaw, George Hackathorne, Al Ferguson, Horace B. Carpenter, Blackie Whiteford, Tom Smith, Carl de Loro.

A Mountie gets on the trail of two men who murdered his partner and then framed another for the crime.

## Rider of the Plains

May 3, 1931, 52 minutes.

*P:* Trem Carr. *D:* J.P. McCarthy. *SC:* Wellyn Totman. *PH:* Archie Stout.

*Cast:* Tom Tyler, Andy Shuford, Lillian Bond, Al Bridge, Gordon DeMain, Ted Adams, Slim Whitaker, Fern Emmett.

A reformed outlaw adopts a young boy but loses custody of him when the townspeople find out about his past.

## Defenders of the Law

May 24, 1931, 76 minutes.

*P:* W. Ray Johnston. *D:* Joseph Levering. *SC:* Hampton Del Ruth & Louis Heifetz. *ST:* Hampton Del Ruth. *PH:* James Brown, Jr. *ED:* Dwight Caldwell. *SD:* Charles Franklin & Neil Jack. *Settings:* Frank Dexter. *Asst Dir:* J.O. Duffy.

*Cast:* Edmund Breese (Police Commissioner Randall), Catherine Dale Owen (Alice Randall), John Holland (Captain Bill Houston), Robert Glecker (Joe Velet/Phil Terry), Mae Busch (Mae Ward), Al Cooke (Cookie), Joseph Girard (Police Chief), Philo McCullough (Gangster), Paul Panzer (Taroni), Kit Guard (Kit), Nick Thompson (Tom Muldoon).

Opening with silent footage with the title "Without Glory" superimposed over it, *Defenders of the Law* then settles down to tell its story of Los Angeles Police Commissioner Randall (Edmund Breese) waging a war against local gangsters. One member of the force is Captain Bill Houston (John Holland), a former fighter of the Riffs in North Africa, who is romancing Alice Randall (Catherine Dale Owen), the commissioner's daughter. Bill is assigned to stop notorious Eastern gangster Velet (Robert Glecker), who is coming West to set up operations. At the airport Velet meets local mobster Taroni (Paul Panzer) but is arrested for carrying a gun and is taken to headquarters. There he meets Bill who recognizes him as Phil Terry, his former sergeant and friend. Velet has apparently become a hoodlum because crime provides him with a lucrative income in deference to the small salary ("cigarette money") paid to law enforcers. Velet is extradited back East for two killings, but his hoodlums pretend to be policemen and he manages to escape. Bill sends out the best men on the force to find Velet, who challenges him to a face-to-face confrontation. At the Silver Slipper Club Velet and his gang arrive to stick up the place, and in a shootout he kills Taroni, whose girl Mae (Mae Busch), really an undercover policewoman, informs on him. Velet again escapes and vows to get even with Bill, who has rounded up most of his gang in a raid on the club. Velet has Alice kidnapped and taken to his hideout, a tenement building in a slum area, and the commissioner orders Bill removed from the case. With only one hour to act, Bill takes some men and locates Velet's hideout, and there is a shootout. Bill manages to corner Velet and free Alice. In a fight between the two former pals, Velet is killed.

The popularity of gangster pictures in the early 1930s resulted in a plethora of such screen fare with *Defenders of the Law* being one of the lesser efforts in the genre from this period. Slow moving, it is a preachy affair against gangland and its denizens with one of the cops announcing of hoodlums: "They're a plague like rats and they will have to be wiped out like rats." Top billing went to Edmund Breese and Catherine Dale Owen as the police commissioner and his daughter. Neither have large roles. Owen, although very beautiful, apparently had her part kept to a minimum because of a distinct lack of Thespian ability. She had a brief vogue in the early talkies in major films like *The Rogue Song* for MGM in 1930, but by 1931 her film career was on the wane. John Holland is not much better as the wooden hero, but Robert Glecker is very good as the gangster who likes to cut out silhouettes. Silent stars Paul Panzer and Mae Busch handle their roles in good form as a rival gangster and his girl (who is actually a police undercover agent), and Al Cooke has some amusing scenes as a clumsy, incompetent news photographer.

## God's Country and the Man

June 7, 1931, 61 minutes.

*P:* Trem Carr. *D:* J.P. McCarthy. *SC:* J.P. McCarthy, Al Bridge & Wellyn Totman. *PH:* Archie Stout. *ED:* Charles Hunt. *AD:* E.R. Hickson. *Prod Mgr:* Charles A. Post. *Asst Dir:* Paul Malvern

*Cast:* Tom Tyler, Betty Mack, Al Bridge, Ted Adams, George Hayes, Julian Rivero, John Elliott, William Bertram, Carmen LaRoux, Merrill McCormack, Slim Whitaker, Henry Rocquemore, Blackie Whiteford, Al Haskell, Tom Smith, Al Taylor.

A government agent and his pal go into Mexico to apprehend a gunrunner wanted for murder. Originally called *God's Country* and reissued as *Man's Country* and *Rose of the Rio Grande*.

## A Son of the Plains

July 5, 1931, 59 minutes.

*P:* Trem Carr. *D-SC:* Robert North Bradbury. *PH:* Archie Stout. *SD:* Balsley & Phillips.

*Cast:* Bob Custer (Tom Brent), Doris Phillips (Ann Farrell), J.P. McGowan (Dan Farrell), Edward Hearn (Brokaw), Gordon DeMain (Sheriff), Al St. John (Drunk), Art Mix, Blackie Whiteford, Eve Humes, Artie Ortego, Jack Evans, Jane Crowley, Bob Burns.

**Bob Custer, Doris Phillips and J.P. McGowan in** *A Son of the Plains* **(Syndicate, 1931).**

The notorious Polka Dot Bandit has been carrying out a series of robberies, and as deputy sheriff, Tom Brent (Bob Custer) is appointed to catch the badman. The bandit holds up the local express office and shoots its operator but in his getaway loses the money he has stolen. It is found by rancher Dan Farrell (J.P. McGowan), who is shot and wounded as he returns to his home. As a result, the locals suspect Dan of being the bandit while Tom thinks he may be giving sanctuary to the outlaw. Complicating the problem is the fact that Tom loves Dan's daughter Ann (Doris Phillips), and the girl believes that Tom is trying to railroad her father. Tom continues to investigate the case as several other suspects surface, and eventually he is able to capture the Polka Dot Bandit, prove Dan Farrell innocent and rewin Ann's love.

*A Son of the Plains* is a very poor entry in the Bob Custer western series for Syndicate, shoddily made and badly acted, especially by its star. One amusing sequence does take place in a tacky dive called the Yucca Saloon (!) where a rather long-in-the-tooth chanteuse warbles Paul Dresser's "On the Banks of the Wabash." About the only other good point in the feature is a few amusing moments with Al St. John as a barfly. Interestingly, director-writer Robert North Bradbury remade the story three years later as *Blue Steel*, one of the Lone Star Westerns producer Paul Malvern made starring John Wayne. It too was photographed by Archie Stout and was a big improvement over the original.

Bob Custer's real name was Raymond Glenn, a monicker he used in the silent days before becoming a cowboy star. When riding cinema trails, however, he became Bob Custer, working first for Films Booking Offices (FBO) in a series in 1924. He stayed with the company, forming Bob Custer Productions in 1927. He joined Syndicate in 1928 and made twenty westerns for them through 1931, after which he went to work for Big 4 (q.v.). Of all the low-budget western stars, Custer was probably the most stoic. Rarely laughing or even smiling, Custer had minimal acting ability and fewer facial expressions. He simply carried out his hero's task as quickly as possible, seemingly oblivious to the fact that his actions seemed ridiculous on many occasions. He was often cast in parts for which he was totally unfit, such as the outlaws' young protégé in *Law of the Rio Grande* (1931). Like other western heroes, Bob Custer had been popular in the silent days because he need not be heard and because his features moved quickly. Sound, however, slowed up that process, leaving fans to wonder how he could have stayed around so long. Despite his severe screen limitations, however, Custer lingered on through a brief series for Reliable (q.v.) that ended in 1937.

## Call of the Rockies

July 12, 1931, 71 minutes.
    *P:* Leon Goetz & Albert Dezel. *D:* Raymond K. Johnson. *PH:* King Gray & H.H. Brownell. *ED:* George McQuire. *Mus:* Dell Youngmeyer. *Orchestra:* James G. Henshel.
    *Cast:* Ben Lyon, Marie Prevost, Gladys Johnson, Anders Randolph, Russell Simpson, Jim Mason, The Four Night Hawks.

The story of the settlement of a valley in the Rocky Mountain foothills. Also called *West of the Rockies.*

## Law of the Rio Grande

August 9, 1931, 57 minutes.
    *P:* Harry S. Webb & F.E. Douglas. *D:* Forrest Sheldon. *SC:* Betty Burbridge & Bennett Cohen. *PH:* Herbert Kirkpatrick. *ED:* Fred Bain. *SD:* Balsey & Phillips.
    *Cast:* Bob Custer, Betty Mack, Carlton King, Nelson McDowell, Harry Todd, Edmund Cobb, Lafe McKee, Fred Burns, Hank Bell.
    After he is shot an outlaw gang leader pretends to be dead so that his protégé will lead an honest life.

## Lightnin' Smith Returns

August 16, 1931, 59 minutes.
    *P-D-SC:* Jack Irwin. *PH:* Amos Stillman. *ED:* Earl Turner. *SD:* Herb Eicke.
    *Cast:* Buddy Roosevelt, Barbara Worth, Tom London, Nick Dunaev, Jack Richardson, Sam Tittley, Fred Parker, Pee Wee Holmes, William Bertram.
    A writer of western stories is invited to visit a ranch and through a prank gets involved in a holdup.

## Law of the Tong

December 20, 1931, 56 minutes.
    *P:* Willis Kent. *D:* Lew Collins. *SC:* Oliver Drake. *PH:* William Nobles.
    *Cast:* Phyllis Barrington, Jason Robards, John Harron, Frank Lackteen, Mary Carr, Dot Farley, William Mahlen, Richard Alexander.
    A dance hall hostess and a government agent find themselves in the middle of a tong war in San Francisco. Also called *Law of the Tongs.*

## The Lone Trail

March 13, 1932, 61 minutes.

*P:* Harry S. Webb & F.E. Douglas. *D:* Harry S. Webb & Forrest Sheldon. *SC:* Betty Burbridge & Bennett Cohen. *PH:* William Nobles & Herbert Kirkpatrick. *ED:* Fred Bain. *Asst Dir:* Melville DeLay.

*Cast:* Rex Lease, Virginia Brown Faire, Joe Bonomo, Jack Mower, Josephine Hill, Al Ferguson, Robert Walker, Edmund Cobb, Harry Todd, Billy O'Brien, Jack Perrin, Muro.

When his sister is murdered, a ranger sets out to get revenge on the killer. Feature version of the serial *The Sign of the Wolf* (Metropolitan, 1931).

## Four Aces

February 24, 1933, 65 minutes.

*Cast:* Private C.K. Slack, General John J. Pershing.

Various filmclips and newsreel footage are used to show the history of World War I.

## Money Talks

August 12, 1933, 66 minutes.

*D:* Norman Lee. *SC:* Norman Lee, Frank Miller & Edwin Greenwood. *PH:* Walter Harvey.

*Cast:* Julian Rose, Judy Kelly, Bernard Ansell, Kid Berg, Lena Maitland, Gladys Sewell, Griffith Jones, Gus McNaughton, Mary Charles, Hal Gordon, Jimmy Godden, Rich & Galvin.

In order to inherit a fortune a man must give up all of his possessions. Produced in England and released there in 1932 by British International Pictures; running time, 73 minutes.

## Secrets of Chinatown

February 20, 1935, 63 minutes.

*P:* Kenneth J. Bishop. *D:* Fred Newmeyer. *SC:* Guy Morton, from his novel. *PH:* William Beckway. *ED:* William Austin. *Mus:* Li-Young. *SD:* Wallie Hamilton.

*Cast:* Nick Stuart, Lucille Browne, Raymond Lawrence, James Flavin, Harry Hewitson, James McGrath, Reginald Hincks, John Barnard, Arthur Legge-Willis.

A detective, trying to solve a series of killings in Chinatown, finds out his friend and the girl he loves have disappeared. Filmed in Canada by Commonwealth Productions.

## The Merry Monarch

July 16, 1935, 58 minutes.

*D:* Alexis Granowsky. *SC:* Pierre Louys. *PH:* Rudolf [Rudolph] Mate. *Mus:* Carl Rathaus.

*Cast:* Emil Jannings, Sidney Fox, Josette Day, Jose Noguerro, Armand Bernard.

English language version of the 1933 German feature *Der Abenteuer des Konigs Pausole [The Adventures of King Pausole].*

## Timberesque

July 8, 1937, 41 minutes.

*P-D:* King Guidice. *SC:* William Berke & Robert St. Clair. *PH:* Robert Cline. *Ed:* Arthur Brooks.

*Cast:* Barry Norton, Vyola Vonn, Flash the Dog, Harold Nelson, Paul Ellis, Christina Montt, William G. Steuer, Enrique DeRosas.

Giving up his life as a famous singer, a man heads to the northwoods with his dog to find peace of mind. Also released in French and Spanish language versions each running 68 minutes.

## Manhattan Shakedown

October 27, 1939, 57 minutes.

*P:* Kenneth J. Bishop. *D:* Leon Barsha. *SC:* Edgar Edwards. *PH:* George Meehan. *ED:* William Austin. *SD:* Herb Eicke. *Supv:* Jack Fier.

*Cast:* John Gallaudet, Rosalind Keith, George McKay, Reginald Hincks, Bob Rideout, Phyllis Claire, Donald Douglas, Michael Heppell, James McGrath, Grant MacDonald, John Caird.

After a friend is murdered, a columnist-radio commentator tries to prove a noted psychiatrist is the killer. Filmed in Canada in 1937 by Central Films.

## Special Inspector

November 1, 1939, 65 minutes.

*P:* Kenneth J. Bishop. *D:* Leon Barsha. *SC:* Edgar Edwards. *PH:* George Meehan. *ED:* William Austin. *AD:* Lionel Banks. *Asst Dir:* George Rhein.

*Cast:* Charles Quigley, Rita Hayworth, George McKay, Edgar Edwards, Eddie Laughton, Bob Rideout, Grant MacDonald, Bill Irving, Virginia Coomb, Fred Bass, Vincent McKenna, Donald Douglas.

Working undercover on a hijacking operation, two men team with a beautiful woman to expose the gang. Filmed in Canada in 1937 by Central Films.

# Tiffany Productions

During its more than a decade of existence, Tiffany used several titles: from 1922 to 1927 it was Tiffany Productions, and from 1927 to 1930 it was Tiffany-Stahl Productions. From 1930 until its demise as a production company it was Tiffany Productions again, and in 1932-33 when it leased its lot for the production of World Wide (q.v.) product it was dubbed California Tiffany Studios. Whatever its name, Tiffany was considered perhaps the apex of independent motion-picture making in Hollywood. As Don Miller noted in *B Movies* (1973), "It might be said that Tiffany Pictures was the MGM of the independents." Certainly Tiffany turned out high-grade productions, and its product was popular with distributors in both the silent and sound eras.

Tiffany Studios went into the movie business in 1921 and the next year launched its own production program with distribution through Metro Pictures, which may account for its rapid rise among the Hollywood independents. L.A. Young was president of Tiffany Productions, William Saal vice president and general manager. Catering mainly to urban audiences, the studio majored in society stories and melodramas, and in its first year it scored a big hit with Mae Murray in *Peacock Alley*. The popular Miss Murray continued to turn out top-grossing movies for the studio, which remained very successful. In 1927, however, Metro joined with Goldwyn to form Metro-Goldwyn (later to become Metro-Goldwyn-Mayer [MGM]) and Tiffany was forced to set up its own distribution system. That year M.H. Hoffman headed Tiffany, and director John M. Stahl became a partner in the operation as the company moved to the former Fine Art Studios at 4500 Sunset Boulevard in Hollywood where it became known as Tiffany-Stahl Productions.

As Tiffany-Stahl the company made the difficult move into the sound era with the part-talkie *Lucky Boy*, starring George Jessel, in January of 1929. Jessel had played the lead in "The Jazz Singer" when it was on Broadway, but the movie role went to Al Jolson in 1927 at Warner Brothers, where Jolson made movie history with the first sound film. Today, Jessel's effort is forgotten except for the fact it provided him with his theme song, "My Mother's Eyes," which he successfully recorded at the time for Victor Records. Tiffany-Stahl continued to struggle through 1929 with a lackluster group of mostly part-talking efforts, including two Belle Bennett-Joe E. Brown starrers, *Molly and Me* and *My Lady's Past*. In 1930 Mae Murray attempted a comeback with a remake of *Peacock Alley*, but *Photoplay* noted, "She shouldn't have done it." The company also made expensive products like *The Lost Zeppelin* and *Mamba*, the latter an early Technicolor product. Neither managed to jolt public response but a coproduction with the British company Gainsborough brought Tiffany-Stahl its greatest prestige when it made *Journey's End*, released in the spring of 1930. A faithful screen adaptation of the austere R.C. Sheriff play about a British unit in the trenches during the World War, it made most of the top ten lists for best film of the year, launched the directorial career of James Whale and made a bundle of money for Tiffany-Stahl.

While *Journey's End* was the high point of the company's existence, it was also the beginning of its decline because Tiffany-Stahl could not come up with a successor in box-office appeal. In the summer of 1930 the company attempted to make a star of Benny Rubin in *Sunny Skies* and *Hot Curves*, but both bombed. No better was a feeble effort starring Jack Benny called *The Medicine Man* with its Jewish stereotypes. Old-timer Kenneth Harlan headlined (and sang!) in *Paradise Island*, and one-time child star Wesley Barry attempted to try young adult roles with *The Thoroughbred* while silent star Leatrice Joy emoted in *The Love Trader* with Henry B. Walthall, Barbara Bedford and Noah Beery. The most popular player to emerge at Tiffany-Stahl in 1930 was Rex Lease, who proved to be a good utility actor in a variety of features like *Troopers Three*, *Sunny Skies*, *Hot Curves*, *Wings of Adventure*, *Borrowed Wives* and *The Utah Kid*, where he found his niche as a western hero. Declining box office, no doubt, caused the company to turn to sagebrush yarns, something it had previously shunned. In 1930, however, the company signed two of the most popular cowboy stars, Ken Maynard and Bob Steele, each for a series of westerns.

John M. Stahl pulled out of the company in 1930, and it reverted to Tiffany Productions. Stahl, who had been a producer-director since 1918, went to Universal where he worked until the end of the decade in features like *Back Street* (1932), *Imitation of Life* (1934), *Magnificent Obsession* (1935) and *When*

*Tomorrow Comes* (1939). He spent the 1940s at 20th Century-Fox directing such movies as *The Immortal Sergeant* (1942), *The Keys of the Kingdom* (1944), *The Foxes of Harrow* (1947) and *Oh, You Beautiful Doll* (1949) before his death in 1950 at the age of 64.

Another activity for Tiffany in 1930 was its short subject program, which included six two-reelers in its "The Tiffany Talking Chimps" series produced by Sigmund Neufeld, twenty-six one-reelers in its popular "The Voice of Hollywood" group and a half-dozen Paul Hurst comedy two-reelers. That year the company also made six one-reel "Musical Fantasies," a half-dozen "Forbes Randolph's Kentucky Jubilee Singers" musicals, three one-reelers and three two-reelers, and six one-reel "Multicolor Subjects." The Tiffany Chimp Series used chimps as actors dressed as humans and filmed among small sets with human voices dubbed in for the dialogue. "The Voice of Hollywood" offered a different star host for each segment which came from a fictional radio station, STAR. The shorts were a hodgepodge of music, comedy and public events footage, and many big names made fleeting appearances in the series. Unfortunately, the movies were cheaply made and not overly entertaining or well done. In *The Great Movie Shorts* (1972), Leonard Maltin called "The Voice of Hollywood," "One of the most preposterous short-subject series of all time.... 'The Voice of Hollywood' shorts serve an academic purpose—to illustrate just how bad a short subject can be." "The Voice of Hollywood" continued in 1931 with another baker's dozen one-reelers while six more "The Tiffany Talking Chimps" one-reelers were also produced along with another half-dozen "Football for the Fan" one-reel shorts before the company folded its short-subject program that year.

In 1931 Sam Bischoff took over as president of Tiffany, but by this time the company was beginning to struggle to keep its head above water. The company turned out the expensive *Aloha* starring Ben Lyon and Raquel Torres that year along with the wonderfully entertaining old-fashioned melodrama *Drums of Jeopardy*, starring Warner Oland, June Collyer and Lloyd Hughes. James Cruze Productions made several carefully budgeted dramas (*Command Performance, Hell Bound, Salvation Nell, Women Go On Forever*) for the company, but its real moneymakers were the westerns with Ken Maynard and Bob Steele. Between 1930 and 1932 Ken Maynard headlined eleven oaters for Tiffany while Bob Steele made his sound debut with the company in 1930 in *Near the Rainbow's End*. He made seven more features with producer Trem Carr at Tiffany before the two moved to World Wide in 1932. Another production unit working at Tiffany was William Saal's Quadruple Pictures, which in 1932 turned out the remainder of the Maynard series (Phil Goldstone had produced eight of the eleven westerns) with *Hell-Fire Austin, Texas Gunfighter* and *Whistlin' Dan* plus the dramas *Hotel Continental, Lena Rivers, The Man Called Back* and *Strangers of the Evening*.

Following the release of *The Man Called Back* in the summer of 1932, Tiffany ceased to exist as a motion picture production company. Since the beginning of that year World Wide had assumed the distribution of its product. In 1932 Burt Kelly, Sam Bischoff and William Saal formed a company known variously as K.B.S. Film Company, K.B.S. Film Corporation and K.B.S. Productions, Inc. Using what was now called the California Tiffany Studios as its base, the outfit produced films for World Wide release including eight Ken Maynard westerns and features like *The Constant Woman*, *The Last Mile*, *The Death Kiss* (which used the studio for its background) and *A Study in Scarlet*. By this time, however, World Wide was also in financial difficulty and ceased operations. Its unreleased features like *A Study in Scarlet* were distributed by Fox. In 1932 K.B.S. became Admiral Productions.

Like its smaller contemporaries Tiffany Pictures simply could not withstand the inroads of the Depression. After hitting its peak with *Journey's End* in 1930, the studio quickly deteriorated and, despite several attempts to reorganize, it was history by the beginning of 1932.

## Broadway Fever

January 6, 1929, 6 reels, Silent.

*D:* Edward Cline. *SC:* Lois Leesson. *Titles:* Frederick Hatton, Fanny Hatton & Paul Perez. *ST:* Viola Brothers Shore. *PH:* John Boyle. *ED:* Byron Robinson. *Sets:* George Sawley. *AD:* Harvey Libbert.

*Cast:* Sally O'Neil, Roland Drew, Corliss Palmer, Calvert Carter.

A stagestruck young girl becomes the maid to an important theatrical producer.

## Lucky Boy

January 6, 1929, 10 reels, Part-Talkie.

*D:* Norman Taurog, Charles C. Wilson & Rudolph Flothow. *SC:* Isadore Bernstein & George Jessel. *Titles:* Harry Braxton & George Jessel. *ST:* Viola Brothers Shore. *PH:* Harry Jackson & Frank Zucker. *ED:* Desmond O'Brien & Russell Shields. *Sets:* George Sawley. *AD:* Harvey Libbert. *Mus:* Hugo Riesenfeld. *Songs:* L. Wolfe Gilbert, Abel Baer, Lewis Young, William Ast, Irving Caesar, Cliff Friend, Al Jolson, B.G. DeSylva & Joseph Meyer.

*Cast:* George Jessel, Gwen Lee, Richard Tucker, Margaret Quimby, Gayne Whitman, Rosa Rosanova, William Strauss, Mary Doran.

When he fails to make a success of his singing career, a young man goes to San Francisco where he becomes a sensation and falls in love with a young girl.

## The Spirit of Youth

March 10, 1929, 7 reels, Silent.

*D:* Walter Lang. *SC:* Eve Unsell & Elmer Harris. *Titles:* Frederick Hatton & Fanny Hatton. *PH:* John Boyle. *ED:* Desmond O'Brien.

*Cast:* Dorothy Sebastian, Larry Kent, Betty Francisco, Maurice Murphy, Anita Femault, Donald Hall, Douglas Gilmore, Charles Sullivan, Sidney D'Albrook.

A boxing champion in the navy promises to be true to his librarian girlfriend but falls for an heiress.

## The Rainbow

March 17, 1929, 68 minutes, Sound Effects.

*D:* Reginald Barker. *SC:* L.G. Rigsby. *Titles:* Frederick Hatton & Fanny Hatton. *PH:* Ernest Miller. *ED:* Robert J. Kent. *AD:* Harvey Libbert. *Sets:* George Sawley. *Mus:* Joseph Littau.

*Cast:* Dorothy Sebastian, Lawrence Gray, Sam Hardy, Harvey Clarke, Paul Hurst, Gino Corrado, King Zany.

A miner falls for a girl involved with gangsters who have staged a fake gold strike near Death Valley.

## The Devil's Apple Tree

March 24, 1929, 7 reels, Silent.

*D:* Elmer Clifton. *SC:* Lillian Ducey. *Titles:* Frederick Hatton & Fanny Hatton. *PH:* Ernest Miller. *ED:* Frank Sullivan.

*Cast:* Dorothy Sebastian, Larry Kent, Edward Martindel, Ruth Clifford, George Cooper, Cosmo Kyrle Bellew.

Traveling to the Tropics to meet her fiancé, a young woman assumes the identity of a rich girl she thinks is dying.

## Molly and Me

April 7, 1929, 8 reels, Part-Talkie.

*D:* Albert Ray. *SC:* Lois Leeson. *Titles:* Frederick Hatton & Fanny Hatton. *ST:* Harold Riggs Durant. *PH:* Frank Zucker & Ernest Miller. *ED:* Russell Shields. *SD:* Rudolph Flothow. *Mus:* Hugo Riesenfeld. *Song:* I. Wolfe Gilbert & Abel Baer.

*Cast:* Belle Bennett, Joe E. Brown, Alberta Vaughn, Charles Byer.

Two vaudevillians split when the husband finds success and falls in love with his costar.

## Two Men and a Maid

August 4, 1929, 7 reels, Part-Talkie.

*D:* George Archainbaud. *SC:* Frances Hyland. *Titles:* Frederick Hatton & Fanny Hatton. *ST:* John Francis Natteford. *PH:* Harry Jackson. *ED:* Desmond O'Brien. *Mus:* Hugo Riesenfeld. *Song:* I. Wolfe Gilbert.

*Cast:* William Collier, Jr., Alma Bennett, Eddie Gribbon, George E. Stone, Margaret Quimby.

When he falsely believes his new wife had a previous lover a man enlists in the Foreign Legion.

## New Orleans

August 11, 1929, 8 reels, Part-Talkie.

*D:* Reginald Barker. *SC:* John Francis Natteford. *Titles:* Frederick Hatton & Fanny Hatton. *PH:* Harry Jackson. *Mus:* Hugo Riesenfeld & Irvin Talbot. *Song:* Hugo Riesenfeld, Ted Shapiro & John Raphael.

*Cast:* Ricardo Cortez, Alma Bennett, William Collier, Jr.

A jockey and a racetrack manager, once good friends, have a falling out over a woman they both love.

## My Lady's Past

August 24, 1929, 9 reels, Part-Talkie.

*D:* Albert Ray. *SC:* Frances Hyland. *Titles:* Frederick Hatton & Fanny Hatton. *PH:* Harry Jackson. *ED:* George Merrick. *Mus:* Hugo Riesenfeld.

*Cast:* Belle Bennett, Joe E. Brown, Alma Bennett, Russell Simpson, Joan Standing, Billie Bennett, Raymond Keane.

When a writer finally gets a novel published he deserts his long-time fiancée for his typist.

## Midstream

September 15, 1929, 8 reels, Part-Talkie.

*D:* James Flood. *SC:* Frances Guihan. *Titles:* Frederick Hatton & Fanny Hatton. *ST:* Bernie Boone. *PH:* Jackson Rose. *ED:* Desmond O'Brien. *Mus:* Hugo Riesenfeld. *Song:* I. Wolfe Gilbert & Abel Baer.

*Cast:* Ricardo Cortez, Claire

Windsor, Montagu Love, Larry Kent, Helen Jerome Eddy, Leslie Brigham, Louis Alvarez, Genevieve Schrader, Florence Foyer.

After getting a rejuvenation operation, a Wall Street financier pretends to be a young man to win the affections of a pretty girl.

## Whispering Winds

September 29, 1929, 7 reels, Part-Talkie.

*D:* James Flood. *SC:* Jean Plannette & Charles Logan. *PH:* Harry Jackson & Jack MacKenzie. *ED:* James Morley. *Mus:* Erno Rapee.

*Cast:* Patsy Ruth Miller, Malcolm McGregor, Eve Southern, Eugenie Besserer, James Marcus.

A fisherman marries a local girl after the woman he loves leaves to go to New York and become a popular singer.

## Mister Antonio

December 8, 1929, 8 reels.

*D:* James Flood & Frank Reicher. *SC:* Frederick Hatton & Fanny Hatton, from the play by Booth Tarkington. *PH:* Ernest Miller. *ED:* Arthur Roberts.

*Cast:* Leo Carrillo, Virginia Valli, Gareth Hughes, Frank Reicher, Eugenie Besserer, Franklin Lewis.

A street musician befriends the cousin of a politician whose reputation may hurt the latter's reelection campaign.

## Party Girl

January 5, 1930, 90 minutes.

*D:* Victor Halperin. *SC:* Monte Katterjohn, George Draney & Victor Halperin, from the novel *Dangerous Business* by Edwin Balmer. *PH:* Henry Cronjager & Robert Newhard. *ED:*

Russell Schoengarth. *SD:* Roy S. Clayton. *Mus:* Harry Stoddard.

*Cast:* Douglas Fairbanks, Jr. (Jay Roundtree), Jeanette Loff (Ellen Powell), Judith Barrie (Leetha Cather), Marie Prevost (Diana Hoster), John St. Polis (John Roundtree), Sammy Blum (Sam Matten), Harry Northrup (Robert Lowry), Almeda Fowler (Mrs. Maude Lindsay), Hal Price (Lew Albans), Charles Giblyn (Lawrence Doyle), Sidney D'Albrook (Investigator), Lucien Prival (Paul Newcast), Florence Dudley (Miss Manning), Earl Burnett's Biltmore Orchestra & Trio (Themselves).

Mrs. Laude Lindsay (Almeda Fowler) runs a party girl racket supplying young women to act as "hostesses" at business functions to lure prospective clients. Two of her girls are Leetha (Judith Barrie), who is pregnant by married businessman Newcast (Lucien Prival), and plump Diana (Marie Prevost), the roommate of a former party girl, Ellen (Jeanette Loff), who now works as the secretary of glass manufacturer John Roundtree (John St. Polis) and is engaged to his playboy son Jay (Douglas Fairbanks, Jr.). Jay and some of his fraternity pals crash a party where he meets Leetha, and she gets him drunk and makes him think he seduced her. The next day he agrees to marry her, after meeting her mother, who is really Mrs. Lindsay who is in on the scheme. For keeping quiet about who is really the father of her child, Leetha forces Newcast to sign a million-dollar deal with Jay's father. Jay becomes upset when he learns the truth, and the elder Roundtree, who abhors the party girl racket, disapproves of the marriage. Leetha tells him the truth about her marriage and the business deal with Newcast and promises to smear the name of Roundtree all over the front pages. Distraught at Jay's marriage, Ellen accepts a businessman's (Hal Price) invitation to return to the party life. Meanwhile Leetha is questioned by the police about her racket and in trying to escape falls from a sixth floor fire escape. Before dying she tells Jay there will be a raid on the party Ellen is attending, and he is able to save her from the law, thanks to Miss Manning (Florence Dudley), an undercover agent getting evidence against the party girl racket.

"A would-be sensational story with a moral ending obviously thrown in as a sop to the censors" is how *Photoplay* summed up *Party Girl*, an exploitation feature from Tiffany-Stahl dressed in the refinements of a good budget. Based on the 1927 novel *Dangerous Business* (the title under which the movie was previewed) by Edwin Balmer, it was subtitled "An Expose of Modern Business." *Party Girl* exposed a form of the prostitution racket used to lure clients into business deals. Produced by Victory Pictures (no relation to Sam Katzman's company of the same name which operated from 1935-40), the movie barely stayed on the edge of good taste and some of its scenes were almost ribald. In particular is the sequence where overweight Marie Prevost (a one-time Mack Sennett Bathing Beauty) is hauled into another room by two middle-aged business men and is obviously made the object of a gang bang as the other party goers look on in amusement. In another scene Prevost tells reformed roommate Jeanette Loff that she can move to the country with her man if she wants but that Prevost would rather remain in the big city and "make whoopee." The acting in *Party Girl* is uniformly good, especially Judith Bar-

rie as the party girl gone wrong, but the direction is stilted and overall the feature is on the slow side. It was also issued in a shorter silent version.

In the course of the movie Jeanette Loff sang "Oh, How I Adore You" and "Farewell."

When *Party Girl* was released in 1930 it was as a major production and it made its New York City debut at the Gaiety Theatre (later the Victoria) with seats going for two dollars each. In 1938, however, the film was picked up by an independent distributor and released on the states' rights market as an exploitation picture. As a result, director Victor Halperin demanded his name be removed from the picture and the nom de plume of Rex Hale was used. Since Marie Prevost had committed suicide the previous year, her name was removed from the reissue prints' credits.

## The Lost Zeppelin

February 9, 1930, 73 minutes.

*D:* Edward Sloman. *SC:* Frances Hyland & Charles Kenyon. *ST:* John Francis Natteford. *PH:* Jackson Rose. *ED:* Martin G. Cohn & Donn Hayes. *SD:* Jerry Eisenberg & John Buddy Myers. *Sets:* George Sawley. *AD:* Harvey Libbert. *Effects:* Jack Robson & Kenneth Peach.

*Cast:* Conway Tearle (Commander Donald Hall), Virginia Valli (Miriam Hall), Ricardo Cortez (Lieutenant Tom Armstrong), Duke Martin (Lieutenant James Wallace), Kathryn McGuire (Nancy), Winter Hall (Mr. Wilson), George Cleveland, Richard Cramer (Radio Announcers).

Commander Donald Hall (Conway Tearle) is about to lead a dirigible expedition to the South Pole, a feat he considers "child's play" thanks to modern inventions. He attends a banquet in

Washington, D.C., in his honor with his wife Miriam (Virginia Valli) and his best friend, Lt. Tom Armstrong (Ricardo Cortez), also a member of the expedition. After the festivities Hall spots his wife and Tom kissing on the terrace, and later, at home, he admits to them what he has seen and says to forget about the incident. Miriam confesses to Donald that she loves Tom and wants a divorce. Before leaving on the expedition, Donald agrees to give Miriam anything she wants. The dirigible *Explorer* leaves for the South Pole and experiences success until getting caught in a tropical storm which disables two of its motors. The expedition continues, however, and passes the base camp and goes over the South Pole. Then the ship is caught in a blinding snowstorm and, weighted down by ice and snow, begins to lose altitude. Finally the zeppelin crashes, and the commander decides to send men in different directions to find rescue planes. Hall and Tom go together but get caught in a blizzard and a third companion is killed. Eventually the two men make it back to the crashed ship to find the rest of the crew frozen to death. A rescue plane piloted by Lt. Wallace (Duke Martin) finds them and Hall orders that Tom be returned for the sake of Miriam's happiness. In Washington, D.C., Armstrong is given a hero's welcome but announces that Wallace has been lost in an attempt to rescue the commander. He then goes to see Miriam, who admits it was her husband she really loved. The two hear a radio announcement that Wallace's plane has landed safely at the South Pole base camp and that Hall has been rescued. Miriam then sends her husband a message confirming her love for him.

*The Lost Zeppelin* is, in many ways,

two separate films. Its beginning and ending sequences are long, talky and stagebound, showing many of the deficiencies of early sound features. On the other hand the middle sequence of the film with the dirigible's journey to the South Pole and its crashing there are exceedingly well done as are the scenes with stars Conway Tearle and Ricardo Cortez fighting a terrible snowstorm as they try to find rescuers. At the time of the film's release *Photoplay* noted, "This has lots of good points, but the plot isn't one of them. Some fascinating scenic effects." The acting in the feature is also quite uneven. Conway Tearle and Ricardo Cortez handle the male leads in good fashion, Tearle especially being effective as the stalwart but wronged husband. On the other hand, Virginia Valli's histrionics are laughable as the wife in the middle of a love triangle. The remaining roles are minor although one can easily recognize the voices of George Cleveland and Richard Cramer as radio announcers giving news flashes on the progress of the zeppelin's expedition and its aftermath. Tiffany-Stahl, billing itself as "The Better Entertainment," spent a bundle on this disaster epic, but it proved to be a box-office flop, adding to the company's financial woes.

## Painted Faces

February 2, 1930, 8 reels.

*D:* Albert S. Rogell. *SC:* Frederick Hatton & Fanny Hatton. *ST:* Frances Hyland. *PH:* Benjamin Kline & Jackson Rose. *ED:* Richard Cahoon. *Song:* Abner Silver.

*Cast:* Joe E. Brown, Helen Foster, Richard Tucker, William B. Davidson, Barton Hepburn, Dorothy Gulliver, Lester Cole, Sojin, Jack Richardson, Howard Truesdell, Baldy Belmont,

Jerry Drew, Walter Jerry, Russ Dudley, Purnell B. Pratt, Clinton Lyle, Alma Bennett, Mabel Julienne Scott, Florence Midgley, May Wallace.

A young man is accused of murdering a vaudeville performer but a member of the jury votes for acquittal.

## Peacock Alley

February 9, 1930, 63 minutes, Part-Color.

*D:* Marcel De Sano. *SC:* Frances Hyland, Wells Root & Carey Wilson. *ST:* Carey Wilson. *PH:* Benjamin Kline & Harry Zech. *ED:* Clarence Kolster. *AD:* Harvey Libbert. *SD:* Buddy Myers.

*Cast:* Mae Murray, George Barraud, Jason Robards, Richard Tucker, W.L. Thorne, Phillips Smalley, E.H. Calvert, Arthur Hoyt, Billy Bevan.

A chorus girl marries a longtime sweetheart after being rejected by the man she loves. A remake of the 1922 film.

## Troopers Three

February 27, 1930, 80 minutes.

*D:* Norman Taurog & E. Reeves Eason. *SC:* John Francis Natteford. *ST:* Arthur Guy Empey. *PH:* Ernest Miller, Benjamin Kline & Jackson Rose. *ED:* Clarence Kolster. *SD:* Dean Daily. *Song:* George Waggner & Abner Silver.

*Cast:* Rex Lease, Dorothy Gulliver, Roscoe Karns, Slim Summerville, Tom London, Joseph Girard, Walter Perry.

By mistake three down-and-out actors end up enlisting in the army.

## Mamba

March 16, 1930, 78 minutes, Color.

*D:* Albert S. Rogell. *SC:* Tim Miranda & Winifred Dunn. *ST:* Ferdinand Schumann-Heink & John Reinhardt. *PH:* Charles Boyle. *Mus:* James C. Bradford. *AD:* Andre Chautin. *SD:* Louis J. Myers.

*Cast:* Jean Hersholt, Eleanor Boardman, Ralph Forbes, Josef Swickard, Claude Fleming, Will Stanton, William Von Brincken, Noble Johnson, Hazel Jones, Andres de Segurola, Arthur Stone, Torben Meyer, Edward Martindel.

In German East Africa a new bride finds herself repulsed by her rich planter husband and drawn to a young officer.

## High Treason

March 25, 1930, 90 minutes.

*P:* L'Estrange Fawcett. *D:* Maurice Elvey. *SC:* L'Estrange Fawcett, from the play by Noel Pemberton-Billing.

*Cast:* Jameson Thomas, Benita Hume, Basil Gill, Humberston Wright, Henry Vibart, James Carew, Hayford Hobbs, Milton Rosmer, Judd Green, Alf Goddard, Irene Rooke, Clifford Heatherley, Wally Patch, Raymond Massey.

In 1940 women unite to stop corrupt businessmen from instigating another world war. Made in England and released there in 1929 by Gaumont.

## Journey's End

April 13, 1930, 130 minutes.

*P:* George Pearson. *AP:* Gerald L.G. Samson. *D:* James Whale. *SC:* Joseph Moncure Marsh, from the play by R.C. Sheriff. *PH:* Benjamin Kline. *ED:* Claude Berkeley. *AD:* Harvey Libbert. *SD:* Buddy Myers.

*Cast:* Colin Clive, Ian MacLaren, David Manners, Anthony Bushell, Billy Bevan, Charles Gerrard, Robert A'Dair, Thomas Whitely, Jack Pitcairn, Walter Klinger, Leslie Sketchley.

A war-weary British army officer is unhappy to find his fiancée's brother a member of his unit. Coproduced with the British studio. Gainsborough Productions.

## Border Romance

May 25, 1930, 66 minutes.

P: Lester F. Scott, Jr. D: Richard Thorpe. SC: John Francis Natteford. PH: Harry Zech. ED: Richard Cahoon. AD: Ralph DeLacy. SD: John Stransky. Songs: Will Jason & Val Burton.

Cast: Armida, Don Terry, Marjorie "Babe" Kane, Victor Potel, Wesley Barry, Nita Martan, J. Frank Glendon, Harry von Meter, William Costello.

After killing a man in self defense, a horsetrader tries to evade the law below the Mexican border.

## The Swellhead

June 15, 1930, 70 minutes.

D: James Flood. SC: Adele Buffington & James Gleason. ST: A.P. Younger. PH: Jackson Rose & Art Reeves. ED: Richard Cahoon. SD: Dean Daily.

Cast: James Gleason, Johnny Walker, Marion Shilling, Natalie Kingston, Paul Hurst, Freeman Wood, Lillian Elliott.

A young factory girl has faith in the man she loves, a third-rate boxer.

## Sunny Skies

June 18, 1930, 75 minutes.

D: Norman Taurog & Ralph DeLacy. SC: Earle Snell & George Cleveland. ST: A.P. Younger. PH: Arthur Reeves. ED: Clarence Kolster. SD: Buddy Myers.

Cast: Benny Rubin, Marceline Day, Rex Lease, Marjorie "Babe" Kane,

Greta Granstedt, Wesley Barry, Robert Randall, James Wilcox.

A college freshman romances an astute coed while his shy roommate tries to emulate his lifestyle.

## Hot Curves

July 6, 1930, 71 minutes.

D: Norman Taurog. SC: Earle Snell, Frank Mortimer & Benny Rubin. ST: A.P. Younger & Frank Mortimer. PH: Max Dupont. ED: Clarence Kolster. Mus: Violinsky & Silverstein. SD: Buddy Myers.

Cast: Benny Rubin, Rex Lease, Alice Day, Pert Kelton, John Ince, Mary Carr, Mike Donlin, Natalie Moorhead, Paul Hurst.

Two buddies become star baseball players but one almost ruins his career when he becomes involved with a flirt.

## Near the Rainbow's End

July 6, 1930, 56 minutes.

P: Trem Carr. D: J.P. McGowan. SC: Sally Winters & Charles A. Post. PH: Hap Depew & T.E. Jackson. ED: Charles J. Hunt. AD: E.R. Hickson. SD: Neil Jackson & C.F. Franklin. Song: Murray Mencher, Billy Moll & Harry Richman.

Cast: Bob Steele, Louise Lorraine, Al Ferguson, Lafe McKee, Alfred Hewston, Merrill McCormack, Hank Bell.

The son of a cattle rancher is falsely accused of killing a rival sheepherder, the father of the girl he loves.

## Kathleen Mavourneen

July 20, 1930, 65 minutes.

D: Albert Ray. SC: Frances Hyland, from the play by Dion Boucicault. PH: Harry Jackson.

Cast: Sally O'Neil, Charles

Delaney, Robert Elliott, Aggie Herring, Walter Perry, Francis Ford.

A young Irish girl comes to New York City to marry her plumber fiancé but falls in love with a politician.

## Paradise Island

July 20, 1930, 68 minutes.

*D:* Bert Glennon. *SC:* Monte Katterjohn. *ST:* M.B. Derring. *PH:* Max Dupont. *ED:* Byron Robinson. *Songs:* Val Burton & Will Jason. *SD:* Dean Daily.

*Cast:* Kenneth Harlan, Marceline Day, Tom Santschi, Paul Hurst, Betty Boyd, Victor Potel, Gladden James, Will Stanton.

After coming to a Pacific isle to marry her fiancé, a young woman finds he is heavily in debt and is attracted to a devil-may-care sailor.

## The Medicine Man

August 3, 1930, 57 minutes.

*D:* Scott Pembroke. *SC:* Layde Horton & Eve Unsell, from the play by Elliott Lester. *PH:* Art Reeves & Max Dupont. *ED:* Russell Schoengarth. *SD:* Dean Daily.

*Cast:* Jack Benny, Betty Bronson, E. Alyn Warren, Eva Novak, Billy Butts, Adolph Milar, George E. Stone, Tommy Dugan, Vadim Uraneff, Caroline Rankin, Dorothea Wolbert.

Not wanting to marry the man her father picks for her, a country girl falls for a traveling medicine show performer.

## Wings of Adventure

August 10, 1930, 65 minutes.

*D:* Richard Thorpe. *SC:* Harry Fraser & Zella Young. *PH:* Art Reeves. *ED:* Clarence Kolster. *SD:* John Stransky.

*Cast:* Rex Lease, Armida, Clyde

Cook, Fred Malatesta, Nick De Ruiz, Eddie Boland.

A captured aviator and his pilot help a young woman held for ransom by a Mexican bandit.

## The Thoroughbred

August 31, 1930, 57 minutes.

*D:* Richard Thorpe. *SC:* John Francis Natteford. *PH:* Max Dupont. *ED:* Clarence Kolster. *AD:* Ralph DeLacy. *SD:* Dean Daily.

*Cast:* Wesley Barry, Nancy Dover, Pauline Garon, Larry Steers, Robert Homans, Walter Perry, Onest Conly, Mildred Washington, Madame Sul-Te-Wan.

Two rival racehorse owners and trainers try to get the services of a young jockey and his retainer.

## Oklahoma Cyclone

September 14, 1930, 64 minutes.

*P:* Trem Carr. *D:* John P. McCarthy. *SC:* J.P. McCarthy & Ford Beebe. *PH:* M.A. Anderson. *ED:* Fred Allen. *Mus:* Jack Scholl. *AD:* E.R. Hickson. *SD:* John Stransky. *Asst Dir:* Perry Murdock. *Prod Mgr:* Charles A. Post.

*Cast:* Bob Steele, Nita Ray, Al St. John, Charles King, Hector Sarno, Slim Whitaker, Shorty Hendricks, Emilio Fernandez, John Ince, Fred Burns, Cliff Lyons.

Trying to find his sheriff father, a young man infiltrates the gang keeping him a prisoner.

## The Land of Missing Men

October 5, 1930, 52 minutes.

*P:* Trem Carr. *D-ST:* John P. McCarthy. *SC:* John P. McCarthy & Bob Quigley. *PH:* Harry Neumann. *SD:* John Stransky. *AD:* E.R. Hickson. *Prod Mgr:* Charles A. Post.

Al St. John, Caryl Lincoln and Bob Steele in *The Land of Missing Men* (Tiffany, 1930).

*Cast:* Bob Steele (Steve O'Neil), Al St. John (Buckshot), Edward [Eddie] Dunn (Sheriff Bower), Caryl Lincoln (Nita Madero), Al Jennings (John Evans), Fern Emmett (Marth Evans), Emilio Fernandez (Lopez), Noah Hendricks (Texas), C.R. Dufau (Senor Madero), S.S. Simon (Express Agent), Jim Corey (Deputy Slim), Hank Bell (Horse Tender), Iron Eyes Cody (Indian).

Small ranchers are having their cattle driven off, their cowhands murdered and their women abducted. The new sheriff, Bower (Edward Dunn), tells his predecessor Evans (Al Jennings) that cowboy Steve O'Neil (Bob Steele) is behind the activities since his father was shot as a cattle rustler. Evans and Senor Madero (C.R. Dufau) do not believe Bower but instead feel that Lopez (Emilio Fernandez), the foreman for a new cattle syndicate, may be behind the crimes. Bower and his deputy, Slim (Jim Corey), ride out to Steve's camp and tell him and his sidekick Buckshot (Al St. John) to get out of the country. Deciding to ride away, Steve and Buckshot stop at a saloon to ask directions, but they find all the men there murdered except Madero, who tells Steve that Lopez did the killings. Dying, Madero also asks Steve to rescue his daughter Nita (Caryl Lincoln) for an incoming stage so Lopez cannot get her. Steve rides to the town from which the stage is leaving and gets on as a passenger. Later he robs the stage of its gold, and he and Buckshot take Nita to a camp of friendly Indians. There Steve tells Nita the truth about her father's death, but in the night she escapes. Meanwhile one of Lopez's men robs the stage also, but they find the gold is already gone. Steve believes that Lopez is really the Black Coyote, the man behind all the robberies, and he and Buckshot take the gold and go to Devil's Rock, the hideout for the outlaw gang. There they meet Lopez, who admits he is the bandit, and Bob and Buckshot give him the gold in return for sanctuary. The next day the stage arrives in town and Nita soon follows with the story about Lopez murdering her father. She begs the sheriff to form a posse to save Steve from Lopez, but Bower rides instead to warn the bandit that Evans is leading a group of both men and women to Devil's Rock. Lopez then vows to hang Steve, and he and Buckshot are badly hurt holding off the gang. The townspeople arrive, the gang members are killed in a shootout and Lopez is captured. The bandit then tells Steve and the others that it was Bower who killed Steve's father by shooting him in the back and that the lawman also paid him to silence Madero. Evans leads the group in giving Bower a necktie party while the badly hurt Steve and Buckshot are taken back to town.

Bob Steele made his talking debut at Tiffany in *Near the Rainbow's End* in the summer of 1930 and *The Land of Missing Men*, the fourth of the eight films he did for the studio, followed that fall. *The Land of Missing Men* is one of Steele's best features, a sturdy combination of both dialogue and action. Filled with somewhat austere but attractive desert surroundings, it tells its tale of betrayal and revenge in a forthright and entertaining manner. Although mainly long and medium shots, with some overhead camera angles, the feature avoids being stagy by using effective camera movement and varying sound perspectives. Star Bob Steele and sidekick Al St. John make the most of their roles, and Steele sings "Way Out at the Prairie's End"

several times in the proceedings. Much has been made of the somber opening of the John Wayne Monogram-Lone Star western *Randy Rides Alone* (1934) when Duke arrives at a saloon to find all the inhabitants murdered. The same scene precedes that one by four years in *The Land of Missing Men*, and it is staged much better. Here Bob Steele and Al St. John arrive at the saloon at night as a player piano drones out "After the Ball." When they walk in, the camera stays on their faces as they register the horror of seeing everyone inside either dead or dying. The finale is also compelling, with both the hero and his sidekick surviving a brutal beating by the outlaw gang and being held in the arms of the leading lady and another woman as they are driven home.

Two noted names appear in the supporting cast of *The Land of Missing Men*, Al Jennings and Emilio Fernandez. Al Jennings was a small-time bandit in the west, and after serving time in prison he became a lawyer and politician and later a movie star. He made low-budget efforts for his Al Jennings Feature Film Company and in the sound era turned to character parts. In 1950 Columbia starred Dan Duryea in the title role of the highly fictionalized *Al Jennings of Oklahoma*. Jennings died in 1962 at the age of 98. Emilio Fernandez had a varied career as an actor but later became one of Mexico's best-known film directors for features like *Flor Silvestre* (1943), *La Perla* (1946), *Rio Escondido* (1947), *El Rapto* (1952), *La Rosa Blanca* (1954) and *Una Cita de Amor* (1956). He remade his 1946 feature *Enamoradoa* in Hollywood four years later as *The Torch*. Fernandez acted in both Mexican and Hollywood features and in 1966 served as assistant director for *The Night of the*

*Iguana.* He also worked in Cuba, Spain and Argentina in the 1950s.

## Borrowed Wives

October 12, 1930, 71 minutes.

*D:* Frank R. Strayer & Leander De Cordova. *SC:* W. Scott Darling. *PH:* Andre Barlatier. *ED:* Byron Robinson. *AD:* Ralph DeLacy. *SD:* Buddy Myers.

*Cast:* Rex Lease, Vera Reynolds, Nita Martan, Paul Hurst, Robert Randall, Charles Sellon, Dorothea Wolbert, Sam Hardy, Harry Todd, Tom London, Eddie Chandler.

A man must wed in order to get a huge inheritance and he is persuaded to marry another woman when his fiancée's flight is delayed.

## Just Like Heaven

October 19, 1930, 70 minutes.

*D:* Roy William Neill. *SC:* Adele Buffington. *PH:* Max Dupont. *ED:* Charles Hunt. *AD:* Ralph DeLacy. *SD:* Dean Daily. *Tech Dir:* Andre Chotin.

*Cast:* Anita Louise, David Newell, Yola D'Avril, Gaston Glass, Thomas Jefferson, Mathilde Comont, Albert Roccardi, Torben Meyer, Emile Chautard.

A Parisian balloon vendor falls in love with a dancer and finances dancing lessons for her without her knowledge.

## Under Montana Skies

November 2, 1930, 60 minutes.

*D:* Richard Thorpe. *SC:* Bennett Cohen & James A. Aubrey. *ST:* James A. Aubrey. *PH:* Harry Zech. *ED:* Carl Himm. *SD:* John Stransky. *AD:* Ralph DeLacy.

*Cast:* Kenneth Harlan (Clay Conning), Slim Summerville (Sunshine), Dorothy Gulliver (Mary), Nita Martan (Blondie), Ethel Wales (Martha Jenkins), Harry Todd (Abner Jenkins), Lafe McKee (Sheriff Pinky), Christian J. Frank (Frank Blake), Charles King (Brag Blake), Slim Whitaker (Joe), Bob Reeves, Tom Bay (Henchmen).

Horse thief Blake (Charles King) and his gang attack cowboy Clay Conning (Kenneth Harlan), who was responsible for sending Blake to jail. Clay's pals come along and rescue him, and he and Sunshine (Slim Summerville) head into town to see a theatrical troupe which plans to put on a show. In Red Rock they learn the show folk are in jail because they cannot pay their hotel rent. Clay tries to raise the money to get them out but fails, so he gets the sheriff (Lafe McKee) to let singer Blondie (Nita Martan) go free. He then uses her to arrange a compromise with hotel owner Abner Jenkins (Harry Todd), convincing him to drop the charges against the performers. Clay is attracted to one of the show girls, Mary (Dorothy Gulliver), and he plans to put on the show himself until Abner's wife, Martha (Ethel Wales), refuses to let the troupe use her opera house. When Sunshine fails to convince Martha to let them do the show, Clay pretends to romance the older woman. Mary spies them and feels rejected. When Clay takes Martha for a ride, Blake and his cronies attack him and tie him up before heading to town to rob the box office during the show. Clay, however, manages to escape and captures Blake, retrieving the money following the holdup. As the troupe tries to leave town, Clay intercepts the stage and proposes to Mary.

A strange admixture of comedy and drama with music and dancing in a western setting, *Under Montana Skies* is a rough-hewn production that moves quickly and proves fairly entertaining.

Star Kenneth Harlan was nearing the end of his headlining days but proved to be a virile hero, while Slim Summerville added some amusing moments as his somewhat tipsy and thoroughly bumbling sidekick. Also good in the humor department was Ethel Wales as the allegedly prudish wife of the town skinflint (Harry Todd). In reality she has a yen for Harlan, and she refers to her husband as "an old fossil" when the cowboy pretends to romance her. Dorothy Gulliver is quite fetching as the leading lady and Nita Martan is also appealing as the vampish but strong willed Blondie. The scenes in which she thoroughly whips the befuddled Slim Summerville are quite amusing. Five songs are included in the film including the title tune. In addition Nita Martan sings "Crying Blues" and "A Man Like That" and she also does an exotic dance which is interrupted when Charles King tries to steal the show receipts. There is also a chorus line rendition of "Harlem Hop" featuring Dorothy Gulliver as the lead dancer.

## She Got What She Wanted

November 9, 1930, 81 minutes.

*P:* Samuel Zierler. *D:* James Cruze. *SC:* George Rosener. *PH:* E. Edgar Schoenbaum.

*Cast:* Betty Compson, Lee Tracy, Alan Hale, Gaston Glass, Dorothy Christy, Fred Kelsey.

Coming to New York City with her struggling writer husband, a young woman gets involved with a gambler.

## The Third Alarm

November 16, 1930, 69 minutes.

*D:* Emory Johnson. *SC:* Frances Hyland & John Francis Natteford. *ST:* Emilie Johnson. *PH:* Max Dupont.

*AD:* George Sawley & Ralph DeLacy. *SD:* Buddy Myers.

*Cast:* Anita Louise, James Hall, Paul Hurst, Jean Hersholt, Hobart Bosworth, Mary Doran, Nita Martan, George Billings, Walter Perry, Aileen Manning.

Wanting to care for two orphans, a couple of firemen decide to find brides in order to keep the children.

## The Love Trader

November 23, 1930, 76 minutes.

*P:* Joseph Henabery & Harold Shumate. *D:* Joseph Henabery. *SC:* Harold Shumate. *PH:* Ernest Miller & Pliny Goodfriend. *SD:* R.S. Clayton & Ted Murray.

*Cast:* Leatrice Joy, Roland Drew, Henry B. Walthall, Barbara Bedford, Noah Beery, Chester Conklin, Clarence Burton, William Welsh, Tom Mahoney.

On a South Seas island a young woman, the wife of a bigoted sea captain, falls in love with a local man, the grandson of an American.

## The Utah Kid

November 23, 1930, 57 minutes.

*D:* Richard Thorpe. *SC:* Frank Howard Clark. *PH:* Art Reed. *ED:* Billy Bolen. *SD:* Corson Jowett.

*Cast:* Rex Lease, Dorothy Sebastian, Tom Santschi, Mary Carr, Walter Miller, Lafe McKee, Boris Karloff, Bud Osborne, Jack Rockwell, Fred Burns, Al Taylor, Blackie Whiteford, Bob Card.

After marrying a young woman to protect her from a gang leader, an outlaw vows to reform but his pals believe he has double-crossed them.

## Extravagance

December 7, 1930, 65 minutes.

*D:* Phil Rosen. *SC:* Adele Buffington, Frances Hyland & Phil Rosen. *ST:* A.P. Younger. *PH:* Max Dupont. *ED:* Charles K. Harris. *SD:* Buddy Myers. *AD:* Ralph DeLacy.

*Cast:* June Collyer, Lloyd Hughes, Owen Moore, Dorothy Christy, Jameson Thomas, Gwen Lee, Robert Agnew, Nella Walker, Martha Mattox, Arthur Hoyt, Davis Hawthorne, Lawrence Baskcomb.

A businessman struggles to keep his finances in check because of the spending habits of his wife.

## Fighting Thru: Or California in 1878

December 25, 1930, 71 minutes.

*P:* Phil Goldstone. *D:* William Nigh. *SC:* John Francis Natteford. *PH:* Art Reed. *ED:* Earl Turner.

*Cast:* Ken Maynard, Jeanette Loff, Wallace MacDonald, Carmelita Geraghty, William L. Thorne, Charles King, Fred Burns, William Nestell, Tommy Bay, Jack Fowler, Chuck Baldra, Art Mix, Bud McClure, Jack Kirk, Jim Corey, Tarzan.

A miner is accused of the murder of his partner and he tries to persuade the man's sister, the girl he loves, of his innocence.

## Headin' North

December 28, 1930, 58 minutes.

*P:* Trem Carr. *D-SC:* John P. McCarthy. *ED:* Fred Allen.

*Cast:* Bob Steele, Barbara Luddy, Perry Murdock, Walt Shumway, Eddie Dunn, Fred Burns, Gordon DeMain, Harry Allen, J. Gunnis Davis, S.S. Simon, Jack Henderson, Jim Welsh.

A man is befriended by the son of a rancher as he attempts to find the gambler who cheated his father.

## Caught Cheating

January 4, 1931, 63 minutes.

*P:* Phil Goldstone. *D:* Frank R. Strayer. *SC:* W. Scott Darling & Frances Hyland. *ST:* W. Scott Darling. *PH:* Max Dupont. *ED:* Edgar Adams.

*Cast:* Charlie Murray, George Sidney, Nita Martan, Robert Ellis, Dorothy Christy, Bertha Mann, Fred Malatesta, George Regas, Tenen Holtz.

A man gives a ride to a young woman who turns out to be the moll of a jealous gangster and the hoodlum vows to shoot him.

## Command Performance

January 18, 1931, 72 minutes.

*P:* Samuel Zierler. *D:* Walter Lang. *SC:* Maude Fulton & Gordon Rigby, from the play by C. Stafford Dickens. *PH:* Charles Schoenbaum.

*Cast:* Neil Hamilton, Una Merkel, Helen Ware, Albert Gran, Vera Lewis, Lawrence Grant, Thelma Todd, Mischa Auer, Burr McIntosh, William Von Brincken, Murdock MacQuarrie.

An actor, a lookalike for a prince, is recruited to court a princess in order to cement a royal marriage and stop a war.

## Aloha

February 1, 1931, 85 minutes.

*P-D:* Albert S. Rogell. *SC:* Thomas H. Ince, J.G. Hawks, Adele Buffington, Wellyn Totman & Leslie Mason. *PH:* Charles Stumar. *ED:* Richard Cahoon. *SD:* H.R. Hobson. *Prod Mgr:* Rudolph Flothow. *Asst Dir:* Edgar G. Ulmer.

*Cast:* Ben Lyon, Raquel Torres, Robert Edeson, Alan Hale, Thelma Todd, Marian Douglas, Otis Harlan, T. Roy Barnes, Robert Ellis, Donald Reed, Al St. John, Dickie Moore, Marcia Harris, Addie McPhail, Phyllis Crane, Rita Rey.

A half-caste native girl refuses to marry a man of her tribe because she loves the son of a copra plantation owner. A remake of *Aloha Oe* (Kay-Bee, 1915).

## The Single Sin

February 15, 1931, 73 minutes.

*P:* Phil Goldstone. *D:* William Nigh. *SC:* Frances Hyland. *ST:* A.P. Younger. *PH:* Max Dupont. *ED:* Charles Harris.

*Cast:* Kay Johnson, Bert Lytell, Paul Hurst, Matthew Betz, Holmes Herbert, George Mitchell, Sandra Ravel, Charles McNaughton, Lillian Elliott, Robert Emmett O'Connor.

A former actress and bootlegger marries a rich man but is blackmailed by her ex-partner who believes she is responsible for sending him to jail.

## Hell Bound

March 1, 1931, 67 minutes.

*P:* Samuel Zierler. *D:* Walter Lang. *SC:* Julian Josephson. *PH:* Charles Schoenbaum. *ED:* Rose E. Loewinger. *AD:* Albert D'Agastino. *SD:* W.C. Smith & Frederick Lau. *Prod Mgr:* Bernard McEveety. *Song:* Russ Columbo.

*Cast:* Leo Carrillo, Lloyd Hughes, Ralph Ince, Lola Lane, Helene Chadwick, Richard Tucker, Gertrude Astor, Frank Hagney, Harry Strang, Luke Cosgrove, Murdock McQuarrie, William Lawrence, Marty Faust, Jack Grey, William O'Brien.

A gangster falls in love with a woman rescued from a shooting and gets her job as a singer but rivals plan to kill both of them. Reissued as *The Law and the Killer* by Screen Attractions in 1934.

## The Drums of Jeopardy

March 8, 1931, 65 minutes.

*P:* Phil Goldstone. *D:* George B. Seitz. *SC:* Florence Ryerson, from the novel by Harold MacGrath. *PH:* Arthur Reed. *ED:* Otto Ludwig. *AD:* Fay Babcock & Ralph DeLacy. *SD:* Corson Jowett. *Mus:* Val Burton.

*Cast:* Warner Oland, June Collyer, Lloyd Hughes, George Fawcett, Ernest Hilliard, Wallace MacDonald, Hale Hamilton, Florence Lake, Mischa Auer, Clara Blandick, Ann Brody, Murdock McQuarrie, Harry Semels, Edward Homans, Ruth Hall.

A young woman gets mixed up with a man who is a member of a Russian royal family blamed by a crazed chemist for the death of his daughter. A remake of the 1923 TruArt feature. Reissued as *Mark of Terror.*

## The Sunrise Trail

March 29, 1931, 63 minutes.

*P:* Trem Carr. *D:* John P. McCarthy. *SC:* Wellyn Totman. *PH:* Archie Stout. *AD:* E.R. Hickson. *Prod Mgr:* Charles A. Post.

*Cast:* Bob Steele, Blanche Mehaffey, Jack Clifford, Germaine De Neel, Eddie Dunn, Fred Burns, Dick Alexander, Jimmy Aubrey.

While working undercover to expose cattle thieves, a young man befriends an outlaw and falls in love with a girl who is running from the law.

## The Ridin' Fool

May 31, 1931, 64 minutes.

*P:* Trem Carr. *D:* John P. McCarthy. *SC:* Wellyn Totman. *PH:* Archie Stout. *ED:* Charles Hunt. *AD:* E.R. Hickson. *SD:* John Stransky. *Prod Mgr:* Charles A. Post.

*Cast:* Bob Steele, Frances Morris,

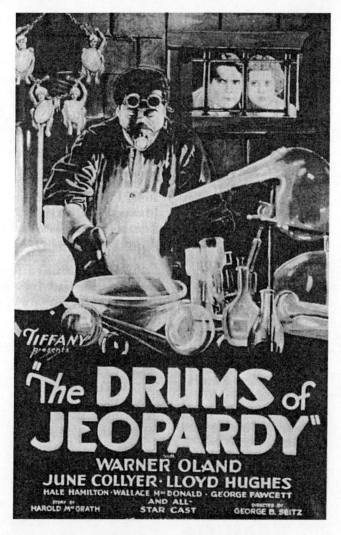

Poster for *The Drums of Jeopardy* (Tiffany, 1931).

Florence Turner, Ted Adams, Al Bridge, Eddie Featherstone, Gordon DeMain, Jack Henderson, Fern Emmett, Josephine Velez, Artie Ortego.

A cowboy saves his gambler pal from being lynched for a murder he did not commit, although they both love the same girl.

## The Two Gun Man

June 7, 1931, 63 minutes.

*P:* Phil Goldstone. *D:* Phil Rosen. *SC:* John Francis Natteford & Earle Snell. *PH:* Arthur Reed. *ED:* Martin G. Cohn. *AD:* Ralph DeLacy.

*Cast:* Ken Maynard, Lucille Powers, Charles King, Nita Martan, Murdock McQuarrie, Lafe McKee, Tom

London, Walter Perry, Will Stanton, William Jackie, Ethan Allen, Jim Corey, Buck Bucko, Roy Bucko, Blackjack Ward, Tarzan.

A gunman, really a government agent, saves a young woman from being shot during an argument between her father and a cattle company owner who is using hired guns to run small ranchers off their range.

## Alias—The Bad Man

June 28, 1931, 62 minutes.

*P:* Phil Goldstone. *D:* Phil Rosen. *SC:* Earle Snell. *ST:* Ford Beebe. *PH:* Arthur Reed. *ED:* Martin G. Cohn. *AD:* Ralph DeLacy.

*Cast:* Ken Maynard, Virginia Brown(e) Faire, Frank Mayo, Charles King, Robert Homans, Irving Bacon, Lafe McKee, Ethan Allen, Jack Rockwell, Earl Dwire, Jim Corey, Tarzan.

When his father and another rancher are killed by rustlers, a cowboy tries to find the culprits but is blamed for the death of the other rancher by the man's daughter.

## Salvation Nell

July 5, 1931, 78 minutes.

*P:* Samuel Zierler. *D:* James Cruze. *SC:* Walter Woods & Selma Stein, from the play by Edward Sheldon. *PH:* Charles Schoenbaum. *ED:* Rose Loewinger. *AD:* Albert D'Agostino. *SD:* W.C. Smith & Frederick Lau. *Prod Mgr:* Bernard McEveety.

*Cast:* Ralph Graves, Helen Chandler, Sally O'Neil, Jason Robards, DeWitt Jennings, Charlotte Walker, Matthew Betz, Rose Dione, Wally Albright.

A young woman gets mixed up with a no-good loafer and after he is sent to prison she must choose whether to work in a brothel or join the Salvation Army.

## Women Go On Forever

August 16, 1931, 67 minutes.

*P:* Samuel Zierler. *D:* Walter Lang. *SC:* Ralph Murphy, from the play by Daniel N. Rubin.

*Cast:* Marion Nixon, Clara Kimball Young, Paul Page, Thomas Jackson, Yola D'Avril, Eddie Lambert, Nellie V. Nichols, Morgan Wallace, Maurice Black, Maurice Murphy, Lorin Baker, Madame Sul-Te-Wan.

When a taxi driver is framed on a murder charge and sent to jail he makes his fiancée believe he has deserted her.

## The Arizona Terror

September 29, 1931, 64 minutes.

*P:* Phil Goldstone. *D:* Phil Rosen. *SC:* John Francis Natteford. *PH:* Arthur Reed. *ED:* Martin G. Cohn. *AD:* Ralph DeLacy.

*Cast:* Ken Maynard (The Arizonian), Lina Basquette (Kay Moore), Hooper Atchley (Cole Porter), Michael Visaroff (Emilio Vasquez), Nena Quartero (Lola), Murdock MacQuarrie (Joe Moore), Charles King (Hite), Edmund Cobb (Zeke), Tom London (Chuck Wallace), Fred Burns (Sheriff), Jim Corey (Deputy), Tarzan (Himself).

An outlaw gang led by Cole Porter (Hooper Atchley) buys cattle from ranchers then ambushes them and takes back their money. They do this to the Arizonian (Ken Maynard), leaving him for dead after killing his partner. The Arizonian's horse Tarzan (Himself) helps him to escape, and he is found by Kay Moore (Lina Basquette), whose father (Murdock MacQuarrie) is the next intended victim of the Porter gang. After tending to the Arizonian's wounds, Kay takes the money from the sale of her father's cattle to the bank. Not knowing she has gone to town with the money, Porter sees Kay and orders his henchmen (Charles King, Edmund Cobb, Tom London) to go to the Moore ranch for the cash. There they murder Moore but are seen by the Arizonian, who chases them, but Porter frames him for the killing. Unable to return to the ranch, The Arizonian hides in the hills where he is accosted by the bandit Emilio Vasquez (Michael Visaroff). Vasquez, however, befriends the cowboy when he learns he is running from the law and takes him to his hideout which he shares with his girlfriend, pretty Lola (Nena Quartero), who is attracted to the Arizonian. Realizing he loves Kay, the Arizonian returns to the ranch, but she only pretends to believe his story and then helps Porter capture him. The cowboy, however, escapes, and he and Vasquez make plans to capture Porter. When Lola tries to seduce the Arizonian, Vasquez spanks her, and the angry girl goes to the sheriff (Fred Burns) with information on how to capture her lover. Vasquez sells cattle to Porter, who then plans to ambush him. He and the Arizonian, however, abduct Kay and Porter and dress the latter in Vasquez' clothes. The outlaws mistake Porter for Vasquez and kill him, thus making Kay realize that the Arizonian did not shoot her father. When the gang tries to capture Kay, Vasquez saves her but is mortally wounded. Lola grieves over the loss of her man while Kay offers the Arizonian the job of running the ranch.

After leaving Universal in 1930 Ken Maynard signed with Tiffany, and in the next two years he made eleven features for the company, *The Arizona Terror* being the fourth. Like many westerns of the period, the film is a good example of the transition period between silent pictures and sound. There are long stretches of action and then places where there is a concentration of dialogue. Ken Maynard and his horse Tarzan handle the action well, and Ken was becoming used to sound techniques by this time. Michael Visaroff, as the good-badman, however, steals the film with his florid acting style. Leading ladies Lina Basquette and Nena Quartero handle their roles in good fashion, and Hooper Atchley is in his usual fine fettle as the villain, called Cole Porter! Overall the film marks Ken Maynard's progression back to the top of the western field at the beginning of the sound era, and , while not his best Tiffany outing, it is more than a reasonably entertaining one.

## Murder at Midnight

September 20, 1931, 69 minutes.

*P:* Phil Goldstone. *D:* Frank R. Strayer. *SC:* W. Scott Darling & Frank R. Strayer. *PH:* William Rees. *ED:* John Rawlins. *AD:* Ralph DeLacy. *Mus:* Val Burton.

*Cast:* Aileen Pringle (Esme Kennedy), Alice White (Millie Scripps), Hale Hamilton (Philip Montrose), Robert Elliott (Inspector Taylor), Clara Blandick (Aunt Julia Kennedy), Brandon Hurst (Lawrence the Butler), Leslie Fenton (Walter Grayson), William Humphrey (Mr. Colton), Tyrell Davis (English Party Guest), Aileen Carlisle (Ella the Maid), Kenneth Thomson (Jim Kennedy), Robert Ellis (Duncan Channing), Vernon Dent (Peanuts).

During a game of charades at a house party, wealthy Jim Kennedy (Kenneth Thomson) shoots his secretary Duncan Channing (Robert Ellis), although he thought the gun he used was loaded with blanks. Among the guests at the party hosted by Kennedy and his wife, Esme (Aileen Pringle), are his Aunt Julia (Clara Blandick) and noted criminologist Philip Montrose (Hale Hamilton). Just after the murder Police Inspector Taylor (Robert Elliott) and his men arrive on the scene having been told there were two murder victims in the house. Lawrence (Brandon Hurst), the butler, tells Taylor there was animosity between the victim and his employer, but soon Jim Kennedy is found murdered and his will and a letter he has written are missing. Since the will was to disinherit Mrs. Kennedy, her brother, Walter Grayson (Leslie Fenton), who lived off the Kennedys, is suspected of the latest killing. A maid, Millie (Alice White), finds the will and letter and hides them before trying to blackmail Grayson into marrying her. When he refuses she phones Taylor, telling him she has information on the case, but when he arrives the next day to interrogate her, she too is found dead. Grayson is arrested for Millie's killing, and while he is at police headquarters Lawrence calls Taylor to say he has found the will and letter. Arriving back at the Kennedy mansion, the police find Lawrence has been murdered. Montrose shows Taylor that the butler died from a needle fired from a telephone receiver. Aunt Julia next finds the will and letter and Esme asks her to burn the missive, but she refuses and takes the items to Montrose. During her visit to the detective, Taylor arrives, and the murderer and the motive for the killings are revealed.

Filmed as *The Monster Kills*, *Murder at Midnight* proved to be a flavorful old-house murder mystery spiced with witty dialogue and a fistful of red herrings. Frank R. Strayer's direction is nicely paced and William Rees' photography beautifully captures the rather posh mansion setting of the homicides. The movie's greatest asset, however, is its fine cast. While top-billed Aileen Pringle and Alice White really have little to do, they handle their roles nicely and are most decorative. Hale Hamilton also does well as the detective, although it is Robert Elliott who has the lion's share of the footage as the rather thick-skulled investigator who looks into the web of killings in a methodical, workmanlike fashion. Clara Blandick has some good lines as the serpent-tongued Aunt Julia, while Brandon Hurst is memorable as the gaunt butler. Vernon Dent does a good job as the police inspector's peanut-eating assistant.

Scripter W. Scott Darling later reworked the plotline of *Murder at Midnight* into *The Mystery of Mr. Wong* (1939) starring Boris Karloff, and again in *The Chinese Ring* (1947), headlining Roland Winters as Charlie Chan. Both features were made by Monogram.

## Leftover Ladies

October 18, 1931, 65 minutes.

*P:* Sam Bischoff. *D:* Erle C. Kenton. *SC:* Robert R. Presnell. *ST:* Ursula Parrott. *PH:* John Stumar. *ED:* Arthur Huffsmith. *AD:* Ralph DeLacy. *SD:* John Stransky.

*Cast:* Claudia Dell, Marjorie Rambeau, Walter Byron, Alan Mowbray, Dorothy Revier, Rita LaRoy, Roscoe Karns, Selmer Jackson, Franklyn Farnum, Bert Roach, Buster Phelps.

Following her divorce a society girl plans a writing career and falls in love with a novelist whose wife has left him.

## Range Law

November 1, 1931, 63 minutes.

*P:* Phil Goldstone. *D:* Phil Rosen. *SC:* Earle Snell. *PH:* Arthur Reed. *ED:* Earl Turner. *AD:* Ralph DeLacy.

*Cast:* Ken Maynard, Frances Dade, Frank Mayo, Aileen Manning, Jack Rockwell, Lafe McKee, Charles King, Tom London, Tarzan.

Escaping from prison to find the man who framed him, a cowboy is hired to work at a ranch by its pretty owner.

## Near the Trail's End

November 24, 1931, 53 minutes.

*P:* Trem Carr. *D:* Wallace Fox. *SC:* George Arthur Durlam. *ST:* Robert Quigley. *PH:* Archie Stout & Faxon Dean. *ED:* J.S. Harrington. *AD:* E.R. Hickson. *Prod Mgr:* Charles A. Post. *Asst Dir:* Paul Malvern.

*Cast:* Bob Steele, Marion Shockley, Hooper Atchley, Jay Morley, Si Jenks, Murdock McQuarrie, Henry Rocquemore, Artie Ortego, Fred Burns.

Coming west to see her father, a young woman is kidnapped by two bandits but rescued by a cowboy and his pal.

## Nevada Buckaroo

November 29, 1931, 64 minutes.

*P:* Trem Carr. *D:* John P. McCarthy. *SC:* Wellyn Totman. *PH:* Faxon Dean. *ED:* Len Wheeler. *AD:* E.R. Hickson. *SD:* John Stransky. *Prod Mgr:* Charles A. Post. *Asst Dir:* Gordon Griffith.

*Cast:* Bob Steele, Dorothy Dix, Ed Brady, George Hayes, Artie Ortego, Glen Cavender, Billy Engle, Merrill McCormack, Blackie Whiteford.

An outlaw vows to go straight because of the love of a girl but is blamed for a stagecoach holdup.

## Branded Men

December 13, 1931, 63 minutes.

*P:* Phil Goldstone. *D:* Phil Rosen. *SC:* Earle Snell. *PH:* Arthur Reed. *ED:* Earl Turner. *SD:* Corson Jowett. *AD:* Ralph DeLacy.

*Cast:* Ken Maynard, June Clyde, Irving Bacon, Charles King, Billy Bletcher, Hooper Atchley, Donald Keith, Gladden James, Robert Homans, Edmund Cobb, Jack Rockwell, Slim Whitaker, Roy Bucko, Buck Bucko, Al Taylor, Bud McClure, Tarzan.

A cowboy becomes a sheriff and promises a young woman he will look out for her younger brother who is being blackmailed.

## X Marks the Spot

December 13, 1931, 72 minutes.

*P:* Sam Bischoff. *D:* Erle C. Kenton. *SC:* Warren B. Duff, Gordon Kahn & F. Hugh Herbert. *PH:* Gil Warrenton. *ED:* Arthur Huffsmith. *AD:* Ralph DeLacy. *SD:* Corson Jowett.

*Cast:* Lew Cody, Sally Blane, Wallace Ford, Mary Nolan, Fred Kohler, Charles Middleton, Virginia Lee Corbin, Joyce Coad, Richard Tucker, Clarence Muse, Helen Parrish.

When his younger sister is hurt in an auto accident and needs an expensive operation, a newspaper reporter is forced to turn to a gangster for help.

## Morals for Women

December 22, 1931, 70 minutes.

*P:* Phil Goldstone. *D:* Mort Blumenstock. *SC:* Frances Hyland & Gene Lewis. *PH:* Max Dupont. *ED:* Martin G. Cohn. *AD:* Ralph DeLacy.

*Cast:* Bessie Love, Conway Tearle, Emma Dunn, Natalie Moorhead, Lina Basquette, Virginia Lee Corbin, June Clyde, David Rollins, John Holland,

Edmund Breese, Crauford Kent, Otis Harlan, Walter Perry, Ethan Allen.

When her old boyfriend appears, a secretary cannot bring herself to tell him she is the mistress of her employer, a wealthy businessman.

## The Pocatello Kid

December 30, 1931, 61 minutes.
*P:* Phil Goldstone. *D:* Phil Rosen. *SC:* Earle Snell & W. Scott Darling. *ST:* W. Scott Darling. *PH:* Arthur Reed. *ED:* S. Roy Luby. *SD:* John Stransky. *AD:* Ralph DeLacy.

*Cast:* Ken Maynard, Marceline Day, Richard Cramer, Charles King, Lew Meehan, Jack Rockwell, Lafe McKee, Bob Reeves, Bud Osborne, Bert Lindley, Blackjack Ward, Tarzan.

Changing identities with his murdered lookalike brother, an outlaw falls for a pretty girl and becomes a lawman.

## Sunset Trail

Tiffany/World Wide, January 17, 1932, 62 minutes.
*P:* Phil Goldstone. *D:* B. Reeves Eason. *SC:* Bennett Cohen. *PH:* Arthur Reed. *ED:* S. Roy Luby. *AD:* Ralph DeLacy. *SD:* John Stransky.

*Cast:* Ken Maynard, Ruth Hiatt, Frank Rice, Philo McCullough, Buddy Hunter, Richard Alexander, Jack Rockwell, Frank Ellis, Bud Osborne, Lew Meehan, Bud McClure, Slim Whitaker, Tarzan.

Taking a job as a cowboy in order to get money to raise a friend's orphaned son, a man finds his new boss, a pretty woman, is being harassed by rustlers.

## Whistlin' Dan

Tiffany/World Wide, March 13, 1932, 64 minutes.
*P:* William Saal. *D:* Phil Rosen.

*SC:* Stuart Anthony. *PH:* Ira Morgan. *ED:* Rose Loewinger. *AD:* Ralph DeLacy. *SD:* John Stransky.

*Cast:* Ken Maynard, Joyzelle Joyner, Georges Renavent, Harlan E. Knight, Don Terry, Jack Rockwell, Jessie Arnold, Lee Meehan, Merrill McCormack, Wally Wales, Frank Ellis, Bud McClure, Hank Bell, Roy Bucko, Buck Bucko, Wesley Giraud, Iron Eyes Cody, Jim Corey, Tarzan.

In order to save the life of a friend held captive by a wanted bandit, a man and his pal rob the local bank to get the ransom money.

## Hotel Continental

Tiffany/World Wide, March 20, 1932, 67 minutes.
*P:* Sam Bischoff. *D:* Christy Cabanne. *SC:* F. Hugh Herbert, Paul Perez & Warren B. Duff. *PH:* Ira Morgan. *ED:* Rose Loewinger, Stanley Kolbert & Zella Young. *Mus:* Val Burton. *SD:* Corson Jowett & Hans Weeren. *AD:* Ralph DeLacy.

*Cast:* Peggy Shannon, Theodore Von Eltz, Alan Mowbray, J. Farrell MacDonald, Rockliffe Fellows, Ethel Clayton, Henry B. Walthall, Bert Roach, William Scott, Harry Edwards, George Humbert, Mary Carlisle, Wedgewood Newell.

As a hotel is about to close a convict is paroled to obtain money he hid there five years before.

## Lena Rivers

Tiffany/World Wide, April 3, 1932, 67 minutes.
*P:* Sam Bischoff. *D:* Phil Rosen. *SC:* Stuart Anthony & Warren B. Duff, from the novel by Mary Jane Holmes. *PH:* Ira Morgan. *ED:* Maurice Wright. *Mus:* Val Burton. *SD:* Corson Jowett. *AD:* Ralph DeLacy.

*Cast:* Charlotte Henry, James Kirkwood, Beryl Mercer, Morgan Galloway, Joyce Compton, Betty Blythe, John St. Polis, Clarence Muse, Russell Simpson, John Larkin, The Kentucky Jubilee Singers.

A young woman of questionable birth moves with her grandmother to Kentucky to live with relatives and attracts the attention of the man courting her cousin. Reissued on December 1, 1938, by Monogram as *The Sin of Lena Rivers.*

## Strangers of the Evening

Tiffany/World Wide, May 8, 1932, 71 minutes.

*P:* Sam Bischoff. *D:* H. Bruce Humberstone. *SC:* Stuart Anthony & Warren B. Duff, from the novel *The Illustrious Corpse* by Tiffany Thayer. *PH:* Arthur Edeson. *ED:* Dave Berg. *Mus:* Val Burton. *AD:* Ralph DeLacy. *SD:* Corson Jowett.

*Cast:* ZaSu Pitts, Eugene Pallette, Lucien Littlefield, Tully Marshall, Miriam Seegar, Theodore Von Eltz, Warner Richmond, Harold Waldridge, Mahlon Hamilton, Alan Roscoe, Charles Williams, William Scott, James Burtis, Francis Sayles, Hal Price.

A man disappears after he finds out his daughter plans to marry a man he does not like and the prospective son-in-law vows to find him. Reissued in 1942 as *The Hidden Corpse.*

## Texas Gun Fighter

Tiffany/World Wide, May 31, 1932, 63 minutes.

*P:* William Saal. *D:* Phil Rosen. *SC:* Bennett Cohen. *PH:* Jackson Rose. *ED:* Jerry Webb. *AD:* Ralph DeLacy. *SD:* John Stransky.

*Cast:* Ken Maynard, Sheila Mannors, Harry Woods, Lloyd Ingraham, Jim Mason, Frank Hall Crane, Bob Fleming, Edgar Lewis, Jack Rockwell, Bob Burns, Bud McClure, Frank Ellis, Blackjack Ward, Roy Bucko, Buck Bucko, Steve Clark, Tarzan.

Leaving his outlaw gang, a gunman falls in love with a girl and becomes a lawman but his old gang leader tries to get him to take part in a robbery.

## Hell-Fire Austin

Tiffany/World Wide, June 6, 1932, 70 minutes.

*P:* William Saal. *D-ST:* Forrest Sheldon. *SC:* Betty Burbridge. *PH:* Ted McCord & Joe Novak. *ED:* Dave Berg. *AD:* Ralph DeLacy. *SD:* H.R. Hobson & Don Peters. *Song:* Walter Donaldson & Gus Kahn.

*Cast:* Ken Maynard, Ivy Merton, Nat Pendleton, Alan Roscoe, Jack Perrin, William Robyns, Fargo Bussey, Lafe McKee, Charles LeMoyne, Lew Meehan, Jack Rockwell, Ben Corbett, Jack Pennick, Blackjack Ward, Bud McClure, Slim Whitaker, Jim Corey, Tarzan.

Down on his luck, a cavalry man ends up on a chain gang but is hired to ride in a big race and finds out his employer plans to cheat a young woman who has the better horse.

## The Man Called Back

Tiffany/World Wide, July 15, 1932, 74 minutes.

*P:* Sam Bischoff. *D:* Robert Florey. *SC:* Robert Presnell, from the novel *Silent Thunder* by Andrew Soutar. *PH:* Henry Sharp. *ED:* Rose Loewinger. *AD:* Ralph DeLacy. *SD:* Joseph Kane. *Asst Dir:* Edwin L. Marin. *Songs:* Val Burton & Corynn Kiehl.

*Cast:* Conrad Nagel, Doris Kenyon, John Halliday, Juliette Compton,

Reginald Owen, Mona Maris, Alan Mowbray, Gilbert Emery, Mae Busch, John T. Murray, Edgar Norton, Lionel Belmore, Clarissa Selwynne, Winter Hall, May Beatty, George Pearce.

A drunken doctor is given a second chance because of his feelings for a young woman, only to discover she is the wife of his benefactor.

# Times Exchange

Times Exchange was a New York City-based states' rights distributing company that handled eleven feature films from 1936 through 1940. Unlike Capital Film Exchange and First Division (qq.v.) earlier in the decade, Times apparently did not invest financially in any of the motion pictures it distributed. Three of the releases were British imports, while another three were reissues. Four features were made by other companies, two each from Metropolitan and Progressive (qq.v.). The other Times Exchange feature was an independently made documentary, *American Gang Busters* (1940).

The first release for Times Exchange was *Trouble Ahead* in the fall of 1936. A British comedy starring Charles Farrell, the company had originally planned to issue it under its British title, *Falling in Love*. It was not until the beginning of 1938 that Times had another release, a second British comedy, *The Girl Thief*, starring Marian Marsh. Again, the film was retitled, this time from *Love at Second Sight*. That year the company also handled the distribution of *Delinquent Parents* and *Rebellious Daughters* for Jed Buell's revived Progressive Pictures, and it closed out the year with the Frank Fay comedy *Meet the Mayor*. This feature had been written and produced by Fay in 1932, and Warner Brothers at the time picked it up for release under the title *A Fool's Advice*. In 1939 Times handled the distribution of two features made by Harry S. Webb's Metropolitan Pictures, *Port of Hate* and *Daughter of the Tong*. It closed out the year with still another British import comedy, *Two's Company*, starring Ned Sparks and Mary Brian.

Nineteen forty found Times Exchange handling a trio of features, two reissues and a documentary. The latter was *American Gang Busters*, an anthology which told such diverse stories as the Lindberg kidnapping case and the careers of gangsters Pretty Boy Floyd, Alvin Karpis and Machine Gun Kelly. The reissues were *Killers of the Wild* and *Men with Steel Faces*. The former had been made in 1938 by Pennant Pictures and called *Topa Topa*. It was filmed on location in the Rocky Mountains, and the small child in the production was portrayed by Jill L'Estrange, the daughter of the film's coproducer Dick L'Estrange. The Times release was the third for the picture since it had been picked up for reissue by Grand National in 1939 as *Children of the Wild. Men with Steel Faces* was a feature version of the 1935 Mascot serial *The Phantom Empire*, which had launched Gene Autry to screen stardom. No doubt this reissue was contrived to take advantage of his immense popularity; in 1940 the *Motion Picture Herald* not only named him the most popular western movie star, but he ranked fourth in the top ten of all money-making stars, behind only Mickey Rooney, Spencer Tracy and Clark Gable. Ironically, Nat Levine, the man who originally made *The Phantom Empire* for his Mascot Pictures, also fashioned a feature version of the serial called *Radio Ranch*. It too was released that year via the states' rights market carrying the Mascot logo, although the studio had officially been defunct for five years.

## Trouble Ahead

September 23, 1936, 74 minutes.
   *P:* Howard Welsch. *D:* Monty Banks. *SC:* Fred Thompson, Miles Malleson & John Paddy Carstairs. *ST:* Lee Loeb, E. Bard & A. Hyman.
   *Cast:* Charles Farrell, Margot Grahame, Gregory Ratoff, Mary Lawson, H.F. Maltby, Diane Napier, Cathleen Nesbitt, Pat Aherne, Sally Stewart, Monty Banks, Carroll Gibbons and His Orchestra.
   A publicity agent tries to stop his client, a Hollywood star, from adopting an orphan. Produced in England in 1934 and released there by Vogue as *Falling in Love*; running time, 80 minutes.

## The Girl Thief

January 14, 1938, 65 minutes.
   *P:* Jules Haimann. *D:* Paul Merzbach. *SC:* Frank Miller & Jack Davies. *ST:* Harold Simpson. *PH:* Jack Cox & Philip Grindrod.
   *Cast:* Marian Marsh, Anthony Bushell, Claude Hulbert, Ralph Ince, Joan Gardner, Stanley Holloway, Neil Kenyon, Vivian Reynolds.
   When a man invents a match that will last forever, a match manufacturer's daughter pretends to fall in love with him. Produced in England in 1934

and released there by Radius as *Love at Second Sight*; running time, 72 minutes.

## Meet the Mayor

October 17, 1938, 62 minutes.
   *P:* Frank Fay. *D:* Ralph Ceder. *SC:* Walter DeLeon & Charles Belden. *ST:* Frany Fay. *PH:* William Rees. *ED:* Don Hayes. *Mus:* Edward Ward. *Prod Mgr:* Harvey C. Leavitt.
   *Cast:* Frank Fay, Ruth Hall, Nat Pendleton, Berton Churchill, Hale Hamilton, George Meeker, Eddie Nugent, Franklin Pangborn, Esther Howard, Nick Copeland, Eddie Borden, Al Hill, Mike Donlin, Sidney Harvis.
   An elevator operator invents a machine which causes the defeat of a crooked politician in a mayoral election. Originally released by Warner Brothers in 1932 as *A Fool's Advice*. Also called *His Honor the Mayor*.

## Port of Hate

Metropolitan, August 22, 1939, 57 minutes.
   *P-D:* Harry S. Webb. *SC:* Joseph O'Donnell. *ST:* Forrest Sheldon. *PH:* Edward Kull. *ED:* Robert Jahns. *SD:* Hans Weeren. *Mus:* Johnny Lange & Lew Porter. *Prod Mgr:* Dallas M. Fitzgerald. *Tech Dir:* Harry Gordon. *Asst Dir:* Edward M. Saeta.

Grant Withers (center) and Evelyn Brent in *Daughter of the Tong* (Times Exchange, 1939).

*Cast:* Polly Ann Young, Kenneth Harlan, Carleton Young, Monte Blue, Frank LaRue, Shia Jung, Richard Adams, Reed Howes, Jimmy Aubrey, Bruce Dane, Edward Cecil, John Elliott.

After finding a black pearl bed on a remote island, two men are attacked by thugs who want to steal their claim.

## Daughter of the Tong

Metropolitan, August 28, 1939, 56 minutes.

*P:* Lester F. Scott, Jr. *AP:* Harry S. Webb. *D:* Raymond K. Johnson. *SC:* Alan Merritt. *ST:* George H. Plympton. *PH:* Elmer Dyer. *ED:* Charles Kiltz. *Mus:* Lee Zahler. *SD:* Cliff Ruberg. *Asst Dir:* Ray Nazarro.

*Cast:* Evelyn Brent (Carney), Grant Withers (Ralph Dickson/Gallagher), Dorothy Short (Marion Morgan), Dave O'Brien (Jerry Morgan), Richard Loo (Wong), Dirk Thane (Slade), Harry Harvey (Harold "Mugsy" Winthrop), Budd Buster (Lefty/McMillan), Robert Frazer (Division Chief Williams), Hal Taliaferro [Wally Wales] (Agent Lawson), James Coleman (Hardy).

When a government agent is killed while investigating an alien smuggling operation in Chinatown, the division chief (Robert Frazer) of the FBI assigns agent Ralph Dickson (Grant Withers) to investigate. The Agency has intercepted a letter from Tong leader Carney (Evelyn Brent) to a gangster who has been hired as a hitman for the organization. Since Dickson is a lookalike for the hoodlum, whose name is Gallagher, he is assigned to impersonate the man and infiltrate the gangland operation. Ralph also has a score to settle with Carney since the murdered agent was his best friend. The FBI wants evidence to convict Carney on federal charges, not knowing she is a woman. Posing as Gallagher, Ralph is met at the bus depot by gang henchman Mugsy (Harry Harvey), and there he also meets a young woman, Marion Morgan (Dorothy Short), who is obviously in distress. Mugsy takes Ralph to the Oriental Hotel, where Carney is headquartered, and again he meets Marion, who has come there to bring money to free her brother Jerry (Dave O'Brien), a one-time partner of Carney in an importing business. When Marion is taken prisoner by the gang, Ralph helps her to get free and later takes her to FBI headquarters where she tells about her honest brother being held prisoner by the gang. Eventually Ralph is able to help Jerry escape but the two are captured by the gang after a car chase. Back at the hotel, Carney and hotel clerk Wong (Richard Loo) torture Ralph to make him tell where he has hidden the ransom money brought for Jerry. Meanwhile Agent Lawson (Hal Taliaferro), Marion and FBI men arrive on the scene and rescue Ralph and after a fight the gang is arrested. Ralph is then offered the job as FBI chief on the West Coast and agrees to stay along with Marion.

Metropolitan Pictures Corporation (q.v.) under the auspices of Harry S. Webb continued to function as a producer of motion pictures after dropping out of the states' rights market under its own banner. *Daughter of the Tong* is one of the features produced by Metropolitan, and like *Port of Hate* from the same year, is was distributed by Times Exchange. The film opens with a prologue tribute to the Federal Bureau of Investigation and its efforts to bring an end to the activities of major criminals. Unfortunately the film itself does not live up to its send-off proving to be just another cheaply made Poverty Row effort, which moves along quickly enough to fill up its one hour dual bill berth. Padded with stock footage of a police chase and hampered by tacky sets, the movie is likable enough in its limited fashion. Grant Withers is the quarter-flipping FBI agent out to avenge the murder of a pal and Harry Harvey supplies some amusement in a semi-comedy relief role. Evelyn Brent in the title role is the film's best asset; she makes a very sexy villain. In the film she is known as "The Illustrious One" with the code name Carney.

## Two's Company

December 28, 1939, 64 minutes.

*P:* Paul Soskin. *D:* Tim Whelan. *SC:* Tom Geraghty, Roland Pertwee, J.B. Morton, John Paddy Carstairs & Tim Whelan, from the novel *Romeo and Julia* by Sidney Horler.

*Cast:* Ned Sparks, Mary Brian, Gordon Harker, Patric Knowles, Harry Holman, Olive Blakeney, Morton Selten, Robb Wilton, Gibb McNaughton, H.F. Maltby, Syd Crossley, Edmond Breon, Lawrence Hanray.

When his son falls in love with the daughter of a rich American, a snobbish earl tries to stop the affair. Made in England in 1936 by British and Dominion Film Corporation; running time, 74 minutes. Reissued in England in 1943 by Equity British Film Producers.

## American Gang Busters

April 3, 1940, 60 minutes.

*P-D-ED:* Captain A.F. Dion.

The history of some of the most notorious crimes in the 20th Century, including newsreel footage.

## Killers of the Wild

Fine Arts, April 3, 1940, 65 minutes.

*P:* Dick L'Estrange, William M. Vogel & William Steiner. *D:* Vin Moore & Charles Hutchison. *SC:* Arthur Hoerl & Hilda May Young. *ST-ED:* Charles Diltz. *PH:* Robert Doran. *SD:* Corson Jowett. *Prod Mgr:* Dick L'Estrange. *Mus:* Dr. Edward Kilenyl. *Songs:* Rudy Sooter.

*Cast:* Joan Valerie, James Bush, LeRoy Mason, Ruth Coleman, Jill L'Estrange, Trevor Bardette, Fred Santley, Lyons Wickland, Helen Hughes, Patsy Moran, Silver Wolf, Goldie.

A wolf dog is falsely accused of the murder of a trapper, a crime committed by the man who lusts for his daughter. Originally released in 1938 by Pennant Pictures Corporation as *Topa Topa* and reissued by Grand National in 1939 as *Children of the Wild.*

## Men with Steel Faces

Mascot, April 3, 1940, 70 minutes.

*P:* Nat Levine. *D:* Otto Brower & Breezy [B. Reeves] Eason. *SC:* John Rathmell & Armand L. Schaefer. *ST:* Wallace MacDonald, Gerald Geraghty & H. Freeman. *PH:* Ernest Miller & William Nobles. *ED:* Earl Turner. *SD:* Terry Kellum. *Supv:* Armand L. Schaefer.

*Cast:* Gene Autry, Frankie Darro, Betsy King Ross, Smiley Burnette, Dorothy Christy, Wheeler Oakman, Charles K. French, Warner Richmond, J. Frank Glendon, William Moore, Ed Peil, Sr., Jack Carlyle, Frankie Marvin, Wally Wales, Buffalo Bill, Jr., Fred Burns, Stanley Blystone, Frank Ellis, Henry Hall, Jim Corey.

Framed on a murder charge, a radio singer is taken prisoner by the minions of the lost world Murania. Feature version of the 1935 Mascot serial *The Phantom Empire.*

# Tower Productions

Headquartered at 220 West 42nd Street in New York City, Tower Productions was formed in 1931, and through 1934 it released a dozen feature films on the states' rights market with distribution through Capital Film Exchange (q.v.). Joseph Simmonds was president of the company, and eleven of its twelve releases were made by the Premier Attractions studio run by producer Sigmund Neufeld. The other Tower release, *The Big Bluff* (1933), was made by producer George Weeks, who had just left Mayfair Pictures (q.v.). The Tower releases were no more than fodder for dual bills and the small-town trade, but they were compactly made and had an air of class about them despite budget limitations. Each also carried a headliner for box-office appeal. Names like Lois

Wilson, Natalie Moorhead, Marion Shilling, Lila Lee, Merna Kennedy, Marian Marsh, Reginald Denny, Regis Toomey, Johnny Mack Brown and Sally O'Neil headlined Tower features.

Sigmund Neufeld launched his career as an independent producer in 1931 with Tower after having spent 18 years with Universal in various capacities. His younger brother Samuel Neufeld, better known as Sam Newfield (also Sherman Scott and Peter Stewart), made his directorial debut at Tower with *Reform Girl* (1933). After Tower's demise in 1934, Sigmund Neufeld teamed with Leslie Simmonds to produce the Tim McCoy series of westerns at Puritan (q.v.) for the 1935-36 season. Sam Newfield directed these sagebrush ventures. Throughout the 1940s the Neufeld brothers turned out scores of cheap productions for Producers Releasing Corporation (PRC) with Sigmund producing and Sam directing. The most prolific series in this grouping were the "Billy Carson" westerns starring Buster Crabbe and Al St. John. The brothers continued to collaborate and in 1956 made the syndicated television series "Hawkeye and the Last of the Mohicans," starring John Hart and Lon Chaney.

Tower Productions ceased activity in 1934. Like many other Poverty Row outfits of the time, the return from its features probably did not compensate enough for production costs to continue operations.

## Discarded Lovers

January 3, 1932, 59 minutes.

*D:* Fred Newmeyer. *SC:* Edward T. Lowe. *ST:* Arthur Hoerl. *PH:* William Hyer. *ED:* Charles Hunt. *SD:* Corson Jowett.

*Cast:* Natalie Moorhead, Russell Hopton, J. Farrell MacDonald, Barbara Weeks, Jason Robards, Roy D'Arcy, Sharon Lynn, Fred Kelsey, Robert Frazer, Jack Trent, Allen Dailey.

A police captain and a reporter try to solve the murder of a disliked movie star with many lovers.

## Shop Angel

March 6, 1932, 67 minutes.

*P:* Morris R. Schlank. *D:* E. Mason Hopper. *SC:* Edward T. Lowe. *PH:* William Hyer. *ED:* Lou Sackin. *Mus:* Val Burton. *SD:* Corson Jowett. *Supv:* Sigmund Neufeld.

*Cast:* Marion Shilling, Holmes Herbert, Anthony Bushell, Walter Byron, Dorothy Christy, Creighton Hale, Hank Mann.

A dress designer is desired by her boss but she is attracted to his daughter's fiancé.

## Drifting Souls

August 9, 1932, 63 minutes.

*P:* Morris P. Schlank. *Supv:* Sigmund Neufeld. *D:* Louis King. *SC:* Douglas Doty and Norman Houston, from the novel by Barbara Hunter. *PH:* William C. Hyer. *ED:* Irving Birnbaum. *SD:* Corson Jowett.

*Cast:* Lois Wilson (Linda Lawrence), Theodore Von Eltz (Joe Robson), Raymond Hatton (Scoop), Gene Gowling (Ted Merritt), Shirley Grey (Greta Janson), Gwynn [Guinn] Williams (Bing), Edmund Breese (Brad Martin), Mischa Auer (Skeets), Bryant Washburn (Littlefield), Edward LeSaint (Doctor), Blanche Payson (Landlady).

**Raymond Hatton and Shirley Grey in** *Drifting Souls* **(Tower, 1932).**

Lawyer Linda Lawrence (Lois Wilson) learns that her father needs a costly operation in order to live. She goes to a big city and places an advertisement in a newspaper offering herself in marriage to anyone who will pay her five thousand dollars, the price needed for the surgery. Newspaperman Scoop (Raymond Hatton) gets on the story, which results in the headline, "New Love Racket." Meanwhile, crook Joe Robson (Theodore Von Eltz) wants his girlfriend Greta (Shirley Grey) to trick reckless playboy Ted Merritt (Gene Gowling) into marriage so they can fleece him of his fortune. They go joyriding with Ted, who is drunk, and Joe takes the wheel and hits a road worker, killing the man. Joe makes Ted believe he is responsible for the homicide while Greta takes it on the lam. Needing an alibi for Ted, Joe convinces Linda to marry the playboy, which she agrees to do for the set financial fee.

After the marriage of convenience, Linda sends the money for her father's operation, which is a success. Scoop investigates the hit-and-run accident and finds out that Linda has married Ted. Greta returns and Joe decides on another blackmail scheme, and at a party given by Ted, Joe tells Linda that Greta was engaged to Ted and that she was his alibi in the hit-and-run killing. Scoop arrives with the law, and Ted is arrested for the crime. Joe hires Brad Martin (Edmund Breese) to defend him, knowing the shyster will lose the case. During the trial, Martin quits and Linda takes over Ted's defense. Scoop, who realizes that Linda is on the level, finds the hiding Greta and the latter testifies that it was Joe, not Ted, who drove the death vehicle. Joe is arrested, Ted is placed in the custody of Linda and the newlyweds decide to consummate their marriage.

Tower Productions' *Drifting Souls*

is a fairly interesting dual biller high-lighted by a fine performance by Lois Wilson in the lead role and good supporting work from Raymond Hatton as a good-hearted newshound, Shirley Grey as a bad girl, and Guinn "Big Boy" Williams in the role of a protective chauffeur. Theodore Von Eltz, however, appears miscast as the slimy villain; he seems better suited for the role of the victimized playboy. An off-shoot of the Cinderella theme, *Drifting Souls* does contain some solid dialogue. At the beginning, the lawyer heroine is told by a kindly doctor that the people in their small town would not trust their legal affairs to a girl. Later, when she offers to sell herself in marriage to get the money for the operation that will save her (unseen) father's life, the newspaperman tells her, "You're just putting a new twist on the oldest racket in the world." Production-wise *Drifting Souls* is acceptably done although its plot contrivances cannot bear close scrutiny.

## Exposure

August 20, 1932, 71 minutes.
*P:* Morris R. Schlank. *AP:* Sigmund Neufeld. *D-SC:* Norman Houston. *PH:* Harry Forbes. *ED:* Irving Birnbaum. *SD:* R.C. Clarke.
*Cast:* Lila Lee, Walter Byron, Mary Duran, Bryant Washburn, Tully Marshall, Spec O'Donnell, Lee Moran, Pat O'Malley, Nat Pendleton, Sidney Bracey.
A hard drinking newspaperman convinces a young woman to carry on her father's faltering business and the two fall in love.

## Red Haired Alibi

October 15, 1932, 75 minutes.
*P:* Sigmund Neufeld. *D:* Christy

Cabanne. *SC:* Edward T. Lowe, from the novel by Wilson Collison. *PH:* Harry Forbes. *ED:* Irving Birnbaum. *SD:* Corson Jowett.
*Cast:* Myrna Kennedy, Theodore Von Eltz, Grant Withers, Purnell Pratt, Huntley Gordon, Fred Kelsey, Arthur Hoyt, Paul Porcasi, John Vosburgh, Shirley Temple, Marion Lessing, Spec O'Donnell.
A young woman comes to the big city where she is hired to be a man's companion, not knowing he is a gangster.

## Reform Girl

March 4, 1933, 65 minutes.
*P:* Sigmund Neufeld. *D:* Sam [Newfield] Neufeld. *SC:* George W. Sayre. *PH:* Harry Forbes. *ED:* Lou Sackin. *SD:* Corson Jowett.
*Cast:* Noel Francis, Skeets Gallagher, Hale Hamilton, Robert Ellis, Dorothy Peterson, Stanley Smith, Ben Hendricks, Jr., De Witt Jennings.
Getting out of prison a young woman is paid to smear a politician by appearing to be his long, lost daughter. Reissued in 1952 as *Vice Raid*.

## Daring Daughters

March 25, 1933, 63 minutes.
*P:* Sigmund Neufeld. *D:* Christy Cabanne. *SC:* Barry Barringer & F. Hugh Herbert. *ST:* Sam Mintz. *PH:* Harry Forbes. *ED:* Irving Birnbaum. *SD:* Corson Jowett.
*Cast:* Marian Marsh, Kenneth Thomson, Joan Marsh, Bert Roach, Allen Vincent, Lita Chevret, Richard Tucker, Arthur Hoyt, Florence Roberts, Bryant Washburn, Jr., Charlotte Merriam.
A young woman tries to protect her younger sister from the ways of men in the big city. Reissued in 1955 as *City Virgin*.

# The Important Witness

September 6, 1933, 64 minutes.
*P:* Sigmund Neufeld. *D:* Sam Newfield. *SC:* Douglas Doty. *ST:* Gordon Morris. *PH:* Harry Forbes. *ED:* Al Clark. *SD:* Otto Blinn. *AD:* Ralph DeLacy. *Asst Dir:* Leslie Simmonds.

*Cast:* Noel Francis, Dorothy Burgess, Donald Dillaway, Noel Madison, Robert Ellis, Charles Delaney, Paul Fix, Ben Hendricks, Jr., Harry Myers, Franklin Pangborn, Sarah Padden, Ethel Wales, Gladys Blake, Mary Dunn, John Deering.

A public stenographer is arrested for murder when found at the scene of the crime where she was hired to work.

# The Big Bluff

October 11, 1933, 58 minutes.
*P:* George W. Weeks. *D-ST:* Reginald Denny. *SC:* Faith Thomas. *PH:* James S. Brown, Jr. *ED:* Byron Robinson. *Mus:* Lee Zahler. *AD:* Paul Palmentola. *SD:* C.S. Franklin. *Asst Dir:* Leigh Smith.

*Cast:* Reginald Denny, Claudia Dell, Jed Prouty, Cyril Chadwick, Donald Keith, Philip Tead, Alden Gay, Lucille Ward, Ethel Wales, Eric Wilton, Ben Hall, Rhea Mitchell.

A small town snob hires an actor to portray British royalty at her party to show up a rival.

# Big Time or Bust

January 10, 1934, 62 minutes
*P:* Sigmund Neufeld. *D:* Sam Newfield. *SC:* George W. Sayre. *PH:* Harry Forbes. *ED:* Al Clark. *AD:* Ralph DeLacy. *SD:* L.E. Tope.

*Cast:* Regis Toomey, Gloria Shea, Walter Byron, Nat Carr, Charles Delaney, Edwin Maxwell, Hooper Atchley, Paul Porcasi.

Two carnival performers wed and then head to Broadway with the wife attracting the attention of a playboy.

# Marrying Widows

May 18, 1934, 65 minutes.
*P:* Sigmund Neufeld. *D:* Sam Newfield. *SC:* Adele Buffington. *PH:* Harry Forbes. *SD:* L.E. Tope. *Asst Dir:* Leslie Simmonds.

*Cast:* Judith Allen, Johnny Mack Brown, Minna Gombell, Lucien Littlefield, Bert Roach, Sara Padden, Virginia Sale, Nat Carr, Arthur Hoyt, Otto Hoffman, Syd Saylor, Gladys Blake, George Grandee.

A widow moves to New York City where she falls for a man who only wants to marry her for her alleged fortune.

# Beggar's Holiday

August 17, 1934, 60 minutes.
*P:* Sigmund Neufeld. *D:* Sam Newfield. *SC:* Adele Buffington. *PH:* Harry Forbes. *SD:* L.E. Tope.

*Cast:* Hardie Albright, Sally O'Neil, J. Farrell MacDonald, Barbara Barondess, George Grandee, William Franklin.

A young woman falls in love with a man not knowing he is an embezzler who plans to leave the country.

# Victory Pictures Corporation

Sam Katzman operated Victory Pictures Corporation from 1935 to 1940. In that time the company turned out two serials and thirty feature films, including western series starring Tom Tyler and Tim McCoy. The Katzman unit consisted mainly of directors Bob Hill, Al Herman and Sam Newfield, with Katzman himself occasionally directing. Most modern-day yarns were scripted by Al Martin while Basil Dickey wrote the westerns. Camera work was done by Bill Hyer with art director Fred Preble dressing the sets. Edward W. Rote served as production manager for Victory throughout its existence. Victory productions were shot in three to five days at rented studio space like the Bryan Foy and Talisman studios and at Monogram. The westerns produced by Katzman were usually filmed outdoors at locales like the Lazy A Ranch in Chatsworth, California, with minimum indoor shooting. Other features were also done on location, like *Bars of Hate* (1936), which was shot at United Airport in Burbank, California.

With a reputation for budget parsimony, Sam Katzman (1901-1973) started working at Fox in 1914 and remained there in various capacities until 1931. He then worked with First National and Cosmopolitan before becoming production manager for Showmen's Productions (q.v.) in 1933. From there he worked with other independents like Supreme Pictures (q.v.) before forming Victory. His features were turned out on budgets of less than $10,000 each with minimum wages paid to his supporting casts and technical crews. His features were hurriedly shot, cut and edited, and he even hired the process laboratory on a percentage basis for negatives and prints. The Victory product, however, proved successful. For example, his Tim McCoy westerns were shot on a budget of $8,000 each (half that going to the star's salary), and their domestic gross was between $40,000 and $60,000 per picture.

Victory kicked off its release schedule in the fall of 1935 with a series of action adventures based on the short stories of popular writer Peter B. Kyne. Eight movies were done in this series through 1937 although all had been filmed the previous two years. In 1936 Katzman turned to westerns and hired popular sagebrush star Tom Tyler to headline eight oaters, several of which were filmed simultaneously. In this series Tyler mostly played the role of an agent for the Cattlemen's Association, Tom Wade. During the filming of the series Tyler married Jeanne Martel, who costarred with him in *Orphan of the Pecos* and *Lost Ranch*, and upon completion of filming he toured with the Wallace Brothers Circus. Upon Tyler's departure Katzman acquired the services of veteran range hero Tim McCoy for another series of eight westerns. In these

McCoy enacted the role of government agent Lightnin' Bill Carson, a role he originated in a film of the same name for Puritan (q.v.) in 1936. Tim McCoy had a penchant for wearing disguises in his features, and he played this to the hilt in his Victory outings, variously portraying a Mexican, Oriental and Gypsy while carrying out his heroics. Ben Corbett costarred in this series as Carson's pal Magpie. All the McCoy features were directed by Sam Newfield and when the western star left Victory in 1940 he went to work at Producers Distributing Corporation (PDC), later Producers Releasing Corporation (PRC), for Newfield's brother, Sigmund Neufeld, who had earlier coproduced his Puritan series. Sam Newfield, who also helmed the Puritans, continued as director but under the name Peter Stewart.

Another series turned out by Victory was with Olympic decathlon champion Herman Brix, who earlier had starred in the Burroughs-Tarzan (q.v.) serial *The New Adventures of Tarzan* (1935). Brix applied himself well to these tattered actioners, but their low-grade quality nearly sank his acting career before he changed his name to Bruce Bennett. Brix headlined five features for Sam Katzman as well as costarring with Bela Lugosi in the fifteen-chapter serial *Shadow of Chinatown* (1936). Its plot was complicated and the story moved slowly; more fast-paced was a feature version which had a different ending than the cliffhanger. Victory also made another chapterplay, *Blake of Scotland Yard* (1937), starring Ralph Byrd with Herbert Rawlinson in the title role. This fun mixture of sleuthing, horror and science fiction "was an out-and-out action thriller with far more excitement than many of his (Katzman's) later efforts," wrote James Stringham in *Film Fan Monthly* (March, 1967). It too was released in a feature version.

With the release of *Straight Shooter*, the final Tim McCoy western for the company in 1940, Victory ceased operations. Sam Katzman moved to Monogram where, from 1940 to 1947, he produced more than three dozen features including a horror-thriller series with Bela Lugosi, the Teen Agers series and the East Side Kids and early Bowery Boys features. In 1947 he joined Columbia where he produced scores of cheap features and serials. It was there he earned the moniker "Jungle Sam" because of his penchant for tacky backlot jungle pictures. Katzman specialized in fad movies, mainly in the musical, science fiction and crime fields, plus the old reliable, westerns. According to the highbrow periodical *Cahiers du Cinéma*, "His films beat all records for speed of shooting, modesty of budget, and artistic nullity." Surprisingly, Katzman became a producer at Metro-Goldwyn-Mayer in the late 1950s, and later in the 1960s his production company, Four Leaf, made films like *Riot on the Sunset Strip* (1967) and *Angel, Angel Down We Go* (1969) for American International.

**Danger Ahead**

July 19, 1935, 65 minutes.

*P:* Sam Katzman. *D:* Al Herman. *SC:* Al Martin, from the story "One Eighth Apache" by Peter B. Kyne. *PH:*

Bill Hyer. *ED:* Dan Milner. *SD:* Herb Eicke. *AD:* Fred Preble. *Asst Dir:* Glen Glenn.

*Cast:* Lawrence Gray, Sheila Mannors, J. Farrell MacDonald, Fuzzy Knight, Bryant Washburn, Fred Kelsey, John Elliott, Eddie Phillips, Arthur Loft, J. Herschel Mayall, Gordon Griffith, Earl Dwire, Richard Cramer, George Chesebro.

A newspaperman comes to the rescue of a sea captain and his daughter when thieves try to take their money from a silk cargo sale.

## Hot Off the Press

October 9, 1935, 57 minutes.

*P:* Sam Katzman. *D:* Al Herman. *SC:* Victor Potel & Gordon Griffith, from the story "The New Pardner" by Peter B. Kyne. *PH:* Bill Hyer. *ED:* Dan Milner. *SD:* Herb Eicke. *Prod Mgr:* Edward W. Rote. *AD:* Fred Preble.

*Cast:* Jack LaRue, Virginia Pine, Monte Blue, Fuzzy Knight, James C. Morton, Fred Kelsey, Mickey Rentschler, William Gould, Edward Hearn, Gordon Griffith, Henry Hall.

The circulation manager of a newspaper quits to join a rival operation and finds himself in the middle of a circulation war.

## A Face in the Fog

February 1, 1936, 66 minutes.

*P:* Sam Katzman. *D:* Bob Hill. *SC:* Al Martin, from the story "The Great Mono Miracle" by Peter B. Kyne. *PH:* Bill Hyer. *ED:* Earl Turner. *SD:* J.S. Westmoreland. *AD:* Fred Preble.

*Cast:* June Collyer, Lloyd Hughes, Lawrence Gray, Al St. John, Jack Mulhall, Jack Cowell, John Elliott, Sam Flint, Forrest Taylor, Ed Cassidy, Robert Williams, The Ramsdell Dancers, Donna Lee Trio.

When a pretty newspaper reporter writes a story about a mysterious fiend who has murdered two actors in a play the madman comes after her for revenge.

## Fighting Coward

May 1, 1936, 55 minutes.

*P:* Sam Katzman. *D:* Dan Milner. *SC:* Al Martin, from the story "The Last Assignment" by Peter B. Kyne. *PH:* Bill Hyer. *ED:* Jack Milner. *AD:* Fred Preble. *SD:* J.S. Westmoreland. *Prod Mgr:* Edward W. Rote.

*Cast:* Ray Walker, Joan Woodbury, William Farnum, Earl Dwire, Syd Saylor, Matthew Betz, Clara Kimball Young, Reed Howes, Roger Williams.

When a district attorney is murdered, a young policeman resigns because he believes the killer is his father. Made as *Wanted Men* and reissued as *The Last Assignment*.

## Rio Grande Romance

May 1, 1936, 60 minutes.

*P:* Sam Katzman. *D:* Bob Hill. *SC:* Al Martin, from the story "One Day's Work" by Peter B. Kyne. *PH:* Bill Hyer. *ED:* Dan Milner. *AD:* Fred Preble. *SD:* Johnny Eilers. *Prod Mgr:* Edward W. Rote.

*Cast:* Eddie Nugent, Maxine Doyle, Fuzzy Knight, Lucille Lund, Don Alvarado, Nick Stuart, George Walsh, Joyce Kay, George Cleveland, Forrest Taylor, Ernie Adams, Ed Cassidy, Ivo Henderson, John Cowell, Richard Cramer.

When his brother-in-law is charged with murder and bond theft, a federal agent gets himself sent to prison to uncover the truth. Reissued by Principal Pictures on October 3, 1936, as *Put on the Spot*.

Advertisement for *A Face in the Fog* (Victory, 1936).

## Prison Shadows

July 18, 1936, 67 minutes.

*P:* Sam Katzman. *D:* Bob Hill. *SC:* Al Martin. *PH:* Bill Hyer. *ED:* Dan Milner. *AD:* Fred Preble. *Prod Mgr:* Edward W. Rote.

*Cast:* Eddie Nugent, Joan Barclay, Monte Blue, Lucille Lund, Forrest Taylor, Syd Saylor, John Elliott, Jack Cowell, Willard Kent, Walter O'Keefe.

After serving a prison sentence for killing another man in a boxing match, a prize fighter is unknowingly lured into the same situation again by a siren, the moll of a gangster.

## Kelly of the Secret Service

July 22, 1936, 69 minutes.

*P:* Sam Katzman. *D:* Bob Hill. *SC:* Al Martin, from the story "On Irish Hill" by Peter B. Kyne. *PH:* Bill Hyer. *ED:* Dan Milner. *SD:* Hans Weeren. *AD:* Fred Preble. *Prod Mgr:* Edward W. Rote.

*Cast:* Lloyd Hughes, Sheila Mannors, Fuzzy Knight, Jack Mulhall, Syd Saylor, Forrest Taylor, John Elliott, Mike Morita, Jack Cowell.

After the plans for a radio-controlled bomb are stolen, a Secret Service agent gets on the case.

## Shadow of Chinatown

October 10, 1936, 15 chapters.

*P:* Sam Katzman. *D:* Bob Hill. *SC:* Isadore Bernstein, Basil Dickey & William Buchanan. *ST:* Rock Hawkey [Bob Hill]. *PH:* Bill Hyer. *ED:* Charles Henkel. *SD:* Hans Weeren. *AD:* Fred Preble. *Prod Mgr:* Edward W. Rote.

*Cast:* Bela Lugosi (Victor Poten), Herman Brix [Bruce Bennett] (Martin Andrews), Joan Barclay (Joan Whiting), Luana Walters (Sonya Rokoff), Maurice Liu (Willy Fu), Charles King (Grogan), William Buchanan (Healy), Forrest Taylor (Captain Walters), James B. Leong (Wong), Henry F. Tung (Dr. Wu), Paul Fung (Tom Chu), George Chan (Old Luee), John Elliott (Ship Captain), Moy Ming (Wong's Brother), Jack Cowell, Denver Dixon (Henchmen), Henry Hall (Psychiatrist), Roger Williams (Harrison), Lester Dorr.

*Chapter Titles:* The Arms of the God, The Crushing Walls, Ferguson Alley, Death on the Wire, The Sinister Ray, The Sword Thrower, The Noose, Midnight, The Last Warning, The Bomb, Thundering Doom, Invisible Gas, The Brink of Disaster, The Fatal Trap, The Avenging Powers.

Because Oriental imports have

Lobby card for *Shadow of Chinatown* (Victory, 1936) picturing Luana Walters and Bela Lugosi.

been drastically cut due to the tourist trade, European businessmen hire Sonya Rokoff (Luana Walters) to close down San Francisco's Chinatown. She in turn obtains the services of Eurasian Victor Poten (Bela Lugosi), who hates both whites and Orientals and plans to start his own race by destroying the other two peoples. When his thugs cause several disturbances, novice newspaper reporter Joan Whiting (Joan Barclay) thinks a Tong war has started and she enlists the aid of writer Martin Andrews (Herman Brix). When she disappears, Andrews, his servant Willy Fu (Maurice Liu) and police Captain Walters (Forrest Taylor) all search for her and find she has been a prisoner of the people behind the trouble. When more problems occur, Walters thinks Andrews is to

blame because several incidents have been described in his books. When Joan is again captured, Andrews is able to stop Poten's henchman Grogan (Charles King) and rescue her. Sonya, who is upset at Poten's tactics persuades him to go to Los Angeles and they travel on a boat. Upset that Grogan wants Sonya for himself, Poten tries to kill him and then turns his subordinate into a zombie. Andrews and Willy Fu are also on the boat, but Poten gives them the slip when it docks. In Los Angeles, Poten is on the loose as Sonya reveals his true nature to the authorities. Later, he places a gas bomb in his laboratory as Andrews, Joan, Sonya and the authorities arrive, but they manage to escape without injury. Later Poten orders Grogan to kill Andrews, but it is the henchman who dies. Joan and Willy Fu go with Sonya to Andrews's home, not knowing Poten and another henchman (William Buchanan) have taken sanctuary there. The two tie up Joan and Willy Fu and set a trap for Andrews, but when he returns, it is Sonya who is killed by a falling chandelier. Andrews then gives chase to Poten in his car, and the latter's vehicle goes off the rail into the Los Angeles harbor, where he is presumed to have drowned. At a dinner given by the Chinese merchants to celebrate the end of Poten's reign of terror, the madman is recognized as one of the waiters and is arrested by Captain Walters. Later Andrews tells Joan she is giving up the newspaper business to become his bride.

Billed as a Carmel Production, *Shadow of Chinatown* (later issued as *Yellow Phantom*) was Sam Katzman's initial Victory serial and the first of his many outings in the cliffhanger field. Shot in about two weeks at Culver City, it is a rather slow affair which greatly benefits from the villainy of Bela Lugosi as the racist madman Victor Poten. Not only does the actor chew up the scenery and dialogue as Poten, but he is also allowed to masquerade as an old man, a Chinaman and a telephone repairman, as well as the waiter trying to poison the wine at the finale. Hampered by exceedingly tacky sets, the serial did benefit from some sci-fi gadgets such as a futuristic television device, but Poten's laboratory is a shoddy affair. Impressive is a character called "The God," a hypnotized man made up to appear as an idol which dispatches Poten's enemies into a pit.

The rest of the cast does well, especially the heroics of Herman Brix (later Bruce Bennett) and Luana Walters as the seductive Sonya, who at midstream forsakes villain Poten and falls for the hero. Joan Barclay plays the newshawk as a featherhead while Forrest Taylor does well as the harried police captain. Charles King and William Buchanan (who wrote special dialogue for the serial) are okay as the henchmen and Roger Williams has a small, but good, role as the newspaper editor who spurs his former society writer to get onto the Chinatown crime story.

Victory also released a 65-minute feature version of *Shadow of Chinatown*, and like most films of its ilk it moves much more quickly than its parent. Interestingly, the feature and the serial have different endings. The serial has Poten being arrested while the feature has his character terminated following the crash of his vehicle into the Los Angeles harbor.

## Rip Roarin' Buckaroo

October 15, 1936.

*P:* Sam Katzman. *D:* Bob Hill. *SC:* William Buchanan. *PH:* Bill Hyer. *ED:* Charles Henkel. *AD:* Fred Preble. *SD:* Herb Eicke. *Prod Mgr:* Edward W. Rote.

*Cast:* Tom Tyler, Beth Marion, Sammy Cohen, Forrest Taylor, Charles King, John Elliott, Richard Cramer, Theodore Lorch, Wally West, Bud Pope, Wimpy the Dog.

After leaving the ring, a boxer becomes a ranch hand and agrees to ride a prize horse in a big race.

## Bars of Hate

November 11, 1936, 57 minutes.

*P:* Sam Katzman. *D:* Al Herman. *SC:* Al Martin, from the story "Vengeance of the Lord" by Peter B. Kyne. *PH:* Bill Hyer. *ED:* Dan Milner. *AD:* Fred Preble. *SD:* Herb Eicke. *Prod Mgr:* Edward W. Rote.

*Cast:* Regis Toomey, Sheila Terry, Molly O'Day, Robert Warwick, Fuzzy Knight, Snub Pollard, Gordon Griffith, Arthur Loft, John Elliott, Jack Cowell.

Two men try to help a young woman prove her brother is not guilty of a crime actually committed by hoodlums.

## Phantom of the Range

November 28, 1936, 58 minutes.

*P:* Sam Katzman. *D:* Bob Hill. *SC:* Basil Dickey. *PH:* Bill Hyer. *ED:* Charles Henkel. *AD:* Fred Preble. *SD:* Herb Eicke. *Prod Mgr:* Edward W. Rote.

*Cast:* Tom Tyler, Beth Marion, Sammy Cohen, Solidad Jiminez, Forrest Taylor, Charles King, John Elliott, Richard Cramer.

Hoping to buy a ranch, a cowboy learns that a ghost is allegedly haunting the area.

## Blake of Scotland Yard

1937, 15 chapters.

*P:* Sam Katzman. *D:* Bob Hill. *SC:* Basil Dickey & William Buchanan. *ST:* Rock Hawkey [Bob Hill]. *PH:* Bill Hyer. *ED:* Holbrook N. Todd & Fred Bain. *AD:* Fred Preble. *SD:* Hans Weeren. *Prod Mgr:* Edward W. Rote. *Supv:* Robert Stillman.

*Cast:* Ralph Byrd, Herbert Rawlinson, Joan Barclay, Lloyd Hughes, Dickie Jones, Nick Stuart, Lucille Lund, Sam Flint, Gail Newbury, Jimmy Aubrey, Theodore Lorch, George DeNormand, Bob Terry, William Farrell, Frank Wayne, Dick Curtis.

*Chapter Titles:* The Mystery of the Blooming Gardenia, Death in the Laboratory, Cleared Mysteries, Mystery of the Silver Fox, Death in the River, The Criminal Shadow, Face to Face, The Fatal Trap, Parisian House Tops, Battle Royal, The Burning Fuse, The Roos of Limehouse, Sting of the Scorpion, The Scorpion Unmasked, The Trap is Sprung.

When a newspaper reporter-inventor and his girlfriend develop a death ray it is sought by a grotesque masked killer called the Scorpion. Also released in a 73-minute feature version.

## Cheyenne Rides Again

January 1, 1937, 56 minutes.

*P:* Sam Katzman. *D:* Bob Hill. *SC:* Basil Dickey. *PH:* Bill Hyer. *ED:* Charles Henkel. *AD:* Fred Preble. *SD:* Herb Eicke. *Prod Mgr:* Edward W. Rote.

*Cast:* Tom Tyler, Lucille Browne, Carmen LaRoux, Lon Chaney, Jr., Roger Williams, Jimmie Fox, Ed Cassidy, Theodore Lorch, Slim Whitaker, Merrill McCormack, Jack Smith, Bud Pope, Francis Walker, Bob Hill, Oscar Gahan, Wilbur McCauley.

A cowboy is suspected of being a stage robber but one of his posse members hides evidence proving that fact.

## Taming the Wild

January 27, 1937, 55 minutes.

*P:* Sam Katzman. *D:* Bob Hill. *SC:* Al Martin, from the story "Shipmates" by Peter B. Kyne. *PH:* Bill Hyer. *ED:* Earl Turner. *SD:* Johnny Eilers & J.S. Westmoreland. *Prod Mgr:* Edward W. Rote.

*Cast:* Rod La Rocque, Maxine Doyle, Bryant Washburn, Barbara Pepper, Donald Kerr, Zella Russell, Reed Howes, Vincent Dennis.

After she is involved in a car accident, a lawyer tries to keep watch on a society girl who then gets mixed up with a gangster.

Advertisement for *Cheyenne Rides Again* (**Victory, 1937**).

## Feud of the Trail

May 1, 1937, 56 minutes.
  *P:* Sam Katzman. *D:* Bob Hill. *SC:* Basil Dickey. *PH:* Bill Hyer. *ED:* Holbrook N. Todd. *SD:* Hans Weeren. *AD:* Fred Preble.
  *Cast:* Tom Tyler (Tom Wade/Jack Granger), Harlene [Harley] Wood (Sheila Granger), Milburn Morante (Jerry MacLaine), Roger Williams (Lance Holcomb), Vane Calvert (Ma Holcomb), Lafe McKee (John Granger), Dick Alexander, Jim Corey, Francis Walker (Holcomb's Henchmen), Steve Clark (Robbery Victim), Slim Whitaker (Sheriff).
  Cattlemen Association agents

Tom Wade (Tom Tyler) and Jerry MacLaine (Milburn Morante) help a man (Steve Clark) who has been robbed, and they chase the outlaws, shooting one of them. The dying man is Jack Granger (Tom Tyler), a look-alike for Wade, who had planned to go straight and return home and help his father and sister save their ranch from greedy neighbors. When Jack dies, Tom puts on his clothes and captures his henchmen and then travels to the Pecos to tell the Granger family that Jack is dead. Meanwhile Lance Holcomb (Roger Williams) has been thwarted by Jack's sister Sheila (Harlene Wood) and his mother (Vane Calvert) tells him to buy out John Granger (Lafe McKee), Sheila's father, because there is gold on his ranch. Mr. Granger accepts the money, but on the way to the bank he is ambushed and robbed by Lance. Tom comes along and wings the robber as he flees. Mr. Granger thinks Tom is his son, and back at the ranch Sheila mistakes him for her brother. Tom decides to keep up the false identity to help the Grangers get back their ranch. He goes to the Holcomb ranch for the deed but a fight ensues, and Jerry comes along and pretends to arrest him. Back at the ranch, Tom tells Mr. Granger and Sheila the truth about his identity and what happened to Jack. He then tells them to go to town for protection while he trails the Holcomb gang to Yellow Horse Canyon, the location of the gold mine. Just as the crooks plan to blow up the mine to open a gold vein, Tom stops them and a fight ensues. Jerry and the sheriff (Slim Whitaker) come along with a posse, and Mr. Granger and Sheila lead them to the mine. An explosion stops the fight and Tom handcuffs the gang as the posse arrives. Later, as Tom and

Jerry take the Holcomb gang to jail, Tom tells Sheila he plans to return to her.

In the majority of the eight westerns Tom Tyler did for Victory Pictures he portrayed Tom Wade, a member of the Cattlemen's Association. *Feud of the Trail*, the fourth in the series, had him playing not only this part but also Wade's outlaw lookalike. Photographed at the Lazy A Ranch in Chatsworth, California, in the early spring of 1937, *Feud of the Trail* is a modern-day western that was obviously quickly made but one that is aided by fairly good characterizations by its cast. Tom Tyler is naturally the stalwart hero, while Harlene [Harley] Wood is the attractive leading lady, and Milburn Morante supplies the comic relief as Wade's braggart fellow agent. On the villainous side, Roger Williams is the bumbling bad guy who is a disappointment to his larcenous mother, nicely played by Vane Calvert who usually portrayed kind old women in westerns. Bad guys Dick Alexander, Jim Corey and Francis Walker have little to do as henchmen, and Lafe McKee is his reliable self as the heroine's father. Filled with the usual fisticuffs, chases and shootings, *Feud of the Trail* is a passable western vehicle for Tom Tyler. Its lowest ebb are a couple of badly dubbed scenes of Milburn Morante singing "The Old Chisholm Trail."

## Mystery Range

May 1, 1937, 60 minutes.

*P:* Sam Katzman. *D:* Bob Hill. *SC:* Basil Dickey. *PH:* Bill Hyer. *ED:* Holbrook N. Todd. *AD:* Fred Preble. *SD:* Hans Weeren.

*Cast:* Tom Tyler, Jerry Bergh, Milburn Morante, Jim Corey, Dick Alexander, Roger Williams, Slim Whitaker, Lafe McKee.

A Cattlemen's Association agent and his pal try to help a girl whose uncle is trying to take away her property.

## Orphan of the Pecos

June 5, 1937, 55 minutes.

*P-D:* Sam Katzman. *SC:* Basil Dickey. *PH:* Bill Hyer. *ED:* Holbrook N. Todd. *AD:* Fred Preble. *SD:* Hans Weeren. *Prod Mgr:* Edward W. Rote.

*Cast:* Tom Tyler, Jeanne Martel, Roger Williams, Theodore Lorch, Howard Bryant, Slim Whitaker, Forrest Taylor, Marjorie Beebe, Lafe McKee, John Elliott.

A cowboy is falsely accused of the murder of a rancher, the crime having been committed by the man's foreman.

## Brothers of the West

June 30, 1937, 55 minutes.

*P-D:* Sam Katzman. *SC:* Basil Dickey. *PH:* Bill Hyer. *ED:* Holbrook N. Todd. *AD:* Fred Preble. *SD:* Hans Weeren. *Prod Mgr:* Edward W. Rote.

*Cast:* Tom Tyler, Lois Wilde, Dorothy Short, Lafe McKee, Bob Terry, Dave O'Brien, Roger Williams, Jim Corey, James C. Morton, George Morrell, Tiny Lipson.

A Cattlemen's Association agent learns his brother disappeared and is accused of a killing and he decides to investigate.

## Lost Ranch

July 10, 1937, 56 minutes.

*P-D:* Sam Katzman. *SC:* Basil Dickey. *PH:* Bill Hyer. *ED:* Holbrook N. Todd. *AD:* Fred Preble. *SD:* Hans Weeren. *Prod Mgr:* Edward W. Rote.

*Cast:* Tom Tyler, Jeanne Martel, Marjorie Beebe, Howard Bryant,

Theodore Lorch, Slim Whitaker, Forrest Taylor, Lafe McKee, Roger Williams, Harry Harvey, Jr., Bud Pope.

When her father is kidnapped a young woman and her friend try to find him and are aided by a Cattlemen's Association agent.

## Two Minutes to Play

October 16, 1937, 61 minutes.

*P:* Sam Katzman. *D:* Bob Hill. *SC:* William Buchanan. *PH:* Bill Hyer. *ED:* Charles Henkel. *SD:* Herb Eicke. *AD:* Fred Preble. *Prod Mgr:* Edward W. Rote.

*Cast:* Herman Brix [Bruce Bennett], Betty Compson, Jeanne Martel, Eddie Nugent, Grady Sutton, Duncan Renaldo, David Sharpe, Sammy Cohen, Forrest Taylor, Richard Tucker, Sam Flint.

Two pals want the same girl and she tries to get one of them to go out for the football team.

## Million Dollar Racket

November 15, 1937, 63 minutes.

*P:* Sam Katzman. *D:* Bob Hill. *SC:* Basil Dickey. *PH:* Bill Hyer. *ED:* Holbrook N. Todd. *AD:* Fred Preble. *Prod Mgr:* Edward W. Rote.

*Cast:* Herman Brix [Bruce Bennett], Joan Barclay, Bryant Washburn, Dave O'Brien, Frank Wayne, Vane Calvert, Sam Adams, Bob Terry, Jimmy Aubrey, Monte Carter, Lyn Arden.

A wealthy man gets a job working for a newly rich family and thwarts crooks who try to rob them.

## Amateur Crook

Royal, January 12, 1938, 62 minutes.

*P-D:* Sam Katzman. *SC:* Basil Dickey. *PH:* Bill Hyer. *ED:* Holbrook N. Todd. *AD:* Fred Preble. *Prod Mgr:* Edward W. Rote.

*Cast:* Herman Brix [Bruce Bennett], Joan Barclay, Monte Blue, Jack Mulhall, Vivian Oakland, Jimmy Aubrey, Fuzzy Knight, Henry Rocquemore, Edward Earle, Fern Emmett.

An artist gets mixed up with a girl who has stolen a gem, belonging to her father, from loan sharks.

## Flying Fists

Treo Exchange, February 25, 1938, 62 minutes.

*P:* Sam Katzman. *D:* Bob Hill. *SC:* Basil Dickey. *ST:* Rock Hawkey [Bob Hill]. *PH:* Bill Hyer. *ED:* Holbrook N. Todd. *AD:* Fred Preble. *SD:* Hans Weeren. *Prod Mgr:* Edward W. Rote.

*Cast:* Herman Brix [Bruce Bennett], Jeanne Martel, Fuzzy Knight, J. Farrell MacDonald, Guinn Williams, Dickie Jones, Charles Williams, John Elliott, Billy Benedict, Tiny Lipson, Buster, Friday.

A young man trains to become a boxing champion and is billed as mean and cruel although in reality he is just the opposite.

## Silks and Saddles

Treo Exchange, April 13, 1938, 63 minutes.

*P:* Sam Katzman. *D:* Bob Hill. *SC:* William Buchanan & Basil Dickey. *PH:* Bill Hyer. *ED:* Charles Henkel. *AD:* Fred Preble. *Prod Mgr:* Edward W. Rote.

*Cast:* Herman Brix [Bruce Bennett], Toby Wing, Fuzzy Knight, Trixie Friganza, Frank Melton, Bess Flowers, Robert McClung, Roy Thompson, William Buchanan, Roger Williams, Flash the Horse.

A college student sells shares in his race horse which is wanted by a rich girl with whom he falls in love. Filmed in 1936.

## Lightning Carson Rides Again

October 10, 1938, 59 minutes.

*P:* Sam Katzman. *D:* Sam Newfield. *SC:* E.R. D'Dasi. *PH:* Marcel LePicard. *ED:* Holbrook N. Todd. *AD:* Fred Preble. *SD:* Hans Weeren. *Prod Mgr:* Edward W. Rote. *Asst Dir:* Charles Henry.

*Cast:* Tim McCoy, Joan Barclay, Ted Adams, Bob Terry, Forrest Taylor, Ben Corbett, Slim Whitaker, Frank Wayne, Jane Keckley, Karl Hackett, Reed Howes, Frank LaRue, James Flavin, Sherry Tansey, Wally West.

A Justice Department agent investigates reports his nephew has disappeared after committing a bank shipment robbery.

## Six-Gun Trail

November 25, 1938, 59 minutes.

*P:* Sam Katzman. *D:* Sam Newfield. *SC:* Joseph O'Donnell. *PH:* Marcel LePicard. *ED:* Holbrook N. Todd.

*Cast:* Tim McCoy, Nora Lane, Ben Corbett, Ted Adams, Alden Chase, Don Gallaher, Karl Hackett, Kenne Duncan, George Morrell, Jimmy Aubrey, Bob Terry, Frank Wayne, Sherry Tansey, Hal Carey.

On the trail of stolen jewels, a government agent impersonates an Oriental in order to bring in the thieves.

## Code of the Cactus

February 25, 1939, 56 minutes.

*P:* Sam Katzman. *D:* Sam Newfield. *SC:* Edward Halperin. *PH:* Marcel LePicard. *ED:* Holbrook N. Todd. *SD:* Hans Weeren. *Mus:* Johnny Lange & Lew Porter. *AD:* Fred Preble. *Prod Mgr:* Edward W. Rote, *Asst Dir:* Bert Sternbach.

*Cast:* Tim McCoy, Dorothy Short, Ben Corbett, Ted Adams, Alden Chase, Dave O'Brien, Forrest Taylor, Bob Terry, Slim Whitaker, Frank Wayne, Art Davis, Kermit Maynard, Jimmy Aubrey, Carl Mathews, Jack King, Clyde McClary, Carl Sepulveda, Lee Burns, Rube Dalroy.

A government agent agrees to help a girl and her partner oppose rustlers using trucks and machine guns.

## Texas Wildcats

April 10, 1939, 57 minutes.

*P:* Sam Katzman. *D:* Sam Newfield. *SC:* George Plympton. *PH:* Marcel LePicard. *ED:* Holbrook N. Todd. *AD:* Fred Preble. *SD:* Glen Glenn. *Prod Mgr:* Edward W. Rote. *Asst Dir:* Bert Sternbach.

*Cast:* Tim McCoy, Joan Barclay, Ben Corbett, Forrest Taylor, Ted Adams, Avando Renaldo, Bob Terry, Dave O'Brien, Frank Ellis, Reed Howes, Slim Whitaker, George Morrell, Carl Mathews, Sherry Tansey, Wally West, Frank Wayne.

A government agent takes on the guise of masked phantom to bring in the man who killed his best friend.

## Outlaws' Paradise

April 19, 1939, 56 minutes.

*P:* Sam Katzman. *AP:* Bert Sterbach. *D:* Sam Newfield. *SC:* Basil Dickey. *PH:* Marcel [Le] Picard. *ED:* Holbrook N. Todd. *AD:* Fred Preble. *SD:* Glen Glenn. *Prod Mgr:* Edward W. Rote. *Song:* Johnny Lange & Lew Porter.

*Cast:* Tim McCoy (Captain William "Lightning Bill" Carson/Trigger Mallory), Joan Barclay (Jessie Treadwell), Benny [Ben] Corbett (Magpie McGillicudy), Ted Adams (Slim Marsh), Bob Terry (Steve), Don Gallagher (Mort), Dave O'Brien (Meggs), Jack Mulhall (Warden), Wally West (Blake), Jack C. Smith (Guard), George Morrell, Carl Mathews (Gamblers).

Trigger Mallory's (Tim McCoy) old gang, led by Slim Marsh (Ted Adams), pulls off a $30,000 negotiable bond robbery, shooting two U.S. mail guards. Mallory is about to be let out of prison after serving a three-year term, but his lookalike, Captain William "Lightning Bill" Carson (Tim McCoy) of the Department of Justice, persuades the warden (Jack Mulhall) to hold him for further investigation. Carson plans to palm himself off as Mallory to capture the rest of the gang and retrieve the stolen bonds. Working with him on the scheme is his pal Magpie (Benny Corbett). Masquerading as Mallory, Carson returns to the bordertown where the gang hides out, but Slim is suspicious and plans to get Mallory out of the way and take over the operation. Carson is able to ingratiate himself with Mallory's girlfriend, singer Jessie Treadwell (Joan Barclay), who thinks he really is her lover. When she overhears Slim's plans she warns Carson, thinking he is Mallory, and in a shootout Carson reinforces Mallory's hold on the gang. The gang then plans to rustle a big herd of cattle, and Carson gets all the gang together so he can arrest them all at the same time. Meanwhile Mallory breaks out of jail and returns to town, proving his true identity to Jessie. Magpie also arrives and overhears their conversation and is captured by Mallory but manages to escape. When Slim hears Carson calling FBI headquarters, he tries to get the drop on him but Carson shoots and kills him. Mallory returns to his gang with Jessie and lays a trap for Carson who is captured upon his return. Carson, however, manages a getaway with the aid of Magpie and the two are able to capture the gang members, although Carson lets Jessie go free.

Tim McCoy originated the character he played in the Victory series earlier in Puritan's *Lightnin' Bill Carson* (1936). The role gave him more acting freedom than the traditional cowboy part, and in *Outlaws' Paradise*, the fifth of eight series entries, he not only portrayed the lawman but also the villain, replete with a facial scar. McCoy does a sturdy job in the dual roles and is especially impressive as the bad guy. Fortunately, sidekick Ben Corbett has little to do in this entry while Ted Adams does well as the doublecrossing henchman. Joan Barclay is lovely as the leading lady, but in an offbeat characterization, she is really a villainess, the girlfriend of the outlaw. Only at the end does she show any remorse when lawman Bill Carson allows her to go free. At one point in the film she sings the song "A Rainbow Is Riding the Range"; otherwise, the music on the soundtrack is canned. Although made cheaply and quickly, the western is competently produced and directed and smoothly edited. Like the others in the Tim McCoy-Victory series, it was done in three days—one for outdoor shooting and two more for indoor shots on rented space at the Monogram studios.

## The Fighting Renegade

September 1, 1939, 54 minutes.

*P:* Sam Katzman. *D:* Sam Newfield. *SC:* William Lively. *PH:* Art Reed. *ED:* Holbrook N. Todd. *SD:* Hans Weeren. *Prod Mgr:* Edward W. Rote. *Asst Dir:* Bert Sternbach.

*Cast:* Tim McCoy, Joyce Bryant, Ben Corbett, Ted Adams, Dave O'Brien, Budd Buster, Forrest Taylor, Reed Howes, John Elliott, Carl Mathews, Wally West, Chick Hannon, Dan White.

Disguised as a Mexican bandit, a government agent leads an archaeological expedition into dangerous country in search of buried Indian treasure.

## Trigger Fingers

December 20, 1939, 55 minutes.

*P:* Sam Katzman. *D:* Sam Newfield. *SC:* Basil Dickey. *PH:* Bill Hyer. *ED:* Holbrook N. Todd. *Prod Mgr:* Edward W. Rote. *Asst Dir:* Bert Sternbach.

*Cast:* Tim McCoy, Joyce Bryant, Ben Corbett, Jill Martin, Carleton Young, Ralph Peters, Bud McTaggert, John Elliott, Kenne Duncan, Forrest Taylor, Ted Adams, Carl Mathews, Bob Terry, Budd Buster, Tex Palmer.

Three government agents pose as gypsies in order to investigate a series of cattle thefts.

## Straight Shooter

January 31, 1940, 54 minutes.

*P:* Sam Katzman. *D:* Sam Newfield. *SC:* Basil Dickey & Joseph O'Donnell. *ST:* Basil Dickey. *PH:* Art Reed. *ED:* Holbrook N. Todd. *Prod Mgr:* Edward W. Rote. *Asst Dir:* Bert Sternbach.

*Cast:* Tim McCoy, Julie Sheldon, Ben Corbett, Ted Adams, Reed Howes, Forrest Taylor, Budd Buster, Carl Mathews, Wally West.

When thieves believe a fortune in stolen bonds is hidden in a ranch house they try to obtain the treasure but are opposed by a federal agent.

# Index

Index